THE ROUGH GUIDE TO
VIETNAM

This ninth edition updated by

Ron Emmons, Rachel Mills and Martin Zatko

**ROUGH
GUIDES**

Contents

OPPOSITE LANTERN-MAKER IN HOI AN **PREVIOUS PAGE** WOMAN COLLECTING WATER LILIES IN THE MEKONG DELTA

Introduction to
Vietnam

One has to admire Vietnam – despite its tumultuous recent history, this resilient nation has bounced back to become a big-hitter on the Southeast Asian travel circuit. As one would expect from a country so long and skinny, there's plenty of variety on offer – it's a land of emerald paddy fields and white-sand beaches, full-tilt cities and venerable pagodas, vast caves, craggy mountains and friendly minority communities. Visitors are met with warmth, curiosity and a seemingly irrepressible desire to connect; add in some of the region's most nuanced cuisine, and you're onto a winner.

The reunification of North and South Vietnam in 1975 ended twenty years of bloody civil war, and was followed by a decade or so of hardline rule from which only the shake-up of **doi moi** – Vietnam's equivalent of *perestroika*, beginning in 1986 – could awaken the country. This signalled a renaissance for Vietnam, and today a high fever of commerce grips the nation, seen in its flash new shopping malls and designer boutiques, and the hustle and bustle of its street markets.

There's a marked difference between **north and south**, a deep psychological divide that was around long before the American War, and is engrained in Vietnamese culture. Northerners are considered reticent, thrifty, law-abiding and lacking the dynamism and entrepreneurial know-how of their supposedly more worldly wise southern compatriots. Not surprisingly, this is mirrored in the broader economy: the south is Vietnam's growth engine, boasting lower unemployment and higher average wages, and increasingly glitzy Ho Chi Minh City (HCMC) looks more to Bangkok and Singapore than it does to the policy-makers in Hanoi.

Many visitors find more than enough to intrigue and excite them in Hanoi, HCMC and the other major centres, but despite the cities' allure, it's the country's striking **landscape** that most impresses. Vietnam occupies a narrow strip of land that hugs the eastern borders of Cambodia and Laos, hemmed in by rugged mountains to the west, and to the east by the South China Sea – or the East Sea, as the Vietnamese call it. To the north and south of its narrow waist, it fantails out into the splendid deltas of the Red

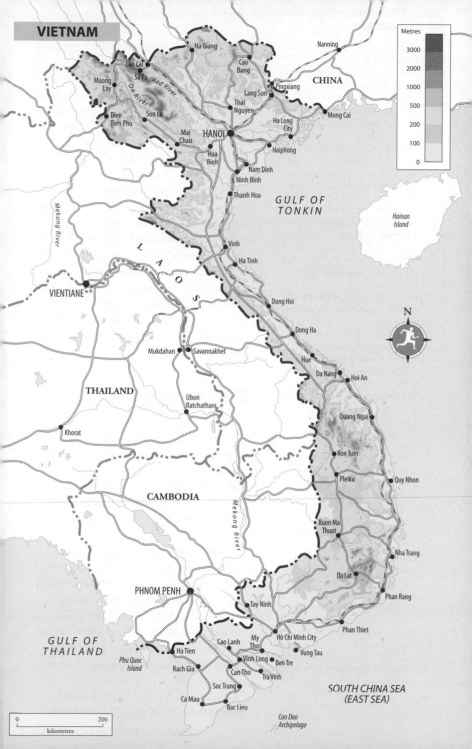

FACT FILE

• The Socialist Republic of Vietnam, the capital of which is Hanoi, is one of the world's last surviving one-party **Communist states**. The others include China, North Korea, Laos and Cuba.

• Vietnam has a **population** of 95 million, of which around two-thirds live in the countryside, giving Vietnam one of the highest rural population densities in Southeast Asia. Despite this, the country has a literacy rate of around 95 percent.

• **Tourist numbers** to Vietnam have risen from just two million in 2000 to ten million in 2016, with a year-on-year increase of ten to thirty percent.

• The Vietnamese **language** is the only language in Indochina to use a Romanized script. However, its complex use of diacritical marks and six separate tones to indicate meaning make it very difficult for foreigners to learn.

• The Vietnam War is known to Vietnamese as the **American War** to distinguish it from other unwelcome incursions by the French, the Chinese and the Japanese.

• The **motorbike** is the preferred form of transport for around ninety percent of Vietnamese; there are currently about forty million motorbikes on the road (including 7.5 million in HCMC alone).

• In 2013 Vietnam became the world's largest **exporter** of cashew nuts, though it has since lost its crown to India. It also ranks number two globally for coffee production, and number four for rice exports.

• Though the *ao dai* is universally recognized as Vietnam's **national dress**, it did not come into popular use until the 1930s.

• Vietnam is home to a tremendous diversity of **plant and animal life**, including some of the world's rarest species, such as the Asiatic black bear, Sarus crane and golden-headed langur.

River and the Mekong, and it's in these regions that you'll encounter the paddy fields, dragonflies, buffaloes and conical-hatted farmers that constitute the classic images of Vietnam.

In stark contrast to the pancake-flat rice land of the deltas, Ha Long Bay's labyrinthine network of **limestone outcrops** loom dramatically out of the Gulf of Tonkin – a magical spectacle in the early morning mist. Any trip to the remote upland regions of central and northern Vietnam is likely to focus on the **ethnic minorities** who reside there. Elaborate tribal costumes, age-old customs and communal longhouses await those visitors game enough to trek into the sticks. As for **wildlife**, the discovery in recent years of several previously unknown species of plants, birds and animals speaks volumes for the wealth of Vietnam's biodiversity and makes the improving access to the country's **national parks** all the more gratifying.

Where to go

Vietnam is bigger than you might assume – if you want to travel the length of the country at some leisure, see something of the highlands and the deltas and allow for a few rest days, you'll really need a month. With only two weeks at your disposal, you can hopscotch between the main draws along the coast, or – perhaps better – concentrate on one region and enjoy it at your own pace. Internal flights can speed up an itinerary substantially, and aren't too expensive.

For the majority of visitors, **Ho Chi Minh City** provides a head-spinning introduction to Vietnam. The city's breakneck pace of life translates into a stew of bizarre characters and unlikely sights and sounds, and ensures that almost all who come here quickly fall for its singular charm.

Easily reached from Ho Chi Minh City is the **Mekong Delta**, where one of the world's truly

OPPOSITE ETHNIC MINORITY WOMAN AT BAC HA MARKET

mighty rivers finally offloads into the South China Sea; its skein of tributaries and waterways has endowed the delta with a lush quilt of rice paddies and abundant orchards. Tucked away to the west of the delta, **Phu Quoc Island** is the perfect place to rest after the rigours of a road journey through Vietnam, or as a quick escape by plane from Ho Chi Minh City.

Sitting at an altitude of 1500m, **Da Lat** is the usual gateway to the **central highlands**, and the fresh breezes that fan this oddly quaint hillside settlement provide the best natural air-conditioning in Vietnam. To sense the region's remoteness you'll need to push further north to the modest towns of **Buon Ma Thuot**, **Pleiku** and **Kon Tum**, which are surrounded by E De, Jarai and Bahnar communities.

Heading northeast of Ho Chi Minh City, Highway 1 is the country's jugular, and carries the lion's share of traffic up towards Hanoi. For many, the first stop is at the delightful beach and sand dunes of **Mui Ne**, which is fast becoming one of Vietnam's top coastal resorts. Further north, **Nha Trang** offers the chance to party all night and sleep all day, or explore idyllic beach hideaways. North again, **Quy Nhon** is one of the country's least touristed beach resorts, while the memorial at **Son My** village near Quang Ngai commemorates one of the ghastliest incidents in the American War.

Once a bustling seaport, the diminutive town of **Hoi An** perches beside an indolent backwater, its narrow streets of wooden-fronted shophouses and weathered roofs making it an enticing destination; just inland, the war-battered ruins of **My Son**, the greatest of the Cham temple sites, lie mouldering in a steamy, forest-filled valley. **Da Nang**, just up the coast, lacks Hoi An's charm, but good sleeping and eating options make it a convenient

> ## WATER PUPPETS
>
> Vietnam's unique contribution to the world of marionettes, **water puppetry** is a delightfully quirky form of theatre in which the action takes place on a stage of water. The tradition was spawned in the rice paddies of the northern Red River Delta, where performances still take place after the spring planting. Obscured by a split-bamboo screen, puppeteers standing waist-deep in water manipulate the wooden puppets which are attached to the end of long poles concealed beneath the surface. Dragons, ducks, lions, unicorns, phoenixes and frogs spout smoke, throw balls and generally cavort on the watery stage – miraculously avoiding tangled poles. In the more sophisticated productions staged for tourists in Hanoi and Ho Chi Minh City, even fireworks emerge to dance on the water, which itself takes on different characters, from calm and placid to seething and furious, during naval battles.

base for the area. From Da Nang, an extremely scenic train ride along the Hai Van Pass brings you to the aristocratic city of **Hue**, where the Nguyen emperors established their capital in the nineteenth century on the banks of the languid Perfume River; the temples and palaces of this highly cultured city still testify to these past splendours.

Only 100km north of Hue, the tone changes as war sites litter the Demilitarized Zone (**DMZ**) which once cleaved the country in two. There's then little to detain you on the northward trek to Hanoi, bar the glittering limestone caverns of **Phong Nha**, which include the world's largest known cave. Then, on the very fringes of the northern Red River Delta, lie the ancient incense-steeped temples of **Hoa Lu** and, nearby, the mystical landscapes of **Tam Coc** and **Van Long**, where paddy fields lap at the feet of limestone hummocks.

Anchored firmly in the Red River Delta, **Hanoi** has served as Vietnam's capital for over a thousand years. It's a decidedly proud city – think pagodas and dynastic temples, tamarisk-edged lakes and boulevards lined with French-era villas – but it's also being swept along by the tide of change as Vietnam forges its own shiny, high-rise capital.

From Hanoi, you can strike out east to spend a leisurely day or two drifting among the thousands of whimsically sculpted islands anchored in the aquamarine waters of **Ha Long Bay**; its most appealing gateway is mountainous **Cat Ba Island**, which defines the bay's southwestern limits.

To the north and west of Hanoi lie dramatic mountain landscapes, which are home to a patchwork of ethnic minorities. The bustling market town of **Sa Pa**, set in a spectacular location close to the Chinese border, makes a good base for exploring nearby minority villages. Southwest of Hanoi, the stilthouse-filled valley of **Mai Chau** offers opportunities to stay in a minority village.

When to go

Vietnam has a tropical monsoon **climate**, dominated by the south or southwesterly monsoon from May to September, and the northeast monsoon from October to April. Within this basic pattern there are marked differences according to altitude and latitude; temperatures in the south remain equable all year round, while the north experiences distinct seasonal variations.

OPPOSITE FROM TOP RICE TERRACES, NINH BINH PROVINCE; FACE MASKS FOR TET CELEBRATIONS

AVERAGE TEMPERATURE AND RAINFALL

	Jan	Feb	Mar	Apr	May	Jun	Jul	Aug	Sep	Oct	Nov	Dec
HO CHI MINH CITY												
Temperature (°C)	27	28	29	30	29	29	28	28	27	27	27	27
Rainfall (mm)	15	3	13	43	221	330	315	269	335	269	114	56
DA NANG												
Temperature (°C)	22	23	24	27	29	30	30	30	28	26	25	23
Rainfall (mm)	102	31	12	18	47	42	99	117	447	530	221	209
HANOI												
Temperature (°C)	17	18	20	24	28	30	30	29	28	26	22	19
Rainfall (mm)	18	28	38	81	196	239	323	343	254	99	43	20

In **southern Vietnam** the dry season lasts from December to late April or May, and the rains from May through to November; most rain falls in brief afternoon downpours, though flooding can cause problems in the Mekong Delta and central highlands. Daytime temperatures in the region rarely drop below 20°C, occasionally hitting 40°C during the hottest months (March to May). The climate of the central highlands generally follows the same pattern, though temperatures are cooler, especially at night.

Along the **central coast** the rainfall pattern reverses under the influence of the northeast monsoon. Around Nha Trang the wet season is relatively short (November to December); further north, around Hue and Da Nang, the rains last a bit longer, so it pays to visit these two cities in the spring (February to May). Temperatures reach their maximum (often in the upper 30°C) from June to August, when it's pleasant to escape into the hills. The northern stretches of this coastal region experience a shorter rainy season (peaking in September and October) and a hot, dry summer. The coast of central Vietnam is the zone most likely to be hit by typhoons, bringing torrential rain and hurricane-force winds (generally between August and November).

Northern Vietnam sees fairly chilly winters (December to March), accompanied by persistent mists that can last for several days. Temperatures then build to summer maximums, which occasionally hit 40°C between May and August, and this is also the rainy season, when heavy downpours render the low-lying delta area almost unbearably hot and sticky, and flooding is a regular hazard. In the northern mountains temperatures are considerably cooler and higher regions see ground frosts, or even a rare snowfall, during the winter.

With such a complicated weather picture, there's no one particular season to recommend as the **best time** for visiting Vietnam. Overall, autumn (September to December) and spring (March and April) are probably the most favourable seasons if you're covering the entire country.

Author picks

From the breathtaking remoteness of the mountain communities in the north to the bustling floating markets of the Mekong, our authors travelled by bike, bus, boat and on foot to cover every corner of Vietnam for this new edition. Aside from the major sights, here are their personal picks.

Spectacular views Between Dong Van and Meo Vac in the country's extreme north, the mountain road snakes through the Ma Pi Leng Pass, where the views down to the Nho Que River and across into China will make you gasp (p.422).

Rural life The Bong Lai Valley is a gloriously far-flung destination, 10km east of Phong Nha town, where rural life continues much as it has for generations, with a remote homestay or rustic restaurant the only concession to tourism (p.311).

Stilthouse stays The Pu Luong Nature Reserve is as yet comparatively unknown to outsiders, so you can trek amid magnificent rice terraces, help prepare a tasty dinner and bed down in a stilthouse without swarms of foreigners spoiling the experience (p.314).

Hoi An delicacies Little Hoi An has an almost bewildering selection of mouthwateringly good restaurants, but *Morning Glory* just about takes the biscuit. For a reasonable price you can eat your fill of superbly prepared Hoi An specialities – only this time in an elegant restaurant, rather than a kindergarten-style plastic chair (p.255).

Musical performances You will be mesmerized by *ca tru*, an ancient form of chamber music that is described by UNESCO as an intangible heritage, at weekly performances in Hanoi (p.379).

Saigon nights Sip a cocktail with a sunset view from one of HCMC's venerable old hotels, then prom with the locals along newly gentrified Nguyen Hue (p.74).

Banh mi Don't leave Vietnam without trying this quintessential street snack – a baguette filled with a choice of meats and whatever other goodies the vendor is carrying in their portable stand. Foreign travellers often end up enjoying *banh mi* as a proxy kebab after a night on the town (p.40).

> Our author recommendations don't end here. We've flagged up our favourite places – a perfectly sited hotel, an atmospheric café, a special restaurant – throughout the Guide, highlighted with the ★ symbol.

27

things not to miss

It's not possible to see everything that Vietnam has to offer in one trip – and we don't suggest you try. What follows, in no particular order, is a selective taste of the country's highlights: outstanding scenery, lively festivals, ancient sites and colonial architecture. Each entry has a page reference to take you straight into the Guide, where you can find out more. Coloured numbers refer to chapters in the Guide section.

1 HOI AN
Page 245

With its rich cultural heritage, beautifully preserved merchants' houses and slow pace of life, Hoi An is a captivating place to spend a few days.

2 DONG VAN KARST PLATEAU GEOPARK
Page 419

Vietnam's most impressive mountainscapes are located in remote Ha Giang province, near the Chinese border.

3 DA LAT
Page 172

The pretty, occasionally chilly hill-town of Da Lat is the de facto travel capital of Vietnam's beautiful central highlands.

4 CU CHI TUNNELS & CAO DAI TEMPLE
Pages 106 & 108

So tiny are the Cu Chi tunnels that it's hard to believe they were inhabited during the war. They're easily visited in combination with the colourful high temple of Vietnam's most charismatic indigenous religion.

5 BEER
Pages 101 & 379

Experience both sides of Vietnam's take on beer – hit Hanoi's bia hoi stalls for some of the world's cheapest draught, then try some fancy ales in one of Ho Chi Minh City's craft-beer dens.

6 THE CITADEL, HUE
Page 276

The former capital's historic citadel, mausoleums and gardens are idiosyncratic enough to impress even the most jaded traveller.

7 WATER PUPPETS
Page 8

Enjoy a performance of *mua roi nuoc*, an art form developed in the Red River Delta around Hanoi.

8 EXPRESS SILK TAILORING
Page 256

Visit one of the many Hoi An tailors who can rustle up a made-to-measure silk dress or suit in just a few hours.

9 MOUNT FAN SI PAN
Page 402

Ride the record-breaking cable car from Sa Pa and stand on top of Vietnam's highest mountain.

10 CHILL OUT ON PHU QUOC
Page 159

Beaches lined with coconut trees circle this holiday island, whose surrounding waters provide some of the finest snorkelling in Vietnam.

11 PO KLONG GARAI
Page 220
These beautifully preserved brick towers are probably the finest example of Cham architecture in the country.

12 TAM COC
Page 316
Slow the pace down with a boat trip in the countryside among dramatic karst landscapes.

13 ETHNIC MARKETS
Pages 404 & 405
Spectacular traditional dress and a lively atmosphere make the ethnic minority markets a must – especially those in Bac Ha and Can Cau.

14 CYCLING AROUND CHAU DOC
Page 131
This is the way to enjoy the Mekong Delta – pedalling between rice fields on the cusp of Cambodia, surrounded by classic Vietnamese scenery.

15 HOP ON A HONDA
Page 178
Vietnam has almost as many motorbikes as people, and if you can't beat them, join them – take an "Easy Rider" tour, rent one or take a ride on a xe om.

14

15

16 A BOAT TRIP IN HA LONG BAY
Page 337
The thousands of limestone islands jutting out of these smooth waters have been dubbed the eighth natural wonder of the world.

17 TET
Page 51
The most important festival in the Vietnamese calendar, Tet sees the New Year ushered in with colourful flower markets, spectacular fireworks and exuberant dragon dances.

18 RIDE THE REUNIFICATION EXPRESS
Page 30
Put honking bus journeys out of your mind as you kick back and relax on the leisurely train journey between Ho Chi Minh City and Hanoi.

19 COLONIAL ARCHITECTURE
Pages 74 & 356
The legacy of French rule can be found in umpteen impressive examples of colonial architecture, such as the opera houses in Hanoi and HCMC.

20 TRADITIONAL MUSIC
Page 476
Music is the most important of all Vietnam's performing arts, and a traditional performance should feature on every itinerary.

21 BROWSE THE MARKETS
Page 83
Markets like Ho Chi Minh City's Binh Tay are good stomping grounds for snacks and souvenirs alike.

22

23

24

25

22 ADVENTURE SPORTS
Page 330

Kitesurfing, kayaking and mountain biking are just a few of the heart-pumping activities awaiting thrill-seekers, though rock climbing in Cat Ba is perhaps the highlight.

23 PHO
Page 40

Make friends with pho – usually eaten for breakfast, this is Vietnam's slurpworthy signature dish.

24 BAHNAR VILLAGES
Pages 195 & 466

Spend the night in a thatched communal house (*rong*), where timeless ceremonies are performed and village decisions made.

25 THIEN MU PAGODA, HUE
Page 287

Vietnamese temples and pagodas reflect the country's diverse range of religions: Thien Mu Pagoda in Hue is a good example.

26 STREET FOOD
Page 375

Soak up the atmosphere at a street kitchen, and have your plate piled high with a selection of fresh food for next to nothing – Hanoi is your best bet.

27 NHA TRANG
Page 223

Take a snorkelling trip in the crystalline waters of the outlying islands around Nha Trang, or simply chill out on the beach.

26

Itineraries

The following itineraries will take you right around Vietnam, combining the classic tourist sites and busy cities with laidback beaches, quiet temples and remote mountain villages, where you'd be hard-pushed to find another visitor. Don't worry about seeing everything – each of these routes will give you a good taste of the country.

THE GRAND TOUR

The classic tour for visitors to Vietnam, and with good reason – following this route gives you easy access to superb historical sights, high-octane nightlife, pristine beaches, mountain-dwelling minority groups and much more. It can easily eat up the full month of your visa.

❶ Ho Chi Minh City Although it's not the capital, most would agree that this buzzing, cosmopolitan city is the true hub of Vietnam – its range of bars, restaurants, shops and hotels is unsurpassed. **See p.64**

❷ Da Lat This mile-high mountain city is highly popular with travellers, and not just for its fresh air or cooler temperatures. Its relaxed atmosphere lends itself to a leisurely exploration of nearby sights, which include some wonderful minority villages. **See p.172**

❸ Mui Ne It's all about the beach at Mui Ne, a curl of sand now fringed with top-drawer resorts. Even so, there are still a few cheap places to stay and a couple of bars maintaining that old-fashioned backpacker vibe. **See p.2123**

❹ Nha Trang Another place famed for its beach life, but with a totally different character. This is one of Vietnam's party capitals, with bars galore attracting revellers with astonishingly long happy hours. Those who wake up before nightfall can hit the nearby Cham ruins, then sink into a mud bath. **See p.223**

❺ Hoi An This small city draws almost universally positive reactions from visitors. Its food is the best in the country, its lantern-lit buildings are truly spellbinding at night, the nearby sea is great for diving and the majestic Cham ruins of My Son are close by. **See p.245**

❻ Hue Notably relaxed for its size, Hue was the capital of Vietnam's last dynasty, the Nguyen empire. Cross the Perfume River to the old Imperial City, a maze of opulent buildings that were home to emperors as recently as 1945. **See p.274**

❼ Hanoi The Vietnamese capital provides a truly startling contrast to Ho Chi Minh City, with a far more traditional air and some superb examples of colonial-era architecture. That said, its bars and restaurants are excellent too. **See p.342**

❽ Ha Long Bay There are few better ways to round off a Vietnamese tour than with a trip to Ha Long Bay, a dizzying mass of limestone peaks jutting from the sea. Most visitors spend a night at sea on a wooden junk after a feast of seafood and cocktails. **See p.336**

UNSEEN MEKONG DELTA

Eager to leave the tourist hordes behind? You'll rarely spot another foreigner at the following locations, and the whole lot can be seen in the space of a week.

ABOVE KHAI DINH MAUSOLEUM

❶ Sa Dec flower nurseries Apart from being the former home of French novelist Marguerite Dumas, Sa Dec is the base of over a hundred flower nurseries – a horticulturalist's dream. **See p.129**

❷ Hang Pagoda near Tra Vinh This Khmer-style pagoda, painted in subtle pastel shades, is home to hundreds of storks roosting in the treetops. **See p.124**

❸ Ca Mau Peninsula Hit Vietnam's southernmost point, where an observation tower offers views over mangrove swamps and the endless ocean. **See p.148**

❹ Highway 63 This narrow road from Ca Mau to Rach Gia passes classic delta scenes of commerce being conducted on canals and locals crossing precarious monkey bridges. **See p.151**

❺ Tra Su Bird Sanctuary Located near Chau Doc, this bird sanctuary is a wonderland of cajuput trees and waterways covered with lily pads, which attract flocks of birds like egrets, cormorants and water cocks. **See p.134**

❻ Hon Chong Peninsula The beach doesn't compare with those on Phu Quoc, but it's perfect on weekdays when you might be the only one swinging in a hammock beneath the casuarina trees. **See p.158**

ETHNIC CULTURE TOUR

Most of Vietnam's 54 ethnic minority groups live in the rugged hills of the north, and a circular journey from Hanoi passes several of the most interesting groups. It's possible to get around the north in a week, though a fortnight would allow more time for relaxing.

❶ White Thai in Mai Chau Women with waist-length hair don traditional costumes and perform lively song and dance routines, then invite guests to share a huge jar of rice wine. **See p.414**

❷ Black Thai in Son La The most remarkable aspect of Black Thai clothing is the headdress, which features delicately embroidered panels. **See p.411**

❸ Red Dao near Sa Pa Easily spotted by their bright red headgear, the Red Dao are one of the most colourful tribes in the north and cling fiercely to their traditional ways. **See p.401**

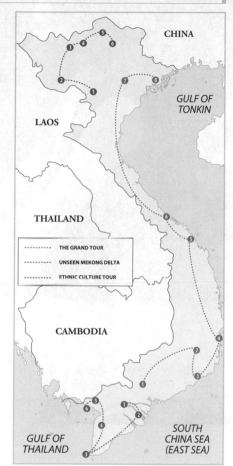

❹ Flower Hmong around Bac Ha These are hands down the north's most flamboyant dressers, and the women are constantly looking for new accoutrements at local markets. **See p.403**

❺ White Hmong near Dong Van Satins and sequins are highly favoured by this group, who live in one of the north's most inhospitable, yet also stunningly scenic, settings. **See p.419**

❻ Tay near Ba Be Lake The Tay are the most numerous of all ethnic groups in Vietnam, and have a rich tradition of song and dance, which they occasionally perform for tourists. **See p.423**

CYCLIST IN HO CHI MINH CITY

Basics

Getting there

The number of international flights heading to Vietnam has been steadily increasing of late – a fair sign of the country's burgeoning popularity as a tourist destination. The vast majority of visitors fly into Ho Chi Minh City and Hanoi, though there are also direct services to Da Nang, Hai Phong, Nha Trang and Phu Quoc from other (largely Asian) destinations. However, a fair chunk of visitors still take the cheaper option of an indirect flight routed through Bangkok, Singapore or Hong Kong; a stay in one of these cities can be factored into your schedule, often at no extra cost.

You may well save even more by taking a bargain-basement flight to Bangkok, Kuala Lumpur or Singapore, and a separate ticket through one of the region's **low-cost carriers**, such as Jetstar (ⓦjetstar.com) and AirAsia (ⓦairasia.com), for the Vietnam leg.

Major long-haul airlines usually fly in and out of both Hanoi and Ho Chi Minh City; they can sometimes sell you an open-jaw ticket, which allows you to fly into one city and out of the other, leaving you to travel up or down the country under your own steam. **Vietnam Airlines** (ⓦvietnamairlines.com) is the national flag-carrier, and currently flies to over fifty destinations in almost twenty countries; it's a quality operator, and part of the SkyTeam group.

Airfares always depend on the **season**, with the highest generally being July to August, during the Christmas and New Year holidays and around Tet, the Vietnamese New Year; fares drop during the shoulder season (September to mid-December) and the low season (January to June), when you'll get the best prices.

You can often cut costs by going through a **specialist flight agent** – either a consolidator, who buys up blocks of tickets from the airlines and sells them at a discount, or a **discount agent**, who in addition to dealing with discounted flights may also offer special student and youth fares and a range of other travel-related services such as travel insurance, rail passes, car rentals, tours and the like.

Lastly, combining Vietnam with other Southeast Asian countries is becoming increasingly popular – and a lot cheaper and easier – thanks to some good-value regional air deals (see p.29 for more information).

Flights from the UK and Ireland

Vietnam Airlines (ⓦvietnamairlines.com) flies from **London** to Ho Chi Minh City and Hanoi (both around 12hr); there are no direct flights from **Ireland**. Note that you may save money by flying with a Middle Eastern or Southeast Asian carrier such as Qatar (ⓦqatarairways.com), Emirates (ⓦemirates.com), Malaysia Airlines (ⓦmalaysiaairlines.com) or Singapore Airlines (ⓦsingaporeair.com), via the airline's hub city; scheduled low-season return **fares** from London start at just over £400, rising to £700 or more at peak periods.

A good place to look for the best deals is the travel sections of the weekend newspapers and in regional listings magazines. Students and under-26s can often get **discounts** through specialist agents such as STA (ⓦstatravel.co.uk) or USIT in Ireland (ⓦusit.ie). Whoever you buy your ticket through, check that the agency belongs to the travel industry bodies ABTA or IATA, so that you'll be covered if the agent goes bust before you get your ticket.

Flights from the US and Canada

Amazingly, no direct flights exist between Vietnam and **North America** – studies have shown that LA to Ho Chi Minh City is the busiest air route in the world lacking a direct service. In 2004, United Airlines (ⓦunited.com) broke a flight embargo in place since 1975, but their service (which ran via Hong Kong) was discontinued in 2016; at the time of research, Vietnam Airlines (ⓦvietnamairlines.com) were clearing the regulatory hurdles necessary to make their first-ever foray into US airspace. Until then, you'll have to catch one of the many flights to a regional hub (such as Bangkok, Singapore or Hong Kong), and continue from there. Scheduled return flights starting from **New York** or **Los Angeles** can dip under US$600 if you're in luck (though be prepared to pay double this), while fares bottom out at around CAN$900 from **Vancouver** and CAN$1300 from **Toronto** (again, it's usually double).

Note that some routes require an **overnight stay** in another city, and often a hotel room will be included in your fare – ask the airline and shop around, since travel agents' policies on this vary. Even when an overnight stay is not required, going to Vietnam can be a great excuse for a stopover somewhere: many airlines will allow you one free stopover in either direction.

Flights from Australia and New Zealand

Direct flights between **Australia** and Vietnam are in surprisingly poor supply, with Vietnam Airlines (ⓦvietnamairlines.com) operating routes from Ho Chi Minh City to Melbourne and Sydney (both 8–9hr). One reason for the dearth of direct services has been the profusion of far cheaper alternate routes, making use of the region's many budget airlines – you can fly AirAsia (ⓦairasia.com), Cebu Pacific (ⓦcebupacificair.com) or Jetstar (ⓦjetstar .com) all the way via Southeast Asia, with one-way prices starting at around AUS$200. The resulting competition means that you can often get decent deals on "proper" airlines, with tickets on Malaysia Airlines (ⓦmalaysiaairlines.com), Singapore Airlines (ⓦsingaporeair.com) and Thai Airways (ⓦthaiair ways.com) via Bangkok all costing AUS$1100–1500 if you book at the right time of year.

There are no direct flights from **New Zealand**, and budget-airline options are a little more restrictive; AirAsia (ⓦairasia.com) fly from Auckland to Kuala Lumpur and thence to Vietnam (from as little as NZ$350 one-way), but you'll often get cheap-as routings via Australia too. As for flag carriers, low-season fares with Malaysia Airlines, Thai Airways, Qantas (ⓦqantas.com) and Singapore Airlines all start at around NZ$1500–2200 return.

Flights from neighbouring countries

Regional air connections are becoming better and better – you can fly from many cities in

Cambodia, **Laos**, **Malaysia** and **Thailand**, while options are also profuse from **South Korea**, **Japan** and mainland **China**. Budget options are increasing every year: from **Singapore** you can choose from Jetstar (ⓦjetstar.com), Scoot (ⓦflyscoot.com), Silk Air (ⓦsilkair.com) and Vietjet Air (ⓦvietjetair.com), and from Bangkok you can try AirAsia (ⓦairasia.com), Jetstar, Lion Air (ⓦlionairthai.com), Nok Air (ⓦnokair.com) or Vietjet – and there are also plenty of options from Kuala Lumpur. As with all discount airlines, prices depend on availability, so the earlier you book the better – prices can start as low as US$20. Otherwise, you're dependent on flag carriers such as Cambodia Angkor Air (ⓦcambodiaangkorair.com) and Lao Airlines (ⓦlaoairlines.com), though Vietnam Airlines (ⓦvietnamairlines.com) occasionally offers some competitive deals.

Overland

It's simple to enter Vietnam **overland** from China, Laos or Cambodia, and this option means you can see more of the region than you would if you simply jetted in.

At the time of research, the border in **China** was open to foreigners at Lao Cai (see p.398), Thanh Thuy near Ha Giang (see p.417), Dong Dang near Lang Son (see p.427) and Mong Cai (see p.333). Direct train services to Hanoi (39hr) leave Beijing on Thursdays and Sundays at 3.45pm, though these days it's easy to get a high-speed train from more or less anywhere in China to the southern city of Nanning, and then catch the daily 6.10pm service to Hanoi (11hr). Note that only soft-sleeper tickets are available on these cross-border trains, and that if travelling to China from Vietnam you can board the train only in Hanoi. Always bring your passport when buying tickets.

From **Laos**, six border crossings are currently open to foreigners: Lao Bao (see p.301), the easiest and most popular, some 80km west of Dong Ha; Cau Treo and Nam Can, to the north and northwest of Vinh (see p.313); Na Meo, northwest of Thanh Hoa (though this isn't worth the hassle); Tay Trang, just west of Dien Bien Phu (see p.410); and Bo Y, northwest of Kon Tum (see p.196). While it's perfectly possible – and cheaper – to use local buses to and from the borders, international bus services also run from Savannakhet and Vientiane to Hanoi, Dong Ha, Vinh, Da Nang and other destinations in Vietnam;

these direct services are recommended, as reports of extortion or unnecessary difficulties continue to come in from those crossing independently.

From **Cambodia** you can travel by air-conditioned bus from Phnom Penh straight through to Ho Chi Minh City, via the Moc Bai crossing. Cheaper operators tend to use old buses and usually get you to switch at the border. Many tour companies in Phnom Penh or Ho Chi Minh City will be able to organize boat-plus-bus services, which are a fun way to make the trip (see p.88). There are two crossings in the Mekong Delta area – Vinh Xuong and Tinh Bien – which are respectively 30km north and 25km west of Chau Doc. There are also border crossings at Xa Xia, on the coast west of the delta, which is useful if you are heading to or from Kampot, Kep or Sihanoukville on the Cambodian coast, and at Le Thanh in the central highlands, making it possible to go from Banlung in northeast Cambodia straight through to Pleiku.

As long as you have a valid **visa**, crossing these borders is generally not a problem, though you may still find the odd Vietnamese immigration official who tries to charge a "processing fee" (typically $1); on the Cambodian side, this bribe is usually around $5. Most border gates are open from around 7am to 5pm, and they may close for an hour over lunch.

SPECIALIST TOUR OPERATORS ABROAD
WORLDWIDE
Abercrombie & Kent UK ☎ 01242 547 760, US ☎ 1 800 554 7016, Australia ☎ 1300 797 010; W abercrombiekent.co.uk. Luxury tour specialist; trips featuring Vietnam come as part of a greater trip through Indochina.

Backyard Travel International freephone ☎ 800 2225 9273, W backyardtravel.com. Though based in Bangkok, these Asia specialists certainly know the ropes in Vietnam, with tours focusing on everything from Hanoi street food and cultural experiences to "the footsteps of Marguerite Duras" (see p.129), as well as the usual pan-country trips.

Intrepid Travel UK ☎ 0808 274 5111, US ☎ 1 800 970 7299, Australia ☎ 1300 364 512, New Zealand ☎ 0800 600 610; W intrepidtravel.com. Affordable small-group trips, usually focusing on low-impact, cross-cultural contact. Tours can cover bits of Vietnam, the whole country or wider Indochina.

Peregrine Adventures UK ☎ 0845 004 0673, Australia ☎ 3 8601 4444; W peregrineadventures.com. Good local knowledge for an outfit that goes everywhere. Most tours are small-group and adventure-based, often with a focus on trekking, cycling or even food.

STA Travel UK ☎ 0800 819 9339, US ☎ 1 800 781 4040, Australia ☎ 134 782, New Zealand ☎ 0800 474 400, South Africa ☎ 0861 781 781; W statravel.com. Worldwide specialists in independent travel, student IDs, travel insurance, car rental, rail passes and more. Good discounts for students and under-26s.

World Expeditions UK ☎ 020 8545 9030, US & Canada ☎ 1 800 567 2216, Australia ☎ 1300 720 000, New Zealand ☎ 0800 350 354; W worldexpeditions.com. Adventure company with a wide variety of programmes, including cycle tours from Hue to Ho Chi Minh City, and kayaking in Ha Long Bay. Also offers community project trips, where participants help renovate a local school, for example, and arrange charity challenges.

AUSTRALIA AND NEW ZEALAND
Griswalds Vietnamese Vacations Australia ☎ 02 9430 6426, W vietnamvacations.com.au. Long-running Vietnam specialist offering small-group, tailor-made itineraries – the website still looks a bit mid-1990s, but the tours are top notch.

UK AND IRELAND
Exodus UK ☎ 0845 287 7644, W exodus.co.uk. Adventure-tour operator taking small groups on specialist programmes that take in trekking, biking, kayaking and cultural trips.

G Adventures UK ☎ 0344 272 2060, W gadventures.co.uk. There are plenty of cross-Vietnam and wider Indochina tours on offer from this well-regarded operator – some include hiking, biking and kayaking.

Imaginative Traveller UK ☎ 0845 287 2855, W imaginative-traveller.com. Affordable, small-group adventure tours from a responsible travel operator – their food-based tours are particularly interesting.

InsideVietnam UK ☎ 0117 370 9758, W insideasiatours.com. Well-run small-group or tailored individual packages from an operator now expanding its scope across Asia. Their ten-night highlights tour is a popular option.

Regent Holidays UK ☎ 020 3131 6202, W regent-holidays .co.uk. Any operators that can organize good tours to North Korea will surely find Vietnam a piece of cake. Good-value, tailor-made tours available, as well as off-the-shelf itineraries like the twelve-day "Highlights of Vietnam" trip.

US AND CANADA
Artisans of Leisure ☎ 1 800 214 8144, W artisansofleisure.com. Luxury private and individually tailored tours, which often include cooking classes and spa therapy sessions.

Backroads ☎ 1 800 462 2848, W backroads.com. Cycling and hiking linking Vietnam and Cambodia, with the emphasis on going at your own pace.

Journeys International ☎ 1 800 255 8735, W journeys international.com. Prestigious, award-winning operator focusing on ecotourism and small-group trips.

VeloAsia ☎ 1 888 681 0808, W veloasia.com. Indochina specialist with a range of organized and tailor-made cycling adventure tours. Their famed 12-day "Highlights of Vietnam" tour connects Hanoi and Ho Chi Minh City.

Visas and entry requirements

Most foreign nationals need a **visa** to enter Vietnam – citizens of some Asian and Nordic nations get 15–30 days visa-free, and from 2016 the government allowed the same of passport-holders from the UK, France, Germany, Italy and Spain (at the time of research this was going to last until mid-2018, but may be extended or reintroduced at a later date).

Tourist visas are generally valid for thirty days from your specified arrival date, though longer durations can be arranged; visitors can **make their applications** in any Vietnamese embassy or consulate, or through specialist visa or tour agents, but these days it's more convenient for most people to get their "visa on arrival" online. If you apply in person at an embassy or consulate, processing normally takes around a week, though many embassies also offer a more expensive "express" service. By contrast, the normal service for an online visa is just three working days, and some agencies even quote fees for two working hours.

Applying through an embassy, consulate or travel agency

Standard visas cost $25–90, depending on where you apply (Bangkok, Phnom Penh and Jakarta are at the cheap and speedy end of the spectrum). Three-month visas are also available for $100 to $145; both types take three to ten days to process, though some agencies and embassies (see opposite) offer an express one-day service.

To apply for **tourist visas**, you have to submit an application form with one or two passport-sized photographs (procedures vary) and the fee. The visa shows specific start and end dates indicating the period of validity within which you can enter and leave the country. The visa is valid for entry via Hanoi, Ho Chi Minh City and Da Nang international airports and any of Vietnam's land borders open to foreigners (see p.26).

Business visas are valid for one month upwards and can be issued for multiple entry, though you'll need a sponsoring office in Vietnam to underwrite your application.

One-year **student visas** are relatively easy to get hold of; for example, if you enrol on a Vietnamese language course at one of the universities, though you'll be required to attend a minimum number of classes per week to qualify. It's easiest to arrange it in advance, but you can enter Vietnam on a tourist visa and apply for student status later – the only downside is that you may have to leave the country in order to get the visa stamp.

Special circumstances affect **overseas Vietnamese** holding a foreign passport: check with the Vietnamese embassy in your country of residence for details.

Applying for a visa on arrival

There are several **websites** offering Vietnamese visa online services, and most, including ⓦ vietnamvisacenter.org, are reliable. Though in reality more "pre-arranged" than "on arrival", they can be helpful for people with no Vietnamese consulate in their home country, or those strapped for time – note that they can only be picked up at Hanoi, Ho Chi Minh City or Da Nang airports, not at land border crossings. **Prices** start at US$20 plus a US$25 "stamping fee" for a one-month, single-entry visa, rising to US$70 plus US$50 stamping fee for a three-month, multiple-entry one. On receipt of your fee, you'll be sent an **approval letter** to print out and present to immigration on arrival, along with an application form (also available at airport desks), photographs (they'll take one at the airport for around US$10) and the stamping fee. The process is very efficient and requires only a short wait on arrival; if you follow this route, look out for the **visa on arrival desk** at the airport before you pass through immigration.

Visa extensions

Thirty-day extensions can be arranged at travel agencies in Hanoi, Ho Chi Minh City, Nha Trang, Da Nang, Hue and Hoi An. In general they take three days to process and cost from US$25 for the first one-month extension; since it's now easy to apply for a three-month visa in the first place, few visitors require this service.

Holders of **business visas** can apply for an extension only through the office that sponsored their original visa, backed up with reasons as to why an extension is necessary.

Overstaying your visa will result in a fine of US$10–25 per day, and is not recommended – border staff at the airport may well insist that you head back into whichever city you're closest to, in order to pay the fine at a dedicated immigration office.

Vietnamese embassies and consulates

A full list of Vietnamese embassies and consulates is available at ⓦ vietnamtourism.com.

Australia Timbarra Crescent, O'Malley, Canberra, ACT 2606 ☎ 02 6286 6059, ⓦ vietnamembassy.org.au; Suite 205, Level 2 Edgecliff Centre, 202–233 New South Head Rd, Edgecliff, Sydney, NSW 2027 ☎ 02 9327 1912.

Cambodia 440a Monivong Blvd, Phnom Penh ☎ 023 726 274; Sihanoukville ☎ 034 934 039; Road No.3, Battambang ☎ 053 952 894.

Canada 55 Mackay St, Ottawa K1M 2B2 ☎ 613 236 0772, ⓦ vietnamembassy.ca.

China 32 Guanghua Lu, Chaoyang, Beijing ☎ 10 6532 1155; 2F B Building North, Landmark Hotel, Qiaoguang Rd, Guangzhou ☎ 20 8330 5916; 15F Great Smart Tower, 230 Wanchai Rd, Hong Kong ☎ 852 2835 9318; 507 Hong Ta Mansion, 155 Beijing Rd, Kunming 65001 ☎ 871 351 5889.

Laos 23 Singha Rd, Vientiane ☎ 021 413 400; 31 Ban Pha Bat, Pakse ☎ 031 212 827; 118 Sisavangvong Rd, Savannakhet ☎ 06 212 418.

Malaysia 4 Persiaran Stonor, 50450 Kuala Lumpur ☎ 03 2148 4036.

New Zealand Level 21, Grand Plimmer Tower, 2 Gilmer Terrace, Wellington ☎ 04 473 5912, ⓦ vnembassy-wellington.mofa.gov.vn.

Singapore 10 Leedon Park, Singapore 267887 ☎ 06 462 5938.

Thailand 83/1 Wireless Rd, Bangkok 10330 ☎ 02 251 5836; 65/6 Chatapadung, Khonkaen 40000 ☎ 043 242 190.

UK 12–14 Victoria Rd, London W8 5RD ☎ 020 7937 1912, ⓦ vietnamembassy.org.uk.

US 1233 20th St NW, Suite 400, Washington DC 20036 ☎ 202 861 0737, ⓦ vietnamembassy-usa.org; 1700 California St, Suite 430, San Francisco, CA 94109 ☎ 415 922 1707, ⓦ vietnamconsulate-sf.org.

Getting around

Though still a little rough around the edges, Vietnam's transport network is continuing to improve. Most travel takes place on the roads, which are largely of decent quality surface-wise, though it must be said that almost every vehicle on them is seemingly overtaking or being overtaken at any given point in time – accidents are common.

The vehicles themselves are in pretty good condition, however, with air-conditioned coaches ferrying tourists (and an increasing number of locals) up and down Highway 1 – which is not really a highway at all, but a desperately narrow and shockingly busy thoroughfare that runs from Hanoi to Ho Chi Minh City, passing through Hue, Da Nang and Nha Trang en route. Trains run alongside Highway 1, and their sleeper berths are far more comfortable than buses for longer journeys. Lastly, the domestic flight network continues to evolve, and the cheap, comfortable services may save you days' worth of travel by road or rail.

By plane

Flying comes into its own on longer journeys, and can save you precious hours or even days – the two-hour journey between **Hanoi** and **Ho Chi Minh City**, for instance, compares favourably with the two days you would spend on the train, and prices are often lower. Other useful, regular services from Hanoi and Ho Chi Minh City fly to Hue, Da Nang, Nha Trang and Phu Quoc Island, and there are now even some direct flights not involving the two main cities at all – Hue, for example, has connections with Da Lat and Nha Trang, while Da Nang has flights to and from Buon Ma Thuot, Pleiku, Hai Phong and Nha Trang. Note that you'll need your passport with you when taking internal flights.

The Vietnamese national carrier Vietnam Airlines (ⓦ vietnamairlines.com) operates a reasonably cheap, efficient and comprehensive network of domestic flights, with both of the main hubs – Ho Chi Minh City and Hanoi – linked to almost all major cities and destinations across Vietnam, bar the closest ones accessible to each by bus or train. Competition is keeping prices low on these domestic services, as a number of **budget carriers** have entered the arena, and an ever-growing middle-class is increasing demand across the board year-on-year – Jetstar (ⓦ jetstar.com) now rivals Vietnam Airlines for local coverage, as does Vietjet Air (ⓦ vietjetair.com). Lastly, Vasco (ⓦ vasco.com.vn) also flies from Ho Chi Minh City to Con Dao and Ca Mau, but it's better to book through its codeshare partner Vietnam Airlines.

By rail

Given the amazing prices and frequencies of the various bus services on offer, few travellers opt for the train. However, **rail journeys** are still well worth considering for several reasons. Firstly, major roads tend to be lined in their entirety with ramshackle cafés, petrol pumps, snack stands and mobile phone shops, and if you take the train you'll avoid these and actually see a bit of the countryside, since the tracks don't always follow the roads. Secondly, you'll be involved in far fewer near-collisions with trucks, motorbikes and dogs. Thirdly, you're almost guaranteed to get talking to a bunch of friendly locals.

Vietnam Railways (Ⓦdsvn.vn) runs a single-track **train network** comprising more than 2500km of line, stretching from Ho Chi Minh City all the way to the Chinese border. Much of it dates back to the colonial period, and though it's gradually being upgraded, most of the services are still relatively slow. Keep a particularly close eye on your belongings on the trains, be especially vigilant when the train stops at stations, ensure your money belt is safely tucked under your clothes before going to sleep, and check that your luggage is safely stowed.

The most **popular routes** with tourists are the shuttle from Da Nang to Hue (2–3hr) – which provides a picturesque yet acceptably short sampler of Vietnamese rail travel – and the overnighters from Hue to Hanoi (11–16hr) and from Hanoi up to Lao Cai (for Sa Pa; 8–9hr).

Services

The country's **main rail line** shadows Highway 1 on its way from Ho Chi Minh City to Hanoi, passing through Nha Trang, Da Nang and Hue en route. From Hanoi, three branch lines then strike out towards the northern coast and Chinese border. One line traces the Red River northwest to **Lao Cai**, just an hour by bus from Sa Pa and also the site of a border crossing into China's Yunnan province; the rail on the Chinese side resumed service in 2014 after many years in disrepair, and though no trains actually cross the border here, taxis bridge the connection between the Chinese and Vietnamese networks. Another rail spur runs north to **Dong Dang**; this is the route taken by twice-weekly trains linking Hanoi and Beijing, though there are also daily services between Hanoi and Nanning. The third branch, a shorter spur, links the capital with **Haiphong**, and this route is good if you're heading to or from Ha Long Bay.

There are over a dozen services heading daily between Hanoi and Ho Chi Minh City (taking 30–40hr), but most travellers use the four main "**Reunification Express**" services (officially numbered SE1 to SE8, with even and odd numbers heading north and south respectively). Note that some roll into Hanoi and Ho Chi Minh City at wretchedly early times in the morning, so pay attention when booking; the fantastic Seat 61 website (Ⓦseat61.com) keeps their Vietnam train schedule information easy-to-read and up-to-date.

On the **northern lines**, three trains per day make the run from Hanoi to Haiphong (2hr 30min) and two go to Dong Dang (4hr 30min); there are also two night trains and a day service to Lao Cai (8–10hr). For those hoping to take the **southern lines**, there are two morning services from Ho Chi Minh City to Phan Thiet (3hr 30min), which is within easy moto-taxi distance of Mui Ne.

Trains usually leave on schedule from their departure points, and though delays can stack up further down the line, they're rarely too severe – though Tet holidays are a notable exception to this rule.

Classes

When it comes to choosing which class to travel in, you may have a choice of seats or sleepers, but it's usually wise to aim high. At the bottom of the scale are **hard seats**, which are just as it sounds though bearable for shorter journeys; these filthy carriages, in which one can actually feel like a caged animal, are slowly being phased out. **Soft seats** offer more comfort and are now almost entirely set in air-conditioned carriages, some of which are double-decker; the newer berths sometimes have flatscreen TVs operating at an ear-splitting volume.

On overnight journeys, you'd be well advised to invest in a berth of some description. The **hard-berth** compartments are quite comfortable and have six bunks, three on either side – the cramped top ones are the cheapest, and the bottom ones are the priciest. Linen is provided, though you may have to ask for fresh linen if you're joining a service that started elsewhere. Roomier **soft-berth** compartments, containing only four bunks, are always comfortable, particularly on the routes numbered SE1 to SE4. **"Luxury" carriages** are also still attached to some regular services between Hanoi and Da Nang, and their fancier fittings and comfier beds make them worth the splurge if you're heading on one of the night routes from Hanoi to Lao Cai (for Sa Pa).

Facilities

Most trains now have **air-conditioning**, and are theoretically **non-smoking**; the rules are obeyed, by and large, in the sleeper rooms, though in hard-seat class even the guards may be puffing away.

All train carriages have **toilets**, which are usually fine, if a little grubby; many are squat in nature, and these are far more likely to be dirty and devoid of paper or running water. You'll find proper sit-down toilets in the sleeper carriages, which are comparatively clean.

Simple **meals** are often included in the price of the ticket, but you might want to stock up with goodies of your own. You'll also have plenty of opportunities to buy snacks from the carts that ply the aisles, and there are kiosks selling the same at more or less every station.

Tickets

It's generally wise to **book ahead** – the further ahead the better – especially if you intend to travel at the weekend or during the holiday periods (when the lower sleeper berths are often sold as six seats, resulting in chaos). Sleeping compartments should be booked at least a day or two before departure, and even further ahead for soft-sleeper berths on the Hanoi–Hue and Hanoi–Lao Cai routes. It's not possible to buy through tickets and break your journey en route; each journey requires you to buy a separate ticket from the point of departure. Getting tickets at the station is usually pretty painless, and in theory it's now possible to book on the national rail booking site (Ⓦdsvn.vn) – in practice, there have been substantial teething problems with international card payments, so it's often still best to book through your hotel or a travel agency for a fee (sometimes as low as 50,000đ, though often much more).

Fares, which have actually decreased in recent years, vary according to the class of travel and the train you take; as a rule of thumb, the faster the train, the more expensive it is. Prices are always quoted in dong, and on the most expensive services from Hanoi to Ho Chi Minh City you'll pay around 1,400,000đ for a soft-sleeper berth, 1,250,000đ for a hard sleeper, 1,000,000đ for a soft seat or 650,000đ for a hard seat. The equivalent fares for Hanoi to Hue are from 800,000đ down to 360,000đ. Prices to Lao Cai generally range from 140,000đ for a hard seat on the day train to 385,000đ for a soft sleeper.

By bus

Vietnam was once famed for bus drivers ripping off foreigners and cramming as many bodies as possible into their vehicles, but almost all routes now have tickets with fixed prices, and the advent of luxury **open-tour buses** on the main tourist trail saw comfort levels rocket – and the birth of similar services now used by locals themselves. On the longer stretches, many buses are **sleeper-berth** for their whole length, though getting forty winks can be tough – the nature of local roads means that emergency stops are common, and Vietnamese drivers use their horn liberally, which can become grating very quickly on a long journey. **Security** remains an important consideration – never fall asleep with your bag uncovered, and never leave your belongings unattended.

Interestingly, many travellers use buses to get around Vietnam – but never actually see a bus station. This is because a fair chunk of tourist journeys are made on the private open-tour buses, which usually operate not from stations but the offices of their respective companies. The term comes from the fact that such companies typically sell through-tickets between Ho Chi Minh City and Hanoi, with customers free to stop off for as long as they like at the main points en route – Da Lat, Mui Ne, Nha Trang, Hoi An, Da Nang, Hue and Ninh Binh. There are drawbacks to doing this, though (see box, p.32). Away from these private affairs, **national bus services** link all major cities in Vietnam, and most minor towns too.

Private buses

On the whole, buses run by **private operators** (including the "open-tour" variety) are a reasonably comfortable way to get around Vietnam: they have air-conditioning, limited seating and fixed time-tables, which instantly gives them the edge over the national services. In addition, the fact that they don't stop as much en route makes them faster too, and fierce competition keeps prices low. Open-tour buses also call at occasional **tourist sights**, such as the Marble Mountains and Lang Co, which can save considerable time and money when compared with doing the same thing independently. Buses are usually quite decent, but don't expect too much legroom, or any on-board toilets – some of the more expensive services have them, but the vast majority will pull in every few hours for a combined loo-and-snack break. This tends to be at mediocre and overpriced restaurants; it's a good idea to arm yourself with snacks before your journey. Sometimes you'll get free bottles of water when boarding, but don't count on it.

Services tend to run on time, and some longer trips take place overnight. Most of the overnight buses are filled with **sleeper berths**, which sound nice and comfortable at first, though you should keep in mind that this is still Vietnam, the land of seemingly continuous overtaking – don't expect to get too much sleep, especially if you're at the front of the bus, near the horn. Also note that some operators have very poor standards of service, and that some are more reliable than others – Futa (Ⓦfutabus.vn) and Mai Linh (Ⓦmailinhexpress.vn) both have good reputations and are recommended.

Ticket prices (always quoted in dong) vary widely depending on which company you choose, though they're usually in the region of 50,000₫ per hour for point-to-point journeys. Many companies run services from their own dedicated terminals, and some (such as the aforementioned Futa) offer free pick-up from and drop-off to your hotel. In such instances, the reception desk at your accommodation can be an invaluable resource, since they're usually able to confirm your ticket for free by phone (you'll pay at the terminal), and arrange a pick-up time.

For open-tour tickets, you'll pay only once, the price (usually quoted in dollars) dependent on your beginning and end points, and occasionally also on how many stops you'd like to make en route; sample prices are US$45 and up from Ho Chi Minh City to Hanoi, US$32 from Ho Chi Minh City to Hue, and US$6 from Hue to Hoi An. You can either make firm bookings at the outset or opt for an open-dated ticket for greater flexibility, in which case you may need to book your onward travel one or two days in advance to be sure of a seat. Alternatively, you can buy separate tickets as you go along, which is recommended (see box below). Each main town on the itinerary has an agent (one for each operator) where you can buy tickets and make onward reservations. To avoid being sold **fake tickets** or paying over the odds, it's best to buy direct from the relevant agent rather than from hotels, restaurants or unrelated tour companies.

State-run buses

On the national bus network, the government has been busy upgrading **state buses**, replacing the rickety old vehicles with air-conditioned models. Progress can still be agonizingly slow, with buses stopping frequently to pick up passengers or have meal breaks.

Tickets are bought at bus stations, where **fares** are clearly indicated above the ticket windows. Prices are usually also marked on the tickets themselves, though there are still occasional cases of tourists being overcharged, particularly in more rural destinations such as those from the Lao border. Prices vary, but are usually around sixty percent of the private-company prices (see opposite), or around 30,000₫ per hour travelled. For long journeys, it's best to buy your ticket a day in advance since many routes are heavily over-subscribed.

Privately owned **minibuses** compete with public buses on most routes; they sometimes share the local bus station, or simply congregate on the roadside in the centre of a town. You can also flag them down on the road. If anything, they squeeze in even more people per square foot than ordinary buses, and often drive interminably around town, touting for passengers. On the other hand, they do at least run throughout the day, and serve some routes not covered by public services. Such services are ticketless, so try to find what the correct fare should be and agree a price before boarding – having the right change will also come in handy. You may also find yourself dumped at the side of the road before reaching your destination, and having to cram onto the next passing service.

Most major cities have their own **local bus networks**, though prices and standards vary. Try to ascertain the correct price and have the exact money ready before boarding, lest unscrupulous fare collectors attempt to take advantage of your captive position.

By boat

As you'd expect of a country with such a lengthy coastline, there are plenty of **boat services** for you to take advantage of in Vietnam – and they're often the best (or at least the most enjoyable) way to access places such as Ha Long Bay or Phu Quoc Island.

Boat tours

A tour around Ha Long Bay is highly recommended – this is not only one of Vietnam's most enjoyable

---

THE DOWNSIDE OF OPEN-TOUR THROUGH TICKETS

Many travellers opt for one-way **through tickets** with one of the umpteen open-tour companies, which enable you to traverse the whole country with just one ticket. However, this course of action is not without its drawbacks: if you lose your ticket, there's no refund; if you choose a bad company, you'll be saddled with them the whole way; and you'll be obliged to stick to your chosen company's daily schedule. Buying separate tickets en route will only cost a little more (if anything at all), yet will give you far more freedom. Another downside to open-tour buses is that you'll be encouraged to book into the company's own or affiliated hotels (usually right next to the drop-off point), though there's nothing to stop you staying elsewhere.

trips (see box, p.337), but a highlight of Southeast Asia in general. These tours can be made on "junks", which approximate the traditional designs of yore, or alternatively on luxuriant cruise vessels; there are also some (occasionally debauched) services aimed at backpackers. Cruise ships also navigate the larger arms of the Mekong Delta, though prices can be stratospheric – hundreds of dollars per night.

Ferries

Scheduled **ferries** sail year-round (weather permitting) to the major islands off Vietnam's coastline, including Phu Quoc, Cat Ba and Con Dao. In addition, ferry and **hydrofoil** services run from Haiphong to Cat Ba, and there are also hydrofoils from Ho Chi Minh City to Vung Tau, and from Ha Long City to Mong Cai and Bai Tu Long. Though they are gradually being replaced by gargantuan bridges, a few **river ferries** still haul themselves from bank to bank of the various strands of the Mekong.

Conditions on board vary widely, but Vietnam has, in general, higher safety and comfort standards in these regards than most of its neighbours. The Mekong Delta barges are an exception, as they're essentially just floating chunks of metal with space for vehicles and gantries for passengers; the hydrofoil services, on the other hand, can be quite comfortable, with small snack-bars, cushioned seating and TV programmes to enjoy (or endure).

By car

Self-drive in Vietnam is not yet a viable option for tourists and other short-term visitors. However, it's easy to hire a car, jeep or minibus **with driver** from the same companies, agencies and tourist offices that arrange tours. This can be quite an economical means of transport if you are travelling in a group. Moreover, it means you can plan a trip to your own tastes, rather than having to follow a tour company's itinerary.

Prices vary wildly so it pays to shop around, but expect to pay in the region of US$60 per day for a car, and US$110 per day for a jeep or other 4WD, depending on the vehicle's size, age and level of comfort; Da Lat usually has the best (and cheapest) selection of jeeps. When negotiating the price, it's important to clarify exactly who is liable for what. Things to check include who pays for the driver's accommodation and meals, fuel, road and ferry tolls, parking fees and repairs, and what happens in the case of a major breakdown. There should then be some sort of contract to sign showing all the details, including an agreed itinerary, especially if you are renting for more than a day – make sure the driver is given a copy in Vietnamese. In some cases you'll have to settle up in advance, though, if possible, it's best if you can arrange to pay roughly half before and the balance at the end.

By motorbike

Motorbike rental is possible in most towns and cities regularly frequented by tourists, and pottering around on one can be an enjoyable and time-efficient method of sightseeing. Lured by the prospect of **independent travel** at relatively low cost, some tourists cruise the countryside on motorbikes, but inexperienced bikers would do well to think very hard before undertaking any long-distance biking: the appalling road discipline of most Vietnamese drivers means that the risk of an **accident** is very real, with potentially dire consequences should it happen in a remote area. Well-equipped hospitals are few and far between outside the major centres, and there'll probably be no ambulance service.

On the other hand, many people ride around with no problems and thoroughly recommend it for both day-trips and touring. The **best routes** can be found in the northern mountains, the central highlands and around the Mekong Delta, while the Ho Chi Minh Highway offers pristine tarmac plus wonderful scenery. Some also do the long haul up Highway 1 from Ho Chi Minh City to Hanoi (or vice versa), a journey of around two weeks, averaging a leisurely 150km per day.

Rental and purchase

There's no shortage of motorbikes **for rent** in Vietnam's major tourist centres; the average rate is 150,000–200,000đ, with discounts for longer periods. You'll sometimes be asked to pay in advance, sign a rental contract and/or leave some form of ID (a photocopy of your passport should suffice). If you're renting for a week or more, you may be asked to leave a deposit – often the bike's value in dollars, though it might also be your air ticket or departure card. In the vast majority of cases, this shouldn't be a problem.

Although it's technically illegal for non-residents to own a vehicle, there's a small trade in **second-hand motorbikes** in the two main cities – look at the noticeboards in hotels, travellers' cafés and tour agents for adverts. So far the police have ignored the practice, but check the latest situation before committing yourself. The bike of choice is usually a **Minsk 125cc**, particularly for the mountains – it's sturdy, not too expensive, and the easiest to get repaired outside the main cities.

Practicalities

Whether you're renting or buying, remember to check everything over carefully, especially brakes, lights and horn. Wearing a **helmet** is now a legal requirement, and most rental outlets have helmets you can borrow, sometimes for a small charge, though they may not afford much protection in the event of a crash.

Note that international driving licences are not valid in Vietnam, but you will need your home **driving licence** and bike registration papers. You also need at least third-party **insurance**, which is available (with the aforementioned documentation) at Bao Viet insurance offices.

Though **road conditions** have improved remarkably in recent years, off the main highways they can still be highly erratic, with pristine asphalt followed by stretches of spine-jarring potholes, and plenty of loose gravel on the sides of the road. **Repair shops** are fairly ubiquitous – ask for *sua chua xe may* (motorbike repairs) – but you should still carry at least a puncture-repair kit, pump and spare spark plug. **Fuel** (*xang*) is cheap and widely available at the roadsides, often from bottles. If you want to get off the main highways, it really pays to take a guide; at the very least, try to travel in the company of one or more other bikes in case one of you gets into trouble.

By bicycle

Cycling is an excellent way of sightseeing around towns, and you shouldn't have to pay more than 50,000đ per day for the privilege, even outside the main tourist centres.

While you can now buy decent Japanese-made bikes in Vietnam, if you decide on a **long-distance cycling** holiday, you should really bring your own bike with you, not forgetting all the necessary spares and tools. Hardy **mountain bikes** cope best with the country's variable surfaces, though tourers and hybrids are fine on the main roads. Bring your own helmet and a good loud bell; a rear-view mirror also comes in handy.

When it all gets too much, or you want to skip between towns, you can always put your bike on a train (though not on all services – check when buying your ticket) for a small fee; take it to the station well ahead of time, where it will be packed and placed in the luggage van. Some open-tour buses will also take bikes – it's free if it goes in the luggage hold (packed up), otherwise you'll have to pay for an extra seat.

If you want to see Vietnam from the saddle, but don't fancy going it alone, note that there are several companies that offer specialist **cycling tours**. In addition to a few of the international tour operators (see p.27), there are local outfits such as Phat Tire (🌐 phattireventures.com).

RULES OF THE ROAD

There's no discernible method to the madness that passes as the **traffic** system in Vietnam, so it's extremely important that you don't stray out onto the roads unless you feel completely confident about doing so. The theory is that you **drive on the right**, though in practice motorists and cyclists swoop, swerve and dodge wherever they want, using their **horn** as a surrogate indicator and brake. Unless otherwise stated, the **speed limit** is 60kph on highways and 40kph or less in towns.

Right of way invariably goes to the biggest vehicles on the road, which means that motorbikes and bicycles are regularly forced off the highway by thundering trucks or buses; note that overtaking vehicles assume you'll pull over onto the hard shoulder to avoid them. It's wise to use your horn to its maximum and also to avoid being on the road after dark, since many vehicles either don't have functioning headlights or simply don't bother to turn them on. In addition, contrary to unwritten rules in many countries, flashing headlights in Vietnam don't mean "after you" – it's more like "there's no way on earth that I'm stopping".

On the whole the **police** seem to leave foreign riders well alone, and the best policy at roadside checkpoints is just to drive by slowly. However, if you are involved in an **accident** and it was deemed to be your fault, the penalties can involve fairly major fines.

When **parking** your bike, it's advisable to leave it in a parking compound (*gui xe*) – the going rate is from 5000đ for a motorbike and 2000đ for a bicycle – or pay for someone to keep an eye on it. If not, you run the risk of it being tampered with.

Organized tours

Ever-increasing numbers of tourists are seeing Vietnam through the window of a minibus on **organized tours**. Ranging from one-day jaunts to two- or three-week trawls across the country, tours are ideal if you want to acquaint yourself speedily with the highlights of Vietnam, and they can also work out much cheaper than car rental. On the other hand, by relying on tours you'll have little chance to really get to grips with the country and its people, or to enjoy things at your leisure.

Hordes of state-owned and private **tour companies** compete for business – see our lists of well-established agents in Ho Chi Minh City (see p.88) and Hanoi (see p.367). While a few companies now put together more innovative itineraries, the vast majority offer very similar tours. However, it pays to shop around since **prices** vary wildly, depending on how many people there are in a group, the standard of transport, meals and accommodation, whether entry fees are included and so forth.

You'll also need to check carefully that the operator is financially sound, reliable and can deliver what is promised – *never* deal with a company that demands cash upfront or refuses to accept payment by credit card, and get references if you can. Check exactly what is included in the price, the maximum number of people on the trip and whether your group will be amalgamated with others if you don't want to be travelling around in a great horde. Bear in mind, as well, that you're far better off dealing directly with the company organizing the tour, rather than going through a hotel or other intermediary. Not only are you more likely to get accurate information about the details of the tour, but you'll also be in a much stronger position should you have cause for complaint.

The other alternative is to set up your own **custom-made tour** by gathering together a group and renting a car, jeep or minibus plus driver (see p.33).

Local transport

In a country with a population so adept at making do with limited resources, it isn't surprising to see locals getting from A to B using wildly diverse types of **local transport**. While taxis are increasingly ubiquitous and a number of cities now boast reasonable bus services, elsewhere you'll be reliant on a host of two- and three-wheeled vehicles for getting around.

Xe om

Most common by far are the motorbike taxis known as **xe om**. In the cities you'll rarely be able to walk twenty yards without being offered a ride; since xe om are unregulated and the profession only requires a motorbike (which almost all Vietnamese have anyway), the number you'll see touting for custom tends to oscillate with the prevailing rate of employment. Prices tend to start at around 10,000đ for very short runs, though this goes up after dark (as does the possibility of extortion – though the vast majority of drivers are fine). At all times the rules of bargaining apply: when haggling, ensure you know which currency you are dealing in (five fingers held up, for instance, could mean 5000đ, 50,000đ or US$5), and whether you're negotiating for a single or return trip, and for one passenger or two – it's always best to write the figures down. Should a difference of opinion emerge at the end of a ride, having the exact fare ready to press into an argumentative driver's hand can sometimes resolve matters.

Cyclos

Xe om have almost entirely replaced the **cyclo**, that quintessential Vietnamese mode of transport. These three-wheeled rickshaws comprise a "bucket" seat attached to the front of a bicycle that can carry one person, or two people at a push, and are now only really found in tourist areas (though locals use them just as much as foreigners). Prices vary by area, and there are continuous stories of cyclo drivers charging outrageous sums for their services, so to avoid getting badly **ripped off**, find out first what a reasonable fare might be from your hotel; if the first driver won't agree to your offer, simply walk on and try another.

Taxis

Taxis are now a common sight on the streets of all major cities. The vast majority are **metered** (with prices in dong) and fares are not expensive; a short ride within central Hanoi, for example, should cost around 50,000đ. In fact, it's often wise to consider taxis as an option for moving from city to city, especially if you're travelling in a small group – a journey that can take well over an hour by bus, plus extra time to get to and from the stations, can often be done in half the time by cab, for a very reasonable price; hotel reception staff can often make the call and arrange a pick-up time for you. Though **standards** have been improving with greater competition, some drivers still need persuading to use their meters, while others dawdle along as the meter spins suspiciously fast, or take you on an unnecessarily long route. When arriving in a town, beware of drivers who insist the hotel you ask for is closed; this is usually a commission scam, so be firm with your directions. In general, smarter-looking taxis and those waiting outside big hotels tend to be more reliable; the **Mai Linh** network has by far the best reputation, and you'll see their green cabs all across the land, while the white-coloured **Vinasun** armada are not far behind.

Accommodation

The standard of accommodation in Vietnam is, by and large, excellent. In the main tourist areas the range caters to all budgets, and though prices are a little expensive by Southeast Asian standards, the quality is generally good. Competition is fierce – great for the traveller, as it keeps prices low and service standards high. There has been a massive increase in the number of luxury resorts along the coast (mainly aimed at the Asian package tour market), while backpackers and those travelling off the tourist trail will find good budget accommodation throughout the country.

Reservations

Supply continues to exceed demand across the country, and even among international-class hotels there are some bargains to be had; however, **booking in advance** is a must around the Tet festival in early spring (see box, p.51), and remains a good idea throughout peak season (December to February).

It's increasingly simple to **book online**, and even some smaller towns are well represented on the major booking engines. One thing to be aware of is

that Vietnam is full of **copycat** businesses – to avoid being taken to a similarly named hotel, it's best to write down the street name and show it to your driver. This is often a good idea in any case, since the Vietnamese pronunciations of Western-sounding hotel names, and foreigners' pronunciation of Vietnamese road names, can leave a lot to be desired. If showing hotel names or a map to your driver on a smartphone, they'll usually try to grab the device off you – this is nothing to be overly afraid of.

If you're searching for a hotel on the ground, look at a range of rooms before opting for one, as standards can vary hugely within the same establishment. You'll also need to double-check the bed arrangement, since there are many permutations in Vietnam. A "**single**" room could have a single or twin beds in it, while a "**double**" room could have two, three or four single beds, a double, a single and a double, and so on.

Practicalities

When you **check in** at a Vietnamese hotel or guesthouse, you'll be asked for your **passport**, which is needed for registration with the local authorities. Depending on the establishment, these will be either returned to you after the salient details are written down or photocopied (this can take some time), or kept as security until you check out. If you're going to lose sleep over being separated from your passport, say that you need it for the bank or an embassy visit; many places will accept photocopies of your picture and visa pages. It's normally possible to pay your bill when you leave, although a few budget places ask for payment in advance.

Room rates fluctuate according to demand, so it's always worth bargaining – making sure, of course, that it's clear whether both parties are talking per person or per room. Your case will be that much stronger if you are staying several nights.

ROOM RATES AND TAXES

Room rates are generally quoted in dong at hotel receptions, but since this often makes nightly rates run into the millions, we've converted them to US$ throughout the Guide, based on the prices found for the cheapest double room in high season.

All hotels charge ten percent **government tax**, while top-class establishments also add a **service charge** (typically five percent). These taxes may or may not be included in the room rate, so check to be sure.

Increasingly, **breakfast** is included in the price of all but the cheapest rooms, and throughout the Guide it has only been mentioned when it's not included, only available for a fee or particularly noteworthy; in budget places it will consist of little more than bread with jam or cheese and a cup of tea or coffee, while those splashing out a little more may be greeted by a gigantic morning buffet.

TOP FIVE HOTELS
Caravelle, Ho Chi Minh City See p.91
Konklor, Kon Tum See p.197
Mui Ne Backpacker Village, Mui Ne See p.216
Phong Nha Farmstay, Phong Nha-Ke Bang National Park See p.311
Sofitel Legend Metropole, Hanoi See p.373

Dangers and annoyances

Bear in mind that hotel security can be a problem: never leave valuables lying about, and consider keeping important documents with you at all times in a money pouch. High-end places might have safes; elsewhere you might be able to leave items in a locked drawer at reception (put everything in a sealed envelope and get a receipt). In the cheapest places, where the door might only be secured with a padlock, increase your security by using your own lock.

Hygiene can also be a problem at the budget end of things, with cockroaches and even rats making occasional unwelcome appearances; you can at least minimize health risks by not bringing foodstuffs or sugary drinks into your room. You may become an expert at sniffing out rat poison during your stay in Vietnam – some budget hotels positively reek of the stuff, and it's a good first sign that the establishment is infested.

Types of accommodation

Grading accommodation isn't a simple matter in Vietnam. The names used (guesthouse, mini-hotel, hotel and so on) can rarely be relied on to indicate what's on offer, and there are broad overlaps in standards. Vietnam's older hotels tend to be austere, state-owned edifices styled on unlovely Eastern European models, while many private mini-hotels make a real effort. Some hotels cover all bases by having a range of accommodation, from simple fan-cooled rooms with cold water, right up to cheerful air-conditioned ones with satellite TVs, fridges and minibars. As a rule of thumb, the newer a place is, the better value it's likely to represent in terms of comfort, hygiene and all-round appeal.

There is a burgeoning number of **"resorts"** appearing across the country. In contrast to the Western image of an all-inclusive complex, in Vietnam these are simply hotels, usually with pretty landscaped gardens, located on the beach or in the countryside. All that's included in the rate

is breakfast, though it is possible to eat all your meals here.

Budget accommodation

The very cheapest form of accommodation in Vietnam is a bed in a **dormitory**, though as yet very few cities have such facilities – there are dedicated hostels in Hanoi, Ho Chi Minh City, Hue and Nha Trang, where you can expect to pay US$6–10 for a bed, sometimes sharing common facilities. Do note that while most of these have private rooms, you'll pay less elsewhere. In the two main cities there are also a fair few budget guesthouses equipped with "backpacker" dorms – you'll generally find these around the De Tham enclave in Ho Chi Minh City (see p.91), and the Old Quarter in Hanoi (see p.370).

If you prefer having your own privacy, you'll find simple fan-cooled rooms in either a guesthouse (nha nghi) or **hotel** (khach san), with prices starting at around US$15; these are likely to be en suite, although you might not get hot water at this price level in the warmer south. Add air-conditioning, satellite TV and slightly better furnishings, maybe even a window, and you'll be paying up to US$25. Upgrading to US$25–35 will get you a larger room with better-standard fittings, usually including a fridge and bathtub, and possibly a balcony. Note that while many hotels advertise satellite TV, the channels you actually get vary wildly, and so can the quality of reception – check first if it matters to you.

Mid- and upper-range accommodation

For upwards of US$35 per room per night, accommodation can begin to get quite rosy. Rooms at this level will be comfortable, reasonably spacious and well appointed with decent furniture, air-conditioning, hot water, fridges, phones and satellite TVs in all but the most remote areas.

Paying US$35–80 will get you a room in a **mid-range hotel** of some repute, with an in-house restaurant and bar, booking office, room service and so on. At the **upper range** the sky's the limit. Most of the international-class hotels are located in the two major cities, which also have some reasonably charismatic places to stay, such as the Metropole in Hanoi (see p.373) and Ho Chi Minh's Continental (see p.91). However, in recent years developers have targeted Nha Trang, Hoi An, Da Nang and Ha Long City, all of which now boast upmarket resort hotels. Off the main trail, there are usually one or two mid- or upper-range hotels in each main city, though very few exist in the countryside.

Village accommodation and camping

As Vietnam's minority communities have become more exposed to tourism, staying in stilthouses or other **village accommodation** has become more feasible.

In the north of the country, notably around Sa Pa and in the Mai Chau Valley, you can either take one of the tours out of Hanoi that includes a homestay in one of the **minority villages**, or make your own arrangements when you get there (see box, p.397). In the central highlands, the Pleiku and Kon Tum tourist offices can also arrange a stilthouse homestay for you.

Accommodation usually consists of a mattress on the floor in a communal room. Those villages more used to tourists normally provide a blanket and mosquito net, but it's advisable to take your own net and sleeping bag to be on the safe side, particularly as nights get pretty cold in the mountains. Prices in the villages are US$5–15 per person per night, depending on the area and whether meals are included.

Where boat trips operate in the Mekong Delta, notably around Vinh Long, tour operators in Ho Chi Minh City or the local tourist board can arrange for visitors to stay with owners of **fruit orchards**, allowing a close-up view of rural life (see box, p.128).

Virtually no provisions exist in Vietnam for **camping** at the present time. The exceptions are at Nha Trang and Mui Ne, where some guesthouses offer tents for a few dollars a night when all rooms are full. Some tour companies also offer camping as an option when visiting National parks.

Food and drink

Light, subtle in flavour and astonishing in variety, Vietnamese food is generally boiled or steamed rather than stir-fried, as is more common elsewhere in Southeast Asia. In addition, rather than throwing in handfuls of spices, huge emphasis is placed on a wide range of fresh herbs and seasoning – no great surprise in this land of diverse climates.

In the south, **Indian** and **Thai** influences add curries and spices to the menu, while other regions have evolved their own array of specialities, most notably the foods of Hue and Hoi An. Buddhism introduced a **vegetarian** tradition to Vietnam, while much later the **French** brought with them bread, dairy products, pastries and café culture. The major tourist centres now provide travellers – and, increasingly, the local *nouveau riche* – with everything from street hawkers to Western-style restaurants, and sometimes even trendy places like colonial-style eateries and bars selling craft beer.

When it comes to the range of eating establishments, you'll find **hawkers** peddling their dish of the day from shoulder poles or handcarts, **street kitchens** – inexpensive joints aimed at locals – and proper sit-down **restaurants** ranging from simple places serving unpretentious Vietnamese meals to top-class establishments offering high-quality Vietnamese specialities and international cuisine. The quality and variety of food is generally better in the main towns than off the beaten track, where restaurants of any sort are few and far between. That said, you'll never go hungry; even in the back

---

DINING PRACTICALITIES

Travellers to Vietnam will soon notice that the country runs to a somewhat different **schedule** – everything happens earlier here, and this goes for mealtimes, too. Outside the major cities and tourist areas, food stalls and street kitchens rarely stay open beyond 8pm, though they do stay open later in the south, especially in Ho Chi Minh City; restaurants, on the other hand, are usually open until fairly late.

You'll also get the chance to brush up your **chopstick-handling skills**, although other utensils are usually available, especially in Western-style restaurants or places frequented by tourists.

The use of **monosodium glutamate** (MSG) can be excessive, especially in northern cooking, and some people are known to react badly to the seasoning. A few restaurants in the main cities have cottoned on to the foibles of foreigners and advertise MSG-free food; elsewhere, try saying *"khong co my chinh"* ("without MSG"), and keep your fingers crossed. Note that what looks like salt on the table is sometimes MSG, so taste it first.

Lastly, when it comes to **paying**, the normal sign language will be readily understood in most restaurants. In street kitchens you pay as you leave – either proffer some dong to signal your intentions, or ask *"bao nhieu tien?"* ("how much is it?").

of beyond, there's always some stall selling a noodle soup or rice platter and plenty of fruit to fill up on.

Throughout the Guide we've given phone numbers and opening hours. While most eating establishments stay open throughout the year, some close over Tet (see p.51). Lastly, note that this guide includes a glossary of food and drink terms (see p.495).

Street kitchens

Eating on the street may not be to everyone's taste, but those willing to take the plunge usually put it up among their favourite experiences in the country – the food is often better to that found in restaurants, it's much cheaper and a whole lot more fun. It's worth using a bit of judicious selection, however – look for places with a fast turnover, where the ingredients are obviously fresh. A bit of basic vocabulary will certainly help (see p.490).

Street kitchens range from makeshift food stalls, set up on the street around a cluster of pint-size stools, to eating houses where, as often as not, the cooking is still done on the street but you either sit in an open-fronted dining area or join the overspill outside. Both tend to have fixed locations, though only the eating houses will have an address – which usually doubles as their name. Some places stay open all day (7am–8pm), while many close once they've run out of ingredients, and others only open at lunchtime (10.30am–2pm). To be sure of the widest choice and freshest food, it pays to get there early (as early as 11.30am at lunchtime, and by 7pm in the evening) – note that the best places will be packed around noon.

Most specialize in one type of food, generally indicated (in Vietnamese only) on a signboard outside, or they offer the ubiquitous **com** (rice dishes) and **pho** (noodle soups). *Com binh dan* (people's meals) are also popular; here you select from an array of prepared dishes displayed in a glass cabinet or on a buffet table, and pile your plate with such things as stuffed tomatoes, fried fish, tofu, pickles or eggs, plus a helping of rice –

TOP FIVE RESTAURANTS
Ancient Hue, Hue See p.282
Essence, Hanoi See p.370
Morning Glory, Hoi An See p.255
Nha Hang Ngon, Ho Chi Minh City See p.97
The Spice House, Phu Quoc See p.165

BREAKFAST
Vietnamese traditionally breakfast on **pho** or some other noodle soup, reasoning that these provide enough energy to get through the day – and many foreigners eventually come around to this way of thinking. You may also find early-morning hawkers peddling *xoi*, a wholesome mix of steamed **sticky rice** flavoured with soya beans, sweetcorn or peanuts. Simple **Western breakfasts** (such as bread with jam, cheese or eggs and coffee) are usually available in backpacker cafés or hotels. More upmarket places increasingly stretch to cereals and fresh milk, while some top-class hotels (and a whole bunch of cheaper ones) lay on the full works in their breakfast buffets. In towns, you could always buy jam and bread or croissants for a **do-it-yourself** breakfast.

expect to pay from around 25,000đ for a good plateful. Though it's not a major problem at these prices, some street kitchens overcharge, so double-check when ordering.

In a similar vein to street kitchens are **bia hoi outlets** (see box, p.379). Though these are primarily drinking establishments, many provide good-value snacks or even main meals as well.

Restaurants

If you're after more relaxed dining, then head for a proper **restaurant** (*nha hang*), which will have chairs rather than stools, a name and a menu, and will often be closed to the street. In general these places serve a more varied selection of Vietnamese dishes than the street kitchens, plus a smattering of international – generally European – dishes. **Menus** at this level show prices, particularly in areas popular with tourists.

In the main tourist haunts, you'll find cheap and cheerful **cafés** aimed at the backpacker market, serving often mediocre Western and Vietnamese dishes – from burgers and banana pancakes to spring rolls, noodles and other Vietnamese standards. Should you crave a reasonably priced Western-style breakfast, fresh fruit salad or a mango shake, these are the places to go.

As you move up the price scale, the decor and the cuisine become more sophisticated and the menu more varied. Some places have menus priced in dollars, and more and more accept credit cards.

Usually menus indicate if there's a **service charge**, but watch out for an additional 3–4 percent on credit card payments. These restaurants can be relatively fancy places, with at least a nod towards decor and ambience, and their prices can be correspondingly high.

The most popular **foreign cuisine** on offer is French, though larger cities boast some pretty good international restaurants, including Thai, Chinese, Tex-Mex, Indian and Italian. You'll find these international cuisines, and upper-class Vietnamese restaurants, in Hanoi, Ho Chi Minh City, Hue, Da Nang, Hoi An and Nha Trang, and though they're scarce in the rest of the country, you'll occasionally find the odd surprise entry if you keep your eyes peeled.

Vietnamese food

The staple of Vietnamese meals is **rice**, with noodles a popular alternative at breakfast or as a snack. Typically, rice will be accompanied by a fish or meat dish, a vegetable dish and soup, followed by a green tea digestive. The most commonly used **flavourings** are shallots, coriander and lemon grass. Ginger, saffron, mint and anise also feature strongly, and coconut milk gives some southern dishes a distinctive richness.

Even in the south, Vietnamese food tends not to be overly spicy; instead, chilli sauces or fresh chillies are served separately. Vietnam's most famous seasoning is the ubiquitous **nuoc mam**, a dark-brown, fermented, nutrient-packed fish sauce that is added during cooking or forms the base for various dipping sauces. Foreigners usually find the smell of the sauce pretty rank, but most soon acquire a taste for its distinctive salty sweetness.

Soups and noodles

Though it originated in the north, one dish you'll find throughout Vietnam is **pho** (pronounced as the British say "fur"), a noodle soup eaten at any time of day but primarily at breakfast. The basic bowl of pho consists of a light beef broth, flavoured with ginger, coriander and sometimes cinnamon, to which are added broad, flat rice-noodles, spring onions and slivers of chicken, pork or beef. At the table you add a squeeze of lime and a sprinkling of chilli flakes or a spoonful of chilli sauce.

Countless other types of soup are dished up at street restaurants. **Bun bo** is another substantial beef and noodle soup eaten countrywide, though most famous in Hue; in the south, **hu tieu**, a soup of vermicelli, pork and seafood noodles, is best taken in My Tho. **Chao** (or *xhao*), on the other hand, is a thick rice gruel served piping hot, usually with shredded chicken or filleted fish, flavoured with dill and with perhaps a raw egg cooking at the bottom; it's often served with fried breadsticks (*quay*). Sour soups are a popular accompaniment for fish; while **lau**, a standard in local restaurants, is more of a main meal than a soup, where the vegetable broth arrives at the table in a steamboat (a ring-shaped metal dish on live coals or, nowadays, often electrically heated). You cook slivers of beef, prawns or similar in the simmering soup, and then drink the flavourful liquid that's left in the cooking pot.

TEN VIETNAMESE FOODS TO TRY

Banh mi Baguette sandwich filled with greens and a choice of fillings including paté and freshly made omelette.

Banh xeo Fried pancake containing shrimp, pork, bean sprouts and egg.

Bun cha Seasoned, charcoal-grilled pork served with rice noodles and assorted foliage.

Ca kho to Caramelized fish in a clay pot.

Cha ca Butter-sautéed, dill-flavoured fish served with rice noodles.

Com tam Street-stand favourite consisting of barbecued beef served with rice and a fried egg.

Goi cuon Translucent spring rolls packed with greens, coriander and various combinations of minced pork, shrimp or crab. In some places they're served with a bowl of lettuce and/or mint. A southern variation has barbecued strips of pork wrapped up with green banana and star fruit, then dunked in a rich peanut sauce – every bit as tasty as it sounds.

Mi quang Unheralded noodle dish – ingredients vary by establishment, but expect shrimp, peanuts, mint and quail eggs.

Nom hua chuoi Banana-flower salad: a great veggie option.

Pho Noodles in broth: the national dish, though at its best in Hanoi.

Fish and meat

Among the highlights of Vietnamese cuisine are its succulent **seafood** and freshwater **fish**. Invented in Hanoi, *cha ca* is the most famous of these dishes: white fish sautéed in butter at the table with dill and spring onions, then served with rice noodles and a sprinkling of peanuts. Another dish found in more expensive restaurants is *chao tom* (or *tom bao mia*), consisting of savoury shrimp pâté wrapped round sweet sugar-cane and fried. *Ca kho to*, fish stew cooked in a clay pot, is a southern speciality.

Every conceivable type of meat and part of the animal anatomy finds itself on the Vietnamese dining table, though the staples are straightforward beef, chicken and pork. **Ground meat**, especially pork, is a common constituent of stuffing, for example in spring rolls or the similar *banh cuon*, a steamed, rice-flour "ravioli" filled with minced pork, black mushrooms and bean sprouts; a popular variation uses prawns instead of meat. Pork is also used, with plenty of herbs, to make Hanoi's *bun cha*, small **hamburgers** barbecued on an open charcoal brazier and served on a bed of cold rice-noodles with greens and a slightly sweetish sauce. One famous southern dish is *bo bay mon* (often written *bo 7 mon*), meaning literally **beef seven ways**, consisting of a platter of beef cooked in different styles.

Vegetables and vegetarian food

It is possible to find **vegetarian food** in Vietnam, though not always easily. Most restaurants offer a smattering of meat-free dishes, from stewed spinach or similar greens, to a more appetizing mix of onion, tomato, bean sprouts, various mushrooms, peppers and so on; places used to foreigners may be able to oblige with vegetarian spring rolls (*nem an chay* or *nem khong co thit*). At street kitchens you're likely to find tofu and one or two dishes of pickled vegetables, such as cabbage or cucumber, while occasionally they may also have aubergine, bamboo shoots or avocado, depending on the season.

Note that unless you go to a **specialist** vegetarian outlet, it can be tricky finding genuine veggie food: soups are usually made with beef stock, morsels of pork can sneak into otherwise innocuous-looking dishes and animal fat tends to be used for frying. The phrase to remember is *an chay* (vegetarian), or seek out a vegetarian rice shop (*tiem com chay*). Otherwise, make the most of the first and fifteenth days of the lunar month when many Vietnamese Buddhists spurn meat – you're more likely to find a range of vegetarian dishes on offer.

CULINARY ADVENTURE TOURISM

There are lots of unusual meats on offer in Vietnam. **Dog meat** (*thit cay* or *thit cho*) is a particular delicacy in the north, where "yellow" dogs (sandy-haired varieties) are considered the tastiest. Winter is the most popular season for dog meat – it's said to give extra body heat, and is also supposed to remove bad luck if consumed at the end of the lunar month. Worryingly, at some rural snack-shacks in the north you may get dog even if you've ordered something else. **Snake** (*thit con ran*) is supposed to improve male virility. Dining on snake is surrounded by a ritual, which, if you're the guest of honour, requires you to swallow the still-beating heart (see p.377). Another one strictly for the strong of stomach is *trung vit lon*, embryo-containing **duck eggs** boiled and eaten only five days before hatching – bill, webbed feet, feathers and all.

Snacks

Vietnam has a wide range of **snacks and nibbles** to fill any yawning gaps, from huge rice-flour crackers sprinkled with sesame seeds to all sorts of dried fish, nuts and seeds. *Banh bao* are white, steamed dumplings filled with tasty titbits, such as pork, onions and tangy mushrooms or strands of sweet coconut. *Banh xeo*, meaning sizzling pancake, combines shrimp, pork, bean sprouts and egg, all fried and then wrapped in rice paper with a selection of greens before being dunked in a spicy sauce. A similar dish, originating from Hue – a city with a vast repertoire of snack foods (see box, p.284) – is *banh khoai*, in which the flat pancake is accompanied by a plate of star fruit, green banana and aromatic herbs, plus a rich peanut sauce.

Markets are often good snacking grounds, with stalls churning out soups and spring rolls or selling intriguing banana-leaf parcels of pâté (a favourite accompaniment for bia hoi), pickled pork sausage or perhaps a cake of sticky rice.

A relative newcomer on the culinary scene is **French bread**, made with wheat flour in the north and rice flour in the south. Known as *banh mi*, baguettes – sometimes sold warm from streetside stoves – are sliced open and stuffed with pâté, soft cheese or ham and pickled vegetables.

Fruit

With its diverse climate, Vietnam is blessed with both tropical and temperate **fruits**, including dozens of banana species. The richest orchards are in the south, where pineapple, coconut, papaya, mango, longan and mangosteen flourish. Da Lat is famous for its strawberries, while the region around Nha Trang produces the peculiar dragon fruit (*thanh long*). The size and shape of a small pineapple, the dragon fruit has skin of shocking pink, studded with small protuberances, and smooth, white flesh speckled with tiny black seeds. The slightly sweet, watery flesh is thirst-quenching, and so is often served as a drink, crushed with ice.

A fruit that is definitely an acquired taste is the durian, a spiky, yellow-green, football-sized fruit with an unmistakeably pungent odour reminiscent of mature cheese and caramel, and a taste like an onion-laced custard. Jackfruit looks worryingly similar to durian but is larger and has smaller spikes. Its yellow segments of flesh are deliciously sweet.

Sweet things

Vietnam is not strong on desserts – restaurants usually stick to ice cream and fruit, although fancier international places might venture into tiramisu territory. Those with a sweet tooth are better off hunting down a bakery – there'll be one within walking distance in any urban area – or browsing around street stalls where there are usually candied fruits and other Vietnamese **sweetmeats** on offer, as well as sugary displays of French-inspired cakes and pastries in the main tourist centres.

Green-coloured *banh com* is an eye-catching local delicacy made by wrapping pounded glutinous rice around sugary, green-bean paste. A similar confection, found only during the mid-autumn festival, is the "earth cake", *banh deo*, which melds the contrasting flavours of candied fruits, sesame and lotus seeds with a dice of savoury pork fat. **Fritters** are popular among children and you'll find opportunistic hawkers outside schools, selling *banh chuoi* (banana fritters) and *banh chuoi khoai* (mixed slices of banana and sweet potato).

In all cities you'll find **vendors** selling tubs or sticks of the local ice creams in chocolate, vanilla or green-tea flavours, though it's prudent to buy only from the larger, busier outlets and not from street hawkers. More exotic tastes can be satisfied at the European- and American-style ice-cream parlours of Hanoi and Ho Chi Minh City, while excellent yoghurts are also increasingly available at ice-cream parlours, and even some restaurants.

Somewhere between a drink and a snack, **che** is made from taro flour and green beans, and served over ice with chunks of fruit, coloured jellies and even sweetcorn or potato; in hot weather it provides a refreshing sugar-fix, and you'll find vendors selling the stuff at many local markets.

Drinks

Giai khat means "quench your thirst" and you'll see the signs everywhere, on stands selling fresh juices, bottled cold drinks or outside cafés and bia hoi (draught beer) outlets. Many drinks are served with ice, which is usually reliable in hotels, bars and restaurants, though less so from street-stands; if in doubt, saying *"dung bo da, cam on"* ("no ice, thanks") should do the trick.

Water and soft drinks

Tap water is not safe to drink in Vietnam, and since **bottled water** is both cheap and widely available, there's no need to take the risk anyway. When buying bottled water check that the seal is unbroken and the water is clear, as bottles are occasionally refilled from the tap (we're looking at you, Ha Long Bay). Tap water in Hanoi and Ho Chi Minh City is chlorinated and most travellers use it

---

WATCH OUT FOR THE WEASELS

Since Vietnam is one of the world's foremost producers of **coffee**, a bag of aromatic beans makes an ideal gift for friends back home, or even something for your own kitchen to remind you of sitting in Vietnamese cafés. Most coffee vendors sell something they call **weasel coffee** (*caphe chon* in Vietnamese), which is produced by passing the beans through the digestive system of civet cats. This results in a distinctive taste – slightly smoky, with a hint of chocolate – and the beans often fetch up to $100 a kilo. Not surprising, then, that some clever coffee-producers have managed to mimic the taste using biotechnology, so it's difficult to know whether you're getting the real thing. Some countries like Australia now ban the import of this coffee, mostly for ethical reasons – coffee beans aren't a natural civet cat food, and the massive caffeine intake drastically shortens their lifespans, so it's best to think twice before buying some to take home.

BIA HOI KNOW-HOW

Though they're on the wane thanks to the profusion of canned beer, there are still plenty of **bia hoi** (draught beer) outlets in most major cities in Vietnam, ranging from beer gardens to a few ankle-high stools gathered round a barrel on the pavement. Bia hoi differs from other local draught beer in that it's unpasteurised – and, therefore, made to be consumed quickly, since it'll usually taste off by the following day. Quality tends to be more consistent at the larger outlets supplied by major breweries such as Hanoi Beer and Halida (under the name Viet Ha), rather than the smaller places that usually buy their beer from microbreweries. On the whole, the more expensive – and colder – the beer, the better it is.

Bia hoi culture is all about enjoying a few beers with a group of friends – it's still an almost completely **male activity**, though in the cities you'll see a few local women (and female travellers won't be judged for joining in). The Vietnamese almost never drink alone and rarely drink without eating, so many places serve a range of snacks and more extensive dishes.

Menus, if they exist, will be in Vietnamese only, so a few classic bia hoi dishes have been listed below. They normally give a price range for each dish, so you order a small, medium or large amount, for example, depending on the size of your group. To maximize the variety, it makes sense to order small quantities of several dishes and share. If no prices are indicated on the menu, be sure to ask when ordering. Usually a note with the running total is left on the table, so you can keep track of how much you're spending.

bo luc lac	cubed spicy beef and green pepper stir-fry
ca bo lo	oven-cooked fish
dau chien ron	fried tofu
dau tu xuyen	tofu in a Chinese pork and tomato sauce
de tai chanh	lightly cooked goat with green banana, pineapple and lemon
dua chuot che	sliced cucumber
ech chien bo	deep-fried battered frogs' legs
ech xao mang	frogs' legs with bamboo shoots
ga xe phay	shredded chicken salad with bean peanuts and basil
khoai tay ran	chips/French fries
lac	peanuts
muc chien bo	squid fried in butter
muc kho	dried squid
muc tam bot	battered squid
nem chua	minced spicy cured pork wrapped in banana leaf
nom du du	papaya salad
nom hoa chuoi	banana-flower salad
nom ngo sen	lotus-stem salad
oc xao xa ot	stir-fried snail, lemongrass and chilli
rau bi xaoi	leaf fried with garlic
tho quay	roast rabbit
tom hap bia	shrimps steamed in beer
tom nuong	grilled shrimps

for brushing their teeth without problems, but this is not recommended in rural areas, where water is often untreated. Particular care should be taken anywhere where there is flooding, as raw sewage may be washed into the water system. To play it safe, avoid drinks with ice, or those that may have been diluted with suspect water.

On sale just about everywhere, locally made **soft drinks** are tooth-numbingly sweet, but cheap and safe – as long as the bottle or carton appears well sealed. The Coke, Sprite and Fanta hegemony also means you can find fizzy drinks in surprisingly remote areas. Oddly, canned drinks are usually more expensive than the equivalent-sized bottle, whether it's a soft drink or beer – apparently it's less chic to drink from the old-fashioned bottle.

A most effective thirst-quencher is fresh coconut juice, though this is difficult to find in the north. Fresh juices such as orange and lime are also delicious – just make sure they haven't been mixed with tap water. Sugar-cane juice (mia da) is safer, since it's pressed right in front of you, and it's quite delicious. Pasteurized milk, produced by Vinamilk, is now sold in the main towns and cities.

A TRADITIONAL TIPPLE

While beer and imported spirits are drunk throughout Vietnam, the traditional tipple is **ruou can**, or rice-distilled liquor. Until recently, *ruou can* was regarded as decidedly downmarket, the preserve of labourers, farmers and ethnic minorities. Nowadays, however, it's becoming popular among the middle class and especially young urban sophisticates – including a growing number of women – as city-centre bars and restaurants begin to offer better-quality *ruou can*.

Recipes for *ruou can* are a closely guarded secret, but its basic constituents are regular or glutinous rice, the latter of which is said to be more aromatic and have a fuller, smoother taste. Selected herbs and fruits are sometimes steeped in the liquor to enhance its flavour and, supposedly, to add all sorts of medicinal and health benefits. You'll also see jars containing snakes, geckos and even whole crows. Traditionally, the basic ingredients are heated together and buried in the ground for a month or more to ferment. Nowadays, more modern – and hygienic – techniques are used to produce *ruou can* for general consumption. Look out for the high-quality rice-distilled liquors marketed under the Son Tinh brand (Ⓦ sontinh.com).

The **ethnic minorities** of the northwest (Thai and Muong) concoct their own home-distilled *ruou can*, sometimes known as stem alcohol. Visitors are often invited to gather round the communal jar to drink the liquor through thin, bamboo straws. In more traditional villages it's regarded as a sacred ritual, and it would be an insult to refuse. You will hear the toast *"chuc suc khoe"* ("your health") and, for more serious drinking sessions, *"tram phan tram"* ("down in one")!

Tea and coffee

Tea is part of the social ritual in Vietnam. Small cups of refreshing, strong green tea are often presented to guests or visitors: water is well boiled and safe to drink, as long as the cup itself is clean, and it's considered rude not to take at least a sip. Although your cup will be continually replenished to show hospitality, you don't have to carry on drinking; the polite way to decline a refill is to place your hand over the cup when your host is about to replenish it. Green tea is also served during or at the end of many restaurant meals, particularly in the south, and is usually provided free.

Coffee production has boomed in recent years, largely for export, with serious environmental and social consequences. The Vietnamese drink coffee very strong and in small quantities; traditionally, it's filtered at the table by means of a small dripper balanced over the cup or glass (usually 8000–15,000đ at simple local cafés), and at local markets you'll be able to purchase the same apparatus in order to make Vietnamese-style coffee back at home. Locals usually take their coffee with a large dollop of condensed milk at the bottom of the cup, but places accustomed to tourists increasingly run to fresh (pasteurized) milk. In addition, across the land you'll now find fancy Western-style cafés turning out decent lattes and cappuccinos (though prices vary widely; expect to pay anything from 20,000–90,000đ). *Highland Coffee* has become Vietnam's very own *Starbucks*-style chain, but there are some lovely independent affairs in Hanoi and Ho Chi Minh City; even out in the sticks, you'll likely still have a couple of excellent cafés to choose from.

Alcoholic drinks

In Vietnam, drinking alcohol is a social activity to be shared with friends. Locals rarely drink alone, and almost never without eating. Be prepared for lots of toasts to health, wealth and happiness, and no doubt to international understanding, too. It's the custom to fill the glasses of your fellow guests – someone else will fill yours.

Canned and **bottled beers** brewed under licence in Vietnam include Tiger, Heineken, Carlsberg and San Miguel, but there are also plenty of very drinkable – and cheap – local beers around, such as Halida, 333 (Ba Ba Ba) and Bivina. Some connoisseurs rate Bière la Rue from Da Nang, though Saigon Export, Hanoi Beer and BGI are also fine brews. Many other towns boast their own local beers; in many places, such as Haiphong and Thanh Hoa, it's simply named after the town, while Hue has a few brands including Huda and Hue Beer – they're all worth a try.

Roughly forty years ago technology for making **bia hoi** (draught beer) was introduced from Czechoslovakia and it is now quaffed in vast quantities, particularly in the north. Bia hoi may taste fairly weak, but it measures in at up to four percent alcohol. It's also ridiculously cheap –

around 5000đ a glass – and supposedly unadulterated with chemicals, so in theory you're less likely to get a hangover. Bia hoi has a 24-hour shelf life, which means the better places sell out by early evening, and that you're unlikely to be drinking it into the wee hours. In the south, you're more likely to be drinking **bia tuoi** ("fresh" beer), a close relation of bia hoi but served from pressurized barrels. Outlets are usually open at lunchtime, and then again in the evening from 5 to 9pm.

Ale-lovers will be delighted to hear that Vietnam has become one of the latest dominoes to fall in the global **craft-beer** revolution. Ho Chi Minh City seemingly sees a new bar dedicated to the stuff opening every month, and some have been known to employ Vietnamese ingredients such as jasmine and dragon fruit in their creations.

Rice wine, known as **ruou**, is the national spirit, and is especially popular in rural areas, where it's often home-made – it's basically local moonshine. It can be dangerous if it's prepared either incorrectly or in an unsanitary environment. The bottled versions are safer, though at 40 percent alcohol by volume they certainly pack a punch, which you'll most likely still be feeling the next morning.

Wine of the conventional kind is becoming increasingly popular in Vietnam – even in small towns, you'll easily track some down, and imported bottles continue to crop up in the most unexpected places. Local production dates from the French era, and is centred around Da Lat – the main producer is Vang Da Lat, bottles of which will cost from 70,000đ in a shop, and often double that at a restaurant. Only at top hotels, restaurants or specialist shops will you find decent imported bottles that have been properly stored – you'll be paying premium prices for these.

Health

Vietnam's health problems read like a dictionary of tropical medicine. Diseases that are under control elsewhere in Southeast Asia have been sustained here by poverty, dietary deficiencies, poor healthcare and the disruption caused by half a century of war. The situation is improving rapidly, however, and by coming prepared and taking a few simple precautions while in the country, you're unlikely to come down with anything worse than a cold or a dose of travellers' diarrhoea.

Before you go

When planning your trip it's wise to visit a **doctor** as early as possible, preferably at least two months before you leave, to allow time to complete any recommended courses of **vaccinations**. It's also advisable to have a troubleshooting **dental check-up** – and remember that you generally need to start taking **antimalarial tablets** at least one week before your departure.

For up-to-the-minute information, contact a specialized **travel clinic**; most clinics also sell travel-associated accessories, including mosquito nets and first-aid kits.

Vaccinations

No **vaccinations** are required for Vietnam (except yellow fever if you're coming directly from an area where the disease is endemic), but typhoid, diphtheria and hepatitis A jabs are recommended; it's also worth ensuring you're up to date with boosters such as tetanus and polio. Additional injections to consider, depending on the season and risk of exposure, are hepatitis B, Japanese encephalitis, meningitis and rabies. All these immunizations can be obtained at international clinics in Hanoi, Ho Chi Minh City and Da Nang, but it's less hassle and usually cheaper to get them done at home. Get all your shots recorded on an International Certificate of Vaccination and carry this with your passport when travelling abroad.

For protection against **hepatitis A**, which is spread by contaminated food and water, the vaccine is expensive but extremely effective – an initial injection followed by a booster after six to twelve months provides immunity for up to ten years. **Hepatitis B**, like the HIV virus, can be passed on through unprotected sexual contact, blood transfusions and dirty needles. The very effective vaccine (three injections over six months) is recommended for anyone in a high-risk category, including those travelling extensively in rural areas for prolonged periods, with access to only basic medical care. It's also now possible – and cheaper – to have a combined vaccination against both hepatitis A and B; the course comprises three injections over six months.

The risk of contracting **Japanese encephalitis** is extremely small, but, as the disease is untreatable, those travelling for a month or more in the countryside, especially in the north during and soon after

AVIAN FLU

Avian flu or **bird flu** is a contagious disease normally limited to birds and, less commonly, pigs. However, the virus can spread to humans by direct contact with infected poultry or with contaminated surfaces. In the 2004–05 outbreak in Vietnam of the highly contagious **H5N1** strain of the disease, there were around sixty confirmed cases involving humans, of which some forty were fatal, according to the World Health Organization. The vast majority of people infected had direct contact with diseased birds. Since the initial outbreak, 123 cases have been reported, the most recent in 2012.

Evidence of human-to-human transmission has yet to be confirmed but the indications are that, if it is possible, it is extremely rare and has so far been limited to close family members. The main fear among health experts is that the virus will mutate into a form that is highly infectious to, and easily spread among, humans.

At present the risk to travellers visiting infected areas remains low. As a precaution, however, you are advised to avoid contact with live poultry and pigs, including live animal markets, and to eat only well-cooked poultry and eggs. Check the latest with your doctor or travel health specialist prior to travel. You can find the latest information at ⓦ who.int/influenza.

the summer rainy season (June to October), should consider immunization. The course consists of two or three injections over a month with the last dose administered at least ten days before departure. Note that it is not recommended for those with liver, heart or kidney disorders, or for multiple-allergy sufferers. If your plans include long stays in remote areas, your doctor may also recommend vaccination against **meningitis** (a single shot) and **rabies** (currently three shots).

Mosquito-borne diseases

Both the Red River and Mekong deltas (including Hanoi and Ho Chi Minh City) have few incidences of mosquito-borne **malaria**. The coastal plain north of Nha Trang is also considered relatively safe. Malaria occurs frequently in the highlands and rural areas, notably the central highlands, as well as the southern provinces of Ca Mau, Bac Lieu and Tay Ninh. The majority of cases involve the most dangerous strain, *Plasmodium falciparum*, which can be fatal if not treated promptly. If you'll be spending time in the highlands, you should consider taking a course of antimalarial drugs; check with your doctor before travelling to Vietnam.

Mosquitoes are also responsible for transmitting dengue fever, zika and Japanese encephalitis. **Dengue** is carried by a variety of mosquitoes active in the daytime (particularly two hours after sunrise and several hours before sunset) and occurs mostly in the Mekong Delta, including Ho Chi Minh City, though the chances of being infected remain small. There is a more dangerous version called dengue haemorrhage fever, which primarily affects children but is extremely rare among foreign visitors to Vietnam. If you notice an unusual tendency to

bleed or bruise, seek medical advice immediately. Japanese encephalitis causes similar symptoms to dengue, and can also be fatal, while zika hit Vietnam as part of a global pandemic in 2016, and remains an issue.

The key **preventive** measure for all these conditions is to avoid getting bitten by mosquitoes in the first place. Mosquitoes are most active at dawn and dusk, so at these times wear long sleeves, trousers and socks, avoid dark colours and perfumes, which attract mosquitoes, and put repellent on all exposed skin. Sprays and lotions containing around thirty to forty percent DEET (diethyltoluamide) are effective and can also be used to treat clothes, but the chemical is toxic: keep it away from eyes and open wounds.

Many hotels and guesthouses provide mosquito nets over beds or meshing on windows and doors. Air-conditioning and fans also help keep mosquitoes at bay, as do mosquito coils and knockdown insecticide sprays (available locally), though none of these measures is as effective as a decent net.

Bites and creepy-crawlies

Bed bugs, fleas, lice or scabies can be picked up from dirty bedclothes, though this is relatively unusual in Vietnam. Try not to scratch bites, which easily become septic. Ticks picked up walking through scrub may carry a strain of typhus; carry out regular body inspections and remove ticks promptly – you can use tweezers, making sure to remove the tick's head and clean the area thoroughly afterwards.

Rabies is contracted by being bitten, or even licked on broken skin or the eyes, by an infected mammal. The best strategy is to give all animals, especially dogs, cats and monkeys, a wide berth.

Vietnam has several poisonous **snakes** but in general snakes steer clear of humans and it's very rare to get bitten. Avoid walking through long grass or undergrowth, and wear boots when walking off-road. If bitten, immobilize the limb (most snake bites occur on the lower leg) to slow down absorption of the venom and remove any tight-fitting socks or other clothing from around the wound. It's important to seek medical assistance as quickly as possible. It helps if you can take the (dead) snake to be identified, snap a photo, or at least remember what it looked like.

Leeches are more common and, though harmless, can be unpleasant. Long trousers, sleeves and socks help prevent them getting a grip. The best way to get rid of a leech is to slide a credit card or your fingernail under its sucker, and quickly flick it away once it's detached; alternatively, you can simply wait until it drops off of its own accord, which can take up to twenty minutes.

Parasitic worms enter the body either via contaminated food, or through the skin, especially the soles of the feet. You may notice worms in your stools, or experience other indications such as mild abdominal pain leading, very rarely, to acute intestinal blockage (roundworm, the most common), an itchy anus (threadworm) or anaemia (hookworm). An infestation is easily treated with worming tablets from a pharmacy.

Heat trouble

Don't underestimate the strength of the tropical sun: **sunburn** can be avoided by restricting your exposure to the midday sun and liberal use of high-factor sunscreens. Drinking plenty of water will prevent **dehydration**, but if you do become dehydrated – the signs are infrequent or irregular urination – drink a salt and sugar solution.

Heatstroke is more serious and may require hospital treatment. Indications are a high temperature, lack of sweating, a fast pulse and red skin. Reducing your body temperature with a lukewarm shower will provide initial relief.

High humidity often causes **heat rashes**, **prickly heat** and **fungal infections**. Prevention and cure are the same: wear loose clothes made of natural fibres, wash frequently and dry off thoroughly afterwards. Talcum powder helps, particularly zinc oxide-based products (prickly heat powder), as does the use of mild antiseptic soap.

Sexually transmitted diseases

Until recently Vietnam carried out very little screening for sex workers, injecting drug users and other high-risk groups. As a result, **sexually transmitted diseases** such as gonorrhoea, syphilis and HIV had been flourishing, though fortunately awareness is growing and the number of HIV victims, at least, is levelling out. It is, therefore, extremely unwise to contemplate casual unprotected sex, and bear in mind that Vietnamese **condoms** (*bao cao su*) are often poor-quality – more reliable imported varieties are available in major cities.

Getting medical help

Pharmacies can generally help with minor injuries or ailments and in major towns you will usually find a pharmacist who speaks English. The selection of reliable Asian and Western products on the market is improving rapidly, and Ho Chi Minh City and Hanoi now have well-stocked pharmacies. That said, drugs past their shelf life and even counterfeit medicines are rife, so inspect packaging carefully, check use-by dates, and bring anything you know you're likely to need from home, including **oral contraceptives**. **Tampons** are sold in Hanoi and Ho Chi Minh City, but don't count on getting them easily elsewhere.

Local **hospitals** can also treat minor problems, but in a real emergency your best bet is to head for Hanoi or Ho Chi Minh City. Hospitals in both these cities can handle most eventualities and you also have the option of one of the excellent international medical centres. Addresses of clinics and hospitals can be found in our "Listings" sections for major towns throughout the book. Note that doctors and hospitals expect immediate cash payment for health services rendered; you will then have to seek reimbursement from your insurance company (make sure you get receipts for any payments you make).

The media

The media in Vietnam falls under tight government control. There have been slight glimmers of less draconian censorship, with an increasing number of stories covering corruption at even quite senior levels and more criticism of government policies and ministers,

albeit very mild by Western standards; in addition, 2012 saw the first foreign press bureau opened up in Vietnam. However, if anything the situation has worsened in recent years, with the government tightening restrictions to prevent the spread of non-sanctioned information online – one newspaper had its licence to publish online revoked; journalists and bloggers have been harassed and detained by police; and in 2015 three activists were imprisoned for articles posted on Facebook.

Newspapers and magazines

Vietnam has several English-language **newspapers and magazines**, of which the daily *Viet Nam News* has the widest distribution. It provides a brief – and very select – rundown of local, regional and international news, as well as snippets on art and culture. Though short on general news, the weekly *Vietnam Investment Review* (@vir.com.vn) covers issues in greater depth and is worth looking at for an insight into what makes the Vietnamese economy tick.

Several free magazines publish excellent restaurant and nightlife **listings**, mainly covering Hanoi and Ho Chi Minh City, and they feature articles on culture and tourist destinations. Best of the bunch are *The Word* (@wordvietnam.com), *Saigoneer* (@saigoneer.com) and *Oi Vietnam* (@oivietnam .com), which all carry listings of bars and restaurants as well as articles on aspects of Vietnamese culture; though the websites are updated regularly, you can also look out for their magazines in restaurants and bars that cater to foreigners.

Foreign publications such as the *International New York Times, Time, Newsweek, The Financial Times* and the *Bangkok Post* are sold by street vendors and at some of the larger bookshops, as well as on the newsstands of more upmarket hotels in Ho Chi Minh City and Hanoi.

Televison

Vietnamese **television** airs a mix of government-approved films, music shows, news programmes, soaps, sport and foreign (mostly American, Korean and Japanese) imports. VTV1, the main domestic channel, occasionally presents a news summary in English. However, most hotels provide satellite TV, offering BBC, CNN, MTV and HBO as standard.

Crime and personal safety

Vietnam is a relatively safe country for visitors, including women travelling alone. In fact, given the country's recent history, many tourists (particularly Americans) are pleasantly surprised at the warm reception that foreign travellers receive. That said, petty crime is on the rise – though it's still relatively small-scale and shouldn't be a problem if you take common-sense precautions. Generally, the hassles you'll encounter will be the milder sort of coping with pushy vendors and overenthusiastic touts and beggars.

Petty crime

As a tourist, you're an obvious target for thieves (who may include your fellow travellers): carry your passport and other valuables in a concealed **money belt**. Don't leave anything important lying about in your room and use a safe, if you have one. A cable lock, or **padlock** and chain, comes in handy for doors and windows in cheap hotels, and is useful for securing your pack on trains and buses. It's also not a bad idea to keep US$100 or so separate from the rest of your cash, along with insurance policy details and photocopies of important documents, such as the relevant pages of your passport including your visa stamp.

At street level it's best not to be ostentatious: forego eye-catching jewellery and flashy watches, try to be discreet when taking out your cash, and be particularly wary in **crowds** and on **public transport**. If your pack is inside or on the top of a bus, keep an eye on it during the most vulnerable times – before departure, at meal stops and on arrival at your destination. On trains, either cable-lock your pack or put it under the bottom bench-seat, out of public view. The odd

---

EMERGENCY PHONE NUMBERS

The following numbers apply throughout Vietnam. If possible, get a Vietnamese-speaker to call on your behalf.
Police ☎113
Fire ☎114
Ambulance ☎115

instance has been reported of travellers being drugged and then robbed, so it's best not to accept food or drink from anyone you don't know and trust. Bear in mind that when walking or riding in a cyclo you are vulnerable to moped-borne **snatch-thieves**; don't wear cameras or expensive sunglasses hanging round your neck, and keep a firm grip on your bags. If you do become a target, however, it's best to let go rather than risk being pulled into the traffic and suffering serious injury.

The place you are most likely to encounter street crime is in **Ho Chi Minh City**, which has a fairly bad reputation for bag-snatchers, pickpockets and con artists. Be wary of innocent-looking kids and grannies who may be acting as decoys for thieves – especially in the bar districts and other popular tourist hangouts.

Petty crime, much of it drug- and prostitution-related, is also a problem in **Nha Trang**, where you should watch your belongings at all times on the beach. Again, be wary of taking a cyclo after dark and women should avoid walking alone at night.

It's important not to get paranoid, however: crime levels in Vietnam are still a long way behind those of Western countries, and violent crime against tourists is extremely rare.

If you do have anything stolen, you'll need to go to the nearest **police** station to make a report in order to claim on your insurance. Try to recruit an English-speaker to come along with you – someone at your hotel should be able to help.

"Social evils" and serious crime

Since liberalization and *doi moi*, Vietnamese society has seen an increase in prostitution, drugs – including hard drugs – and more serious crimes. These so-called "**social evils**" are viewed by some as a direct consequence of reduced controls on society and ensuing Westernization. The police once imposed midnight closing on bars and clubs, mainly because of drugs, but also to curb general rowdiness; however, this was patchily enforced, and even in conservative Hanoi the curfew was later extended to 2am in 2016.

Having anything to do with **drugs** in Vietnam is extremely unwise. At night there's a fair amount of drug-selling on the streets of Ho Chi Minh City, Hanoi, Nha Trang and even Sa Pa, and it's not unknown for dealers to turn buyers in to the police. Fines and jail sentences are imposed for lesser offences, while the **death penalty** is regularly imposed for possessing, trading or smuggling larger quantities.

Military hazards and UXO

Not surprisingly, the Vietnamese authorities are sensitive about **military installations** and strategic areas – including border regions, military camps (of which there are many), bridges, airports, naval dockyards and even train stations. Anyone taking photographs in the vicinity of such sites risks having the memory card (or offending images) removed from their camera or being fined.

Unexploded ordnance from past conflicts still poses a threat in some areas; over 40,000 Vietnamese have been killed by UXO since the war ended. The problem is most acute in the Demilitarized Zone, where each year a number of local farmers, scrap-metal scavengers and children are killed or injured. Wherever you are, stick to well-trodden paths and never touch any shells or half-buried chunks of metal.

Beggars, hassle and scams

Given the number of disabled and unemployed in Vietnam, there are surprisingly few **beggars** around. Most people try very hard to earn a living somehow, and many day-tours include a visit to a factory that employs disabled workers to produce handicrafts or local products.

Online accommodation booking has largely put an end to the old taxi driver scam, whereby new arrivals in town are told that the hotel they asked for is closed or has moved, and are taken to a commission-paying establishment instead. Taxi agency standards have also increased substantially of late, with rigged meters also having largely gone the way of the dodo.

A more sustained complaint is that organized **tours** don't live up to what was promised. Sometimes there are more people on the tour than first stated, for example, or the room doesn't have air-conditioning, or the guide's English is limited. If it's a group tour and you've paid up front, unfortunately there's very little you can do beyond complaining to the agent on your return; you may be lucky and get some form of compensation, but it's unlikely. As always, you tend to get what you pay for, so avoid signing up for dirt-cheap tours.

Women travellers

Vietnam is generally a safe country for women to travel around alone. Most Vietnamese will simply be curious as to why you are on your own and the chances of encountering any threatening behaviour are extremely rare. That said, it pays to take the normal precautions, especially **late at night** when there are few people on the streets; avoid taking a cyclo by yourself, and use taxis from a reputable agency – you will find recommendations for these throughout this guide.

These days most young Vietnamese women **dress** much as their Western counterparts do, but topless sunbathing, even beside a hotel pool, remains a complete no-no.

Festivals and religious events

The Vietnamese year follows a rhythm of festivals and religious observances, ranging from solemn family gatherings at the ancestral altar to national celebrations culminating in Tet, the Vietnamese New Year. In between are countless local festivals, most notably in the Red River Delta, honouring the tutelary spirit of the village or community temple.

The majority of festivals take place in spring, with a second flurry in the autumn months. One festival you might want to make a note of, however, is **Tet** (see box opposite); not only does most of Vietnam close down for the week, but either side of the holiday local transport services are stretched to the limit and international flights are filled by returning overseas Vietnamese.

Many Vietnamese festivals are **Chinese** in origin, imbued with a distinctive flavour over the centuries, but minority groups also hold their own specific celebrations. The ethnic **minorities** continue to punctuate the year with rituals that govern sowing, harvest or hunting, as well as elaborate rites of passage surrounding birth and death. The **Cao Dai** religion (see p.458) has its own array of festivals, while **Christian** communities throughout Vietnam observe the major ceremonies. Christmas is marked as a religious ceremony only by the faithful, though it's becoming a major event for all Vietnamese as an excuse to shop and party, with sax-playing Santas greeting shoppers in front of malls.

The ceremonies you're most likely to see are **weddings** and **funerals**. The tenth lunar month is the most auspicious time for weddings, though at other times you'll also encounter plenty of wedding cavalcades on the road, their lead vehicle draped in colourful ribbons. Funeral processions are recognizable from the white headbands worn by mourners, while close family members dress completely in white. Both weddings and funerals are characterized by streetside parties under makeshift marquees, and since both tend to be joyous occasions, it's often difficult to know what you're witnessing, unless you spot a bridal gown or portrait of the deceased on display.

Most festivals take place according to the **lunar calendar**, which is also closely linked to the Chinese system with a zodiac of twelve animal signs. The most important times during the lunar month (which lasts 29 or 30 days) are the full moon (day one) and the new moon (day fourteen or fifteen). Festivals are often held at these times, which also hold a special significance for Buddhists, who are supposed to pray at the pagoda and avoid eating meat during the two days. On the eve of each full moon, Hoi An now celebrates a **Full-Moon Festival**: traffic is barred from the town centre, where traditional games, dances and music performances take place under the light of silk lanterns.

All Vietnamese calendars show both the lunar and solar (Gregorian) months and dates, but to be sure of a festival date it's best to check locally.

A FESTIVAL CALENDAR

Tet Late January to mid-February. The most important date in the Vietnamese festival calendar is New Year (see box opposite).

Tay Son Festival Late January to mid-February. Martial arts demonstrations in Tay Son District (near Quy Nhon) plus garlanded elephants on parade.

Water-Puppet Festival February. As part of the Tet celebrations a festival of puppetry is held at Thay Pagoda, west of Hanoi.

Lim Singing Festival February to March. Two weeks after Tet, Lim village near Bac Ninh, in the Red River Delta, resounds to the harmonies of "alternate singing" (quan ho) as men and women fling improvised lyrics back and forth.

Hai Ba Trung Festival March. The two Trung sisters (see p.430) are honoured with a parade and dancing at Hanoi's Hai Ba Trung temple.

Perfume Pagoda March to April. Vietnam's most famous pilgrimage site is Chua Huong, west of Hanoi. Thousands of Buddhist pilgrims flock to the pagoda for the festival, which climaxes on the full moon (fourteenth or fifteenth day) of the second month, though the pilgrimage continues for a month either side.

Den Ba Chua Kho March to April. The full moon of the second month sees Hanoians congregating at this temple near Bac Ninh, to petition the goddess for success in business.

Thanh Minh April. Ancestral graves are cleaned and offerings of food, flowers and paper votive objects are made at the beginning of the third lunar month.

Phat Dan May. Lanterns are hung outside the pagodas and Buddhist homes to commemorate Buddha's birth, enlightenment and the attainment of Nirvana.

TET: THE VIETNAMESE NEW YEAR

"Tet", simply meaning "festival", is the accepted name for Vietnam's most important annual event, properly known as **Tet Nguyen Dan**, or festival of the first day. Tet lasts for seven days and falls sometime between the last week of January and the third week of February, on the night of the new moon. This is a time when families get together to celebrate renewal and hope for the new year, when ancestral spirits are welcomed back to the household and when everyone in Vietnam becomes a year older – age is reckoned by the new year and not by individual birthdays.

There's an almost tangible sense of excitement leading up to midnight on the eve of Tet, though the welcoming of the new year is now a much more subdued – and less dangerous – affair since firecrackers were banned in 1995. Instead, all the major cities hold fireworks displays.

PREPARATIONS

Tet is all about **starting the year afresh**, with a clean slate and good intentions. Not only is the house scrubbed, but all debts are paid off and those who can afford it have a haircut and buy new clothes. To attract favourable spirits, good-luck charms are put in the house, most commonly in the form of cockerels or the trinity of male figures representing prosperity, happiness and longevity.

The crucial moments are the first minutes and hours of the new year, as these set the pattern for the whole of the following year. People strive to avoid arguments, swearing or breaking anything – at least during the first three days when a single ill word could tempt bad luck into the house for the whole year ahead. The first visitor on the morning of Tet is also vitally significant: the ideal is someone respected, wealthy and happily married who will bring good fortune to the family; the bereaved, unemployed, accident-prone and even pregnant, on the other hand, are considered ill-favoured. This honour carries with it an onerous responsibility, however: if the family has a bad year, it will be the first-footer's fault.

ONG TAU

Tet kicks off seven days before the new moon with the festival of **Ong Tau**, the god of the hearth (23rd day of the twelfth month). Ong Tau keeps watch over the household throughout the year, wards off evil spirits and makes an annual report of family events, good or bad, to the Jade Emperor. In order to send Ong Tau off to heaven in a benevolent mood, the family cleans its house from top to bottom, and makes offerings to him, including pocket money and a new set of clothes. Ong Tau returns home at midnight on the first chime of the new year and it's this, together with welcoming the ancestral spirits back to share in the party, that warrants such a massive celebration.

FEASTS AND GOOD FORTUNE

The week-long festival is marked by **feasting**: special foods are eaten at Tet, such as pickled vegetables, candied lotus seeds and sugared fruits, all of which are first offered at the family altar. The most famous delicacy is *banh chung* (*banh tet* in the south), a thick square or cylinder of sweet, sticky rice that is prepared only for Tet. The rice is wrapped round a mixture of green-bean paste, pork fat and meat marinated in *nuoc mam*, and then boiled in banana leaves, which impart a pale green colour. According to legend, an impoverished prince of the Hung dynasty invented the cakes over two thousand years ago; his father was so impressed by the simplicity of his son's gift that he named the prince as his heir.

Tet is an expensive time for Vietnamese families, many of whom save for months to get the new year off to a good start. Apart from special foods and new clothes, it's traditional to give children red envelopes containing *li xi*, or lucky money, and to decorate homes with spring blossoms. In the week before Tet, flower markets grace the larger cities: peach blossoms in the north, apricot in Hue and mandarin in the south. Plum and kumquat (symbolizing gold coins) are also popular, alongside the more showy, modern blooms of roses, dahlias or gladioli.

Chua Xu Festival May. The stone statue of Chua Xu at Sam Mountain, Chau Doc, is bathed, and thousands flock to honour her.

Tet Doan Ngo Late May to early June. The summer solstice (fifth day of the fifth moon) is marked by festivities aimed at warding off epidemics brought on by the summer heat. This is also the time of dragon-boat races.

Trang Nguyen (or Vu Lan) August. The day of wandering souls is the second most important festival after Tet. Offerings of food and clothes are made to comfort and nourish the unfortunate souls without a home, and all graves are cleaned. This is also time for the forgiveness of faults, when the King of Hell judges everyone's spirits and metes out reward or punishment as appropriate. Until the fifteenth century prisoners were allowed to go home on this day.

Do Son Buffalo-fighting Festival August. Held in Do Son village, near Haiphong.

Kate Festival September to October. The Cham New Year is celebrated in high style at Po Klong Garai and Po Re Me, both near Phan Rang.

Trung Thu September to October. The mid-autumn festival, also known as Children's Day, is when dragon dances take place and children are given lanterns in the shape of stars, carp or dragons. Special cakes, *banh trung thu*, are eaten at this time of year. These are sticky rice cakes filled with lotus seeds, nuts and candied fruits and are either square like the earth (*banh deo*), or round like the moon (*banh nuong*) and contain the yolk of an egg.

Whale Festival September to October. Crowds gather at Lang Ca Ong, Vung Tau, to make offerings to the whales.

Oc Bom Boc Festival November to December. Boat-racing festival in Soc Trang.

Da Lat Flower Festival Late December/New Year. An annual extravaganza in which the city shows off the abundance of blooms grown locally.

Christmas December 24. Midnight services at the cathedrals in Hanoi and Ho Chi Minh City, and much revelry in the streets.

Sports and outdoor activities

Though Vietnam was slow to develop its huge potential as an outdoor adventure destination, things have really changed in the last few years. Apart from trekking in the mountainous north, visitors can now also go rock climbing, canyoning, sea-kayaking or kitesurfing, among other activities. Da Lat has emerged as Vietnam's adventure sports capital and Mui Ne as its surf city, though some sports like mountain biking can be done throughout the country.

Trekking

The easiest and most popular areas for **trekking** are in the northwest mountains around Sa Pa (see p.395) and Mai Chau (see p.414). Sa Pa is also the starting point for ascents of the country's highest peak, Fan Si Pan, though climbing has become slightly less rewarding since the recent opening of a cable car to the summit. Other options include hiking around Kon Tum (see p.194) or Da Lat (see p.172) in the central highlands, or in one of Vietnam's many national parks, including Phong Nha-Ke Bang, Cat Ba, Cuc Phuong, Bach Ma, Cat Tien and Yok Don. If you'd like to steer clear of the tourist hordes, a trek in the Pu Luong Nature Reserve (see p.314) is a good way to go.

There's no problem about striking out on your own for a day's hiking. However, for anything more adventurous, particularly if you want to overnight in villages, you'll need to **make arrangements in advance**. This is easily done either before you arrive in Vietnam or through local tour agents, most of which offer organized tours and homestay accommodation. In most cases you can also make arrangements through guesthouses and guides on the spot. Note that it's essential to take a guide if you are keen to get off the beaten track: even in this day and age, many areas remain sensitive to the presence of foreigners.

Cycling and motorbiking

Mountain biking is becoming increasingly popular in Vietnam. The classic ride is from Hanoi to Ho Chi Minh City, a journey of between two and three weeks; thankfully, these largely avoid Highway 1 and the battles with trucks and buses that would ensue. Some tour companies offer excursions down the Ho Chi Minh Highway, which runs along the western Truong Son mountain chain and remains largely free of heavy traffic; this route is also popular among motorbike enthusiasts.

The area around Sa Pa is a focus for biking activity, with tour operators offering excursions to suit all levels of experience and fitness. You can choose from half-day excursions to multiday outings including overnighting in minority villages. Other good areas for exploring by bike include Mai Chau, Bac Ha, Da Lat and the Mekong Delta. If you prefer to ride mostly on the flat, note that Mai Chau and the delta are the best places.

North Vietnam is also popular among the **motorbiking** fraternity. Specialist outfits in Hanoi (see p.367) organize tailor-made itineraries taking you way off the beaten track. Two of the most popular motorbike adventures in the country are the Northwest Loop (from Hanoi to Sa Pa and back) and the Dong Van Karst Plateau Geopark (from Hanoi to

Ha Giang province and back). If you enjoy motorbike trips but don't fancy riding yourself, hook up with the Easy Riders in Da Lat (see p.178), who can arrange short or long itineraries anywhere in the country for reasonable prices.

Watersports

With its 3000km coastline, Vietnam should be a paradise for watersports, but the options remain fairly limited at present for a variety of reasons. One is simply a matter of access: the infrastructure is not yet in place (though this is changing fast). More crucial is the presence of potentially dangerous **undercurrents** along much of the coast, accompanied by strong winds at certain times of year. Many of the big beach resorts have guards or put out flags in season indicating where it's safe to swim. Elsewhere, you should check carefully before taking the plunge.

While many of the beaches along the coast are great for **swimming**, the best are those around Mui Ne and Nha Trang, with Hoi An and Da Nang close behind. There are also some delightfully quiet beaches around Ca Na (see p.219) and to the south of Quy Nhon (see p.234). Mui Ne is the country's top venue for **windsurfing** and **kitesurfing**, both of which are now hugely popular; in fact, Mui Ne hosts an international kitesurfing competition each spring (usually in February).

Phu Quoc Island (see p.159), off Vietnam's southern coast, is also famed not only for its fabulous beaches but also as the country's top spot for **snorkelling** and **scuba diving**. The Con Dao Islands and Nha Trang are other popular places to don a snorkel or wet suit, but wherever you dive it's worth noting that standards of maintenance aren't always great, so check equipment carefully and only go out with a properly qualified and registered operator that you trust.

Heading inland, the rivers and waterfalls around Da Lat provide good possibilities for **canyoning** and **rock climbing**, though Cat Ba Island is a good alternative if you'd like to combine rock climbing with sightseeing in Ha Long Bay.

In north Vietnam Ha Long Bay is the watersports centre, while rock climbing here is big as well, and best organized on Cat Ba. Most boat tours of the bay allow time for **swimming** and kayaking – weather permitting – while there are decent beaches on Cat Ba and better still on remote Quan Lan Island. A few tour agents offer **sea-kayaking** trips on the bay, sometimes overnighting in a basic hut on a deserted beach (see p.330).

Other activities

Vietnam has some 800–900 species of birds including several that have only been identified in the past few years. The best places for **birdwatching** are the national parks, including Cuc Phuong (famous also for its springtime butterfly displays), Bach Ma and Cat Tien. The rare Sarus crane, among many other species, spends the dry

---

RESPONSIBLE TOURISM

Though domestic tourism has the greatest impact through sheer weight of numbers, international travellers can play a positive role by setting examples of **responsible behaviour**. Various NGOs and groups involved in the travel industry have developed **guidelines** for tourists and travel companies.

Some of the most important points are: to avoid buying souvenirs made from endangered species or that damage the environment – notably tortoiseshell, ivory and coral in Vietnam; as far as possible, to eat in local restaurants, buy local produce, employ local guides and stay in homestays or locally owned hotels – not only is it usually a lot more fun, but also your money is more likely to benefit smaller communities; to be sensitive to the local culture, including appropriate standards of dress; and to adopt a responsible attitude towards drugs, alcohol and prostitution. Finally, when booking tours, ask how much – if anything – the tour company contributes to conservation and community development at its chosen destinations.

Tour agents in Vietnam with a reputation for their conscientious approach include Handspan, Buffalo Tours, Sinhbalo, Footprint and Ethnic Travel. Intrepid also has a long track record of engaging in sustainable tourism. Among other initiatives, the Netherlands Development Organization (SNV; Ⓦ snvworld.org) has been working with local authorities to draw up tourism development plans and to raise awareness of sustainable development issues, while conservation body Flora and Fauna International (FFI; Ⓦ fauna-flora.org) is also active in Vietnam, helping develop community-based ecotourism. •

season in and around the Tram Chim National Park in the Mekong Delta. For more information, check out Ⓦ vietnambirding.com.

Finally, there are now dozens of excellent **golf** courses in Vietnam – around Ho Chi Minh City, Hanoi, Phan Thiet, Da Nang and Da Lat among others – all with much cheaper green fees than in the West.

Shopping

Souvenir-hunters will find rich pickings in Vietnam, whose eye-catching handicrafts and mementoes range from colonial currency and stamps to fabrics and basketware crafted by the country's ethnic minorities, and from limpet-like conical hats to fake US Army-issue Zippo lighters. Throughout the Guide we've highlighted places to shop, but in general you'll find the best quality, choice and prices in Ho Chi Minh City, Hanoi and Hoi An. Though you'll find more shops now have fixed prices, particularly those catering to tourists, in markets and rural areas prices remain open to negotiation (see box opposite).

Clothing, arts and crafts

Many Western tourists leave Vietnam donning the near-obligatory **conical hat**, or *non la*, sewn from rain- and sun-proof palm fronds; at around 50,000đ for a basic version, they're definitely an affordable keepsake. From the city of Hue comes a more elaborate version, the **poem hat**, or *non bai tho*, in whose brim are inlays which, when held up to the light, reveal lines of poetry or scenes from Vietnamese legend. Vietnamese women traditionally wear the **ao dai** – baggy silk trousers under a knee-length silk tunic slit up both sides. Extraordinarily elegant, *ao dai* can be bought off the peg anywhere in the country for around US$30, or, if you can spare a few days for fitting, you can have one tailor-made for US$50–100, depending on the material.

Local **silk** is sold by the metre in Vietnam's more sizeable markets and in countless outlets in Hoi An, along Dong Khoi in Ho Chi Minh City and on Hanoi's Hang Gai. These same shops also sell ready-made clothes and accessories, including embroidered silk handbags and shoes, and most also offer tailoring. In general, Hoi An's tailors have the best reputation, either working from a pattern book or copying an item you take along. Be sure to allow plenty of time for fittings.

Embroidered **cotton**, in the form of tablecloths, sheets and pillowcases, also makes a popular souvenir. Meanwhile, the sartorial needs of backpackers are well catered for in major tourist destinations, where **T-shirt**-sellers do brisk business. Predictably popular designs include a portrait of Uncle Ho, and the yellow Communist star on a red shirt, though a few stores have expanded into small chains after finding success with edgy or comical designs.

Traditional handicrafts

Of the many types of traditional handicrafts on offer in Vietnam, **lacquerware** (*son mai*) is among the most beautiful. It is also incredibly light, so won't add significantly to your baggage weight. Made by applying multiple layers of resin onto an article and then polishing vigorously to achieve a deep, lustrous sheen, lacquer is used to decorate furniture, boxes, chopsticks and bangles and is sometimes embellished with eggshell or inlays of **mother-of-pearl** (which is also used in its own right, on screens and pictures) – common motifs are animals, fish and elaborate scrolling. More recently, the lacquerware tradition has been hijacked by more contemporary icons, and it's now possible to buy colourful lacquerware paintings of Mickey Mouse, Tin Tin and Batman. Imported synthetic lacquer has also made an appearance. These brightly coloured, almost metallic, finishes may not be for the purist, but they make for eye-catching bowls, vases and all sorts of household items.

Bronze, **brass** and **jade** are also put to good use, appearing in various forms such as carvings, figurines and jewellery. In Hue, brass and copper teapots are popular. Of the porcelain and ceramics available across the country, thigh-high ceramic elephants and other animal figurines are the quirkiest buys – though decidedly tricky to carry home. Look out, too, for boxes and other knick-knacks made from wonderfully aromatic cinnamon and camphor wood. For something a little more culturally elevated, you could invest in a water puppet or a traditional musical instrument (see box, p.478).

Vietnam's **ethnic minorities** are producing increasingly sophisticated fare for the tourist market. Fabrics – sometimes shot through with shimmering gold braid – are their main asset, sold in lengths and also made into purses, shoulder bags and other accoutrements. The minorities of the

THE ART OF BARGAINING

The Vietnamese, not unreasonably, see tourists as wildly rich (how else could they afford to stop working and travel the world?) and a **first quoted price** is usually pitched accordingly. It makes sense, therefore, to be prepared.

First of all, do your homework. Find out the approximate going rate for the item that interests you, either from your hotel or fellow travellers, or from one of the increasing number of fixed-price shops – remembering to take into account the difference in quality, for example, between mass-produced and hand-crafted goods.

The trick then is to remain **friendly** and amused, but also to be realistic: traders will quickly lose interest in a sale if they think you aren't playing the game fairly. Any show of aggression, and you've lost it in more ways than one. If you feel you're on the verge of agreement, **moving away** often pays dividends – it's amazing how often you'll be called back.

Keep a sense of **perspective**. If a session of bargaining is becoming very protracted, step back and remind yourself that you're often arguing the toss over mere pennies – nothing to you, but a lot to the average Vietnamese.

central highlands are adept at basketwork, fashioning backpacks, baskets and mats, as well as bamboo pipes. Hanoi probably has the greatest variety of **minority handicrafts** on sale, though you'll also find plenty available in Ho Chi Minh City. In the far north, Sa Pa is a popular place to buy Hmong clothes, bags and skull-caps, and you'll find lengths of woven fabrics or embroidery in markets throughout the northern mountains.

Paintings

A healthy fine arts scene exists in Vietnam, and **painting** in particular is thriving. In the galleries of Hanoi, Ho Chi Minh City and Hoi An you'll find exquisite works in oil, watercolour, lacquer, charcoal and silk weaving by the country's leading artists. Hanoi is the best single place to look for contemporary art.

For the top names you can expect to pay hundreds or even thousands of dollars. Buyer beware, however: many artists find it lucrative to knock out multiple copies of their own or other people's work. You'll need to know what you're doing, or to buy from a reputable gallery.

A cheap alternative is to snap up a reproduction of a famous image by Dalí or Van Gogh, while something essentially Vietnamese are reproductions of Communist **propaganda posters**, which are on sale almost everywhere.

Memorabilia, trinkets and food

Army surplus gear is still a money-spinner, though fatigues, belts, canteens and dog tags purportedly stolen from a dead or wounded GI are bound to be fakes. The green **pith helmets** with a red star on the front, worn first by the NVA during the American War and now by the regular Vietnamese Army, find more takers. Other items that sell like hot cakes, especially in the south, are fake **Zippo lighters** bearing such pithy adages as "When I die bury me face down, so the whole damn army can kiss my ass" and "We are the unwilling, led by the unqualified, doin' the unnecessary for the ungrateful", though they're not at all authentic GI issue. In Ho Chi Minh City, extravagant wooden **model ships** are sold in a string of shops on Hai Ba Trung, at the east side of Lam Son Square.

Finally, **foodstuffs** that may tempt you include coffee from the central highlands, candied strawberries and artichoke tea from Da Lat, coconut candies from the Mekong Delta, preserved miniature tangerines from Hoi An and packets of tea and dried herbs and spices from the northern highlands. As for **drinks**, most snake wine, rice alcohol etc is securely bottled. The Soc Tinh range of rice-distilled liquor makes an attractively packaged souvenir.

Travelling with children

Travelling through Vietnam with children can be challenging and fun. The Vietnamese adore kids and make a huge fuss of them, with fair-haired children coming in for even more manhandling than usual.

The main concern will probably be **hygiene**: Vietnam can be distinctly unsanitary, and children's stomachs tend to be especially sensitive to unfriendly bacteria. Avoiding spicy foods will help while their stomachs adjust, but if children do become sick it's crucial to keep up their fluid intake, so as to avoid dehydration. Bear in mind, too, that **healthcare facilities** can remain basic outside Hanoi and Ho Chi Minh City, so make sure your travel insurance includes full medical evacuation.

Long bus journeys are tough on young children, so wherever possible take the train or plane – at least the kids can get up and move about in safety. There are reduced fares for children on domestic flights, trains and open-tour buses. On trains, for example, it's free for under-5s (as long as they sit on your lap) and half-price for children aged 5 to 10. Open-tour buses follow roughly the same policy, though children paying a reduced fare are not entitled to a seat; if you don't want them on your lap you'll have to pay full fare. Tours are usually either free or half-price for children.

Many budget **hotels** have family rooms with one double and two single beds, which are generally good value. At more expensive hotels under-12s can normally stay free of charge in their parents' rooms, and baby cots are becoming more widely available.

Activities

One activity that kids love as much as adults is playing on the beach, and Vietnam has some superb **beaches** with affordable resorts in places like Phu Quoc Island (see p.159), Nha Trang (see p.223) and Hoi An (see p.258). Many beach resorts offer boat rides or watersports such as kayaking and some such as the *Anantara Hoi An* (see p.253), also provide hands-on activities such as lantern making.

Some of the better-organized **national parks**, like Cuc Phuong (see p.320) and Cat Tien (see p.172), have well-marked trails and offer the possibility of spotting rare animals as well as a host of unusual tropical plants.

Vietnam has some of the world's most impressive **cable cars** taking visitors to fun destinations. Take the kids to check out a long one (over 3km) to Vinpearl Land Amusement Park on Hon Tre near Nha Trang (see p.227), or a high one (over 1300m altitude gain) to Ba Na Hill Station (see p.268) on a day-trip from Da Nang.

All big cities have **amusement parks** and **water parks**, which are a great way to beat the heat; these include the Dam Sen Water Park in Ho Chi Minh City (see p.91), and the Dak Lak Water Park in Buon Ma Thuot (see p.188). While on the topic of water, the one unmissable activity for kids in Vietnam is a performance of **water puppets**, either in Hanoi (see p.380) or Ho Chi Minh City (see p.79).

Travel essentials

Addresses

Locating an **address** is rarely a problem in Vietnam, but there are a couple of conventions it helps to know about. Where two numbers are separated by a slash, such as 110/5, you simply make for no. 110, where an alley will lead off to a further batch of buildings – you want the fifth one. Where a number is followed by a letter, as in 117a, you're looking for a single block encompassing several addresses, of which one will be 117a. Vietnamese cite addresses without the words for street, avenue and so on; we've followed this practice throughout the Guide except where ambiguity would result.

Costs

With the average Vietnamese annual income hovering around £1400/US$1800/€1600, daily expenses are low, and if you come prepared to do as the locals do, then food and drink can be incredibly cheap – even accommodation needn't be too great an expense. **Bargaining** is very much a part of everyday life, and almost everything is negotiable, from fruit in the market to a room for the night (see box, p.55).

By eating at simple com (rice) and pho (noodle soup) stalls, picking up local buses and opting for the simplest accommodation, there's no reason why you shouldn't be able to adhere to a **daily budget** in the region of £15–20/US$20–25/€18–23. Upgrading to more salubrious lodgings with a few mod cons, eating good food followed by a couple of beers in a bar and signing up for the odd minibus tour and visiting a few sights could bounce your expenditure up to a more realistic £32–40/US$40–50/€35–44. A fair mid-level budget, treating yourself to three-star hotels and more upmarket restaurants, would lie in the £40–80/US$50–100/€45–90 range, depending on the number and type of tours you take. And if you stay at the ritziest city hotels, dine at the swankiest restaurants and rent cars with drivers wherever you go, then the sky's the limit.

Admission charges

Admission charges are usually levied at museums, historic sights, national parks and any place that attracts tourists – sometimes even beaches. The good news is that amounts are low, starting at just a few thousand dong, rising to 15,000đ for most museums, and topping out at 150,000đ for the Cham ruins at My Son or Hue's citadel. Note that there's often a hefty additional fee for **cameras** and **videos** at major sights.

Apart from those with some historical significance, **pagodas and temples** are usually free, though you'll notice locals leaving donations of a few thousand dong in the collection box or on one of the altar plates – it doesn't hurt to do the same, though such actions are not expected or requested of foreign visitors.

Culture and etiquette

With its blend of Confucianism and Buddhism, Vietnamese society tends to be both conservative and, at the same time, fairly tolerant. This means you will rarely be remonstrated with for your **dress** or behaviour, even if your hosts disapprove of it. By following a few simple rules, you can minimize the risk of causing offence. This is particularly important in rural areas and small towns where people are less used to the eccentric habits of foreigners.

As a visitor, it's recommended that you err on the side of caution. Shorts and sleeveless shirts are fine for the beach, but less welcome in pagodas, temples and other religious sites. When dealing with officialdom, it also pays to look as neat and tidy as possible – anything else may be taken as a mark of disrespect.

Women in particular should dress modestly, especially in the countryside and ethnic minority areas, where revealing too much flesh is regarded as offensive. It's also worth noting that **nudity**, either male or female, on the beach is absolutely beyond the pale.

When entering a Cao Dai temple, the main building of a pagoda or a private home it's the custom to remove your **shoes**. In some pagodas nowadays this may only be required when stepping onto the prayer mats – ask or watch what other people do. In a pagoda or temple you are also expected to leave a small donation.

Officially, **homosexuality** is regarded as a "social evil", alongside drugs and prostitution. However, there is no law explicitly banning homosexual activity and, as long as it is not practised openly, it

> ### DOLLARS OR DONG?
>
> In Vietnam, some of the larger costs (such as accommodation and transport) are quoted in **US dollars**, but can be paid for in either currency; everything else is usually paid in **dong**. Throughout the Guide we've priced accommodation and certain transport expenses (such as tours) in dollars, and all other expenses in dong.

is largely ignored. Indeed, the number of openly gay men has increased noticeably in recent years, particularly in Ho Chi Minh City and Hanoi, and homosexuality is discussed more frequently in the media, although the lesbian scene remains very low-key. Although outward discrimination is rare, this is still a very traditional society and it pays to be discreet in Vietnam. For more information, consult the excellent Utopia Asia website, Ⓦ utopia-asia.com.

As in most Asian countries, it's not normal to get outwardly angry, and it certainly won't get things moving any quicker. Passing round cigarettes (to men only) is always appreciated and is widely used as a social gambit aimed at progressing tricky negotiations, bargaining and so forth.

Tipping, while not expected, is always appreciated; in general, a few thousand dong should suffice. Smart restaurants and hotels normally add a service charge, but if not ten percent is the norm in a restaurant, while the amount in a hotel will depend on the grade of hotel and what services they've provided. If you're pleased with the service, you should also tip the guide, and the driver where appropriate, at the end of a tour.

Other social conventions worth noting are that you shouldn't touch **children** on the head and, unlike in the West, it's best to ignore a young baby rather than praise it, since it's believed that this attracts the attention of jealous spirits who will cause the baby to fall ill.

Electricity

The **electricity** supply in Vietnam is 220 volts. Plugs generally have two round pins, though you may come across sockets accepting two flat pins and even some that take three pins. Adaptors can be found in electrical shops around the land, though as always it's often best to come prepared. Power supplies can be erratic in the sticks, so be prepared for cuts and surges.

Insurance

It is essential to have a good **travel insurance policy** to cover against theft, loss and illness or injury. It's also advisable to have medical cover that includes evacuation in the event of serious illness, as the local hospitals aren't that great. Most policies exclude so-called dangerous sports unless an extra premium is paid: in Vietnam this can include scuba diving, whitewater rafting, kitesurfing, rock climbing and trekking. If you're doing any motorbike touring, you are strongly advised to take out full medical insurance including emergency evacuation; make sure the policy specifically covers you for motorbiking in Vietnam, and ascertain whether benefits will be paid as treatment proceeds or only after you return home, and whether there is a 24-hour medical emergency number. If you need to make a claim, you should keep receipts for medicines and medical treatment, and in the event that you have anything stolen, you must obtain an official statement from the police.

Internet

Going online in Vietnam will present you will few problems, though it is still monitored and controlled by a government fearful of this potentially subversive means of communication. Social networking sites like Facebook have occasionally been blocked.

In the major cities and tourist centres, most cafés and hotels provide **wi-fi**, while the same is becoming true even in smaller towns around the country. Unfortunately, some top-end hotels still charge a hefty fee for the privilege of getting online. Wi-fi has only been mentioned in the Guide's accommodation listings when it's not available, not free or otherwise restricted in some way.

Laundry

Most top- and mid-range hotels provide a **laundry service**, and many budget hotels do too, but rates can vary wildly so it's worth checking first. In the bigger cities, especially in tourist areas, you'll find laundry shops on the street, where the rate is usually 10,000–20,000đ per kilo. Clothes are often given a rigorous scrubbing by hand, so don't submit anything delicate.

Maps

The best **maps** of Vietnam are online – the country is well covered on Google Maps and local site ⓦ diadiem.com, as well as on smartphone apps such as the excellent ⓦ maps.me. Alternatively, the locally produced maps you'll find on sale in all the major towns and tourist destinations in Vietnam aren't bad, and you'll most likely be able to pick up free versions of them at your accommodation.

Money

Vietnam's unit of currency is the **dong**, which you'll see abbreviated as "đ", "d" or "VND" after an amount. Notes come in a wide variety of denominations – the main ones of 20,000đ, 50,000đ, 100,000đ, 200,000đ and 500,000đ are all polymer, while 1000đ, 2000đ and 5000đ are about the only paper ones you'll still see. Coins are next to invisible, though they come in denominations from 200–500đ. In addition to the dong, the **American dollar** operates as a parallel, unofficial currency (see box, p.57) and it's a good idea to carry some dollars as a back-up to pay large bills. On the whole, though, it's more convenient to operate in dong.

Dong are not available outside Vietnam at present, but there are **ATMs** in all international airports and at the major border crossings – xe om and taxi drivers will accept small dollar bills, and

EXCHANGE RATES

At the time of research, the **exchange rate** was around 30,000đ to £1; 23,000đ to US$1; 26,000đ to €1; 17,500đ to CAN$1; 17,000đ to AUS$1; and 16,500đ to NZ$1. Thankfully, inflation rates have stabilized in recent years, but for the latest exchange rates, go to ⓦxe.com.

once you've reached a town of any size, there'll be ATMs all over the place. Most ATMs accept Visa, MasterCard and American Express cards issued abroad, and more and more accept other cards too, including Cirrus, Plus and Union Pay. The maximum withdrawal is between two and five million dong at a time (depending on the bank), with a charge of 20,000–30,000đ per transaction (in addition to whatever surcharges your own bank levies). In Hanoi and Ho Chi Minh City you'll also find ATMs operated by ANZ and HSBC, which accept a wider range of cards.

Banks and **exchange bureaux** rarely levy charges for changing foreign currency into dong; banks in major cities will accept euros and other major currencies, but elsewhere may only accept dollars. Some tour agents and hotels will also change money, though at a less attractive rate than the banks, and some jewellery shops in Vietnam will exchange dollars at a slightly better rate. Wherever you change money, ask for a mix of denominations (in remote places, bigger bills can be hard to split), and refuse really tatty banknotes, as you'll have difficulty getting anyone else to accept them.

Major **credit cards** – Visa, MasterCard and, to a lesser extent, American Express – are accepted in Vietnam's main cities and major tourist spots. All top-level and many mid-level hotels will accept them, as will a growing number of restaurants, though some places levy surcharges of three to four percent.

Having **money wired** from home via MoneyGram (UK ☎0800 026 0535, US ☎1 800 666 3947; ⓦmoneygram.com) or Western Union (US ☎1 800 325 6000, ⓦwesternunion.com) is never cheap, and should be considered a last resort. It's also possible to have money wired directly from a bank or post office in your home country to a bank in Vietnam, although this has the added complication of involving two separate institutions; money wired this way normally takes two working days to arrive, and charges vary according to the amount sent.

Opening hours

Basic **hours of business** are 7.30–11.30am and 1.30–4.30pm, though after lunch nothing really gets going again before 2pm. The standard closing day for **offices** is Sunday, and many now also close on Saturdays, including most government offices.

Most **banks** tend to work Monday to Friday 8–11.30am and 1–4pm, though some stay open later in the afternoon or may forego a lunch break. In tourist centres you'll even find branches open on evenings and weekends. **Post offices** keep much longer hours, in general staying open from 6.30am through to 9pm, sometimes with no closing day. Some sub-post offices work shorter hours and close at weekends.

Shops and **markets** open seven days a week and in theory keep going all day, though in practice most stallholders and many private shopkeepers will take a siesta. Shops mostly stay open late into the evenings, perhaps until 8pm or beyond in the big cities.

Museums tend to close one day a week, generally on Mondays, and their core opening hours are 8–11am and 2–4pm. **Temples** and **pagodas** occasionally close for lunch but are otherwise open all week and don't close until late evening.

Post

Post can take anything from four days to four weeks in or out of Vietnam, depending largely where you are. Services are quickest and most reliable from the major towns, where eight to ten days is the norm. **Overseas postal rates** are reasonable: a postcard costs 20,000–30,000đ, while the price of a letter is in the region of 45,000đ for the minimum weight. **Express Mail Service** (EMS) operates to most countries and certain destinations within Vietnam; the service cuts down delivery times substantially and the letter or parcel is automatically registered. For a minimum-weight dispatch by EMS (under

PUBLIC HOLIDAYS

January 1 New Year's Day
Late January/mid-February (dates vary each year): Tet, Vietnamese New Year (see box, p.51)
10th day of 3rd lunar month (usually April): Vietnamese Kings Commemoration Day (aka Hung Kings Festival)
April 30 Liberation of Saigon, 1975
May 1 International Labour Day
September 2 National Day

500g), you'll pay around US$40 to the UK or the US, and US$25 to Australia.

When **sending parcels** out of Vietnam, take everything to the post office unwrapped since it will be inspected for any customs liability and wrapped for you, and the whole process, including wrapping and customs inspection, will cost you upwards of 50,000đ. It's advisable to register any package containing valuable items.

Telephones

Mobile phones are as ubiquitous in Vietnam as they are everywhere else. However, transport centres like airports and bus stations still maintain a few functioning landline booths, which accept only pre-paid phone cards, not coins. All post offices also operate a public phone service, where the cost is displayed as you speak and you pay the cashier afterwards. Local calls are easy to make and are often free, though you may be charged a small fee of a few thousand dong for the service if, for example, you use the phone in a hotel lobby.

Mobile phones

If you want to use your own **mobile phone** in Vietnam, the simplest – and cheapest – thing to do is to buy a SIM card locally (or even a phone, if your own is locked). Since a governmental crackdown on unregistered cards, it is now best to go to stores run by the major operators – you'll find them at the

---

major international airports (bring your passport, too). The best option at the time of research was Viettel (Ⓦviettel.com.vn), particularly for travellers also heading to Cambodia and/or Laos, since the company removed roaming charges in 2017. The other big phone companies, Vinaphone (Ⓦvinaphone.com.vn) and Mobifone (Ⓦmobifone.vn), also offer English-language support and similar prices, though Vinaphone has the edge for geographical coverage (which extends pretty much nationwide). At the time of research, a SIM card with 5GB of data cost around 100,000đ; further data is available from as little as 10,000đ to 500,000đ, and you can top up at any store or kiosk featuring your provider's logo.

The other, more expensive, option is to stick with your home service-provider – though you'll need to check beforehand whether it offers international roaming services. In many cases it could work out cheaper to just buy a simple mobile phone in Vietnam for around US$20 and give everyone your new number.

Time

Vietnam is seven hours ahead of London, twelve hours ahead of New York, fifteen hours ahead of Los Angeles, one hour behind Perth and three hours behind Sydney – give or take an hour or two when summer time is in operation.

Tourist information

Tourist information on Vietnam is at a premium. The Vietnamese government maintains a handful of **tourist promotion offices** and a smattering of accredited travel agencies around the globe, most of which can supply you with only the most basic information. You'll generally find far better information online – a couple of the more useful and interesting sites are Ⓦtravelfish.org, which is a regularly updated online guide to Southeast Asia, and Ⓦrustycompass.com, which offers candid reviews of attractions, hotels and restaurants by an expat resident. In addition, many English-language **magazines** (see p.48) have tandem websites that include restaurant and event listings, as well as feature articles – they're excellent sources of info.

In Vietnam itself there's a frustrating dearth of free and impartial advice. The state-run **tourist offices** – under the auspices of either the Vietnam National Administration of Tourism (Ⓦvietnamtourism.com) or the local provincial organization – are thinly disguised, profit-making tour agents, which don't take kindly to being treated as information bureaux

---

DIALLING CODES

All phone numbers in Vietnam consist of nine to eleven digits, with the first two to four digits representing the area code and the remaining digits the specific number. The complete number must be dialled whether you are phoning locally or long distance.

To **call Vietnam from abroad**, dial your international access code, then ❶84, then the number minus its first 0.

To **call abroad from Vietnam**, dial ❶00 followed by the country code (see below), then the area code (minus the first 0, if there is one), then the number.

Australia ❶61
Canada ❶1
Ireland ❶353
New Zealand ❶64
South Africa ❶27
UK ❶44
US ❶1

(though their official websites often have a lot of useful information about destinations and practicalities such as visas). In any case, Western concepts of information don't necessarily apply here – you won't find any information on bus timetables, for example.

You'll generally have far more luck approaching hotel staff or one of the many **private tour agencies** operating in all the major tourist spots, as staff there have become accustomed to Westerners' demands for advice. There's also a government-run **telephone information service** (☎1080), which has some English-speaking staff who will be able to answer all manner of questions – if you can get through, since the lines are often busy.

Travellers with special needs

Although Vietnam is home to so many war-wounded, few provisions are made for the disabled, so you'll have to be pretty self-reliant. It's important to contact airlines, hotels and tour companies as far in advance as possible to make sure they can accommodate your requirements.

Getting around can be made a little easier by taking internal flights, or by renting a private car or minibus with a driver; taxis are also widely available in all cities. Even so, the roads with speeding traffic and the cluttered and uneven pavements – if the pavements even exist – can pose real problems. Furthermore, relatively few buildings are equipped with ramps and lifts.

When it comes to **accommodation**, Vietnam's new luxury hotels usually offer one or two specially adapted rooms. Elsewhere, the best you can hope for is a ground-floor room, or a hotel with a lift.

One, albeit expensive, option is to ask a tour agent to arrange a **customized tour**. Contact one of the recommended agents in Ho Chi Minh City (see p.88) or Hanoi (see p.367) for more information.

Working and studying in Vietnam

Without a prearranged job and work permit, you shouldn't bank on finding work in Vietnam. That said, you could try approaching some of the Western companies operating in Hanoi and Ho Chi Minh City if you have specific skills to offer.

Otherwise, **English-language teaching** is probably the easiest job to land, especially if you have a TEFL, TESOL or CELTA qualification. Universities are worth approaching, though you'll find that pay is better at private schools, where qualified teachers earn upwards of US$20 an hour. In either case, you'll need to apply for a work permit, sponsored by your employer, and then a working visa. Private tutoring is an unwieldy way of earning a crust, as you'll have to pop out of the country every few months to procure a new visa. Furthermore, the authorities are clamping down on people working without the proper authorizations.

The main English-language teaching operations recruiting in Vietnam include the British Council (🖥britishcouncil.vn), ILA Vietnam (🖥www.ilavietnam .com), Language Link Vietnam (🖥languagelink.edu .vn) and RMIT International University (🖥rmit.edu.vn). The TEFL website (🖥tefl.com) and Dave's ESL Café (🖥eslcafe.com) also have lists of English-teaching vacancies in addition to lots of other useful information.

There are also opportunities for **volunteer work**. Try contacting the organizations listed below, or check the websites of the NGO Resource Centre Vietnam (🖥ngocentre.org.vn) and Volunteer Abroad (🖥volunteerabroad.com).

STUDY, WORK AND VOLUNTEER PROGRAMMES

Australian Volunteers International 🖥 avi.org.au. Offers postings for up to two years, focusing on rural development, vocational education and capacity building.

Bamboo 🖥 wearebamboo.com. Born out of the Global Volunteer Network, this NGO supports the work of local communities through the placement of international volunteers.

British Council 🖥 britishcouncil.org. The British Council's TEFL vacancies are posted on the Jobs section of their website.

Brockport Vietnam Project 🖥 brockportabroad.com. Opportunities for American undergraduates and graduates to study in Da Nang, and to participate in community service activities.

Council on International Educational Exchange (CIEE) 🖥 ciee.org. This nonprofit organization runs semester and academic-year programmes in Vietnam.

Earthwatch Institute 🖥 earthwatch.org. Long-established international charity with environmental and archeological research projects worldwide, including Vietnam. Participation mainly as a paying volunteer, but fellowships for teachers and students are available.

Voluntary Service Overseas (VSO) 🖥 vsointernational.org. A British government-funded organization that places volunteers in various projects around the world.

Volunteers for Peace US ☎ 802 540 3060, 🖥 vfp.org. Nonprofit organization with links to a huge international network of "workcamps", which are two- to four-week programmes that bring volunteers together from many countries to carry out needed community projects. Most workcamps are in summer, with registration by April or May.

Ho Chi Minh City and around

HO CHI MINH CITY

1

Ho Chi Minh City and around

Reverberating with the whirr of a million motorbikes, Ho Chi Minh City (HCMC) is a metropolis on the move. By turns chaotic, elegant, exotic and zestful, this has long been one of Asia's more interesting cities, ever since the days when it answered to the evocative name of Saigon. National reunification ushered in a far less evocative moniker (Thanh Pho Ho Chi Minh, to give it the full Vietnamese title), and more than eight million people now live in this effervescent city, making it more populous than Hanoi. Compared to the more romantic, mellow national capital, Ho Chi Minh City comes across as a hyper-commercial flurry of sights and sounds, and functions as the crucible in which Vietnam's rallying fortunes are boiling. All the accoutrements of economic success are here – fine restaurants, flashy hotels, glitzy bars and clubs, and shops selling imported luxury goods – adding a glossy veneer to the city's hotchpotch landscape of French colonial architecture, venerable pagodas and austere, Soviet-style housing blocks.

Few corners of the city afford respite from the cacophony of **construction work** casting up new office blocks and hotels with logic-defying speed. An increasing number of cars and minibuses jostle with an organic mass of state-of-the-art SUVs, choking the tree-lined streets and boulevards. Amid this melee, the local people go about their daily life: smartly dressed schoolkids wander past streetside baguette-sellers; shoppers and businessfolk ride motorbikes clad in gangster-style bandanas to protect their skin from the sun and dust; while teenagers in designer jeans take selfies of each other with their smartphones. Much of the fun of being in Ho Chi Minh City derives from the simple pleasure of absorbing this **flurry of activity** – something best done from a roadside café or restaurant, or perhaps with an evening stroll down the newly pedestrianized Nguyen Hue.

For some visitors, the American War is their primary frame of reference, and such historical hotspots as the **Reunification Palace** rank highly on their itineraries. In addition, ostentatious reminders of French rule abound, among them such memorable buildings as **Notre Dame Cathedral** and the grandiose **Hotel de Ville** – but even these look spanking-new when compared to gloriously musty edifices like **Quan Am Pagoda**

BURNING INCENSE, JADE EMPEROR PAGODA

Highlights

❶ Evening prom along Nguyen Hue The city finally has a decent pedestrianized area, and it's a real beaut – come around sundown to see locals enjoying a simple stroll. **See p.74**

❷ Bitexco Tower Enjoy the superlative views from the upper levels of the city's tallest building. **See p.75**

❸ War Remnants Museum The city's most moving museum, a stark reminder of man's inhumanity to man. **See p.78**

❹ Jade Emperor Pagoda Beautifully carved woodwork, an eclectic collection of deities and a constant fog of incense all combine to make this the city's most fascinating temple. **See p.81**

❺ Cho Lon Take an improvised wander around the streets of "big market" – the city's occasionally manic Chinatown. **See p.82**

❻ Ben Thanh Street Food Market Named after the regular market just alongside, this fantastic new venue hosts umpteen street food stalls, and is proving tremendously popular with foreigners and locals alike. **See p.98**

❼ Craft beer HCMC has got into craft beer in a big way, and at bars such as Pasteur Street Brewing Company you can quaff local ales. **See p.101**

❽ A day-trip north Two of the biggest draws for travellers to HCMC – the Cu Chi tunnels and Cao Dai temple – are actually outside the city itself, and best tackled on a day-tour. **See p.105**

HIGHLIGHTS ARE MARKED ON THE MAP ON P.66, P.68 AND P.70

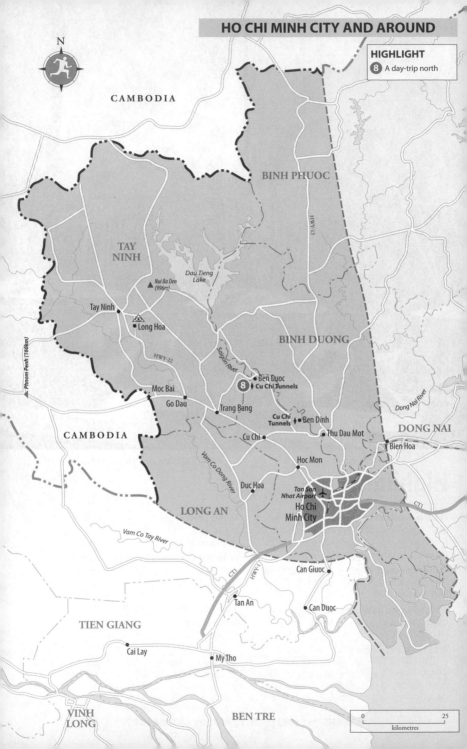

HO CHI MINH CITY AND AROUND

HIGHLIGHT
8 A day-trip north

N

CAMBODIA

BINH PHUOC

HWY-13

TAY NINH

Dau Tieng Lake

Nui Ba Den (996m)

Tay Ninh

Long Hoa

Saigon River

BINH DUONG

HWY-22

Ben Duoc
8 Cu Chi Tunnels

Moc Bai

Go Dau

Trang Bang

Cu Chi Tunnels   Ben Dinh

Phnom Penh (160km)

CAMBODIA

Vam Co Dong River

Cu Chi   Thu Dau Mot   DONG NAI

Bien Hoa

Dong Nai River

CT1

Hoc Mon

Duc Hoa

Tan Son Nhat Airport

Ho Chi Minh City

LONG AN

Vam Co Tay River

CT1

CT1

Can Giuoc

Tan An

Can Duoc

TIEN GIANG

Cai Lay

My Tho

VINH LONG

BEN TRE

0   25
kilometres

1

and the **Jade Emperor Pagoda**, just a couple of the many captivating places of worship across the city. And if the chaos becomes too much, you can escape to the relative calm of the **Botanical Gardens** – also home to the city's **History Museum** and **zoo**. Most of these sights are strewn between three component wards of central **District One** – Ben Nghe, Pham Ngu Lao and Ben Thanh.

It's one of Ho Chi Minh City's many charms that once you've exhausted, or been exhausted by, all it has to offer, paddy fields, beaches and wide-open countryside are not far away. The most popular trip out of the city is to the **Cu Chi tunnels**, where villagers once dug themselves out of the range of American shelling. The tunnels are often twinned with a tour around the beautiful **Cao Dai Great Temple** in Tay Ninh.

The best time to visit tropical Ho Chi Minh City is in the dry season, which runs from December through to April. During the wet season, between May and November, there are frequent tropical storms, though these won't disrupt your travels too much. Average temperatures, year-round, hover between 26°C and 29°C, though March, April and May are the hottest months.

Brief history

Knowledge of Ho Chi Minh City's early history is sketchy at best. Between the first and sixth centuries, the territory on which it lies fell under the nominal rule of the **Funan Empire** to the west. Funan was subsequently absorbed by the Kambuja peoples of the pre-Angkor **Chen La Empire**, but it is unlikely that these Imperial machinations had much bearing on the sleepy fishing backwater that would later develop into Ho Chi Minh City.

Khmer fishermen eked out a living here, building their huts on the stable ground just north of the delta wetlands, which made it ideal for human settlement. Originally named **Prei Nokor**, it flourished as an entrepôt for Cambodian boats pushing down the Mekong River, and by the seventeenth century it boasted a garrison and a mercantile community that embraced Malay, Indian and Chinese traders.

Such a dynamic settlement was bound to draw attention from the north. By the eighteenth century, the Viets had subdued the kingdom of Champa, and this area was swallowed up by Hue's **Nguyen dynasty**. With new ownership came a new name, **Saigon**, thought to have derived from the Vietnamese word for the kapok tree. During the **Tay Son Rebellion**, which started in 1771, Nguyen Anh bricked the whole settlement into a walled fortress, the eight-sided **Gia Dinh Citadel**. The army that put down the Tay Son brothers included an assisting French military force, who grappled for several decades to undermine Vietnamese control in the region and develop a trading post in Asia. Finally, in 1861, they seized Saigon, using Emperor Tu Duc's persecution of French missionaries as a pretext. The 1862 **Treaty of Saigon** declared the city the capital of French Cochinchina.

Colonial-era Saigon

Ho Chi Minh City owes much of its form and character to the **French colonists**: channels were filled in, marshlands drained and steam tramways set to work along its regimental grid of boulevards, which by the 1930s sported names like Boulevard de la Somme and Rue Rousseau. Flashy examples of European architecture were erected, cafés and boutiques sprang up to cater for its new vermouth-sipping, baguette-munching citizens and the city was imbued with such an all-round Gallic air that Somerset Maugham, visiting in the 1930s, found it reminiscent of "a little provincial town in the south of France, a blithe and smiling little place". The French colonials bankrolled improvements to Saigon with the vast profits they were able to cream from exporting Vietnam's **rubber** and **rice** out of the city's rapidly expanding seaport.

On a human level, however, French rule was invariably harsh; dissent crystallized in the form of strikes through the 1920s and 1930s, but the nationalist movement hadn't

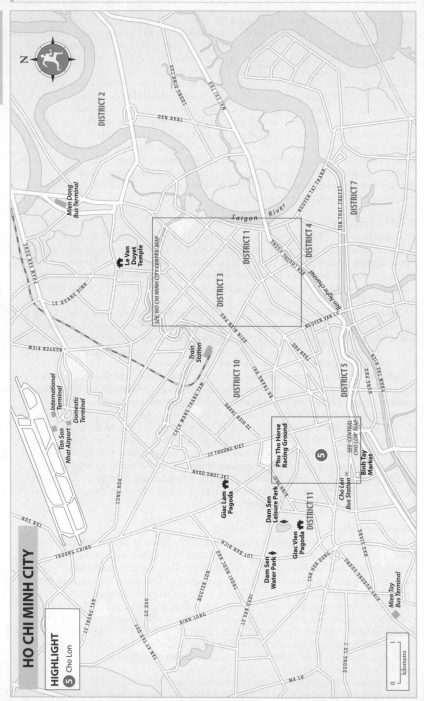

HO CHI MINH CITY

HIGHLIGHT

5 Cho Lon

HO CHI MINH CITY ORIENTATION

HCMC is divided into 24 districts, though tourists rarely travel beyond districts One, Three and Five. **District One** constitutes the centre of the city, while **District Three** lies between the centre and the airport, and **District Five** is home to the most interesting parts of Cho Lon (see p.82).

These districts are in turn divided up into wards, though these are only really relevant to travellers in District One. **Ben Nghe Ward** makes up much of District One's bulk, hugging the west bank of the Saigon River; traditionally the French Quarter of the city, this area is still widely known as Saigon. It's filled to near bursting point with hotels (mostly mid- to upper-range), shops and restaurants, and boasts a fair few sights, including some lovely examples of colonial architecture.

Just to the southwest is **Pham Ngu Lao Ward** – its official title is based on the name of a major road, though many refer to the area as Bui Vien or De Tham on account of the other two important local thoroughfares here. Facing a pleasant stretch of quasi-parkland, Pham Ngu Lao is the largest and busiest of the three roads; parallel to the south, Bui Vien is a small street that fills up with beer-guzzling backpackers and locals each evening, while De Tham connects the two and is the drop-off point for most of those arriving in HCMC on an open-tour bus.

North of the backpacker zone is **Ben Thanh Ward**, home to the Reunification Palace, one of the city's best sights and surrounded by other appealing places to visit. North of the centre, you'll find some great Buddhist monuments, as well as a good museum.

Way out west across an uninspiring stretch of no-man's-land is the area known as **Cho Lon**, famed for its large Chinese population and the many colourful temples and shrines built by their ancestors. Elsewhere, there are a couple of areas of note: **District Four**, just south across the channel from District One, is increasingly popular for its street food; and **District Two**, east across the Saigon River, is now home to many expats and the Saigonese *nouveau riche*.

gathered any real head of steam before **World War II**'s tendrils spread to Southeast Asia. At its close, the **Potsdam Conference** of 1945 set the British Army the task of disarming Japanese troops in southern Vietnam. Arriving in Saigon two months later, they promptly returned power to the French. So began thirty years of war, though Saigon itself saw little action during this conflict.

Saigon in the American War

Following the partition of Vietnam in 1954 (see p.440), Saigon was designated the capital of the **Republic of South Vietnam** by President Diem. In the mid-1960s, the city became the nerve centre of the American war effort – as well as its R&R capital, with a slew of sleazy bars along Dong Khoi (known then as Tu Do) catering to GIs on leave from duty. Despite the Communist bomb attacks and demonstrations by students and monks that periodically disturbed the peace, local entrepreneurs prospered on the back of the tens of thousands of Americans posted here. The gravy train ran out of steam with the withdrawal of American troops in 1973, and two years later the **Ho Chi Minh Campaign** rolled into the city and through the gates of the presidential palace, and the Communists were in control. Within a year, Saigon had been renamed **Ho Chi Minh City**.

Post-reunification

The **war years** extracted a heavy toll: American carpet-bombing of the Vietnamese countryside forced millions of refugees into the relative safety of the city, and ill-advised, post-reunification policies triggered a social and economic stagnation whose ramifications still echo like ripples on a lake. Persecution of southerners with links to the Americans saw many thousands sent to re-education camps. Millions more fled the country by boat.

1

Le Van Duyet Temple (800m)

HO CHI MINH CITY CENTRE

Tan Son Nhat Airport (5km)

Mien Dong Bus Station (2.8km)

0   500
metres

N

TAN DINH

Jade Emperor Pagoda

History Museum

DA KAO

Botanical Gardens and Zoo

Le Van Tam Park

Train Station (700m) & An Suong Bus Station (12km)

SEE 'BEN NGHE' MAP FOR DETAIL

War Remnants Museum

BEN NGHE

Xa Loi Pagoda

Golden Dragon Water Puppet Theatre

Reunification Palace

Cong Vien Van Hoa Park

BEN THANH

Sri Mariamman Hindu Temple

Ben Thanh Market

Veggy's
Ben Thanh Bus Station

NGUYEN THAI BINH

Saigon River

Cho Lon (4km)

Cong Vien

Fine Art Museum

PHAM NGU LAO

Ben Nghe Channel

SEE 'PHAM NGU LAO' MAP FOR DETAIL

CAU ONG LANH

■ ACCOMMODATION
Della Boutique	10
Emm	1
Fusion Suites	4
Himalaya Phoenix Hostel	11
Lavender	3
New World	9
Nguyen Shack	7
Pullman	12
Sanouva	5
Silverland Central	6
Sofitel Plaza	2
Townhouse 50	8

● SHOPPING
Fine Arts Museum	2
Tay Son	1

● EATING
An Vien	5
Au Parc	8
Banh Xeo	3
Ben Thanh Street Food Market	11
Cuc Gach Quan	1
Huynh Hoa	12
Loving Hut	2
Milkbar	9
Nam Giao	10
Napoly Café	7
Ngoc Suong	14
Pho 79	13
Pho Hoa	4
Quan Nem	6
San Fu Lou	16
Vatel	15

■ DRINKING
Lush	1
Saigon Soul Pool Party	5
Vespa Sofar	6
Vung Oi	2
Vuvuzela	4
Yoko	3

HIGHLIGHTS
1 Evening prom along Nguyen Hue
2 Bitexco Tower
3 War Remnants Museum
4 Jade Emperor Pagoda
6 Ben Thanh Street Food Market
7 Craft beer

Only in 1986, when *doi moi* (the **economic liberalization**) was established and a market economy reintroduced, did the fortunes of the city show signs of taking an upturn. Today the city's resurgence is well advanced, as made evident by the legions of new high-rise buildings sprouting up in the city centre and beyond – it's almost impossible to believe that the 92m-high Sunwah Tower, sat humbly on Nguyen Hue (see map, p.72), was the city's tallest building as recently as 1995. There are now over forty taller structures around the city, with the same number again under construction at the time of research – the Landmark 81 building (due to be completed in 2018) will soon top the lot at 460m, and it's set to be the eleventh-tallest building in the world upon completion. These immense construction projects hint at the size of HCMC's **burgeoning middle class**. In addition, the city's culinary options and cultural make-up are growing ever more cosmopolitan, while major streets are being beautified and pedestrian-friendly areas are being created. Even the city's signature motorbike mayhem may soon be reduced once the brand-new subway system is up and running (see p.90). All in all, it's no surprise that the Saigonese are eyeing the future with unprecedented optimism.

Ben Nghe

Ho Chi Minh City's de facto city centre is **Ben Nghe**, a busy area dotted with prime specimens of **colonial-era architecture** (see box, p.74). Bisecting the zone is **Dong Khoi**, one of the city's main streets. Though it is currently undergoing massive changes, with entire blocks being razed and towering monoliths transforming its image further still, the street still has some character in the form of chic boutiques with eye-catching window displays and cute cafés in which to pause between shopping and sightseeing.

One block west of Dong Khoi is **Nguyen Hue**, created when Saigon's French administrators laid Charner Boulevard over a filled-in canal and down to the Saigon River. Their brief was to replicate the elegance of a tree-lined Parisian boulevard, and in its day this broad avenue was known as the Champs Elysées of the East; following the American War it became somewhat run-down and scruffy, though things are looking up once more with the addition of a new **pedestrian promenade** (see p.74).

Both Dong Khoi and Nguyen Hue end at the **Saigon River**. In colonial times, the quay hugging its confluence with the Ben Nghe Channel provided new arrivals with their first real glimpse of Indochina: scores of coolie-hatted dock-workers lugging sacks of rice off ships; shrimp farmers dredging the shallows; and junks and sampans bobbing on the tide under the vigilant gaze of *colons* imbibing at nearby cafés.

The sights listed here follow a general route southeast from the cathedral at the top of Dong Khoi. You can spend half a day mopping them up – and enjoying the odd coffee or snack – on your way south to **Me Linh Square**, where a statue of Tran Hung Dao points across the river.

DONG KHOI: STREET OF MANY NAMES

Slender **Dong Khoi**, running for just over 1km from Le Duan to the Saigon River, has long mirrored Ho Chi Minh City's changing fortunes. The French knew the road as **Rue Catinat**, a tamarind-shaded thoroughfare that constituted the heart of French colonial life. Here the *colons* would promenade, stopping at chic boutiques and perfumeries and gathering in cafés such as the *Taverne Alsacienne* for a vermouth, before hailing a *pousse-pousse* (a hand-pulled variation on the cyclo) to run them home. With the departure of the French in 1954, President Diem saw fit to change the street's name to **Tu Do** ("Freedom"), and it was under this guise that a generation of young American GIs came to know it as they toured the glut of bars – *Wild West*, *Uncle Sam's*, *Playboy* – that sprang up. After Saigon fell in 1975, the more politically correct moniker of **Dong Khoi** ("Uprising") was adopted, but the street quickly went to seed in the dark, pre-*doi moi* years, and by the Seventies had gone, in the words of Le Ly Hayslip, from "bejewelled, jaded dowager to shabby, grasping bag lady".

1

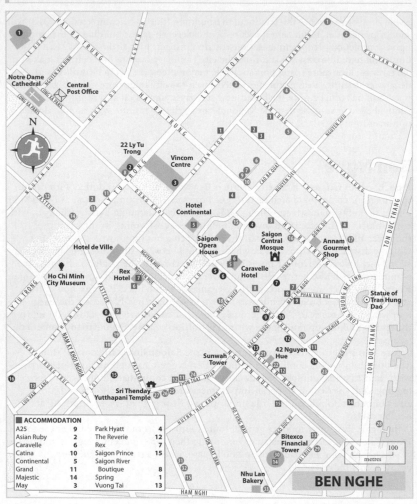

BEN NGHE

0		100
	metres	

■ ACCOMMODATION

A25	9	Park Hyatt	4
Asian Ruby	2	The Reverie	12
Caravelle	6	Rex	7
Catina	10	Saigon Prince	15
Continental	5	Saigon River	
Grand	11	Boutique	8
Majestic	14	Spring	1
May	3	Vuong Tai	13

● EATING

3T Quan Nuong	26	Le Jardin	3
Banh Mi 24	29	Lemongrass	18
Banh Mi Nieu Lan	33	Matsuzakaya	4
Café Eon	30	Modern Meets Culture	13
Camargue	9	Namo	10
Cha Ca La Vong	24	Nha Hang Ngon	12
Cong	8	Quan Bui	2
Elbow Room	31	Refinery	7
Fanny's	25	Royal Pavilion	22
Gartenstadt	20	Saigon Oi	21
Highlands Coffee	15	Secret Garden	14
Hoa Tuc	6	Skewers	5
Hoi An	1	Temple Club	27
Hum	17	Tuk Tuk	11
Jake's	32	Xu	16
Jaspa's	23		
Kem Bach Dang	19		
La Perle de l'Orient	28		

■ DRINKING

Apocalypse Now	4
Blanchy's Tash	3
Broma: Not a Bar	13
Dublin Gate	1
Eon Heli Bar	14
Hangover	11
La Fenetre Soleil	2
Level 23	8
Malt Saigon	7
Number 5 Bar	15
Pasteur Street	
Brewing Company	9
Phatty's	12
Rooftop Garden	6
Saigon Saigon	5
Sax n' Art	10

● SHOPPING

Art Arcade	6
Artbook	14
Diamond Plaza	1
Fahasa	13
Ipa-nima	12
Khai Silk	9
Libé	2
Lotus Gallery	11
Nagu	5
Saigon Centre	15
Saigon Kitsch	10
T&V	7
Vincom Centre	3
Vo Viet Chung	16
Yen Loan	4
Zakka	8

Notre Dame Cathedral

Off the top end of Dong Khoi • Daily 5.30am–5pm; weekday Mass 5.30am & 5.30pm, seven Sunday Mass 5.30am–6.30pm • Free

Up at Dong Khoi's northern end, the twin compass-point spires of **Notre Dame Cathedral** have, for decades, been one of Saigon's handiest landmarks. An attractive redbrick building of late nineteenth-century vintage, its interior boasts only scant decoration bar the few stained-glass windows above and behind its altar, and its marble relief Stations of the Cross. There's plenty of scope for people-watching, however, as a steady trickle of Catholics pass through in their best silk tunics and black trousers, fingering rosary beads, their whispered prayers merging with the incessant murmur of the traffic outside. A statue of the Virgin Mary provides the centrepiece to the small **park** fronting the cathedral, where cyclo drivers loiter and kids hawk postcards and maps. Make sure you take a close look at Mary's face, as locals swear they have seen her shed tears.

Ho Chi Minh City Museum

65 Ly Tu Trong • Daily 7.30am–6pm • 15,000đ • ☎ 028 3829 9741, ⓦ hcmc-museum.edu.vn

Of all the buildings thrown up in Vietnam by the French, few are more eye-catching than the former **Gia Long Palace**, built a block west of the Hotel de Ville in 1886 as a splendid residence for the governor of Cochinchina. Homeless after the air attack that smashed his own palace, Diem decamped here in 1962, and it was in the tunnels beneath the building that he spent his last hours of office, before fleeing to Cha Tam Church in Cho Lon where he finally surrendered (see p.83). It now houses the **Ho Chi Minh City Museum**, which makes use of photographs, documents and artefacts to trace the struggle of the Vietnamese people against France and America. Even if you're not desperate to learn more about the country's war-torn past, you're likely to be enchanted by the grandeur of the building, and you might even witness couples posing for wedding photographs as the regal structure and well-tended gardens are a favourite backdrop for photographers.

The collection

The **downstairs** area has a hotchpotch of ancient artefacts and antique collections, along with a section on nature and another featuring ethnic clothing and implements. The museum shifts into higher gear **upstairs**, where the focus turns to the American War. The best exhibits are those showcasing the ingenuity of the Vietnamese – bicycle parts made into mortars, a Suzuki motorbike in whose inner tubes documents were smuggled into Saigon, a false-floored boat in which guns were secreted, and so on. Look out, too, for jumpers knitted by female prisoners on Con Dao Island bearing the Vietnamese words for "peace" and "freedom". Elsewhere, there's a cross-sectional model of the Cu Chi tunnels, and a rewarding gallery of photographs of the Ho Chi Minh Campaign and the fall of Saigon.

As with many of Vietnam's museums, the hardware of war is on display in the **gardens**. Tucked away behind the frangipanis and well-groomed hedges out back are a Soviet tank, an American helicopter and an antiaircraft gun, while out front are two sleek but idle jets.

22 Ly Tu Trong

Daily 24hr • Free • Lift ride 5000đ

An innocuous-looking, five-storey block stands at **22 Ly Tu Trong**; few who walk past it – even locals – are aware that this was the backdrop for one of the most famous photos ever taken of HCMC. During the war, this building served as a CIA safe-house, and just before the Fall of Saigon (see box, p.77) its staff were evacuated via a helicopter perched precariously on the roof, atop the block that still houses the lift apparatus.

1

Dutch photographer Hubert van Es took a few photos, one of which went on to become a defining image of the war. The building has become decidedly trendy of late (see box, p.93), with clothing boutiques, cafés (including *Cong*, p.96) and cookery schools now occupying its elegantly aging floors.

Nguyen Hue

Daily 24hr • Free • No food, drink or heavy petting allowed on pedestrian area

The former Hotel de Ville (see box below) faces a **statue of Ho Chi Minh** to the south; together they form the centrepiece of the extremely pleasing **Nguyen Hue** redevelopment, and make for fabulous photos around sunset when both are artfully illuminated. A pedestrianized zone runs down the middle of the boulevard, passing a fountain system on the way south, and the whole area has free wi-fi. At the time of research, whistle-toting security guards (some on rollerblades) were keeping a keen eye out for anyone riding motorbikes or hawking goods along this stretch. Since there are few other places for a decent stroll in the city, it fills up each evening with a mix of promenading Saigonese and foreign visitors.

ON THE HUNT FOR COLONIAL SAIGON

On a walk along and around Dong Khoi, you'll see myriad examples of HCMC's extant colonial architecture. The **Notre Dame Cathedral** is the most pertinent example (see p.73), and just off its southeastern corner is the **Central Post Office** (daily 6am–10pm), a classic colonial edifice unchanged since its completion in the 1880s. It's worth a peek inside for the nave-like foyer, which is lent character by two huge map-murals, one charting Saigon and its environs in 1892, the other the telegraphic lines of southern Vietnam and Cambodia in 1936.

Further south, the stately edifice that stands at Nguyen Hue's northern extent is the former **Hotel de Ville**, the city's most photographed icon. Built between 1902 and 1908 as the city's administrative hub, this wedding cake of a building today houses the People's Committee behind its showy jumble of Corinthian columns, classical figures and shuttered windows. Just south of the Hotel de Ville is the **Rex Hotel**, which despite its colonial-style charm has only existed in its current incarnation since 1976; during the 1960s it billeted American officers, and before that it was used as a garage for the Renaults and Peugeots of the city's French expat community. Its *Rooftop Garden* bar (see p.101) yields a superb view of the whirl of life on the street below, while at night a giant crown lights up on the terrace, providing the city with one of its best-known landmarks.

Heading just to the east across Lam Son Square, you'll soon spot the cyclopean, domed entrance of the **Saigon Opera House**, completed in 1899. The National Assembly was temporarily housed here in 1955, but today, lovingly restored to its former glory, it once again presents operatic performances and the like (see p.102).

Two classic hotels face the opera house. To its north rises the **Hotel Continental**, once a bastion of French high society and still one of the city's premier addresses. Somerset Maugham followed his nose for a story to the hotel's famous terraces in the mid-1920s, declaring that "at the hour of the aperitif, they are crowded with bearded, gesticulating Frenchmen drinking sweet and sickly beverages… and they talk nineteen to the dozen in the rolling accent of the Midi." Sadly, the terraces no longer exist. On the other side of the opera house is the 1958-built, and now grandiosely revamped, **Caravelle Hotel**, which in a former incarnation found favour with Western journalists assigned to cover the war – its terrace bar saw many a report drafted over a stiff drink. A stroll to the river from here will take you past two of the city's more venerable hotels, the lovingly restored **Grand** (see p.91) on the left, followed thirty metres later on the right by the lavish, riverfront **Majestic** (see p.92).

Saigon Central Mosque

66 Dong Du • Daily 4.30am–9.30pm • Free

Though glitzy boutiques predominate along Dong Khoi below the *Caravelle*, they haven't yet managed to entirely eradicate the past and it's still possible to winkle out relics of old Saigon. South of Lam Son and just off Dong Du lie the white- and blue-washed walls of the 1930s **Saigon Central Mosque**, now towered over by the *Sheraton*. The rounded curves of its arches and its slender minarets make a stark contrast to the utilitarian design of the hotel next door, and there's a reassuring sense of peace that's enhanced by the slumbering worshippers lazing around the complex.

Sri Thenday Yutthapani Temple

66 Ton That Thiep • Daily 7.30am–7.30pm • Free

With its colourful sculpted gate tower (known as a *gopuram*), the peaceful **Sri Thenday Yutthapani Temple** looks out of place on Ton That Thiep, a trendy strip of boutiques and bars. The place manages a certain rag-tag charisma, the lavish murals normally associated with Hindu temples replaced by faded paintings of Jawaharlal Nehru, Mahatma Gandhi and various deities from the Hindu pantheon, plus a ceiling gaily studded with coloured baubles and lamps. Steps beyond the topiary to the right of the main sanctuary lead to a roof terrace that's dominated by a weather-beaten tower of deities, whose ranks have been infiltrated by two incongruous characters dressed like public schoolboys in braces, shorts and striped ties.

Bitexco Financial Tower

2 Hai Trieu • Daily 9.30am–9.30pm; last ticket 45min before closing • 200,000đ • ☎ 028 3915 6868, ⓦ bitexcofinancialtower.com

With its tapered shape and distinctive helipad protruding like a tongue near the top, the sleek, glass **Bitexco Financial Tower** is already one of Saigon's most memorable icons, despite only having being completed in 2010. Its base is an uninteresting mix of mall space and offices, but visitors flock to take in the sweeping views from the **Saigon Skydeck** on the 49th floor, 178m above the ground. Look upwards and you'll see the lip of the helipad on the floor above; look down and you should spot a few familiar sights, such as Ben Thanh Market, the Hotel de Ville, the Opera House and the tips of the spires of Notre Dame Cathedral far below.

A little money-saving tip for you: there's a decent **café** on the floor above the Skydeck, where the coffee, drinks and ice cream are overpriced but still cost less than tickets for the deck itself – it's free to take the lift to this level, where you'll essentially get the same view with a free latte, and some change to boot.

Pham Ngu Lao

Referred to by most backpackers as "the backpacker area", the atmospheric jumble of streets around **Pham Ngu Lao** (also the name of one of its most important thoroughfares) do indeed contain the overwhelming majority of the city's budget accommodation options. There are pricier places here too, and the same goes for the area's many places to eat – everything from trendy restaurants serving foreign nosh to streetside shacks whipping up exactly what you see in and on their various tubs and shelves. If you've been to Bangkok's Khaosan Road, you may remark on a certain similarity – it's most evident during the evening, when Bui Vien finds itself crammed with locals and not-so-locals drinking **cheap beer** on tiny chairs. Further north, the

1

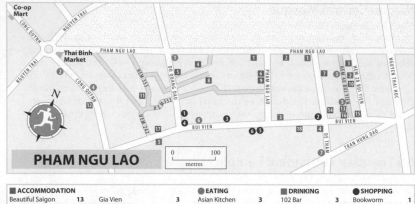

■ ACCOMMODATION				● EATING		■ DRINKING		● SHOPPING	
Beautiful Saigon	13	Gia Vien	3	Asian Kitchen	3	102 Bar	3	Bookworm	1
Bich Duyen	4	Hong Han	17	Baba's Kitchen	6	Allez-Boo	1	Ginkgo	2
Bizu	14	Liberty Parkview	1	Beautiful Saigon	5	Go 2	4	Nam Phoung	5
Cat Huy	11	Luan Vu	18	Café Zoom	7	Le Pub	2	Nhut Van	6
C-Central	15	Madam Cuc	12	Dinh Y	2	The View	5	Saigon Jane	4
Cozy	9	Ngoc Minh	8	Espy	4			Sapa Village	3
Eco Backpackers	7	Ngoc Thao Guesthouse	6	Pho Quynh	1				
Elios	2	Pink Tulip	16						
Flipside Hostel	10	Vinh Chung	5						

park fronting Pham Ngu Lao (this time the road) is a pleasant place by day, and a bit of a pick-up spot by night, particularly for elements of the city's gay community.

Fine Art Museum

97 Pho Duc Chinh • Tues–Sun 9am–5pm • 10,000đ • ☏ 028 3829 4441

Set in a grand colonial mansion, Ho Chi Minh City's **Fine Art Museum** is worth a visit to view some of the country's best Cham and Oc Eo relics (see box, p.430). The first floor hosts temporary exhibitions, while the courtyard out back is given over to artworks for sale (see p.104). Revolutionary art dominates the second floor, relying heavily on hackneyed images of soldiers, war zones and Uncle Ho, though a few offerings capture the anguish and turmoil of the conflicts. Things get better on the third floor, where there's an impressive collection of Oc Eo and Cham statues, gilt Buddhas and other antiquities.

Ben Thanh

Bustling **Ben Thanh Ward** is most famous for its eponymous **market**, and nowadays also the near-eponymous **street-food** version (see p.98). Many visitors end up staying in this teeming area, since it's within walking distance of a fair number of the city's best sights. One of Ho Chi Minh City's most popular and important sights is the **Reunification Palace**, set in a patch of parkland just to the west of the city centre, and within walking distance. The area has enough to keep you occupied for at least half a day: poke east and you'll find yourself at the hulking, redbrick **Notre Dame Cathedral**, head northwest and you'll soon hit the **War Remnants Museum**, while a walk west will take you through **Cong Vien Van Hoa Park** towards **Xa Loi Pagoda**.

Ben Thanh Market

Junction of Le Loi and Le Lai • Dawn to dusk • Free

Sitting under a pillbox-style clock tower, **Ben Thanh Market** has been the city's busiest and most important market for almost a century. After growing during colonial times –

it was known to the French as the Halles Centrales – Ben Thanh's dense knot of trade has caused it to burst at the seams, disgorging stalls onto the surrounding pavements. Inside the main body of the market, a tight grid of aisles, demarcated according to produce, teems with shoppers; if it's souvenirs you're after, a reconnaissance here will reveal conical hats, basketware, bags, shoes, lacquerware, Da Lat coffee and Good Morning Vietnam T-shirts. Sadly, all stalls are now designated "fixed price", so there's no more good-natured bargaining, and prices are generally a bit higher than elsewhere.

Walk through to the wet market along the back of the complex, and you'll find buckets of eels, clutches of live frogs tied together at the legs, heaps of pigs' ears and snouts and baskets wedged full of hens, among other gruesome sights. If you can countenance the thought of eating after seeing – and smelling – this patch of the market, com, pho and baguette vendors proliferate towards the back of the main hall. In the evenings, food stalls specializing in seafood set up along the sides of the market, attracting a mixed crowd of locals and tourists; things are generally more pleasant at the nearby Ben Thanh Street Food Market (see p.98).

Sri Mariamman Hindu Temple

45 Truong Dinh • Daily 7.30am–7.30pm • Free

A block west of Ben Thanh, the aroma of jasmine and incense replaces the stench of butchery at Truong Dinh's **Sri Mariamman Hindu Temple**. Less engaging than Sri Thenday Yutthapani (see p.75), Sri Mariamman's imposing walls are sometimes lined with vendors selling oil, incense and jasmine petals. The walls are topped by a colourful *gopuram*, or bank of sculpted gods. Inside, the gods Mariamman, Maduraiveeran and Pechiamman reside in stone sanctuaries reminiscent of the Cham towers upcountry, and there are more deities set into the walls around the courtyard.

The Reunification Palace

135 Nam Ky Khoi Nghia • Daily 7.30–11am & 1–5pm • 30,000đ, tour groups 200,000đ

Walk five minutes north up Nam Ky Khoi Nghia from the Ho Chi Minh City Museum, and you'll soon spot a red flag billowing proudly above the **Reunification Palace**. A whitewashed concrete edifice with all the charm of a municipal library, the complex occupies the site of the former Norodom Palace, a colonial mansion

---

THE TAKING OF THE PRESIDENTIAL PALACE

The **Reunification Palace** is of enormous significance to the Vietnamese – on April 30, 1975, the storming of its gates by a tank belonging to the Northern Army became the defining moment of the **fall of Saigon** and the South. These days, two tanks stand in the grounds as a reminder of the incident.

Of the many Western journalists on hand to witness the spectacle, none was better placed than English journalist and poet **James Fenton**, who conspired to hitch a ride on the tank that first crashed through the gates:

"The tank speeded up, and rammed the left side of the palace gate. Wrought iron flew into the air, but the whole structure refused to give. I nearly fell off. The tank backed again, and I observed a man with a nervous smile opening the centre portion of the gate. We drove into the grounds of the palace, and fired a salute. An NLF soldier took the flag and, waving it above his head, ran into the palace. A few moments later, he emerged on the terrace, waving the flag round and round. Later still, there he was on the roof. The red and yellow stripes of the Saigon regime were lowered at last."

Inside the palace, **Duong Van Minh** ("Big Minh"), sworn in as president only two days before, readied to perform his last presidential duty. "I have been waiting since early this morning to transfer power to you," he said to General Bui Tin, to which the general replied: "Your power has crumbled. You cannot give up what you do not have."

1

erected in 1871 to house the governor-general of Indochina. After the French departure in 1954, Ngo Dinh Diem commandeered this extravagant monument as his presidential residence, but after sustaining extensive damage in a February 1962 assassination attempt by two disaffected Southern pilots, the place was condemned and pulled down. The present building was named the Independence Palace on its completion in 1966, only to be retitled the Reunification Hall when the South fell in 1975 (see box, p.77). The reversion to the label "Palace" was doubtless made for its tourist appeal.

The interior

Spookily unchanged from its working days, much of the building's **interior** is a time capsule of Sixties and Seventies kitsch; as you're pacing its airy banqueting rooms, conference halls and reception areas, it's hard not to think you've strayed into the arch-criminal's lair in a James Bond film. Most interesting is the **third floor**, where, as well as the presidential library (with works by Laurens van der Post and Graham Greene alongside heavyweight political tomes), there's a curtained projection room, and an entertainment lounge complete with tacky circular sofa and barrel-shaped bar. Nearby, a set of sawn-off elephant's feet add an eerie touch to the decor. Perhaps the most atmospheric part of the building is the **basement** and former command centre, where wood-panelled combat staff quarters yield archaic radio equipment and vast wall maps.

War Remnants Museum

28 Vo Van Tan • Daily 7.30am–5pm • 15,000đ • ☎ 028 3930 6664, ⓦ baotangchungtichchientranh.vn

A block north of Cong Vien Van Hoa Park, the **War Remnants Museum** is a highly popular attraction, though not one for the faint-hearted. Unlike at the Ho Chi Minh City Museum, you are unlikely to be distracted here by the building that houses the heart-rending exhibits – a distressing compendium of the horrors of modern warfare. Some of the instruments of destruction are on display in the courtyard outside, including a 28-tonne howitzer and a ghoulish collection of bomb parts. There's also a guillotine that harvested heads at the Central Prison on Ly Tu Trong, first for the French and later for Diem.

The collection

Inside, a series of halls present a grisly portfolio of **photographs** of mutilation, napalm burns and torture. Most shocking is the gallery detailing the effects of the 75 million litres of defoliant sprays dumped across the country: beside the expected images of bald terrain, hideously malformed foetuses are preserved in pickling jars. A gallery that looks at international opposition to the war as well as the American peace movement adds a sense of balance, and makes a change from the self-glorifying tone of most Vietnamese museums. Accounts of servicemen – such as veteran B52 pilot Michael Heck – who attempted to discharge themselves from the war on ethical grounds are also featured. Artefacts donated to the museum by returned US servicemen add to the reconciliatory tone, while upstairs you'll find a pretty hard-hitting exhibition of war pictures, taken by photographers killed on both sides of the conflict.

At the back of the museum is a grisly mock-up of the **tiger cages**, the godless prison cells of Con Son Island (see p.203), which could have been borrowed from the movie set of *Papillon*.

Cong Vien Van Hoa Park

Adjoining the western edge of the Reunification Palace's grounds, **Cong Vien Van Hoa Park**, also known as Tau Dan Park, is a municipal space whose tree-shaded lawns are pleasant for a stroll and heave with life each Sunday. During the colonial era, the park's northernmost corner was home to one of the lynchpins of French expat society, the **Cercle Sportif**, a Westerners-only sports club where the *colons* gathered to swim and play tennis before sinking an aperitif and discussing the day's events. Today it functions as the Workers' Sports Club, and also houses the Golden Dragon Water Puppet Theatre (see below).

Golden Dragon Water Puppet Theatre
55b Nguyen Thi Minh Khai • Shows daily 5pm, 6.30pm and occasionally 7.45pm; 50min • 200,000đ • ☎ 028 3840 4027

If you sink into the depths of depression upon leaving the War Remnants Museum, you can cheer yourself up at this **water puppet theatre**; few people fail to be enchanted at their first encounter with these waterborne buffoons. The tradition of water puppetry (see p.476) is much stronger in the north, but it's such an appealing aspect of Vietnamese culture that there's plenty of demand for shows in the south as well. The early evening timing of the shows here make them a fun activity for the kids before bed or dinner; they consist of a dozen or so sketches on themes like rearing ducks, catching foxes and boat racing.

Xa Loi Pagoda
89 Ba Huyen Thanh Quan • Daily 6–11.30am & 2–9pm • Free

Vapid **Xa Loi Pagoda**, a short walk west of the War Remnants Museum, became a hotbed of Buddhist opposition to Diem in 1963. The austere, 1956-built complex is unspectacular, its most striking component a tall **tower** whose unlovely beige blocks lend it a drabness that even six tiers of Oriental roofs can't quite dispel. The main **sanctuary**, accessed by a dual staircase (men scale the left-hand flight, women the right), is similarly dull: beyond a vast joss-stick urn inventively decorated with marbles and shards of broken china, it's a lofty hall featuring a huge gilt Buddha and fourteen murals that narrate his life. Turn left and around the back of the Buddha, and you'll come across a shrine commemorating **Thich Quang Duc** and the other monks who set fire to themselves in Saigon in 1963 (see box below). Quang Duc's is the ghostly figure holding a set of beads, to the left of the shrine.

North of the centre
North of Notre Dame Cathedral, **Le Duan Boulevard** runs between the Botanical Gardens and the grounds of the Reunification Palace. Known as Norodom Boulevard to the French, who lined it with tamarind trees to imitate a Gallic thoroughfare, it soon became a residential and diplomatic enclave with a crop of fine pastel-hued colonial

---

THE SELF-IMMOLATION OF THICH QUANG DUC

In the early morning of June 11, 1963, a column of Buddhist monks left the Xa Loi Pagoda and proceeded to the intersection of Cach Mang Thang Tam and Nguyen Dinh Chieu. There, **Thich Quang Duc**, a 66-year-old monk from Hue, sat down in the lotus position and meditated as fellow monks doused him in petrol and then set light to him in protest at the repression of Buddhists by President Diem, who was a Catholic. As flames engulfed the impassive monk and passers-by prostrated themselves before him, the cameras of the Western press corps rolled, and by the next morning the grisly event had grabbed the world's headlines. More self-immolations followed, and Diem's heavy-handed responses at Xa Loi – some four hundred monks and nuns were arrested and others cast from the top of the tower – led to mass popular demonstrations against the government. Diem, it was clear, had become a liability. On November 2, he and his brother were assassinated after taking refuge in Cho Lon's Cha Tam Church (see p.83), the victims of a military coup.

1

villas to boot. Its present name doffs a cap to Le Duan, the secretary-general of the Lao Dong, or Workers' Party, from 1959 until his death in 1986. Turn northeast from the top of Dong Khoi and the sense of harmony created by Le Duan's graceful colonial piles ends abruptly with a number of brand-new edifices. There's ample sightseeing potential here, however: the **Jade Emperor Pagoda** and **Le Van Duyet Temple** are undervisited, if anything, while closer to the centre, the city's **Botanical Gardens**, **zoo** and **History Museum** all sit in the same swathe of land.

The Botanical Gardens

Junction of Le Duan and Nguyen Binh Khiem • Daily 7am–6pm • 50,000đ

The pace of life slows down considerably – and the odours of cut grass and frangipani blooms replace the smell of exhaust fumes – when you duck into the city's **Botanical Gardens**, accessed by a gate at the far eastern end of Le Duan, and bounded to the east by the Thi Nghe Channel. Established in 1864 by two *colons*, the gardens' social function has remained unchanged for decades, and their tree-shaded paths still attract as many courting couples and promenaders as when Norman Lewis followed the "clusters of Vietnamese beauties on bicycles" and headed there one Sunday morning in 1950 to find the gardens "full of these ethereal creatures, gliding in decorous groups, sometimes accompanied by gallants". In its day, the gardens harboured an impressive collection of tropical flora, including many species of orchid. Post-liberation the place went to seed, but nowadays a bevy of gardeners keep it reasonably well tended.

The zoo

Forming part of the gardens is the city **zoo**, home to camels, elephants, crocodiles and big cats, and also komodo dragons – the latter a gift from the government of Indonesia. Unfortunately, conditions here are rather poor and some animals look half-crazed, so it could be a harrowing experience if you're an animal lover. There's also an **amusement park** that is sometimes open, and you can get an ice cream or a coconut from one of the several **cafés** sprinkled around the grounds.

OPERATION FREQUENT WIND

Located at 4 Le Duan, the nondescript building that houses the US Consulate was built right on top of the site of the infamous former **American Embassy**, where a commemorative plaque is now the only reminder of its existence and significance in the American War. Two events immortalized the former building on this site, in operation from 1967 to 1975 and left standing half-derelict until 1999 as a sobering legacy. The first came in the pre-dawn hours of January 31, 1968, when a small band of **Viet Cong commandos** breached the embassy compound during the nationwide Tet Offensive. The fact that the North could mount such an effective attack on the hub of US power in Vietnam was shocking to the American public. In the six hours of close-range fire that followed, five US guards died, and with them the popular misconception that the US Army had the Vietnam conflict under control.

Worse followed seven years later during "**Operation Frequent Wind**", the chaotic helicopter evacuation that marked the US's final undignified withdrawal from Vietnam. The embassy building was one of thirteen designated landing zones where all foreigners were to gather upon hearing the words, "The temperature in Saigon is 105 degrees and rising" on the radio followed by Bing Crosby singing *White Christmas*. At noon on April 29, 1975, the signal was broadcast, and for the next eighteen hours scores of helicopters shuttled passengers out to the US Navy's Seventh Fleet off Vung Tau. Around two thousand evacuees were lifted from the roof of the embassy alone, before Ambassador Graham Martin finally left with the Stars and Stripes in the early hours of the following morning. In a tragic postscript to US involvement, as the last helicopter lifted off, many of the Vietnamese civilians who for hours had been clamouring at the gates were left to suffer the Communists' reprisals.

The History Museum

2 Nguyen Binh Khiem • Tues–Sun 8–11am & 1.30–4.30pm • 15,000đ • ☎ 028 3829 8146 • Water puppetry shows on the hour from 10am–4pm, except 1pm; 40,000đ

A pleasing, pagoda-style roof crowns the city's **History Museum**, next to the Botanical Gardens. It houses fifteen galleries illuminating Vietnam's past from primitive times to the end of French rule by means of a decent if unastonishing array of artefacts and pictures. Dioramas of defining moments in Vietnamese military history – including Ngo Quyen's 938 AD victory at Bach Dang (see box, p.152) – lend the collection some cohesion.

Should you tire of Vietnamese history, try exploring other halls, focusing on such disparate subjects as Buddha images from around Asia; seventh- and eighth-century Champa art; and the customs and crafts of the ethnic minorities of Vietnam. There's also a room jam-packed with exquisite ceramics from Japan, Thailand and Vietnam, and you could round off your visit at the **water puppetry theatre**.

Jade Emperor Pagoda

73 Mai Thi Luu • Daily 7am–6pm • Free

A few blocks northwest of the Botanical Gardens, the **Jade Emperor Pagoda**, or Chua Phuoc Hai, was built by the city's Cantonese community at the beginning of the twentieth century. If you visit just one temple in town, make it this one, with its exquisite panels of carved gilt woodwork, and its panoply of weird and wonderful deities, both Taoist and Buddhist, beneath a roof that groans under the weight of dragons, birds and animals.

The main building

To the right of the temple's tree-lined front **courtyard** is a grubby pond whose occupants have earned the temple its alternative moniker of Turtle Pagoda. Once over the threshold, look up and you'll see Chinese characters announcing: "The Only Enlightenment is in Heaven" – though only after your eyes have adjusted to the fug of joss-stick smoke. A statue of the **Jade Emperor** lords it over the main hall's central altar, sporting an impressive moustache, and he's surrounded by a retinue of similarly moustached followers.

A rickety flight of steps in the chamber to the right of the main hall runs up to a **balcony** looking out over the pagoda's elaborate **roof**. Set behind the balcony, a neon-haloed statue of Quan Am (see box, p.452) stands on an altar. Left out of the main hall, meanwhile, you're confronted by Kim Hua, to whom women pray for fertility; judging by the number of babies weighing down the female statues around her, her success rate is high. The Chief of Hell resides in the larger chamber behind Kim Hua's niche. Given his job description, he doesn't look particularly demonic, though his attendants, in sinister black garb, are certainly equipped to administer the sorts of punishments depicted in the ten dark-wood reliefs on the walls before them.

Le Van Duyet Temple

Dinh Tien Hoang • Dawn to dusk • Free

A national hero is commemorated at the **Le Van Duyet Temple**, known locally as Lang Ong and sited at the top of Dinh Tien Hoang, in the region of the city where the **Gia Dinh Citadel** once stood. A military mandarin and eunuch, Le Van Duyet (1764–1832) succeeded in putting down the Tay Son Rebellion, and later became military governor of Gia Dinh.

The temple itself, which underwent extensive renovations in 2008, stretches through three halls behind a facade decorated with unicorns assembled from shards of chinaware. Inside, a bronze statue of the marshal sits in front of an altar, flanked by an

1

ancient pair of tusks. A steady stream of visitors pay their respects by burning incense, while the ringing of a brass bell adds to the pious mood. On the first day of the eighth lunar month, to coincide with the marshal's birthday, a **theatre** troupe dramatizes his life, and there's more activity around Tet, when crowds of pilgrims gather to ask for safekeeping in the forthcoming year. Strolling around the grounds reveals the **tombs** in which the marshal and his wife are buried.

South of the centre

Across the Ben Nghe Channel from the city centre, **District Four** has become a popular tour-group stop of late – though there's nothing much to see here, it's a great place for **street food**, with snails and shellfish a major drawcard for locals and tourists alike. A few kilometres further south again (and just over 100,000đ from the centre by taxi), **District Seven** is the diametric opposite, a fancy new area filled with high-rises, small tracts of parkland, shopping boutiques and stylish cafés. Home to much of the city's *nouveau riche*, and a growing number of international residents, this area is likely to become more and more important to visitors in time. For now, the only real draws are **The Crescent**, a large shopping mall complex, and the **Starlight Bridge**, a pedestrian crossing that is beautifully lit up at night.

Cho Lon

The dense cluster of streets comprising the Chinese ghetto of **Cho Lon** was once distinct from Saigon, though it now blends seamlessly into present-day Ho Chi Minh City as **Districts Five** and **Six**, and is linked to the centre by the five-kilometre-long umbilical cord of Tran Hung Dao. The distinction was already somewhat blurred by 1950, when

---

THE HISTORY OF CHO LON

The **ethnic Chinese**, or **Hoa**, first began to settle at Cho Lon around 1900; many came from existing enclaves in My Tho and Bien Hoa. The area soon became the largest Hoa community in the country, a title it still holds, with a population of over half a million. Residents gravitated towards others from their region of China, with each congregation commissioning its own places of worship and clawing out its own commercial niche – thus the Cantonese handled retailing and groceries, the Teochew dealt in tea and fish, the Fukien were in charge of rice, and so on.

The great wealth that Cho Lon generated had to be spent somewhere. By the early twentieth century, sassy restaurants, casinos and brothels existed to facilitate this. Also prevalent were **fumeries**, where nuggets of opium were quietly smoked from the cool comfort of a wooden opium bed. Among the expats and wealthy Asians who frequented them was Graham Greene, and he recorded his experiences in *Ways of Escape*. By the 1950s, Cho Lon was a potentially dangerous place to be, its vice industries controlled by the **Binh Xuyen** gang. First the French and then the Americans trod carefully here, while Viet Minh and Viet Cong **activists** hid out in its cramped backstreets – as journalist Frank Palmos found to his cost, when the jeep he and four other correspondents were riding in was ambushed in 1968.

Post-reunification, Cho Lon saw hard times. As Hanoi aligned itself increasingly with the Soviet Union, Sino–Vietnamese tensions became strained. Economic **persecution** of the Hoa made matters worse, and, when Vietnam invaded Chinese-backed Cambodia, Beijing launched a punitive **border war**. Hundreds of thousands of ethnic Chinese, many of them from Cho Lon, fled the country in unseaworthy vessels, fearing recriminations. Today, the business acumen of the Chinese is valued by the local authorities, and the distemper that gripped Cho Lon for over a decade is a memory.

1

Norman Lewis found the city's Chinatown "swollen so enormously as to become its grotesque Siamese twin", and the steady influx of refugees into the city during the war years saw to it that the two districts eventually became joined by a swathe of urban development. A short stroll around Cho Lon (whose name, meaning "**big market**", couldn't be more apposite) will make clear that, even by this city's standards, the mercantile mania here is breathtaking; most visitors make a bee-line for the historic **Binh Tay Market**, though there are larger ones catering to more genuine local needs such as home furnishings, farming equipment and so on.

Cho Lon's greatest architectural treasures are its temples and pagodas, many of which stand on or around **Nguyen Trai**, whose four-kilometre sweep northeast to Pham Ngu Lao starts just north of **Cha Tam Church**. However, you may get more out of the area simply by losing yourself in its amorphous mass of life: amid the melee, streetside barbers briskly clip away, bird-sellers squat outside tumbledown **pagodas and temples**, heaving markets ring with fishwives' chatter and stores display mushrooms, dried shrimps and rice paper.

Binh Tay Market

Hau Giang · Dawn to dusk

First impressions of **Binh Tay Market**, with its multitiered, mustard-coloured roofs stalked by serpentine dragons, are of a huge temple complex. Once inside, however, it quickly becomes obvious that only mammon is deified here. If any one place epitomizes Cho Lon's vibrant commercialism, it's Binh Tay, its well-regimented corridors abuzz with stalls offering products of all kinds, from dried fish, pickled vegetables and chilli paste to pottery piled up to the rafters, and the colourful bonnets that Vietnamese women so favour. Beyond Binh Tay's south side, stalls provide cheap snacks for shoppers and traders, though these could well end up moving as the market was closed for wholesale renovation at the time of research. It should be open again by the beginning of 2018, and mercifully it looks like the iconic architectural style will be retained.

Cha Tam Church

25 Hoc Lac · Dawn to dusk · Free, but small tip appreciated

The slender spire of **Cha Tam Church** peers down from above the eastern end of cramped Tran Chanh Chieu, but you'll have to walk round to Tran Hung Dao to find the entrance. It was in this unprepossessing little church, with its Oriental outer gate and cheery yellow walls, that President Ngo Dinh Diem and his brother Ngo Dinh Nhu holed up on November 1, 1963, during the coup that saw them chased out of the Gia Long Palace (see p.73). Early the next morning, Diem phoned the leaders of the coup and surrendered. An M-113 armoured car duly picked them up, but they were shot dead by ARVN soldiers before the vehicle reached central Saigon.

1

SHOPS ON HAI THUONG LAN ONG

Walk five minutes towards the river from the Cha Tam Church, along Tran Hung Dao and through the cloth market, and you'll eventually reach the eastern end of the street. Shops specializing in Chinese and Vietnamese **traditional medicine** have long proliferated here, identifiable by the sickly sweet aroma that hangs over them. Named after a famous herbalist who practised and studied in Hanoi two centuries ago, the street is lined by dingy shophouses banked with cabinets whose wooden drawers are crammed full of herbs. Step over the sliced roots laid out to dry along the pavement and peer inside any one of the shops, and you'll see rheumy men and women weighing out prescriptions on ancient balances. Steepled around them are boxes, jars and paper bags containing anything from dried bark to antler fur and tortoise glue. Predictably popular is **ginseng**, the Oriental cure-all said to combat everything from heart disease to acne. You may also still see monkey-, tiger- and rhino-based medicines – despite a government ban on these products.

With clearance from the janitor (who's usually hanging around somewhere, hoping for a tip) you can clamber up into the **belfry** and under the bells, Quasimodo-style, to join the statue of St Francis Xavier for the fine views he enjoys of Cho Lon. The janitor can also point out the pew where Diem and his brother sat praying as they awaited their fate.

Quan Am Pagoda

12 Lao Tu • Dawn to dusk • Free

North of Nguyen Trai's junction with Chau Van Liem, on tiny Lao Tu, **Quan Am Pagoda** is the pick of the bunch in this part of town. Set back from the bustle of Cho Lon, it has an almost tangible air of antiquity, enhanced by the film of dust left by the incense spirals hanging from its rafters. Don't be too quick to dive inside, though: the pagoda's ridged roofs are impressive enough from the outside, their colourful crust of "glove-puppet" figurines, teetering houses and temples from a distance creating the illusion of a gingerbread house. Framing the two door gods and the pair of stone lions assigned to keeping out evil spirits are gilt panels depicting petrified scenes from traditional Chinese court life – dancers, musicians, noblemen in sedan chairs, a game of chequers being played.

When Cho Lon's Fukien congregation established this pagoda in the early nineteenth century, they dedicated it to the Goddess of Mercy, but it's **A Pho**, the Queen of Heaven, who stands in the centre of the main hall, beyond an altar tiled like a mortuary slab. A pantheon of deities throngs the open courtyard behind her, decked out in sumptuous apparel and attracting a steady traffic of worshippers. Twin ovens, flanking the main chamber, burn a steady supply of fake money offerings and incense sticks.

Phuoc An Hoi Quan Pagoda

Hung Vuong • Dawn to dusk • Free

Three minutes' walk north of the Quan Am Pagoda, **Phuoc An Hoi Quan Pagoda** (aka Minh Huong Pagoda) is a disarming place. Beyond the menacing dragons and sea monsters patrolling its roof, and the superb woodcarving depicting a king being entertained by jousters and minstrels hanging over the entrance, is the temple's **sanctuary**, in which a stately statue of Quan Cong sits, instantly recognizable by his blood-red face, fronted by two storks standing on top of turtles fashioned from countless plectrum-shaped ceramic shards.

1

Thien Hau Pagoda

Nguyen Trai • Dawn to dusk • Free

Thien Hau Pagoda is popular with women making offerings to Me Sanh (Goddess of Fertility) and to Long Mau (Goddess of Mothers and Newborn Babies). When Cantonese immigrants established the temple towards the middle of the nineteenth century, they named it after Thien Hau, Goddess of Seafarers. New arrivals from China would have hastened here to express their gratitude for a safe passage across the South China Sea. Three statues of her stand on the altar, one behind the other, while a large mural on the inside of the front wall depicts her guiding wildly pitching ships across a storm-tossed sea. The temple's most attractive aspect is its roof, bristling with so many figurines you wonder how those at the edge can keep their balance.

North of Cho Lon

Two of Ho Chi Minh City's oldest and most atmospheric places of worship, the **Giac Lam** and **Giac Vien pagodas**, are tucked away in Districts Ten and Eleven, a hinterland to the north of Cho Lon; also nearby is **Dam Sen leisure park** (including a water park; see p.91). The best way to get to these destinations is by xe om or taxi, as they are hidden away in the backstreets.

Giac Lam Pagoda

118 Lac Long Quan • Dawn to dusk • Free

You'll see the gate leading up to **Giac Lam Pagoda** on Lac Long Quan, a couple of hundred metres northeast of its intersection with Le Dai Hanh. From the gate, a short track passes a newish tower (its seven levels are scaleable and afford good city views) and a cluster of monks' tombs on its way to the actual pagoda. Built in 1744, and believed to be the oldest in HCMC, rambling Giac Lam is draped over 98 hardwood pillars, each inscribed with traditional *chu nom* characters (Vietnamese script, based on Chinese ideograms). From its terracotta floor-tiles and extravagant chandeliers to the antique tables at which monks sit to take tea, Giac Lam is characterized by a clutter that imbues it with an appealingly fusty feel, and a reassuring sense of age.

The funerary chamber

The entrance to the temple is at the back right of the building, which takes you through to the funerary chamber, flanked by row upon row of gilt tablets above photos of the deceased. The many-armed goddess that stands in the centre of the chamber is **Chuan De**, a manifestation of Quan Am. A right turn leads to a **courtyard-garden** around which runs a roof studded with blue and white porcelain saucers.

The classroom

Monks occasionally sit studying on the huge wooden benches in the peaceful old **classroom** at the back of the complex. The panels in this chamber depict the ten Buddhist hells; study them carefully, and you'll see sinners being variously minced, fed to dogs, dismembered and disembowelled by fanged demons.

The main sanctuary

To the left of the funerary chamber as you enter the pagoda is the **main sanctuary**, whose multitiered altar dais groans under the weight of the many Buddhist and Taoist statues it supports. Remember to take off your shoes before entering. Elsewhere in this chamber, you'll spot an ensemble of oil lamps balanced on a Christmas-tree-shaped wooden frame. Worshippers pen prayers on pieces of paper, which they affix to the tree and then feed the lamps with an offering of oil. A similar ritual is attached to the bell across the chamber, though in this case people believe that their prayers are hastened to the gods by the ringing of the bell.

Giac Vien Pagoda

Lac Long Quan • Dawn to dusk • Free

Hidden away in a maze of backstreets, **Giac Vien Pagoda** was founded in the late eighteenth century, and is said to have been frequented by Emperor Gia Long. On entering its red doors daubed with yellow *chu nom* characters, visitors are confronted by banks of old photos and funerary tablets flanking long refectory-style tables. The two rows of black pillars lend an arresting sense of depth to this first chamber, which is dominated by a panel depicting a ferocious-looking red lion. Continue around the stone walls (crafted, incongruously, in classical Greek style) and into the **main sanctuary**, and you'll find a sizeable congregation of deities, as well as a tree of lamps similar to the one at Giac Lam. The monks residing in Giac Vien are hospitable to a fault, and you may well be invited for a cup of tea before you leave.

ARRIVAL AND DEPARTURE   HO CHI MINH CITY

The lion's share of new arrivals to Vietnam fly into Ho Chi Minh City's **Tan Son Nhat Airport**, which is also a major hub for domestic flights – these can be even cheaper than the buses, and are perfect for visitors spending a short time in the country. **Arriving overland**, you'll end up either at the train station, a short distance north of the downtown area, at one of a handful of bus terminals inconveniently scattered across the city, or right in the centre on De Tham at the end of an open-tour bus ride.

BY PLANE

Tan Son Nhat Airport (ⓦ hochiminhcityairport.com) is 7km northwest of the city centre, though it backs right onto the urban area – the impossibility of expansion means that a huge new airport is set to replace it to the east, though this won't happen before 2025. Facilities at Than Son Nhat include a post office (daily 9am–10pm) and two left-luggage depots – the one in the domestic terminal is markedly cheaper (daily 7.30am–10pm; from 25,000đ per bag per day).

Destinations Buon Ma Thuot (3–4 daily; 1hr); Ca Mau (daily; 1hr); Con Dao (7 daily; 1hr); Da Lat (6–7 daily; 50min); Da Nang (1–3 hourly; 1hr 10min); Haiphong (1–2 hourly; 2hr); Hanoi (2–4 hourly; 2hr); Hue (1–2 hourly; 1hr 20min); Nha Trang (1–2 hourly; 1hr 10min); Phu Quoc (1–2 hourly; 1hr); Pleiku (4 daily; 1hr 15min); Quy Nhon (7 daily; 1hr 10min).

GETTING INTO THE CITY

By taxi The taxi journey downtown from the airport takes 30–45min and costs between 130,000–200,000đ, depending on your destination. Make sure your driver switches on the meter, since many still wrongly ask for $25 claiming it'll be the same in the end. Also watch out for drivers who insist you pay the 10,000đ entrance fee both on their way in and out of the airport, even though they only have to stump up the cash once, on exit. If in doubt, Mai Linh (ⓣ 028 3838 3838) and Vinasun (ⓣ 028 3827 2727) are the best companies to go with. If you're set on a particular hotel, ensure your driver knows exactly where you want to go (show them in writing if possible). Alternatively, many hotels offer a pick-up service for advance bookings, typically in the 400,000–500,000đ range.

By xe om These will run you into town for about 100,000đ, but you'll have to bargain hard. To find one, walk around a hundred metres or so outside the airport gates.

TO AND FROM CAMBODIA

The closest border crossing into Cambodia from HCMC is 64km away at **Moc Bai–Bavet**. Buses between HCMC and Phnom Penh use this crossing, and any travel agency in the Pham Ngu Lao area will sell you a ticket ($10–15, 6hr). The crossing is generally painless, though you'll need to have arranged a Vietnamese visa in advance (see p.28) if you're crossing from Cambodia. Going the other way, visas are available on arrival ($30), but be warned there's also a near-obligatory $5 bribe – and refusal can hold up the whole bus.

1

TOUR AGENTS

Tour agencies abound in Ho Chi Minh City and offer a range of itineraries, from one-day whistle-stop tours around the region to lengthy trips upcountry including accommodation. Most of the recommended operators here can lay on tailor-made itineraries, private cars and personal guides for you, but be aware that we receive numerous reports of inefficient and **unscrupulous companies**, so it's worth choosing your agent carefully. Provisos and tips on signing up for a tour in Vietnam are listed in Basics (see p.35).

Ann Tours 58 Ton That Tung ☎028 3833 2564, ⊛anntours.com. Highly recommended, offering good-value, tailor-made tours.

★**Buffalo Tours** 157 Pasteur ☎028 3827 9170, ⊛buffalotours.com. This Western-managed setup specializes in customized tours throughout Indochina, and many run from HCMC. They have shorter trips available too, including the Story of Saigon day-tour ($35).

Exo Travel New World Saigon, 76 Le Lai ☎028 3824 3759, ⊛exotravel.com. Offers an extensive tour programme that includes special interests such as culinary options and Vespa journeys (both around $75) and a four-day "Unseen HCMC" option. Also adept at making spec hotel bookings across the country.

GoGo Vietnam 40/7 Bui Vien ☎090 311 9200, ⊛gogo-vietnam.com. Small, well-located operator specializing in cheap Mekong tours ($10 for a day-trip, $25 overnight including hotel), as well as hotel bookings, train tickets and the like – the small stuff that can end up being rather important.

Innoviet 199 Nguyen Van Huong ☎096 793 1670, ⊛innoviet.com. This company runs ecofriendly, small-group bike and boat tours of the delta (most around $75 for a day-trip) as well as half-day city trips.

Kim Travel 189 De Tham ☎028 3920 5552, ⊛kimtravel.com. A veteran of the independent travel scene, this operator offers open-tour buses, flight and rail bookings, car and minibus rental and guides. Their day-trips to My Tho and Ben Tre in the Mekong Delta are super cheap ($19).

Sinhbalo Adventure Travel 283/20 Pham Ngu Lao ☎028 3837 6766, ⊛sinhbalo.com. Super-efficient setup specializing in customized tours such as bicycle expeditions along the Ho Chi Minh Trail (⊛cyclingvietnam.net), motorbike tours, long-distance boat cruises and kayaking in the Mekong Delta. They also offer a wealth of reliable travel info.

The Sinh Tourist 246–248 De Tham ☎028 3838 9597, ⊛thesinhtourist.com. Offers cut-price organized tours of Vietnam such as dinner cruises ($20), open-bus tours, guides, visa services, buses and boats to Cambodia, and vehicle rental. Beware of copycat operators with similar names.

TNK Travel 220 De Tham ☎028 3920 4767, ⊛tnktravelvietnam.com. This operator offers cheap tours to destinations across the country, including trips to the Mekong Delta (from $19). It generally gets good feedback.

★**Vespa Adventures** 169a De Tham ☎093 850 0997, ⊛vespaadventures.com. This one is up there with the most popular tours in the city. Each night a fleet of Vespas takes to the streets under the charge of charismatic locals; meals, snacks, live music and rather a lot of alcohol are included in the $93 price. There's also plenty of booze on offer on the nightly craft-beer tour ($89), though dry daytime options are available too.

XO Tours 611/111 Dien Bien Phu ☎093 3028 3727, ⊛xotours.vn. Xe om rides with a difference – this company is the first all-female motorbike tour operator in Vietnam, and runs an interesting range of city tours that include food ($75), shopping ($48) and Saigon-by-night ($48) options.

By bus If you don't have much baggage, you can get the #152 a/c bus (every 15min–1hr; 5000đ) from the domestic terminal to Dong Khoi and Pham Ngu Lao. Shuttle buses (which don't have numbers) are a slightly more luxurious option (every 30min; 20,000đ), and "limousine" service #109 heads to some of the major hotels (every 30min; 40,000đ).

BY TRAIN

Trains from the north pull in at HCMC's Station (☎028 3843 6528), 3km northwest of town on Nguyen Thong. Since it's a few kilometres from the centre, it's best to take a taxi from there (70,000–85,000đ) – though you may be able to save money with a xe om driver.

Tickets Vietnamese trains are oversubscribed, so book as far ahead as possible – particularly for a sleeping berth. It's now possible to make reservations online (⊛dsvn. vn), but the site has had teething problems with foreign cards – you may have to resort to booking through a HCMC tour operator (see box above) or direct from the station itself.

Destinations Da Nang (15 daily; 15–20hr); Hanoi (11 daily; 30–41hr); Hue (15 daily; 21–23hr); Muong Man (5 daily; 3–4hr); Nha Trang (15 daily; 6–7hr); Ninh Binh (8 daily; 34–37hr); Phan Thiet (for Mui Ne; daily; 4hr); Quang Ngai (5 daily; 13–16hr); Thap Cham (16 daily; 5–6hr); Vinh (5 daily; 29–33hr).

BY BUS

Regular buses stop at the two main stations, though some companies have started using their own dedicated terminals, mostly in the wide area between Pham Ngu Lao and Mien Tay bus station. You can buy tickets at one of dozens of agencies around De Tham, and staff at your accommodation will also be able to help you make bookings.

Mien Dong bus station Buses to and from the north arrive at this sprawling station, 5km northeast of the city on Xo Viet Nghe Tinh. The #26 bus shuttles between here and Ben Thanh bus station, or you can take a taxi for under 100,000đ.

Mien Tay bus station Buses to and from the southwest terminate here, 10km west of the city centre in An Lac District; take a taxi (around 200,000đ) or a #2 bus to Ben Thanh bus station.

Shuttle buses Well-signposted shuttle buses between the Mien Tay (#2) and Mien Dong (#26) terminals make it possible to bypass central Ho Chi Minh City altogether in the event that you want to travel direct from the Mekong Delta to the north, or vice versa.

Destinations Buon Ma Thuot (7hr); Ca Mau (8hr 30min); Can Tho (4hr); Chau Doc (6hr); Da Lat (7hr); Da Nang (21hr); Hanoi (41hr); Ha Tien (9hr); Hue (27hr); My Tho (2hr); Nha Trang (11hr); Phan Thiet (4–5hr); Qui Nhon (13hr); Vung Tau (2hr).

BY OPEN-TOUR BUS

Open-tour buses are generally the simplest way to arrive or depart, since they pick up and drop off on or around De Tham, in the heart of the budget accommodation area; the same goes for the many buses heading to and from Cambodia (see box, p.87). Many of the tour operators concentrated around De Tham sell tickets for the open-tour buses that crisscross the country. Tickets, information and departing buses, which leave daily in the early morning or evening, can also be found at the various companies' offices around De Tham and Pham Ngu Lao. Sample fares from Ho Chi Minh City are as follows, often including stops in intervening destinations: Da Lat $13; Hanoi $40; Hoi An $23; Hue $30; Mui Ne $8; Nha Trang $10; and Phnom Penh $11.

BY BOAT

It's possible to take a boat trip to the Cu Chi tunnels (see p.106) or the Mekong Delta (see box, p.119); these trips leave from various docks along the river, but your fee will include transport to and from your hotel or booking office. There were once hydrofoil services to Vung Tau, but completion of a new highway sadly saw their demise in late 2016.

GETTING AROUND

Faint-hearted visitors to Ho Chi Minh City will blanch upon first encountering the chaos that passes for its **traffic system**. Thousands of motorcycles, bicycles and cyclo fill the city's streets and boulevards in an insectile swarm that is now supplemented by a burgeoning number of cars and minibuses, most with their horns constantly blaring.

By cyclo A leisurely cyclo ride around HCMC adds a uniquely Vietnamese touch to the experience. They are a dying breed here, since the local government is in the process of phasing them out. They are already forbidden to enter many key streets in the city centre, so if your rider seems to be taking a circuitous route, he may not be doing so to bump up the fare. Scams, however, are commonplace. Agree on a rate of 70,000–100,000đ an hour (showing notes if possible, to avoid any zero- or dollar-related misunderstandings). You'll likely have to haggle. Though it's feasible to have two (very small) passengers on a cyclo, the corresponding rise in cost and lessening of comfort make this a false economy.

By taxi Taxis are inexpensive and worth considering, if only to avoid interminable haggling over fares. They're easy to flag down on the street, though it's just as easy to call for a pick-up wherever you are. The flag fare is 12,000đ, but you can still traverse a decent chunk of the city for 40,000đ – which is worth it, especially given the pollution levels of the city's streets. It's best to stick with reliable companies like Mai Linh (☏ 028 3838 3838) and Vinasun (☏ 028 3827 2727), though these days most of the branded taxis are fine.

By xe om Expect to pay around 30,000đ for a short ride around town.

On foot The majority of the city's attractions are conveniently clustered despite its urban sprawl, so it's quite feasible to discover many of them on foot. But first you have to learn to cross the streets where the traffic never stops. There's an art to crossing the street in Vietnam: besides nerves of steel, a steady pace is required – motorbike riders are used to dodging pedestrians, but you'll confuse them if you stop in your tracks. Also note that during rush hour, motorbikes use some pavements as temporary roads (see box, p.90).

By bus Few visitors ever take a public bus, though it's relatively easy to hop on one to Cho Lon from the backpacker district. When leaving the city, Ben Thanh bus station is a useful point of departure, linking other long-distance bus stations in Ho Chi Minh City as well as offering direct services to Vung Tau and other places. It'll cost 5000–7000đ per ride.

By bike or motorbike This is a cheap way to get around HCMC, though you'll need skill and bravery to survive in the traffic. Most hotels and guesthouses can arrange a motorbike for you (150,000đ/day), and while bicycles (40,000đ/day) are a bit more difficult to track down, your accommodation should be able to point you in the right

1

HOPE YET FOR PEDESTRIANS IN MOTORBIKE CITY?

It has to be said: Ho Chi Minh City is an absolute nightmare for **pedestrians**. Walking along the pavements can feel something akin to tackling a military obstacle course, and you'll often find yourself having to step into the road as shop signs get in the way, street vendors spray their seats clean and trees are planted in unnecessarily impedimentary positions. Then, of course, there are the motorbikes, which deliver a quadruple whammy – those parked where they shouldn't be, those driving where they shouldn't be (a particular problem during rush hour), those being sold outside motorbike shops and the drivers who (assuming you couldn't possibly be walking from A to B) pester you for a ride. All in all, it can feel like the whole city is against you.

For most Vietnamese this is not much of an issue, since almost everyone has a motorbike and few people actually walk anywhere. However, this does not fit the image that the city and national governments would like to present to the world, and changes are afoot. The newly pedestrianized **Nguyen Hue** is the most pertinent example (see p.74), and "Music Street" (see p.103) closes to traffic on weekends. In addition, in early 2017 city officials started a drive to remove shop signs, parked bikes and other **pavement clutter** from many streets in District One; other district councils are considering similar actions. Lastly, the new city **metro** system (see p.103) will soon see Saigonese commuting underground in their hundreds of thousands; this will have the effect of relieving the traffic on the streets, but to what extent remains to be seen.

direction. One reputable organisation is the Saigon Scooter Centre (@ saigonscootercentre.com), which has an array of classic-style scooters for around 300,000đ/day (minimum three days).

By car Many tour operators and hotels offer car rental plus driver for $60–100/day, depending on the vehicle and the driver's proficiency in English.

By metro The first two lines of the city's metro system – the first in the country – are set to be up and running by 2020, with another four lines to follow in due course. Line 1 will start by Ben Thanh Market, then stop at the Opera House (both areas were eyesores at the time of research) before rising overground and heading east; Line 2 will go west from Ben Thanh. Neither are likely to be much use for tourists, but they'll hopefully alleviate some of the city's traffic (see box above).

INFORMATION

Tourist information For practical information with no strings attached, enquire at your guesthouse or hotel. Your hosts should also be able to provide you with a basic map of the city centre, though Google Maps and offline smartphone apps such as @ maps.me work very well here.

Listings For information about what's going on in Ho Chi Minh City, check out *The Word* (@ wordhcmc.com), *Oi Vietnam* (@ oivietnam.com) or *Saigoneer* (@ saigoneer .com), which also come in print form; you'll find them in many hotels and foreigner-oriented bars and cafés.

ACTIVITIES

If you're done with HCMC's sights, there are plenty of other ways to increase (or lower) your pulse across the city. Most of the upmarket hotels have gym facilities, some of which can be used by non-guests for a fee. For unbridled pampering, check out @ spasvietnam.com for the lowdown on the many spas and treatments on offer here.

DANCE CLASSES

La Salsa 212 Nguyen Dinh Chieu ☎ 091 377 1989, @ lasalsa.vn. The city's best salsa classes, with a good mix of local and foreign attendees. A block of six lessons costs 450,000đ, usually spread across a week each month.

GOLF

Vietnam Golf and Country Club Long Thanh My Village, District Nine ☎ 028 6280 0124, @ vietnamgolfcc .com. Two 18-hole courses (one designed by Lee Trevino) and a driving range. Membership isn't required, and weekdays are cheaper at $110 for a round.

ICE-SKATING

Saigon Centre 65 Le Loi. Ice-skating in HCMC? Well yes, but only in November and December. It'll cost 120,000đ for 45min. Nov & Dec daily 9am–9pm.

MASSAGE AND SPAS

L'Apothiquaire 64a Truong Dinh ☎ 028 3932 5181, @ spasaigon.com. Now, this is the full works. The mansion-like setting (slightly out of the centre in District Three) enhances the pampering experience, with sauna and pool facilities as well as all sorts of massages, herbal baths and more to choose from. They've a slightly less elegant branch in District One, at 100 Mac Thi Buoi. Daily 9am–9pm.

RUNNING

Hash House Harriers ⊛ saigonh3.com. For runners and walkers, the Hash House Harriers meet at the *Caravelle Hotel* (see below). There's a fee of 220,000đ. Sun 1.30pm.

SWIMMING AND LEISURE FACILITIES

Beautiful Saigon 40/13 Bui Vien ☏ 028 3836 4852. Non-guests can use the open-air, centrally located pool at this hotel (see p.93) for 100,000đ. There's a restaurant here, and alcohol is available too.

Dai The Gioi Water Park 600 Ham Tu, Cho Lon ☏ 028 3853 7867. This attractive park has pools (50,000đ) and slides (55,000đ). Combined entry is 85,000đ for adults and 60,000đ for children. Daily 8am–9pm.

Dam Sen Water Park 3 Hoa Binh, Cho Lon ☏ 028 3858 8418. This is another fun water park, perhaps a little bit fancier than Dai The Gioi, and correspondingly pricier at 140,000đ. There's a slight discount after 4pm. Mon–Sat

8am–6pm.

Hotel Pools Park Hyatt, Renaissance and Sofitel. For a daily fee of 150,000–250,000đ you can use the facilities at these pools if you are not a guest. Some include the use of a sauna and steam bath.

Vincom Centre 70–72 Le Thanh Ton. This shopping centre (see p.103) also has a pool; 600,000đ will get you a day's use of this and the fitness centre.

Labour Culture Palace 55 Nguyen Thi Minh Khai ☏ 028 3930 9254. Best for budget travellers, this place will only charge you 30,000đ for admittance to the pool, which is filled with locals and surrounded by vaguely Art Deco-style architecture. Daily 5.30am–7pm.

Lan Anh Country Club 291 Cach Mang Thang ☏ 028 3862 7144, ⊛ lananhclub.vn. Favoured by expats, this place has a relatively cheap pool (50,000đ), international-standard tennis courts, squash courts and a gym (from 70,000đ). Daily 6am–9pm.

ACCOMMODATION

There are thousands of hotel rooms in Ho Chi Minh City, ranging from windowless cupboards to sumptuous suites. The best hotels are located around **Dong Khoi** in the city centre, and there are some smart mini-hotels on nearby **Mac Thi Buoi**. Ho Chi Minh City's budget enclave centres around Pham Ngu Lao, De Tham and Bui Vien, though there are some smarter options here, too. The area sits roughly 1km west of the city centre, but is still convenient for visiting most city attractions; in addition, restaurants, bars and shops tend to be cheaper out here. If the De Tham region is too crowded for you, note that there's a smaller clutch of budget hotels in an alley a few blocks south off Co Giang.

BEN NGHE

A25 35 Mac Thi Buoi ☏ 028 3827 3637; map p.72. Nicely furnished mini-hotel, bookended at the bottom by an extremely brown lobby and at the top by a restaurant with a view of the bustle around Dong Khoi. Staff are friendly and helpful, and discounts are available for longer stays. $30

Asian Ruby 26 Thi Sach ☏ 028 3827 2838, ⊛ asianrubyhotel.com; map p.72. This centrally located mid-range hotel is the first of a growing chain with a winning combination of convenient location, comfy rooms and helpful staff. Rooms feel welcoming, with bedside control panels, thick mattresses and bright artwork. $70

★**Caravelle** 19 Lam Son Square ☏ 028 3823 4999, ⊛ caravellehotel.com; map p.72. The city's most prestigious hotel is steeped in history, and since it opened in 1959 its fortunes have echoed those of the country. A new 24-storey wing was opened in 1998, and since then it has led the pack with its luxurious rooms and suites, impeccable service and fine dining options. A sundowner at the *Saigon Saigon* bar on the rooftop of the old building (see p.101) is an essential experience. Breakfast is not included in the rates; also note that prices go down a bit on weekends, sometimes even under $100. $185

Catina 109 Dong Khoi ☏ 028 3829 6296, ⊛ hotelcatina .com.vn; map p.72. A nice little option that's right in the heart of Dong Khoi, though there's nothing special about the decor, which is smart yet a little soulless – this place is

all about location. Superior rooms are rather cramped and usually windowless, so it's worth paying the $15 extra for a deluxe room. $70

Continental 132–134 Dong Khoi ☏ 028 3829 9201, ⊛ continentalvietnam.com; map p.72. The grandly carpeted staircases, marbled floors and dark-wood furnishings of this venerable address's halls convey a colonial splendour that doesn't quite extend to its rooms, though some boast commanding views down Dong Khoi. The rack rates have been slashed of late, which is great news. $122

★**Della Boutique** 67 Ham Nghi ☏ 028 6857 8798, ⊛ dellahotel.com; map p.70. There are few places to stay on busy Ham Nghi, which makes this odd venue stand out all the more. The intricately designed rooms here are quite delightful, yet this place is suitable for backpackers as well as mid-rangers since they include what are without doubt the swankiest dormitories in the city (you climb stairs to the upper bunks!). There's also a rooftop bar with killer views – all things considered, this is a fantastic choice. Dorms $10, doubles $60

Grand 8 Dong Khoi ☏ 028 3823 0163, ⊛ grandhotel .vn; map p.72. This restored 1930s hotel has over two hundred rooms; the large, comfortable suites in the old wing are best, with comfortable furnishings and polished wooden floors. Modern facilities include a swimming pool and jacuzzi. Expect to get big discounts from the overly high rack rates. $169

1

ACCOMMODATION ESSENTIALS

Most of the general travel advice for Vietnamese accommodation (see p.91) also rings true in Ho Chi Minh City, especially regarding breakfast (all places listed here include it, unless otherwise stated) and pricing (some places quote in dollars and some in dong, yet all will accept either as payment). However, there are a couple of things that are worth being aware of.

ADVANCE BOOKINGS

In HCMC it's advisable to book accommodation in advance – this will save you hauling your bags around the city, and might even secure you a pick-up from the airport or station. In addition, the city is so popular that accommodation can be difficult to find, especially in December and January.

HOSTELS

Until recently, there were very few dorm beds to be found in HCMC, but a glut of guesthouses featuring such facilities have popped up in the De Tham area. Few of them exude a truly hostel-like vibe. Also note that many are unofficial operations that do not pay tax, and therefore risk being closed down at any moment.

TRAFFIC NOISE

This is a big issue in HCMC, and many hotels are fitting double glazing in an attempt to block it out; keep this in mind when choosing a room if you're a light sleeper.

★**Majestic** 1 Dong Khoi ☎028 3829 5517, ⓦ majesticsaigon.com; map p.72. This is a historic 1920s riverfront hotel that oozes character. All the rooms are charming, especially those with river views, and the staff fall over themselves to be helpful. There's a first-floor pool and rooftop bar, too. $225

May 28–30 Thi Sach ☎028 3823 4501, ⓦ mayhotel .com.vn; map p.72. With a good downtown location, this place features a pool, spa and fitness centre. Rooms are bright affairs with solid furnishings. $80

★**Park Hyatt** 2 Lam Son ☎028 3824 1234, ⓦ saigon .park.hyatt.com; map p.72. Enjoying a prime spot on Lam Son Square, and staring down over the Municipal Theatre, this place simply exudes class, with over 250 classically elegant rooms, two stylish restaurants as well as a pool and spa. $275

★**The Reverie** 22–36 Nguyen Hue ☎028 3823 6688, ⓦ thereveriesaigon.com; map p.72. Move over at the top – Saigon's accommodation has a new king of the hill. Ostentatious from top to toe, the profusion of marble and mosaics here is reminiscent of similar constructions in the Middle East. The suites are particularly palatial, with chandeliers and sculpted ceilings. For a cheap-ish taste of what it's like to live the high-life, visit the on-site *Royal Pavilion* restaurant (see p.97). $400

Rex 141 Nguyen Hue ☎028 3829 2185, ⓦ rexhotel vietnam.com; map p.72. A series of recent makeovers have re-established this as one of the city's most appealing options, though the plush rooms and central location don't quite justify the price tag unless you can score a discount (book on-site for the best deals). A sundowner on the fifth-floor terrace is a memorable treat whether you're staying here or not (see p.101). $165

Saigon Prince 63 Nguyen Hue ☎028 3822 2999, ⓦ saigonprincehotel.com; map p.72. There are nearly two hundred spacious, coffee-colour-carpeted rooms in this classy hotel. Each is equipped with a big desk and a tub in the bathroom, and the hotel also boasts a restaurant and a great outdoor pool. You'll save around $20 if you forgo breakfast. $125

Saigon River Boutique 58 Mac Thi Buoi ☎028 3822 2828, ⓦ saigonriverhotel.com; map p.72. With boutiquey flourishes from top to toe, this is a popular budget spot in pricey Dong Khoi. Rooms are large for the price, and some have balconies; also check out the wonderful rooftop bar area. $35

Spring 44–46 Le Thanh Ton ☎028 3829 2738, ⓦ springhotelvietnam.com; map p.72. With its spiral staircase and Roman-style statuary and columns, this place is the epitome of budget chic. Having apparently got over a few cleanliness issues, this place is now a Dong Khoi steal, with top-quality services, a convenient location and carpeted rooms. $45

Vuong Tai 20 Luu Van Lang ☎028 3521 8597, ⓦ vuongtaihotel.com; map p.72. Small hotel set on a shoe-shop-lined street east of the market; you can't miss its gleaming, gold-coloured lobby. Rooms are pretty, if simple, with nice bathrooms; some of the cheaper ones have smaller windows, but better views. $40

BEN THANH

★**Fusion Suites** 3–5 Suong Nguyet Anh ☎028 3925 7257; map p.70. This is a winning recent addition to the area, and the city in general. The lemongrass aroma hits as soon as you step into the lobby, while rooms feature floor-to-ceiling windows and prints of whimsical Vietnamese scenes. The wood-panelled bathrooms are also so nice that you may actually want to sleep in them. Breakfast is usually only included with suites, though it is available as a free addition on some booking sites. $130

Himalaya Phoenix Hostel 7/12 Nguyen Trai ☎090 765 3230; map p.70. Somewhat removed from the main backpacker area (it's on the other side of the park), this is a popular choice. Dorms look a bit institutional, but they're clean and get the job done; the private rooms are cheerier places to sleep. All in all, it's the generous welcome that will tempt you to stay on another night or three. Dorms $8, doubles $24

★ **Lavender** 208–210 Le Thanh Ton ☎028 2222 8888, ⓦlavenderhotel.com.vn; map p.70. Situated in a prime shopping spot, just along the road from the Ben Thanh Market, this friendly, professionally run hotel (now one of a small chain of three) features smallish but cosy, carpeted rooms with full facilities. Expect to see purple trims all over the place. $65

New World 76 Le Lai ☎028 3822 8888, ⓦsaigon .newworldhotels.com; map p.70. This has been a benchmark on the HCMC hotel scene since it opened in 1993. Over five hundred luxurious rooms are complemented by impressive sports and leisure facilities, cutting-edge restaurants and a business centre. $225

★ **Nguyen Shack** 6/15 Cach Mang Thang Tham ☎028 3822 0501, ⓦnguyenshack.com; map p.70. Now this is something rather different. After the success of their "countryside" hostels in Can Tho and Ninh Binh, the owners attempted to transport the concept to the big city – and with a great deal of success. There's bamboo all over the place and a general air of calm, yet you're within walking distance of basically everywhere of note in HCMC. In addition, they run regular bicycle tours, and some of the proceeds go towards paying school fees for impoverished local children. Great stuff. $49

Sanouva 177 Ly Tu Trong ☎028 3827 5275, ⓦsanouvahotel.com; map p.70. There's a lot of mid-market competition around Ben Thanh Market, but this place stands out due to its spacious and well-appointed rooms, decent breakfasts, ever-cheery staff and the extremely useful convenience store joined to the lobby. You're unlikely to pay much more than half the rack rate. $80

Silverland Central 14–16 Le Lai ☎028 3827 2738, ⓦsilverlandhotels.com; map p.70. One of a chain of mini-hotels offering comfortable, if cramped, mid-range rooms. This one is right next to Ben Thanh Market, meaning it's ideal for shopping and well positioned to get to most sights; some rooms have great views, thanks to the wide-open area in front of the hotel. $60

★ **Townhouse 50** 50e Bui Thi Xuan ☎028 3925 0210; map p.70. This is a super little spot, and one that gives off a "flashpacker" vibe. It's a little way north and west of the action at the end of a tiny alley, though still within easy walking distance of the bars. Upon entry you'll be left wondering whether you're in the right place or a fancy café, though rows of backpacks betray the clientele who stay in a series of immaculate dorms and private rooms. Sells out quickly. Dorms $10, doubles $32

PHAM NGU LAO

Beautiful Saigon 62 Bui Vien ☎028 3836 4852; map p.76. This place may well tempt you to splash out in the most literal sense – it's got a great pool downstairs by the excellent restaurant (see p.99). Rooms are comfy affairs with swish bathrooms. Call them up, rather than booking online, and you can sometimes get good discounts. $43

Bich Duyen 283/4 Pham Ngu Lao ☎028 3837 4588, ⓦbichduyenhotel.net; map p.76. Great-value rooms on a quiet sidestreet, with friendly, English-speaking staff – what more could you possibly need? Perhaps a window – you'll need to pay a little more if you want one. Breakfast not included. $19

PIMP MY TOWER: ALL CHANGE AT 42 NGUYEN HUE

Nguyen Hue is turning into a seriously cool place. Not only does it have the pedestrian boulevard down the middle (see p.74), new drinking spots like *Broma: Not a Bar* (p.100) and the *Eon Heli Bar* (p.101) presiding over the lot, but it also has what's going on at **#42**. Formerly a run-down apartment block with some pretty nice views, it has recently been pimped to the nines, with every floor featuring an array of sushi restaurants, cafés (like *Saigon Oi*, p.97), clothing boutiques, gallery spaces and the like (note that there's a nominal charge to take the lift up). While the place – in this iteration, at least – is still in its infancy, things should settle soon, and it's primed to be even cooler; the views of the building from outside are already pretty spectacular. Something similar is going on to the north at **22 Ly Tu Trong**, which has its own fascinating wartime history (see p.73) and is now home to cafés (like *Cong*, p.96), shopping boutiques (including *Libé*, p.103), art galleries and more. Hopefully this trend continues, and HCMC will start to make similar use of some of its most idiosyncratic buildings.

1

Bizu 183 De Tham ☎028 3920 8986, ⓦbizuboutique hotel.com; map p.76. Spotless, spacious, tiled rooms with crisp sheets in a fantastic central location. The receptionists are particularly helpful. $32

Cat Huy 353/28 Pham Ngu Lao ☎028 3920 8716, ⓦcathuyhotelvn.com; map p.76. One has to admire the chutzpah of a place billing itself "maybe the best one-star hotel you've ever stayed in". And it really is good for the price, with nice rooms and attentive service. It's signed off Pham Ngu Lao, down an alley that initially looks forbidding, but gets better as you go along. $30

★**C-Central** 40 Bui Vien ☎028 3823 5234; map p.76. A great new addition to the area, this boutique-style hotel has given its rooms relaxed yet classy stylings, as well as tubs in all the bathrooms. Easy to find, and the location is ideal. Rooms on the street side are brighter and noisier, but correspondingly cheaper. $60

★**Cozy** 265/7 Pham Ngu Lao ☎028 3925 3214; map p.76. A real winner at this price range, filled with passable impressions of "proper" hotel rooms and presided over by the cheery type of characters you could only really find at a guesthouse. Breakfast not included. $20

Eco Backpackers 264 De Tham ☎028 3836 5836; map p.76. We're not sure where the "eco" bit comes in, but the individual pods in the dorms give some measure of privacy, the location is as central as can be and the private rooms, though dark, are clean and spacious. Dorms $7, doubles $20

Elios 231–235 Pham Ngu Lao ☎028 3838 5584, ⓦelioshotel.vn; map p.76. This swish place, with over ninety snug rooms, is a good example of how things are changing in the city's main budget district. Staff are efficient and helpful, and there's also a rooftop restaurant; the main drawback is the busy road outside. $65

★**Flipside Hostel** 175/24 Pham Ngu Lao ☎028 3920 5656, ⓦflipsideadventuretravel.com; map p.76. This Kiwi-owned hostel has been a real backpacker hit, thanks to decent dorms, a buzzing atmosphere, great service and that hostel holy of holies – a rooftop pool. Tours are rather pricey here, so compare the costs elsewhere. Dorms $6, doubles $30

Gia Vien 174/4 Pham Ngu Lao ☎028 3920 9988, ⓦgiavienhotel.com; map p.76. The best venue on one of De Tham's more gentrified streets – expect restaurants, bars and moto-pests galore, but it's actually quite nice. Rooms here are comfy and fair value for the price; their bathrooms have been decorated with rare attention. $32

Hong Han 238 Bui Vien ☎028 3836 1927, ⓦhonghanhotelhcm.com; map p.76. Agreeable place on De Tham's main nightlife thoroughfare; rooms at the front can be a bit noisy, but they're all nicely decorated with artwork and the like. The balcony-style breakfast area is a nice bonus. $35

Liberty Parkview 265 Pham Ngu Lao ☎028 3836 4556, ⓦodysseahotels.com; map p.76. One of the nicer venues on Pham Ngu Lao itself, this place offers stylish rooms with satellite TV and tea- and coffee-making facilities, plus a decent buffet breakfast served in its ninth-floor restaurant. Rooms with park views cost a bit more, but it's certainly worth considering the splurge. $45

★**Luan Vu** 35/2 Bui Vien ☎028 3837 7185; map p.76. Located down an alley away from the traffic, this hotel has pleasantly furnished rooms, awesome breakfasts and helpful staff – the attention to detail places this amiable establishment a cut above the rest. $22

Madam Cuc 127 Cong Quynh ☎028 3836 8761, ⓦmadamcuchotels.com; map p.76. Long-running spot with plain, reliably cheap rooms. Staff are well informed and helpful, and they will also collect you from the airport. If this place is full, note they have three more branches where you'll find a similarly warm welcome. $25

Ngoc Minh 283/11–13 Pham Ngu Lao ☎028 3837 6407; map p.76. Located in a narrow alley and tucked away from the honking horns on Pham Ngu Lao, this place has a range of competitively priced rooms, all with a/c, cable TV and en-suite facilities. $25

Ngoc Thao Guesthouse 241/4 Pham Ngu Lao ☎028 3837 0273, ⓦngocthaoguesthouse.hostel.com; map p.76. Super-friendly guesthouse with comfortable dorms and rather plain private rooms, all en suite, and a lovely location on one of the area's most charming back-alleys. Dorms $7, doubles $17

Pink Tulip 40/11 Bui Vien ☎028 3837 3567, ⓦpinktuliphotel.com; map p.76. This family-run establishment is just about the cheapest place in town to boast a functional lift – a nice little surprise, as are the pleasantly decorated rooms, amiable staff and excellent breakfasts. $25

★**Pullman** 148 Tran Hung Dao ☎028 3838 8686, ⓦpullmanhotels.com; map p.70. Visible from much of the Pham Ngu Lao area, this place is a relatively new stab at luxury, and one that has really paid off. The rooms have been lovingly designed with pleasing artwork and docks for audio devices, there's an excellent on-site spa and the views from the rooftop restaurant are quite superb. Very fair value for what you get. $90

★**Vinh Chung** 283/26 Pham Ngu Lao ☎028 3837 9865, ⓦvinhchunghotel.com; map p.76. The owner of this hotel bends over backwards to accommodate her guests. Some rooms come with balcony, some come with cable TV and the beds are a tad softer than the usual hard-as-rock variety you find around these parts. $20

NORTH OF THE CENTRE

★**Emm** 157 Pasteur ☎028 3936 2100, ⓦemmhotels .com; map p.70. Forget the scruffiness of the surrounding area – this place is a steal. The lobby and the rooms themselves are sleek affairs dotted with splashes of lime and fuchsia, and this colour scheme extends to the plates used for their delicious rooftop buffet breakfasts. $45

★**Sofitel Plaza** 17 Le Duan ☎028 3824 1555, Ⓦsofitel.com; map p.70. One of the jewels in HCMC's crown, firmly established as a favourite with business travellers. The high-tech, open-plan lobby is a masterpiece, the rooftop pool is simply stunning, and its rooms and facilities boast luxurious elegance with the most modern trimmings. $170

EATING

Ho Chi Minh City has more **culinary sophistication** than anywhere else in Vietnam, including Hanoi. A mouthwatering array of international cuisine awaits: the regular French, Italian and Indian options, mixed up with Korean, Japanese, German and far more. Most importantly, there's a gut-busting gamut of good local food, from budget eats to fine dining. Aside from lower-end street stalls, recent years have seen a crop of gentrified places selling similar food in greater comfort: some are cheap chain operations, others offer a more sophisticated experience. At the other end of the scale, some of the swankier restaurants lay on reasonably priced set menus, and also live traditional music, in order to lure diners. Finally, **café culture**, introduced by the French, is still very much alive in Ho Chi Minh City, and there are numerous places at which to linger over a coffee or sundae and watch the world go by. Many of the corner buildings in the stylish area east of Nguyen Hue now have cafés, often featuring balconies with wraparound seating.

BEN NGHE

3T Quan Nuong 29–31 Ton That Tiep ☎090 835 7530; map p.72. This hugely popular rooftop spot serving Vietnamese barbecue is located right above *Fanny's* ice cream parlour (see p.96). Order your choice of meat, seafood and veg, and cook it to your taste at the table. Best to go with a group, and make sure you book ahead at weekends. Most dishes 70,000–150,000đ. Daily 5–11pm.

Banh Mi 24 31 Hai Trieu; map p.72. Tiny place serving novel takes on the humble *banh mi*, all freshly made to order and with a heated bun to boot – try the beef-and-Philly-cheese one (22,000đ). Daily 6am–10pm.

Banh Mi Nieu Lan 66 Ham Nghi, ☎028 3914 1338; map p.72. One of the cheapest popular places in the area, this long-running local legend serves freshly baked bread, cheap fruit juices and simple Viet staple meals (most around 45,000đ) – something for everyone. Daily 6am–10.30pm.

DINING PRACTICALITIES

The bulk of travellers eat in two main areas: the city centre, with its profusion of quality establishments; and the budget area, concentrated around De Tham, Pham Ngu Lao and Bui Vien, where many establishments cater exclusively to tourists.

COOKING CLASSES AND TOURS

Why not take some Vietnamese cooking skills home with you? You could start by trying the half-day classes at *Hoa Tuc* restaurant (see p.96; Ⓦsaigoncookingclass.com), which cost $45 including a market tour and allow you to whip up three dishes and a dessert (Tues–Sun 10am–1pm or 2–5pm). Alternatively, visit the Vietnam Cookery Center (26 Ly Tu Trong Ⓦvietnam-cooking-class-saigon.com), which runs two three-hour sessions each day for $37 (or $42 including a visit to the market for provisions), as well as twelve-dish three-session marathons for $180. It's also possible to go on culinary tours of the city: Saigon Streeteats (Ⓦsaigonstreeteats.com) does half-day trips from $35 per person, while XO (Ⓦxotours.vn) and Vespa Adventures (Ⓦvespaadventures.com) offer evening motorbike tours, with plenty of culinary treats, from $70 or so.

INFORMATION

There are several websites (see p.90) and blogs on hand to guide you through Saigon's maze of eating options, though being expat-focused, they tend to highlight places away from the main tourist areas. As well as the websites of the main local magazines, there are other food-oriented options like Ⓦeatingsaigon.com.

VEGETARIANS

HCMC is a little better endowed with veggie restaurants than most Vietnamese cities, though the choice is still sparse. As well as dedicated establishments like *Loving Hut* (see p.100), *Hum* (see p.96) and *Dinh Y* (see p.99), places such as *Asian Kitchen* (see p.99) and Indian restaurant *Baba's Kitchen* (see p.99) have veggie components to their menus.

BEST OF HCMC

Best pho *Pho Hoa* (p.100).
Best banh mi *Huynh Hoa* (p.98).
Best aroma *Cha Ca La Vong* (p.96).
Best ice cream *Fanny's* (p.96).
Best for veggies *Hum* (p.96) or *Loving Hut* (p.100).
Best for colonial splendour *Nha Hang Ngon* (p.97), *Quan Bui* (p.97) or *Temple Club* (p.98).
Best for evening atmosphere Ben Thanh Street Food Market (p.98).
Best hipster café *Saigon Oi* (p.97) or *Cong* (p.96).
Best craft beer *Pasteur Street Brewing Company* (p.101).
Best for drinks with a view *Broma: Not a Bar* (p.100) or *Eon Heli Bar* (p.101).

Café Eon 50F Bitexco Tower, 2 Hai Trieu ☎028 6291 8750; map p.72. The highest café in the city boasts accordingly lofty prices – 150,000₫ for a coffee may seem ridiculous, as may 180,000₫ for a fruit juice, though notably they're still both lower than the ticket price to the observation deck one level down (see p.75). Daily 8am–midnight.

Camargue 191 Hai Ba Trung ☎028 3824 3148; map p.72. A colonial-style, modern villa with rattan furniture and wooden ceiling fans sets the scene of a bygone era for this expensive French restaurant. The menu is constantly changing, but features dishes like beef carpaccio and lamb tenderloin with couscous. It's set back from the main road down a narrow lane. Main courses 250,000–500,000₫. Daily 6–11pm.

★**Cha Ca La Vong** 36 Ton That Thiep ☎028 3915 3343; map p.72. You'll find love at first smell in this restaurant, whose Hanoi counterpart is one of the oldest in the country. Take a step inside and you'll instantly be hit by the dill-heavy aroma of a secret combination of herbs and spices used with their signature (only) dish: *cha ca la vong*, or fried fish, cooked at the table for 180,000₫ a portion and served with noodles and other sides. Daily 11am–2pm & 5–10pm.

Cong 26 Ly Tu Trong ☎028 3737 3274, ⌨congcaphe .com; map p.72. First came the *Starbucks*-like chains, and then came the glut of faux-colonial ones. *Cong* are starting something a little different, with their ever-growing number of cafés all individually styled by local artists (this one: industrial chic), and no Western-style coffee on the menu. Vietnamese coffees cost from 30,000₫, and there's also juice, ice cream and more. Daily 7am–10.45pm.

Elbow Room 52 Pasteur ☎028 3821 4327; map p.72. This cosy diner specializes in comfort food such as eggs Benedict (198,000₫) or Philly cheese steak (242,000₫)

– just open the door and see if you can resist the delicious smells emanating from the kitchen. There's also a well-stocked bar and live music on Friday evenings. Daily 8am–11pm.

★**Fanny's** 29–31 Ton Thap Thiep; map p.72. This ice cream specialist serves up slurp-worthy scoops of heaven (65,000₫ each), served with tiny Vietnamese hats. In addition to the regular flavours, you can have a crack at ginger, black sesame, passion fruit, cinnamon or salted caramel. With wrought-iron chairs and magazines to read, this is a great place to kick back and cool off for an hour or two. Daily 8am–11pm.

Gartenstadt 34 Dong Khoi ☎028 3822 3623; map p.72. This German bar-restaurant is smaller, more atmospheric and more authentic than similar options around town. Schnitzels and sausages (a dozen types of the latter, including ostrich) start at 220,000₫, and soups are a bargain at 75,000₫. There's also a good selection of German beers, some on draught. Daily 10.30am–midnight.

Highlands Coffee 7 Con Truong Lam Son ☎028 3822 5017, ⌨highlandscoffee.com.vn; map p.72. Snuggling into the back of the opera house, this is the best located of this major national chain (see p.98). The coffee's passable; have it Viet-style for 29,000₫, or with an Italian name from 44,000₫. Daily 7.30am–11pm.

Hoa Tuc 74 Hai Ba Trung ☎028 3825 1677, ⌨hoatuc .com; map p.72. Wedged into a lovely, expat-heavy enclave of expensive eateries, this is the best looking of the bunch yet surprisingly cheap; check out starters like tofu with mint, pepper and lime (55,000₫) and cheap rice or noodle mains, or splash out on something like battered squid in tamarind sauce (175,000₫). They also run excellent cooking classes (see p.95). Daily 11am–11pm.

Hoi An 11 Le Thanh Ton ☎028 3823 7694; map p.72. Refined, traditional Vietnamese food served in a sumptuous wooden house. It's not cheap, with spring rolls going for 200,000₫ and seafood mains from 250,000₫; if you're in a real dong-splashing mood, opt for one of the huge sets (from 740,000₫). It's wise to book ahead. Daily 11am–2pm & 5.30–11.30pm.

Hum 2 Thi Sach ☎028 3823 8920, ⌨humvietnam.vn; map p.72. There's nothing ho-hum about this place, a veggie paradise with a fruit-and-foliage wall of sorts, soft piano music and even a small pool. The menu is heavy on tofu, taro and the like, and explains the health benefits of most dishes (usually in the 90,000–130,000₫ range). Also present and correct is a huge range of salads and fruit juices. Daily 10am–10pm.

★**Jake's** 50 Pasteur ☎028 3825 1311, ⌨jakesamerican bbq.com; map p.72. This all-American eatery has, in a few short years, become a real fixture with HCMC's expat set. With "football" (the type you don't play with your feet) on the TV and giant burgers (from 240,000₫) and pulled pork sandwiches (200,000₫) in front of happy customers, it's just like being in South Carolina, rather than South Vietnam. Daily 10.30am–1pm.

Jaspa's 33 Dong Khoi ☎028 3822 9925; map p.72. Classy venue, whose menu features international fusion cuisine (mains from 325,000đ) such as lemon sea bass with wasabi mash; the weekday lunch sets cost 245,000đ for two courses, plus 40,000đ for optional dessert. They've another branch serving similar meals at 74/7 Hai Ba Trung. Daily 8.30am–midnight.

Kem Bach Dang 26 & 28 Le Loi ☎028 3829 2707; map p.72. Twin open-fronted ice-cream parlours, revered for their extravagant creations (80,000đ or so), some of which feature fruits from Da Lat. The one that's open to the road is a magnet for beggars, who periodically stray inside; the other is sealed off and occasionally stinks of durian, but has good evening views from its upper floors. Daily 9am–11.30pm.

La Perle de l'Orient Off Ton Duc Thang ☎028 3827 5050; map p.72. The best looking of the flotilla of ship-restaurants that sets sail every evening. Set courses only available (from 339,000đ), but it's more about the experience than the food. Daily 7–9.15pm.

Le Jardin 31 Thai Van Lung ☎028 3825 8465; map p.72. Excellent French food at reasonable prices (from 80,000đ) served in a pleasant garden setting. Very popular, and not very big, so advance booking is advisable; the door is also a little hard to find. Daily 11am–2pm & 6–9pm.

Lemongrass 4 Nguyen Thiep ☎028 3822 4005; map p.72. A decent, upmarket establishment where the highly rated Vietnamese food is eaten under illuminated parasols. You should be able to fill up for under 300,000đ. Come at 7pm, and you'll be able to listen to traditional live music. Daily 11am–2pm & 5–10pm.

Matsuzakaya 17/34a Le Thanh Ton; map p.72. Tucked into a wonderfully calm residential enclave that many a Japanese expat calls home, this pair of restaurants sells cheap, passable food from the Land of the Rising Sun. The one further from the main road is best; try the *karaage* (fried chicken; 120,000đ) or *yakisoba* (fried noodles; 80,000đ). Daily 11am–10pm.

Modern Meets Culture 44b Ly Tu Trong ☎028 3822 2495; map p.72. You'll see haircuts galore at this hipster hangout – it's a good (not to mention smoke-free) place to meet some of Saigon's more characterful youngsters. Coffees are fine (45,000đ and up), though their smoothies are even better (particularly the banana peanut butter and cacao one), and the avocado ice cream is fab, too. Daily 7.30am–10.30pm.

Namo 74/6 Hai Ba Trung ☎028 3822 7988, ⓦnamopizza.com; map p.72. Now here's where you go to get a proper Napoli-style pizza (from 200,000đ); they also do decidedly non-traditional "fried" versions, which sound weird and aren't great for your health, but do taste pretty great. Daily 11am–11pm.

★**Nha Hang Ngon** 160 Pasteur ☎028 3827 7131; map p.72. Be sure to take at least one meal in this wonderful venue, spectacularly set in a yellow-and-white cream-cake of a colonial building – take your seat inside by the pool, or outside amid palm leaves and chunky yellow pillars. Two lines of chefs whip up all sorts of Vietnamese specialities in no time at all; the only surprise is that they're incredibly cheap, with most dishes weighing in at 50,000–80,000đ. It's very popular, so be prepared to wait for a table at peak eating times. Daily 7am–midnight.

★**Quan Bui** 17a Ngo Van Nam ☎028 3829 1515; map p.72. What a pleasant place – the pretty floor-tiling and gentrified atmosphere contrast nicely with the occasional noise from the bikes racing past. The food's cheap for somewhere so fancy-looking, and the menu's varied; try the chicken sautéed in tamarind (89,000đ), or flash-fried tofu in a passion-fruit dressing (59,000đ). Daily 7am–midnight.

Refinery 74 Hai Ba Trung ☎028 3823 0509, ⓦtherefinerysaigon.com; map p.72. Set back from busy Hai Ba Trung, this cute little bistro has a relaxed, almost colonial-era air, and is extremely popular with local expats. It serves an appealing range of dishes, many home-made, such as swordfish with lime and parsley mash (250,000đ), as well as a range of filling salads. To round things off, you can choose from beers, cocktails and a good selection of wines. Daily 11am–late.

Royal Pavilion 4F Times Square Building, 22–36 Nguyen Hue ☎028 3823 6688, ⓦthereveriesaigon.com; map p.72. Set in a building also housing the fancy *Reverie* hotel (see p.92), this Chinese restaurant has been designed with similar extravagance – gold-and-plum tables and chairs, lacquered folding screens, dark-wood panelling on the walls and (this is important) a no flip-flop policy. If you can afford it, come whenever and order as much seafood as you want; if you're a penny-pincher out for the high-roller experience, come on weekday lunchtimes and eat a few plates of *dim sum* (from 78,000đ each). Daily 11am–2pm & 6–10pm.

Saigon Oi 42 Nguyen Hue ☎093 897 0809, ⓦfacebook.com/saigonoicafe; map p.72. The best of the many, many trendy cafés to have sprung up in this gentrified residential block, filled with stylish young locals from morning to night. Try a coffee (45,000đ) or flavoured yoghurt (35,000đ) and soak up views that are even more spectacular at sunset. Daily 7am–9pm.

Secret Garden 158 Pasteur ☎090 990 4621; map p.72. Secret indeed – this surprisingly stylish place is located on the rooftop of an elevator-less building, down a hard-to-spot alley filled with motorbikes. The menu is filled with fantastic Vietnamese home cooking, and most mains are just 75,000đ. A word to the wise: think for a second before you order any chicken dishes, lest the regular (genuine) cock-a-doodle-doos become cock-a-doodle-don'ts. Daily 8am–10pm.

1

SAIGONESE CHAIN RESTAURANTS

One tell-tale sign that HCMC is on the up is the sudden prevalence of **chain restaurants** – not just Western favourites, but places serving local food at budget prices. Locals and expats may sneer at some of these offerings, but for better or worse they're becoming an integral part of the local culinary scene, and are therefore deserving of a little attention.

Highlands Coffee Vietnam's answer to *Starbucks* has branches all over the city, serving a mixture of Viet- and espresso-style coffees as well as cakes and sandwiches. There's a good one around the back of the opera house (see p.96).

Mon Hue In keeping with the budget-boutique trend, this chain serves good Hue food in a bright, cheerful atmosphere. Most are here for the *bun bo hue* noodle soup (65,000đ), though the menu's full of tasty options and there's also cheap fruit juice (from 18,000đ).

Pho 24 If the thought of eating from a street stall makes you shudder, sample your first bowl of pho (from 49,000đ), the nation's signature dish, in these spotless diners. The chain boasts over a dozen branches in District One alone.

Wrap & Roll Specialist spring roll chain, serving street food (most dishes 35,000–78,000đ) in a sanitized, a/c environment. Choose from a host of ingredients, peel off the rice wrapper and get rolling.

Skewers 9a Thai Van Lung ☎028 3822 4798, ⓦskewers-restaurant.com; map p.72. Superlative Mediterranean cuisine – everything from French to Levantine – made using simple and healthy ingredients. Try the pan-fried salmon with nicoise salad (300,000đ), pastas (130,000đ) or all manner of yummy dips; be sure to check the blackboard for daily specials. Mon–Fri 11.30am–2pm & 6–10pm, Sat & Sun 6–10pm.

Temple Club 29–31 Ton That Thiep ☎028 3829 9244, ⓦtempleclub.com.vn; map p.72. Like a step back into the world of Indochina – excellent, MSG-free Vietnamese food (around 200,000đ a dish), served in a wonderful, relaxed atmosphere amid tasteful decor. There's also a comfy lounge bar out back, which is the perfect spot for a glass of wine. Daily 11.30am–midnight.

Tuk Tuk 38 Ly Tu Trong ☎028 3823 1188, ⓦtuktukthaibistro.com; map p.72. By far the most attractive Thai restaurant in town, this sleek, modern spot is no slouch in the kitchen department either – as well as green curries and *tom yum* soup, there's plenty of more adventurous fare on the menu (mains around 120,000đ). Daily 10am–10.30pm.

Xu 71–75 Hai Ba Trung ☎028 3824 8468, ⓦxusaigon .com; map p.72. This super-cool, minimalist venue is revered as one of the city's most innovative fusion restaurants – think coconut-braised pork belly (250,000đ) and lotus seed falafel (120,000đ). Most dishes are prepared to be shared; it's best to go with a small group. The main restaurant is upstairs, while downstairs is more a lounge bar, where a DJ spins tunes on weekends. Daily 11.30am–midnight.

BEN THANH

★**Ben Thanh Street Food Market** 26–30 Thu Khoa Huan; map p.70. It was going to take something special to lure backpackers north of their Bui Vien comfort zone,

and this place *is* that good. Hordes of foreigners and young Vietnamese descend on this covered, market-like venue to browse street food from over twenty stalls. It's cheap, tasty and fun, with reasonable beer and occasional live music – a superb addition to the HCMC dining scene. Daily 9am–11pm.

Huynh Hoa 26 Le Thi Rieng ☎028 3925 0885; map p.70. This is the semi-official holder of the best *banh mi* in town, with reams of travellers popping by every day to sample the Vietnamese sandwich (33,000đ). The secret? Fresh ingredients, and a far greater attention to hygiene than normal – this is one place where you won't find hairs in your food. Daily 2.30pm–midnight.

Milkbar 5 Le Quy Don ☎091 808 0707; map p.70. Milk and suitably dairy-heavy desserts are on offer at this cute café, shaped like a wooden house with a tiny second floor for good measure. Try the crème brûlée (30,000đ). Daily 7am–10pm.

Nam Giao 136/15 Le Thanh Ton ☎028 3825 0261; map p.70. Excellent Hue food is served in this atmospheric yet simple place, tucked away down a manicure-heavy alley behind Ben Thanh Market. Join the throng of locals and smattering of tourists to sample the famous *bun bo hue*, or a tasty *banh khoai*; most things on the menu are 58,000đ. Daily 7.45am–10pm.

Ngoc Suong 106 Suong Nguyet Anh ☎028 3925 6939; map p.70. This giant, mansion-like place is the most atmospheric branch of this hugely popular chain of seafood restaurants, and draws big crowds every evening. Figure on around 300,000đ per head, before drinks; reservations recommended. Daily 10am–10.30pm.

Pho 79 79 Syong Nguyet Anh ☎028 3926 2929; map p.70. This restaurant is popular with groups of young men, who frequent it most afternoons and evenings – you can expect cheap beer and very pretty waitresses. The food's good and not too expensive, with a compendium of

Vietnamese staples (100,000đ and up) as well as some interesting additions such as frog and crocodile. Daily 10am–10pm.

San Fu Lou New World Hotel, 76 Le Lai ☎028 3823 9513; map p.70. Affordable Cantonese food in a classy setting. There are a few *dim sum* choices on the menu, but mostly there are options like chilled chilli aubergine with chicken, and dried noodles with BBQ pork (both 79,000đ). Dishes are small, so it's best to share a few. Daily 7am–3am.

Vatel 120 Suong Nguyet Anh ☎028 5404 2220; map p.70. The most urbane café on this particularly urbane road, with a leafy, shaded courtyard as well as good coffee from just 25,000đ, plus some tasty cheesecakes. Mon–Sat 7.30am–10pm.

PHAM NGU LAO

★**Asian Kitchen** 185/22 Pham Ngu Lao ☎028 3836 7397; map p.76. Tucked away down a pleasant, narrow alley east of De Tham, this place has a surprisingly wide menu with Western dishes like a large English breakfast (85,000đ) as well as tasty Vietnamese and Japanese options. For a fusion of the latter two, try the delectable crocodile sashimi (99,000đ). Cheap beer, too. Daily 7am–11.30pm.

Baba's Kitchen 164 Bui Vien ☎028 3838 6661, ⓦbabaskitchen.in; map p.76. The most authentic of several Indian options hereabouts, with curries hovering

around the 100,000đ mark; pay a little more at lunchtime and you'll get a full thali set. Daily 10.30am–10.30pm.

Beautiful Saigon 62 Bui Vien ☎028 3836 4852, ⓦbeautifulsaigonhotel.com; map p.76. Eat by the pool at this hotel restaurant, and you can jump in for just 100,000đ. The food's surprisingly affordable too, with mostly Vietnamese staples – try the DIY spring rolls (89,000đ). Daily 6am–11pm.

Café Zoom 169a De Tham ☎093 850 0997; map p.76. The starting point for Vespa tours (see box, p.88) comes with a close-up view of the action at one of the city's busiest junctions. Coffee's only served Vietnamese-style (25,000đ), while there are all sorts of snacks to munch on, including German sausage, sourdough toast and Tex-Mex options. Daily 7am–2am.

Dinh Y 171b Cong Quynh ☎028 3836 7715; map p.76. Expect cheap but tasty vegetarian food prepared by Cao Dai adherents in a convenient location by Thai Binh Market. Dishes start at 22,000đ – there are very few options over 50,000đ. Daily 6.30am–9pm.

Espy 154 Cong Quynh ☎028 3837 7555; map p.76. New York-style pizza by the slice, on the cheap (45,000đ) – it's no wonder this place is always teeming with backpackers. Daily 10am–11pm.

Pho Quynh 323 Pham Ngu Lao ☎028 3836 8515; map p.76. This gets a lot of local custom for a backpacker-zone eatery, and is the place to head if you feel the need to slurp

BUYING YOUR OWN FOOD: MARKETS AND SUPERMARKETS

With staples like baguettes, cheese and fruit in such abundant supply in Vietnam, whipping up a picnic is easy. All the basics can be found at any of the city's **markets**, though if you're homesick for peanut butter, Vegemite or other such exotica, you'll need to head for a specialist **supermarket** or **provisions store**.

MARKETS

A stroll through a wet or fresh market in Vietnam, gazing at all the familiar and unfamiliar items on sale, is an essential activity for every visitor to the country. The handiest one for De Tham is **Thai Binh Market**, down at the southwestern end of Pham Ngu Lao, though it's not terribly interesting. Just about as near, and larger, is **Ben Thanh Market** (see p.76), the central market in the city centre. Cho Lon is served by **Binh Tay Market** (see p.83), on its southwestern border.

SUPERMARKETS AND PROVISIONS STORES

Annam Gourmet Shop 16–18 Hai Ba Trung ⓦannamgourmet.com; map p.72. Huge downtown deli, pandering to the whims of expats and visitors alike.

Circle K ⓦcirclek.com.vn. Branches of this 24-hour convenience store are ubiquitous across the city, and they're great for cheap late-night snacks and alcoholic drinks.

Co-op Mart 189c Cong Quynh ⓦco-opmart.com.vn; map p.76. This is a large, Western-style supermarket within easy walking distance of De Tham, selling clothes, toys, household goods, cosmetics and a good selection of food. There's also a large branch at 168 Nguyen Dinh Chieu.

Nhu Lan Bakery 66–68 Ham Nghi; map p.72. Famed bakery selling a range of bread, croissants and cakes. It's also a restaurant of sorts.

Veggy's 29a Le Thanh Ton; map p.70. Well stocked with imported meats, cheeses and cereals, this place is a popular shopping spot for local expats. At the time of research, it was expected to move to a new spot near the *New World* hotel (see p.93).

Vincom Plaza 72 Le Thanh Ton; map p.72. On the basement level of this shopping mall is a supermarket selling the city's best range of imported goods.

down a bowl of beef noodle soup (50,000đ), which is up there with the best in town. Daily 24hr.

NORTH OF THE CENTRE

An Vien 178a Hai Ba Trung ☎ 028 3824 3877; map p.70. Tucked away from the main road, this place is extremely intimate with lots of different alcoves and corners across three floors, all sumptuously decorated. There's high-quality Vietnamese food to match, and a lovely park just around the corner if you want to walk the calories off afterwards. Main courses 140,000–200,000đ. Daily 9am–11pm.

Au Parc 23 Han Thuyen ☎ 028 3829 2772; map p.70. This is a stylish place (you've got to dig the Socialist Realist mural), conveniently located between Notre Dame Cathedral and Reunification Palace. It serves up a couple of great breakfasts (150,000đ and up) and salads (120,000đ or so), and there's also a good deli counter and a few nice Turkish options. Mon–Sat 7.30am–10.30pm, Sun 8am–5pm.

★**Banh Xeo** 46a Dinh Cong Trang ☎ 028 3824 1110; map p.70. This street-side restaurant off Hai Ba Trung specializes in the eponymous Vietnamese pancakes (75,000đ), stuffed with a mixture of shrimps, pork, beans, bean sprouts and egg. They're so tasty that the place has become a must-visit spot for many travellers. Daily 10am–9pm.

Cuc Gach Quan 9 & 10 Dang Tat ☎ 028 3848 0144; map p.70. Facing off across a quiet road, these twin venues have exploded in popularity since a certain Brangelina popped by on their visit to 'Nam. Long since cleaved neatly in half, the two-headed publicity hound chose well, for what's on offer is a splendidly simple take on local cuisine (most dishes 90,000–140,000đ), served in a tranquil, down-to-earth environment. Daily 10am–11pm.

★**Loving Hut** 38 Huynh Khuang Ninh ☎ 028 3820 9702; map p.70. On a sidestreet near the Jade Emperor Pagoda (see p.81), this is a great find for veggies and vegans. The bulk of the menu is in the 45,000–70,000đ range, and the dishes are absolutely delicious – even carnivores would enjoy their fabulous pho. The photo-roster of well-known vegetarians on the wall is a nice touch, and just about the only place you'll see Pamela Anderson flanked by Socrates and Gandhi. Daily 9.30am–2pm & 4.30–9pm.

Napoly Café 7 Pham Ngoc Thach ☎ 028 3829 0583; map p.70. A short stroll northwest of the cathedral, this place is hugely popular among locals after a short coffee break or live music in the evening. Choose from a selection of ice creams, cakes, pastries and sundaes, or indulge in the *mangia e bevi* – a sensational blend of ice cream, orange juice and fresh fruit (68,000đ). There's also a Red Bull smoothie (85,000đ). Daily 7.30am–11pm.

★**Pho Hoa** 260c Pasteur ☎ 028 3829 7943; map p.70. This restaurant serves up generous portions of pho (65,000đ), with far-bigger-than-usual slices of beef or chicken and piles of fresh greens – it's by far the best you'll find in HCMC, and even more popular with locals than it is with overseas visitors. Daily 7am–10pm.

Quan Nem 15e Nguyen Thi Minh Khai ☎ 028 6299 1478; map p.70. Though a bit far from the centre, it's worth the trip north to this popular place. There are only two things on the menu: *nem cua ben* (fried, fist-sized crab spring rolls; 46,000đ) and *bun cha hanoi* (barbecued beef; 60,000đ), served with dipping sauce and a miniature forest of salad leaves. Daily 10am–10pm.

DRINKING AND NIGHTLIFE

Ho Chi Minh City boasts a good range of **nightlife**, although there are often restrictions on opening late. The magazine websites (see p.48) carry listings, plus features on the hottest new bars and clubs; for even more up-to-the-minute notifications, try Everyone's a DJ (ⓦ facebook.com/everyonesadj). **Prices** vary wildly: a Saigon beer at a streetside spot in De Tham will cost you around 15,000đ, but you can multiply that by five or more in an upmarket place on Dong Khoi. One way to economize while downtown is to take advantage of early-evening happy hours.

BEN NGHE

Apocalypse Now 2c Thi Sach ☎ 028 3824 1463, ⓦ apocalypsesaigon.com; map p.72. Dark and cavernous, with two dancefloors, "Apoc Lip" (as it's known to locals) is a real pioneer of the city's nightlife scene. It's always rowdy and sweaty at weekends with an eclectic crowd, though it can be rather dull during the week. There's a 150,000đ cover charge on weekends, which includes one free drink. Daily 7pm–2am.

Blanchy's Tash 95 Hai Ba Trung ☎ 090 902 8293, ⓦ blanchystashsaigon.com; map p.72. Super-cool cocktail lounge that's one of the most popular places in the area, especially on the occasions when international DJs drop by for a spin (think Pete Tong and Grand Master Flash). Wednesday is ladies' night, while Thursdays are the male equivalent. Daily 5.30pm–3am.

★**Broma: Not a Bar** 41 Nguyen Hue ☎ 028 3823 6838; map p.72. Not a bar, they say? Well it certainly is, and it's a cracker too. Try one of their signature martinis (165,000đ), such as the one made with lychee and lemongrass, while also drinking in the stunner of a rooftop view out towards the Bitexco Tower. Daily 5.30pm–2am.

Dublin Gate 74a 19 Thai Van Lung ☎ 028 3822 1720, ⓦ thedublingateirishpub.com; map p.72. This is just about the most authentic of the city's myriad Irish and English pubs, and is very popular with expats for its lively atmosphere, well-stocked bar and comforting Western menu. Try the full English or Irish breakfasts (150,000đ and 170,000đ respectively). Daily 7am–midnight.

Eon Heli Bar Bitexco Tower, 2 Hai Trieu ☎028 6291 8752, ⓦeon51.com; map p.72. By far the loftiest bar in the city, peering out from floor 52 – the helipad level – of the Bitexco Tower (see p.75). Views are predictably good, though prices aren't as high as you might expect; cocktails are 250,000đ and beers go from 160,000đ. Entry is free – and remember a visit to the observation deck two floors down would cost you 200,000đ anyway. Daily 10.30am–1am.

Hangover 38 Ton That Thiep ☎028 3915 2853; map p.72. On trendy Ton That Thiep, this is a pretty decent choice if you're looking for a "girlie" bar – it's common to see female travellers and expats visiting regularly. They offer a huge array of shooters and cocktails, and a full range of beers. There's usually sport on the TV, and some kind of Seventies or Eighties song playing on the sound system. Daily 5pm–2am.

La Fenetre Soleil 1F, 44 Ly Tu Trong ☎028 3824 5994; map p.72. Functioning as a chilled-out café during the day, this little gem turns its hand to mixing cocktails and filling shisha pipes by night. Daily 11.30am–midnight.

Level 23 Sheraton Hotel, 88 Dong Khoi ☎028 3827 2828, ⓦlevel23saigon.com; map p.72. This is a great spot for after-dinner cocktails (215,000đ) while enjoying panoramic views of the city, and there's often a live band playing if you're in the mood for dancing. Daily 7pm–midnight.

Malt Saigon 46 Mac Thi Buoi ☎091 848 4763, ⓦmaltsaigon.com; map p.72. Duck down below street level to this bar, which functions as a one-stop shop for the city's best craft beer – check out the latest run-down of what's on offer on the blackboard. Daily 5pm–2am.

Number 5 Bar 44 Pasteur ☎090 380 1676; map p.72. When is 130,000đ for a beer a good deal? When it's free flowing, that's when – swing by between 3pm and 7pm and you can refill your glass with as much San Miguel as you like. Even outside these times prices are cheap, though it becomes a girlie bar in the evening. Daily 3pm–midnight.

★**Pasteur Street Brewing Company** 144 Pasteur ☎028 3823 9562, ⓦpasteurstreet.com; map p.72. The best of the many new microbreweries in town, with creations including beer flavoured with jasmine, passion fruit, jackfruit and other local ingredients. The atmosphere is convivial, and the venue acceptably stylish. Daily 11am–11pm.

Phatty's 46–48 Ton That Tiep ☎028 3821 0796; map p.72. This sports bar and grill is regularly packed with punters watching rugby or Aussie Rules. There are enough screens, it seems, for every customer to be watching a different channel, even if the result is a bit cacophonous. Spirits from 99,000đ, beers from 50,000đ and huge cocktail jugs from 270,000đ. Daily 9am–11pm.

Rooftop Garden Rex Hotel, 141 Nguyen Hue ☎028 3829 2185; map p.72. A drink amid the fairy-lit topiary and clumsy model animals of the *Rex* fifth-floor terrace is still *de rigueur* on a trip to the city – at least for those who can afford it, as beers start at 150,000đ and cocktails at 270,000đ. Daily 6am–1am.

Saigon Saigon Caravelle Hotel, 19 Lam Son Square ☎028 3823 4999; map p.72. Located on the tenth floor of the *Caravelle*, this bar is one of the city's best sunset spots, with dreamily romantic views if the weather is deciding to cooperate. There are two for-one drinks specials around this time, though it's still fairly pricey (think 250,000đ for

HCMC: WHERE TO DRINK

Bars and pubs in Ho Chi Minh City range from hole-in-the-wall dives to elegant cocktail lounges that would not look out of place in a European capital. The area around Dong Khoi is predictably well endowed with fancy spots, and hotels such as the *Rex* and *Caravelle* have bars that wouldn't look out of place in colonial times. **Craft beer** bars have been a welcome recent addition to the city's nightlife scene, and you'll see in-the-know expats flocking en masse to each one's grand opening.

The city also has plenty of drinking spots at the lower end of the scale. Most popular with locals are the **street cafés** and cheap **restaurants**, whose plastic tables often end up creaking under the weight of umpteen beer bottles. In these sorts of places, you're not even required to purchase food, and you'll see those on Bui Vien absolutely heaving with boozy foreigners.

In the middle of the scale are the cheery watering holes around Bui Vien and the **girlie bars**, which hark back to the raunchy GI haunts of the 1960s. In such places, male customers will often quickly find themselves with an attractive, talkative young lady for company, and one is expected – though not obliged – to purchase their drinks. You'll find stacks of these bars around Thon That Thiep and Pasteur, and most are perfectly harmless (not to mention entertaining) for female visitors.

1

an Aperol Spritz, or other cocktails). There's also live music each evening from 9pm. Daily 9am–midnight.

Sax n' Art 28 Le Loi ✆028 3822 8472; map p.72. Slick, atmospheric jazz club with mellow sounds from the house band, led by saxophonist Tran Manh Tuan. The live music starts at 9pm, and sometimes features a range of good vocalists. Cover charge 100,000đ. Daily 5pm–midnight.

BEN THANH

★**Saigon Soul Pool Party** New World Hotel, 76 Le Lai ✆0122 734 8128, ⊛saigonsoul.com; map p.70. On Saturday nights from November to May, the rooftop pool at this plush hotel (see p.93) becomes *the* "it" venue in town (entry 150,000đ). Cool beats pulse out while hundreds drain cold beers, push each other off inflatable rafts and do all sorts of other stuff that their parents wouldn't be proud of. It's bloody brilliant fun. Jan–May & Nov–Dec Sat 2–10pm.

Vespa Sofar 99 Pham Ngu Lao ✆093 880 1498; map p.70. This is something a little out of the ordinary. Take the short walk from the tourist masses to reach this Vespa-themed bar, where you can try cocktails (90,000đ) or beer (from 20,000đ) served from the front of a VW camper van and enjoy them on a motorbike-seat chair. Daily 8am–2am.

Vuvuzela 54 Nguyen Trai ✆028 3207 5588; map p.70. One of nine branches (and counting), this bar atop Zen Plaza has commanding views from its outdoor seats, and the beer isn't all that pricey (from 37,000đ). It may be a bit weird to say this, but guys… you'll love the views from the urinals. Daily 10am–midnight.

★**Yoko** 22a Nguyen Thi Dieu ✆028 3933 0577; map p.70. If you get fed up with the lack of variety in music bars, head on round to *Yoko*, named after John Lennon's missus, where you'll catch talented bands pumping out blues/rock, reggae and jazz from 9pm every night of the week. Add to this the warm atmosphere of the place and decent drinks (cocktails 120,000đ; draft Pasteur beer 90,000đ), and you've got one of HCMC's best live music venues. Daily 8am–midnight.

PHAM NGU LAO

★**102 Bar** 102 Bui Vien; map p.76. For many backpackers, this is the abiding memory of HCMC – sitting en masse on tiny plastic chairs outside this shop pretending

to be a bar, with motorbikes zooming way too close, and a bottle of 15,000đ beer in hand. Daily 5pm–late.

Allez-Boo 187 Pham Ngu Lao ✆028 3837 2505; map p.76. One of the biggest foreigner magnets in town, this attractive venue doesn't quite live up to its reputation and pleasing bamboo-and-thatch decor. While the food isn't great, it remains a good drinking hole (beers from 75,000đ), and the upper floors turn into dancefloors of a sort if there's a big crowd in. Daily 24hr.

Go 2 187 De Tham ✆028 3836 9575; map p.76. This large, four-storey bar and restaurant on the corner of Bui Vien is packing them in, with a little help from a small army of touts who steer passers-by inside. The outdoor seats are popular with people-watchers, and on some evenings the rooftop space turns into a grill area. Daily 24hr.

★**Le Pub** 175/22 Pham Ngu Lao ✆028 3837 7679; map p.76. The clue's in the name here – a winning mix of French bar and English pub, tucked away down a charming lane off Pham Ngu Lao. Moodily attractive it may be, but there's often some serious drinking going on, perhaps best evidenced by the nightly promotions and large cocktail jugs (250,000đ). Daily 9am–late.

The View 195 Bui Vien ✆028 3920 6991; map p.76. HCMC has no shortage of bars with a view, but the prices are generally sky-high too. Hurrah, then, for this standby atop the *Duc Vuong* hotel, since a beer is still only 30,000đ despite recent price increases, and the views are still superb. Daily 10am–1am.

NORTH OF THE CENTRE

Lush 2 Ly Tu Trong ✆028 3824 2496, ⊛facebook.com /LushSaigon; map p.70. This elegant club is one of the top places for the city's movers and shakers to let their hair down at the weekend, when it gets packed. On weekdays it can be pretty dead, though Ladies' Night on Tuesdays and Latin Thursdays (free entry, plus two-for-one specials) usually draw a crowd. Daily 6pm–late.

★**Vung Oi** 17 Ngo Thoi Nhiem ✆028 2215 7813; map p.70. A little out of the way, but what a find this is, offering live music of a rather more refined ilk than the stuff played at the majority of HCMC's bars. You'll forget that you're in Saigon at all – this is almost like a hipster hangout somewhere like Lisbon, with jazz and blues taking place nightly from 9pm, and best enjoyed over a glass of wine. Daily 6–10.30pm.

ENTERTAINMENT

Cinema If you feel like a movie, head to the Lotte Cinema complex on the thirteenth floor of Diamond Plaza (see p.103; ✆028 3822 7897), the CGV in Vincom Plaza (see p.103; ✆1900 6017), or Galaxy Cinema, 116 Nguyen Du (✆028 3822 8533) – all show films in English with Vietnamese subtitles. You'll pay around 110,000đ for a ticket.

Classical music and opera The Conservatory of Music (112 Nguyen Du ✆028 3824 3774) showcases both Western and Vietnamese classical music, performed by the HCMC Youth Chamber Music Club. Saigon Opera House (Lam Son Square ✆028 3829 9976) hosts all sorts, including ballet, opera and classical music. Shows at this delightful venue (see box, p.74) rotate every few months, and can often be very entertaining. Tickets tend to start at 630,000đ, and you'll usually get 10% off by booking at the theatre itself.

Live music Many bars feature live music either every night or at the weekend, with bands performing well-rehearsed covers of current hits and old favourites. There's also a growing base of local musicians who are making a name for themselves in venues like *Yoko*. At the time of research,

the city authorities had just branded Alexandre de Rhodes St "Music Street" (see map, p.70), and were intending to close it to traffic and feature multiple live performances every weekend. It isn't unheard of for big showbiz names from the West to make appearances in HCMC, so check out the local press for details.

Water puppetry This can be seen at the Golden Dragon Theatre (see p.79) or for far less money at the History Museum (see p.81).

SHOPPING

HCMC can be a dangerous place to go shopping, as you'll likely buy more than you intended once you see the prices. For cheap and cheerful **souvenirs** (see box, p.104), head for Ben Thanh Market, Le Loi or De Tham (be prepared to bargain); for something precious and pricey, browse the upmarket boutiques around Dong Khoi, Dong Du and Mac Thi Buoi. Lastly, the air-conditioned **shopping malls** tend to attract the masses with their glitz and glamour, and often offer some distractions in the form of cinemas and bowling alleys.

DEPARTMENT STORES AND SHOPPING MALLS

Diamond Plaza 34 Le Duan; map p.72. Probably the city's most diverse mall, featuring a department store, supermarket, fitness centre, hospital, swimming pool, bowling alley, cinemas and serviced apartments. Daily 10am–9.30pm.

Saigon Centre 65 Le Loi; map p.72. You'll find cafés, souvenir shops, clothing boutiques, Western-brand stores, a small department store and a supermarket in this highly convenient spot between downtown and the budget area. Popular with youngsters on photo-frenzy dates and group meets. Daily 9am–9pm.

Vincom Centre 70–72 Le Thanh Ton; map p.72. One of HCMC's newer malls, containing a selection of Western and Vietnamese designer labels, and housing a few cafés and restaurants. Daily 9.30am–10pm.

BOOKS, NEWSPAPERS AND MAGAZINES

Artbook 43 Dong Khoi ☎028 3822 0838; map p.72. Titles are well displayed in this attractive store. Most books here are art- or architecture-related, but there's plenty more on offer as well. Daily 9am–9pm.

Bookworm 4 Do Quang Dao ☎028 3838 9487; map p.72. There are lots of secondhand books to choose from at this small café, which also has board games for you to play while making your choice or enjoying a hot drink. Daily 7am–11.30pm.

Fahasa 40 Nguyen Hue ☎028 3775 2987; map p.72. Large bookstore with a few English-language novels and magazines. Daily 9am–8pm.

CLOTHING AND BAGS

Ginkgo 54–56 Bui Vien ☎028 3837 3077; map p.76. The Bui Vien area is chock-full of places selling T-shirts, but this chain is a cut above the rest with a wide range of colourful, Vietnam-centric designs – occasionally

humourous or artistic. They also claim to be ecofriendly. On top of this one, there are three more branches across the city. Daily 8am–11pm.

★**Ipa-nima** 77–79 Dong Khoi ☎028 3822 3277, ⓦ ipa-nima.com; map p.72. With branches in Singapore, Berlin, Tokyo and Kuala Lumpur, this is perhaps the best-known Vietnamese fashion brand overseas, even if the designer herself is from Hong Kong. She specializes in fabulous handbags, which range from subtle to exaggeratedly ostentatious. They're actually pretty affordable, at least in relation to the handbag price tags of the West. Daily 10am–8pm.

Khai Silk 101 Dong Khoi ☎028 3829 1146; map p.72. One of several downtown outlets for the creations of one of the city's top designers, selling exclusive outfits at high prices. The designs are a tasteful fusion of Western and Vietnamese motifs, and even a shawl is likely to set you back a couple of million dong. You'll find smaller (and usually pricier) stores from the same chain in some of the city's top hotels. Daily 9.30am–10pm.

Libé 26 Ly Tu Trong ☎090 940 8169, ⓦfacebook.com /libeworkshop; map p.72. Tucked into this newly trendy building is this ladieswear outlet, which is proving extremely popular with young, local women. Daily 10am–9pm.

Saigon Jane 214 Bui Vien ☎028 3831 3928; map p.76. Another fun T-shirt place, whose Viet-themed wares vary in style from Joy Division album covers to socialist takes on Roy Lichtenstein. Daily 9am–11pm.

★**Vo Viet Chung** 205 Ly Tu Trong ☎028 3914 2008, ⓦvovietchung.com; map p.72. VOV, as he's often referred to, is one of Vietnam's top designers, and the man most responsible for bringing the *ao dai* into the international fashion realm. There are more "regular" items on sale in his Saigon showroom, though each and every item here is an innovative little work of art. Bring lots of money. Daily 9am–8pm.

1

SAIGON SOUVENIRS

Saigon is one of Asia's great souvenir-hunting destinations. Paintings on rice paper, silk *ao dai*, lacquerware, embroidered cloth, musical instruments and ethnic garments are all popular choices, as are **curios** such as opium pipes, antique watches, French colonial stamps and banknotes, while the cheapest items include the ubiquitous T-shirts and conical hats. Visitors interested in Vietnam's history will find a wealth of copied **books** on the subject, sold in tourist areas by wandering vendors with a metre-high stack on their hip. For something different, intriguing **model ships** are sold on Cao Ba Quat, north of the Municipal Theatre, just east of the *Caravelle Hotel* facing the *Highland Coffee*.

MARKETS AND SHOPPING STREETS

Ho Chi Minh City's biggest market is **Ben Thanh Market** (see p.76), which has a huge variety of cheap clothes (including *ao dai* under 800,000đ) and all kinds of souvenirs like chopstick sets and carved seals.

   Dan Sinh Market, behind the Phung Son Tu Pagoda at 104 Yersin, has a section specializing in army surplus, both American and Vietnamese. Here you can pick up khaki gear, Viet Cong pith helmets, old compasses and Zippo lighters embossed with pearls of wisdom coined by GIs, such as "We are the unwilling, led by the unqualified, doing the unnecessary for the ungrateful." Keep in mind that none of this equipment is likely to be original, even if it looks a bit battered.

   Across the road from the Fine Art Museum (see p.76), **Le Cong Kieu** is a road rather than a market, yet one lined with "antique" shops selling Oriental and colonial bric-a-brac such as opium weights and vases – though your chances of finding genuine antiques are slim. Keep in mind when shopping here that the Vietnamese are very good at making new things look old.

   For other smaller souvenirs, check out the shops along **Le Loi** and **Dong Khoi** for old coins, stamps, notes and greetings cards featuring typical Vietnamese scenes hand-painted onto silk.

HANDICRAFTS, FABRICS AND ANTIQUES

Art Arcade 151 Dong Khoi; map p.72. A number of stands selling paintings, lacquerware and ceramics, plus Buddha statues, old watches and trinkets. In addition, there are usually a few quirky goods being sold outside by vendors who disappear whenever the police are around. Daily about 8am–8pm.

★**Nagu** 155 Dong Khoi ☎028 3936 9379, ⊛zantoc.com; map p.72. Twee it may be, but this great shop contains some perfect gift material – teddy bears made from Vietnamese-style patterned fabric, wearing tiny conical hats (from 220,000đ). Some of them wear *ao dai* too, and you can have names sewn into the feet. Daily 9am–10pm.

Saigon Kitsch 43 Mac Thi Buoi ☎028 3821 8019; map p.72. The clue's in the name here – humorous souvenirs on sale, including Mr Binh and iPho T-shirts, cups, notepads and the like. Daily 8am–9pm.

Sapa Village 209 De Tham ☎028 3836 5163; map p.76. Attractive garments and artefacts, some genuinely designed along the lines of Vietnamese ethnic minority group costumes and trinkets, others mere facsimiles of "ethnic-style" fashion. Daily 8am–11pm.

Tay Son 198 Vo Thi Sau ☎028 3932 5708, ⊛tayson.vn; map p.70. Frequented by tourist groups, who arrive to watch the making of lacquerware and browse the large warehouse of furniture, wooden carvings and lacquered art. It's a bit out of the way, but prices are usually far lower than you'd pay for the same things on Bui Vien or Dong Khoi. Daily 8am–6pm.

Yen Loan 9 Nguyen Sieu ☎097 612 8152; map p.72. The most attractive of several shops on this road selling wooden model ships – a foot-long one will cost around $25, and they can arrange shipping for the larger items. Daily 8am–8pm.

Zakka 73 Pasteur ☎028 3829 1516; map p.72. This is a high-quality tailor selling divine ready-to-wear silk creations, perhaps more notable for the lovely trinkets, including fabric pins (75,000đ) and silken bags (400,000đ). Daily 10am–8pm.

PAINTINGS

Fine Arts Museum 97 Pho Duc Chinh; map p.70. The basement level of this museum (see p.76) is devoted to commerce, in the form of artworks on sale by various city galleries. If you're in the market for a piece of Vietnamese art, it's worth checking these places out as standards are high and some prices are affordable. Tues–Sun 9am–5pm.

Lotus Gallery 67 Pasteur ☎028 3829 2695; map p.72. If you're hunting for original Vietnamese art, be it traditional or contemporary, there's a good range on show here over two floors. This place has been around since 1981. Daily 9am–6pm.

Nam Phoung 105 Bui Vien ☎028 3837 1281; map p.76. One of many artists making a living by reproducing classic images in the travellers' quarter. You can expect good work and reasonable prices. Daily 8am–9pm.

TAILORS

Nhut Van 107 Bui Vien; map p.76. Long-standing tailor in the budget district with many satisfied customers. Shirts can go for as little as $15. Daily 8am–9pm.

★**T&V** 39 Dong Du ☎028 3824 4556, ⊚triciaandverona .com; map p.72. Slightly more expensive than the bulk of the city's tailors, but worth it for the fresh and original designs. Some staff speak English, which makes everything easier. Shirts are around $50, suits more like $180–250, and there are plenty of ladieswear choices. Daily 9am–7pm.

DIRECTORY

Banks and exchange There are ATMs all over the city, and most banks can exchange cash. Sacombank at 211 Pham Ngu Lao (Mon–Fri 7.30–11.30am & 1–4.30pm, Sat 7.30–11am) is one of the most convenient. Otherwise, foreign exchange kiosks on Nguyen Hue and Le Loi have extended daily opening times.

Consulates Australia, Vincom Centre, 45 Ly Tu Trong ☎028 3821 8100; Cambodia, 41 Phung Khac Khoan ☎028 3829 2751; Canada, 10F Metropolitan Building, 235 Dong Khoi ☎028 3827 9899; China, 175 Hai Ba Trung ☎028 3829 2457; Indonesia, 18 Phung Khac Khoan ☎028 3825 1888; Laos, 93 Pasteur ☎028 3829 7667; Malaysia, 2 Ngo Duc Ke ☎028 3829 9023; New Zealand, Suite 804, 8F Metropolitan Building, 235 Dong Khoi ☎028 3822 6907; Singapore, Saigon Centre, 65 Le Loi ☎028 3822 5174; Thailand, 77 Tran Quoc Thao ☎028 3932 7637; UK, 25 Le Duan ☎028 3825 1380; US, 4 Le Duan ☎028 3820 4200.

Courier services DHL, 3 Nguyen Van Binh ☎028 3844 6203; FedEx, 146 Pasteur, close to the *Rex Hotel* ☎028 3829 0995.

Dentists Starlight Dental Clinic, 2 Cong Truong Quoc Te (☎028 3822 6222, ⊚starlightdental.net), is an international-standard dental clinic.

Emergencies Dial ☎113 for the police, ☎114 in case of fire or ☎115 for an ambulance; if possible, get a Vietnamese speaker to call on your behalf.

Hospitals and clinics Raffles Medical, 167a Nam Ky Khoi Nghia (☎028 3824 0777, ⊚rafflesmedicalgroup.com), has international doctors, can arrange emergency evacuation and has a 24hr emergency service (☎028 3829 8520).

Columbia Saigon, 8 Alexandre De Rhodes (☎028 3823 8455, ⊚colombiaasia.com), has multinational doctors with 24hr emergency and evacuation cover. Family Medical Practice, Diamond Plaza, 34 Le Duan (☎028 3822 7848, ⊚vietnammedicalpractice.com), is an international clinic with multinational doctors and specialist knowledge of vaccinations, as well as 24hr emergency and evacuation cover.

Laundry Most hotels and guesthouses will wash clothes for you, and some higher-end venues dry-clean too, but rates vary wildly so check first. There are also a number of laundry and dry-clean operators around Pham Ngu Lao, where rates are from 20,000đ per kilo.

Pharmacies There are several pharmacies in and around the De Tham area, such as at 65 Bui Vien. The one at 389 Hai Ba Trung is reputed to have the best stock in the city.

Police The main police station is at 73 Yersin ☎028 3829 7073, but before coming here you must first go to the police station in the ward where the crime took place to obtain an initial report. Try to avoid lunchtime visits, as there's likely to be nobody on duty.

Post offices The GPO (daily 6am–10pm) is beside the cathedral at the top of Dong Khoi; poste restante is kept here.

Visas Visa extensions and re-entry visas must be organized through an agent or tour operator; GoGo Vietnam (see box, p.88) is adept at the process, which takes about four days and usually costs $40 for an extra month.

Around Ho Chi Minh City

Once Ho Chi Minh City's blaring horns and pushy vendors become too much for you, you'll find you can get quite a long way **out of the city** in a day. With public transport slow and erratic, day-trips are best arranged through a tour operator (see box, p.88). The most popular trips out of the city take in one or both of Vietnam's most memorable sights: the **Cu Chi tunnels**, which were used as bolt holes for twenty years, first for Viet Minh agents and later for Viet Cong cadres; and the weird and wonderful **Cao Dai Great Temple** at Tay Ninh, the fulcrum of the country's most charismatic indigenous religion. While it's possible to see both places in a day (indeed, most people do), be prepared to spend most of your time on the road.

By bus tour By far the easiest way of reaching the Cu Chi tunnels and the Cao Dai temple is to take a guided bus tour with one of the innumerable travel agencies operating around the Pham Ngu Lao area. In fact, it's often possible to book such a trip without leaving the comfort of your accommodation – most guesthouses team up with a particular agency, and though they'll want their own piece of the pie, the extra fee is usually small if it exists at all. Hotels are a different matter; many run their own tours, and the prices are usually a fair bit higher than those given here. In general, signing up through your accommodation will give you some kind of come-back should things go wrong. Most agencies charge in the region of 130,000đ per person for a half-day trip to the tunnels, and 180,000đ for a full-day sojourn to the tunnels and temple. This will include an English-speaking guide and admission fees to the tunnels, though it'll cost extra for lunch. Tours usually leave at 8am, with half-dayers returning at 3pm or so, and full-day trips finishing around 6pm.

By boat tour An interesting option is to take a boat tour to the tunnels with Les Rives (☎ 0128 592 0018, ⓦ lesrivesexperience.com) from Bach Dang pier. It'll cost $84/person, including lunch and hotel pick-up, and it's $140 including the Cao Dai temple.

By taxi Some people prefer to go by taxi, which will set you back around $70 including the main tunnels, the temple and waiting time.

By bus A few budget travellers try to hit the temple or tunnels by bus, though it's usually not worth the bother as some tours are so cheap that you'd end up saving hardly anything at all. If you'd rather go it alone, take one of the infrequent buses to Tay Ninh, which depart from HCMC's An Suong station, north of the airport; ask the driver to drop you off at the front gates of the temple.

The Cu Chi tunnels

Both sites daily 7am–5pm • 110,000đ for Ben Dinh; 90,000đ for Ben Duoc • Shooting ranges from 35,000đ per bullet (min 10 bullets)

During the American War, the villages around the district of **Cu Chi** supported a substantial **Viet Cong (VC)** presence. Faced with American attempts to neutralize them, they quite literally dug themselves out of harm's way, and the legendary **Cu Chi tunnels** were the result. Today, tourists can visit a short stretch of the tunnels, drop to their hands and knees and squeeze underground for an insight into life as a tunnel-dwelling resistance fighter. Some sections of the tunnels have been widened to allow passage for the fuller frame of Westerners, but it's still a dark, sweaty, claustrophobic experience, and not one you should rush into unless you're confident you won't suffer a subterranean freak-out.

There are two sites where the tunnels can be seen – **Ben Dinh** and, 15km beyond, **Ben Duoc**, though most foreigners get taken to Ben Dinh.

Ben Dinh

Guided **tours** of Ben Dinh kick off in a thatched hut, where a map of the region, a cross-section of the tunnels and a black-and-white movie bristling with national pride fill you in on the background. From there, you head out into the bush, where your guide will point out lethal booby-traps, concealed trap doors and an abandoned tank. There are several models showing how unexploded ordnance was ingeniously converted into lethal mines and traps, and a demonstration of how smoke from underground fires was cleverly dispersed far from its source.

When you reach the **shooting range**, you have the chance to shoulder an M16 or AK47 and shoot off a few rounds, or stop at the adjacent souvenir and snack stalls. Finally, you get the chance to stoop, crawl and drag yourself through a section of the tunnels that's about 140m long (with frequent escape routes for anyone who can't hack it). It only takes 10–15min to scramble through, but the pitch blackness and intense humidity can be discomforting – when you emerge, you'll be glad you don't have to live down there for weeks on end as the VC did.

Ben Duoc

The tunnel experience at **Ben Duoc** is similar to that at Ben Dinh, but it has fewer foreign tourists and a cheesier atmosphere – it's better if you're claustrophobic, though scores fewer points for authenticity. The original tunnels have been expanded, and for

CU CHI: A HISTORY

When the first spades sank into the earth around Cu Chi, the region was covered with a rubber plantation tied to a French tyre company. Anticolonial **Viet Minh** dug the first tunnels here in the late 1940s; intended primarily for storing arms, they soon became valuable hiding places for the resistance fighters themselves. Over a decade later, VC activists controlling this staunchly antigovernment area, many of them local villagers, followed suit and went to ground. By 1965, 250km of tunnels crisscrossed Cu Chi and surrounding areas – the notorious guerrilla power base known as the **Iron Triangle** was just across the Saigon River – making it possible for the VC guerrilla cells in the area to link up with each other and to infiltrate Saigon at will. One section daringly ran underneath the Americans' Cu Chi Army Base.

Though the region's compacted red clay was perfectly suited to tunnelling, and lay above the water level of the Saigon River, the **digging parties** faced a multitude of problems. Apart from the snakes and scorpions they encountered as they laboured, there was the problem of inconspicuously disposing of the soil by spreading it in bomb craters or scattering it in the river under cover of darkness. American bombing made timber scarce, so the tunnellers had to resort to stealing iron fence posts from enemy bases. Tunnels could be as small as 60cm wide and 80cm high, and were sometimes four levels deep; **vent shafts** (to disperse smoke and aromas from underground ovens) were camouflaged by thick grass and termites' nests. In order to throw the Americans' dogs off the scent, pepper was sprinkled around vents, and sometimes the VC even washed with the same scented soap used by GIs.

TUNNEL LIFE

Living conditions below ground were appalling for these "human moles". Tunnels were foul-smelling, and became so hot by the afternoon that inhabitants had to lie on the floor in order to get enough oxygen to breathe. The darkness was absolute, and some long-term dwellers suffered temporary blindness when they emerged into the light. At times it was necessary to stay below ground for weeks on end, alongside bats, rats, snakes, scorpions, centipedes and fire ants. Some of these unwelcome guests were co-opted to the cause: boxes full of scorpions and hollow bamboo sticks containing vipers were secreted in tunnels, where GIs might unwittingly knock them over.

Within the multilevel tunnel complexes, there were latrines, wells, meeting rooms and dorms. Rudimentary **hospitals** were also scratched out of the soil. Operations were carried out by torchlight using instruments fashioned from shards of ordnance, and a patient's own blood was caught in bottles and then pumped straight back using a bicycle pump and a length of rubber hosing. The medical supplies that existed were secured by bribing ARVN soldiers in Saigon. Doctors also administered herbs and acupuncture – even honey was used for its antiseptic properties. **Kitchens** cooked whatever the tunnellers could get their hands on. With rice and fruit crops destroyed, the diet consisted largely of tapioca, leaves and roots, at least until enough bomb fragments could be transported to Saigon and sold as scrap to buy food.

THE END OF THE LINE

American attempts to **flush out** or destroy the tunnels proved ineffective – one frustrated soldier compared the task to filling "the Grand Canyon with a pitchfork". GIs would lob down gas or grenades or else go down themselves, armed only with a torch, a knife and a pistol. Booby traps made of sharpened bamboo stakes awaited them in the dark, as well as "bombs" made from Coke cans and dud bullets found on the surface. Tunnels were low and narrow, and entrances so small that GIs often couldn't get down them, even if they could locate them.

Another American tactic aimed at weakening the resolve of the VC guerrillas involved dropping leaflets and broadcasting bulletins that played on the fighters' fears and loneliness. Although this prompted numerous desertions, the tunnellers were still able to mastermind the **Tet Offensive** of 1968 (see p.444). Ultimately, the Americans resorted to more strong-arm tactics to neutralize the tunnels, sending in B52s to level the district with **carpet bombing**. The VC's infrastructure was decimated by Tet, but by this time the tunnels had played their part in proving to America that the war was unwinnable. At least twelve thousand Vietnamese guerrillas and sympathizers are thought to have perished here during the American War, and the terrain was laid waste – pockmarked by bomb craters, devoid of vegetation, the air poisoned by lingering fumes.

1

an extra fee you'll be able to don soldier gear to crawl through them. Afterwards, you'll be able to fire off a few rifle rounds. These tunnels are further from HCMC and often best attacked by taxi.

Cao Dai Great Temple

Daily dawn to dusk; services at 6am, noon & 6pm • Free

A few kilometres off Highway 22, in the town of Long Hoa, sits the enigmatic **Cao Dai Great Temple**, or Cathedral, of the Holy See of Tay Ninh. A grand gateway marks the entrance to the grounds of the 1927-built structure. At first sight, the temple seems to be subsiding (an optical illusion created by the rising steps inside it), but your initial impressions are more likely to be dominated by what Graham Greene described as a "Walt Disney fantasia of the East, dragons and snakes in Technicolor".

Despite its Day-Glo hues and rococo clutter, this gaudy construction somehow manages to bypass tackiness. Two square, pagoda-style **towers** bookend the front facade, whose central portico is topped by a bowed, first-floor balcony and a **Divine Eye**. The most recurrent motif in the temple, the eye is surrounded by a triangle, as it is on the American one-dollar bill. A figure in semi-relief emerges from each tower: on the left is Cao Dai's first female cardinal, Lam Huong Thanh, and on the right is Le Van Trung, its first pope.

The interior

The eclectic ideology of Cao Dai (see p.458) is mirrored in the **interior**. Part cathedral and part pagoda, it draws together a potpourri of icons and elements under a vaulted ceiling, and daubs them all with the primary colours of a Hindu temple. Men enter the main building through an entrance in the right wall, women by a door to the left, and all must take off their shoes. Inside the lobby, a **mural** shows the three "signatories of the Third Alliance between God and Mankind": French poet Victor Hugo and the fifteenth-century Vietnamese poet, Nguyen Binh Khiem, are writing the Cao Dai principles of "God and humanity, love and justice" in French and Chinese onto a shining celestial tablet. Beside them, the Chinese nationalist leader Sun Yat Sen holds an inkstone, a symbol of "Chinese civilization allied to Christian civilization giving birth to Cao Dai doctrine", according to a nearby sign.

The nave

Apart from service times, tourists are welcome to wander through the **nave** of the cathedral, as long as they remain in the aisles, and don't stray between the rows of **pink pillars**, entwined by green dragons, that march up the chamber. Cut-away windows punctuate the outer walls, their grillework consisting of the Divine Eye, surrounded by bright pink lotus blooms. Walk up the shallow steps that lend the nave its litheness, and you'll reach an **altar** that groans under the weight of assorted vases, fruit, paintings and slender statues of storks.

PHAN THI KIM PHUC

Several kilometres northwest of Cu Chi, Highway 22 slices through idyllic paddy flatlands before reaching **Trang Bang**, where the photographer Nick Ut captured one of the war's most horrific and enduring images – that of a naked girl, severely burnt, running along the highway, fleeing a napalm attack. Now married and living in Canada, **Phan Thi Kim Phuc** was named a goodwill ambassador for UNESCO in 1997. Despite third-degree burns covering half of her body, she remains remarkably unembittered, stating "I am happy because I am living without hatred."

The **papal chair** stands at the head of the chamber, its arms carved into dragons. Below it are six more chairs, three with eagle arms and three with lion arms, for the cardinals. Dominating the chamber, though, and guarded by eight scary silver dragons, is a vast, duck-egg-blue **sphere**, speckled with stars, resting on a polished, eight-sided dais. The ubiquitous Divine Eye peers through clouds painted on the front. You'll see more spangly stars and fluffy clouds if you look up at the sky-blue **ceiling**, which has mouldings of lions and turtles.

The Mekong Delta

BOAT TRIP IN THE MEKONG DELTA

The Mekong Delta

From its lofty source in the Tibetan Himalayas, the mighty Mekong River tumbles down through China's Yunnan province, squeezes between Thailand and Laos, then slides through Cambodia before reaching Vietnam. Here, in a flat, comma-shaped delta protruding from the south of the country, the river fragments and spreads out into innumerable tributaries and rivulets, all meandering slowly seawards. It's in and around the delta's myriad waterways that you'll find some of Vietnam's most iconic images: shimmering emerald paddy fields, endless horizons punctuated by coconut trees, cone-hatted farmers hauling fruit and sugar cane from the ground, and markets run from colourfully painted boats. Keep an eye out and you'll also see children riding on the backs of water buffalo, bright yellow incense sticks drying at the roadside, and locals scampering over monkey bridges or rowing boats on the delta's maze of channels.

To the Vietnamese, this region is known as Cuu Long, or "**Nine Dragons**", a reference to the nine tributaries of the Mekong River that dovetail across plains fashioned by millennia of flood-borne alluvial sediment. These rich soils have turned the delta into Vietnam's rice bowl, an agricultural miracle that pumps out more than a third of the country's annual food crop – not just rice, but also sugar cane, coconut and fruit – from just ten percent of its total landmass. Such bounty has come at a cost, since this is now also one of Vietnam's most **densely populated** areas: you may notice, when travelling between the various settlements by road, that the traffic is almost city-like in nature, and that the surrounding countryside is rarely visible behind twin ranks of housing, shops, cafés and more – travelling by bus can be slow and tedious. There is also a relative dearth of actual tourist sights – not really a problem, since you'll likely be visiting for the area's unique culture and topography, in any case.

Southwest of Ho Chi Minh City, buses emerge from the city's unkempt urban sprawl and into the pastoral surrounds of the Mekong Delta's **upper plains**. The delta is too modest to flaunt its full beauty so soon, but glimpses of rice fields hint at things to come, the brilliant emerald green dotted with the occasional white ancestral grave. There are over a dozen towns in the delta with facilities for tourists, though most are rarely visited.

Closest to HCMC is the town of **My Tho**. This is well geared up for boat tours, and near enough to Ho Chi Minh City to be seen on a day-trip: it affords an appetizing glimpse of

PHU QUOC ISLAND

Highlights

❶ Khmer pagodas Marvel over the rich colours and fancy script of Cambodian-style temples around Tra Vinh. **See p.123**

❷ An Binh Island Take a cheap ferry ride from Vinh Long to this delightfully untouristed island, whose maze of waterways and low-rise housing depict the delta area in miniature. **See p.126**

❸ Homestays Spend the night amid rural communities, observing daily aspects of Vietnamese culture and getting to know your hosts. **See box, p.128**

❹ Chau Doc Visit a Cham village and the fish farms on the river, or explore nearby Sam Mountain. **See p.131**

❺ Boat trips Drift along a series of narrow canals, visiting the floating markets and fruit orchards around Can Tho. **See p.144**

❻ Hillside rail-ride Unleash your inner child on an odd rail-car system, which runs up a hillside near the charming coastal town of Ha Tien. **See p.156**

❼ Phu Quoc Island Sprawl on Phu Quoc's gorgeous beaches, ride a motorbike through its mountainous interior and dive or snorkel around the coastline. **See p.159**

HIGHLIGHTS ARE MARKED ON THE MAP ON P.114

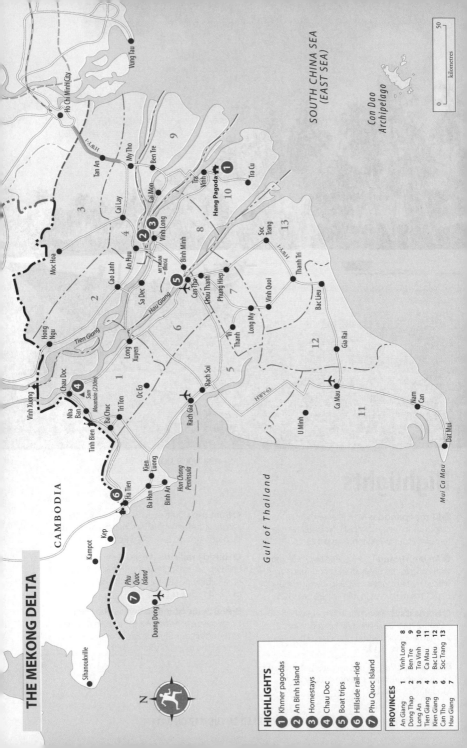

THE MEKONG DELTA

N

CAMBODIA

SOUTH CHINA SEA
(EAST SEA)

Con Dao
Archipelago

0 ____ 50
kilometres

Gulf of Thailand

Sihanoukville
Kampot
Kep
Vinh Xuong
Chau Doc (4)
Nha Ban
Tinh Bien
Ha Tien (6)
Ba Hon
Binh An
Kien Luong
Hon Chong Peninsula
Phu Quoc Island (7)
Duong Dong
Rach Gia
Rach Soi
Oc Eo
Tri Ton
Ba Chuc
Sam Mountain (230m)
Hong Ngu
Moc Hoa
Cao Lanh
Sa Dec
Long Xuyen
An Huu
Cai Lay
Tan An
Ho Chi Minh City
Vung Tau
My Tho
Ben Tre
Cai Mon
Vinh Long (2) (3)
Binh Minh
Can Tho (5)
Chau Thanh
Phung Hiep
Vi Thanh
Long My
Vinh Quoi
Bac Lieu
Gia Rai
Soc Trang
Thanh Tri
Tra Vinh
Hang Pagoda (1)
Tra Cu
Ca Mau
U Minh
Nam Can
Dat Mui
Mui Ca Mau
Tien Giang
Hau Giang
HWY-1
HWY-63

the delta's northernmost main arm, the Tien Giang. From My Tho, laidback **Ben Tre** and the bounteous fruit orchards besieging it are only a hop and a skip away. Further south, across a major arm of the Mekong, is modest **Tra Vinh**, whose surrounds are dotted with spectacular Cambodian temples. To the west is **Vinh Long**, another jumping-off point for boat trips and a pleasant town to boot. Heading west again, there's little of interest until you hit the ebullient town of **Chau Doc**, near the Cambodian border; nearby **Sam Mountain** provides a welcome undulation in the surrounding plains, while the opening of the border here has brought a steady stream of travellers going on to Phnom Penh by boat, and several of them rest up a few days here before leaving the country.

Southeast of Chau Doc is **Can Tho**, the delta's largest city and yet another popular base for boat-trips and visits to **floating markets**. From here it's possible to take a loop-trip around the southern half of the delta area; first up is the Khmer stronghold of **Soc Trang**, a visit to which is especially rewarding if your journey coincides with the colourful Oc Om Bok festival (November or December), during which the local Khmer community takes to the river to stage spectacular longboat races. Further on, at the foot of the delta, the swampland that surrounds **Ca Mau** can be explored by boat. A boat-ride north is the charming, unassuming town of **Rach Gia**, while pressing on northwest to the border will bring you to **Ha Tien**, a remote frontier town surrounded by Khmer villages, which is the best place to hop on a boat to Phu Quoc. The town has also become popular for its **international border crossing**, which allows beach bums to slide along the coast to Sihanoukville in Cambodia or vice versa. Last, but not least, is **Phu Quoc Island** itself – though developing at speed and growing more popular with each passing year, it remains one of the best beach destinations in the land.

Given its seasonal flooding, **the best time to visit** the delta is, predictably enough, in the dry season, which runs from December to May.

Brief history

It may come as a surprise to learn that agriculture gripped the Mekong Delta area relatively recently. Under **Cambodian** sway until the close of the seventeenth century, the region was sparsely inhabited by the Khmer krom, or "downstream Khmer", whose settlements were framed by swathes of marshland. The eighteenth century saw the Viet **Nguyen** lords steadily broaden their sphere of influence to encompass the delta, though by the 1860s **France** had taken over the reins of government. Sensing the huge profits to be gleaned from such fertile land, French *colons* spurred Vietnamese peasants to tame and till tracts of the boggy delta; the peasants, realizing their colonial governors would pay well for rice harvests, were quick to comply. Ironically, the same landscape that had served the French so well also provided valuable cover for the Viet Minh resistance fighters who sought to overthrow them; later it did the same for the Viet Cong, who had well-hidden cells here – inciting the Americans to strafe the area with bombs and defoliants.

THE MEKONG RIVER

By the time it reaches Vietnam, the **Mekong River** has already covered more than 4000km from its source high on the Tibetan Plateau; en route it traverses southern China, skirts Myanmar (Burma), then hugs the Laos–Thailand border before cutting down through Cambodia and into Vietnam – a journey that makes this the world's twelfth-longest waterway.

Flooding has always blighted the delta; ever since Indian traders imported their advanced methods of irrigation more than eighteen centuries ago, networks of canals have been used to channel the excess water, but the rainy season still claims lives from time to time.

It's difficult to overstate the influence of the river: the lifeblood of the rice and fruit crops grown in the delta, it also teems with craft that range in size from delicate rowing boats to hulking sampans, all painted with distinctive eyes on the prow. These continue an ancient tradition and were originally intended to scare off "river monsters", probably crocodiles.

Most travellers take a bus to the delta, usually from HCMC or Cambodia, though flying in is also possible. Once you're there, the best way to experience life on the river is by boat. Day-trips and multi-day journeys are perfectly easy to organize, and needn't break the bank.

BY PLANE
You can cut a fair bit of travel time by taking a flight to or from the delta – Phu Quoc Island has the most connections, with services to the mainland cities of Can Tho, Rach Gia and Ca Mau as well as some from within the delta area itself (see p.162).

BY BUS
There are plenty of bus services to and around the delta, though journeys can be long, and the scenery samey and uninspiring. Traffic has to stop occasionally at the ferries that make road travel in the delta possible, though completion of some long-awaited bridges has sped up travel times. Futabus (⊚futabus.vn) is by far the most popular operator in these parts, and pleasingly (especially since the bus terminals can be somewhat remote) they usually run free transfers to and from your accommodation – ask your hotel to book onward tickets, and you'll barely have to lift a finger to get from A to B.

BY MOTORBIKE AND BICYCLE
With the main roads clogged with traffic, it's a great idea to get your own pair of wheels – in this way you'll be able to fully immerse yourself in the languid life of the region. Motorbikes and bicycles can be rented at pretty much every major town in the area, and once you've got one you'll soon be out in the fields and rivulets. Phu Quoc Island is perhaps the most enjoyable place for a motorbike ride, while for bicycles you can't beat the area between Chau Doc and the Cambodian border. Dedicated two-wheel tours are available – try Sinhbalo Adventure Travel (⊚sinhbalo .com), Vespa Adventures (⊚vespaadventures.com) or Vietnam Backroads (⊚mekongbiketours.com).

BY BOAT
Locals used to do much of their travelling on the cargo boats that still crawl around the delta's waterways, but the increased prevalence of motorbikes has led to many routes being cut, and this is no longer a viable way of getting around for visitors. Bar the hydrofoils to Phu Quoc from Ha Tien and Rach Gia (see p.162), the only decent route is the delightful backwater passage linking Rach Gia and Ca Mau (see p.154).

BY BOAT TOUR
Day-trips can be organized in HCMC, My Tho, Cai Be, Vinh Long, Can Tho or Chau Doc, while some tour operators offer two- or three day liveaboard trips as well as homestays (see box, p.128); some of the pricier ones chug all the way upriver into Cambodia, just like Martin Sheen in *Apocalypse Now* (but without most of the weirdness). Since most day-tours follow a similar itinerary (a visit to a floating market and stops at cottage industries on the shore), you'll probably want to choose just one. Though Can Tho is most popular for its good range of hotels and restaurants, you're likely to see more tourists than locals in the nearby floating markets. A good alternative is Vinh Long, from where boats head out in many different directions through the canals of An Binh Island to the floating market at Cai Be – though this market is slowly dying a death (see box below).

Aqua Expeditions ⊚aquaexpeditions.com. If you really want to do the delta in style, sign up for a multi-day trip aboard this operator's luxury cruise ships, which come with on-board pools, games rooms, restaurants and the like. Figure on at least $3000 for a three-day excursion.

Bassac ☎0292 382 9540, ⊚transmekong.com. Former rice barges have been converted into floating hotels, which offer a cosy cabin and gourmet meals to accompany the

---

THE DELTA'S DYING MARKETS
Unfortunately, time and tide are catching up with one of the Delta area's most absorbing drawcards: its wonderful **floating markets**, where cone-hatted salespeople hawk their wares on sticks while both they and their customers maintain their balance with practiced ease. The main reasons behind the death of these oddly transport-based bazaars are also rooted in **transportation** – bridges and bikes. The area's drivers have long been forced to queue to cross its countless channels on slow, lumbering ferries, but many routes have now been strung together with huge bridges, shortening journey times considerably; the first went up in 2000, and several have been added since then. Compounding this, these days most delta folk have motorbikes, so it's now simpler for them to head to a land-based market for buying or selling.

As such, if you want to see the floating markets, **now's your time**; even if attendances are plummeting, they still make for absorbing visits. Check out the two great markets near Can Tho (p.144), the good one at Cai Be near Vinh Long (p.126), or the one just across the waters from central Chau Doc (p.131).

classic delta sights. The most popular trip is from Cai Be to Can Tho, stopping off at a few rural villages along the way and joining the throng at Cai Rang's floating market in the morning (around $250, including a night on board).

Mango Cruises ☎ 096 768 3366, ⓦ mangocruises.com. Offers affordable trips on classy vessels, with stacks of options from day-trips to multi-day adventures (two-day-one-night trips including cycling cost $350).

Mekong Eyes ☎ 0292 378 3586, ⓦ mekongeyes.com.

Named with a nod to the eyes you'll spot on Vietnam's traditional wooden boats, this operator offers plenty of routes, including round-trips from HCMC (two-day delta tour $262), and others finishing in Phu Quoc or even Cambodia.

Victoria ☎ 0286 290 9720, ⓦ victoriahotels.asia. This luxury hotel chain has establishments in Chau and Can Tho, and offers suitably opulent vessels linking the two and heading further around the delta.

My Tho

Seventy kilometres out of Ho Chi Minh City lies **MY THO**, an amiable market town that nestles on the north bank of the Mekong River's northernmost strand, the Tien Giang, or Upper River. My Tho's proximity to Ho Chi Minh City means that it receives the lion's share of day-trippers to the delta, resulting in a scrum of pushy vendors crowding round each tour bus that arrives. Nevertheless, the town can come as a great relief after the onslaught of manic HCMC, its uncrowded boulevards belying a population of around a quarter of a million, and you can easily escape the melee by hopping onto a boat, wandering into the backstreets or merely staying the night – the

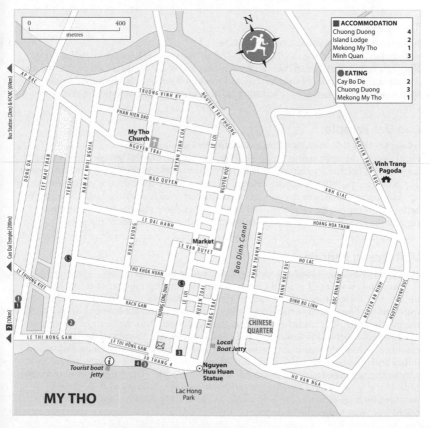

ACCOMMODATION	
Chuong Duong	4
Island Lodge	2
Mekong My Tho	1
Minh Quan	3

EATING	
Cay Bo De	2
Chuong Duong	3
Mekong My Tho	1

MY THO

2

vast majority of visitors to the town sleep elsewhere, lending the place a pleasingly local atmosphere in the evenings.

The river's **traffic**, which ranges from elegant sampans to vast, lumbering cargo boats, unpainted and crude, is best viewed from Lac Hong Park at the eastern end of 30 Thang 4, where you're sure to catch sight of the most characteristic feature of the boats in the delta – staring eyes painted onto their prows. In the evenings, especially at weekends, this corner of town is packed as families stroll up and down, interspersed with sellers of balloons, popcorn and even tropical fish. At night, young lovers huddle on their motorbikes, while men play shuttlecock football on the street under the intent gaze of a statue of nineteenth-century anti-French hero Nguyen Huu Huan, who studied in My Tho.

Brief history

My Tho's daily influx of visitors seems rather appropriate, given the town's history. Following the collapse of the Ming dynasty in the late seventeenth century, Chinese immigrants fleeing Taiwan (then known as Formosa) established the town, along with a Vietnamese population keen to make inroads into a traditionally Khmer-dominated region. Two centuries later the French, wooed by the district's abundant rice and fruit crops, rated it highly enough to post a garrison here and to lay a (now-defunct) rail line to Saigon. The American War also saw a consistent military presence in town. Today My Tho's commercial importance is as pronounced as ever, something a walk through the town's busy market amply illustrates.

The market

Between Le Dai Hanh and Thu Khoa Huan streets • Dawn to dusk • Free

Follow the direction of the canal up along Trung Trac and you'll soon be gobbled up by My Tho's vast **market**, which covers several blocks and is at its busiest early in the morning. As well as the usual piles of fruit, cereals and tobacco, several stalls sell ships' chandlery, their heaped fishing nets almost indistinguishable from the fresh noodles on sale nearby.

Cao Dai Temple

Ly Thuong Kiet • Daily 7.30–10.30am & 1.30–5.30pm; services usually noon & 6pm • Free

Head west of the town centre on Ly Thuong Kiet for the **Cao Dai Temple**, which is worth a look for its colourful architecture. It is, in effect, a small-scale replica of the Holy See in Tay Ninh (see p.108), with an all-seeing Divine Eye above the entrance, dragons writhing up columns and images of the odd mix of characters – such as Victor Hugo and Sun Yat Sen – that comprise the religion's pantheon of saints. Note also the herb garden to the right of the temple, which is used to concoct remedies for ailments of the poor.

Vinh Trang Pagoda

60a Nguyen Trung Truc • Daily 9–11.30am & 1.30–5pm • Free • Xe om from centre about 30,000đ

A worthwhile side-trip if you're in town is to make the short journey on foot or cyclo up Nguyen Trung Truc to the attractive **Vinh Trang Pagoda**, with its rajah's palace-style front facade. Since its construction in 1849 it has been renovated several times, most recently in 2002. The entrance, round to the right, leads into the heart of the temple, where a tiny courtyard is flanked by the cubicles where the monks sleep. The main chamber, beyond the miniature mountain to your left, is characterized by dark-wood pillars and tonnes of gilt woodwork, but of more interest are the eclectic influences at play in the pagoda's decor – classical pillars, Grecian-style mouldings of urns and bowls of fruit and glazed tiles. Outside, the tombs of several monks stand near a pond patrolled by huge elephant-ear fish, while a tall standing Buddha, and a more jovial seated one, watch over the front gate.

ARRIVAL AND DEPARTURE

By bus Most buses terminate at Tien Giang station, 3km northwest of town, from where xe om (about 40,000đ) and taxis (65,000đ) shuttle visitors into the centre. Services to and from HCMC have been expedited by a new highway, though traffic in HCMC itself will still form a fair chunk of your journey. To get to Vinh Long, you may have to jump off a service bound for Can Tho; coming from Vinh Long can be trickier, though the main terminal there (see p.127) can advise.

Destinations Ben Tre (30min); Can Tho (2hr 30min); Cao Lanh (2hr); HCMC (1hr 15min).

By tour The bulk of visitors to My Tho arrive on a tour from HCMC. These usually include the bus rides in and out, boat rides to some nearby islands, a village walk, lunch, and a boat trip to a sweet factory in the nearby Ben Tre area (see p.121) – figure on around 220,000đ/head, all in. You can also arrange similar boat tours in My Tho itself (see box below for details).

By taxi By far the most convenient means of travelling between My Tho and Ben Tre is by taking a cab across the river bridge, as it negates the necessity of heading to and from the bus station and taking (the often super-slow) local buses – the 15km trip is over in a flash, and usually works out at around 260,000đ from centre to centre.

ACCOMMODATION

Chuong Duong 10, 30 Thang 4 ☎ 0273 387 0875; map p.117. Based beside the river and boasting excellent views, this place is pretty good value for a "proper" (if scrubby) hotel. Its rooms all have a/c, hot water and TVs, and those upstairs have waterfront balconies that make wonderful places for morning coffees or nightcaps from the minibar. **$22**

Island Lodge 390 Ap Thoi Binh ☎ 0273 651 9000, ⓦ theislandlodge.com.vn; map p.117. This is a luxury option, based on an island west of town. With manicured lawns, a great restaurant and a pool facing the river, it's an undeniably charming spot, though the square patterns on the rooms' colonial-chic floor tiling can start to make your eyes feel funny after a while. **$165**

★**Mekong My Tho** 1a Tet Mau Than ☎ 0273 388 7777, ⓦ mekongmythohotel.net.vn; map p.117. Now the top dog in town, this fancy new high-rise still feels a bit empty at times – hopefully more of the city's day-trippers will choose to stay the night soon, especially at these prices. The carpeted corridors feel pleasingly out of place in My Tho, the rooms are just lovely and there's a good pool and rooftop café (see p.120). Rooms usually cost a bit more on booking sites, so try giving them a call. **$30**

Minh Quan 69, 30 Thang 4 ☎ 0273 397 9979; map p.117. Tall and skinny, this charming guesthouse has rooms with tasteful furnishings and modern fittings, and its staff are pleasingly cheery. Rooms at the front have good river views, as does the nice little café/bar up top. **$17**

EATING

Though there's nowhere to get very excited about in town, tour groups will get taken to one of a couple of **places to eat** just outside My Tho; if you've any leeway over what's served, ask for the locally famous elephant-ear fish. If you're staying on in town, make sure you go for a stroll around the **night market**, which opens up each evening beside the tour boat offices on 30 Thang 4.

★**Cay Bo De** 22 Nam Ky Khoi Nghia ☎ 0273 388 3528; map p.117. This is one of three eponymous restaurants located almost side by side (this one's in the middle, and the prettiest), serving filling and nutritious bowls of *hu tieu* (noodles with seafood and meat, though there's also a vegetarian version). Locals usually eat these noodles for breakfast, though *Cay Bo De's* popularity means they're now enjoyed well into the evening. You'll fill up for 60,000đ/head. Daily 6am–7.30pm.

Chuong Duong 10, 30 Thang 4 ☎ 0273 387 0875; map p.117. This hotel restaurant, which specializes in seafood, serves large, reasonably priced portions served on a breezy terrace overlooking the Mekong. It's very popular among locals and domestic visitors, so it can be crowded at times.

BOAT TRIPS

Several companies offer boat trips from the tourist boat centre (6–8, 30 Thang 4) to the islands in the Mekong; most tours head for Thoi Son, Phung and Qui islands. **Tien Giang Tourist Company** (☎ 0273 387 3184, ⓦ tiengiangtourist.com) is the most reliable, charging 200,000–350,000đ per person for a tour of around three hours, depending on how many people are in the group. You may be interested in their two-day options, which are more or less the same but include one night in a homestay for an extra 250,000đ. Local boats, which you can find at the small jetty on Trung Trac, are much cheaper, and 350,000đ should get you an entire boat for a two- to three-hour trip. However, bear in mind that the owners of these boats are not licensed or insured to carry tourists, so it's a bit of a risky business – you're far more liable to get ripped off.

Mains 60,000đ–140,000đ. Daily 6am–11pm.
Mekong My Tho 1a Tet Mau Than ☎ 0273 388 7777, ⓦ mekongmythohotel.net.vn; map p.117. The café atop this hotel (see p.119) is a grand place to have a drink with a view, whether you choose a coffee (from 20,000đ), a strawberry shake (39,000đ), or even a cocktail (50,000đ). Daily 6am–10pm.

Around My Tho

Day-trippers tend to see little of My Tho as they disgorge from tour buses and embark on a boat trip (see box, p.119) round two or three of the **islands** in the Tien Giang branch of the Mekong River. Arranging trips locally tends to lead to a more relaxed and enjoyable experience, but you'd probably need to sleep over at least one night. Note that some tours also include a visit to the floating market at **Cai Be**, which is far closer to Vinh Long (see p.124).

Thoi Son (Unicorn Island)

Thoi Son (Unicorn Island) is the largest of the four islands, and many of the organized tours out of Ho Chi Minh City stop here for lunch and fruit sampling. Narrow canals allow boats to weave through its interior; gliding along these slender waterways, overhung by handsome water-palm fronds that interlock to form a cathedral-like roof, it's easy to feel you're charting new territory. Swooping, electric-blue kingfishers and sumptuously coloured butterflies add to the romance. Local tours do not always include **lunch** in the price, but all tours will stop somewhere you can get refreshment.

Con Phung (Phoenix Island)

Complex daily 8–11.30am & 1.30–6pm • 5000đ

Con Phung (Phoenix Island) is famed as the home of an offbeat religious sect set up three decades ago by the eccentric **Coconut Monk**, Ong Dao Dua (see box below), although there's not much left to see from his era, and only the skeleton of the open-air **complex** he established remains. Amid its mesh of rusting staircases and platforms, you'll spot the rocket-shaped elevator the monk had built to whisk him up to his private meditation platform. Elsewhere are nine dragon-entwined pillars, said to symbolize the Mekong's nine tributaries and betraying a Cao Dai influence. The Coconut Monk's story is told (in Vietnamese) on a magnificent **urn**, which he is said to have crafted himself out of shards of porcelain from France, Japan and China.

ONG DAO DUA, THE COCONUT MONK

Ong Dao Dua, the **Coconut Monk**, was born in 1909 as Nguyen Thanh Nam in the Mekong Delta. Aged 19, he travelled to France where he studied chemistry until 1935, and then he returned home, married and fathered a child. During a lengthy period of meditation at Chau Doc's Sam Mountain (see p.133) he devised a new religion, a fusion of Buddhism and Christianity known as **Tinh Do Cu Si**. By the 1960s, this new sect had established a community on Phoenix Island, where the monk lorded it over his followers from a throne set into a man-made grotto modelled on Sam Mountain. The monk became as famous for his idiosyncrasies as for his doctrine: his name, for instance, was coined after it was alleged he spent three years meditating and eating nothing but coconuts.

Unfortunately, the Coconut Monk never got to enjoy his "kingdom" for long: his belief in a peaceful reunification of North and South Vietnam (symbolized by the map of the country behind his grotto, on which pillars representing Hanoi and Saigon are joined by a bridge) landed him in the **jails** of successive South Vietnamese governments, and the Communists were no more sympathetic to his beliefs after 1975. Ong Dao Dua died in 1990.

Tan Long (Dragon Island)

Beyond its chaotic shoreline of stilthouses and boatyards, **Tan Long (Dragon Island)**, the least frequently visited island, boasts bounteous sapodilla, coconut and banana plantations, as well as highly regarded longan orchards. As with the other islands, Tan Long is sparsely inhabited, by small communities of farmers and boat-builders.

Con Qui (Turtle Island)

Con Qui (Turtle Island) is the newest of the group, having been formed by sediment in the river then stabilized by planting mangroves, and is overflowing with longans, dragon fruit, mango, papaya, pineapple and jackfruit. There is a small, family-run **coconut candy factory**, just opposite here along the Ben Tre coastline, where you can watch the coconut being pressed and the extracted juice being mixed with sugar and heated, then dried and cut into bite-size pieces. You can buy a box to take home.

2

Ben Tre

The few travellers who push on beyond My Tho into Ben Tre province are rewarded with some of the Mekong Delta's most breathtaking scenery. **BEN TRE** itself is a pleasant and industrious town displaying none of the wounds of its past (apart from a heavily populated cemetery and proud war memorial), and makes an agreeable contrast to the tourist bustle of nearby My Tho. Though short on specific sights, the surrounding countryside is lush and photogenic. It's a relaxing and friendly place to hole up for a couple of days, with a buzzing **market** and a new **riverside promenade**, which makes a pleasant place to stroll in the morning or evening. With a bicycle or motorbike, you can explore the maze of trails on both sides of the river. For more of an adventure, head out of town on a boat trip along the **Ben Tre coastline**, where labyrinthine creeks afford marvellous scope for exploring, and sometimes include stops at apiaries, rice-wine and sugar-processing workshops.

2

Brief history

Famed for its fruit orchards and coconut groves (the Vietnamese call it the "coconut island"), Ben Tre province has proved just as fertile a breeding ground for revolutionaries, first plotting against the French, and later against the Americans, and was one of the areas seized by the Viet Cong during the Tet Offensive of 1968. Of the US bombing campaign against the provincial capital itself, a US major was quoted as saying, "It became necessary to destroy the town in order to save it" – a classic wartime analysis. Until recently the province was isolated by the Mekong's wide arms, but the Rach Mieu Bridge from My Tho, opened in 2009, is starting to bring a rush of visitors; this increase in popularity has, as yet, had little effect on scruffy Ben Tre town, though change cannot be far away.

ARRIVAL AND DEPARTURE   BEN TRE

By bus Almost all visitors arrive in Ben Tre by road: buses terminate at the new bus station on Highway 60, about 2km northwest of the town centre (35,000đ by taxi), though some companies use their own dedicated terminals. Most buses head to and from HCMC; city buses to My Tho leave from the road outside, though these stop everywhere and it can take up to 45min for the 15km journey.

Destinations Can Tho (2hr); HCMC (1hr 45min–2hr 15min); My Tho (30min); Tra Vinh (1hr 30min); Vinh Long (2hr).
By taxi Cabs are the fastest way to travel between My Tho and Ben Tre, and you can expect to pay around 260,000đ from centre to centre.

GETTING AROUND AND TOURS

By car or bicycle Located at 65 Dong Khoi to the north of the centre, Ben Tre Tourist Company (daily 7–11am & 1–5pm; ☎0275 382 9618) can organize car rental, bicycle rental and some tours, including boat trips.

Tours Mango Cruises, the travel arm of *Mango Home* (see below) runs good half-day trips. A nice mix of cycling and rowing, the tours cost around $75/person (plus $15 for lunch), and most of the proceeds are funnelled to local businesses.

ACCOMMODATION

TOWN CENTRE
Ben Tre Riverside Resort 708 Nguyen Van Tu ☎0275 355 4888, ⓦbentreriverside.com; map p.121. On the very western periphery of town, at the confluence of the Ben Tre channel and the mightier Ham Luong arm, this is a stylish new hotel with a delightful pool, decent breakfasts, and well-appointed rooms – try to get one with a river view. It's a bit out of the way, but the location is relatively peaceful, and you can make use of the free bicycles if you want to get to the town area. In-the-know staff round off a pleasing picture. $70
Phuong Hoang 16 Hai Ba Trung ☎0275 357 5377; map p.121. Ben Tre has very little at the budget end of the scale, though there are a few cheapies on the north bank of Truc Giang Lake. This is the pick of a sorry bunch – the management are hardly switched on, while rooms are bare and you may end up sharing them with a cockroach or two. $7
Viet Uc 144 Hung Vuong ☎0275 251 1888,

ⓦhotelvietuc.com; map p.121. The rooms at this fancy-looking riverside spot aren't exactly huge, but they're well equipped; all have a/c and TVs, while some have bathtubs and river views (the latter for a slightly higher price). There's also a smart café abutting the lobby. $28

OUT OF TOWN
★**Mango Home** My Thanh village ☎0275 351 1958, ⓦmangohomeriverside.com; map p.121. This family-run, community-focused place is located around 6km from town in the middle of semi-rural nowhere. To get there, you'll have to take a taxi, following the hotel's instructions, and then either walk or call for a pick-up –it takes a bit of an effort, though you'll be rewarded in full. The collection of charming rooms is arrayed around an idyllic stretch of riverbank, and they also run tours (see above). Given the dearth of anywhere else to eat in the nearby area, it's a nice surprise that the food served here is both tasty and fairly priced. $45

EATING

Ben Tre's hitherto dismal culinary scene has improved slightly of late, but there are only a few places worthy of special attention. Dong-pinchers should make a beeline for the grimy **market** area, where you'll find a range of cheap noodles and other simple fare.

Sau Cong 160c Hung Vuong ☎091 544 4861; map p.121. Just west of the centre, after a tiny bridge, this cute, neighbourly little place specializes in *hu tieu* (noodles with seafood and meat) for just 30,000đ, and *banh canh* (noodles with veggies and all-sorts) for a shade more. Make sure you wash it down with some sugar cane juice (8000đ). Often closes earlier than advertised. Daily 7am–7pm.

★**Thuy Pasta & Pizza** 186 Hung Vuong ☎0129 983 3999; map p.121. You don't expect authentic Italian food in Ben Tre – what a nice surprise this place is. With checked tablecloths and scooters parked outside, it's almost like being in Italy (especially if you're lucky enough to nab one of the street tables), and the pasta dishes in particular are pretty outstanding – try the baked lasagne (50,000đ). Other tempting treats include club sandwiches, Cajun rice, nasi goreng and Caesar salad; they're all in the 30,000–60,000đ range, and beer's cheap too. Daily 3–11pm.

TTC Floating Restaurant 60 Hung Vuong, 3km west of the centre ☎0275 382 2492; map p.121. Ship-shape in more ways than one, this is a fine venue for a sunset drink, and not bad at all for seafood – the prices (mains from 90,000đ) aren't really all that different to those you'd find at "regular" restaurants, let alone floating ones. Daily 10am–10pm.

Tra Vinh and around

TRA VINH is an outback market town whose 800-metre-square grid of broad, tree-lined streets and smattering of colonial piles have yet to see tourists in any numbers. Most visitors come here to watch the storks at nearby **Hang Pagoda** (see p.124), although the town's low-key charm makes it a pleasant place to spend a day or two. At the very least, Tra Vinh is worth a half-day detour from Vinh Long, especially since the area between the two towns is a real delta rarity. Largely devoid of roadside clutter or heavy traffic, you can actually see plenty of countryside from the bus here: vivid green rice paddies, fringed by coconut and water palms. This is Khmer country; as you get nearer to Tra Vinh, distinctive pagodas begin to appear beside the road, painted in rich pastel shades of lilac, orange and turquoise, their steep horned roofs puncturing the sky. Altogether there are over 140 **Khmer pagodas** scattered around the province.

The pagodas and church

Just south of the market, at the junction of Pham Thai Buong and Tran Quoc Tuan, the Chinese **Ong Pagoda** is well worth a visit, as it's a very active place of worship and there's always something interesting going on. North of the town centre up Le Loi, the **Ong Met Pagoda** is very different, sporting a distinctive Khmer-style roof above colonial arches and shutters: you're assured of a friendly reception here from the monks studying at its English school. Immediately north is the pretty **Tra Vinh Church**, an imposing buttressed construction; it's fronted by a statue of Christ above the entrance.

Ba Om Pond

Daily 24hr • Free • 5km southwest of town, a signposted road on the left runs down to the pond; buses to and from Vinh Long pass the short approach road here, minibuses can usually drop you off directly, while a xe om from the centre of Tra Vinh costs around 50,000đ

Ba Om Pond is beloved of Tra Vinh picnickers and courting couples. Around the pond, drinks and snack vendors lie in wait for visitors, but although it can get crowded at weekends, on weekdays it is usually restful. Bordered by grassy banks, and shaded by towering, aged trees whose roots clutch at the ground, Ba Om is cloaked with plants that attract flocks of birds in the late afternoon.

Ang Pagoda

Behind Ba Om Pond • Dawn to dusk • Free

The area across the far side of the pond has been a Khmer place of worship since the eleventh century, and today it's occupied by **Ang Pagoda**. Steep roofed and stained with age, the pagoda makes an affecting sight, especially when it echoes with the chants of its resident monks. Fronting it is a nest of stupas guarded by stone lions, while murals inside depict scenes from the Buddha's life. In season, rice from the pagoda's paddy fields is heaped next to the altar, where it's watched over by an impressive golden Sakyamuni image and a host of smaller ones. Several Cambodian monks are resident here, and you'll find them eager to practise their English with visitors.

2

Hang Pagoda

6km south of Tra Vinh along Dien Bien Phu • Daily 24hr • Free • Xe om about 75,000đ for the return trip

The sight of the hundreds of **storks** that nest in the grounds of this Khmer pagoda is one that will linger in the memory. Timing, however, is all-important, and you should aim to catch these magnificent creatures before dusk, when they wheel and hover over the treetops, their snowy wings catching the evening's sunlight. It's a stirring sight, though you might find yourself distracted by the saffron-robed monks who clamour to practise their English. They may also show you their woodcarving workshop, where there's usually someone at work on a wooden tiger. Hang Pagoda itself is nothing to write home about; dominating it is a **Sakyamuni statue**, hooped by a halo of fairy lights.

ARRIVAL AND INFORMATION   TRA VINH AND AROUND

By bus and minibus The main bus station is a full 5km south of town on Highway 54 – the eventual continuation of Dien Bien Phu, which heads south from the town centre. Buy your ticket in town (ask at your accommodation, or the tourist information office) and you may get a free transfer there. Minibuses from Vinh Long terminate about 800m southwest of the town centre, running to no set schedule and no set price – figure on 40,000–75,000đ, depending on how many other passengers there are, and how fast you'd like to get there.

Destinations Ben Tre (1hr 30min); Can Tho (2hr); Ho Chi Minh City (4hr); Vinh Long (1hr 30min).

Tourist information The extremely helpful Tra Vinh Tourism at 64–66 Le Loi (0294 385 8556) can provide local information, and can also book – or at least advise on – bus and ferry tickets. There's usually some English spoken here.

ACCOMMODATION

Hoan My 105a Nguyen Thi Minh Khai 0294 386 2211. Set on the main road just west of town (you may spot it on the bus-ride in), this mini-hotel looks very ordinary from the outside, but inside it has tastefully furnished rooms, some with massage showers. The most expensive rooms are huge and have private balconies. If it's full, note that there are similar options you could try in the nearby area. $15

Palace 3 Le Thanh Ton 0294 386 4999. Pink as a fairytale palace, this is one of the smartest places in the town centre, and located just off the corner of a pleasant park. You might wonder whether it's been transported from a bygone era, thanks to its chunky traditional furniture, high ceilings and all-round mock-colonial air; even the polite welcome from the staff harks back to a time when courtesy counted above all. If full, note that they now have an annexe a few blocks away down Pham Ngu Lao. $16

EATING

★**Café de Paris** 200 Pham Ngu Lao 094 515 0234, facebook.com/cafedeparistravinh. Finally, two new adjectives – "different" and "stylish" – can be added to the Tra Vinh culinary scene! There's a tempting range of coffees, juices and yummy cakes (and sometimes even *crème brûlée*; 25,000đ), and it's even a cheery place for your morning noodles. Daily 6am–10pm.

Thanh Tra 1 Pham Thai Buong. The top-floor restaurant of the otherwise so-so *Thanh Tra* hotel serves an unexciting but reliable range of Vietnamese staples (40,000đ for simple rice or noodle dishes; 100,000–200,000đ for meats), and boasts modest views from the windowside tables. It may not offer gourmet food, but it's one of the few places in town with an English menu, and it's in a very convenient location in the town centre. Daily 6am–9pm.

Vinh Long and around

Ringed by water and besieged by boats and tumbledown stilthouses, the island that forms the heart of the town of **VINH LONG** has the feel of a medieval fortress. However, if you find yourself yearning for a peaceful backwater, first impressions will be a letdown; central Vinh Long is hectic and noisy, its streets a blur of buses and motorbikes. Make for the waterfront, though, and it's a different story, with hotels, restaurants and cafés conjuring up something of a riviera atmosphere. From here you can watch the **Co Chien River** roll by, dotted with sampans, houseboats and the odd raft of river-weed. Though there's little to see or do in town, Vinh Long offers some of the most interesting **boat trips** in the delta – the Cai Be floating market, coconut candy workshops, fruit orchards and a variety of homestays are all within reach.

Vinh Long Museum

Phan Boi Chau • Tues–Thurs 8–11am & 1.30–4.30pm, Fri & Sat 6–9pm • Free

Of Vinh Long's few specific sights, the **Vinh Long Museum**, facing the waterfront, is worth a look if you haven't already visited war museums elsewhere. Displays in various buildings include historical finds from the region, farming implements and musical instruments, as well as a gruesome photographic catalogue of the province's pummelling during the American War. In the gardens are tanks, a helicopter and planes from the war, as well as a guillotine from French colonial times.

Cau Lac Bo Huu Tri

Le Van Tam

West of the Vinh Long Museum stands the impressive French colonial building **Cau Lac Bo Huu Tri**. This oddly shaped mansion, with its red-tiled roof and shuttered windows topped by mouldings of garlands, conjures the ghosts of French *colons* and rice merchants. The place is now run by the government as a social club for retirees, and they won't mind you peeking in through the front door at the fancy furnishings – look out for the mother-of-pearl inlay and the bust of Uncle Ho.

Van Thanh Mieu Temple

Off Tran Phu • Daily 5–11am & 1–7pm • Free

The **Van Thanh Mieu Temple** sits 2km south of the centre, down the road that runs parallel to the Rach Long Canal. If you wander into the tiny lanes that back onto the river along the way, you can watch tiles and coffins being made in the simplest of surroundings, and you might even be invited to take tea with the friendly locals.

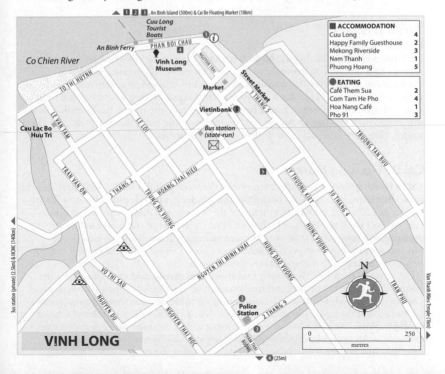

2

PHAN THANH GIAN

Born in Vinh Long province in 1796, the mandarin diplomat **Phan Thanh Gian** was destined to be involved in a chain of events that shaped over a century of Vietnamese history.

On August 31, 1858, French naval forces attacked Da Nang, citing persecution of Catholic missionaries as their justification. The French colonial land-grab, that would culminate in 1885 in the total conquest of Vietnam, had begun. By 1861, the three eastern provinces of Cochinchina had been conquered by the **French Expeditionary Corps**, and although there were popular anti-French uprisings, Emperor Tu Duc sold out the following year, when the three provinces were formally ceded to the French by the **Treaty of Saigon**, which was signed by Phan Thanh Gian. A year later he had the opportunity to redress the situation, when he journeyed to Paris as ambassador to Emperor Napoleon III to thrash out a long-term peace – the first Vietnamese ambassador ever to be despatched to Europe.

However, efforts to reclaim territory given up under the terms of the treaty failed, and by 1867 France moved to take over the rest of Cochinchina. Unable to persuade the spineless Tu Duc to sanction popular uprisings, Phan Thanh Gian embarked on a hunger strike in protest at French incursions and Hue's ineffectuality. When, after fifteen days, he had still not died, he swallowed **poison**, and his place among the massed ranks of Vietnamese heroes was assured.

The temple itself, located at the end of an avenue of tall trees, is dedicated to Confucius – unusually for southern Vietnam – and a heavily bearded portrait of him watches over proceedings, while a wooden statue of Chu Van An (1292–1370), one of his disciples, stands in front of the altar. Another temple at the front of the compound honours local mandarin Phan Thanh Gian (see box above), who is pictured in red robes and flanked by slender storks. Fronting the temple are two cannons that rained fire on the French in 1860. Unfortunately, both temples are often kept locked, though the gardener or caretaker may be able to open them for you (for which a small donation would be appreciated).

An Binh Island

Ferry from centre 5min • 5000đ

Sometimes called Minh Island, **An Binh Island** is a jigsaw of bite-sized pockets of land, skeined by a fine web of channels and gullies that eventually merge, to the east, with the province of Ben Tre. This idyllic landscape is crisscrossed by a network of dirt paths, which makes it ideal for a morning's rambling or cycling, though you'll need to take your own refreshments. You're best advised to take the minor road heading west just as you hit **Chua Tien Chau**, the first temple from the jetty; this is a pleasingly calm stretch with very little traffic, and plenty of curious locals.

Cai Be Floating Market

Cai Be Floating Market has long been one of the most popular in the delta, and also the most distinctive because of its backdrop of a slender cathedral spire. However, it's in danger of becoming yet another victim of the area's burgeoning bridges and bikes (see box, p.116) – the boats, which once filled the waters of the Tien Giang each morning, are now very few in number. For now it's still an enjoyable experience, but you shouldn't go in expecting much more than a simple, charming view of trade being conducted from a sparse array of small boats.

Day-trippers from HCMC mostly find themselves shepherded onto boats for a few hours of exploring the market and fruit orchards on the nearby islands, before zipping back to the city. While this may be convenient for those who are short of time, it's all a bit rushed and the midday heat can be oppressive. If you have a more relaxed schedule, consider taking one of the longer tours (some of which meander through the picturesque channels of An Binh Island between Vinh Long and Cai Be market); alternatively, overnight in a homestay (see box, p.128) before visiting the market in the morning.

ARRIVAL AND DEPARTURE

By bus State-run buses, including jalopies to Sa Dec, pull into the bus station on 3 Thang 2 in the centre of town, which is also used as a base for private minibuses to Tra Vinh. Private buses use the main bus station, 2km west of town on Nguyen Hue; from here take a xe om (about 30,000đ) or taxi (50,000đ or so) into the centre. Also note that from HCMC or elsewhere around the delta, you may end up buying tickets for buses that merely pass by, rather

VINH LONG AND AROUND

than stop in, Vinh Long; in this case, you'll likely be dumped unceremoniously at a roundabout near to the main bus station.

Destinations Can Tho (1hr); HCMC (3hr); Sa Dec (50min); Tra Vinh (1hr 30min).

By taxi The only place within affordable taxi range is Sa Dec (see p.128); it'll cost around 400,000đ from centre to centre.

2

INFORMATION

Tourist information For information about boat trips or homestays, check out the state-run Cuu Long Tourist (☎0270 382 3616, ⓦcuulongtourist.com), whose main office is in the *Cuu Long* hotel: they charge 600,000đ to send two people on a three-hour tour of Cai Be floating market, fruit orchards and the narrow waterways of An

Binh Island; shell out another 250,000đ and you'll get yourself an English-speaking guide, a dance-and-music performance and another hour in the boat.

Services Vietinbank at 143 Le Thai To has an ATM. The post office is in the middle of town at 12c Hoang Thai Hieu.

ACCOMMODATION

Most of Vinh Long's accommodation options are located near the **boat jetty** on the northern edge of town. The local tourist board can also arrange for visitors to stay with the owners of **fruit orchards**, allowing a close-up view of rural life (see box, p.128) – though these days you'll also find plenty of them listed on online booking engines.

TOWN CENTRE

Cuu Long Phan Boi Chau ☎0270 382 3656; map p.125. This government-run place is looking rather faded now, and its polyester sheets and thin aluminium doors fail to impress, but it is still decent value for money. The location is ideal, while some rooms have fine views of the Vinh Long riviera. All rooms include satellite TV, a/c and hot water, and you can enjoy breakfast looking out over the river. $28

Phuong Hoang 2h Hung Vuong ☎0270 382 5185; map p.125. This mini-hotel represents some of the best value in town. It has a dozen or so rooms with varying sizes and facilities, all with chintzy furnishings, and the staff are very friendly. No breakfast. $12

AN BINH ISLAND

★ **Happy Family Guesthouse** 53/4 Phu My ☎090 921 0177, ⓦguesthousemekong.com; map p.125. Way up on the north side of the island, and therefore most quickly accessed from Cai Be town, this is by far the most distinctive guesthouse hereabouts – it's the only one with a pool (which is absolute heaven on hot days), and meals can be taken on a deck overlooking the river. Massages are available, there's a small "gym" on site, and staff can organize river excursions. $25

Nam Thanh 172/9 Binh Luong ☎0270 385 8883; map p.125. If you want that DIY feeling, head to this simple, homely guesthouse on An Binh Island (see opposite). It sits in a gorgeous location, a short, signed walk from the ferry jetty. Prices include free bike rental and two meals. $14

BOAT TRIPS FROM VINH LONG

The cheapest and simplest way to cruise the river is to hop on the An Binh ferry on Phan Boi Chau, and cross the Co Chien River (5min; 5000đ) to reach **An Binh Island** (see opposite). However, most people fork out for a day or half-day **boat trip** to take in the colourful tapestry of everyday delta life, organized through Cuu Long Tourist (see above), or through local boatmen on the lookout for customers near the tourist jetty. These tours often include the option of overnighting in a **homestay** (see box, p.128) in a totally rural environment, though some have started to resemble guesthouses as they've increased in popularity, with visitors put up in custom-built bamboo huts separated from the family home.

Most tour itineraries also head upriver to the floating market at **Cai Be** (see opposite), stopping to visit fruit orchards, rice-paper factories and candy factories en route; some tours add a fish lunch at a rural outpost. Watching the river traffic, from the tiny rowing boats to huge sampans loaded with rice husks (fuel for the nearby brick kilns), is fascinating, and stepping ashore from time to time reveals insights into the lifestyles of the locals – a simple, unhurried existence quite at odds with the bustle of the delta towns.

2

HOMESTAYS IN THE DELTA

While the Vietnamese are generally gregarious people, it's unusual for foreigners to be invited into their homes. However, most visitors are curious about local culture, so it's not surprising that **homestays** are becoming ever more popular, and those located on tranquil islands of the delta, surrounded by acres of orchards, are particularly attractive.

For around $15 per head, plus $10 for the boat, you'll be transported to your host's (usually isolated) abode, shown around the gardens, given a tasty dinner – most likely including the delicious elephant-ear fish, a delta speciality – and lodgings for the night, either in a bed or hammock in a spare room. Bathroom facilities are basic, sometimes with squat toilets and bucket baths, but generally clean. If you book your homestay with a tour operator like Sinhbalo Adventures (see p.88), you can also spend the day kayaking between water palms along narrow canals, or cycling along narrow lanes between coconut, mango and papaya trees.

CAI BE

Mekong Riverside Hoa Qui, west of Cai Be ☎ 0273 392 4466, ⍟ mekongriversideresort.com; map p.125. The most luxuriant accommodation in the wider Vinh Long area is a few kilometres west of Cai Be town, an area where the only sounds you'll hear are the putt-putts of occasional riverboats. The wide compound is taken up with an array of highly pleasant villas (those facing the river are best, though they usually cost a bit more), and there's a swimming pool, restaurant and bar to keep you occupied in this remote location. **$120**

EATING

★ **Café Them Sua** 87 Trung Nu Vuong ☎ 091 389 9904; map p.125. A pleasing little café that wouldn't look out of place in HCMC – the downstairs level is surprisingly smart, while its tree-surrounded rooftop vies with the riverfront for Vinh Long's best views. It'll set you back 20,000đ for most juices, and 25,000đ for shakes or something resembling an Orange Julius. It's located on an alley just off the main road. Daily 7am–10pm.

Com Tam He Pho 14 Phan Thai Buong ☎ 091 389 9904; map p.125. Buzzing with locals every night, this is the friendliest of several cheap *com tam* places abutting the road just over the bridge from the police station. Plates of their delicious grilled pork and rice go from just 15,000đ; a 50,000đ note will get you two, plus a few bangers and a can of pop. Daily 3–10pm.

Hoa Nang Café 1 Thang 5; map p.125. With a long river frontage, this is the perfect place to sip a cool drink while watching the sun sink over the Mekong. Occasionally, this place plays host to screaming karaoke soon afterwards. Coffees from 10,000đ. Daily 7am–11pm.

Pho 91 91, 2 Thang 9; map p.125. Slurp-worthy pho in the town's best noodle joint; the greens are nice and fresh, the broth is both sweet and meaty, and the atmosphere is typically Vietnamese. Bowls go from just 20,000đ. Daily 6am–9pm.

Sa Dec

A cluster of brick and tile kilns on the riverbank announces your arrival in the dusty town of **SA DEC**, a little over 20km upriver of Vinh Long. French novelist Marguerite Duras lived here as a child (see box opposite), and decades later the town's stuccoed shophouse terraces, riverside mansions and remarkably busy stretch of the rumbling Mekong provided the backdrop for the movie adaptation of her novel *The Lover*. Elements of such whimsy remain, but in general Sa Dec feels little different to most other delta towns – and it's far from beautiful.

Huynh Thuy Le Old House

255a Nguyen Hue • Daily 8am–5pm • 30,000đ • ☎ 0277 377 3937

Sa Dec's best place for a wander is Nguyen Hue, whose umbrella-choked lanes hide an extensive riverside market. Waterfront comings and goings are observed by rheumy old men playing chequers, while women squat on their haunches, selling fruit from wicker baskets.

Nestled among the tumbledown riverside houses stands the former home of **Huynh Thuy Le**, who became the lover of Marguerite Duras in the 1930s (see box below). The old family home, now administered by Dong Thap Tourism, features some elaborate carved panels and lashings of gold lacquerwork, as well as some photos of the couple in question, though interestingly none of them together.

Tu Ton Rose Garden

Off Le Loi • Daily 8–11am & 1–5pm • Free • Xe om about 40,000đ

A few kilometres north of town by the river, Sa Dec's famed flower nurseries consist of more than a hundred farms cultivating a host of ferns, fruit trees, shrubs and flowers. The expansive grounds of **Tu Ton Rose Garden** get the lion's share of tourists visiting the area. In addition to the varieties of rose cultivated here (among them the Brigitte Bardot, the Jolie Madame and the Marseille), over 580 species of plant are grown, ranging from orchids, carnations and chrysanthemums, through to medicinal herbs and pines grown for export around Asia. Bear in mind that tourists from Ho Chi Minh City overrun the nurseries on Sundays, as they come to pose for photos among the blooms; things get particularly busy and colourful in the run-up to Tet, as farms prepare to transport their stocks to the city's flower markets.

ARRIVAL AND DEPARTURE
SA DEC

By bus Buses terminate 300m southeast of the town centre. It's quite walkable, and just after you cross the bridge the town's three main arteries – riverside Nguyen Hue, then busier Tran Hung Dao and Hung Vuong – branch off one after another to your right.

Destinations Cao Lanh (1hr); Chau Doc (3hr 30min, including ferry); HCMC (3hr 30min); Long Xuyen (2hr, including ferry); Vinh Long (50min).

By taxi The only place within affordable taxi range is Vinh Long (see p.124); it'll cost around 400,000đ from centre to centre.

ACCOMMODATION AND EATING

Com Thuy 439 Hung Vuong ☎ 0277 386 1644. A popular lunch spot serving Vietnamese staples; there are no prices on its English menu, so ask when ordering. Try some spring rolls, a steamy soup or a stir-fry; it's 50,000đ or under for most dishes. Daily 7am–9pm.

★**My Ngoc** 150 Hung Vuong ☎ 0277 386 2379. A friendly clutch of ladies serves up delectable *banh canh*, a hearty noodle soup featuring meat, quail eggs, bamboo shoots and much more. It's just 50,000đ/bowl. Daily 5am–9pm.

Thao Ngan 2 An Duong Vuong ☎ 0277 377 4255. More or less the only decent place to stay in town, with a friendly owner and an elevator to hoist you up to the plain (but clean) rooms, which are fair value for the price. $14

MARGUERITE DURAS

Marguerite Duras (1914–96) was born to French parents in a suburb of Saigon, and lived in various locations in Vietnam and Cambodia before going, aged 18, to study at the Sorbonne in France. She wrote many novels, plays and film scripts, including the fictionalized autobiographical novel *The Lover* (1984), which sold over three million copies and was translated into forty languages. Its subject is an interracial affair between a 15-year-old French girl and her middle-aged Chinese lover, set in 1930s Indochina. Duras had little sympathy for her peers, of whom she wrote, "I look at the (French) women in the streets of Saigon. They don't do anything, just save themselves up… Some of them go mad… some are deserted for a young maid." Duras clearly had no intention of letting life pass her by in this way, even if it meant becoming the subject of the town's gossip.

Though her novels are principally about the inner thoughts of her characters, she also describes the landscape around Sa Dec as it still appears today: "In the surrounding flatness, stretching as far as the eye can see, the rivers flow as if the earth slopes downward." If you visit Sa Dec with a tour guide, they will almost inevitably take you to look at her former house beside the river – an old colonial villa that now belongs to the People's Committee.

2

Cao Lanh and around

Modest **CAO LANH** is one potential stop – or, given the distances involved, an overnight base – for those heading to or from Chau Doc. The town is far from an oil painting, and offers little unless you're charmed by **wading birds**; its location beside the western edge of the **Plain of Reeds** makes it an ideal launching pad for trips out to the storks and cranes that nest in the nearby swamplands. Coming from Ho Chi Minh City, you'll pass the two great concrete tusks (intended to resemble lotus petals) of the **war memorial** as you veer onto the main drag, Nguyen Hue – one tusk bears a hammer and sickle, the other a Vietnamese red star. South of town, another whopping great bridge was nearing completion at the time of research, and this will improve access greatly. If you're stuck for something to do in town, head for **Van Thanh Mieu**, a pretty park just north of the centre.

The burial place of Nguyen Sinh Sac

Pham Huu Lau, about 1km west of the town centre • Daily 24hr • Free

On the southwestern outskirts of town, a landscaped park contains a monument, shaped like an open clam, which marks the burial place of Ho Chi Minh's father, **Nguyen Sinh Sac**. The park's area has recently been expanded to include several examples of stilted houses typical of the south, as well as a replica of Ho Chi Minh's house in Hanoi. With a lake and benches in shady areas, it's a pleasant place to pass an hour or so.

Dong Thap Museum

Just off Pham Huu Lau, to the left beyond the first bridge • Mon 7–11.30am, Tues–Sun 7–11.30am & 1.30–5pm • Free

While in town, it's worth having a look around the **Dong Thap Museum**. Though there are no English signs, this place has a well-organized display of fossils, skulls, farming tools, fishtraps, basketware and textiles, as well as the inevitable paintings of heroic Vietnamese forces repelling French and American troops.

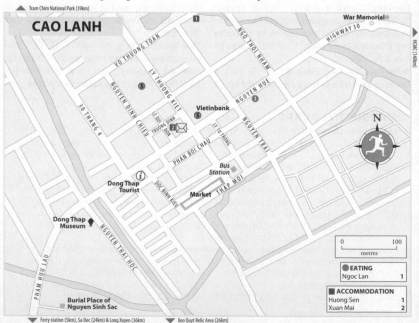

Tram Chim National Park

45km northwest of Cao Lanh • 450,000đ return from Cao Lanh by xe om, including 2hr waiting time; park tours 200,000–300,000đ/boat

Of the 220 species of bird nesting at **Tram Chim National Park** (previously Tam Nong Bird Sanctuary), it's the sarus cranes, with their distinctive red heads, which most visitors come to see. In flight above the marshland of the sanctuary, the slender grey birds reveal spectacular black-tipped wings. **Cranes** feed from the land, so when the spate season (July to November) waterlogs the delta, they migrate to Cambodia.

Visiting the park can be quite expensive, so this is a trip for committed bird enthusiasts only – if you're keen, ask at the office of Dong Thap Tourist in Cao Lanh for details (see below). Most people do the rounds of the park by boat, though there's not much to be seen outside the months of December to May.

Xeo Quyt Relic Area

30km southeast of Cao Lanh • Daily 7am–4pm • 10,000đ • 300,000đ return from Cao Lanh by xe om, including waiting time

You'll most likely need to go through the local tourist office (see below) if you want to take a trip out to **Xeo Quyt Relic Area**, which conceals former Viet Cong bunkers deep in the cajeput forest 30km southeast of Cao Lanh. The district's dense cover provided the perfect bolthole for Viet Cong guerrillas during the American War, and from 1960 to 1975 the struggle against America and the ARVN was masterminded from here. The boggy nature of the terrain made a tunnel system similar to that of Cu Chi (see p.106) unfeasible, so they made do with six submerged metal chambers sealed with tar and resin.

ARRIVAL AND INFORMATION

CAO LANH AND AROUND

By bus Buses to and from Cao Lanh stop at one of two bus stations – the main one across the river, 2km east of the centre, and the scruffy local one right in the middle of things. In general, you'll be dropped at the former if coming from HCMC or other non-local destinations; with the opening of the bridge to the south of town, more and more services are also likely to use this terminal. Destinations HCMC (3hr 30min); Sa Dec (50min); Vinh Long (1hr 20min).

Tourist information Dong Thap Tourist (daily 7–11.30am & 1.30–5pm; ☎067 385 5637, ⓦdongthap tourist.com), whose office is at 2 Doc Binh Kieu (just off the main road, Nguyen Hue), is the place for information about the nearby bird sanctuaries. They often have an English-speaker on hand, but dedicated twitchers might be better off approaching tour operators in HCMC.

ACCOMMODATION

Huong Sen Vo Truong Toan ☎0277 354 6789, ⓦhuongsenhoteldt.com; map opposite. This is the nicest accommodation in town, for what it's worth. It's in a decent spot, overlooking the park, and the rooms are excellent value, even if they don't quite live up to the promise of the snazzy lobby. $23

Xuan Mai 33 Le Qui Don ☎0277 385 2852; map opposite. Just west of the post office on a back alley, and one of the only acceptable budget choices around, this place has been subject to a half-hearted makeover – make sure you check your room first, as some are still very dingy. Its larger rooms have bathtubs. $9

EATING

Ngoc Lan 210 Nguyen Hue ☎0277 385 1498; map opposite. If you walk down Cao Lanh's main street at lunchtime, this simple place is likely to be the most crowded. They have plenty of cheap rice and noodle dishes (try the sour basa-fish soup for 35,000đ), and you can wash it all down with a carrot juice or coffee (from 15,000đ). There are no prices on the English menu, but they're honest sorts. Daily 7am–10pm.

Chau Doc and around

Sitting merrily on the languid banks of the Hau Giang, **CHAU DOC** is the only delta town bar Can Tho in which you are likely to see foreigners in any significant numbers. Since the opening of the border to Cambodia a few kilometres north of town, the place has boomed in popularity, and it makes a decent bookend to a stay in Vietnam.

As with many delta towns, there's little of sightseeing interest here bar a market and a couple of temples. Around said market, stalls are crammed into narrow alleyways that run towards the river, where you'll be greeted by a multitude of bobbing boats and waterside activities. If you wander south from here, you'll find a narrow park bordering the river; featuring a tall statue celebrating the local catfish, it makes a pleasant place for a breezy morning or evening stroll.

There are several places of interest to visit in the surrounding area, including a thriving **Cham community** and the brooding **Sam Mountain** with its kitsch pagodas. Further afield you'll find a bird sanctuary, a battlefield from the American War and the harrowing scene of a Khmer Rouge massacre.

Brief history

The town was actually once part of Cambodia, until it was awarded to the Nguyen lords in the mid-eighteenth century for their help in putting down a localized rebellion. The area still sustains a large Khmer community, which combines with local Cham and Chinese groups to form a diverse social melting pot. Just as diverse is Chau Doc's religious make-up: as well as Buddhists, Catholics and Muslims, the region supports an estimated 1.5 million devotees of the indigenous Hoa Hao religion (see box, p.138).

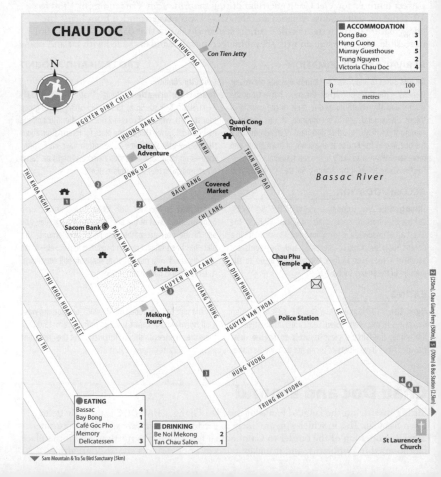

CHAU DOC

N

Con Tien Jetty

TRAN HUNG DAO

NGUYEN DINH CHIEU

THUONG DANG LE

LE CONG THANH

Quan Cong
Temple

Delta
Adventure

DONG DU

BACH DANG

Covered
Market

TRAN HUNG DAO

Bassac River

THU KHOA NGHIA

CHI LANG

Sacom Bank

PHAN VAN VANG

Futabus

NGUYEN HUU CANH

PHAN DINH PHUNG

Chau Phu
Temple

THU KHOA HUAN STREET

QUANG TRUNG

NGUYEN VAN THOAI

LE LOI

Mekong
Tours

Police Station

CU TRI

HUNG VUONG

TRUNG NU VUONG

St Laurence's
Church

ACCOMMODATION	
Dong Bao	3
Hung Cuong	1
Murray Guesthouse	5
Trung Nguyen	2
Victoria Chau Doc	4

0 ——————— 100
metres

2 (250m), Chau Giang Ferry (500m); 5 (700m) & Bus Station (2.5km)

● EATING	
Bassac	4
Bay Bong	1
Café Goc Pho	2
Memory Delicatessen	3

DRINKING	
Be Noi Mekong	2
Tan Chau Salon	1

▼ Sam Mountain & Tra Su Bird Sanctuary (5km)

Forays by Pol Pot's genocidal Khmer Rouge into this corner of the delta led to the Vietnamese invasion of Cambodia in 1978.

The covered market

Main entrance on Quang Trung • Daily 7am–6pm • Free

The obvious place to begin an exploration of Chau Doc is at its **covered market**, where the overspill of stalls and street vendors spreads from Quang Trung to Tran Hung Dao, and from Dong Du to Nguyen Van Thoai. This is one of the delta's biggest markets and is packed with a phenomenal range of produce, much of which is unfamiliar to Western eyes. Even if you have explored other markets in the region, it's well worth picking your way through the rows of neatly stacked stalls of fresh produce, household goods, fish and flowers.

Quan Cong Temple

Tran Hung Dao • Dawn–dusk • Free

A four-tiered gateway deep in the belly of the open market announces **Quan Cong Temple**. Beyond the courtyard, two rooftop dragons oversee its entrance and the outer walls' vivid murals. Inside the temple is the red visage of Quan Cong, sporting a green robe and bejewelled crown, and surrounded by a sequin-studded red velvet canopy.

Chau Phu Temple

Cnr Tran Hung Dao and Nguyen Van Thoai • Dawn–dusk • Free

A few steps southeast through the covered market stalls along Tran Hung Dao, the lofty chambers of **Chau Phu Temple** offer a cool respite from the heat outside, and fans of gilt woodwork will find much to divert them. It was built in 1926 to honour Thoai Ngoc Hau (1761–1829), a local hero whose elaborate tomb is located at the base of Sam Mountain (see below).

Chau Doc Floating Market

Opposite tourist jetty on Bassac River • Daily 5–9am • Most visit by tour (see p.135), but local boatmen will row you there for a small fee

Since this floating market was established relatively recently, you have to wonder whether it's more for the benefit of tourists than locals. Nevertheless, if you've managed to get this far through the delta without visiting any of the other floating markets along the way, it's certainly worth a look. As usual, boats advertise their products by hanging a sample from a stick on the deck. Tours to the market also often stop at a cluster of **fish farms** floating on the river next to Con Tien Island, above cages of catfish that are fed through a hatch in the floor.

Chau Giang District

Ferries depart regularly from a busy jetty just south of the *Victoria Chau Doc* hotel (10min; 1000đ)

The **Chau Giang District** and its Cham community can be visited independently by ferry. Amid the traditional wooden houses, you'll notice the influence of Islam in the sarongs, the white prayer caps and the twin domes and pretty white minaret of the **Mubarak Mosque**.

Sam Mountain

5km west of Chau Doc • Free • 50,000đ from Chau Doc by xe om to base, or 100,000đ to summit

Arid, brooding **Sam Mountain** rises dramatically from an ocean of paddy fields just west of Chau Doc. It's known as Nui Sam to Vietnamese tourists, who flock here in their thousands to worship at its clutch of pagodas and shrines. Even if the temples don't appeal, the journey up to the summit is good fun. As you climb, you'll pass massive boulders that seem embedded in the hillside, as well as some plaster statues of rhinos, elephants, zebras – and even a Tyrannosaurus rex near the top. From the top, the **view** of the surrounding, pancake-flat terrain is breathtaking, though the "mountain" is, in fact, only 230m high. In the rainy season, the view is particularly spectacular, with lush paddy fields scored by hundreds of waterways, though in the dry season the barren landscape is hazy and marginally less inspiring. There's a tiny military outpost at the summit, from which you can gaze into Cambodia on one side, Chau Doc on the other.

Tay An Pagoda

At the foot of Sam Mountain, the first temple you'll see is kitsch **Tay An Pagoda**, built in 1847. It's the pick of the bunch, its frontage awash with portrait photographers, beggars, incense-stick vendors and bird-sellers (releasing one from captivity accrues merit, though some wily vendors train the birds to fly back later). The number of gaudy statues inside exceeds two hundred: most are of deities and Buddhas, but an alarmingly lifelike rendering of an honoured monk sits at one of the highly varnished tables in the rear chamber. To the right of this room an annexe houses a goddess with a thousand eyes and a thousand hands, on whose mound of heads teeters a tiny Quan Am.

Chua Xu Temple

Fifty metres west of Tay An, **Chua Xu Temple** honours Her Holiness Lady of the Country, a stone statue said to have been found on Sam's slopes in the early nineteenth century, though the present building, with its four-tiered, glazed green-tile roof, dates only from 1972. Inside, the Lady sits in state in a marbled chamber, resplendent in colourful gown and headdress. Glass cases in corridors either side of her are crammed to bursting with splendid garb and other offerings from worshippers, who flood here between the 23rd and 25th of the fourth lunar month, to see her ceremonially bathed and dressed. Shops in front of the temple sell colourful baskets of fruit that locals buy to offer to Her Holiness.

Tra Su Bird Sanctuary

23km from Chau Doc, just north of Chi Lang on Highway 948 • Daily 6am–5pm • 120,000đ; 75,000đ/person for a 90min boat ride, or 150,000đ to rent the boat • Around 500,000/300,000đ return by taxi/xe om from Chau Doc

The **Tra Su Bird Sanctuary** consists of a protected forest of cajeput trees and wetlands, which attract a great variety of birds including storks, egrets, cormorants, peafowl and water cocks. Once here, you'll be able to take a boat ride around the sanctuary, combined with a walk to a viewing tower. Even if you're not a dedicated birder, you'd probably enjoy floating around this watery wonderland with its huge lily pads and moss-shrouded trees.

Ba Chuc

40km southwest of Chau Doc • Daily 9am–5pm • Free • Take Highway 91 and then Highway N1 along the border towards Ha Tien, and turn south on to Highway 3T for the last few kilometres; around 800,000đ/400,000đ by taxi/xe om for the return trip from Chau Doc or Ha Tien

A sweep of staggeringly beautiful countryside southwest of Chau Doc conceals a far from peaceful history. Refugees fleeing Pol Pot's Cambodia boosted the Khmer population here in the late 1970s, and pursuit by the Khmer Rouge ended in numerous indiscriminate massacres; a grisly memorial to the worst of these, at the village of **BA CHUC**, stands as testament to that horrific era.

Memorials

The **memorial** in the centre of the village pays homage to the 3157 villagers massacred, most of them clubbed to death, over the course of two weeks during April 1978. Only two villagers survived the tragedy. An unattractive concrete canopy fails to lessen the

ON TO CAMBODIA FROM CHAU DOC

Chau Doc and its arm of the Mekong provide one of the most exciting, and popular, means of connecting Vietnam and **Cambodia**. The border crossing itself is just north of the city, so the "dull" way is to take a direct **bus** from Chau Doc to Phnom Penh (daily 7am; 6hr; $25). The "fun" way (which is also easier to arrange) is to take a **boat ride** all the way to Phnom Penh. You'll be able to buy tickets at various agents around Chau Doc (including those listed below, and usually your accommodation too), and they can be quite affordable. Keep in mind that you will need a **visa**: these are generally easy to find if you're heading into Cambodia, as you can get them at the border for $30 (plus, usually, a $5 bribe), but if you're enterting Vietnam you'll need a visa arranged in advance.

Blue Cruiser ☎083 926 0253, ⓦbluecruiser.com. Relatively luxurious service ($55) leaving the *Victoria* hotel at 7am, then returning from Phnom Penh at 1.30pm; most passengers are on through-tickets to or from HCMC. The price, by the way, includes all-you-can- drink beer.

Hang Chau ☎0296 356 2771, ⓦhangchautourist .com.vn. These speedy boats ($25) leave Chau Doc daily at 7.30am, arriving just after noon; from Phnom Penh they depart at noon.

impact of the eight-sided memorial: behind its glass enclosure, the bleached skulls of the dead of Vietnam's own "killing fields" are piled in ghoulish heaps, grouped according to age to highlight the youth and innocence of many of the dead.

Many of the victims were killed in the adjacent **Phi Lai Pagoda**, where bloodstains on the walls and floor can still be easily seen. A signboard in Vietnamese beside a tiny door below the altar notes that forty villagers perished here when a grenade was thrown into the cramped space.

Between the memorial and the pagoda is a small room, where a horrific set of black-and-white photos taken just after the massacre shows buckled, abused corpses scattered around the countryside. Some of the images on display are extremely disturbing and you should not enter if you are sensitive. There are also a few cafés and food stalls set up to cater to visitors to the site.

ARRIVAL AND DEPARTURE

CHAU DOC AND AROUND

By bus The bus station comes as a nice surprise – it's a large, neat place with free wi-fi. It's roughly 3km southeast of town on Le Loi, and around 30,000đ away by xe om, or 55,000đ by cab. Futa (ⓦfutabus.vn) will give you a free pick-up from their office on Phan Van Vang (see map, p.132), though it's even easier if you go with Hung Cuong, who run buses to HCMC – via Long Xuyen and Sa Dec – from their office inside the eponymous hotel (see below).

Destinations Ca Mau (7hr); Can Tho (3hr); Cao Lanh (3hr 30min); Ha Tien (2hr 30min); HCMC (6hr 30min); Long Xuyen (1hr 30min).
By ferry There are no longer any scheduled domestic passenger services to other towns across the delta, but Chau Doc is visited frequently as part of boat tours. Ferries to Cambodia (see box above) leave from a few different points along the riverfront.

INFORMATION AND TOURS

Tourist information Most hotel and guesthouse owners can help out with local information, and can also arrange local excursions and onward travel, including boat services to and from Phnom Penh.
Tours Delta Adventure (12–14 Quang Trung; ☎0296 358 4222) offers half-day trips to the local floating market, a

fish farm and a Cham village (300,000đ/person). Mekong Tours (14 Nguyen Huu Canh; ☎0296 386 7817, ⓦmekongvietnam.com) run similar trips (400,000đ for two people) from their tiny office, and these work out cheaper if you're in a pair. To get to Tra Su, Tup Duc and Ba Chuc, try enquiring with either of these companies.

ACCOMMODATION

★ **Dong Bao** 21 Phan Van Vang ☎0296 356 9789; map p.132. This city-centre mini-hotel offers some of the cheapest sleeps in town, and unlike most places in this price bracket, it's super-clean – you'll have to take your footwear off upon entry. Rooms are surprisingly easy on

the eye, with cream-coloured walls and dark-wood furnishings – though try to get one with a window. Breakfast extra. $11
Hung Cuong 96 Dong Da ☎0296 356 8111; map p.132. This place is excellent value in the city centre, with sharp

rooms that come with smart bathrooms – and if you pay another few dollars, you can nab a deluxe room with a balcony. The lift will save you a bit of sweat, and all you have to do is walk out the door to pick up services from the bus company operating next to the lobby (see p.135). $22

★**Murray Guesthouse** 11–15 Truong Dinh ☎0296 356 2108, ⓦmurraymekong.com; map p.132. This Kiwi–Viet-run establishment has been a wonderful recent addition to the Chau Doc accommodation scene. Their rooms are very nicely decorated with silky fabrics, local paintings and the like, and the pool table and bar make the guest lounge a great hangout spot – the breakfast pho takes some beating, too. The only slight downside is the location, on a scruffy street south of the centre. $32

Trung Nguyen 86 Bach Dang ☎0296 356 1561; map p.132. Very smart mini-hotel, right in the town centre,

with fifteen smallish but well-furnished rooms, all with small balconies. Staff are very helpful and efficient, and they rent out bicycles and motorbikes too (see below). $17

Victoria Chau Doc 1 Le Loi ☎0296 386 5010, ⓦvictoriahotels-asia.com; map p.132. Just 300m southeast of the town centre, this colonial-style hotel lords it over the river. The rooms are tastefully furnished with Indochinese elegance and some have glorious river views, though one has to say they represent questionable value considering the sky-high prices. They've a lovely restaurant (see below) and bar (see below) on site, as well as a small swimming pool with a river view. Note that there's yet another *Victoria* way up on Sam Mountain (see p.133); linked to the main hotel by occasional shuttle buses (free for guests), this one's preferable if you prefer views of rice paddies and a sense of remoteness. $185

EATING

Chau Doc has more places to eat than most Mekong Delta towns, which cater to diners looking for something tasty and cheap. A snack at one of the **food stalls** around the market, particularly on Tran Hung Dao, Chi Lang or Le Cong Thanh, is also a good option if you're in an adventurous mood.

Bassac Victoria Chau Doc hotel, 1 Le Loi ☎0296 386 5010, ⓦvictoriahotels-asia.com; map p.132. Expect imaginative iterations of Western and Asian dishes (most around 350,000đ), such as roast loin of lamb or roasted duck breast, as well as cheaper meals such as pho, all served in a romantic riverside dining terrace overlooking the Mekong and the hotel pool. Daily 11am–10pm.

★**Bay Bong** 22 Thuong Dang Le ☎0296 386 7271; map p.132. A visit here is a treat after a long day on the move. With its plastic stools and tables, it may look like any other hole-in-the-wall eatery, but the food is wonderfully prepared – go for their speciality, catfish in a clay pot (55,000đ). Daily 7am–9pm.

Café Goc Pho 86 Dong Da ☎0296 626 7888; map p.132. Good option for an espresso or juice (both around 25,000đ), in a place that's about as popular as any in Chau Doc. There's a nice balcony area upstairs. Daily 6.30am–10pm.

Memory Delicatessen 57 Nguyen Huu Canh ☎0296 629 3769; map p.132. If you're in the mood for something different, or just some a/c, give this place a whirl. Their menu is bursting with tempting choices like pizza, spaghetti, burgers and curries (mostly 80,000–150,000đ), and there are plenty of desserts on show – though don't expect maximum authenticity with any of these options. Daily 6am–10pm.

DRINKING

Be Noi Mekong Just south of the tourist jetty on Le Loi ☎0296 356 3810; map p.132. Located on the riverbank, and also known as the *Mekong Floating Restaurant,* this place is popular for its cheap beer and river views. Daily 7am–10pm.

Tan Chau Salon Victoria Chau Doc, 1 Le Loi

☎0296 386 5010, ⓦvictoriahotels-asia.com; map p.132. Yes, it's the *Victoria* yet again – their bar is, without doubt, the town's standout place for a drink. There's a pool table and backgammon, and prices are just about low enough that even a backpacker can pop in for a sundowner (100,000đ). Daily 6am–11pm.

DIRECTORY

Banks Sacombank (88 Dong Du) can exchange foreign currency, and also has an ATM.
Bicycle and motorbike rental Available at *Trung Nguyen* hotel for $2 or $8/day respectively.
Hospital The hospital is based opposite the *Victoria Chau*

Doc on Le Loi.
Pharmacy You'll find a pharmacy at 14 Nguyen Huu Canh.
Post office On the corner of Le Loi and Nguyen Van Thoai (daily 6am–10pm).

2

THE HOA HAO RELIGION

Sited 20km east of Chau Doc, the diminutive village of Hoa Hao lent its name to a unique religious movement at the end of the 1930s. The **Hoa Hao Buddhist sect** was founded by the village's most famous son, Huynh Phu So. A sickly child, Huynh was placed in the care of a hermitic monk under whom he explored both conventional Buddhism and more arcane spiritual disciplines. In 1939, at the age of 20, a new brand of Buddhism was revealed to him in a trance. Upon waking, Huynh found he was cured of his congenital illness, and began publicly to expound his breakaway theories, which advocated purging worship of all the clutter of votives, priests and pagodas, and paring it down to simple unmediated communication between the individual and the Supreme Being. The faith has a fairly strong **ascetic** element, with alcohol, drugs and gambling all discouraged. Peasants were drawn to the simplicity of the sect, and by rumours that Huynh was a faith healer in possession of prophetic powers.

Almost immediately, the Hoa Hao developed a **political agenda**, and established a militia to uphold its fervently nationalist, anti-French and anti-Communist beliefs. The Japanese army of occupation, happy to keep the puppet French administration it had allowed to remain nominally in charge of Vietnam on its toes, provided the sect with arms. For themselves, the French regarded the Hoa Hao with suspicion: Huynh they labelled the "Mad Monk", imprisoning him in 1941 and subsequently confining him to a psychiatric hospital – where he promptly converted his doctor. By the time of his eventual release in 1945, the sect's uneasy alliance with the Viet Minh, which had been forged during World War II in recognition of their common anticolonial objectives, was souring, and two years later Viet Minh agents **assassinated** Huynh.

The sect battled on until the mid-Fifties when Diem's purge of dissident groups took hold; its guerrilla commander, Ba Cut, was captured and beheaded in 1956, and by the end of the decade most members had been driven underground. Though in the early sixties some of these resurfaced in the Viet Cong, the Hoa Hao never regained its early dynamism, and any lingering military or political presence was erased by the Communists after 1975.

Today there are thought to be somewhere around two million Hoa Hao worshippers in Vietnam, concentrated mostly around Chau Doc and Long Xuyen. Some male devotees still sport the distinctive long beards and hair tied in a bun that traditionally distinguished a Hoa Hao adherent.

Long Xuyen and around

The large, spread-out town of **LONG XUYEN** attracts few foreign visitors, though the unusual cathedral, the well-organized museum, Tiger Island and the nearby stork garden are all worth a look if you're passing through – however, with Chau Doc and Can Tho so close, there's precious little reason to stay here. You'll be able to get your bearings from the cathedral, whose distinctive spire is shaped in the form of two upstretched arms whose hands clasp a cross.

My Phuoc Communal Hall

Nguyen Hue • Dawn to dusk • Free

Near the eastern end of Nguyen Hue, the dragon-stalked roofs of the grandest building in town, the **My Phuoc Communal Hall**, shelter carved pillars and embroidered banners in the temple-like interior. Nearby is a very large statue of a meek-looking **Ton Duc Thang**: born locally, he was successor to Ho Chi Minh as president of the Democratic Republic of Vietnam, giving the town its main claim to fame.

Tiger Island

Ferry from the eastern end of Nguyen Hue will cost 1000đ

You can visit Ton Duc Thang's birthplace and childhood home at My Hoa Hung village on **Tiger Island**. Here you will find the Ton Duc Thang Exhibition House (daily 7–11am & 1–5pm; free), which displays well-presented photos and memorabilia such as the leg irons he wore in Con Dao prison, the prime-ministerial bicycle and the plane that took him from Hanoi to Saigon in 1975 to celebrate victory. The island is very tranquil and unspoiled, and homestays here can be arranged (see box, p.128).

An Giang Museum

11 Ton Duc Thang, on the corner of Ly Thuong Kiet • Tues–Sun 7.30–11am & 1.30–5pm • 15,000đ

Also worth a look, particularly for its display of Oc Eo relics (see box, p.140), is the **An Giang Museum**, housed in a grand edifice in the northern part of town. On the first floor the focus is on the different religions practised in the region – Catholicism, Buddhism and Hoa Hao. On the second floor is a treasure-trove of remnants of Oc Eo culture. Among the exhibits are a large lingam and a wooden Buddha, which is now so decayed it is now almost unrecognizable, as well as delicate items of gold jewellery. Other displays focus on minority culture, particularly the Cham, and the inevitable documenting of the local revolutionary movement and battles against the French and Americans.

Bang Lang Stork Garden

About 15km south of Long Xuyen on Highway 9 • Daily 6am–6pm • 10,000đ • Xe om from Long Xuyen 200,000đ return

South of Long Xuyen is one of the Mekong Delta's best stork sanctuaries, the **Bang Lang Stork Garden**, where you can watch thousands of birds wheeling, swooping and

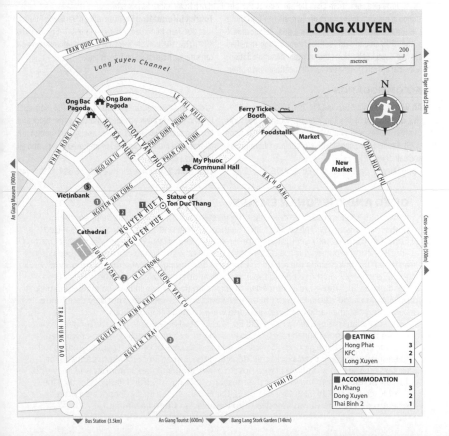

LONG XUYEN

EATING
Hong Phat	3
KFC	2
Long Xuyen	1

ACCOMMODATION
An Khang	3
Dong Xuyen	2
Thai Binh 2	1

squabbling over nesting places at dusk. The most obvious birds here are, in fact, egrets, but there are indeed plenty of Asian openbill storks, along with a few adjutants and black-necked storks; you'll also likely see herons and pelicans. Turn up an hour before sunset to witness the memorable sight – wearing a hat might be wise, since the site is smothered with their droppings.

Oc Eo

40km west of Long Xuyen on Highway 943 • As it's difficult to find, you're best off arranging a trip through An Giang Tourism (see below)

Excavations at the site of the vanished port of **Oc Eo** during the late 1990s uncovered gold jewellery, bowls and skeletons in vases, all dating back over a thousand years to the Funan Empire (see box below) – though, as these precious objects have now been shifted to museums around the country, you'd need to be pretty keen about history to get much from the modest building foundations that remain on-site. The ride here is an enjoyable diversion into the back lanes of the delta, however, passing rice fields, lotus ponds and fruit orchards along the way. It's also possible to continue on Highway 943 to Chau Doc, though it's a bumpy road and progress is slow.

ARRIVAL AND INFORMATION LONG XUYEN AND AROUND

By bus Most buses stop on Pham Cu Luong, off Tran Hung Dao a couple of kilometres south of town, though local buses, including some from Chau Doc, pull up at the bus station about 2km to the north of town, also on Tran Hung Dao. Futa (@futabus.vn) use their own dedicated terminal in the sticks around 5km south of town, though transfers are free if you book a ticket through your accommodation. Note that arrivals from Sa Dec and destinations north often make use of a ferry to cross the Hau Giang.
Destinations Ca Mau (6hr); Chau Doc (1hr 30min); Ha Tien (5hr); HCMC (5hr); Sa Dec (2hr).
Tourist information The main office of An Giang Tourism is at 80e Tran Hung Dao (daily 7–11am & 1–5pm; @076 384 1036); the staff are helpful with local information and can arrange homestays on Tiger Island.

ACCOMMODATION

An Khang 5–9 Thi Sach @0216 394 2551; map p.139. This is a tall, skinny block in a central location, boasting comfy rooms as well as a palatial suite on the top floor ($29). Rooms are equipped with a/c, satellite TVs, minibars and hair dryers. **$17**
Dong Xuyen 9a Luong Van Cu @0216 394 2260, @dongxuyenhotel.com; map p.139. The fanciest-looking place in town occupies almost an entire block and boasts a sauna and jacuzzi, as well as carpeted rooms with all the usual facilities. Service has improved of late, and all in all it's a good deal. **$25**
Thai Binh 2 4–8 Nguyen Hue @0216 384 1859; map

OC EO AND THE FUNAN EMPIRE

Between the first and sixth centuries AD, the western side of the Mekong Delta, southern Cambodia and much of the Gulf of Siam's seaboard came under the sway of the Indianized **Funan empire**, an early forerunner of the great Angkor civilization. The heavily romanticized annals of contemporary Chinese diplomats describe how the Funan empire was forged when an Indian Brahmin visiting the region married the daughter of a local serpent-god, and how the serpent rendered the region suitable for cultivation by drinking down the waters of the flood plains. Such fables are grounded in truth: Indian traders would have halted here to pick up victuals en route from India to China, and would have disseminated not only their Hindu beliefs, but also their advanced irrigation and wet-rice cultivation methods.

One of Funan's major trading ports, **Oc Eo**, was located between Long Xuyen and Rach Gia. In common with other Funan cities, Oc Eo was ringed by a moat and consisted of wooden dwellings raised off the ground on piles. Given the discovery of Persian, Egyptian, Indian and Chinese artefacts (and even a gold coin depicting the Roman Emperor Marcus Aurelius) at Oc Eo sites, the port must have played host to a fair number of traders from around the world. To view **artefacts** from the site, visit the museums at Long Xuyen and Rach Gia, or the Fine Arts Museum in Ho Chi Minh City (see p.76). The Funan empire finally disappeared in the seventh century, when it was absorbed into the adjacent **Chen La** empire.

p.139. You'll find some of the cheapest rooms in town here (though those with a/c cost around double), but don't expect much in the way of service, and try to avoid proximity to the karaoke rooms. Rates exclusive of breakfast. $7

EATING

Hong Phat 242/4 Luong Van Cu ☎ 0216 384 2359; map p.139. Small, simple place with tasty Chinese and Vietnamese fish and meat dishes (most mains 50,000–70,000đ) in a clean, brightly lit dining room. The menu's in English, too – try the ribs stewed with pepper. Daily 9am–9pm.

KFC 59b Ly Tu Trong; map p.139. As a change from local food, or if you just need a/c and a chocolate sundae, you'll find this place – part of a fried chicken chain of some kind, according to staff – near the cathedral. Daily 9am–10pm.

Long Xuyen 19 Nguyen Van Cung ☎ 0216 384 1927; map p.139. The most reliable restaurant in town is at this otherwise disappointing hotel, whose ground-floor restaurant serves tasty dishes such as shrimp fried with cauliflower (80,000đ) and steak and chips for just 50,000đ. Daily 6am–10pm.

DIRECTORY

Banks Vietinbank, just north of the *Long Xuyen* on Luong Van Cu, can exchange money and also has an ATM.

Hospital The town's hospital is north of the centre on Le Loi.

Post office Long Xuyen's post office (daily 6am–10pm) is at 106 Tran Hung Dao, to the north of the centre.

Can Tho and around

At the confluence of the Can Tho and Hau Giang rivers, there's a lot to like about **CAN THO**. Though the delta's largest city by some way, with a population of just over one million, its riverside centre is refreshingly urbane – not to mention something of a surprise, after you've navigated your way through the urban sprawl encasing the town. Can Tho was the last city to succumb to the North Vietnamese Army, a day after the fall of Saigon, on May 1, 1975 – the date that has come to represent the reunification of the country. The former US air base opened up in 2011 to commercial flights, the year after the giant Can Tho bridge was completed, and both of these major projects have enabled the city to become the de facto capital of the delta.

As with so many settlements in the area, Can Tho is a little short on actual sights, although it does boast some of the region's best restaurants, and the bridges to the north and east of the centre provide access to some fantastic walks. In addition, abundant **rice fields** are never far away, and at the intersections of the canals and rivers that thread between them are some of the delta's best-known **floating markets**. All in all, it's perhaps the delta's best place in which to take a **boat trip**.

Can Tho Museum

1 Hoa Binh • Tues–Thurs 8–11am & 2–5pm, Sat & Sun 8–11am & 6.30–9pm • Free

Broad Hoa Binh is the city's backbone and is the site of the impressive **Can Tho Museum**, which presents "the history of the resistance against foreign aggression of Can Tho people" as well as local economic and social achievements. Despite the enormity of the place and the extensive signs in English, it's all a bit drab apart from a few highlights like models of a teahouse and a herbalist treating patients. The whole place was under renovation at the time of research – here's hoping for some more interesting exhibits.

Munirangsyaram Pagoda

36 Hoa Binh • Daily 7.30am–5pm • Free

Southwest of the Can Tho Museum, the 1946-built **Munirangsyaram Pagoda** warrants examination only if the more impressive Khmer pagodas around Tra Vinh or Soc Trang aren't on your itinerary. Entrance into the pagoda compound is through a top-heavy stone gate weighed down with masonry reminiscent of Angkor Wat, but there is little to see inside apart from a few plaster Buddha images.

2

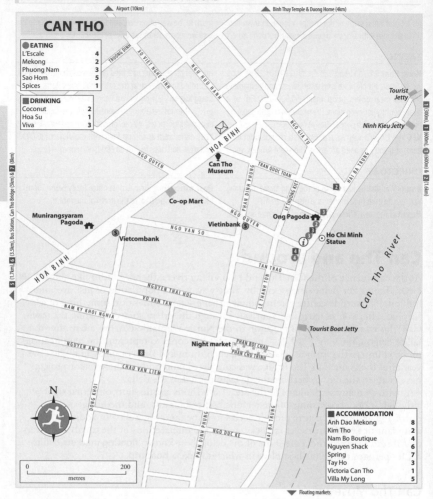

CAN THO

Airport (10km)

Binh Thuy Temple & Duong Home (4km)

● EATING
L'Escale	4
Mekong	2
Phuong Nam	3
Sao Hom	5
Spices	1

■ DRINKING
Coconut	2
Hoa Su	1
Viva	3

TRUONG DINH
VO VIET NGHE TINH
NGU HUU HANH
NGO GIA TU
Tourist Jetty
Ninh Kieu Jetty
HOA BINH
NGO QUYEN
Can Tho Museum
TRAN QUOC TOAN
PHAN DINH PHUNG
HAI BA TRUNG
Co-op Mart
LY THUONG KIET
NGO QUYEN
Ong Pagoda
Munirangsyaram Pagoda
Vietinbank
Ho Chi Minh Statue
Vietcombank
NGO VAN SO
TAN TRAO
HOA BINH
LE THANH TON
NGUYEN THAI HOC
VO VAN TAN
NAM KY KHOI NGHIA
Tourist Boat Jetty
NGUYEN AN NINH
PHAN BOI CHAU
Night market
PHAN CHU TRINH
CHAU VAN LIEM
N
DONG KHOI
PHAN DINH PHUNG
NGO DUC KE
HAI BA TRUNG
Can Tho River

■ ACCOMMODATION
Anh Dao Mekong	8
Kim Tho	2
Nam Bo Boutique	4
Nguyen Shack	6
Spring	7
Tay Ho	3
Victoria Can Tho	1
Villa My Long	5

0 — 200 metres

Floating markets

Ong Pagoda

32 Hai Ba Trung • Daily 6.30am–8pm • Free

Just north of the Uncle Ho statue on the river promenade (see box opposite), **Ong Pagoda** is a colourful place built in the late nineteenth century by wealthy Chinese townsman Huynh An Thai. Inside, a ruddy-faced Quan Cong presides, flaunting Rio Carnival-style headgear. On his left is Than Tai, to whom a string of families come on the first day of every month, asking for money and good fortune. On his right is Thien Hau, the protector of sailors. There's also a small chamber dedicated to Quan Am to the left of the main hall.

The Duong Home

144 Bui Huu Nghia • Daily 8am–noon & 2–5pm • Small donation expected

Down a sidestreet opposite Binh Thuy Temple is the beautiful **Duong Home**, which was used in the 1992 filming of *The Lover* (see box, p.489). A classic example of French colonial architecture, and completed in 1870, its shuttered windows and elaborate stucco decorations conceal a spacious living room featuring period furnishings with mother-of-pearl inlay. Note the intricately carved panels beside the pillars, where a bat sits at the summit of a menagerie of animals; unlike in the West, where bats symbolize vampires, in the East they are seen as a portent of good luck. The current residents are often on hand to show visitors round, and the adjacent orchid garden contains what is thought to be the tallest cactus in the country.

Binh Thuy Temple

Le Hong Phong, 6km north of Can Tho • Daily 7.30–10.30am & 1.30–5.30pm • Free • From 100,000đ return by xe om

Along the road to Long Xuyen, the **Binh Thuy Temple** began life in the nineteenth century as a *dinh*, or communal house for travellers to rest in. The present building dates back to 1909, and immediately catches the eye with its green-tiled eaves framed by frangipani trees. Though it appears small from outside, the cool interior runs very deep, and the walls are decorated with images of Chinese gods and Vietnamese heroes. Between the sturdy wooden pillars are several altars, with some ghoulish characters guarding one of them with axes raised.

ARRIVAL AND DEPARTURE

CAN THO AND AROUND

By plane Can Tho's aiport is at Tra Noc, about 11km northwest of the city centre, and inside you'll find a cafeteria, souvenir shops, currency exchange, hotel booking services and tourist information desks. Taxis (around 180,000đ) and xe om (more like 100,000đ) await arriving planes. Services are slowly being added (bar the one from HCMC, which was taken away); in addition to the following destinations, there are occasional charters from Thailand and Taiwan, and ones from mainland China may follow in due course.

Destinations Con Dao (daily; 1hr); Da Nang (daily; 1hr 30min); Hanoi (4 daily; 2hr); Phu Quoc (daily; 50min).

By bus In 2010 the much-touted bridge across the Hau Giang River to Can Tho was finally completed, cutting travel time to and from Ho Chi Minh City. The main station is a horrid affair on Nguyen Van Linh, 2km southwest of the centre (walkable, or peanuts by taxi or xe om). If travelling with Futa (ⓦ futabus .vn), you'll be dropped at their station about 5km across the river to the east – not so bad if you're coming from the north, but from destinations west and south you might beg to jump off in the city centre, lest you waste almost an hour heading to the station, then back the same way on a free shuttle.

Destinations Bac Lieu (3hr); Ca Mau (4hr); Chau Doc (3hr); Ha Tien (5hr); HCMC (3hr 30min); Long Xuyen (1hr 30min); My Tho (2hr 30min).

TOURS

Can Tho Tourist 50 Hai Ba Trung ☎ 0292 382 7674, ⓦ canthotourist.vn. Organizes all sorts of tours around the area, as well as cooking and city tours closer to the centre, though most of the prices are dependent upon how many book onto a particular tour – ask the day before, and they should have a pretty good idea of what's going on.

GOING FOR A STROLL IN CAN THO

With few sights to pick from, most visitors to Can Tho end up simply going for a nice walk. The main magnet is, inevitably, the city's **riverside promenade**, which features an imposing silver **statue** of a waving Uncle Ho and is now lined by beds of plants and stone seats. As with most delta towns, this riverside area gets crowded in the evenings as locals come out for a stroll in the cooler air. Waterfront **cafés** will rustle up some fresh coconut juice or a pot of green tea, and from your seat you can watch the relentless sampan traffic of the Can Tho River.

Just to the north, a stylish new **pedestrian bridge** (which is beautifully illuminated at night) leads to the *Victoria Can Tho* resort (see p.145), and the path continues along the riverfront for a couple of kilometres – in Vietnam, it's a pleasure to walk for so long without seeing, or hearing, any motorbikes, and you can even drop in at a couple of cafés and restaurants on the way.

Alternatively, take a **ferry** across the river from central Can Tho (2000đ), and turn right along the riverbank; after 2km you'll reach the **river bridge**, which will bring you back to the city centre. This walk is certainly not pedestrianized, but what you'll see on the way is a quintessential slice of Mekong Delta life – locals will be surprised to see foreigners in these parts, and you'll doubtless be tempted to spend some dong at a neighbourhood shop, café or snack shack.

2

CAN THO: BOAT TRIPS AND FLOATING MARKETS

Early every morning, an armada of boats takes to the web of waterways spun across Can Tho province and makes for one of its **floating markets**. While custom is declining at both (though tourism remains the same – see box, p.116), you'll still see all sorts on sale, from haircuts to coffins, though predictably fruit and vegetables make up most of what's on offer. Each boat's produce is identifiable by a sample hanging off a bamboo mast in its bow, but it's difficult to get colourful pictures, as the produce is stored below.

CAI RANG

Just 7km out of Can Tho is **Cai Rang**, the most commonly visited of the two major nearby markets, best visited between 7 and 8am, and particularly active on Sundays. You'll have to be prepared to queue up with all the other tourist boats before you can weave among the fervent waterborne activity, where you'll see drinks vendors clamouring to make a sale – some have made a wonderfully logical attempt to counter the recent decrease in traditional custom by turning their vessels into "floating bars", and selling dawn drinks to bleary-eyed tourists.

PHONG DIEN

Another 10km west from Cai Rang and you're at modest **Phong Dien**, whose appeal is that it sees relatively few tourists and correspondingly friendly locals. Again, custom is decreasing here, but it's still a wonderful spectacle to see huge baskets of fruit or vegetables hoisted from vessel to vessel.

VISITING THE MARKETS

Most **organized tours** take you to Cai Rang or Phong Dien early in the morning, then make a leisurely return to the city via the maze of picturesque canals and orchards that surround it, usually stopping to sample star fruit and sapodilla, longan and rambutan along the way. Agencies charge between 200,000đ and 250,000đ per person for such a tour, depending on the itinerary and type of boat. As usual, **unofficial boat operators** are cheaper, charging about 150,000đ per hour for a simple sampan: women prowl for customers along Hai Ba Trung, and some can be friendly and informative, but be on the lookout for scams. Do note that most boats have no shelter from sun or rain; bring a hat, sun-block and water. Phong Dien is more easily reached by hiring a xe om (about 100,000đ), then renting a sampan locally (about 100,000đ) for an hour's rowing among the buyers and sellers.

Hieu's Tours 27a Le Thanh Ton ☎0292 381 9958, ⓦhieutour.com. Put together good trips including floating market visits (from 565,000đ; prices are lower if you forego the cacao farm option), cycle and motorbike tours (around 900,000đ each), and short (non-market) morning boat trips.

Trans Mekong 144 Hai Ba Trung ☎0292 382 9540, ⓦtransmekong.com. A very reliable operator. Join them for a breakfast cruise in the morning (935,000đ; minimum two) or try the 3pm cycle tour, which will see you dashing through fields and making use of the local ferries (450,000đ).

ACCOMMODATION

Hai Ba Trung and Chau Van Liem together form the axis of Can Tho's thriving **hotel** scene, with the more expensive and mid-range properties clustered around the northern end of Hai Ba Trung, and budget places located around Chau Van Liem and streets further south.

CITY CENTRE

Anh Dao Mekong 70 Nguyen An Ninh ☎0292 381 9501, ⓦanhdaomekonghotel.com; map p.142. This relatively new venue is the city's best "flashpacker" option, with a range of spotless, stylishly designed rooms. 〒30

Kim Tho 1a Ngo Gia Tu ☎0292 222 2228, ⓦkimtho .com; map p.142. Squeezing in beside the established hotels along the riverfront, this twelve-storey place is giving stiff competition with its state-of-the-art fixtures

and fittings, plus sweeping river views. There's a nice café on the ground level. 〒45

Nam Bo Boutique 1 Ngo Quyen ☎0292 381 9138, ⓦnambocantho.com; map p.142. Renovated colonial building that accommodates not only L'Escale restaurant (see opposite), but also a boutique hotel with just seven rooms. While not particularly spacious, they're all suitably plush, and you can head up on to the rooftop restaurant-bar for some lovely river views. 〒130

★**Spring** 22 Khu Dan Cu ☎0292 383 9723; map p.142. Just south of the centre, this is exactly what you want of a cheap guesthouse – attractive rooms, attentive staff, hot water, a little telly, comfy beds, and a sense of security. However, this place does more than merely ticking all the simple boxes – it's a great deal. Breakfast extra. $18

Tay Ho 42 Hai Ba Trung ☎0292 382 3392; map p.142. After a thorough renovation, this cheap and cheerful place right on the riverfront stands out as the best budget deal in town, especially if you can get one of the two rooms with riverfront views ($15). Staff are adept at organizing boat tours, right down to the hand-drawn explanatory maps. No breakfast. $14

Victoria Can Tho Cai Khe Ward ☎0292 381 0111, ⓦvictoriahotels-asia.com; map p.142. Built and furnished in classic French-colonial style, but with all the modern facilities you'd expect from the delta's first international-standard hotel. It's set in a grand riverside location across a bridge to the north of the town centre, and is surrounded by lush tropical growth. $220

OUTSIDE THE CENTRE

★**Nguyen Shack** Thanh My, Thuong Thanh Ward ☎0292 628 8688, ⓦnguyenshack.com; map p.142. A collection of shacks, indeed, but a rather good one – way out in the countryside around 8km south of the city centre, this is an ideal place from which to take the pulse of delta life. The hut-rooms have rather more in the way of amenities than you'd guess from the outside (including fans and even minibars), while the on-site restaurant comes in very handy this far from "regular" civilization. Some of the proceeds go towards educating local children. $22

★**Villa My Long** Nguyen Van Cu, Phong Dien Ward ☎090 300 7811, ⓦvillamylong.com; map p.142. Straddling the boundary between homestay and boutique hotel, this riverside establishment belies its remote location with tidy, a/c rooms. If you want the full experience, take a dip in the communal hot tub, or get picked up from central Can Tho by boat (for an additional fee). $40

EATING

Can Tho is well endowed with good, affordable **restaurants**, most serving Vietnamese food, though there are plenty that also offer international dishes – those along Hai Ba Trung target a primarily foreign clientele, while locals tend to patronize places around the **market** and along Nam Ky Khoi Nghia. A couple of the options listed in the Drinking section (see below) are actually decent restaurants too; also make note of the **ferry-restaurants** that launch from the promenade just before sunset, and the **night market** that fills Phan Boi Chau and Phan Chu Trinh each evening.

L'Escale Nam Bo Boutique, 1 Ngo Quyen ☎0292 381 9138; map p.142. While the *Nam Bo Boutique* has a charming lobby-level restaurant, resplendent with attractive furnishings, swirling fans and the like, its menu is almost the same as (though more expensive than) *Sao Hom* (see opposite). The roof restaurant has different options, with a pleasing French twist – try onion gratin soup (90,000đ) or a *crème brûlée* (65,000đ) with a stunner of a view out over the river. Loads of wine, too. Daily 7am–11pm.

★**Mekong** 38 Hai Ba Trung ☎0292 382 1646; map p.142. This long-established favourite is still hard to top for its cheap, flavoursome Vietnamese, Chinese and Western meals – try a square pizza (those right-angles sure are tasty) for 68,000đ, tacos from 35,000đ, or cheap local staples like *bun xao* or *banh xeo* from 35,000đ. Daily 8am–2pm & 4–10pm.

Phuong Nam 48 Hai Ba Trung ☎0292 381 2077; map p.142. This place enjoys a great riverfront location, and has a few "odd" menu items alongside the cheap local and international favourites – try snake meat, curried or with satay sauce (150,000đ), crocodile steak with fries (160,000đ), or ostrich in steak or sautéed form (150,000đ). Daily 10am–2pm & 5–10pm.

★**Sao Hom** Hai Ba Trung ☎0292 381 5616; map p.142. Most of Can Tho's riverfront restaurants are actually separated from the water by Hai Ba Trung, but this wonderful place, housed under an almost market-like roof, is perched just above the ripples – right next to where hungry tourists disembark from boat trips. Despite this, prices are low and quality very high; the pumpkin flower fritters (70,000đ) and fish fried in tamarind sauce (140,000đ) are recommended, though there are Western items such as quiche, spaghetti and duck à l'orange here too, as well as special steamboat and snake-meat sets. Daily 6am–11pm.

Spices Victoria Can Tho hotel, Cai Khe Ward ☎0292 381 0111; map p.142. Enjoy fine dining in a tastefully decorated interior, or outside nearer the swimming pool – you've got to dig those colonial-style floor tiles. The extensive menu has everything from gazpacho (208,000đ) to salmon gravlax (140,000đ) for starters, while the Viet and Western mains (from 210,000đ) include pasta, lamb shank and the like. Daily 6am–10pm.

DRINKING

Can Tho has few decent dedicated places to drink – most people just add booze to their dinner bill, since many of the restaurants listed here (see p.146) also function as atmospheric drinking spots.

2

Coconut Cai Khe, off Song Hau ☎ 0292 654 6888; map p.142. Ostensibly a seafood restaurant, this place is almost better for a sunset beer (just 15,000đ), or even a coffee or juice. Set on a weird little "beach" at the end of the path leading from the *Victoria Can Tho* (see box, p.143), its cream-yellow-orange tricolore of plastic chairs sit almost entirely unoccupied until evening – kick back and watch the Mekong traffic sliding past. Daily 7am–11pm.

Hoa Su By the pedestrian bridge, off Song Hau ☎ 0292 382 0717; map p.142. Like *Coconut* (see above), this is actually a restaurant, though one which makes a fine place to drink. It's a ramshackle maze of stilthouses, connected with a lattice of creaking boardwalks, so it's quite worthy of a few photos, and particularly pretty at sunset. Beers are just 13,000đ, and the Vietnamese food's pretty good – the stuffed pumpkin flowers (60,000đ) are recommended. Daily 7am–10pm.

Viva 26 Hai Ba Trung ☎ 0292 381 8485; map p.142. For once, this bar *isn't* a restaurant – it's a cheap hotel. But the lobby bar (essentially the main focus of the business) sees customers spilling out into the street most evenings, and it stays open until just before dawn – making it a real backpacker hub. Beers go from just 25,000đ, cocktails for double that, and there are even shishas to puff on for 180,000đ. Daily noon–4am.

DIRECTORY

Banks Try Vietcombank, 7 Hoa Binh (Mon–Fri 7–11am & 1–5pm), or Vietinbank at 9 Phan Dinh Phung (Mon–Fri 7.30am–noon & 1–6pm).

Hospital The general hospital is located 3km west of the centre on Highway 91B.

Pharmacy You'll find pharmacies at 31b Chau Van Liem and 78 Hai Ba Trung.

Police The police station is based at 67–69 Hung Vuong, northwest of the city centre.

Post office Visit 2 Hoa Binh (daily 6am–9pm).

Sports Non-residents can use the swimming pool and tennis courts at *Victoria Can Tho* hotel (floodlit in the evening) for a few dollars.

Supermarket There is a huge Co-op Mart at the junction of Hoa Binh and Ngo Quyen, and another supermarket in the new Vincom Plaza mall off Ba Muoi Thang Tu, south of the centre.

Soc Trang and around

Straddling an oily branch of the Mekong, **SOC TRANG** lacks the panache of other delta towns – but as it has a sizeable population of ethnic Khmer, a visit here is almost like getting a free, short-term Cambodian visa. A waterway running roughly west to east splits Soc Trang in two, though most of the town nestles on the south bank. Hai Ba Trung is the town's backbone, and it runs across the water before morphing into Tran Hung Dao on the southern outskirts.

On the fifteenth day of the tenth lunar month (between November and December), Soc Trang springs into life as thousands converge to see traditional Khmer boats (*thuyen dua*) racing each other during the **Oc Om Boc festival**.

Khleang Pagoda

Nguyen Chi Thanh • Dawn to dusk • Free

Khmer pagodas are ten-a-penny in this region, but the **Khleang Pagoda**, located in the heart of Soc Trang, is one of the most impressive. A two-tiered terrace surrounds it, and its doors and windows are adorned with traditional Khmer motifs in greens, reds and golds. Inside is a wonderful golden Sakyamuni statue, though unfortunately the doors are often locked.

Khmer Museum

23 Nguyen Chi Thanh • Mon–Sat 7.30–11.30am & 1.30–4.30pm • Free

Directly opposite the Khleang Pagoda, the **Khmer Museum** houses some low-key exhibits, including stringed instruments made of snakeskin and coconut husks, and some wonderfully colourful food covers, shaped like conical hats but with a stippled surface.

Dat Set Pagoda

163 Mau Than 68 • Dawn to dusk • Free

Head north from the Khleang Pagoda along Mau Than 68 for a few minutes, and you'll eventually come across the **Dat Set Pagoda** on the right. Also known as the Buu Son Tu Pagoda, it is constructed almost entirely from clay, save for a smart sheet-metal roof to keep the rain off. Dat Set makes a welcome change from the more numerous Khmer pagodas in this region of the delta. Chinese visitors flock here to see the pagoda's impressive and highly colourful collection of clay statues; many are life-size, with animals and figures from Chinese mythology the most popular subjects. The pagoda is also home to some truly gargantuan candles that look like pillars, weigh around 200kg each and are said to last for seventy years of continuous burning.

Mahatup Pagoda

2km south of Soc Trang off Le Hong Phong • Dawn to dusk • Free • Around 50,000đ by xe om, including waiting time; taxis cannot proceed directly to the pagoda

Mahatup Pagoda, aka the Bat Pagoda, is famed for its vast community of golden-bodied **fruit bats**, which spectacularly take to the skies at dusk. A fire in 2007 destroyed much of the main building, but reconstruction proceeded smoothly and a large pond has now been added behind the temple. Plan to get here around 5.30pm – as the drop in temperature wakes the bats, you'll see them spinning, preening and flapping their black wings, which can span as much as 1.5m.

Khmer monks have worshipped at this site for four hundred years, and it is often busy with Vietnamese visitors. Inside, bright murals bearing the names of the Khmer communities around the world that financed them recount the life of the Buddha. Outside, look out for the graves of four pigs behind the large hall to the right opposite the pagoda, each of which had five toenails (pigs usually have four). Since such animals are believed to bring bad luck, they are honoured with well-tended resting places to ward off any evil tendencies. The tombstones are painted with their likenesses and the dates of their passing on.

ARRIVAL AND DEPARTURE
SOC TRANG AND AROUND

By bus The bus station is at the northern end of town on Nguyen Chi Thanh. Buses to Ho Chi Minh City leave every half an hour; services are less frequent to other destinations in the delta, though for Can Tho, Vinh Long and My Tho you can opt to pay the full price to HCMC and travel in comfort before jumping off en route.

Destinations Bac Lieu (1hr 30min); Ca Mau (3hr); Can Tho (1hr 30min); HCMC (5hr); My Tho (3hr 30min); Vinh Long (2hr).

INFORMATION

Tourist information Staff at Soc Trang Tourist, at 104 Le Loi (daily 7–11am & 1.30–5pm; ☎0299 382 2024), can usually help with local information.

Services The post office is in the centre of town at 1 Tran Hung Dao. There's an ATM in front of the *Khanh Hung* hotel.

ACCOMMODATION AND EATING

Khanh Hung 17 Tran Hung Dao ☎0299 382 1026. Located in the centre of town, this place has 53 rooms ranging from basic and cheap up to carpeted suites that have seen better days. Its central location and friendly staff make it a convenient base, but check a few different rooms before deciding. The handy, on-site restaurant won't win any prizes, but it's just about the only place in town with an English menu. ‾$10‾

Phu Qui 3km out of town at Km2127 on Highway 1 ☎0299 361 1811, ⊛phuquihotel.com. Right in the thick of things, this is a very decent option – at least, once you get past the vehicle-filled entry area so beloved of lower-end Vietnamese accommodation. The rooms themselves do the job, and are usually kept super-clean. Breakfast extra. ‾$14‾

Bac Lieu and around

Beyond Soc Trang the landscape becomes progressively more waterlogged, and palms hug the banks of the canals that crisscross it. A little over 40km southwest of Soc Trang, Highway 1 dips south towards the town of **BAC LIEU**, before veering off west to Ca Mau. It may be the back end of nowhere, but even so Bac Lieu's prosperity is evident in the new shopping complexes and upmarket homes around its centre. The source of this prosperity is overseas Vietnamese, many of whom hail from this region. Although there are few sights to set the pulse racing, the town has the only accommodation between Soc Trang and Ca Mau, and is in good proximity to the nearby **Bac Lieu Bird Sanctuary**.

Bac Lieu Bird Sanctuary

Daily 7.30am–5pm • 15,000đ • Arrange transport through Bac Lieu Tourist Company (see below)

Well worth the visit, the **Bac Lieu Bird Sanctuary** is 6km southwest of Bac Lieu, towards the coast. There is an observation tower and a number of paths that crisscross the cajeput forest, along which local guides can lead you. Lots of birds can be seen here from July to December, including herons, egrets and, just possibly, endangered painted storks, but there is little to see from January to June. Guides are necessary and will appreciate a tip, even though their English skills are limited.

ARRIVAL AND DEPARTURE
BAC LIEU AND AROUND

By bus The bus station is 1.5km west of town. There are frequent departures to HCMC, as well as less regular departures to other destinations across the delta; if you'd like to hit Can Tho, My Tho or some of the other towns north, HCMC-bound buses will take you, though you may have to pay the full route fare. Some buses also head west to Ca Mau. Destinations Ca Mau (2hr); Can Tho (3hr); HCMC (6hr); My Tho (4hr 30min).

INFORMATION

Tourist information The Bac Lieu Tourist Company, at 2 Hoang Van Thu (daily 7–11am & 1–5pm; ☎ 0291 382 4272), is next to the *Saigon Bac Lieu* – but don't expect much.

Services Sacombank at 82 Tran Phu can exchange money and has an ATM; the post office is in the centre of town at 20 Tran Phu.

ACCOMMODATION

Cong Tu 13 Dien Bien Phu ☎ 0291 395 3304. For a bit of character, head to this palatial colonial villa on the riverside. It boasts just ten rooms with fancy furnishings and high ceilings, so finds itself quite popular – it's best to book ahead. $18

★**Saigon Bac Lieu** 4–6 Hoang Van Thu ☎ 0291 395 9697. The town's main hotel has recently been brought under the banner of the giant Saigon organization, and is all the better for it. Rooms are a decent size, and come complete with a/c and cable TV, but some of their en-suite bathrooms are – as part of the glass-enclosed plague now spreading around the hotel world – a little visible, and sometimes audible, from the beds. Their restaurant also makes a decent place to eat. $30

EATING AND DRINKING

Cong Tu 13 Dien Bien Phu ☎ 0291 395 3304. The café at this hotel is highly atmospheric, with tables spread around a covered courtyard, and its wide-ranging menu includes lots of fish dishes. Mains from 55,000đ. Daily 7am–10pm.

Kitty Cnr of Ba Trieu and Tran Phu ☎ 0291 399 7777. Your best option for nightlife in Bac Lieu is to join the overseas Vietnamese at this first-floor bar, which wouldn't look out of place in HCMC. They serve cocktails, beers and coffee for national-norm prices, as well as a reasonable range of Vietnamese dishes. Daily 6pm–2am.

Ca Mau and around

A pancake-flat region composed of silt deposited by the Mekong, the **Ca Mau Peninsula** constitutes not only the end of mainland Vietnam, but of former Indochina as well. **CA MAU** itself, Vietnam's southernmost town of any size, has a frontier feel to it, though rapid development has brought many changes since 1989, when travel writer Justin Wintle described it as a "scrappy clutter… a backyard town in a backyard province" – though there are still pockets of squalor here and there. Ca Mau sprawls across a vast area, with broad boulevards connected by potholed lanes and a couple of busy bridges spanning the Phung Hiep Canal that splits the town in two. To the west, the town is bordered by the Ganh Hao River, which snakes past as though trying to wriggle free before the encroaching stilthouses squeeze the life from it.

Although few Western travellers currently visit Ca Mau, there are speedboats that cover the journey to and from Rach Gia in less than three hours, while improvements to Highway 63 have made the journey by road less arduous. Incorporating Ca Mau in a circular tour of the area is now a tempting possibility, as it takes you off the tourist trail and through some classic delta scenes.

The **marshes** encircling Ca Mau form one of the largest areas of swampland in the world, covering about 1500 square kilometres and home to a variety of wading birds. As you might expect, the **waterways** are the most efficient means of travel in this part

2

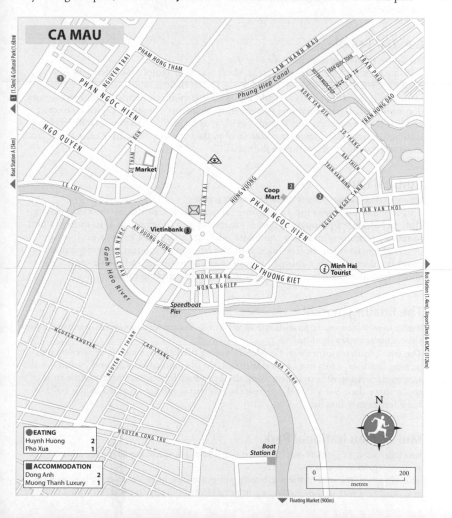

CA MAU

●EATING
Huynh Huong 2
Pho Xua 1

■ ACCOMMODATION
Dong Anh 2
Muong Thanh Luxury 1

0 — 200
metres

N

▼ Floating Market (900m)

of the country – a point pressed home by the slender ferries moored in all the villages the road passes. The Ca Mau Peninsula was once a stronghold of resistance against France and America, and for this it paid a heavy price, as US planes dumped millions of gallons of Agent Orange over it to rob guerrillas of jungle cover. Further damage has been done by the shrimp-farm industry, but resilient pockets of mangrove and cajeput forests remain, inhabited by sea birds, wading birds, waterfowl and also honey bees, attracted by the mangrove blossoms.

The market
Le Loi • Dawn to dusk

Along the north bank of the Phung Hiep Canal, which divides the town, is the rag-tag squall of the **market** that lurks on the banks of the canal. A shantytown of corrugated iron and canvas, it is a bustling centre for packing fish for sale and shipment. As such, it doesn't have the photogenic appeal of most delta markets – though it doesn't have the tourists, either.

Cao Dai Temple
Phan Ngoc Hien • Dawn to dusk; services usually noon & 6pm • Free

Worth a look for its ornate towers, Ca Mau's Cao Dai Temple is evidence of how deeply rooted the religion is in the Mekong Delta; these temples are a distinctive feature of many delta towns and add a playful splash of colour with their Disneyesque decorations. This particular one isn't great, to be honest – it scores high for concrete and low for atmosphere, and if you've made it as far as Ca Mau you'll doubtless have seen better examples. However, a couple of parks opposite the temple offer shady areas to escape the bustle of town near the canal.

Cultural Park
2km west of Ca Mau • Daily 8am–5.30pm • 10,000đ • About 30,000đ by xe om

This is one of the town's most intriguing attractions, at least during the rainy season (July to November), though its name is something of a misnomer. It is, in fact, a **bird sanctuary** teeming with storks and many other birds that nest in the trees in easily observed fenced-off areas. The huge park also has a mini-zoo featuring elephants, monkeys, deer and other animals, as well as lots of pavilions and picnic spots. Arrive about 4pm to explore the park, then watch the birds arriving to roost.

The floating market
Negotiate fee with boatmen; expect to pay around 200,000đ/boat for the 30–40min trip downstream and back • Boats from boat station B, south of town on west bank of Ganh Hao River

The two-kilometre journey to Ca Mau's floating market gives a taste of riverine life, passing factories, a fish market and warehouses, plus lots of flotsam and jetsam, on the way to see a string of boats advertising their produce by suspending a sample from sticks above their bows. A definite risk on this trip is getting splashed in the wake of huge ferries speeding by.

Mui Ca Mau National Park
About 100km south of Ca Mau • 10,000đ • Rent a speedboat or xe om to Dat Mui (see opposite), then either rent a local boat or hop on a xe om (about 60,000đ return) to Mui Ca Mau

This voyage to the end of the earth may not quite be a Jules Verne epic, but it's a fun and satisfying way to pass a day, as you get to visit not only the **southernmost point of**

Vietnam but also the end of mainland Southeast Asia. A road runs to **Mui Ca Mau National Park** from the isolated hamlet of Dat Mui, though to get further into the spirit of things you may prefer to negotiate a fare with a local boatman. The latter is also the best way of navigating the national park itself, though most visitors content themselves with a wander around the paths surrounding the main visitor centre – from these you'll make out wooden houses, shrimping ponds and the odd monkey bridge. You can take a photo of yourself standing beside a boat-shaped monument marking the latitude (8 degrees north) and longitude (104 degrees east) of this remote location, then gaze out over the endless ocean and the mountainous Khoai Island just off the coast. There's even a **lookout tower** from where you can get good views over the mangrove forests, and a restaurant on stilts over the water – the hammocks are a nice touch.

2

ARRIVAL AND DEPARTURE   CA MAU AND AROUND

By plane Vasco Airlines operates a daily flight from HCMC to Ca Mau airport (1hr), a few kilometres southeast of town on Highway 1; it's best to book through Vietnam Airlines (ⓦ vietnamairlines.com). A xe om into town will cost about 40,000đ, and there will be taxis (60,000đ) waiting too.
By bus Almost next door to the airport is the bus station, where buses from HCMC, Can Tho and other destinations pull up. Transport into town is again by xe om (40,000đ).

Destinations Bac Lieu (2hr); Can Tho (5hr); HCMC (8hr); Long Xuyen (5hr); Rach Gia (3hr 30min); Soc Trang (3hr).
By boat The most useful boat services are to be found at the speedboat pier, located on the south side of town at 162 Phan Boi Chau; from here you can get to Rach Gia (3hr; 140,000đ), Nam Can (1hr 15min; 80,000đ) or Dat Mui (for Mui Ca Mau National Park; 3hr; 165,000đ).

ACCOMMODATION

Dong Anh 25 Tran Hung Dao ☏0290 357 6666; map p.149. Those on a budget should aim for Tran Hung Dao in the centre; there are plenty of guesthouses hereabouts, though *Dong Anh* is the pick of the bunch. Breakfast is usually free if you book directly, and extra for booking-engine customers; it's served on an attractive rooftop patio boasting great views of the city centre. As for the rooms, well, they're absolutely fine. **$15**
Muong Thanh Luxury Nam Ky Khoi Nghia

☏0290 222 8888, ⓦluxurycamau.muongthanh.com; map p.149. The snazzy lobby doesn't lie – this is far and away the best place to stay in the whole province. Though it's a little distant from the city centre, those aiming at this price level may actually find this a plus-point; far from the grime and hubbub, you'll be able to soak your stresses away in the pool, or give the on-site spa a go. The views are great from the upper levels of the tower, so room-wise you should aim as high as possible. **$49**

EATING

★**Huynh Huong** Bui Thi Truong ☏0290 357 5566; map p.149. This café comes as a lovely surprise in remote Ca Mau. You'll find a variety of sitting areas, the most interesting one resembling an English garden with its

white-painted metal chairs, leafy canopies, dangling flowerpots, roses on the table, and grass that – though fake – is pleasant to bare feet. Coffees from 12,000đ, fruit juices 20,000–25,000đ. Daily 6am–10pm.

GET YOUR KICKS ON HIGHWAY 63

Of all the roads that crisscross the Mekong Delta, few have such a strong sense of what this watery world is all about as **Highway 63**, which zigzags north from Ca Mau to Minh Luong, just south of Rach Gia – a distance of a little over 100 kilometres. The road is sealed all the way, though it's often no wider than a single track road, and for most of its journey it follows narrow canals that carry a real hotchpotch of vessels going about their business. If you don't have your own transport, take a **bus** from Ca Mau to Rach Gia to follow this highway.

At **Vinh Tuan** it crosses a wide canal, allowing great views of river life, though parking on the bridge is illegal so you will need to park nearby and walk onto it. There are also several **monkey bridges** across the canals – fragile structures consisting of narrow tree trunks, which require the assured balance of a monkey to cross them (hence the name). Like many other aspects of local culture, monkey bridges are disappearing fast, but Highway 63 still offers a fascinating glimpse of traditional life in the delta. Near the end of the highway, you need to cross a wide river by ferry at Tac Cau, where you'll see huge fishing ships loading ice to freeze their catch.

Pho Xua 239 Phan Ngoc Hien ☎0290 356 6666; map p.149. Set in a traditional, wooden-pillared pavilion by a shaded garden, this is the best spot in town for a meal. It has a fairly extensive menu of Vietnamese dishes in English and plenty of appealing seafood options, many of which are priced by the kilo; try the shrimp stir-fry (85,000đ) or sautéed squid (125,000đ). This said, there's nothing wrong with their starters (55,000đ), soups (30,000đ) or rice dishes (from 95,000đ). Daily 8am–midnight.

DIRECTORY

Bank To exchange cash or use an ATM, head to Vietinbank at 94 Ly Thuong Kiet (Mon–Fri 7.30–11am & 1.30–4.30pm), or any number of other banks.

Post office The main post office (daily 6am–10pm) is opposite Vietinbank, on Luu Tan Tai.

Rach Gia

There's something a little special about **RACH GIA**, a thriving port community of around two hundred thousand people, teetering precariously over the Gulf of Thailand. For most foreign visitors it is simply a place to overnight en route to Phu Quoc Island, but stay on for the night and escape from the incessant motorbike buzz of the main streets, and you'll be able to bask in a languid, easygoing air stemming from the town's seaside location.

A small islet in the mouth of the Cai Lon River forms the hub of the town, but the urban sprawl spills over bridges to the north and south of it and onto the mainland. It's worth taking a walk along **Bach Dang** or **Tran Hung Dao** to watch the activity on the boats of all sizes that clutter the port. Men and women darn and fold nets, charcoal-sellers hawk their wares to ships' captains and roadside cafés heave with fishermen – many of whom have seen the bottoms of a few beer bottles – awaiting the next tide.

The museum

27 Nguyen Van Troi • Mon–Fri 7.30–11am & 1.30–5pm • Free

Rach Gia's **museum** is the single worthwhile sight in the town centre, and even that probably won't distract you for more than half an hour. The exterior will likely tempt you to take a few pictures – it's a charming old mansion painted a fetching shade of colonial lemon. Inside, exhibitions include wartime photos and souvenirs, and some relics from nearby Oc Eo – shards of pottery, coins and bones, and the skeleton of a whale in a mesh-fronted shed to the right of the main building. The place has been given a recent refurb, and is now attractively decorated with lacquered panels, though there's still little English-language signage.

THE HEROICS OF NGUYEN TRUNG TRUC

From 1861 to 1868, **Nguyen Trung Truc** spearheaded anti-French guerrilla activities in the western region of the delta: statues in the centre of Rach Gia and at the temple dedicated to him depict him preparing to unsheathe his sword and harvest a French head. In 1861, he masterminded the attack that culminated in the firing of the French warship *Esperance* – an event which, in the minds of many Vietnamese, signified that the tide of the conflict was about to change. As a wanted man, Truc was forced to retreat to Phu Quoc, from where he continued to oversee the campaign. Only after the French took his mother hostage in 1868 did he turn himself in and in October of the same year he was executed by a firing squad in the centre of Rach Gia. Defiant to the last, his final words could have been lifted from a Ho Chi Minh speech: "So long as grass still grows on the soil of this land, people will continue to resist the invaders."

Nguyen Trung Truc Temple

18 Nguyen Cong Tru • Dawn–dusk • Free

Of Rach Gia's handful of pagodas, only the **Nguyen Trung Truc Temple** is really worth making an effort to see. It's also conveniently located right next to the jetty from which hydrofoils leave for Phu Quoc, so if you enter or leave Rach Gia in this manner, it's quite possible to take a quick look on your way.

Inside, a portrait of Nguyen in a black robe and hat provides the main chamber with its centrepiece. Up at the altar, a brass urn flanked by slender storks standing on turtles is said to hold the ashes of local hero **Nguyen Trung Truc** (see box opposite). In front of the temple is a statue of Trung Truc drawing his sword; there's a similar one in the very centre of town (see map above).

ARRIVAL AND DEPARTURE   RACH GIA

By plane Arriving at the airport, it's a 7km taxi ride north into town (about 140,000đ).

Destinations HCMC (1–2 daily; 50min).

By bus Buses to and from points north (such as Ha Tien) pull up at Rach Gia's local bus station on Nguyen Binh Kiem, 500m north of the town centre. Arrivals and departures from other destinations use the bigger bus terminal at Rach Soi, near the airport, 7km southeast of Rach Gia; a taxi will cost around 125,000đ, though Futa (ⓦfutabus.vn) will pick up or drop off for free.

Destinations Ca Mau (3hr 30min); Can Tho (3hr); Ha Tien (2hr); HCMC (6–7hr); Long Xuyen (2hr).

By boat Arriving and departing boats use one of two piers. Daily services to and from Phu Quoc Island depart from the small quay 200m west of the Nguyen Trung Truc Temple; at the time of research, they left Rach Gia at 8am, 1pm & 3pm (250,000đ; 2hr 30min). Buy your ticket the day before, if possible, from the Superdong office near the pier (☎ 0297 387 7742); staff at your accommodation may also be able to help. From Rach Meo quay, 5km south of town on Ngo Quyen, boats leave for and arrive from Ca Mau (3hr; 175,000đ) as well as other destinations in the delta.

ACCOMMODATION

★**Hoa Binh-Rach Gia** 3–7 Co Bac ☎ 0297 355 3355, ⓦ hoabinhrachgiaresort.com.vn; map p.153. Part of the Hoa Binh chain, this new hotel is by far Rach Gia's most appealing accommodation option. Within walking distance of the seafront promenade, it's a relaxed venue with a charming, foliage-surrounded pool, a decent café (see below), and friendly, English-speaking staff. $40

Kim Co 141 Nguyen Hung Son ☎ 0297 738 79610; map p.153. Centrally located, and emblazoned with aquamarine go-faster stripes, this is probably the most convenient budget option in town; its brightly painted, good-sized rooms come with cable TV. No breakfast. $15

Sealight A11, 3 Thang 2 ☎ 0297 625 5777, ⓦ sealighthotel.vn; map p.153. A weird place: towering nineteen storeys over the Rach Gia coastline, it stands out like a sore thumb, and rather bizarrely most windows in its rooms face the city, rather than the sea. There are never anywhere near enough guests, and its echoey lobby seems rather forlorn. However, such bad planning makes for good-value rooms, which are comfy enough, especially at deluxe level ($30) and above. $20

EATING

★**Gio Bien** Off Ton Duc Thang ☎ 0297 387 7865; map p.153. Stuck out on a pier south of the centre, and with far more staff than should be necessary, this is a highly appealing place to eat seafood, and by far the most atmospheric place to drink in town – it's apparently open all night (feel free to put this to the test), and beers are just 14,000đ. Happily for a seafood place, many of their dishes are set-price rather than pay-by-weight; 90,000đ will get you a plate of squid, sea snails or scallops cooked in various ways. Daily 24hr.

Hoa Binh-Rach Gia 3–7 Co Bac ☎ 0297 355 3355; map p.153. The riverside seating area of this charming hotel (see above) is certainly the most urbane place to eat or drink in Rach Gia, and worth a visit even if you're not staying here. The menu is bafflingly extensive, with all kinds of exotic meats such as turtle and venison, but Vietnamese staples like fish in clay pot (55,000đ) are safest. They also do coffee and juices, and serve alcohol. Daily 10am–10pm.

Ha Tien

Small, breezy and extremely likeable, **HA TIEN** is not your typical delta town – here it's the sea, rather than an assortment of rivers and rivulets, that shapes the place. It's now buzzing with Western travellers for two reasons – one, the **hydrofoil** services to Phu Quoc Island, which are faster than those from Rach Gia; and two, the town's proximity not only to the **Cambodian border**, but the popular Cambodian coastal towns of Kampot, Kep and Sihanoukville, which are all a minibus- or taxi-ride away. This town, which until fairly recently had an end-of-the-line feel, is now brimming with commerce, and adjusting to its newfound popularity.

Central Ha Tien still has a few quaint, shuttered **colonial buildings** in its backstreets, though recent beautifications include the new market buildings (which still smell like the old ones), a pleasant boulevard area where the old market once stood, and a fountain and walking paths along the so-called East Lake (Dong Ho). The "lake" is, in fact, a large inlet where the To Chau River flows out to the sea, and its banks now make for an enjoyable place to stroll as you can watch the fishing boats unloading on the opposite bank, and (if you're in luck) enjoy an agreeable breeze.

Brief history

Founded by Chinese immigrant **Mac Cuu** in 1674, with the permission of the local Cambodian lords, **Ha Tien** thrived thanks to its position facing the Gulf of Thailand and astride the trade route between India and China. By the close of the seventeenth century, Siam (later Thailand) had begun to eye the settlement covetously, and Mac

Cuu was forced to petition Hue for support. The resulting alliance, forged with Emperor Minh Vuong in 1708, ensured Vietnamese military protection, and the town continued to prosper. Mac Cuu died in 1735, but the familial fiefdom continued for seven generations, until the French took over in 1867. Subsequently, Ha Tien became a resistance flashpoint, with Viet Minh holing up in the surrounding hills, and even sniping at French troops from the **To Chau Mountain**, to the south.

Tam Bao Pagoda

At junction of Mac Thien Tich and Phuong Thanh • Dawn–dusk • Free

The colourful **Tam Bao Pagoda** is set in tree-lined grounds dominated by an attractive lotus pond, a thirteen-storey tower and a large reclining Buddha. Out the back of the pagoda, said to have been founded by Mac Cuu himself, is a pretty garden tended by the resident nuns, its colourful flowers interspersed with tombs. In the rear chamber of the pagoda, a statue of the goddess with a thousand hands and a thousand eyes sits on a lurid pink lotus, while behind her are photos and funerary tablets remembering the local dead.

Mac Cuu temple and burial place

Off Mac Cuu • Dawn to dusk • Free

Mac Cuu lies buried on a hillside rising from a road named after him, just northwest of the centre. Before ascending the hill, check out his temple at the base; here, electric candles flicker constantly before Mac Cuu's funerary tablet, keeping the memory of Ha Tien's founding father alive. His actual **grave** is further up the hill, guarded by two

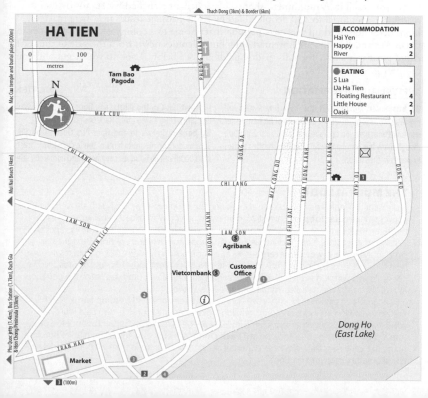

HA TIEN

Thach Dong (3km) & Border (6km)

ACCOMMODATION	
Hai Yen	1
Happy	3
River	2

EATING	
5 Lua	3
Da Ha Tien	
Floating Restaurant	4
Little House	2
Oasis	1

Tam Bao Pagoda

Dong Ho (East Lake)

Agribank

Vietcombank

Customs Office

Market

swordsmen and statues of a white tiger and a blue dragon; you'll be able to ascend further for partial views over the mop-tops of the coconut trees below and down to the sea.

Mui Nai beach

5km west of the centre • 10,000đ beach entry fee usually levied

A pleasant – if not idyllic – 400m-long curve of sand, shaded by coconut palms and backed by lush green hills, **Mui Nai beach** offers reasonable swimming in clean, shallow waters. The beach is very popular among Vietnamese, and there are several resorts here, though they're all overpriced and poorly maintained. There are a few other restaurants and beachside cafés, so you can kick back and crack open a few crabs while enjoying a fresh coconut juice or a refreshing slice of watermelon.

Head away from the beach to the hill rising from its north end, and you'll soon find yourself at the base of a highly enjoyable **rail ride** (daily 9am–3pm; 20,000đ). Pulleys tug your go-kart-like vehicle (which sits one or two passengers) up the hillside, and you're ushered off at the top to take in some superlative views all the way into Cambodia. The way back down is even more fun, since you can control the braking with odd hand-levers – build up some space between yourself and the kart in front, and you can really let yourself fly.

Thach Dong

Off Highway 80, 5km north of town • Daily 6.30am–6pm • 10,000đ

You'll see the 48m-high granite outcrop housing **Thach Dong**, or Stone Cave, long before you reach it. A monument shaped like a defiant clenched fist stands by the roadside, a memorial to 130 people killed by Khmer Rouge forces near here in 1978. From here, steps lead up to a **cave pagoda** that's home to a colony of bats; its shrines to Quan Am and Buddha are unremarkable, but balconies hewn from the side of the rock afford great views over the hills, paddy fields and sea below. Look to your right and you can peer into Cambodia.

ARRIVAL AND INFORMATION HA TIEN

By bus Buses terminate at the new bus station off Highway 80, a couple of kilometres south of Ha Tien. To get into town from here you can take a xe om (about 20,000đ), though many bus companies will offer free shuttle services to and from the station.

Destinations Can Tho (4hr); Chau Doc (4hr); Ho Chi Minh City (9hr); Long Xuyen (4hr); Rach Gia (2hr 30min).
By boat Hydrofoils to and from Phu Quoc Island (1hr 30min), dock on the south bank of the To Chau River. Tickets (230,000đ) can be bought at any hotel and numerous sales

THE MUI NAI LOOP

A pleasant half- or full day can be spent exploring the countryside around Ha Tien, with a convenient **circular loop** northwest of town meaning you won't need to backtrack. This makes an ideal bike ride – and an even better motorbike route – when the weather is good.

Strike off west along Lam Son. At the end of the road, turn left and continue straight at a small roundabout. A **war cemetery** serves as a landmark on the right, 2.5km from town, and here the road forks and branches left, signposted Nui Den (lighthouse). Follow this road to the coast, along a winding stretch of road with some beautiful views, until you reach the entrance to Mui Nai beach and its adjacent rail-bike ride (see above).

Back on the coastal road, you'll weave your way between rice fields, shrimp farms, water buffalo wallowing in ponds and signs reading "Frontier Area". Around 3–4km past Mui Nai, you'll reach the main road where a left turn leads to the Cambodian border (but not the gate); turn right instead and you'll soon be at **Thach Dong** (see above), a 48m-high granite outcrop home to a cave pagoda. From here, continue along the circular road that will bring you, after a few kilometres, back into Ha Tien.

TO CAMBODIA FROM HA TIEN

Ha Tien makes a good start or finish line to a trip through Vietnam, since it's ideally placed for access to the popular Cambodian coastal towns of **Kep**, **Kampot** and **Sihanoukville**. From Ha Tien, **buses** (often minibuses) leave at around 10am for Kep ($9) and Kampot ($10), and some then continue on (often with a change of vehicle) to Sihanoukville ($15). However, taking the buses leaves you more prone to delays at the Xa Xia border crossing, as **Cambodian visas** are available here – though they should cost $30, a "bribe" of $5 is commonly added to the fee, and if one person in your bus disagrees with paying it, you will all have to wait for it to be settled. It's often far better to go by **xe om**, as prices are the same as the bus tickets, you can leave any time you like and you'll enjoy the spectacular scenery all the more, especially since drivers heading to Kep tend to break off across the fields to the coastal road soon after entry into Cambodia. It's a long, bone-shaking haul to Sihanoukville this way, though – think about getting a **taxi**, which can work out just as cheap if you're in a small group ($40 to Kep, $45 to Kampot, $80 to Sihanoukville), if you're after a more comfortable ride.

2

points visible around town; they leave Ha Tien at 7.30am, 8am, 9am and 1.15pm.

Tourist information The best place to ask for tourist information is the *Oasis* restaurant (see below).

Vehicle rental Though nowhere officially rents vehicles, most hotels can help out; ask staff at the *River* hotel or *Oasis* restaurant, who will be able to get you a motorbike for the day for around 200,000đ.

ACCOMMODATION

A word of warning – Ha Tien is dotted with speakers playing **fake birdcalls** at an extraordinary volume. Though the birds it's supposed to fend off rarely treat it as a threat, you'll find these speakers a lot less funny if they're next to your hotel room – pay attention when checking in.

Hai Yen 15 To Chau ☎0297 385 1580; map p.155. An efficiently run place with helpful and informative staff. Their bright, decent-sized rooms are good value, and some on the upper floors have nice views of Dong Ho. $13

Happy 13–14 Hoang Van Thu ☎0297 396 6688; map p.155. Also known as the *Ha Tien Hang Phuc* (words that are far easier to discern on the hotel facade), this is a great budget option, though staff speak zero English. They've four floors of rooms, and though some are windowless and a bit smelly, all are en suite and rather comfy for the price. $11

River Dang Thuy Tram ☎0297 395 5888; map p.155. The town's first upper-end hotel has, so far, proven something of a disappointment, due to shockingly poor management. Rooms are plushly appointed, and some boast superlative river views, but guests still end up full of gripes. On top of the shabbiness of the lobby (which still looks partially under construction, after all these years), you may be pointed to a different place for breakfast every day, and to access their small swimming pool you'll have to exit the hotel and walk down the road (then usually back again, to ask for the key). $45

EATING

In the evening, a **night market** sets up between the river and the main market buildings, some stalls selling souvenirs and others selling seafood, attracting crowds of locals and the odd foreigner.

5 Lua 36 Dang Thuy Tram ☎098 8864 4464; map p.155. By far the busiest place in town, this is an attractive open-air venue that's strung with tiny lanterns. Most come for the hotpots (125,000đ), but there are all sorts of staples (75,000–85,000đ) on the English-language menu, and some even cheaper rice or veggie choices. There's lots of beer, too. Daily 7am–10pm.

Da Ha Tien Floating Restaurant Dang Thuy Tram ☎0297 395 5888; map p.155. Operated by the *River* hotel, this characterful wooden vessel is an equally mixed bag – it's a fun place for cheapish beer, but ask for anything else on the menu and you're likely to be laughed at, since

they won't have it. Daily 7am–10pm.

Little House Cau Cau; map p.155. Popular with young couples and local families, this back-alley courtyard venue is basically the only place in town to have put any effort into its decor – just a few nice photos and some fake flowers, but it makes the world of difference. For food, go for their fried chicken, or Korean-style seafood noodles (both 39,000đ), and wash it down with an ice tea (15,000đ). Daily 10am–10pm.

★**Oasis** 30 Tran Hau ☎0297 370 1553; map p.155. This is an English-run venue that's by far the most popular place in town with visitors, and for several good reasons. Their menu is full of tempting dishes like full English breakfasts

(90,000đ, plus 20,000đ if you want black pudding), omelettes, baguettes and the like, and it's also a cheap place for alcohol (from 12,000đ for local beer, or 30,000đ for a Strongbow). Add in the fact that it's the best place in town for local information, and you'll see why it has become such a foreigner hub. Daily 9am–10pm.

DIRECTORY

Banks There are surprisingly few ATMs around town (which is annoying if you've just come from Cambodia), but the one at the Agribank (37 Lam Son) usually works, and if that fails you can try the Vietcombank, which is just down the road (4 Phuong Thanh).

Post office The post office (daily 6.30am–9pm) is on To Chau, a short walk north of the river.

Hon Chong Peninsula

A string of offshore isles has earned the **Hon Chong Peninsula** the moniker "mini-Ha Long", but it's as a coastal resort that it draws throngs of Vietnamese and a smattering of foreigners. The approach to the peninsula, 30km south of Ha Tien, is blighted by unsightly cement factories belching out clouds of smoke, but head further along and you'll find calm beaches fringed with palms and casuarinas, which remain among the most attractive in the delta. Right at the southern tip of the peninsula, the main area of note is fairly compact (a bay-like stretch of around 6km); with your own wheels it's easy to scoot between the various sights and beaches.

Bai Duong beach

10,000đ when staff are on duty; free otherwise

The most picturesque stretch of sand on the peninsula is right at the end of the main road – **Bai Duong beach**, named after the casuarina trees that line it. After passing pandanus, tamarind and sugar-palm trees, the coastal track ends at a towering cliff, in front of which stands **Sea and Mountain Pagoda** (Chua Hai Son) and a cluster of souvenir and food stalls. Go into the temple grounds, and look for an opening in the rock that leads into **Cave Pagoda** (Chua Hong). A low doorway leads from its outer chamber to a grotto in the cliff's belly, where statues of Quan Am and several Buddhas are lit by coloured lights. The cramped stone corridor that runs on from here makes as romantic an approach to a beach as you could imagine, though the stench of the resident bats somewhat spoils the atmosphere.

As you hit Bai Duong's stretch of sand, the rugged rocks out to sea in front of you constitute **Father and Son Isle** (Hon Phu Tu), though it is now rather a misnomer as "Father", the bigger of the two pillars of rock, crashed into the sea in 2006. The beach here is reasonably attractive, though still too shallow for swimming.

| ARRIVAL AND DEPARTURE | HON CHONG PENINSULA |

By bus and xe om Take one of the irregular buses from Rach Gia (2hr), or take a Rach Gia-bound bus from Ha Tien and get off at Ba Hon, before taking a xe om (about 60,000đ) the last few kilometres to Bai Duong.

By motorbike Perhaps the most pleasurable means of approach is hiring a motorbike from Ha Tien (see p.157); once you're out of the urban area, the journey becomes rather beautiful, and will take around an hour; just remember to take the right-hand fork away from the main road once you're over the bridge in the hamlet of Ba Hon.

ACCOMMODATION

Green Hill Guesthouse On the road running south of the peninsula, towards Bai Duong beach ☎ 0297 385 4369. Perched on the hillside at the western end of the bay, this family-run hotel lives up to its billing, its handful of beautifully furnished rooms all commanding sweeping views of the bay and representing a good deal. $16

★ **Hon Trem Resort** On the road running south of the peninsula, towards Bai Duong beach ☎ 0297 385 4331. Boasts a prime location on a small isthmus poking out from the middle of the bay. All of its compact villas ($60–70) enjoy great views from a steep hillside, and the spacious rooms in a new block are extremely comfortable and well equipped. Add a gorgeous swimming pool and great beach views, and you've got the best spot to lay your head around these parts. Their restaurant is also the best place to eat in the area, with a wide range of Vietnamese dishes at 95,000–250,000đ. $40

Phu Quoc Island

One of Vietnam's most popular holiday destinations, **PHU QUOC ISLAND** rises from the country's slender southern tip like a genie released from a bottle. Its soft-sand beaches, swaying palms and limpid waters have been casting spells on visitors ever since its tourism potential was finally realized in the late 1990s. Progress was initially slow – it's almost impossible to believe that electricity from the mainland only arrived in 2013 – but a recent glut of construction, and a volley of flights arriving from the mainland and beyond, means that Phu Quoc is now challenging Nha Trang as Vietnam's top beach destination.

Phu Quoc is located in the Gulf of Thailand just 15km off the coast of Cambodia, a country that still has territorial claims on the island (which they refer to as Ko Tral). Phu Quoc's isolation made it an attractive hiding place for two of the more famous figures from Vietnam's past. **Nguyen Anh** holed up here while on the run from the Tay Son brothers in the late eighteenth century, and so too did **Nguyen Trung Truc** in the 1860s (see box, p.152). Today, over eighty thousand people – and a sizeable population of indigenous dogs, recognizable by a line of hair running up the spine instead of down – dwell on the island, famous throughout Vietnam for its black pepper and its fish sauce (*nuoc mam*), which is graded like olive oil.

Like Mui Ne, Phu Quoc is a favourite bolthole for **expats** living in Ho Chi Minh City, and its future looks rosy. Yet while resorts and bars are springing up fast and access roads are being sealed, for the moment Phu Quoc still retains something of a pioneer outpost feel; though the island is a spacious 46km long, many places can still only be reached via dirt tracks and the beaches are largely free of vendors. In the rainy season (between May and Oct) Phu Quoc is relatively quiet, and room rates become more easily negotiable, though in peak season (between December and January), accommodation prices can increase sharply and advance booking is necessary.

Western Phu Quoc

Phu Quoc Island's west coast is quite rugged, but the beautiful bays tucked along **Ong Lang Beach** are certainly worth visiting, and a few cosy resorts, separated from each other by rocky headlands, offer the chance to really get away from it all. Ong Lang Beach is much quieter than Long Beach (see p.161), and has a few coral reefs just off the coast, though for really good snorkelling you'd need to join a boat trip to the north or south end of the island. North of Ong Lang, there are a few more attractive beaches

---

SNORKELLING AND DIVING AROUND PHU QUOC ISLAND

There's a reason why visitors come in droves to Phu Quoc from November to May, and why resorts raise their rates then. It's because during those months the waters surrounding the island become limpid and ideal for **diving and snorkelling**. Some visitors snorkel optimistically in front of resorts on Ong Lang beach, but the best locations are around the **An Thoi Islands** to the south or **Turtle Island** off the northwest coast, both of which can be visited by boat trip from Phu Quoc. At these reefs (particularly the former, which is rated by some as the best dive site in Vietnam) you can float above brain and fan corals, watching parrot fish, scorpion fish, butterfly fish, huge sea urchins and a host of other marine life. Most resorts can sort out snorkelling trips, charging around $15–20 per person (depending on the number in the group) and including gear rental, fishing and lunch. Diving will, of course, cost a little more – check out Rainbow Divers (see p.163) for an idea of prices.

2

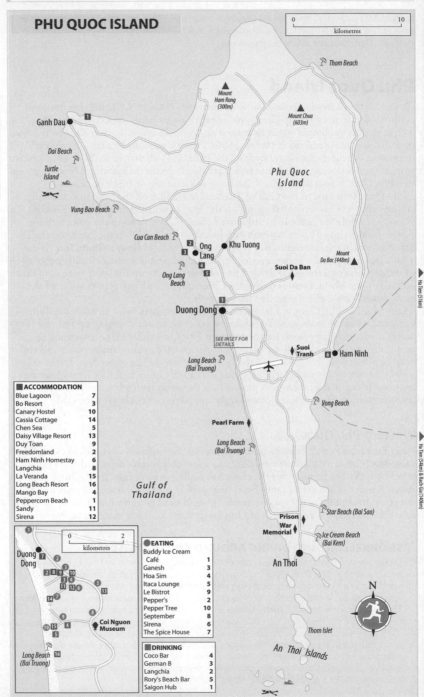

PHU QUOC ISLAND

0   kilometres   10

Thom Beach

Mount Ham Rong (300m)

Mount Chua (603m)

Ganh Dau 1

Phu Quoc Island

Dai Beach

Turtle Island

Vung Bao Beach

Cua Can Beach

Ong Lang 2

Khu Tuong

Mount Da Bac (448m)

3

Ong Lang Beach

4

5

Suoi Da Ban

Duong Dong 1

SEE INSET FOR DETAILS

Suoi Tranh

6 Ham Ninh

Long Beach (Bai Truong)

Ha Tien (51km)

Vong Beach

Pearl Farm

Long Beach (Bai Truong)

Ha Tien (54km) & Rach Gia (140km)

Gulf of Thailand

Star Beach (Bai Sao)

Prison War Memorial

Ice Cream Beach (Bai Kem)

An Thoi

N

ACCOMMODATION

Blue Lagoon	7
Bo Resort	3
Canary Hostel	10
Cassia Cottage	14
Chen Sea	5
Daisy Village Resort	13
Duy Toan	9
Freedomland	2
Ham Ninh Homestay	6
Langchia	8
La Veranda	15
Long Beach Resort	16
Mango Bay	4
Peppercorn Beach	1
Sandy	11
Sirena	12

Duong Dong 7

2

8 9 3

10

3

3

11 12 6

13

14

9

8

Coi Nguon Museum

10 15 4

5

Long Beach (Bai Truong) 16

0   kilometres   2

EATING

Buddy Ice Cream Café	1
Ganesh	3
Hoa Sim	4
Itaca Lounge	5
Le Bistrot	9
Pepper's	2
Pepper Tree	10
September	8
Sirena	6
The Spice House	7

DRINKING

Coco Bar	4
German B	3
Langchia	2
Rory's Beach Bar	5
Saigon Hub	1

Thom Islet

An Thoi Islands

called **Cua Can**, **Vung Bao** and **Dai**. Resorts are beginning to spring up here too, though the region still has a feel of splendid isolation.

Duong Dong

You'll probably find no real need to go into the only town of any size on Phu Quoc – **DUONG DONG** – since most resorts, and the main road linking them, provide all basic needs. However, it's worth dragging yourself off the beach to spend a few hours here – early morning or evening are the best times. There is a small **lighthouse** and **temple** (Dinh Cau) situated on a promontory at the entrance to the harbour, which is of no great consequence but does provide good **views** down the northern part of Long Beach. The town's **market**, on Ngo Quyen, to the left across the rickety bridge in the centre of town, is always bustling and photogenic with its throng of shoppers and displays of fruit and flowers, and is at its best early in the morning. There's also a **night market** that sets up each evening along Vo Thi Sau near the lighthouse, where you can pick up a few souvenirs and check out the good-value Vietnamese food stalls.

Long Beach

The main attractions on Phu Quoc are its fabulous beaches, and the west coast has some of the best. The majority of resorts and guesthouses are strung out to the south of Duong Dong, along **Long Beach** (Bai Truong) – an appropriate name, as it stretches almost to the southern tip of the island some 20km away. Most resorts are fronted by fine stretches of soft yellow sand and coconut palms, and the beach is ideal for sunbathing, sunset-watching and swimming. Beyond the first seven kilometres or so south of town the beach is completely deserted, and the coast road southward provides some classic tropical beach views.

If you're here for rest and relaxation, you need do nothing more than saunter back and forth between your resort and the beach. If you get restless, you can always rent a motorbike to explore the island (see box, p.162) or sign up for a boat trip.

Coi Nguon Museum

149 Tran Hung Dao • Daily 7am–5pm • 20,000đ • ☎ 0297 398 0206

This museum, the only privately owned one in the Mekong Delta, is located on the main road behind the resorts on Long Beach and about 5km south of Duong Dong; it is well worth a visit to get an overview of Phu Quoc's natural and political history. The carefully arranged exhibits include whale, dugong and swordfish skeletons, samples of sand and petrified wood, a fantastic variety of shells, a potted history of the island's past, ceramics from shipwrecks and, if you make it up to the fifth floor, sweeping views along the coast. There are also handicrafts made of local materials on sale, though a shell-encrusted chair might be a bit big for your backpack.

Eastern Phu Quoc

The **east coast** is, so far, largely undeveloped, though it does have a good surfaced road running halfway up it (from An Thoi to Ham Ninh and Duong Dong) that offers some respite from the constant dust kicked up off the dirt roads throughout the rest of the island.

Star Beach

Signposted just north of the T-junction where the road from Long Beach meets the road up the east coast, **Star Beach** (Bai Sao) is a hot contender for best beach on the island. Its dazzling white sand and pale blue water are mesmerizing, and while the waves crash on Long Beach during the monsoons, Star Beach often remains calm. A few **beach restaurants** do a healthy trade, particularly at weekends when the beach gets

2

EXPLORING PHU QUOC BY MOTORBIKE

Phu Quoc is the kind of island that is ideal for exploration, and there is little traffic, making it easy to ride a **motorbike** around. Over seventy percent of the island is forested at present, and the hills of the north are particularly verdant. If you do this, be aware that few roads are surfaced, so you are likely to return to your resort at the end of the day covered in a film of red dust – wearing a helmet is compulsory and a face-mask is a good idea too.

All over the island, and especially in the north, you will pass by **pepper plantations**, the plants easily identifiable as climbers on three-metre-high poles; at places like **Khu Tuong**, a few kilometres inland from Ong Lang beach (see map, p.159), they welcome visitors to look around. There are also two cleansing **streams** in the centre of Phu Quoc: **Suoi Da Ban** and **Suoi Tranh**. A walk beside them reveals moss-covered boulders, tangled vines and small cascades, though they tend to dry up between January and May.

One highly recommended route to follow heads north out of Duong Dong; turn right when you hit the end of Tran Hung Dao, left across the bridge, then right again in the direction of Thom beach. This is a fast, easy road, though things get rather more wild if you turn left at the first main junction you hit (after 12km or so). The red-earth road heading from here to Ganh Dau is absolutely splendid: no traffic, corners and bumps that can cope with a bit of speed, and an ever-present forest aroma. When hitting the end of the road in Ganh Dau, you could turn right and have a meal or fruit juice at the *Peppercorn Beach Resort* (follow the signs). Turning left instead will take you onto a road running along the coast; this area is becoming more developed, but there are plenty of tranquil spots before you rejoin the main road back to Duong Dong.

overrun with locals, and there are even a couple of places offering lodgings (see opposite). In season there are kayaks for rent and half-day snorkelling trips by boat.

Other beaches

A little south of Bai Sao, **Ice Cream Beach** (Bai Kem) is also a blinding white colour, but the military generally prohibit entry to foreigners not arriving on a boat tour.

In the middle of the east coast, **Vong beach** and **Ham Ninh** provide jetties for hydrofoils arriving from Rach Gia and Ha Tien. There's no beach to speak of at Vong beach – just mudflats. The only other beach on the east coast is **Thom beach**, in the extreme northeast of the island, which is only reached after a wearing, 35 kilometre-long motorbike ride over rough roads from Duong Dong, and has virtually nothing in the way of facilities.

ARRIVAL AND DEPARTURE   PHU QUOC ISLAND

Whether you arrive by air or by sea, you will likely be besieged by **touts** trying to drag you off to their favoured hotel or guesthouse, so it's a good idea to have somewhere in mind before arrival. If you have made a prior booking, most resorts provide **free airport transfers**, saving you a lot of hassle and expense.

By plane Flights land at the sparkly Phu Quoc Airport, around 9km south of Duong Dong town and less from many of the resorts lying in between the two; as well as the domestic destinations listed here, China Southern and Lucky Air fly from China, Vietnam Airlines come from Cambodia and Thomson offer flights from London and Stockholm – which gives you an idea of how big Phu Quoc might yet become. Taxis will be able to take you into town from the airport (60,000–120,000đ, from the beginning to the end of the Long Beach "strip") – though do make sure the meter is at zero before the journey begins.
Destinations Can Tho (2 daily; 45min); Hai Phong (4 weekly; 2hr); Hanoi (4–6 daily; 2hr 15min); HCMC (1–2 hourly; 1hr).

By boat Speedboats run to Phu Quoc from Ha Tien and Rach Gia (230,000đ from either destination); the precise jetties used on the island's east coast have been in flux for some time, though wherever you go there'll be taxis (around 230,000đ) and usually minibuses (from 60,000đ) waiting to take passengers to their accommodation. Heading back out, it's best to buy your ticket in advance; ask your hotel or guesthouse to help you, or visit the offices at the top of Tran Hung Dao, just behind the northern end of Long Beach (some offer through-tickets to Cambodian destinations, via Ha Tien); there's often a 60,000đ minibus transfer fee, though some hotels and operators offer it for free so it pays to ask around. Destinations Ha Tien (2–4 daily; 1hr 30min); Rach Gia (2–4 daily; 2hr 30min).

GETTING AROUND

By xe om or taxi There is currently no organized bus service so – unless you hire a motorbike – you'll have to take a taxi or xe om to get around the island.
By motorbike Prices are 150,000–250,000đ/day depending on the type of motorbike you rent. Most resorts and guesthouses rent motorbikes, or will know where to point you – check yours over carefully, as many of these machines are falling apart. Wear a helmet, face-mask (for the dust) and plenty of sunscreen.

TOURS

There are numerous operators strung along the road linking the resorts. Most resorts and guesthouses can also arrange **boat tours**, including visits to the local pearl farm on Long Beach, or an evening's **squid fishing**, using coloured plastic shrimps as bait.

John's Tours 143 Tran Hung Dao ☎091 910 7086, ⓦjohnsislandtours.com. Long-established operator with a wide range of tours, many of which run daily (in season, at least): try snorkelling and fishing ($17/person), a full-day cruise including snorkelling and fishing ($25/person), or night-fishing for squid ($15/person).
Rainbow Divers 11 Tran Hung Dao ☎091 340 0964, ⓦdivevietnam.com. Well-organized operator running diving trips with hotel pick-ups on most days during the diving season (early Nov–late May). It'll be around $30 for snorkelling or $85 for two dives, including all equipment and lunch or fruit. They also offer PADI courses in open-sea (3-day courses; $255) and advanced diving (2-day courses; $375).

ACCOMMODATION

Accommodation options are expanding fast, and many new places were under construction at the time of research. Not all mid-range options include air-conditioning, TVs and fridges, so check before booking if these are important (the first one certainly can be). While resorts on **Ong Lang beach** are quieter, they are separated from each other by headlands, so there's not much choice when it comes to eating – it's certainly not like **Long Beach**. Bear in mind that during the rainy season (May to October), many small places close for several months, and those that are open usually reduce their prices. By contrast, it can be difficult to find a room in the high season, so advance booking is advised.

Blue Lagoon 64 Tran Hung Dao, Long Beach ☎0297 399 4499; map p.160. More of a hotel than a resort, this may appeal to those who favour comfort over the semi-rustic beachside lifestyle. It is on the beach, however, and features a splendid pool, a great restaurant, and well-appointed rooms with quality bedding. $85
Bo Resort Ong Lang beach ☎0297 398 6142, ⓦboresort-phuquoc.com; map p.160. Pleasant, tastefully furnished bungalows made of wood and thatch on a steep hill overlooking a gorgeous stretch of beach, with a well-appointed restaurant too. The bungalows enjoy some privacy, so it's ideal for an escape, but it's a bit of a clamber to the ones at the top of the hill. $65
Canary Hostel 170 Tran Hung Dao, Long Beach ☎0297 399 6772, ⓦcanary-hostel.com; map p.160. One of the best of the many hostels to have opened in recent years – the sizeable pool encourages mingling, while the dorms and private rooms are comfy affairs. Dorms $10, doubles $30
★**Cassia Cottage** West of Tran Hung Dao, Long Beach ☎0297 384 8395, ⓦcassiacottage.com; map p.160. An absolutely beautiful mini-resort, whose airy rooms exude cinnamon, nutmeg and other pleasing aromas – their restaurant (see p.165) isn't called *The Spice House* for nothing. Even the smallest rooms are nice and large, while the swimming pools are a delight. $99

Chen Sea Ong Lang beach ☎0297 399 5895, ⓦchensearesortandspa.com; map p.160. The southernmost and most expensive resort on Ong Lang beach features luxurious rooms in a mixed traditional and modern style, some with private pools. There's also a large, beachfront, communal pool, a diving and watersports centre, a solarium deck, a spa, a mini-library and a recreational activities programme. Expect generous discounts from the stratospheric rack rates. $500
Daisy Village Resort East of Tran Hung Dao, Long Beach ☎0297 384 4412, ⓦdaisyresort.com; map p.160. If you're willing to splash out a bit, rooms here can often be a steal – especially when off-season discounts kick in. Of their two adjoining resorts, the *Daisy Village* is cheaper, with candy-coloured bungalows set around a highly attractive swimming pool; it's just a little bit of a walk out, though this makes for peace and quiet at night. Breakfast is awesome, too. $60
Duy Toan 91/6a Tran Hung Dao, Long Beach ☎0297 384 7666; map p.160. This place offers some of the cheapest private rooms in the Duong Dong area; they're spick and span with small TVs and private facilities. A great deal. $12
★**Freedomland** Ong Lang beach ☎094 468 7071, ⓦfreedomlandphuquoc.com; map p.160. One of the most popular places around Ong Lang, thanks to the

2

charming rooms and common areas that make the place feel more like a Thai-island hipster hangout than something in Vietnam – expect treehouses, outdoor showers, ecofriendliness and a bar selling "secret" alcohol. No a/c, no TV, nobody cares. $30

Ham Ninh Homestay Rach Ham ☎ 090 675 8797; map p.160. For something a little different, head to this cosy little homestay, just a short walk away from where the ferries set down. It's a little far from the beaches, but the friendly owners can help you to get a rental motorbike in no time. $14

Langchia 84 Tran Hung Dao, Long Beach ☎ 093 913 2613, ⓦ langchia-hostel.com; map p.160. This hostel's popularity has meant it has expanded in recent years; the large dorm is perfectly comfortable, and they have fairly pricey private rooms, too. It's fronted by a large bar-like area with a pool table, and backed by a small pool, and its staff run regular tours, movie nights and the like. Dorms $7, doubles $30

★**La Veranda** West of Tran Hung Dao, Long Beach ☎ 0297 398 2988, ⓦ laverandaresort.com; map p.160. The presence of this Accor property on Long Beach is a clear sign of the developers' confidence in the island's appeal. It occupies a lovely, French-colonial-style building with luxurious rooms, a small pool, spa, a delightful restaurant and super-efficient staff. Ask about discounts from the rack rates. $185

Long Beach Resort West of Tran Hung Dao, Long Beach ☎ 0297 398 1818, ⓦ longbeach-phuquoc.com; map p.160. This top-end resort takes ancient architecture as its theme, and indeed the entrance looks like the gateway to Hue's Imperial City. Rooms continue the trend

with traditional furnishings, long drapes and simple tiled floors. At the back of the resort is a pool and bridge leading over a lotus pond to the beach. $165

★**Mango Bay** Ong Lang beach ☎ 090 338 2207, ⓦ mangobayphuquoc.com; map p.160. This place enjoys a lovely, tranquil location and offers spacious, stylish bungalows, made with local soil using ecofriendly techniques, with fans and large verandas (no a/c or TV). The coast is rocky in front but there are deserted sandy bays on each side. $145

Peppercorn Beach Chuong Vic ☎ 0297 398 9567, ⓦ peppercornbeach.com; map p.160. Snuggled in solitude off the island's northwestern flank, this is a grand choice for those wishing to get away from it all. There are only eight rooms here, and they're often taken up for weeks at a time – in season, you'll be lucky to get a booking at less than a month's notice. Mercifully, given its somewhat remote setting, meals at the restaurant are both affordable and of good quality. $150

Sandy West of Tran Hung Dao, Long Beach ☎ 0297 399 8866, ⓦ sandyphuquoc.com; map p.160. A moderately tall hotel – not unusual in mainland Vietnam, but a little bit of an oddity in Phu Quoc. Stuck a little out on its own, it's so close to the beach that you won't even have to don flip-flops, and the rooms are comfy, pleasingly decorated affairs – though you'll have to pay around $15 extra if you want a sea view. $40

Sirena 100c Tran Hung Dao, Long Beach ☎ 0297 399 2256; map p.160. Cheap and central, this simple guesthouse-cum-restaurant (see opposite) offers villa-like rooms that are absolutely fine if you're not too fussy. They have a swimming pool too, if that helps to sweeten the deal. $30

EATING

Duong Dong's **night market** is a great place to sample authentic Vietnamese dishes at very cheap prices (daily 5pm–midnight). Not surprisingly, every beach resort, apart from the cheapest guesthouses, has its own restaurant; most have reasonable menus and some have sea views, but the quality is erratic and prices are often inflated. Bear in mind that if you stay anywhere but **Long Beach**, you'll be more or less limited to your resort's restaurant unless you have a rented motorbike. Long Beach may be busier, but you do get several dining choices in a small area.

Buddy Ice Cream Café 6 Bach Dang ☎ 0297 399 4181; map p.160. This congenial café upped sticks to a new location in recent years – and is all the better for it. It's a highly attractive place where locals pop by for an extended coffee or lunch break. What hasn't changed is the menu: imported New Zealand ice cream (40,000đ/scoop), sublime fruit shakes, fish and chips and toasted sandwiches. Daily 7.30am–11pm.

Ganesh 97 Tran Hung Dao ☎ 0297 399 4917; map p.160. All the quality you'd expect of the pan-Vietnamese Indian chain, with images of Gandhi and colourful Indian architecture peering down at you as you wolf down your meal – most mains cost around 100,000đ (a little more for chicken or lamb), and filling thali sets start at 180,000đ.

Wash it all down with a lassi (40,000đ). Daily 10am–11pm.

Hoa Sim 92 Tran Hung Dao ☎ 094 883 9939; map p.160. Sometimes you just want good Vietnamese food at regular Vietnamese prices. If that's you, head straight to this family-run place, which whips up rice and noodle staples from just 30,000đ, and fancier curries for a little more. Daily 9am–10pm.

Itaca Lounge 125 Tran Hung Dao ☎ 0297 399 2022, ⓦ itacalounge.com; map p.160. Lanterns in the trees and strings of tiny lights subtly illuminate this open-air lounge, which has comfy couches and tables scattered around. The menu is creative international, with an emphasis on Spanish food – try the chorizo-and-egg pizza (210,000đ),

Andalucian fried squid (160,000đ) or paella (310,000đ/person). The service is super-attentive and the ambience just lovely. Daily 6–11pm.

Le Bistrot On the lane leading to La Veranda resort, Long Beach ☎ 0297 398 2200; map p.160. Relaxing place with a pool table offering French and international dishes (from 75,000đ), and there's a children's playground in the garden. It's popular for dining in the day, and you can choose a drink from the well-stocked bar in the evening. Daily 10am–midnight.

Pepper's 89 Tran Hung Dao, on the main road near the north end of Long Beach ☎ 0297 384 8773; map p.160. The place to go for pizzas (from 95,000đ for a medium), grills and jumbo salads; somewhat oddly, there are also a couple of German dishes on the menu. Though it doesn't have beach views, it's a pleasant, breezy spot and staff are very welcoming. They do hotel deliveries too – there's something special about having pizza on your balcony or veranda. Daily 10am–11pm.

Pepper Tree La Veranda resort, Long Beach ☎ 0297 398 2988; map p.160. This classy, first-floor restaurant in a colonial-style building makes an ideal place for a splurge. There's plenty of seafood on offer, such as steamed sea bass with artichokes in clam butter (400,000đ), served in a refined atmosphere. Daily 11.30am–2pm & 6.30–10.30pm.

★**September** Tran Hung Dao ☎ 0168 222 4034; map p.160. A lovely new option near the south end of the strip, where you'll find veggie food served in a simple but elegant environment. Follow your nose to the source of the tantalizing aromas emanating from the open kitchen, and try yummy mains such as sweet pumpkin and peanut curry (75,000đ), or claypot tofu with bitter melon (70,000đ). Daily 1–10pm.

Sirena 100c Tran Hung Dao ☎ 0297 399 2256; map p.160. Open-air, double-decker venue with good seafood at reasonable prices (see what's on ice at the front for an idea of what's freshest); also good for a breakfast croissant or pain au chocolat (both 25,000đ) with coffee. Daily 11.30am–2pm & 6.30–10.30pm.

★**The Spice House** Cassia Cottage ☎ 0297 384 8395; map p.160. Set in what seems for all the world a large, beachside garden, this top-notch hotel restaurant is rarely too busy outside breakfast time. Check the blackboard for daily special sets (255,000đ), or take your pick from tasty treats like seafood, caramelized shrimps and rice, or cheaper Vietnamese veggie staples. Alternatively, come here for a juice (from 60,000đ) or an evening cocktail (145,000đ, including the "Spice House" crafted with cinnamon, apple and coconut). Daily 10am–10pm.

DRINKING

Coco Bar 118/3 Tran Hung Dao ☎ 0121 800 0953; map p.160. Popular watering hole with cheaper booze than its exterior may suggest (including some good home-made rum), as well as miniature shisha pipes – there are loads of flavours available (150,000đ). Daily 9am–midnight.

German B Tran Hung Dao ☎ 0166 405 8380; map p.160. Not exactly the friendliest place in town, this main-road joint is nevertheless a fine place for a beer (20,000đ for a big bottle of Saigon) and some pool. It's super cheap, and the great German bar food sweetens the deal – you'll soon be slavering over one of their tasty *wursts* (from 50,000đ). Daily 9am–10pm.

Langchia Long Beach ☎ 093 913 2613; map p.160. This hostel is fronted by a small bar, which is a cheap and pleasant place to make new travel friends whether you're staying here or not. Closes a bit early, but the beach is just a

short walk away, so buy a couple of bottles (or, if you're feeling cheeky, a 70,000đ cocktail) and sit out a while longer watching the stars. Daily 7am–9pm.

★**Rory's Beach Bar** Next to La Veranda resort, Long Beach ☎ 0125 749 9749; map p.160. Aussie-owned beach venue that's without doubt the best nightlife option in Phu Quoc. Chairs on the beach, campfires, a pool table and decent beer (draught from 40,000đ)… what more could you want? Often stays open later than advertised. Daily 9am–midnight.

Saigon Hub By the night market, Duong Dong ☎ 094 769 4869; map p.160. This fun spot may tempt you into sticking around a while after a night market meal. They've a whole range of interesting house cocktails (from 95,000đ), plus electronic darts, and a nice view out over the boats. Daily 5pm–midnight.

DIRECTORY

Bank The Vietcombank at 20, 30 Thang 4 in Duong Dong will exchange money and has an ATM.

Hospital and pharmacies There is a hospital towards the eastern end of 30 Thang 4, and there are plenty of

pharmacies around, including one along Ngo Quyen beside the market.

Post office The post office (7am–8pm) is also on 30 Thang 4.

The central highlands

DAMBRI WATERFALLS

The central highlands

Vietnam's central highlands are fragrant with flowers for much of the year, and home to thundering waterfalls, immense longhouses and umpteen minority cultures, so it's something of a surprise that they're among the least-visited parts of the country. The bulk of travellers shoot along the coast to the east, and even those who prefer mountains to beaches usually head to the larger, more spectacular ranges in northern Vietnam. True, the central highlands score lower for scenic beauty, and the area's minority groups may be less colourful, but there's still a lot to see here. With the exceptions of majestic Da Lat and enjoyably intimate Kon Tum, the appeal of the area lies outside its urban pockets: there are two national parks to choose between, a wealth of minority home-stay options and barely a tourist in sight.

Bounded to the west by the Cambodian and Lao borders, the central highlands' fertile red soils yield considerable **natural resources**, among them coffee, tea, rubber, silk and hardwood. Not all of the highlands, though, have been sacrificed to plantation-style economies of scale – pockets of **primeval forest** still thrive, where wildlife including elephants, bears and gibbons somehow survived the days when the region was a hunting ground for Saigon's rich and Hue's royalty.

Most visitors who ascend to these altitudes set their sights on **Da Lat**, an erstwhile French mountain retreat that appears very romantic from afar, especially when the mists roll over its pine-crested peaks. Some find it disappointing close-up, with its dreary architecture and tacky tourist trappings, but the city itself is not without its charms, among them a bracing climate, some beguiling colonial buildings, picturesque bike rides and a market overflowing with delectable fruits and vegetables.

Heading northwest from Da Lat, you'll pass pretty **Lak Lake**, an attractive body of water surrounded by minority villages. Then comes a series of gritty highland towns whose reputations rest less on tourist sights than on the villages and open terrain that ring them. First comes **Buon Ma Thuot**, a surprisingly busy place considering its far-flung location. While the city itself has little to detain visitors, the surrounding waterfalls and E De minority villages certainly do, and it's also the gateway for treks into **Yok Don National Park**.

Pleiku to the north is another less-than-lovely city, though again encircled with a ring of delightful minority villages – this time Jarai and Bahnar. Further north again is **Kon Tum**, by far the most attractive and relaxing of these three provincial capitals; you'll be able to take in three **Bahnar villages** on an afternoon's walk from the city centre, and visit several other minority groups farther afield.

Your highland experience will vary enormously depending on **when you visit**. The dry season runs from November through to April. To see the region at its atmospheric best, it's better to go in the wet season between May to October, although bear in mind that the rain can make some outlying villages inaccessible during this time.

COFFEE GROWING

Highlights

❶ **Dambri Waterfalls** The most impressive waterfalls in the highlands – stand right below them and feel the spray on your face. **See p.171**

❷ **Da Lat** Abseil down a waterfall, pose for pictures on a pony or just enjoy some cooler nights in this popular hill city. **See p.172**

❸ **Ride the rails** Chug your way through highland scenery on the short train ride to Trai Mat village, 7km east of Da Lat. **See p.178**

❹ **Lak Lake** Paddle around Lak Lake in a dugout canoe at dawn and watch the sunrise sweep across its surface. **See p.184**

❺ **Coffee country** Enjoy a cup of fresh coffee in Vietnam's capital of caffeine, Buon Ma Thuot. See p.185

❻ **Kon Tum** Kick back in the small, agreeable town of Kon Tum, which deserves more tourists on account of the minority villages on its doorstep. **See p.194**

❼ **Bahnar villages** Overnight in a dramatically tall communal *rong* in a Bahnar village near Kon Tum. **See p.195**

HIGHLIGHTS ARE MARKED ON THE MAP ON P.170

THE CENTRAL HIGHLIGHTS

N

LAOS

QUANG NAM
DA NANG

Dak
Glei

Mount
Ngoc Linh
(2598m)

Quang Ngai

QUANG
NGAI

KON TUM

Bo Y

Dak To

Kon Plong

Mang Den
Pass

BINH
DINH

6 Kon Tum

Kon Kotu

Ialy Reservoir

Giang
Pass

Plei
Phun

7 Bahnar
Villages

An Khe

Quy Nhon

Pleiku

CAMBODIA

Le Thanh

GIA LAI

Ia Drang Valley

HWY-25

HWY-14

PHU
YEN

SOUTH
CHINA
SEA
(EAST SEA)

YOK DON
NATIONAL PARK

Serepok
River

Ban Don

DAK
LAK

HWY-26

5

Buon Ma Thuot

Trinh Nu Falls

Dray Sap
Falls

Dray Nur Falls

4 Lak Lake

Jun Village

Lang Bian
Mountain
(2167m)

KHANH
HOA

Nha Trang

DAK
NONG

Lat Village

Tiger
Falls

HWY-27

BINH
PHUOC

Dong Nai
River

HWY-14

LAM
DONG

Dambri
Waterfalls

1

Bao Loc

Madagui

Di
Linh

2 Datanla
Falls

3 Da Lat

NINH
THUAN

HWY-27

Phan Rang

HWY-20

HWY-28

CAT TIEN
NATIONAL PARK

DONG NAI

La Nga
Lake

Dinh Quan

BINH
THUAN

Dau Giay

Mui Ne

BA RIA
VUNG TAU

Vung Tau

0   100
kilometres

Attapeu (62km) & Pakse (235km)

MINORITY ISSUES IN THE CENTRAL HIGHLANDS

The Jarai and Bahnar are merely the major players in the highlands' patchwork of **ethnic minorities**. Cocooned in woolly jumpers, scarves and bobble hats, the highlanders are the undoubted highlight of a trip through the area. Many groups are now struggling to maintain their identities in the face of persistent pressure from Hanoi to assimilate, and a number of large protests have taken place in the highlands since the turn of the century, with the central government's reactions widely criticized by international governments and human rights groups alike. Sensitive to the minority rights issue, the Vietnamese authorities only opened this region to foreigners in 1993, and while you're free to travel independently between the major cities today, visiting one of the highlands' many minority villages independently can be difficult – in most cases, you'll need to go through a local tourist office (and pay for the privilege). Wherever you go here, it's best to double-check the current regulations, especially concerning **overnight stays** in villages.

Bao Loc and around

3

The vast majority of travellers pass straight from Ho Chi Minh City to Da Lat, but buses sometimes screech to a brief halt on the causeway traversing **La Nga Lake**, from where the houseboats cast adrift on the water are only a zoom lens away. Locals use foot-powered rowing boats to access their homes, which also double as fish farms.

Eventually the hills yield to the tea, coffee and mulberry plantations of the **Bao Loc Plateau**. Here, the town of **BAO LOC** is the best place for a pit stop between Ho Chi Minh City and Da Lat, and it's also a jumping-off point for visits to nearby **Cat Tien National Park** and the **Dambri Waterfalls**. Though there are no sights of interest in the town itself, the undulating hills nearby provide fertile soil for the cultivation of tea and coffee, and locals also grow the mulberry bushes that silkworms are fond of. Those with their own transport will be able to scoot around this highly attractive area; alternatively, rent a taxi or xe om for half a day.

ACCOMMODATION | BAO LOC

★ **Lien Do Star** 905a Tran Phu ☎ 097 936 4993. This snappy little hotel should satisfy even those accustomed to paying much higher rates. The lobby might not look like much, but the rooms are spacious and easy on the eye, and they all boast a/c and en-suite facilities. $12

Memories 193 Tran Phu ☎ 0263 386 4129. Providing good value for the price, this modest hotel just south of central Bao Loc constitutes the default accommodation for the many bikers and Easy Riders who pass through this neck of the woods. The rooms are large, the hot water is reliable and the service is friendly, but note that you'll pay a bit more for a/c. $13

Dambri Waterfalls

18km north of Bao Loc • Daily 7am–5pm • 10,000d; lift 5000d • Xe om from Bao Loc around 280,000d return; from Da Lat, take a tour or "Easy Rider" xe om (see box, p.178)

Surrounded as they are by dense forest, the **Dambri Waterfalls** are much more attractive than any of those in the vicinity of Da Lat, and the only ones worth visiting in the dry season. The road to the falls, which branches north from Highway 20 just east of Bao Loc, bisects rolling countryside carpeted with coffee, tea and pineapple plantations.

Once you arrive, there are **two paths** leading to the falls. The main one to the right leads to the top of the falls, where some ugly fencing stands between you and a precipice over which a torrent of whitewater tumbles 80m. From here, you can descend to the base of the falls by the steep steps or take a **lift**. A second path, to the left by the restaurant, leads down a steep stairway amid towering trees to a superb view of the falls from the front. A bridge links the two paths over the river, and here you're likely to get drenched by the spray even during the dry season. The path continues downstream to a smaller cascade, **Dasara Falls**, but the trail can be slippery after rain.

Cat Tien National Park

Daily 7am–7pm • 60,000đ, payable at park office 100m before the ferry crossing to the park headquarters; park limits visitor numbers, so book ahead • ☎ 0251 366 9228, ⊛ namcattien.vn

The area's outstanding attraction is **Cat Tien National Park**, a protected area situated 150km north of Ho Chi Minh City and about 50km west of Bao Loc. The park covers the largest lowland tropical rainforest in south Vietnam, and hosts nearly 350 species of bird, over 450 species of butterfly and over one hundred mammals, including wild cats, elephants, monkeys and the rare Javan rhinoceros. Don't bank on seeing a rhino, as the few residing here are in a secluded reserve that's closed to visitors. Crocs are a different story, since a clutch resides in an area around 12km from the park entrance (8km by boat, 4km on foot).

ARRIVAL AND DEPARTURE

CAT TIEN NATIONAL PARK

By bus and xe om The buses heading between Da Lat and HCMC's Mien Dong station can drop you off here; tell the driver you want "Vuon Quoc Gia Cat Tien" (Cat Tien National Park), and you'll be dropped at a junction by Tan Phu town. From here, xe om cover the final 24km to the park along a narrow surfaced road (about 170,000đ); alternatively, the park can organize a car for 400,000đ.

By tour Some operators can organize tours that include a visit to the park. Sinhbalo Adventure Travel in HCMC (see p.88) have two-day trips starting at $150, and Phat Tire Ventures in Da Lat (see box, p.177) feature Cat Tien on some itineraries, such as a five-day jaunt ($633) including Da Lat and a bike-ride towards Mui Ne.

GETTING AROUND

By tour The park organizes lots of tours from its visitor centre, including a jaunt to the endangered primate refuge ($40), birdwatching excursions ($15) and a night safari ($15) – although you're unlikely to see much more than a brief glimpse of a panicked creature on the latter.

On foot Over a dozen walking trails crisscross the park,

ranging from 2–26km in length. Keep in mind that you will need to rent a jeep or pick-up from the park HQ to get to the start of most of them (which costs at least $15), as well as a guide if you're hoping to tackle any of the longer trails ($20–25) – needless to say, a day out on foot here can easily cost over $50.

ACCOMMODATION

Forest Floor Lodge 2km from park HQ ☎ 0251 366 9890, ⊛ forestfloorlodges.com. Set inside the park itself, this is a spectacular, resort-style affair, with rooms either in well-appointed wooden lodges or "deluxe tents" that are more like treehouse dwellings. Their *Hornbill Bar* offers tasty meals and cold beers, while staff can also organize a range of park activities, even if you're not staying here. **$120**

★**Green Bamboo Lodge** Across river from park entrance ☎ 097 334 6345, ⊛ greenbamboolodge.net. The best of the small array of decent lodges clustered across the river from the park entrance. Rooms are set in a series of cute "bungalows" approximating local ethnic designs; they

look basic, but have all the facilities you need (even mini-bars and safes). Dorms **$7**, doubles **$12**

Park accommodation ☎ 0251 366 9228, ⊛ namcattien .vn. The park HQ has a few simple rooms with a/c, as well as a campsite with two-person tents. Basic meals available. Camping **$6**, doubles **$17**

Ta Lai Longhouse Ta Lai Village, 12km from park HQ ☎ 097 897 2734, ⊛ talai-adventure.vn. Traditional longhouse establishment in an ethnic Ma hamlet, set a short distance from the park (though free bike hire is available). The single dorm can accommodate up to 25 (pray that nowhere near that many are staying), and meals can be served in addition to the free breakfast. Dorms **$22**

Da Lat

Tucked into the mountainous folds of the **Lang Bian Plateau** at an altitude of around 1500m, the former hill station of **DA LAT** has exploded in popularity of late and is now a lofty chill-out spot for the country's burgeoning number of domestic tourists, especially those on honeymoon. This small city is famed among the Vietnamese for its flowers, and the surrounding area is also a major source of their fruit and vegetables – some things simply grow better at this altitude. Consequently, the country's best-selling brand of wine bears the Da Lat name.

3

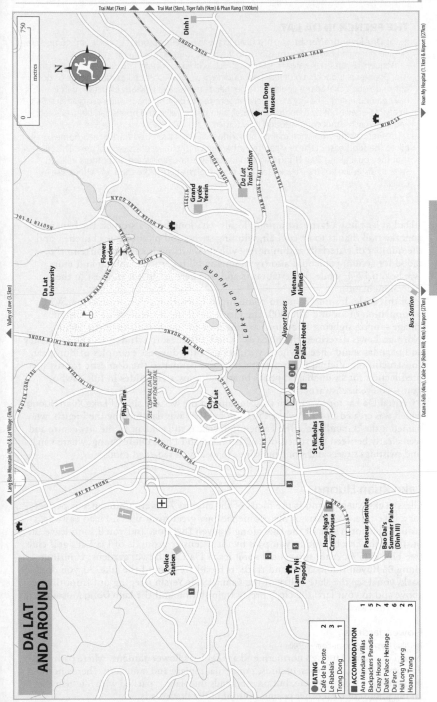

DA LAT AND AROUND

Trai Mat (7km) ▲ ▲ Trai Mat (5km), Tiger Falls (9km) & Phan Rang (100km)

Dinh I

HUNG VUONG

HOANG HOA THAM

Lam Dong Museum

Hoan My Hospital (1.1km) & Airport (27km) ▶

MIMOSA

QUANG TRUNG

Da Lat Train Station

TRAN HUNG DAO

PHAM HONG THAI

Grand Lycée Yersin

YERSIN

BA HUYEN THANH QUAN

NGUYEN TU LUC

Flower Gardens

B A HUYEN THANH QUAN

Da Lat University

TRAN NHAN TONG

Xuan Huong Lake

Valley of Love (3.5km) ◀

Vietnam Airlines

Airport buses

Bus Station ▶

PHU DONG THIEN VUONG

DINH TIEN HOANG

I THANG 4

Dalat Palace Hotel

Datanla Falls (4km), Cable Car (Robin Hill; 4km) & Airport (27km) ▶

Lang Bian Mountain (9km) & Lat Village (2km) ◀

NGUYEN CONG TRU

BUI THI XUAN

Phat Tire

SEE 'CENTRAL DA LAT MAP' FOR DETAIL

Cho Da Lat

NGUYEN THAI HOC

St Nicholas Cathedral

TRAN PHU

PHAN DINH PHUNG

KHE SANH

HAI BA TRUNG

Police Station

Lam Ty Ni Pagoda

Hang Nga's Crazy House

Pasteur Institute

Bao Dai's Summer Palace (Dinh III)

LE HONG PHONG

TRIEU VIET VUONG

750

metres

0

N

● EATING
Café de la Poste	2
Le Rabelais	3
Trong Dong	1

■ ACCOMMODATION
Ana Mandara villas	1
Backpackers Paradise	5
Crazy House	7
Dalat Palace Heritage	4
Du Parc	6
Hai Long Vuong	2
Hoang Trang	3

THE FRENCH IN DA LAT

It was **Dr Alexandre Yersin** who first divined the therapeutic properties of Da Lat's temperate climate, during an exploratory mission into Vietnam's southern highlands in 1893. His subsequent report on the area must have struck a chord: four years later Governor-General Paul Doumer of Indochina ordered the founding of a convalescent hill station, where Saigon's hot-under-the-collar *colons* could recharge their batteries, and perhaps even take part in a day's game-hunting. The city's Gallic contingent had to pack up their winter coats after 1954's Treaty of Geneva, but by then the cathedral, train station, villas and hotels had been erected, and the French connection well and truly forged.

The French elite who once maintained **villas** in Da Lat preferred to site their homes on a hill to the southeast of the city centre, rather than in the maw of its central area. The villas that they built along Tran Hung Dao survive today, some renovated and others in a sad state of disrepair, but they evoke the feel of the colonial era more than anywhere else in Da Lat.

Da Lat isn't just a favourite among locals – it's long been a stop on the banana pancake trail thanks to its cool air, winding streets and picturesque churches, and the number of waterfalls and minority villages on its periphery. If you're in the mood for action, you could also try mountain biking, rock climbing and more (see box, p.177), while the restaurants and bars here are by far the best in the central highlands.

All this aside, it's important to come to Da Lat without preconceptions. With a population of around 200,000, the city is anything but an idyllic mountain village – upon sighting its forlorn architecture for the first time in the 1950s, Norman Lewis described the place as "a drab little resort". Today, its colonial relics and pagodas stand cheek by jowl with some of the dingiest examples of European construction in Vietnam. Attractions here also pander to the domestic tourist's predilection for swan-shaped pedal-boats and pony-trek guides in full cowboy gear – you've been warned.

Central Da Lat forms a rough crescent around the western side of **Lake Xuan Huong**, which was created in 1919 when the Cam Ly River was dammed by the French, who named it the "Grand Lac". The French influence is still evident in the city centre and seen clearly between the streets of Bui Thi Xuan and Phan Dinh Phung, where you'll find twistings streets and stone buildings topped with red-tiled roofs.

Lake Xuan Huong

Glassy **Lake Xuan Huong** is the focus of the city; its 7km circumference is perfect for a bike ride, and parts of the promenade are great for walkers. Head eastwards around the north side of the lake along **Nguyen Thai Hoc**, and you'll soon leave the bustle of the city behind as you pass by the extensive grounds of Da Lat's golf club (see box, p.177). After this, you'll soon reach Da Lat's flower gardens. Continue along **Ba Huyen Thanh Quan** and trace its broad arc around the lake. As you double back, you'll see the slate belfry of the **Grand Lycée Yersin** peeping out from the trees above and to your left; the city's pretty train station and the **Lam Dong Museum** are just to the east.

Flower gardens

Tran Nhan Tong • Daily 7.30am–5pm • 30,000đ

Near Lake Xuan Huong's northern end are Da Lat's **flower gardens**, where paths lead you past hydrangeas, roses, orchids, poinsettia, topiary and a nursery. There's nothing outstanding on display here, but on weekends the place is packed with Vietnamese taking photos of each other posing in front of the flowerbeds.

Ga Da Lat

Off Quang Trung

East of Lake Xuan Huong, **Ga Da Lat**, the city's train station, dates to 1938 and is a real time capsule. Below its gently contoured red-tiled roof and the multicoloured Art Deco windows striping its front facade, its ticket booths are reminiscent of a provincial French station. Outside, the rail yard is in a charming state of dilapidation, with cattle grazing on the grass and flowers growing amid its tracks and ancient locomotives; one of the trains has been turned into a neat little café of sorts.

Trains ran on the railway linking Da Lat to Thap Cham and beyond from 1933 until the mid-Sixties, when Viet Cong attacks became too persistent a threat for them to continue. Nowadays, the only services are those heading 7km across horticultural land and market gardens to the village of **Trai Mat**, a few kilometres away (see p.182).

Lam Dong Museum

4 Hung Vuong • Mon–Fri 7.30am–4.30pm • 15,000đ

Set on a hill beyond the eastern end of Tran Hung Dao, the **Lam Dong Museum** is the best of its kind in the central highlands. Displays here are thoughtfully laid out, and

3

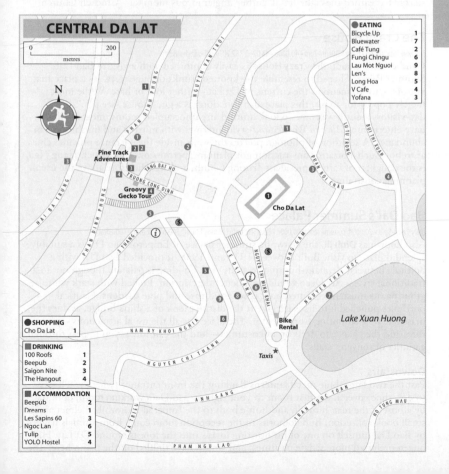

CENTRAL DA LAT

0 — 200
metres

N

● EATING
Bicycle Up	1
Bluewater	7
Café Tung	2
Fungi Chingu	6
Lau Mot Nguoi	9
Len's	8
Long Hoa	5
V Cafe	4
Yofana	3

Pine Track Adventures

Groovy Gecko Tour

Cho Da Lat

Lake Xuan Huong

Bike Rental

Taxis

● SHOPPING
Cho Da Lat	1

■ DRINKING
100 Roofs	1
Beepub	2
Saigon Nite	3
The Hangout	4

■ ACCOMMODATION
Beepub	2
Dreams	1
Les Sapins 60	3
Ngoc Lan	6
Tulip	5
YOLO Hostel	4

provide a tantalizing taste of the region's rich history. Exhibits include Cham artefacts from recent archeological digs, a collection of rice jars, ceramics and jewellery found in tombs, and some vicious-looking spears. The museum also gives a thorough introduction to the lifestyles of the local minority groups such as the Ma, Koho and Churu, along with a map showing their distribution in the province and many of their handicrafts and household implements. Also look out for the display covering the French and American Wars, though it is little different to similar ones found across the rest of the country.

St Nicholas Cathedral

Tran Phu • Dawn to dusk • Free

Across the road from the *Dalat Palace Hotel* and a few steps west along Tran Phu, Da Lat's dusty pink **cathedral** was consecrated in 1931 and completed eleven years later. It's dedicated to St Nicholas, protector of the poor, and you'll see a statue of him standing at the opposite end of the nave to the simple altar, with three tiny children loitering at his feet. The light streaming in from the cathedral's seventy stained-glass windows, mostly crafted in Grenoble, teases a warm, sunny glow from the mellow pink of the interior walls. A tiny metal cockerel perched almost invisibly at the top of the steeple has earned the cathedral its rather unglamorous moniker, "Chicken Church".

The Crazy House

3 Huynh Thuc Khang • Daily 8.30am–7pm • 40,000đ • ☎ 0263 382 2070, ⓦ crazyhouse.vn

Gaudier than Gaudí, the **Crazy House** is easily combined with a visit to Bao Dai's Summer Palace. Shaped to resemble the knotted trunks of huge trees, it's a place that visitors – not to mention the citizens of Da Lat – either love or hate. While most merely pop by for a visit, this place also functions as a guesthouse (see p.179); day-visitors are still welcome to look around any unoccupied rooms, most of which have entertaining *Alice in Wonderland*-style interiors with mirrors and mushrooms in abundance. A selection of photographs on the walls inside the entrance provides clues as to how such a bizarre construction got planning permission – its owner, Hang Nga, is the daughter of former president Truong Chinh, and was therefore above the usual planning constraints.

Bao Dai's Summer Palace

Daily 7am–5pm • 20,000đ; costume rental 90,000đ • Bear left onto Le Hong Phong, 500m west of the cathedral

Also known as **Dinh III**, the erstwhile summer palace of Emperor Bao Dai is a suitably splendid place to visit. Built between 1933 and 1938, it provided Bao Dai with a bolthole between elephant-hunting sessions. The building is palatial, though not in a traditional style – Art Deco would be a better description. Etched with stark white grouting, its mustard-coloured bulk is set amid rose and pine **gardens**. Nautical portholes punched into its walls give it the distinct look of a ship's bridge, as does the mast-like pole sprouting from its roof. The place has all the usual attractions – pony rides and the chance to dress up in costumes – and the exit forces you to pass through a gauntlet of souvenir stalls.

Downstairs

Past the two large, blue metal lanterns flanking the front entrance (where you'll have to don shoe covers), the first room to your right is Bao Dai's **working room**, dominated by a bust of the man himself, and home both to the Imperial motorbike helmet and a small book collection. Buffalo horns in the **reception room** come from animals bagged by Bao Dai himself on one of his hunting forays into the forests around Da Lat. His queen preferred more sedate pastimes, and would have tinkled on the piano here. The

ACTIVITIES IN AND AROUND DA LAT

There is some spectacular scenery in the vicinity of Da Lat, which lends itself to challenging treks, bike rides and other **adventure activities**.

ACTIVITIES

Bike riding There are a number of excellent day- and half-day bike routes around Da Lat. Many head north to Lat Village (see p.184) or south into the countryside, but it's also possible to organize trips to further-flung locations such as Buon Ma Thuot, Nha Trang or even Hoi An.

Canyoning There's a beautiful canyon fifteen minutes from Da Lat by car, though the adventurous climbing course requires ropes and a bit of bravery. Half-day trips go from $30 per person. Groovy Gecko (see below) run full-day ones to the Dasara Falls ($49), whose four cascades range in height from 8–65m. Do note, however, that 2016 saw several tourist deaths from canyoning in the Da Lat area – be sure to go with a fully licensed operator.

Golf The eighteen-hole Da Lat Palace course just north of the lake (ⓦdalatpalacegolf.com) boasts inspiring views from some tees. Fees start at around $60/$95 per person for 9/18 holes, plus a bit more for a caddy.

Hiking Most local tour operators will be able to organize guided hikes, with everything from half-day to week-long walks and treks. You should count on spending around $30 per person per day. Again, Lat Village and the surrounding area is a popular destination, though the operators here will be able to take you into more far-flung territory.

Tennis Both the *Dalat Palace* and *Dalat Du Parc* have tennis courts, available to guests for free and non-guests for a small fee.

Whitewater rafting The operators here run rafting and kayaking trips on routes including rapids of class 2, 3 and 4. Kayaking starts from $39 per person including a hike, while rafting starts from $72 per person.

TOUR OPERATORS

A number of local tour operators can help to organize most of the activities here. Hotel pickup usually comes as part of the package.

★**Groovy Gecko** 65 Truong Cong Dinh ☎0263 383 6521, ⓦgroovygeckotours.net.

Phat Tire Ventures 109 Nguyen Van Troi ☎0263 382 9422, ⓦptv-vietnam.com.

Pine Track Adventures 72b Truong Cong Dinh ☎0263 383 1916, ⓦpinetrackadventures.com.

palace's most elegant common room is its **festivities room** or dining room, though catching a whiff of furniture polish in this dark, echoing chamber, it's hard to imagine the royal revelries that once went on here.

Upstairs

Royal ghosts are far easier to summon upstairs, where the musty **Imperial bedrooms** seem to have just had the dustsheets whipped back for another royal season. Princes and princesses all had their quarters, as did the queen, whose chamber features a chaise longue that looks unnervingly like a dentist's chair. But the finest room, predictably enough, went to Bao Dai, who enjoyed the luxury of a balcony for his "breeze-getting and his moon-watching". Out on the landing, look out for a bizarre mini-sauna, labelled a *Rouathermique*.

ARRIVAL AND DEPARTURE   DA LAT

By plane Lien Khuong Airport (☎0263 384 3373) is 29km south of town, off the HCMC road. Buses meet each flight (and cost around 40,000đ) – as long as your accommodation is fairly central, either the buses or a connecting shuttle can drop you directly there. It's the same story on the way back, though try booking with your accommodation as you may get a free ride. Otherwise, buses depart 2hr before flights from outside the *Ngoc Phat* hotel, south of the lake. Alternatively, a taxi to or from the airport costs around 350,000đ, though they're best arranged with a fixed-fee agreement, since it'll cost more on the meter.

Destinations Da Nang (5 weekly; 1hr 15min); Hanoi (6 daily; 1hr 45min); HCMC (5–6 daily; 50min).

By train The only services from Da Lat station, which constitutes a sight in itself (see p.175), are the irregular ones to Trai Mat village (daily 7.45am, 9.50am, 11.55am, 2pm, 4.05pm; 40min; 124,000đ). Although there is a schedule in place in theory, in practice trains are very unlikely to run with fewer than twenty passengers.

By bus Buses from HCMC, Nha Trang and elsewhere arrive at Da Lat bus station, located about 1km south of the city centre on 3 Thang 4. Most of the reliable open-tour operators run shuttle services into town, but failing that you can walk or take a short xe om or taxi ride. Regular travellers rate *Sinh Café* buses (ⓦthesinhtourist.vn) the best for travelling to and from HCMC, and Orange Bus for the route to and from Nha Trang.

Destinations Buon Ma Thuot (4hr 30min); Da Nang (15hr); HCMC (7hr); Nha Trang (4hr); Phan Rang (3hr).

GETTING AROUND AND INFORMATION

By bicycle or motorbike If you're fit, you might consider renting a bicycle or tandem (for about 100,000đ/day), though a motorbike may make more sense with all the big hills (from 120,000đ/day) – both are available from various hotels and tour operators.

By car Renting a car and driver for the day (also easily arranged through hotels or tour operators) costs around $60, or around $30 for a half-day whizz around the closest sights.

Tourist information The handful of tourist offices in Da Lat can all arrange guides, bus tickets, car hire and tours. If you plan to go trekking to minority villages, you may need to get a permit from the police and be accompanied by a certified guide. You can skirt around the red tape by signing up for a tour of one or several days with one of Da Lat's adventure sports operators, which also offer mountain-biking, rock-climbing and abseiling outings. Phat Tire Ventures is a reliable outfit (see box, p.177).

ACCOMMODATION

Enduringly popular with both Western and domestic tourists, Da Lat has a wide range of **places to stay**, from cheap, windowless rooms to luxury, international-standard hotels. However, if your visit coincides with a public holiday, especially Tet, be warned that prices increase by up to fifty percent, and you'll need either to arrive early or **book ahead**. The densest concentration of budget hotels lies on Phan Dinh Phung; ask for a room at the back, as the main road can be noisy. Several upmarket hotels operate downtown, but there are many more out in the open spaces south and west of the city centre. Check that prices include hot water – a luxury in much of southern Vietnam, but a necessity in Da Lat. Air-conditioning is neither necessary nor usually provided.

CENTRAL DA LAT

Beepub 74 Truong Cong Dinh ☎0263 382 5576; map p.175. Staying in a bar may not seem like such a great idea, but these are by far the most central dorm beds in Da Lat. The rooms are, mercifully, upstairs away from the noise, and they're also surprisingly attractive. No breakfast. Dorms $̶6̶

★**Dreams** 141 Phan Dinh Phung ☎0263 383 3748; map p.175. The default accommodation setting for Da Lat's budget travellers – you're advised to book at least a couple of days ahead. Its good reputation is well deserved, with helpful and highly friendly staff, clean rooms with modern bathrooms, a free jacuzzi and sauna upstairs and

EASY RIDERS

Those travelling through central Vietnam will surely, at some stage, hear references to the famed **Easy Riders**. Though the term is now used to describe pretty much any motorbike driver willing to go beyond day-trip distance, the concept started life in Da Lat. The success of the initial Easy Riders group (ⓦdalat-easyrider.com) spawned a glut of copycat operators (this is Vietnam, after all), many of which now go under totally different names. The "real" ones rarely disappoint, though some copycat operators are just as good – ask around for the latest on-the-ground advice.

The machinations of Vietnamese tourism mean that it's hard to give any cast-iron recommendations. However, the best place to go shopping for a budding Vietnamese Dennis Hopper is the bottom end of **Truong Cong Dinh**, where several competing outfits vie for your affections. Most are able to produce telephone directory-size folders filled with glowing recommendations, but copying is rife so take these with a pinch of salt.

Prices range from around $20 per day for a tour of the main sights in the city to around $75 per day for a longer trip, usually including simple accommodation and entrance fees to sights – feel free to suggest your own itinerary. The standards and prices of local operators change like the wind, but there is a simple trick for those planning to go on a long tour – go on a short one first. Spending a day, or even a half-day, with your prospective driver will give you a good indication of what they'll be like on a week-long trip.

unbeatable breakfasts (complete with Marmite, peanut butter and fresh passion fruit juice). They also have two similar locations on the same road. **$25**

Les Sapins 60 60 Truong Cong Dinh ☎0263 383 0839, ⓦlessapins60dalathotel.com; map p.175. Accessed through an attached ground-floor café, this is a small place with English-speaking staff and cute rooms, some of which have little balconies. A good option if you want to be close to the action, but far away from it at the same time. **$16**

Ngoc Lan 42 Nguyen Chi Thanh ☎0263 382 2136, ⓦngoclanhotel.vn; map p.175. This four-star hotel offers spacious, well-equipped rooms with good views over the lake, and has been plastered with pleasant purple and mauve hues. It's a bit overpriced, though facilities are excellent, and the ground-floor restaurant is a good place to eat whether you're staying here or not. **$92**

★**Tulip** 14 Nguyen Chi Thanh ☎0263 351 0991, ⓦtuliphoteldalat.com; map p.175. This is a nice, new option with partial lake views and lovely rooms – it's excellent value for money. Staff speak little English, but they're willing to please and keep the place spick and span. The popularity of this hotel means it's now part of a small chain of three. **$22**

★**YOLO Hostel** 31 Truong Cong Dinh ☎0263 628 5455; map p.175. Relatively new, this is the pick of the central hostel options, with incredibly low prices for such a looker – though this is perhaps something to do with how tightly the dorm mattresses (not beds) are laid out. The communal areas are the real draw here, particularly the highly attractive rooftop and bar. Dorms **$5**, doubles **$13**

OUTER DA LAT

Ana Mandara Villas Le Lai ☎0263 355 5888, ⓦanamandara-resort.com; map p.172. This new complex of luxury villas is located in spacious grounds just outside the city centre. Though it boasts every conceivable comfort inside, the complex is in a humble village area and offers a good opportunity to connect with local society. **$240**

Backpackers Paradise 13 Tran Le ☎0263 355 6179, ⓦfacebook.com/backpackersparadisedalat; map p.172. Though a little hard to find, it's worth hunting this hostel down south of the centre. Dorms are slightly cramped, but the private rooms are a steal – many of them come with little TVs. Dorms **$5**, twins **$10**

Crazy House 3 Huynh Thuc Khang ☎0263 382 2070, ⓦcrazyhouse.vn; map p.172. Da Lat's quirkiest sight (see p.176) is also its quirkiest place to stay. Rooms are small for the price, and it's worth noting that you'll have tourists crawling around from 7am to 7pm, but it's not too much of a problem if you plan the day accordingly. **$30**

★**Dalat Palace Heritage** 12 Tran Phu ☎0263 382 5444, ⓦroyaldl.com; map p.172. Da Lat's most magnificent colonial pile sits amid manicured grounds, still radiating 1920s splendour. All rooms are lavishly appointed and decked out with period furnishings, including chunky telephones and massive bathtubs. It's gorgeous, but can feel a little empty at times – though this can be a positive thing. Book online for the best deals. **$230**

★**Du Parc** 7 Tran Phu ☎0263 382 5777, ⓦdalathotel duparc.com; map p.172. This sympathetically restored colonial edifice would be an ideal place to stay if your budget won't stretch to a room at the nearby *Dalat Palace*. The cage-lift creaks up to pleasant, well-ventilated rooms with elegant interiors and polished wooden floors. Outside peak season, it's possible to get some superb deals via their website. **$85**

Hai Long Vuong Lot 6, Tran Le ☎090 986 2901; map p.172. The friendliest guesthouse in town, a 10min walk from the centre. The English-speaking owner is always on hand to advise, and most rooms have great views over Da Lat. **$18**

Hoang Trang 5/3 Ba Trieu ☎098 763 9053; map p.172. This place is also known as the *Happy Hostel* and is another excellent option, though it only has private rooms – no dorms. Still, it's cheap as chips, especially if you're travelling as a pair, and the staff here are great at arranging tours and giving general travel advice. **$12**

EATING

Da Lat has abundant food stalls and a broad range of restaurants serving Vietnamese and international cuisines. Head to the **market** for pho, com and the like, as well as for *com chay* from the one or two vegetarian stalls. You can even buy picnic provisions of bread, cheese and cake at the market, complemented by fresh local berries. Note that you'll also see a fair few places serving *bun bo* and other types of Hue cuisine – apparently, sixty percent of Da Lat's current population can trace their origins back to Hue.

RESTAURANTS

Bluewater 2 Nguyen Thai Hoc ☎0263 353 1668; map p.175. Also known as *Thanh Thuy*, this attractive Chinese restaurant is perched over the lake – and considering the location, the food is pretty fair on the wallet. The soups (from 50,000đ) are large affairs made for sharing; try the chrysanthemum and minced pork one, or the sour and

spicy Sichuanese option. The *gong bao* chicken (200,000đ) and spicy *mapo* tofu (110,000đ) are also excellent choices. Daily 6am–11pm.

★**Café de la Poste** 12 Tran Phu ☎0263 382 5777; map p.172. Modern, French-style café opposite the *Dalat Du Parc* hotel. Grand colonial in style, this place is a tad pricey (mains 150,000–200,000đ), yet just about worth the

3

splurge for the good *croques-monsieurs*, pastas and pizzas, as well as the Vietnamese fusion dishes (try the trout in ginger and chive sauce for 240,000đ). You can't miss the large display of affordable cakes and pastries, laid out just by the entrance – it's very hard to leave without trying some. Daily 8am–10pm.

Fungi Chingu Nguyen Thi Minh Khai ☎1900 9400; map p.175. A great recent addition to Da Lat's culinary scene, this Korean-style barbecue hall is almost always packed at mealtimes, which is no surprise since portions of meat (you do your own grilling at the table) can cost as little as 55,000đ. It's not all meat, though – try some *bibimbap* (veggies on rice; 39,000đ), *japchae* (glass noodles with sesame oil; 39,000đ) or a *kimchi* soup (45,000đ). Daily 11am–2pm & 5–10pm.

Lau Mot Nguoi 16b Nguyen Chi Thanh ☎0263 351 5989; map p.175. You'll see "Single Hot Pot" on the sign, and that's just what you get (59,000đ) – a real treat if you've turned up in Da Lat on a chilly evening, and especially convenient for solo travellers. They also sell good squid kebabs (25,000đ each) and a small range of other snacks. Daily 8am–10pm.

Le Rabelais The Dalat Palace Hotel, 7 Tran Phu ☎0263 382 5777; map p.172. This place can be quite a treat, since for much of the day you may have it almost entirely to yourself. Given the palatial setting, replete with waitresses clad in beautiful *ao dai*, this gives one licence to play emperor or empress over High Tea, served 3–5.30pm (330,000đ). Mains from the largely French menu usually go for around the same price in the evening, though you could always just pop in for a coffee, which starts at 70,000đ. Daily 5.30am–9.30pm.

Long Hoa 6, 3 Thang 2 ☎0263 382 2934; map p.175. This is a great place with a French café ambience, attentive staff and superbly made Vietnamese dishes. Kick off with a strawberry wine aperitif, and try the home-made yoghurt for dessert – it takes some beating. As for the mains, figure on spending 80,000đ for veggies or rice dishes, or 120,000đ for meatier options. Daily 11.30am–2.30pm & 5.30–9pm.

★**Trong Dong** 220 Phan Dinh Phung ☎0263 382 1889; map p.172. This is an old favourite with a homely

atmosphere (their tartan-effect tablecloths have been copied by several local restaurants) and fantastic food – try the shiitake mushrooms stuffed with minced shrimp and pork (80,000đ), shrimp in clay pot (100,000đ), or the more adventurous eel, frog or rabbit highland specialities. Daily 11am–3pm & 5–9pm.

★**V Cafe** 1/1 Bui Thi Xuan ☎0263 352 0215, ⓦvcafedalatvietnam.com; map p.175. This is worth tracking down for its cosy atmosphere, affordable prices and good cooking, including some great home-made pies and cakes. Check out the daily specials, but the lasagne (115,000đ), breakfast burritos (105,000đ) and green curries (100,000đ) always go down well. There are some good veggie dishes too, and it's also a good drinking hole. Daily 8am–10pm.

CAFÉS

Bicycle Up 82 Truong Cong Dinh ☎0263 370 0177; map p.175. Filled with maps, violins, weird lampshades and the like, this is an oddball café, but one that's proving very popular with the hipster set. They have a good espresso (25,000đ), syphon coffee (60,000đ) and all sorts of juices and shakes. Daily 7.30am–10pm.

Café Tung 6 Khu Hoa Binh ☎0263 382 1390; map p.175. Leather upholstery, dark varnished wood, lemon walls and tabletops, amber lampshades, 1950s French crooners on the sound system and a smiling Mona Lisa on the wall… this is truly a café lost in time, one reason why it's still almost entirely the preserve of older locals. Daily 6.30am–9.30pm.

Len's 7 Nguyen Chi Thanh ☎094 691 7348; map p.175. The best of the many cafés lining this road (it's the one with the windmill), selling coffee, juices, *banh mi* and the like, all for 35,000–45,000đ, plus some pricier mains such as pizza and pasta. The lake views are pretty good from some tables. Daily 8am–10pm.

Yofana Da Lat Centre, off Phan Boi Chau ☎093 869 7388; map p.175. This café would be considered generic in HCMC, but there's one main draw – frozen yoghurt, priced by weight (25,000đ for 100g). Just keep your fingers crossed that they haven't sold out of the passion fruit option. Daily 7am–9pm.

DRINKING AND NIGHTLIFE

100 Roofs 57 Phan Boi Chau ☎091 309 0204; map p.175. Forget the roofs for a second – at the time of research, this place had seven floors (many a sort of odd temple-treehouse mix), with more potentially on the way. It gets pretty loud some evenings with folks drinking cheap shots (20,000đ) and *mojitos* (50,000đ). Daily 8am–midnight.

★**Beepub** 74 Truong Cong Dinh ☎0263 382 5576; map p.175. This is the most happening place in town,

regularly packed to the rafters with travellers and young Vietnamese. There's plenty to keep people entertained, including live music, DJs and cheapish beer (30,000đ) – you might also like the sign to the toilet (known here as the "beep room"). Daily 6.30am–9.30pm.

Saigon Nite 11a/1 Hai Ba Trung ☎0263 382 0007; map p.175. This bar has been here for decades, and is so laidback that one wonders how the place is still in business.

LAK LAKE (P.184) >

Games of pool can be fun – though space is so tight that you might need to borrow a chopstick to play certain shots. Daily 3pm–midnight.

The Hangout 71 Truong Cong Dinh ☎ 099 333 3664; map p.175. Easy Rider-affiliated place aimed at travellers, with a pool table, cheap beer and motorbikes for rent. A good place to take the pulse of Da Lat and make some local friends, though it has to be said that their beer can taste somewhat dodgy. Daily 9am–midnight.

SHOPPING

Cho Da Lat Nguyen Thi Minh Khai; map p.175. House within a charmless reinforced-concrete structure, the town market nevertheless offers a staggering range of fruit and vegetables. Strawberries, beetroot, fennel, artichokes, avocados, blackberries and cherries grown in the market gardens surrounding the city are all sold here, along with a riot of flowers. Artichoke teabags, with their diuretic properties, make quirky souvenirs, and candied Da Lat strawberries are also sold at many stalls. Montagnards carrying their chattels in backpacks are a diminishing sight but still fairly common, especially early in the morning when they come to trade with stallholders.

DIRECTORY

Banks Vietcombank (6 Nguyen Thi Minh Khai) and Sacombank (Hoa Binh Square) change cash, and have ATMs.
Hospital Hoan My hospital, south of the centre off Mimosa St (☎ 0263 357 7633, ⊛ hoanmy.com), is by far the best place to be sick in provincial Vietnam.
Police 9 Tran Binh Trong ☎ 0263 382 2032.
Post office 14 Tran Phu (daily 7.30am–5.30pm), with poste restante and DHL courier services.

Around Da Lat

The city of Da Lat itself has more than enough to fill up a few days, but you could extend this to almost a week by visiting the best of its surrounding sights, which include vintage train rides, former palaces, waterfalls and minority villages.

East of Da Lat

The wide area to the east of Da Lat conceals some appealing sights, including **Dinh I**, one of several Bao Dai palaces in the area, and **Trai Mat**, a super little village connected to Da Lat by **vintage trains**. These run both infrequently and irregularly; if you'd like to see both sights, take the train out to Trai Mat first, then return by xe om or taxi and pop by the palace on the way.

Dinh I

1 Tran Quang Dieu • Daily 7.30–11.30am & 1.30–4.30pm • 40,000đ, though there were plans to increase this to 150,000đ at the time of research

About 3km east of the train station, a small lane leads south off Hung Vuong to **Dinh I**. A number of its features and 1930s furnishings are very similar to the ones at Bao Dai's Summer Palace (Dinh III; see p.176), but if you're prepared to trek out here you'll find better views over the city, a more peaceful setting and fewer visitors. The building was used as Bao Dai's workplace, and the conference room upstairs, with its large map of the country, has a business-like air to it. There are several evocative photos on the walls of the other rooms, including one of Bao Dai in a racing car and another of his concubines.

Trai Mat

The village of **Trai Mat** is just 7km from Da Lat, and ideally placed for a short excursion. Most head there by **train** (see p.178), the line taking you east past some interesting, if not particularly beautiful, countryside. The village itself rewards exploration – **Linh Phuoc Pagoda** is the main draw, but if you have more time (or are willing to get a xe om back), you can grab a bite to eat or hunt down the beautiful Cao Dai temple on a rise just east of the village.

Linh Phuoc Pagoda

120 Tu Phuoc Thanh • Dawn–dusk • Free

The highlight of Trai Mat is **Linh Phuoc Pagoda**, an incredibly ornate building that showcases the art of tessellation, whereby small pieces of broken china or glass are painstakingly arranged in cement. The first thing to catch the eye is the huge dragon in the courtyard to the right of the main building, constructed from over twelve thousand carefully broken beer bottles. Artwork inside the pagoda is even more intricate, with mosaic dragons entwined around the main hall's pillars, while stairs lead up on the left to colourfully inlaid galleries, shrines and lovely views. The deep sound of resonating bells, rung by devotees, makes the main hall very atmospheric.

South of Da Lat

There are a few great sights in the area just south of Da Lat, all concentrated around the modest rise of **Robin Hill**. Near the summit you'll find a lake and temple, with the **Datanla Falls** thundering (or trickling in drier months) off its eastern flank.

Robin Hill and Lake Tuyen Lam

Cable car daily 7.30–11.30am & 1.30–5pm • 50,000đ each way; boat trips 250,000đ for up to five people • Xe om to base of cable car around 35,000đ

As you leave Da Lat to the south on Highway 20, a slip road leads to the top of **Robin Hill**, crowned by a huge cable car terminus and the appealing **Truc Lam Pagoda**. Rides in the cable car offer decent views over the slopes around the city, and the twelve-minute trip deposits you near **Lake Tuyen Lam**, a placid and attractive expanse of water on which you can take a boat trip.

Datanla Falls

200m east of Lake Tuyen Lam, signposted "Thac Datanla" • Daily 7am–5pm • 20,000đ

The **Datanla Falls** can easily be combined with a visit to nearby Lake Tuyen Tam. In Koho, *datanla* means "water under leaves", and that pretty much sums up the place: from the car park, it's a steep fifteen-minute clamber down to the falls through some splendidly lush forest. The falls themselves are not terribly thrilling, their muddy waters cascading onto a plateau spanned by a wooden footbridge that provides a hackneyed photo opportunity. You can also take the recently constructed "rollercoaster" here, though it's more like a kart on rails (50,000đ one-way, 70,000đ return).

North of Da Lat

The sights clustered to the north of Da Lat are rather more far-flung than those to the east and south, though it's still quite possible to tackle them all in a half-day – or a full one if you choose to ascend **Lang Bian Mountain**. This rises just beyond **Lat Village**, an appealing place in which to experience a little Montagnard culture. Taking a different road north out of Da Lat will soon bring you to the **Valley of Love**, a beautiful, if somewhat schmaltzy, place popular with local tourists.

Valley of Love

5km north of Da Lat • Daily 7am–5pm • 20,000đ

Thung Lung Tinh Yeu, or the **Valley of Love**, was a hunting spot for Bao Dai and his courtiers in the 1950s, before a dam project in 1972 flooded part of the valley and created **Lake Da Thien**. The valley's still waters and wooded hills are actually quite enticing, though the music blasting from souvenir stalls and the buzzing of rented motorboats do not enhance the aura of romance. Kitsch diversions such as pony rides around the lake escorted by a cowboy are also on offer, while just outside the complex there's a small crazy golf course – pretty awful, but still an amusing diversion.

Lat village

14km north of Da Lat along Xo Viet Nghe Tinh • Cycle, or take one of the hourly green buses heading up Phan Dinh Phung in Da Lat (5000đ)

Until recently, a trip up to **Lat village** was almost de rigueur with backpacker visitors to Da Lat, but it now receives plenty of small tour groups and has been over-gentrified. Still, it remains a worthwhile excursion for those interested in seeing minority life. The village's thatch-roofed bamboo stilthouses are occupied by Chill and Ma, but mostly Lat, groups of Koho peoples eking out a living growing rice, pulses and vegetables. The various paths running through the village are easy to follow so a guide is not essential, though one can be easily arranged through any of Da Lat's tour operators (see p.177).

Lang Bian Mountain

20,000đ; add an extra 20,000đ to access the peak itself

From Lat Village, you'll see the peak of **Lang Bian Mountain** (2169m) – now designated a national park – looming above you to the north. It's a four-hour ascent on foot, though by car you can drive up to the canopy of pines on the lower peak. Inevitably, a corny legend has been concocted to explain the mountain's formation. The story tells of two ill-starred lovers, a Lat man called Lang and a Chill girl named Bian, who were unable to marry because of tribal enmity. Broken-hearted, Bian passed away, and the peaks of Lang Bian are said to represent her breast heaving its dying breath. Bian's death seems not to have been wholly in vain: so racked with guilt was her father, that he called a halt to tribal unrest by unifying all of the local factions into the Koho.

Lak Lake

Gong performances $100/group; canoe rides $20

A hundred and fifty kilometres northwest of Da Lat and 40km south of Buon Ma Thuot, Highway 27 passes serene **LAK LAKE**, a charming spot that has become very popular with tourists. Five thousand people, mostly from the Mnong community, once lived on the lake itself, but have since moved into distinctive longhouses in shoreside villages. There are a number of (slightly cheesy) activities available here, including musical gong performances and elephant rides; note that the latter are not recommended, since you'll be sitting atop a metal cage that's doubtless extremely painful for the poor pachyderm. Still, the lake itself is a glorious place, as once attested by Emperor Bao Dai himself – he grabbed some of the best sites in southern Vietnam for his many palaces, so it comes as no surprise to learn that he had one here, in a prime spot on a small hill overlooking the lake. The palace is long gone, but the site is now home to a small hotel (see opposite).

Jun Village

Southern side of the lake, just off the main road

If you're intent on getting the whole minority village experience, complete with grunting pigs and squawking chickens waking you in the morning, head to **Jun Village**, a thriving Mnong community on the west side of the hill, whose longhouses crowd together near the shore. To say hello in the local tongue, use *kuro-me* to men and *kuro-e* to women. The Dak Lak tourist office (see opposite) has a branch here, and a longhouse where it's possible to stay overnight.

ARRIVAL AND INFORMATION
LAK LAKE

By bus Although Lak Lake is mostly geared towards organized tour groups, it's possible to arrive here independently on the inter-city buses heading between Da Lat (3hr 30min–4hr) and Buon Ma Thuot (1hr 30min–2hr).

Unfortunately, it's not easy to arrange onward transport from Lak Lake, or even to pick it up if you've purchased a ticket in advance – ask staff at your accommodation to help make sure that the bus stops for you. Alternatively, there are local buses linking Buon Ma Thuot with the lake approximately once per hour. All buses set down and pick up at Jun Village.

Information For bookings, activities and enquiries, contact Dak Lak tourist office (☎0262 385 2246, ⓦ daklaktourist.com.vn). *Lak Resort* (see below) is also useful for booking certain activities, such as canoe rides (250,000đ), which are best arranged in the early morning.

ACCOMMODATION

The accommodation situation around Lak Lake is pretty dire, and staff at the following will likely speak little English. You will be able to book through Dak Lak tourist office (see above), which operates the following establishments and organizes village stays.

Bao Dai Villa On a rise off the southeastern shore of the lake ☎0262 358 6184. One of Bao Dai's many old palaces, this makes an intriguing and occasionally atmospheric place to stay, though you should come prepared – facilities are next to naught (even the restaurant is usually closed), and there's a general air of neglect. $35

Jun Village To the south of the lake ☎0262 385 2246, ⓦ daklaktourist.com.vn. Accommodation is available at just over a dozen longhouses in Jun Village itself. Mosquito nets and mattresses are provided in the longhouses themselves, and there are outdoor toilet facilities. Note that you're likely to be woken up early by village activity. $9

Lak Resort To the east of the lake ☎0262 358 6184. Snuggled into a protected bay to the east of the hill, this is yet another missed opportunity – the rooms are rarely cleaned properly, the swimming pool is usually green and staff don't really seem to know what's going on. Still, if you don't mind living a little rough, it's not that bad for a night. $25

Buon Ma Thuot

To the Vietnamese, **BUON MA THUOT** means only one thing: **coffee**. Vietnam is the world's second-largest producer of the bean, and this is where most of its best stuff is grown. There's an almost mind-boggling profusion of cafés here, and though no venues are particularly memorable, it would be a pity to leave town without sampling some of its most famous product for yourself.

All this said, and despite the highland location, first impressions of Buon Ma Thuot are unlikely to be all that favourable. A city with a population of around half a million, its sprawl of modern buildings are splayed across a grid of grubby, characterless streets, and there's little to keep you occupied in the way of attractions. However, a range of good accommodation means that, if you're on your way through the highlands, this is a logical place to hunker down for a day or two – some even end up developing an affinity for the place, and staying longer than they'd intended.

Brief history

During French colonial times, Buon Ma Thuot developed on the back of the coffee, tea, rubber and hardwood crops that grew in its fertile soil, and was the focal point for the **plantations** that smothered the surrounding countryside. Plantation owners and other *colons* would amuse themselves by picking off the elephants, leopards and tigers once prevalent in the area. In later years Americans superseded the French, but they were long gone by the time the North Vietnamese Army (NVA) swept through in March 1975, making Buon Ma Thuot the first "domino" to fall in the Ho Chi Minh Campaign. These days, the town is surprisingly affluent with a spate of buildings under construction and flash cars buzzing along its streets. In a neat reversal of the norm, urban renewal is occurring from the outside in, and the centre is still appealingly grubby.

Khai Doan Pagoda

117 Phan Boi Chau • Dawn to dusk • Free

One of central Buon Ma Thuot's few sights is the **Khai Doan Pagoda**, built in 1951 to honour Emperor Khai Dinh's wife, Hoang Thi Cuc, who was also mother of Bao Dai. The complex has undergone substantial renovation in recent years, and although the main building appears overly angular, this is due to an attempt to entwine elements of E De longhouse design with that of Hue Imperial architecture – it doesn't work all that well, but it's still worth popping by for a look.

Ethnographic Museum

Le Duan • Daily 8am–4pm • 20,000đ

To find out more about the cultures of the local minority groups, head to the **Ethnographic Museum**. It's set in a large and intriguingly designed building to the south of the centre, and is a bizarre fusion of tribal and contemporary styles – though one that looks more sloppy and concrete-rich the closer you get.

The interior is split into three sections – people, biodiversity and history. The latter focuses more on modern times, its main angle being the local people's (apparent) dedication to the Ho Chi Minh cause. The biodiversity section features a miniature zoo's worth of stuffed animals, the regular run-down of local wood and rock samples,

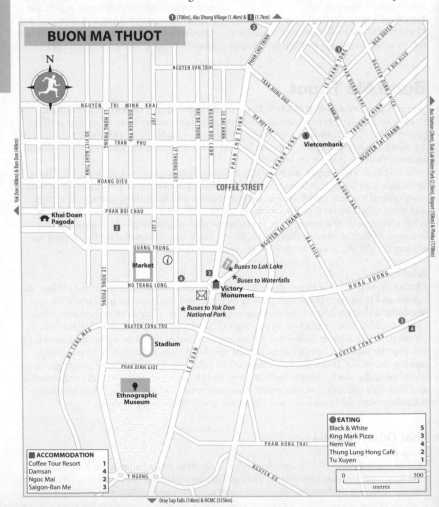

BUON MA THUOT

ACCOMMODATION	
Coffee Tour Resort	1
Damsan	4
Ngoc Mai	2
Saigon-Ban Me	3

● EATING	
Black & White	5
King Mark Pizza	3
Nem Viet	4
Thung Lung Hong Café	2
Tu Xuyen	1

and a rather pathetic coffee display. The ethnographic section is far more diverting, with mock-up miniature longhouses and examples of tribal baskets, clothing and ornaments. Keep your eyes peeled for a waistcoat made of bark, funerary statues of peacocks and tusks, and vicious mahouts' spikes and thorny harnesses – both instruments for taming elephants.

ARRIVAL AND DEPARTURE BUON MA THUOT

By plane Buon Ma Thuot airport is 8km east of town on the road towards Da Lat, and a taxi into town from there costs around 140,000đ.
Destinations Da Nang (daily; 1hr 10min); Hanoi (2–4 daily; 1hr 40min); HCMC (3–4 daily; 1hr).
By bus The bus station (☎0262 387 6833) is 3km northeast of town on Nguyen Tat Thanh, and several a/c

express services arrive daily from Nha Trang and HCMC. There is little in the direction of Pleiku, bar a couple of crowded minibuses. Some companies offer free hotel pick-up, so it's certainly worth enquiring about this with your accommodation.
Destinations Da Nang (12hr); Ho Chi Minh City (7–8hr); Nha Trang (4hr); Pleiku (5hr).

INFORMATION

Tourist information The Dak Lak tourist office is based at 53 Ly Thuong Kiet (☎0262 385 2246, �◯daklaktourist .com.vn), and staff can arrange car rental, guides, visa extensions and tours. You'll also need to check here before visiting the surrounding villages (see p.188): although the

situation in Dak Lak province is fairly relaxed, some villages – particularly those near the Cambodian border – are still theoretically off limits, while others are not permitted to house foreign guests overnight.

3

ACCOMMODATION

There are plenty of places to stay in Buon Ma Thuot, catering for most budgets, though few of them have much character. Most of the cheaper options are clustered along Ly Thuong Kiet, while mid-range hotels are scattered around town.

★**Coffee Tour Resort** 149 Ly Thai Tho ☎0262 357 5575; map opposite. First, the bad news – this place is located a little bit outside the centre. However, in Buon Ma Thuot this bad news is essentially good news too, with the greenery and calm air quite welcome after a day on the road. They've tried to weave E De stylings into the design, particularly in the café out back, and there are loads more cafés (plus some of the coffee trees themselves) in the surrounding area. $22
Damsan 212–214 Nguyen Cong Tru ☎0262 385 1234, ⓦdamsanhotel.com.vn; map opposite. This is a good-value place to stay, though it's based about 1km from the centre – which is no bad thing. Its smart rooms are furnished with tasteful local textiles and most have lovely views across

a lush hillside. There's also a pool and tennis courts. $38
Ngoc Mai 14 Dien Bien Phu ☎0262 385 3406; map opposite. This is pretty much as far down the price scale as you'll want to go, though it does have a range of tidy, a/c rooms – and if you pay a few dollars more, you can have a balcony too. The location is fine, and the staff are surprisingly engaging – they even rent out bicycles. $9
Saigon-Ban Me 30 Nguyen Chi Thanh ☎0262 368 5666, ⓦsaigonbanmehotel.com.vn; map opposite. The most salubrious place to stay in the city, and with a wonderfully central location to boot. Lifts whisk guests up from the neat lobby to even neater rooms, while elsewhere on the complex you'll find a decent restaurant, a fitness centre and a sauna. $65

EATING

Dining in Buon Ma Thuot is unlikely to get the pulse racing, though there are a few quirky options here and there. For budget evening fare, try the stalls on Y Jut and surrounding roads. More importantly, it would also be a crime to visit the heart of Vietnam's **coffee industry** without tasting the product itself, and there are plenty of opportunities in the city's cafés. You'll find them scattered all over town, but there's a particular concentration along the south end of Le Thanh Tong, known to locals as "Coffee Street".

Black & White 171 Nguyen Cong Tru ☎0262 385 6275; map opposite. One of the sharpest-looking cafés in town, its interior decorated along monochrome lines. The prices are pleasingly normal considering the arty ambience – a coffee should set you back around 12,000đ. The fact that the art on display is local, yet almost entirely devoid of predictable

"ethnic" motifs, is another plus. Daily 8am–9pm.
King Mark Pizza 103 Le Thanh Ton ☎097 519 9789; map opposite. There's no shame in admitting that the word "pizza" carries more resonance in a place as remote as Buon Ma Thuot – all the more reason to head to this unobtrusive place, presided over by an actual Sicilian. You'll

pay from 90,000đ for a cheesy, circular homesickness pill. Daily 6am–10pm.

Nem Viet 14–16 Ly Thuong Kiet ☎0262 381 8464; map p.186. The best of the many *nem* (spring roll) joints lined up along this road – or at least the most hygienic. Their tasty *nem* go for around 35,000đ for a portion; you'll get cuts of meat, lots of greens, plenty of sauce and circles of rice paper to roll the lot up in, and the end result is absolutely delicious. Daily 8am–10pm.

★ **Thung Lung Hong Café** 153 Phan Chu Trinh ☎0262 386 5221; map p.186. Snuggled at the base of a steep valley at the end of a side street off Phan Chu Trinh, this oddball café is hugely popular among locals and, given the dearth of nightlife in Buon Ma Thuot, a godsend for visitors too – come for a drink under a constellation of neon and twinkly LED lights. Daily 8am–9.30pm.

Tu Xuyen 245 Phan Chu Trinh, just off junction with Nguyen Dinh Chieu ☎0262 395 3799; map p.186. Locals love this modest-looking goat hotpot venue, and though a little far from the centre, it's well worth the walk or a short xe om ride. Try the curried variety – a little boiling bowl of goodness for just 110,000đ. Daily 8am–10pm.

DIRECTORY

Banks Vietcombank, 6 Tran Hung Dao, changes foreign currency and has an ATM, and there are many more around the town centre.

Post office The post office (daily 7am–8.30pm) is on Le Duan, just south of the Victory Monument.

Around Buon Ma Thuot

The main draw of Buon Ma Thuot is what can be found surrounding it: traditional minority communities (mostly E De people) at **Ako Dhong** and in the surrounding countryside at **Ban Don**; **Yok Don National Park**; and some wonderful **waterfalls**. Between April and July you'll see the city surrounded by millions of lemon-coloured butterflies, wafting through the air like yellow petals.

Ako Dhong
2km north of the city centre

The tidy E De weaving village of **Ako Dhong** is on the city's northern fringes. Don't come expecting any real insights into tribal culture – the sturdy longhouses have clean-swept yards and trimmed hedges, giving the feel of an affluent suburb. However, it's an absorbing place in its own way – the tantalizing aroma of roasting coffee beans often fills the air, and the gentle clack-clack emanating from the buildings signals the weavers at work.

Dak Lak Water Park
Nguyen Chi Thanh, 4km northeast of centre • Daily 8am–5.30pm • 40,000đ • ☎0262 395 0381

If you're in need of cooling down, head for the pools and water flumes of **Dak Lak Water Park**, which can come as a blessed relief on one of Buon Ma Thuot's many scorching summer days. The complex is centred on an artificial mountain, from which the slides race down. Still, it's rather smaller than similar facilities around the world, and it's best to come during the week when it's less busy.

Waterfalls around Buon Ma Thuot

Several **waterfalls** near Buon Ma Thuot are worth visiting, especially in the wet season, though you should be selective unless you're a real falls fan. **Dray Sap** and **Dray Nur**, situated side-by-side, are the most impressive and most popular.

Trinh Nu Falls
Daily 8am–6pm • 30,000đ

Comprising a narrow chute of water approached by a steep path, these small falls are the first you'll come to when approaching from the city – watch out for a signed left-turn. The boulders lining the river here are highly picturesque, though the area is in the process of turning into a resort of sorts – in fact, it may soon make a more appealing place to stay than central Buon Ma Thuot. At the top of the falls is a restaurant with small, inviting pavilions overlooking the river – a good spot to rest up for refreshment or lunch.

Dray Sap and Dray Nur falls
Daily 8am–6pm · 30,000đ ticket gives access to both falls

The crescent-shaped **Dray Sap Falls** and neighbouring **Dray Nur Falls** are among the most spectacular waterfalls in the central highlands. After a short descent down steps from the car park, a wooden **suspension bridge** to the left leads to Dray Nur, which, though not as wide as Dray Sap, carries more water in the dry season; even at such times, it's quite a spectacle to watch the mist swirling around beneath the ledge-like crag the water topples over. On the other hand, at the end of the wet season in September, water levels are usually too high for the short walk to the falls to be accessible.

Almost 15m high and over 100m wide, Dray Sap doesn't mean "waterfall of smoke" for nothing: a fug of invigorating spray hangs in the air around. The area by the falls can get very crowded at weekends and on public holidays, but midweek a trip here makes a pleasant outing for a half- or full day.

ARRIVAL AND DEPARTURE	WATERFALLS AROUND BUON MA THUOT
By tour Most people go as part of a tour, which is certainly the easiest option; the Dak Lak tourist office (see p.187) offers good day-long packages including the falls, Yok Don National Park (see p.189) and Lak Lake (see p.184) for 620,000đ/person. **By bus** The falls are accessible on the hourly bus #13 (20,000đ), which you can pick up on Phan Chu Trinh	(see map, p.186). **By motorbike** You can rent a motorbike from most hotels; figure on around 200,000–250,000đ for a half-day. The falls are based southwest of Buon Ma Thuot; follow Highway 14 for 20km southwest of town, then turn left at the village of Ea Ting. Just 1km down this road, a left turn leads to Trinh Nu Falls; Dray Sap and Dray Nur are a further 9km along.

Yok Don National Park and around
40,000đ · ☎ 0262 378 3049, ⓦ yokdonnationalpark.vn

Vietnam's largest wildlife preserve, **Yok Don National Park**, covers over a thousand square kilometres of land between the hinge of the Cambodian border and the **Serepok River**, about 45km from Buon Ma Thuot. Much of it comprises deciduous forest, though the place can seem surprisingly dry for most of the year. If you start off early in the morning you might see E De and other minority peoples leaving their split-bamboo thatch houses for work in the fields, carrying their tools in raffia backpacks. In addition, over sixty species of animal, including tigers, leopards and bears, and more than 450 types of bird, populate the park; most, however, reside deep in the interior. Of all its wildlife, **elephants** are what Yok Don is best known for; the tomb of the most famous elephant-hunter of them all – Y Thu Knu (1850–1924), who had a lifetime tally of 244 – is located beyond the final hamlet from the park entrance.

Ban Don
The three sub-hamlets that comprise the village of **BAN DON** lie a few kilometres beyond Yok Don's park HQ, on the bank of the crocodile-infested Serepok River. Khmer, Thai, Lao, Jarai and Mnong live in the vicinity, though it's the **E De** that make up the majority. They adhere to a matriarchal social system, whereby a groom takes his bride's name, lives with her family and, should his wife die subsequently, marries one of her sisters so that her family retains a male workforce. Houses around the village, a few of which are longhouses, are built on stilts, and some are decorated with ornate woodwork.

However, village life in Ban Don has become overwhelmingly commercial, as the Ban Don Tourist Centre has organized its residents into a tourist-welcoming taskforce. It's

3

ACTIVITIES IN YOK DON NATIONAL PARK

There are a number of **activities** on offer in Yok Don, an increasingly switched-on national park. Basic **hiking** is the most popular, though you'll need a guide ($40 for a full day, $20 for a half-day); the area in the vicinity of the park office is not terribly interesting, though heading further afield increases the chance of animal sightings considerably. One interesting variation is a guided night hike ($10; seven-person minimum) – at certain times of year, you can shine a torch into the darkness and see the eyes of thousands of frogs staring back at you. Crocodile sightings are another exciting possibility. During daylight hours, it's also possible to take a short **boat-ride** along the Serepok ($20 per boat) or join an **elephant-trekking tour**, though the latter is not recommended owing to the use of metal cages atop the animals.

possible to spend the night here, though you'll only truly appreciate Yok Don by heading further into the park.

ARRIVAL AND DEPARTURE

By tour Most people visit the park on an organized tour. These can be arranged with the Dak Lak tourist office (see p.187), which runs tours from around 320,000đ per person, as well as more popular ones that include the falls near Buon Ma Thuot and Lak Lake (630,000đ).

By bus The hourly public bus #15 (25,000đ) runs from Nguyen Tat Thanh in Buon Ma Thuot (see map, p.186), and

YOK DON NATIONAL PARK AND AROUND

usually terminates a few hundred metres from the park entrance. They occasionally stop further away, and in this case the remaining distance can be easily covered in a xe om.

By taxi A taxi from Buon Ma Thuot costs around $60, including 2hr waiting time – this is what drivers expect of local tourists, but negotiate for longer if you'd like to truly make use of the park.

ACCOMMODATION

Park accommodation Overnight accommodation in the park includes the twin-bedded cabin-style rooms in the guesthouse by the park office, a campground and forest stations in the park. While it's possible to just turn up at the park office, you'll certainly save time by booking through Dak Lak tourist office (see p.187).

Pleiku

It has to be said that **PLEIKU**, the capital of Gia Lai province, is the runt of the central highland litter. It lacks the majesty of Da Lat, the coffee of Buon Ma Thuot and both the beauty and unhindered minority-visiting of Kon Tum, so only crops up on visitors' agendas if they're heading to or from Laos or Cambodia, or merely in need of a rest in between long bus-rides. The city is not terribly easy on the eye either, having been wrecked during the war (see box opposite); so little was left standing that a near-total reconstruction was required when hostilities ceased – in other words, in the very height of 1980s Soviet design. However, many come to enjoy the city's relatively carefree air, as well as the chance to visit a range of fascinating minority villages in the nearby area. The town itself is slowly being polished too, with the visually pleasing **Minh Thanh Pagoda** a neat recent addition to the city's modest roster of sights.

Ho Chi Minh Museum

Phan Dinh Phuong • Mon–Fri 7.30–11am & 1–5pm • Free

The **Ho Chi Minh Museum**, to the north of the town centre, features swords, crossbows, bamboo xylophones, a weaving loom and a pair of Uncle Ho's sandals, but no English signs. Unfortunately, of all the similar museums dotted around the land, this one scores most highly on the glorifying scale – there's a rather distasteful focus on the local ethnic communities' apparently uncompromising adoration for Uncle Ho.

Gia Lai Museum

Tran Hung Dao • Mon–Fri 7.30–11am & 1–5pm • Free

The **Gia Lai Museum** is, mercifully, a little better than its Ho Chi Minh counterpart. Most of the sparse exhibitions on display in this giant building follow the regular proforma for the museums of Vietnamese provincial capitals – a run-down of local rocks, wood and animals (badly stuffed to an almost comical degree, especially the angry dog), together with some clay and metal fragments. Far more interesting are the Cham reliefs, replicas of a Bahnar grave and longhouse, and displays of minority-group weaving. At the time of research the complex was under reconstruction, and its surrounds had been beautified with new grass, ponds and the like – look out for the Ho Chi Minh statue nearby, backed by a curl of Montagnard socialist-realist reliefs.

Minh Thanh Temple

Off Nguyen Viet Xuan • Dawn to dusk • Free

The newest attraction in town is probably its best – the surprisingly spectacular **Minh Thanh Temple**, recently erected a couple of kilometres south of the city centre. Though devoid of any real history, and largely made of concrete rather than wood, it may just tempt you into taking a few pictures – try the sinuous dragons growling from each corner of the main hall's roof. From within, sonorous bells and gongs chime a lovely, almost musical sound if there's a slight breeze. The star of the show, however, is a **nine-tiered pagoda**, resplendent in vermilion and gold. Further down the gentle hillside that the complex calls home, you'll find a few cheery statues, ponds and bridges.

ARRIVAL AND DEPARTURE | PLEIKU

By plane The airport (☎0269 382 5097) lies 7km northeast of the city, from where taxis (about 130,000đ) and xe om (60,000đ) make the journey to the centre.
Destinations Da Nang (3 weekly; 50min); Hanoi (2–3 daily; 1hr 25min); Ho Chi Minh City (4 daily; 1hr 25min).
By bus The bus station is off Ly Nam De, a short way east of the centre; you'll find taxis (55,000đ) and xe om (25,000đ) waiting to take passengers the rest of the way into town.

Note that there are daily international services (departing at 7am or 8am) to Attapeu and Pakse in Laos, and Banlung in Cambodia's Rattanakiri province.
Destinations Buon Ma Thuot (4–5hr); Da Nang (10hr); Kon Tum (1hr 30min); Quy Nhon (4hr).
By taxi If you're headed to or from Kon Tum, consider travelling in style – taxis booked through your accommodation should only cost 250,000đ.

INFORMATION

Tourist office Gia Lai Eco-Tourist (☎0269 376 0898, ⓦgialaiecotourist.com) has a branch at 82 Hung Vuong, and can provide information as well as arrange expensive, tailor-made trekking, battlefield tours and overnight stays

in minority villages (see p.195).
Services Vietcombank at 62 Phan Boi Chau can exchange cash, and has an ATM.

THE ROLLING THUNDER CAMPAIGN

The band of peaks to the west of Highway 14 en route to Pleiku, and the rugged terrain buttressing them, constituted one of the American War's major combat theatres. It was an NVA (North Vietnamese Army) attack on Pleiku, in February 1965, that elicited the "**Rolling Thunder**" campaign (see p.443). The war's first conventional battle of any size was fought in the Ia Drang Valley, southwest of Pleiku, eight months later. Hundreds of Americans died at Ia Drang, but many times more Communists perished, spurring America to claim victory by dint of a higher body count. A decade later, in March 1975, Pleiku was abandoned when NVA troops overran Buon Ma Thuot. As the South's commanding officers flew by helicopter to safety, two hundred thousand southern soldiers and civilians were left to make their own way down to the coast, hounded at every step by NVA shells.

ACCOMMODATION

Accommodation in Pleiku is decidedly uninspiring; there's a smattering of near-identical cheap options in the city centre, though almost nothing at the middle or higher end.

★**Duc Long** 117–119 Tran Phu ☎0269 374 8777. You can't miss the tower housing this hotel – it's one of the tallest buildings in Pleiku, or indeed the entire central highlands. The rooms, mostly located on the high-teen floors, are both large and of reasonable quality, and some have good views over the market area. $\overline{\$20}$

★**HAGL** 1 Phu Dong ☎0269 371 8450, ⓦhaglhotel pleiku.vn. This is by far the most comfortable option around, with spacious rooms that are well equipped with desks and bathtubs – those on the upper floors also have nice views across the countryside. Good value, and a lovely place to treat yourself if you've been on a central highland slog. It's about 1km east of the town centre. $\overline{\$50}$

Tre Xanh 18 Le Lai ☎0269 371 5787. A decent choice bordering the mucky grid of streets facing the city market. Rooms are large enough and service is attentive, and you can use the on-site travel agency to organize a tour of local minority villages. $\overline{\$15}$

EATING

Pleiku's signature dish is *pho kho*, which is a bit like a normal pho but with the noodles served in a different bowl to the broth – the damp noodles are topped with bamboo shoots, minced pork and shallots, and are often so tasty that you don't need the broth at all.

Acacia HAGL hotel ☎0269 371 8450, ⓦhaglhotelpleiku.vn. Offers a good range of Vietnamese dishes, as well as a few Western ones – spaghetti bolognese may suddenly seem very tempting to those who've made it as far as Pleiku. Considering the fact that it's in the city's poshest hotel, prices are surprisingly reasonable (you can eat for under 100,000đ, though most mains are double that), and the service is fast. One major downside is that it's a fair walk from the centre. Daily 9am–9pm.

Café Tennis 61 Quang Trung. This is a reasonable place for a decent coffee. It's located next to a tennis court, and if you come at the right time you may even be able to catch a few games. Daily 8am–10pm.

Hong 22 Nguyen Van Troi ☎0269 382 3307. The best spot for *pho kho* (see above) is this buzzing little joint, which is popular enough to have a second level. It costs just 35,000đ for a generous serving of noodles. Daily 8am–9pm.

Around Pleiku

This far north in the highlands, the **Jarai** (see p.467) and, to a lesser extent, the **Bahnar** (see p.466) outnumber the E De, though many of them have been assimilated into mainstream Vietnamese culture. You'll need a **guide** to tour any of their villages (see p.195).

Plei Phun

Around 34km northwest of Pleiku, **PLEI PHUN** is by far the most commonly visited of the local Jarai villages. Your guide will show you around the headman's house, the local graveyard and village spring. As is common with this particular tribe, the incredibly ornate graveyards are the main focus of interest, and you'll see roughly hewn **hardwood statues** depicting figures in a range of moods placed around each family grave. In the past the Jarai would stick bamboo poles through the earth and into a fresh grave, through which to "feed" the dead, though now they tend to leave fruit and bowls of rice on the top.

Bahnar villages

A group of four secluded but easily accessible **Bahnar villages** lie 38km east of Pleiku, en route to Quy Nhon, where **Dek Tu**, **De Cop**, **De Doa** and **Dek Rol** rub shoulders with one another across a small area of forests and streams. Small split-bamboo and straw houses on stilts are used in these orderly communities, and each one boasts an impressive, steeply thatched *rong*, or communal house, where ceremonies are

performed, local disputes are resolved and decisions taken. As at Plei Phun, the **graveyards** are particularly interesting (especially in Dek Tu), where the practice of feeding the dead is prevalent; unlike the Jarai, however, each of the deceased here has their own grave complete with a small sloping roof. Ladders made out of bamboo poles are leant against the graves to aid the journey to a new life, and some are adorned with surprising ornaments, including wooden American fighter jets.

INFORMATION

Tourist information Gia Lai province is notoriously defensive of its few remaining traditional settlements – authorities don't approve of individuals making forays into the wilds, and insist that you should always be with a licensed guide. If you try to bypass this regulation and just turn up in villages, you'll get little cooperation from the locals, who receive a cut from visitor fees – and face

AROUND PLEIKU

potential punishment from the authorities for your unauthorized intrusion.

Guides To visit the Jarai or Bahnar villages, you can hire an official guide from Gia Lai Eco-Tourist (see p.191) or another agency; these cost from $15 for a half-day and $25 for a whole one, and you'll also have to fund their transportation.

ACCOMMODATION

Home-stays It's possible to arrange a home-stay in the largest Bahnar village, De Cop. Gia Lai Tourist has commandeered a house on stilts here, from where you can

visit each village on a one-day hike. A two-day programme visiting both Plei Phun and these villages works out about $35/person for a group of five people.

Kon Tum

Sitting on the edge of the Dakbla River, the sleepy, friendly town of **KON TUM** could market itself as the Sapa of the South – except the mountains are hills, the weather stays warm and locals don't wear traditional dress. It is, however, the best base in the central highlands for those wanting to understand minority culture, and unlike busy Buon Ma Thuot and concrete-heavy Pleiku, this provincial capital makes a highly pleasant place to stay. It also has a few sights of its own, including some lovely colonial-era architecture – some of the most beautiful buildings in the country. However, most are here to use Kon Tum as a springboard for jaunts to outlying villages of the **Bahnar** and other minorities such as the **Sedang** (see p.468), **Gieh Trieng** and

MINORITY VILLAGES AROUND KON TUM

There are dozens of Bahnar villages encircling Kon Tum (as well as some in the town itself; see p.196). As most are free from the official restrictions that hang over Pleiku, you're at liberty to explore this area at will, although for **overnight stays** it's best to check first with the tourist office (see p.197) – a guided tour would cost you around $25 per person per day. Prices are often a little lower at *Eva Café* (see p.197), whose knowledgeable staff speak excellent English.

All Bahnar villages have a longhouse at their centre known as a **rong**. They're built on sturdy **stilts** with a platform and entrance at either end (or sometimes in the middle), and the interior is generally made of split bamboo and protected by a towering thatched roof, usually about 15m high. The *rong* is used as a venue for festivals and village meetings, and as a **village court** – anyone found guilty of a tribal offence has to ritually kill a pig and a chicken, and must apologize in front of the village.

KON KOTU

About 5km to the east of Kon Tum is the most frequently visited of the Bahnar villages, **Kon Kotu**. Though this place is now linked to Kon Tum by a surfaced road, the route there involves a pleasant walk along country paths (contact the local tourist office for details) and it's possible to overnight in the village *rong*. To get there by road, follow Tran Hung Dao east out of town until you reach a suspension bridge over the river at Kon Klor. Turn left 200m beyond the bridge and follow the road to Kon Kotu. Though the village church is absolutely huge, and fairly pretty to boot, it's still the immaculate *rong* that commands the most attention. No nails were used in the construction of the bamboo walls, floor and the impossibly tall thatch roof of this lofty communal hall. The *rong* also doubles as an occasional **overnight stop** for local trekking tours organized by Kon Tum Tourist (see p.197), in either a simple guesthouse ($12 per person), or the longhouse itself ($10).

PLEI THONGHIA AND KON HONGO

The villages of **Plei Thonghia** and **Kon Hongo**, respectively 1km and 4km west of Kon Tum, are inhabited by members of the Rongao, one of the smaller minority groups in the region. Women are often busy weaving in the shade of their simple, wooden huts, **ox carts** trundle along the dusty road and children splash about in the Dakbla River down below. It's possible to walk to Plei Tonghia – head north from the Dakbla bridge, turn left at Ba Trieu and just keep going (don't be tempted to walk or cycle along the riverbank, since it's a hard slog, mostly the wrong way). Kon Hongo is within cycling distance but a little tricky to find – it's easier to take a xe om there (30,000d) and work your way back on foot.

YA CHIM

About 17km southwest of Kon Tum is the village of **Ya Chim**, where there are a few Jarai cemeteries that can be visited – though it's best to go with a guide from Kon Tum Tourist as they are tricky to find. Wooden posts, some of them carved in the form of mourning figures, surround the graves, and personal possessions such as a bicycle or TV are placed inside. The graves are carefully tended for a period of three to five years after death and offerings are brought to the site daily. At the end of this period a buffalo is sacrificed to make a feast for the villagers and the grave is abandoned in the belief that the spirit of the deceased has now departed.

Rongao. There are about 650 minority villages in the province, of which only a few have been visited by foreigners, so the scope for adventure here is broad.

Kon Tum's riverside promenade along the Dakbla River is a fine place for a stroll – especially on fair-weather evenings, when it seems as if half the town stops by.

Tan Huong Church
92 Nguyen Hue • Dawn to dusk • Free

You can't miss the grand bulk of **Tan Huong Church**, which sports colourful, pastel-shaded bas-reliefs (look out for George slaying a dragon) on its peach-Melba-coloured facade. Considering Kon Tum's remote location, the church is a surprisingly elegant

3

MOVING INTO LAOS: THE BO Y CROSSING

The easiest option to cross to Attapeu or Pakse in Laos is to take a direct bus across the border at **Bo Y**, 86km northwest of Kon Tum. There are daily buses, but companies servicing this route have been in flux for some time, and there's no set pick-up spot in Kon Tum – all buses start an hour south in Pleiku. It's best to get your accommodation to book you a ticket and arrange a pick-up time and place – buses usually pass through Kon Tum daily around 9–10am, hitting Attapeu (170,000đ) after 5–7hr, depending on where the lunch stop is, and then continuing on to Pakse (12hr; 330,000đ). One-month Lao visas are available at the border for about $40, though the price depends on your nationality.

---

building; the original structure was completed in the 1850s, but the place has been restored several times since. Be sure to peek inside the interior, as it's a charming place with dark wooden columns and a couple of stained-glass windows.

Montagnard Church

Nguyen Hue • Dawn to dusk; Mass usually around 4.30pm • Free

Also known as the "Wooden Church", this stunning edifice was built by the French in 1913, and has been frequently restored since then. A statue of Christ stands over the front entrance; below, a stained-glass window neatly fuses the classic Christian symbol of the dove with images of local resonance – a Bahnar village and an elephant. In the grounds is a statue of nineteenth-century French bishop Stephen Theodore Cuenot, who established the diocese of Kon Tum. Mass is held in the Bahnar language – they don't mind curious foreigners popping their heads in, but be respectful if taking any pictures.

Catholic seminary

56 Tran Hung Dao • Dawn to dusk • Free

Kon Tum's **Catholic seminary** is certainly worth a look for its impressive architecture. Set in the middle of garden-filled grounds, its appearance is far more European than Vietnamese. The soft cream colour of the seminary walls is offset by dark wood, and though few of the rooms are open to visitors, the gardens are a great place to relax for half an hour.

Bahnar villages

One good thing about Kon Tum is that you don't have to go far to get a feel of minority culture, since there are a couple of **Bahnar villages** within the town itself. First comes **Kon Harachot**, whose immaculate *rong* faces a football field – if you're lucky, you may even get to see an all-Bahnar game. To get there, head east along Nguyen Hue, and take any right turn up until Hoang Dieu; Ly Thai To will bring you straight to the *rong*. The walk from here to the river is delightful, especially during or after sunset – take any road going west.

Heading the other way, following Nguyen Hue to its eastern end (at one point it stops being the main road and becomes a side street to the right) brings you to **Kon Tum Konam**. This village has a slightly seedier feel, and its *rong* has been given a fetching roof of red corrugated metal. Lastly, following Tran Hung Dao to the east takes you directly to **Kon Tum Kopong**, where there is another wonderful *rong*. Villagers here are big on **basket weaving**, and you might chance upon locals cutting bamboo into thin strips and crafting them into sturdy baskets, which they sell very cheaply in the local market.

ARRIVAL AND DEPARTURE   **KON TUM**

By plane The nearest airport is less than an hour down the road in Pleiku (see p.191), though you'll need to use your initiative to get to Kon Tum without hitting Pleiku first. Highway 14 is around 1km west of the terminal, so you can either wait for one of the irregular Kon Tum-bound buses, or prepare to haggle with a xe om driver.

By bus The bus station is to the northwest of town on Phan Dinh Phung. From here, it's best to take a xe om (30,000đ) to the town centre, which is about 3km away, though it's not an unpleasant walk. Also note that Kon Tum is a port of call for buses heading between Pleiku or Quy Nhon and the Lao towns of Attapeu and Pakse. The exact stopping points have been in a state of flux for some time, so try asking at your accommodation if you'd like to buy a ticket.

Destinations Da Nang (5hr); Pleiku (1hr); Quang Ngai (5hr); Quy Nhon (5hr).

INFORMATION

Tourist information Kon Tum Tourist (2 Phan Dinh Phung; ☎ 0260 386 3334) can, in theory, organize a wide range of tours, including trekking, river trips and traditional dance performances. In practice, there is not always an English-speaker present, and in this case you'll be lucky to get more than a shrug and a smile. *Eva Café* (1 Phan Chu Trinh ☎ 0260 386 2448) is far more useful than the official provincial tourist office, and the range of tours that they organize is almost as extensive.

ACCOMMODATION

Family 235 Tran Hung Dao ☎ 0260 386 2448, ✉ familyhotelkt@yahoo.com; map p.194. This budget option started off well then let things slip, though at the time of research it seemed to have turned the corner and become a decent place to stay once more. The friendly staff speak English and advise on trips in and around town, while the garden area is a marvellously pleasant place in which to relax. **$20**

Hoang Van 1a Hoang Van Thu ☎ 0260 391 7555; map p.194. This friendly little guesthouse is far prettier than you'd expect for the price, rooms are a steal and its well-designed lobby looks, if not always functions, like that of a "real" hotel. The rooms are no different, even though the very cheapest have no windows; all have small tubs and TV. **$14**

Indochine 30 Bach Dang ☎ 0260 386 3335, ⓦ indochinehotel.vn; map p.194. Enjoying a prime riverside location, the town's fanciest hotel is perhaps not as grand as its wistful name may lead you to believe, but it's still decent value. Rooms are cosy and carpeted, and those facing the river have great views – for the price, it's actually quite a bargain. **$35**

★ **Konklor** 155 Bac Can ☎ 0260 386 1555; map p.194. The bad news first: this hotel is pretty far from the centre, a 25,000đ xe om ride to the east (though also walkable with light luggage). The good news is pretty much everything else – it's set in a quiet area by a totally tourist-free Bahnar village (also called Kon Klor), rooms are astonishingly attractive for the price, the grounds are green and pretty, and the staff are just lovely. Breakfast costs extra. **$16**

EATING

3 Ngon 7 Nguyen Dinh Chieu ☎ 090 599 2707; map p.194. The best of a clutch of local venues selling eggs, meat, pate and the like on cow-shaped sizzle-platters – cute, not to mention tasty and cheap (sets from 25,000đ, including salad and a fizzy drink). Daily 8am–10pm.

Benz's House 53 Nguyen Trai; map p.194. If you've made it as far as Kon Tum, you'd be forgiven for wanting something a little different in your diet. Step forward this cheery Korean restaurant, serving cheap and passably authentic "Seoul" food such as *bibimbap* (veggies and egg on rice; 29,000đ). You could also give *soju*, Korea's favourite alcohol, a try. Daily 8am–11pm.

★ **Eva Café** 1 Phan Chu Trinh ☎ 0260 386 2448, ⓦ facebook.com/cafeevakontum; map p.194. This quirky café is an excellent place in which to savour some Kom Tum coffee, and is run by a local sculptor whose work is also displayed here. Built to vaguely resemble a stilthouse, its surrounding garden yields fountains, wooden sculptures of distorted faces and a waterfall trickling down the back wall. The friendly, English-speaking staff also put on excellent tours to surrounding villages (see p.197). Coffees and juices cost 25,000đ or so. Daily 6am–10pm.

Hanoi 166 Nguyen Hue; map p.194. If you're missing the north, slurp your sorrows away with a great bowl of pho (25,000đ) at this simple spot. The staff will most likely make a big fuss of you. Daily 5am–10pm.

Indochine 30 Bach Dang ☎ 0260 386 3335; map p.194. Your eyebrows are likely to go a bit Roger Moore the first time you see this hotel's café – with river views, fish ponds and curved columns of bamboo giving off a neo-forest feel, it would still count as attractive in Hanoi or HCMC. The service doesn't live up to the appearance, but it's still a grand place for coffee (14,000đ), juices (25,000đ) or cute bowls of ice cream (25,000đ); in the evening you can make use of the super-cheap beer prices (from 13,000đ). Daily 6.30am–10pm.

DIRECTORY

Banks It's possible to change money at the BIDV Bank at 1 Tran Phu, where there's also an ATM; there's another at the Agribank at 88 Tran Phu.

Post office You can find the post office at 205 Le Hong Phong.

The southern coast

RED SAND DUNES NEAR MUI NE

The southern coast

Beaches are, for many travellers, the primary reason for a visit to Southeast Asia, and in Vietnam they're most prevalent along the country's convex southern coastline. The main resort areas of Nha Trang and Mui Ne have both seen their popularity go through the roof of late, with ubiquitous Cyrillic- and Chinese-language signage showing that the area's popularity has transcended the West; to sate this demand, each of these places have added plenty of culinary sophistication and top-drawer accommodation to their existing coastal charms. There are also a number of less-heralded beaches to track down, and even a few islands, but the region has ample historical significance too – this was once the domain of the kingdom of Champa, whose magnificent ruins still dot the coast. An Indianized trading empire, Champa was courted in its prime by seafaring merchants from around the globe, but became steadily marginalized from the tenth century onwards by the march south of the Vietnamese.

4

These days a few enclaves around Phan Thiet and Phan Rang are all that remain of the **Cham people**, but the remnants of the towers that punctuate the countryside – many of which have recently been restored – recall Champa's former glory (see p.220).

Despite the influx of tourism, **sea fishing** is the region's lifeblood and provides a living for a considerable percentage of the population. Fleets of fishing boats jostle for space in the cramped ports and estuaries of the coastal towns, awaiting the turn of the tide, and fish and seafood drying along the road are a common sight. The fertile soil also blesses the coastal plains with coconut palms, rice paddies, cashew orchards, sugar cane fields, vineyards and shrimp farms. One of the most commonly seen fruits here, especially around Phan Thiet, is the dragon fruit, which grows on plants with distinctive, octopus-like tentacles.

Vietnam's southernmost beaches are not on the southern coast at all, but on the former French prison islands of the **Con Dao Archipelago**. While many beaches elsewhere are now experiencing high-octane development, Con Dao retains a laidback, unhurried air that tempts many to stay far longer than they'd planned. Back on the mainland, the first place of note is **Vung Tau**, once a French seaside resort, and now a smart, oil-rich town with passable beaches – much better ones can be found further up the coast. In reality, few travellers have the time or inclination to meander along the beaches between Vung Tau and Mui Ne, but with your own transport and an adventurous spirit you'll find somewhere to pace out a solitary set of footprints in the pristine sand.

Just a short way up the coast, you'll find it impossible to be alone in **Mui Ne** itself. It was almost unheard of until very recently, when its transition from being the country's best-kept secret to one of its most high-profile resorts happened almost overnight. It's perhaps a sign of things to come for Vietnamese tourism – slick resorts rubbing shoulders

SNORKELLING OFF THE COAST OF NHA TRANG

Highlights

❶ Con Dao Archipelago These islands once hosted Vietnam's most feared prison, but now welcome divers, trekkers and beach bums alike. **See p.203**

❷ Mui Ne Stay in a fancy resort at Mui Ne and spend your time kitesurfing in the breezy bay. **See p.213**

❸ Ca Na beach Everyone knows about Nha Trang and Mui Ne, but the southern coast still has a few virtually deserted beaches – this pristine stretch being one such example. **See p.219**

❹ Cham architecture Get up close to the impressive Po Klong Garai towers, just outside Phan Rang, or check out the other Cham structures in the region. **See box, p.220**

❺ Underwater activities Snorkel or dive in the clear waters off the islands near Nha Trang. **See box, p.227**

❻ Mud baths Soak in a mud bath at the Thap Ba Hot Springs near Nha Trang. **See p.231**

❼ Quy Nhon Spend time exploring this unsung beach city, which has great seafood, some of the coast's best Cham ruins and a chilled-out vibe. **See p.234**

HIGHLIGHTS ARE MARKED ON THE MAP ON P.202

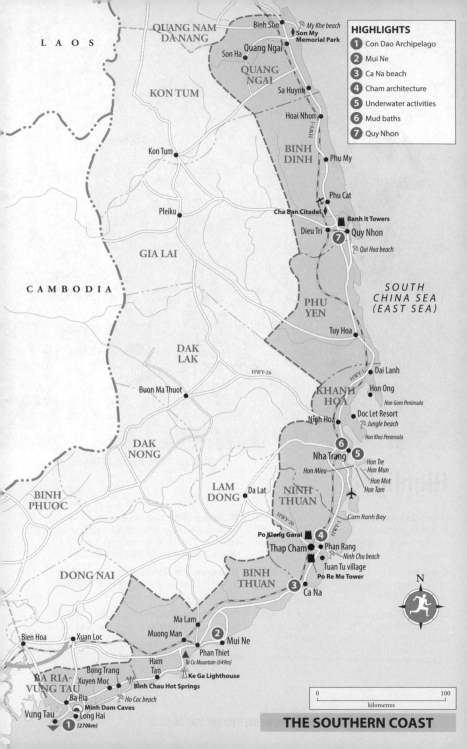

HIGHLIGHTS
1 Con Dao Archipelago
2 Mui Ne
3 Ca Na beach
4 Cham architecture
5 Underwater activities
6 Mud baths
7 Quy Nhon

LAOS

QUANG NAM
DA NANG

Binh Son
Quang Ngai
My Khe beach
Son My Memorial Park
Son Ha
QUANG NGAI
Sa Huynh

KON TUM

Hoai Nhon

BINH DINH

Kon Tum
Phu My

Pleiku
Phu Cat
Cha Ban Citadel
Banh It Towers
Dieu Tri
7 Quy Nhon
Qui Hoa beach

GIA LAI

CAMBODIA

SOUTH CHINA SEA (EAST SEA)

PHU YEN

Tuy Hoa

DAK LAK

HWY-26
Dai Lanh
Hon Ong
HWY-1
KHANH HOA
Hon Gom Peninsula

Buon Ma Thuot
Nigh Hoa
Doc Let Resort
Jungle beach
Hon Khoi Peninsula

DAK NONG
6
5
Nha Trang
Hon Mieu
Hon Tre
Hon Mun
Hon Mot
Hon Tam

BINH PHUOC

LAM DONG
Da Lat
NINH THUAN
Cam Ranh Bay

HWY-20
Po Klong Garai
4
Thap Cham
Phan Rang
Ninh Chu beach
Tuan Tu village
Po Re Me Tower

DONG NAI

BINH THUAN
3
Ca Na

N

Ma Lam
Muong Man
2
Mui Ne

Bien Hoa
Xuan Loc
Phan Thiet
Ta Cu Mountain (649m)

Ham Tan
Ke Ga Lighthouse

BA RIA-VUNG TAU
Bong Trang
Xuyen Moc
Binh Chau Hot Springs
Ba Ria
Ho Coc beach
Minh Dam Caves
Vung Tau
1
Long Hai
(270km)

0   100
kilometres

THE SOUTHERN COAST

along a fine sweep of soft sand, looking out over aquamarine waters. This tourist enclave attracts a steady stream of overseas visitors, and also provides an idyllic short break for Ho Chi Minh City's expats and growing middle-class. Those who feel that a day sunbathing is a day wasted will prefer to rest up around **Phan Rang**, site of **Po Klong Garai**, the most impressive of the many tower complexes erected by the once-mighty Champa empire.

North of Phan Rang, Highway 1 ploughs through sugar-cane plantations, blinding white salt flats and shrimp farms on its way into **Nha Trang**. Here travellers can enjoy the best of both worlds – a combination of Cham towers and beach activities, including diving and snorkelling trips. Nha Trang also has the southern coast's greatest range of accommodation and restaurants, and is a deservedly popular place. Other more secluded beaches that warrant an expedition further north include **Doc Let**, while **Quy Nhon** makes a useful halt above Nha Trang. The scars of war tend not to intrude too much along this stretch of the country, though many visitors make time to visit **Quang Ngai**, where Vietnam's south-central arc of coastline culminates, and view the sombre site of the notorious **My Lai** massacre, perpetrated by US forces in 1968.

The Con Dao Archipelago

Vietnam is book-ended to the south by the unspoiled **Con Dao Archipelago**, a confetti-like spray of sixteen emerald-green islands, cast adrift in the South China Sea some 185km south of Vung Tau. The sleepy nature of the archipelago belies its tumultuous history – under French occupation, Con Dao was home to the most feared prison in the country, and haunting remnants of that time are still visible. However, most come here to get away from such negative thoughts, and since regular flights began recently, the archipelago has taken its first steps towards welcoming tourists.

4

Con Son

The biggest island in the archipelago, **Con Son** is its undisputed hub and the only place with any facilities. Bar dive-trips and jaunts to neighbouring islands, this is the only easily accessible part of Con Dao – no bad thing, since Con Son itself is an arrestingly beautiful place with striking colonial buildings. While you're based here, try **trekking** in the national park (which covers part of the island and its surrounding sea), **diving** off the nearby islands, or lounging on various uncrowded **beaches**.

Brief history

The British East India Company established a **fortified outpost** on Con Son in 1703. Had this flourished, the island may by now have been a more diminutive Hong Kong or Singapore, given its strategic position on the route to China. But within three years, the Bugis mercenaries drafted in to construct and garrison the base from Sulawesi – in Indonesia – had murdered their British commanders, putting paid to this early experiment in colonization. Known then as Poulo Condore, Con Son was still treading water when the American sailor John White spied its "lofty summits" a little over a century later, in 1819. White deemed it a decent natural harbour, though blighted by "noxious reptiles, and affording no good fresh water".

The island finally found its calling when decades later the French chose it as the site of a **penal colony** for anticolonial activists, and Con Son's savage regime soon earned it the nickname **Devil's Island**. Prisoners languished in squalid pits called "tiger cages", which featured metal grilles instead of roofs, from which guards sprinkled powdered lime and dirty water on the inmates. As the twentieth century progressed, the colony developed into a sort of unofficial "revolutionary university". Older hands instructed their greener cell-mates in the finer points of Marxist–Leninist theory, while the dire conditions they endured helped reinforce the lessons.

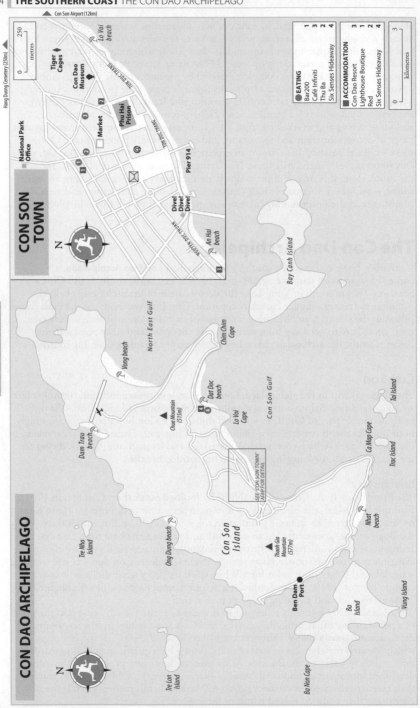

Con Son town

Village-like **CON SON TOWN** is the largest settlement, and home to almost all of the island's accommodation and restaurants. Its peaceful promenade makes a beautiful place for a walk, past the huge gnarled trunks of the malabar almond trees as colourful fishing boats bob in the bay. The promenade is punctuated by **Pier 914**, whose curious name derives from one estimate of the number of prisoners who died during its construction; nowadays it's a great place to listen to the sea at night, perhaps with a beer in hand.

Few come to the archipelago for its sightseeing potential, but there are a few worthy historical sights in and around the town centre.

Con Dao Museum

Nguyen Hue • Mon–Sat 7–11am & 1–5pm • Free

Recently relocated to a larger building, the **Con Dao Museum** is well worth a visit, with various photographic displays illustrating the island's often-traumatic history, including some fascinating snaps from the French colonial period and the American War. The dioramas and interactive displays are a bit cheesier, but all in all it's a pretty good effort, even if the delivery is inevitably one-sided.

Phu Hai Prison

Nguyen Hue • Daily 7.30–11.30am & 1–5pm • 20,000đ

The many cells in the now-defunct **Phu Hai Prison** remain littered with shackles, placed painfully close together. In a couple of exhibition cells, emaciated statues show how the Vietnamese inmates spent their days crowded together, unless they were selected for the "tiger cages" or the "solariums", where they were exposed to the elements in roofless rooms. There are more tiger cages just to the east in a separate, former museum complex, accessible via a path from the main road.

Hang Duong Cemetery

About 1km northeast of town on Nguyen An Ninh • Daily 24hr • Free • No shorts or sleeveless tops

The graves in the **Hang Duong Cemetery** add a tangible layer to the island's tragic past. All are unmarked, but one stands out – brightly coloured combs lie deposited on the grave of Vo Thi Sau, a teenage Viet Minh figher who in 1952 became the first woman to be executed here, at the age of 19. As with many revolutionary heroes and heroines, her name lives on in the form of eponymous streets in pretty much every town in the land. If you're game, try visiting around midnight when locals usually gather to burn offerings to her – it's quite a spectacle.

Con Son's beaches

After visiting the historic monuments and trekking across Con Son, you may want to focus on some serious relaxation. **Lo Voi** and **An Hai** beaches, which front the town, are not bad, though in winter months the bay is often cluttered with fishing boats. Other notable beaches are dotted around the island: **Dam Trau** up north is by far the best looking, with fine sand and a few small eateries; nearby **Ong Dung Beach** is also good, though mostly stones and less appealing; and **Dat Doc Beach** to the east of town is a long, sandy option, amenable to swimming. You'll likely need to rent a motorbike (see box, p.206) or xe om to get to any of them, and you should keep in mind that snorkelling only really gets good far from these beaches, around the outlying islands where most tour operators will take you (see below).

Outlying islands

Renting a boat to explore the other islands can be incredibly tricky, not to mention expensive if you're not travelling in a group; contact Dive! Dive! Dive! (see box, p.206) for advice

You'll find plenty of deserted beaches and healthy coral reefs on some of Con Dao's outlying islands. From June to October it is possible to watch sea turtles laying eggs at

ACTIVITIES ON CON SON

BIKING

Renting a bike here is a piece of cake (see below), and you'll find that the roads are virtually empty, even in the middle of the village, for most of the day. You essentially have two options for a memorable bike ride. The first route involves heading north from Con Son Town, where you'll pass the *Six Senses* resort and the airport before reaching Dam Trau beach, located down a side-trail branching off to the west. Alternatively, it's an easy journey south to Ca Map Cape, and from there you can swing northwest towards the small settlement of Ben Dam, where most of the fishing boats dock. Its population is mostly an interesting mix of sailors and prostitutes.

DIVING AND SNORKELLING

Given Con Dao's remote location, it should be little surprise to hear that its surrounding waters are up there with the top dive sites in Vietnam. The best time for this is between April and May, when visibility can stretch as far as twenty metres. There are two good operators on the island, both of which have a full range of services from snorkelling trips to full PADI courses. The excellent Dive! Dive! Dive! on Nguyen Hue (☎0254 383 0701, ⓦdive-condao.com) offers trips throughout the year, while Rainbow Divers at 40 Ton Duc Thang (☎090 557 7671, ⓦdivevietnam.com) opens its doors between April and August only.

HIKING

A hike along one of the island's many trails in the national park may be more appealing than a tour of the prison. Some trails, such as the one heading straight north from town to Ong Dung Beach, are well marked and can be followed independently, though it's not possible to scale Thanh Gia, the island's highest peak at 577m, since the paths here lead through military land. Keen birdwatchers might be lucky enough to spot rare species such as the red-billed tropicbird or the pied imperial pigeon around the island. Make sure to take plenty of water and food, as there is nothing available outside the town. The Con Dao National Park headquarters is located north of the town centre at 29 Vo Thi Sau (☎0254 383 0669, ⓦcondaopark.com.vn), and can provide information about hiking trails. It's also possible to hire a guide here, though they rarely have any English-speakers on staff.

night on nearby **Bay Canh Island**, though the local authorities have done a poor job with protecting them so far. Few restrictions are placed on groups that are visiting, so it's best to think twice about taking a turtle-tour out here. It's also possible to enjoy occasional sightings of dugongs, which are endearing mammals (also known as sea cows) that feed only on seagrass, grow up to three metres long and weigh up to 400kg.

ARRIVAL AND GETTING AROUND   THE CON DAO ARCHIPELAGO

By plane VASCO (☎0283 842 2790, ⓦvietnamairlines .com) operates a few small, propeller-driven planes to Con Son airport, which is around 15km northeast of town. The airline websites have, for years, shown zero availability for flights that later take off half-full, so if you're unable to book in this manner try asking a travel agent in HCMC (see box, p.88) or elsewhere. Most of the major hotels run shuttle services from the airport, which meet the planes and can drop you back before your return flight; wherever you're staying, you can catch a

ride with one for 50,000đ. The journey into town gives a tantalizing glimpse of the island's rugged beauty and windswept, deserted beaches.

Destinations Can Tho (daily; 50min); HCMC (5 daily; 1hr).

By scooter or bicycle Most hotels charge from 100,000–120,000đ/day for a scooter. Note that your bike will come with almost no fuel, as there are very few petrol stations on the island. Instead, you could try renting a bike from Dive! Dive! Dive! (see above) for 50,000đ/day.

ACCOMMODATION

Be warned: you'll pay far more here than you would for similar facilities on the mainland. The number of traveller-friendly spots has been increasing in recent years, though the middle market is suffering.

Con Dao Resort 8 Nguyen Duc Thuan ☎0254 383 0939, ⓦcondaoresort.vn; map p.204. With perhaps the

best beach location on Con Son, this hotel has a good swimming pool, comfortable rooms and large buffet breakfasts –though it is starting to show its age. Staff can arrange boat trips and vehicle hire. **$70**

Lighthouse Boutique Ho Thanh Tong ☎0164 468 3866; map p.204. This is a good choice in the budget category, with a central location in town, perfectly comfortable rooms and decent standards of service. Sometimes that's all you really need, but they've even thrown in some pleasing decorative frills. **$22**

★ **Red** 17b Nguyen An Ninh ☎096 673 0079; map p.204. The prize fighter in Con Dao's welterweight division, this family-run affair is based right in the thick of the action.

Painted a soothing lemon hue, the rooms here are easy on the eye, and for Con Dao they're pretty easy on the wallet too. **$30**

Six Senses Hideaway Dat Doc Beach ☎0254 383 1222, ⓦsixsenses.com; map p.204. One of Vietnam's most exclusive resorts, a few minutes' drive up the coast from Con Son Town. The modern, timber-framed villas are rather gorgeous, while the bamboo-covered outdoor showers – and the fact that a healthy chunk of the staff are from the island – is a particularly nice touch. There's also a pristine stretch of private beach, and a butler to take care of your every need. **$600**

EATING

Not too long ago, **hotels** were more or less the only reliable places to eat on Con Dao. While this isn't the case any longer, you still shouldn't raise your expectations too high as the scene is still in its infancy.

Bar200 7 Vo Thi Sau ☎0254 363 0024; map p.204. If you want a cheese-loaded pizza with lashings of HP or pesto sauce on top, this is the place for you – just like eating an airline meal, the remoteness of Con Dao somehow makes such things taste great. This restaurant is also good for sandwiches and burgers (figure on around 100,000đ for a light meal), and you can grab a coffee or beer. Daily 10am–2pm & 5–9pm.

★ **Café Infiniti** Corner of Pham Van Dong and Tran Huy Lieu ☎093 359 4246; map p.204. This is hugely popular with visitors and the island's few expats, largely on account of the fact that it's the only place around with decent Western food on the menu – it's 100,000đ for sandwiches, 150,000đ or so for pizzas, and there's ice cream for dessert (or cocktails, later on). The friendly local owner is also a

good source of general Con Dao advice. Daily 7am–11pm.

Six Senses Hideaway Dat Doc beach ☎0254 383 1222, ⓦsixsenses.com; map p.204. This place is so secluded that if you're staying here, you'll be eating here anyway. The luxurious restaurant and juice/cocktail bar are both superb and open to non-guests, but make sure you bring money – cocktails are 275,000đ, and many meals double that. Daily 8am–10pm.

Thu Ba 7 Vo Thi Sau ☎0254 383 0939, ⓦcondaoresort .vn; map p.204. This is the pick of the town's Vietnamese restaurants, especially if you're into seafood. Still, if you've other meals in mind, have a chat with the amiable owner (this is one of the only places on Con Dao in which English is spoken), and they'll rustle up a nice hotpot, curry or veggie dish for you (mains from 70,000đ). Daily 8am–11pm.

DIRECTORY

Bank There are now several ATMs dotted around town (including one outside the Vietinbank, at the junction of Le Duan and Le Van Viet), as well as an Agribank just outside the main market. They're pretty reliable these days, but you

should still consider bringing enough money to cover your stay.

Post office The post office is based at Nguyen Thi Minh Khai.

Vung Tau

VUNG TAU (pronounced more like "boom dow") is one of those places that divide opinion – it's deemed scruffy by some and agreeable by others, and you may well leave town with one foot in both camps. Its popularity stems from its fast connections to Ho Chi Minh City – the promise of beaches and a seaside atmosphere just a quick ride away makes Vung Tau a default weekend bolt hole for stressed-out Saigonese.

Located on a hammer-headed spit of land jutting into the mouth of the Saigon River, Vung Tau was once a thriving riviera-style beach resort; the city's offshore **oil industry** and steadily growing port have transformed it into a more business-oriented conurbation. Locals are fond of swimming from the town's **beaches**, but they're all second-rate despite recent attempts to clean them up. However, the boardwalk along **Sau Beach**, known to seasoned expats as "Back Beach", remains a pleasant place for an evening stroll, and perhaps a light seafood meal. "Front Beach", where the ferries arrive, has more traffic and less appeal.

Brief history

Portuguese ships are thought to have exploited the city's deep anchorage as early as the fifteenth century. By the turn of the twentieth century, French expats, who knew the place as "Cap Saint-Jacques", had adopted it as a retreat from the daily rigmarole of Saigon, and set to work carving colonial villas into the sides of **Nui Lon** and **Nui Nho**, two low hills near the coast. Shifts in Vietnam's political sands duly replaced French visitors with American GIs; with them gone, and the Communist government in power, the city became a favoured launch pad for the vessels that spirited away the **boat people** in the late 1970s (see box, p.448).

Nui Lon

Cable car station on Tran Phu • Daily 7.30am–6pm • 300,000đ return

Just north of the city centre, **Nui Lon** is the highest peak in Vung Tau, and commands predictably sweeping views from its 201m-high summit. While it's possible to walk to the top, or take a xe om, most choose to make the ascent by **cable car**. At the top you'll find a small park, which is particularly good for families; known officially as the Ho May Tourism Resort, it includes a cherry blossom orchard and a peacock garden. There are also a couple of small lakes here – all very pretty, though they are a bit too popular on weekends and holidays.

VUNG TAU

Alternate Port for Hydrofoils, Jetty for Con Dao boats, Ba Ria (31km) & HCMC (94km)

0 — 1 kilometre

■ ACCOMMODATION	
Golden Sea	4
Grand	3
Green	5
Imperial	2
Son Ha	1
The Wind Boutique	6

● EATING	
David	2
Ganh Hao	1
Lan Rung Resort	3

■ DRINKING	
Lucy's Sports Bar	1

Bach Dinh

12 Tran Phu • Daily 7am–5pm • 15,000đ

One of the few remaining colonial structures worth a look is the imposing **Bach Dinh**, a mansion peeping out from behind a vanguard of frangipani and bougainvillea. Built at the end of the nineteenth century, the "White Palace" served as a holiday home to Vietnam's political players, hosting such luminaries as Paul Doumer, governor-general of Indochina (for whom it was originally erected), emperors Thanh Thai and Bao Dai, and President Thieu.

Inside you can see the building's collection of "valuable antique items", excavated from a seventeenth-century shipwreck off Con Dao; among the exhibits are such unmissables as "dry burned fruits", "beard-tweezers" and "pieces of stone in the ship". Upstairs is a display of Cambodian Buddhist statuary and shards of old pottery, but they are eclipsed by the commanding views of the bay.

Nui Nho

Accessible via Hai Dang, a small lane just north of the hydrofoil jetty

The town's lighthouse stands on **Nui Nho** hill. Built in 1910, its design seems to have been based on a child's sketch of a space-rocket, and it's now a popular place for locals out exercising in the morning and evening. The views from here out to sea and across town make for good photos. Note that the foothills in these parts are studded with almost a dozen pagodas, and though they're all accessible to the public, the presence of a large military field can make joining the dots time-consuming.

Giant Jesus

Approach via a stairway from the southern end of Ha Long • Daily 7.30–11.30am & 1.30–5pm • Free

Vung Tau's own little touch of Rio, the 28m-high **Giant Jesus** sits on a low peak a few hundred metres south of Nui Nho. Cherubs wielding harps and trumpets herald your approach to the outstretched arms of the city's most famous landmark. Climb the steps inside the wind-buffeted statue and you can perch, parrot-like, on Jesus's shoulder, from where you'll enjoy giddying views of the surrounding seascape.

Sau Beach

If swimming and sun-seeking brought you to Vung Tau, your best bet is to head for the sands of **Sau Beach** ("Back Beach"), far and away Vung Tau's widest, longest (5km) and best – which is still not saying much. Backed by hotels, it's not exactly a tropical paradise, though it's pleasant enough on weekends when it's cluttered with kids, deckchairs and umbrellas, and the fruit- and seafood-vendors are out in force.

ACTIVITIES IN VUNG TAU

Once you've tried hiking to the top of Nui Lon or Nui Nho, there are a couple more interesting ways to while away the time in Vung Tau.

Lam Son Stadium 15 Le Loi. If you enjoy a wager and are in town on a Saturday or Sunday night, head to Vietnam's only grey-hound racing venue (daily 7.30–10pm; 60,000đ, or 120,000đ for VIP section) – in fact, it's one of the few such places in Southeast Asia.

Paradise Golf Course Off San Beach ☎ 0254 385 9697, ⊛ golfparadise.com.vn. Golfers can take advantage of this decent 27-hole range off San Beach; a round will cost about $95, including caddy.

Vung Tau Beach Club 8 Thuy Van ☎ 0254 526 1101, ⊛ vungtausurf.com. This team rents out watersports equipment, and also offers classes through their "Surf Station".

ARRIVAL AND INFORMATION VUNG TAU

The once-popular hydrofoil connection to HCMC was discontinued in early 2017 – a great pity, though it came about thanks to a new highway slashing times from the city. The nearest airport is in HCMC (see p.87).

By bus All buses terminate at the bus station at 192 Nam Ky Khoi Nghia, where xe om and taxis will be on hand to ferry you to a hotel. Some big-bus services will pick up and drop off from your Vung Tau hotel, and some minibuses do too – and they tend to be faster.

Destinations Da Lat (8hr); Da Nang (11hr); Ho Chi Minh City (1hr 30min); Mui Ne (4hr).

Tourist information For local maps and information, go to Vung Tau Tourist at 29 Tran Hung Dao (☏ 0254 385 6445, ⓦ vungtautourist.com.vn).

GETTING AROUND

By xe om and taxi It's difficult to give specific prices for taxis and xe om given the city's sprawling layout, though you should be able to ascertain the right amount for a journey simply by asking around.

By bike For more independence, you can rent a bicycle (up to 75,000đ/day) or motorbike (from 200,000đ/day) through most hotels.

ACCOMMODATION

There's a wide range of accommodation lining both **Front Beach** and **Back Beach**, and in recent years some appealing, boutiquey options have popped up in between them, which are more of a walk from the sand but worth it for the night-time calm. Both beaches are appealing in their own ways, though in general Front Beach is better for those here to see the sights, and Back Beach has the best stretch of sand. Weekend rates are higher than weekdays, as escapees from HCMC invade the town.

FRONT BEACH

Grand 2 Nguyen Du ☏ 0254 385 6888, ⓦ grandhotel .com.vn; map p.208. This is a swanky place with smart (though slightly old-fashioned) rooms, as well as attentive staff and good facilities for business travellers. The hotel is right on the front, so many of its rooms have delightful sea views. $60

Son Ha 17a Thu Khoa Huan ☏ 0254 385 2356; map p.208. The best budget option on Front Beach, run by a family who genuinely seem to want to make their guests leave with smiles on their faces. Rooms are simple but do the job, there's a good view from the rooftop and breakfasts often feature a lot of yummy fruit. $20

BACK BEACH

Green 147c Thuy Van ☏ 0254 625 1003, ⓦ greenhotel .vn; map p.208. This mid-range, smart hotel provides excellent bang for your buck with its splendidly appointed rooms – most of which offer sea views. $60

Imperial 159–163 Thuy Van ☏ 0254 362 8888,

ⓦ imperialhotel.vn; map p.208. This is one of the most attractive hotels on the Back Beach strip, with Roman stylings in the lobby and smart, modern-looking rooms – the ones on upper floors have good sea views. $150

INLAND

★ **Golden Sea** L9 A Chau ☏ 0254 359 0899; map p.208. Tucked away from the beaches, this place is a budget winner. It's set in a tall, skinny structure rather typical of Vietnamese guesthouses, and the welcome is very warm, the rooms do a decent impression of those at more expensive hotels, and the comfy beds will ensure a good night's sleep. $22

★ **The Wind Boutique** 84 Phan Chu Trinh ☏ 0254 628 9139, ⓦ thewind.com.vn; map p.208. This place occupies a lovely spot near the Big Jesus. You'll find water all over– as well as a stylish communal swimming pool and steam room, some rooms have hot tubs. H2O aside, the rooms are great, and there are free shuttle services to nearby beaches. Amazingly, you can often lop almost half off the rack rate. $115

EATING

With a large number of resident expats, Vung Tau supports a more **cosmopolitan** span of restaurants than your average Vietnamese town; it's possible to find spaghetti, burgers and Aussie pies, as well as delicious Vietnamese seafood – Back Beach is a good place to head for the latter.

★ **David** 92 Ha Long ☏ 0254 352 1012; map p.208. The best Western option in town, selling a pleasing range of meals. They're justly proud of their home-made pasta and wood-fired pizzas, while the sea bass (225,000đ) and oysters (133,000đ) are tasty alternatives. Daily 10am–10pm.

Ganh Hao 3 Tran Phu ☏ 0254 355 909; map p.208. The town's best seafood place, and up there with the most attractive, too – many tables are set on a platform adorned with Buddhist temple motifs, overlooking the ocean. The menu is lengthy, and there's something for all tastes and budgets – you could eat for 60,000đ, or for ten times more

DRIVING THE BA RIA COAST

As you move up the coast of Ba Ria province from Vung Tau, the **beaches** gradually get more enticing. That said, since the region is near Ho Chi Minh City, you have to go quite a way before you escape the hordes of domestic tourists who head for the area on weekends and public holidays – though weekdays can be blissfully quiet. **Public transport** is scarce on this stretch, and you really need a rental vehicle to explore the road that hugs the coast much of the way from Vung Tau to Mui Ne, which provides glimpses of rural life as well as the salty tang of the nearby sea. Keep your eyes open for the photogenic **Ke Ga Lighthouse** along the way, around 30km from Phan Thiet on an island just off the coast (see map, p.202).

than that, depending upon your leanings. Daily 10am–10pm.

Lan Rung Resort 3–6 Ha Long ☎0254 352 6010; map p.208. This hotel may be aimed more at honeymooning locals than foreign tourists, and it may look like a giant wedding cake, but its seafront seafood restaurant is a quality affair – try the oysters (39,000đ each), tilapia (260,000đ) or sea bass (490,000đ). You'll also be tempted to guzzle down a microbrewed beer. Daily 6am–10pm.

DRINKING

Lucy's Sports Bar 138 Ha Long ☎0254 385 8896, ⓦlucyssportsbar.com; map p.208. A great place for an evening beer, not to mention Western food like fried breakfasts (135,000đ), burgers (90,000đ) or shepherd's pie (170,000đ). One other plus point is the location, raised slightly from street level – it's far harder for touts to try to sell you sunglasses. Daily 7am–11pm.

DIRECTORY

Banks Vietcombank, 27 Tran Hung Dao (Mon–Fri 7–11.30am & 1.30–4pm) has a 24hr ATM.

Post office The post office (7am–8.30pm) is at 408 Le Hong Phong.

4

Long Hai and around

LONG HAI sits below a wall of impressive mountains some 25km from Vung Tau. It's very popular with Vietnamese, not least because the beach here is wider and far more appealing than the ones found in Vung Tau. A string of resorts bookend the town to the east; to the west, and sheltered from the sea thanks to its location on the north side of a small peninsula, is the dock area, complete with a huge flotilla of fishing boats and assorted coracles sporting brightly coloured flags.

ARRIVAL AND DEPARTURE
LONG HAI

By bus Long Hai is served by buses from HCMC's Mien Dong station (2hr 30min). Coming from Vung Tau, you'll need to take a bus to Ba Ria (45min) and then change, or take a xe om direct for about 200,000đ.

ACCOMMODATION AND EATING

Few foreigners stay in Long Hai, and those who do so tend to bypass the town altogether and head straight to the **resort area** just east, or the numerous fancy places up the coast. Bear in mind that most places see prices rocket at weekends. Most people eat where they stay, though you're bound to see a few good food-stalls around.

CENTRAL LONG HAI

★**Alma Oasis** Off Route 44A ☎0254 386 8227, ⓦalmaoasislonghai.com. The lovingly restored former residence of Emperor Bao Dai overlooks a stretch of deserted coastline. Its thatch-roofed bungalows are discreetly set among pine-studded hills, and sport gorgeous bamboo furnishings and fittings, as well as huge bathtubs. Facilities also include a business centre, swimming pool and charming open-air terraced restaurant. $165

Seaview Hai Tan ☎0254 386 8386. The pick of Long Hai's budget guesthouses, especially on the many occasions when you can score $10 or more off the rack rates (going on weekdays helps). As this place is one of the newer options, its rooms are as good as you can hope for at this price, and there's also an excellent restaurant. $30

★**Ho Tram Beach Resort** Ho Tram, Xuyen Moc ☎0254 378 1525, ⦿hotramresort.com. A thoroughly classy resort whose characterful rooms boast elegant furnishings and fittings; these are augmented by luxurious spa facilities, as well as a superb restaurant. This place is a full 22km northeast of Long Hai, though the hotel does operate (costly) shuttle buses. $150

Loc An Resort Loc An, Dat Do ☎0254 388 6377, ⦿locanresort.com. Budget resort nestled 14km northeast of Long Hai, beside a lagoon cut off from the sea by a line of sand dunes. It has cosy rooms with all the usual facilities, as well as bicycles and tandems available for guests' use. Unless you have your own wheels, you'll need to take a taxi or xe om to get here. $55

Minh Dam caves

Take the coastal road east from Long Hai, then a signed left turn just beyond *Thuy Duong Resort*

The **Minh Dam caves**, just around the cape from Long Hai, were used as Communist bolt holes from 1948, and from them you can enjoy prodigious views of the rice fields that quilt the coastal plain stretching to the horizon to the northeast, and of the boulder-strewn coastline below. The caves are not much more than gaps between piled boulders, yet with a little imagination it's still possible to picture Viet Minh and Viet Cong soldiers. Bullets have left pockmarks on some of the rocks, and joss sticks are still lodged in crevices in memory of those who fell here. Since there are many forks in the path, however, you really need a guide to find your way around – and they're best organized through one of the nearby resorts.

Binh Chau Hot Springs

20km northeast of Long Hai · 50,000đ; private mud-pools 400,000đ/person · ☎0254 379 1036, ⦿saigonbinhchau.com

The **Binh Chau Hot Springs** have been developed into a kind of theme park with the addition of a golf-driving range, tennis courts, sand volleyball court, billiards and ox-cart rides around the site. The sulphurous waters bubbling hellishly in the streams and wells here all vary greatly in temperature: older people soothe their aching limbs in the foot-soaking stream, while elsewhere visitors boil eggs sold on site to make up ad hoc picnics. You can bathe in the mineral waters of the "Dreaming Lake", a communal **swimming pool**, but renting your own **mini mud-pool** is a more tempting option – though rather costly.

ARRIVAL AND DEPARTURE   BINH CHAU HOT SPRINGS

There's **no public transport** to the springs; guests tend to arrive on package tour buses or with their own vehicle. However, it's only 6km away from Binh Chau village, which is accessible on the highly irregular coastal buses linking Mui Ne and Vung Tau. From here, you can pick up a xe om for the final stretch for 80,000đ or so.

ACCOMMODATION

Binh Chau Hot Springs Binh Chau, Xuyen Moc ☎0254 387 1131, ⦿saigonbinhchau.com. Part of the mammoth Saigon corporation, this is a so-so-spot whose rooms vary considerably in style – try to see a couple before choosing, and grab one with mountain views. Call ahead if you want to arrange pick-up. $60

Phan Thiet

The unassuming capital of Binh Thuan province, **PHAN THIET** has little of interest for foreigners, who tend to prefer the sands of Mui Ne just along the coast (see opposite). However, the very absence of tourists is a draw in itself, and the town is likeable enough. A picture-perfect fleet of fishing boats lies beside the Tran Hung Dao bridge and they make for a truly splendid sight, although they're to blame for the stench – the city is famed for its mammoth **fish sauce** production. Phan Thiet also has **Doi Duong**, a perfectly acceptable stretch of beach, and one very popular with the Vietnamese – to get to the best bit, head around 700m northeast from the main entrance point on Nguyen That Thanh.

Ho Chi Minh Museum

Tues–Sun 7.30–11.30am & 1.30–4.30pm • 15,000đ

Trung Trac skirts the city centre en route to the riverside **Ho Chi Minh Museum**. As with other such museums around the country, its exhibits include memorabilia of Ho's life from his early days abroad up to his death in 1969, such as his white tunic, walking stick, sandals and metal helmet. Next door is a school where Ho once taught; its rooms have remained unchanged since his brief spell here, and effortlessly conjure up another age.

ARRIVAL AND DEPARTURE   **PHAN THIET**

By train Phan Thiet's station – the closest one to Mui Ne (see below) – is served by a small branch line, with two direct connections daily to and from HCMC (3hr 40min); there's occasionally another service on holidays. Otherwise, the nearest mainline stations to Phan Thiet are at Muong Man, 15km to the west, and Ma Lam, 17km north. Both are approximately 250,000đ away by taxi.
Destinations from Muong Man Da Nang (13 daily; 12–17hr); HCMC (13 daily; 3–5hr); Hue (12 daily;

14–18hr); Nha Trang (13 daily; 4–6hr).
By bus The bus station is 2km north of the centre on Tu Van Tu. If you're set on staying here, you should be able to get Mui Ne-bound open-tour buses to drop you off, rather than taking local services. Note that there's also a shuttle bus linking Phan Thiet and Mui Ne (every 15min; 15,000đ).
Destinations HCMC (4hr); Nha Trang (5hr).
By taxi and xe om To Mui Ne (see below) it's 150,000–300,000đ by taxi, or 50,000–150,000đ by xe om.

ACCOMMODATION AND EATING

There are many places to stay in Phan Thiet, though the **culinary scene** isn't terribly exciting. As you'd expect, there's plenty of seafood on offer, but no specific establishments stand out from the crowd.

Ocean Dunes 1 Ton Duc Thang ☏0252 382 2393, ⓦoceandunesresort.com.vn. A mammoth, but attractive, resort with two swimming pools and free use of bicycles, as well as the wonderful *Sea Horse* restaurant. Note that you should be able to lop a fair bit from the over-high rack rates. $185
★**Tay Ho** 401 Tran Hung Dao ☏0252 382 1710,

ⓦkhachsantayho.com. If you're the sort of traveller who actually wants to stay in Phan Thiet rather than Mui Ne, chances are you'll absolutely love this place – it's cheap and cheerful, and the unintentionally hilarious decor in the rooms may well end up forming part of some ironic social media postings. Full marks for effort, though, and it's only a short walk from the river and its colourful flotilla of boats. $16

4

Mui Ne

If you want evidence of how quickly things can change in Vietnam, take a trip to the beach strip of **MUI NE**. Until recently, this was a sleepy yet pristine backwater ignored by domestic and international tourists alike – partly down to the fact that Highway 1 juts inland along this section of coast. However, the secret was unveiled during an eclipse of the sun in the mid-1990s, which had its optimum viewing spot here, and demand immediately began to outstrip supply. While it took a little while for big business to arrive, what you'll see here now is 10km of resorts, sitting almost wall to wall and essentially blocking any view of the beach from the coastal road. More are being built all the time, though thanks to problems with the Russian economy, visitor numbers have actually declined slightly in recent years – unlike in Nha Trang up the coast, the nascent Chinese market hasn't addressed the shortfall. Even so, this remains one of the few places in Southeast Asia in which Cyrillic text vies for supremacy with Roman.

There's no doubt that Mui Ne's laidback atmosphere is one of its best features, but this is also something of a tourist enclave, separated as it is from any Vietnamese community. This probably won't bother you if you're looking for unadulterated beachside relaxation, but if you crave interaction with locals or a higher-octane nightlife scene, you'd be better off heading on up to Nha Trang. Another potential problem at Mui Ne is that the **strong winds** and **surf** tend to erode parts of the beach between August and December, so you might just find the waves lapping the garden of your chosen resort. However, good stretches of soft sand can always be found with a little exploration.

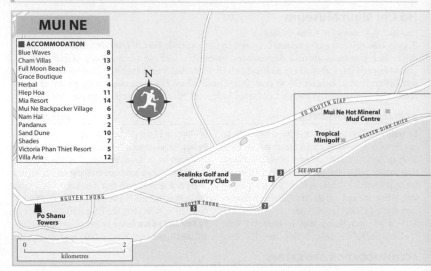

4

Sights, as such, are thin on the ground, bar some **Cham towers** and the almost otherworldly **Fairy Springs**. Instead, this is a place of action and inaction – when you're done lounging around by the hotel pool, go for a spot of crazy golf, head uphill for a mud-bath, then drink the night away.

Po Shanu towers

Off the coastal road, west of Mui Ne • Daily 7am–5pm • 15,000đ • Accessible on buses linking Mui Ne and Phan Thiet (see p.213)

On the western fringe of Mui Ne are the **Po Shanu towers**, Cham ruins that date from the ninth century. While they can't compare with monuments like Po Klong Garai near Phan Rang (see p.220), they are worth a look as the towers – two big, one small – are in reasonable repair, and the site occupies a pretty hilltop location with good views. It's just a pity that they close the place before sunset.

Fairy Spring

North of Mui Ne, signed from the main road • Daily 24hr • Free

Mui Ne's famed **Fairy Spring** is in fact a narrow stream running through a psychedelic landscape of red **sand dunes**, which are accessible via an uphill, inland turn just west of Mui Ne village. You're best advised to kick off your shoes and pad your way along the course of the stream itself – a highly pleasurable, not to mention stunningly beautiful, experience. You'll be able to follow the stream for a couple of kilometres, though most find themselves hiking up the adjacent dunes at some point; the softness of the sand makes them a little tricky to climb (you'll need three steps to travel the distance of one), but the resulting views are ample reward. The sand can also get very

---

MUI NE ORIENTATION

Mui Ne stretches for over 10km along one main road. Resorts make up most of the seaward side, especially to the west of the curl; these peter out further east, where budget hotels start to pop up. All along, the non-seaward side of the road is made up of restaurants and cheap hotels. Heading further east, the beach finally disappears too, before the road reaches the actual village and harbour of Mui Ne, where fishing boats cluster together in their hundreds.

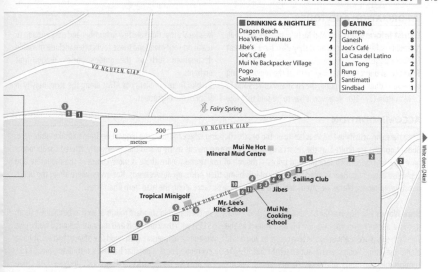

DRINKING & NIGHTLIFE

Dragon Beach	2
Hoa Vien Brauhaus	7
Jibe's	4
Joe's Café	5
Mui Ne Backpacker Village	3
Pogo	1
Sankara	6

EATING

Champa	6
Ganesh	8
Joe's Café	3
La Casa del Latino	4
Lam Tong	2
Rung	7
Santimatti	5
Sindbad	1

hot, so it makes sense to go early or late in the day, when the colours are also at their most spectacular.

White dunes

Northeast of Mui Ne, signed from the main road • Daily 6am–6pm • 15,000đ • Quad-biking and dune-buggying best organized through one of the many agencies in town

In Mui Ne, sand-based fun is not confined to the beach – just north of Mui Ne village, in an area known as the **white dunes**, you'll be able to get your fix of **quad-biking** and **dune-buggying**. You'll likely run into local kids offering **plastic sledges** for hire – great fun in theory, though in practice it's hard to slide for more than a few metres.

ARRIVAL AND DEPARTURE   MUI NE

By bus The majority of travellers arrive in Mui Ne on open-tour buses from HCMC, Nha Trang or central Vietnam, which drop off outside the relevant company offices. Most hotels will be able to book an onward ticket, often for buses that pick up right outside the front door. Local buses are few and far between, bar the shuttle buses linking Phan Thiet and Mui Ne; there are also a couple of juddering services down to Vung Tau.

Destinations Da Lat (4hr 30min); HCMC (5hr); Nha Trang (5hr 30min); Phan Thiet (every 15min); Vung Tau (4hr).

By train Many go by train from HCMC to nearby Phan Thiet (see p.212), which cuts out the stress of traffic jams and delays on the buses. Getting back this way can be hard though, since the station is some distance from the beach and tickets often sell out – buy your return ticket in HCMC if you're sure about your dates. From Phan Thiet it's 150,000–300,000đ by taxi to Mui Ne, depending on your precise destination; by xe om it's 50,000–150,000đ. If you're heading to or from the north, the nearest stations are in Muong Man and Ma Lam (see p.212).

GETTING AROUND

By xe om The Mui Ne strip is long, and tedious to cover on foot, so it's best to hop in a xe om – you'll be endlessly badgered by drivers, who will charge from 20,000đ for a short ride.

By bus Basic buses bump up and down the road every 15min; it'll cost around 13,000đ within the Mui Ne area.

By bike It's easy to rent a bicycle (40,000đ/day) from your resort or guesthouse, but make sure you first check things

like the brakes to avoid any untoward incidents. Also note that, outside the more sheltered resort strip, the area's high winds can often make it tricky to get around on something with just two wheels.

By scooter Things have become a little tricky of late, thanks to a few fatal accidents caused by intoxicated tourists. Ask around and you should still be able to find one for 150,000đ/day or so, but be very careful from sunset on.

4

INFORMATION AND TOURS

Tourist information Give Mui Ne Info and Events a look (ⓦ muine-info-and-events.com); they also have a decent Facebook page.

Tours Local operators offer day-tours of the region taking in the sand dunes, Fairy Spring, the Po Shanu towers and Ta Cu Mountain ($7–10). However, it has to be said that Mui Ne's local attractions are few in number and easy enough to reach on your own, and these tours often include missable destinations such as the guide's uncle's dragon-fruit orchard.

Banks There are plenty of ATMs along the strip, mostly in front of the big resorts.

ACCOMMODATION

Since the main activity in Mui Ne is lazing on the beach, choosing where to stay is the biggest decision to make while here. Budget options are limited, as the resort's **upmarket image** means many places that previously offered cheap rooms have now upgraded their facilities and prices – though of course this means there is more choice in the moderate and expensive categories. Bear in mind that many places bump their prices up at weekends. Not everywhere along the beach has street numbers; places are often identified by kilometre distance along the road from Phan Thiet.

Blue Waves 94a Nguyen Dinh Chieu ☎ 0252 384 7989, ⓦ tiendatresort.com.vn; map p.214. Also known as the *Tien Dat*, this place is about as cheap a resort as you'll find along the strip. Rooms aren't super-swish, but they're comfortable and fairly priced; you'll pay about twenty percent more for those facing the sea. $45

★ **Cham Villas** 32 Nguyen Dinh Chieu ☎ 0252 374 1234, ⓦ chamvillas.com; map p.214. Mini-resort with only a handful of luxurious, well-appointed villas – it just about represents value for money, since everything here is of sky-high quality. A good place to go if you're seeking some peace and quiet; spa treatments are also available. $169

Full Moon Beach 84–90 Nguyen Dinh Chieu ☎ 0252 384 7008, ⓦ fullmoonbeach.com.vn; map p.214. Attractive and sturdy beachfront establishment, featuring thatched bamboo huts with verandas and spacious rooms, some on stilts and with attached bathrooms. Also note that this is the location of *Jibe's*, one of Mui Ne's best bars (see p.218). $70

Grace Boutique 144a Nguyen Dinh Chieu ☎ 0252 374 3357, ⓦ graceboutiqueresort.com; map p.214. One of Mui Ne's friendliest resorts, which is one reason why it has become a real favourite with HCMC-fleeing expats. There are only fourteen rooms here, so it helps to book ahead; prices can be slashed if you do so far in advance. Almost uniquely in Vietnam, smoking is prohibited across the resort, which also features a small infinity pool and an equally minuscule restaurant. $105

Herbal 21 Nguyen Dinh Chieu ☎ 094 242 7911, ⓦ herbalhotelmuinevietnam.com; map p.214. Fourteen spacious bungalows sleeping up to four, overlooking a calm garden area – highly pleasant, and in a nice area. They also offer cheap spa treatments. $19

Hiep Hoa 80 Nguyen Dinh Chieu ☎ 0252 384 7262; map p.214. You'll find just eight smart but basic rooms and a handful of bungalows (around $15 more), some with fans and others with a/c, in this tiny, friendly compound facing a fine stretch of beach. $20

★ **Mia Resort** 24 Nguyen Dinh Chieu ☎ 0252 384 7440, ⓦ miamuine.com; map p.214. Delightfully landscaped resort featuring standard rooms as well as bungalows (from $155) with thatched roofs and mustard-coloured walls, plus imaginative interiors with good use of local textiles. It has a swimming pool, a popular bar and a restaurant, too. $115

★ **Mui Ne Backpacker Village** 137 Nguyen Dinh Chieu ☎ 0252 374 1047, ⓦ muinebackpackervillage.com; map p.214. This friendly, Aussie-run place proved so popular that they upped sticks and moved to a far larger location. The atmosphere is loungey, rather than scroungey – expect comfy a/c dorm rooms (with proper beds, no bunks) and a bunch of beach loungers set around a large swimming pool, which is backed at one end by an awesome bar (see p.219). Staff are great for organizing tours, and helpful when it comes to local information. Dorms $7, doubles $40

Nam Hai 25 Nguyen Dinh Chieu ☎ 0252 374 1789; map p.214. A good option if you want something approximating a hotel room – moderate luxury at a moderate price, and there are super views from the upper-floor rooms. You'll save almost $10 if you choose to do without breakfast, too. $33

Pandanus Km5 ☎ 0252 384 9849, ⓦ pandanusresort.com; map p.214. Sitting in near solitude east of the strip, and indeed east of Mui Ne village itself, this is a smart resort with staff who genuinely seem eager to please. It boasts elegant rooms and a landscaped garden, plus a pool, spa and restaurant overlooking the beach. The breakfasts here are excellent. $135

Sand Dune 117 Nguyen Dinh Chieu ☎ 0252 374 1168; map p.214. At the upper end of budget, this is a neat (and fairly large) place with small but cheery rooms, and a good tour information desk in the lobby. The hotel reception is actually hidden away upstairs – you'll have to ask, and perhaps wait until someone arrives to serve you. $20

★ **Shades** 98a Nguyen Dinh Chieu ☎ 0252 374 3237, ⓦ shadesmuine.com; map p.214. You'll have to book early to stay at this fantastic boutique hotel. There are just eleven individual apartments here, all super-hip in design, with flatscreen TVs and kitchen facilities. $55

Victoria Phan Thiet Resort Km9 ☎ 0252 381 3000, ⓦ victoriahotels-asia.com; map p.214. Set among

MUI NE OUTDOOR ACTIVITIES

Though the number one activity in Mui Ne is relaxing on the beach, there's a lot more to do besides. The place has become hugely popular with **windsurfers** and **kitesurfers**, and there are also a couple of good **golf courses** (including a crazy one) in the area. And, though it's not an activity as such, you may find it hard to pass up the chance to wallow in mud at a local **hot springs**. The sand dunes near town also allow for **quad-biking** and **dune-buggying** excursions – ask any travel agency in town, or even at your accommodation.

WATERSPORTS

Mui Ne is heaving with wind- and kitesurfers when the wind is up between August and April; the strip even hosts an event in the Asian Windsurf Tour each February. There are a number of establishments that offer lessons for windsurfing ($55 per hour) and kitesurfing ($60). It costs less if you'd simply like to rent the equipment, and Mui Ne is the perfect place to hone your skills – the winds here can be gusty and aggressive, so anywhere else will seem easy by comparison.

★**Jibes** 90 Nguyen Dinh Chieu ☎0252 384 7008, Ⓦwindsurf-vietnam.com. Quality operator with savvy instructors (lessons $60/hr), excellent equipment and the best surfing bonhomie in town.

Manta 108 Huynh Thuc Khang ☎090 840 0108, Ⓦmantasailing.org. Dedicated sailing school ($60/hr) with all the relevant international accreditations. They also offer wakeboarding lessons ($100/hr per boat), and have accommodation for longer-term students.

Mr. Lee's Kite School 78 Nguyen Dinh Chieu ☎097 480 4695. Based at the *Xuan Uyen* hotel, this is about the cheapest reliable operator in town (lessons $45/hour). They only have a few instructors, so it's best to contact them well in advance.

Sailing Club 24 Nguyen Dinh Chieu ☎0252 384 7440, Ⓦsailingclubkiteschool.com. A little pricier than the rest (cheapest course $110 for 2hr), but expert instructors and top-end equipment don't usually come cheap.

GOLF

There's a decent golf course in the Mui Ne area, plus a fantastic crazy golf course on the strip itself.

Sealinks Golf and Country Club Km9 Nguyen Thong ☎0252 374 1666, Ⓦsealinkscity.com. Excellent course sprawling across the hills at the entrance to Mui Ne. It boasts fabulous ocean views, and costs a shade under $100/round, including caddy. Daily 8am–8pm.

★**Tropical Minigolf** 97 Nguyen Dinh Chieu. Less refined, though a lot of fun, is the crazy golf "course" here on the strip. It's 100,000đ/person for a round, though (somewhat amazingly) they'll give you a beer to waltz around the course with for 120,000đ –150,000đ can upgrade you to an extraordinarily strong cocktail. Daily 9.30am–midnight.

MUD BATHS

Mui Ne may only have one mud-bath centre compared with Nha Trang's three, but it's a real winner.

Mui Ne Hot Mineral Mud Centre 133a Nguyen Dinh Chieu ☎0252 374 3482, Ⓦbunkhoangmuine .com. Located a short xe om ride north of town, this place is very fancy, right the way down to the underwater seats encircling the pool's cocktail bar. The rates vary depending on what kind of service you'd like

– the regular mud bath will set you back 570,000đ for a couple or 390,000đ for just the one, and you'll get a free swimsuit (if you need one), towel and bottle of water. If you're not into mud and would simply like to use the pool, jacuzzis and sunbeds, you can pay just 80,000đ/person. Daily 6am–9pm.

COOKING CLASSES

With its great restaurant scene, it stands to reason that Mui Ne should form an appropriate place for culinary instruction.

Mui Ne Cooking School 82 Nguyen Dinh Chieu ☎091 665 5241, Ⓦmuinecookingschool.com. This is a hugely popular cooking school, with lessons that follow a pleasing routine – market visit, cooking lesson,

mealtime. Classes ($30) leave at 9am for those wanting the market tour option ($5 extra), and the cooking itself starts at 10am.

4

tropical gardens, the cottages here feature spacious interiors with tasteful European decor and all the mod cons. They surround a couple of excellent pools, and the beach is never more than a short stroll away. Staff can arrange excursions,

and guests have free use of mountain bikes. **$190**

★**Villa Aria** 60a Nguyen Dinh Chieu ☎0252 374 1660, Ⓦvillaariamuine.com; map p.214. This place certainly has a bit of wow factor. The large, bright, airy rooms have been decorated with rare attention; there's a massage pavilion looking onto the swimming pool, which itself looks onto the sea; and the restaurant prides itself on its fresh fruits, veggies and seafood. **$150**

EATING

What Mui Ne lacks in cultural attractions, it makes up for with **gastronomic diversity**. As well as the resorts and hotels, all of which have their own restaurants, there's no shortage of independent eating joints and bars along the strip. Note that you may struggle to find anywhere to eat after 10pm.

★**Champa** 58 Nguyen Dinh Chieu ☎0252 384 7111; map p.214. On a delightful terrace at the *Coco Beach Resort*, this serves top-class French cuisine (dinner only) with impeccable service and prices from about 240,000đ for a main dish. Daily 3–10pm.

Ganesh 57 Nguyen Dinh Chieu ☎0252 374 1330; map p.214. This small but attractive restaurant is still the best Indian option in Mui Ne. Thali platters are a good choice, and start at 165,000đ; alternatively, try the *malai kofta* (minced cottage cheese balls with spices) or fish masala, and wash the lot down with a very tall mango lassi (54,000đ). Daily 11am–10pm.

★**Joe's Café** 86 Nguyen Dinh Chieu ☎0252 384 7177; map p.214. The best Western food on the strip, with a range of great burgers – have them stuffed with mushroom and mozzarella (149,000đ) or beetroot, egg, cheese and spice (139,000đ). The ice cream is awfully tempting on a hot day, especially the passion fruit sorbet (30,000đ). It's also a great bar (see below), and there's some seaside seating – though you do run the risk of a soaking at high tide. Daily 7am–midnight.

La Casa del Latino 117c Nguyen Dinh Chieu ☎0126 425 2487; map p.214. A neat addition to Mui Ne's culinary scene – Mexican cuisine including breakfast burritos and tasty *quesadillas* (100,000đ). Eat them by the pool with a passion-fruit *mojito* (40,000đ). Daily 8am–11pm.

Lam Tong 92 Nguyen Dinh Chieu ☎0252 384 7598; map p.214. This breezy, no-frills place is right on the beach and has some of the lowest prices on the strip (from 60,000đ for squid, shrimp or fish mains). They turn the grills on in the evening, when you'll also likely be enquiring about the cheap beer (15,000đ for a bottle of Saigon). Daily 8am–9.30pm.

Rung 65b Nguyen Dinh Chieu ☎0252 384 7589; map p.214. The name of this restaurant means "forest" in Vietnamese, and thanks to tree-trunk seating, a treehouse atmosphere and other quirky decor, that's exactly what it feels like here. The menu is, suitably, full of creatures to eat – go for the frog, eel, snake, ostrich or crocodile if you're feeling adventurous (most mains 120,000–200,000đ). Daily 2–10pm.

Santimatti 83 Nguyen Dinh Chieu ☎0252 374 1559; map p.214. This place offers by far the best Italian food in town, and is perfect for those with a hankering for pizza as they have plenty of varieties (from 160,000đ). Throw in home-made pasta, bread, tiramisu and limoncello, and you're onto a winner. Daily 11am–11pm.

Sindbad 233 Nguyen Dinh Chieu ☎0169 991 5245; map p.214. Tiny, slightly distant spot selling excellent gyros and shawarma from 60,000đ, and doner wraps for slightly less. Their smoothies are also good value at 29,000đ, but they've stopped making their delectable falafel – in the wider interests of Mui Ne, beg for it to return. Daily 11am–11pm.

DRINKING AND NIGHTLIFE

Mui Ne's nightlife is now pretty kicking, and you'll see rows of taxis disgorging and absorbing passengers outside the most popular spots. Bars often close at dawn in peak season, while at quieter times you may find many of them closed.

★**Dragon Beach** 120/1 Nguyen Dinh Chieu ☎090 304 2566; map p.214. The best party spot in town, as evidenced by the slew of taxis and bikes picking up and dropping off through the night. The huge dancefloor and open-air pool are major draws, and there's pleasing variety to the music on offer, though DJs usually plump for electro and deep house. Daily 1pm–4am.

Hoa Vien Brauhaus 2a Nguyen Dinh Chieu ☎0252 374 1383; map p.214. This restaurant is based a bit far out from the centre, but its microbrewed beer is probably the tastiest alcohol available in Mui Ne. Glasses of the good stuff cost from 40,000đ, and dark and red beers are available too. They also provide meals (there are a couple of Czech dishes, including plates of fried cheese), and there's a great sea view. Daily 8am–10pm.

Jibe's 90 Nguyen Dinh Chieu ☎0252 384 7008; map p.214. The main base of the local kitesurfing community, and for good reason – the drinks are good and cheap (beer from 25,000đ, cocktails 80,000đ), the comfy seating encourages chatting and the atmosphere is uber chilled. The sea views help, too. Daily 10am–11pm.

Joe's Café 86 Nguyen Dinh Chieu ☎0252 384 7177; map p.214. This restaurant also makes a fine place to drink, especially in the evening when there's usually live music. Beers from 25,000đ, or two cocktails for 70,000đ during happy hour. Daily 7am–midnight.

Mui Ne Backpacker Village 137 Nguyen Dinh Chieu ☎0252 384 7047, ⓦmuinebackpackers.com; map p.214. This hostel (see p.216) is also a great drinking hole, whether you're staying here or not. They don't so much have a happy hour as an entire happy evening, and if you can find some time between downing cocktails, you could play some pool or ping pong, or join the people in the slouch space watching films. Daily 7am–late.

★**Pogo** 138 Nguyen Dinh Chieu ☎ 090 738 7600; map p.214. Sometimes hectic and sometimes chilled, this is one of the best bars in the area, with tables right by the sea. Enjoy a beer (25,000đ), cocktail (100,000đ, double that for a bucket) or shisha (150,000đ) while squashing sand in between your toes. It also offers good burgers, while 100,000đ will get you a free flow of rum and coke from 10pm to 1am. Daily 8pm–2am.

Sankara 90 Nguyen Dinh Chieu ☎ 0252 374 1122; map p.214. This rather pricey bar is still the trendiest-looking in Mui Ne, though standards have decreased under new management. Its various nooks and crannies surround an open-air pool, and the whole joint is illuminated with gentle lighting in the evening. Often open later than advertised. Daily 10am–midnight.

Ca Na

Given its proximity to the highway, the small town of **CA NA** is a more relaxing place than you would think – it might even tempt you into staying overnight. Beyond the coracles parked along the **beach**, the water is invitingly clear and snorkelling is a possibility, though you'd be wise to ask locals where to wade in as the coral here is razor sharp. If you crave a little more solitude, a spine of decent dunes back up another good stretch of sand 2km south; the **main village** itself is a fifteen-minute walk east of the resort area, characterized by the coracles and colourful fishing boats typical of coastal Vietnam.

ARRIVAL AND DEPARTURE   CA NA   4

By train Ca Na's station is on the main line, 2km north of the beach and village – around 20,000đ away by xe om. Destinations HCMC (7 daily; 5hr 30min); Nha Trang (7 daily; 2hr 45min).

By bus Buses stop right next to the beach resort. You should be able to get open-tour buses to drop you off, though arranging a pick-up can be troublesome. The only regular services are to Phan Rang (1–2 hourly; 1hr; 20,000đ).

ACCOMMODATION AND EATING

Ca Na has a few cheap places to stay, and that's about it; both establishments listed here have attached restaurants, which are your best bet for food. They lie in between the highway and the beach, a short walk east of the bus stop and about 1.7km south of the train station.

Ca Na ☎ 0259 376 1320. Cheap and a little scruffy, this guesthouse has rooms set in distinctive, high-roofed bungalows – a nice idea, though sloping walls mean that parts of the room are next to inaccessible. $15

Hon Co ☎ 0259 376 0999. A budget resort, at least in layout, this is a surprisingly nice place for somewhere as remote as Ca Na. You can opt to stay in the regular hotel section, rather than the bungalows; the whole place is aimed at domestic tourists, and the karaoke room can get rather noisy. $40

Phan Rang and around

Although **PHAN RANG** is a less than lovely place, whose western limits have fused with the neighbouring town of **Thap Cham**, the area is rich in historical attractions. The name of the latter, meaning "Cham Towers", gives a clue to the primary reason for stopping here. This region of Vietnam once comprised the Cham kingdom of Panduranga (see box, p.220), and the nearby remnants of **Po Klong Garai** are some of the best preserved in the country. The excellent **Po Re Me** towers – which are nearly as good – are also in the area. **Tuan Tu**, one of Vietnam's most appealing Cham villages, lies near Phan Rang, as does **Ninh Chu beach**, a glorious sweep of wide sand that is sometimes deliciously quiet on weekdays, but often overrun with Vietnamese at weekends.

If you'd just like to see Po Klong Garai, you won't need to visit Phan Rang at all – the towers will eat up an hour, at the most, and it's a long day-trip from Mui Ne or Nha

CHAM ARCHITECTURE

The weathered but beguiling **towers** that punctuate the scenery upcountry from Phan Thiet to Da Nang are the legacy of Champa, an Indianized kingdom that ruled parts of central and southern Vietnam for over fourteen centuries (see p.430). From murky beginnings in the late second century, Champa rose to unify an elongated strip from Phan Thiet to Dong Hoi, and by the end of the fourth century it comprised four provinces: **Amaravati**, around Hue and Da Nang; **Vijaya**, centred around Quy Nhon; **Kauthara**, in the Nha Trang region; and **Panduranga**, which corresponds to present-day Phan Thiet and up to Phan Rang. The unified kingdom's first capital, established in the fourth century in Amaravati, was **Simhapura** ("Lion City"); nearby, just outside present-day Hoi An, **My Son**, Champa's holiest site and spiritual heartland, was established (see p.260).

To honour their gods, Cham kings sponsored the construction of the **religious edifices** that still stand today; the red-brick ruins of their towers and temples can be seen all along the coast of south-central Vietnam. While they never attained the magnificence of Angkor, their greatest legacy was a striking architectural style characterized by a wealth of exuberant sculpture. The typical Cham **temple complex** is centred around the *kalan*, or sanctuary, normally pyramidal inside, and containing a *lingam*, or phallic representation of Shiva, set on a dais that was grooved to channel off water used in purification rituals. Having first cleansed themselves and prayed in the *mandapa*, or meditation hall, worshippers would then have proceeded under a gate tower and below the *kalan*'s (normally) east-facing vestibule into the sanctuary. Any ritual objects pertaining to worship were kept in a nearby repository room, which normally sported a boat-shaped roof.

Cham towers crop up at regular intervals all the way up the coast from Phan Thiet to Da Nang, and many of them have been restored in recent years. A handful of sites representing the highlights of what remains of Champa civilization would include: Po Klong Garai towers (see below); Thap Doi towers (see p.236); Po Re Me tower (see p.222); My Son (see p.260); and Po Nagar towers (see p.226).

4

Trang. With some clever scheduling, you can merely get on the next train – there are places to eat around the station.

Quan Cong Temple

In central Phan Rang on Thong Nhat • Dawn to dusk • Free

The only thing to see in Phan Rang itself is the **Quan Cong Temple**, dedicated to the Chinese deity Guan Yu and dating from the 1860s. It has faded, pink-washed walls that rise to three consecutive roofs, each draped on huge red wooden piles imported from China, and laden with fanciful figurines and dragons. Quan Cong himself is at the head of the third and final chamber, framed by ornate gilt woodwork and rows of pikes. There's a decent **market** just south of the temple, one popular with local Cham people.

Po Klong Garai

Daily 7am–5pm • 15,000đ • Xe om from Thap Cham station 20,000đ; xe om from Phan Rang 50,000đ; to walk, head south of town and take the road under the tracks

Elevated with fitting grandeur on a granite mound known as Trau Hill, the **Po Klong Garai** Cham towers are among the most spectacular sights on the southern Vietnamese coast. Dating back to around 1400, after the rule of King Jaya Simhavarman III (to whom it is dedicated), the complex comprises a *kalan*, or sanctuary, a smaller gate tower and a repository, under whose boat-shaped roof offerings would have been placed. It's the 25m-high *kalan*, though, that's of most interest. From a distance its stippled body impresses; up close, you see a bas-relief of six-armed Shiva cavorting above doorposts etched with Cham inscriptions and ringed by arches crackling with stonework flames, while other gods sit cross-legged in niches elsewhere around the exterior walls.

Inside the complex

Push deeper into the *kalan*'s belly and there's a *mukha* lingam fashioned in a likeness of the Cham king Po Klong Garai, after whom the complex is named. In days gone by, the statue of Shiva's bull (Nandi) that stands in the vestibule would have been "fed" by farmers wishing for good harvests; nowadays it gets a feed only at the annual **Kate Festival** (the Cham New Year, see p.52), a great spectacle if you're here around October. On the eve of the festival, there's traditional Cham music and dance at the complex, followed the next morning by a lively procession bearing the king's raiment to the tower.

Po Re Me tower

8km south of Phan Rang and Thap Cham on Highway 1 • Daily 7.30am–6pm • Free • Xe om from Phan Rang 120,000đ return

If Po Klong Garai inspires further interest in Cham structures, you could make the trickier journey out to **Po Re Me tower**. The tower draws its name from the last Cham king and enjoys a fine hilltop location like its near-neighbour, though its four storeys (which taper into a lingam) are sturdier and less finished than at Po Klong Garai. Its highlight is the splendid bas-relief in the *kalan*'s entrance, depicting Shiva manifest in the image of mustachioed King Po Re Me waggling his arms, and watched over by two Nandis. Po Re Me is also a focus of Cham festivities during the Kate Festival (see above).

4 Tuan Tu village

3–4km from central Phan Rang, though unsigned and difficult to find • Xe om around 100,000đ for the round-trip

There's still a Cham presence around Phan Rang; **Tuan Tu village** is home to more than a thousand Cham people, and they are largely **Muslim**, as you'll soon divine from the headcloths that they favour over conical hats. They maintain an unpretentious, 1966-built **mosque** behind a well, to the right of the settlement's only road, and it's free of any trappings – not even a minaret. Also keep an eye out for the distinctive **Cham text**, dotted liberally about the place, which is rather more beautiful than Vietnam's somewhat messy Roman writing. Locals are friendly and not used to seeing visitors – don't be surprised to find yourself invited for tea or coffee.

Ninh Chu beach

Some 5km east of Phan Rang is **Ninh Chu beach**, a more indolent alternative to trekking around Phan Rang's Cham towers. The beach is a reasonably clean and wide crescent of sand – soft, if not exactly golden. Ninh Chu doesn't have the same pulling power for foreigners as Mui Ne or Nha Trang, but it's a popular place for swimming, sunbathing, beach games and jogging. With several resorts located here, it's worth considering as a place to rest up, particularly midweek when it can be very quiet. If you're here at a weekend, be prepared for crowds of families and noisy teenagers.

ARRIVAL AND DEPARTURE   PHAN RANG AND AROUND

Note that though fused together with a few stringy roads, the centres of Phan Rang and Thap Cham are around 7km apart. Trains arrive in Thap Cham to the west, and buses in Phan Rang to the east, and you'd be wise to plan accordingly – the train station is right next to the Cham towers, though the bus station is closer to most accommodation and Tuan Tu Village.

By train The train station (Ga Thap Cham) sits on the main line, though not all services stop here – you'll find out which ones do when booking your ticket.
Destinations HCMC (9 daily; 6hr 30min); Nha Trang (9 daily; 2hr).

By bus The bus station is 300m north of Phan Rang town centre. Local buses to Ca Na leave from outside the *Ho Phong* hotel.
Destinations Ca Na (1hr); Da Lat (3hr); HCMC (7hr); Nha Trang (2hr); Phan Thiet (3hr).

ACCOMMODATION AND EATING

Accommodation in Phan Rang itself is **limited**; you're better off avoiding the town completely and heading for Ninh Chu beach, where the options are much more appealing. There are also a few cheap options near the train station in Thap Cham, though the area is far less appealing than Phan Rang. As for **eating**, there's nothing notable in town, but there are plenty of snack shacks around the train station, and some decent establishments in hotels on Ninh Chu beach itself (see opposite).

PHAN RANG

Ho Phong 353–363 Ngo Gia Tu ☎ 0259 392 0333. The best option in the centre, with bare but spacious rooms and (occasionally) an English-speaker at reception. It's at the south end of town, near the bridge – it's easy to spot at night, when the decorative lights come on. Breakfast not included. $20

NINH CHU BEACH

Minh Duc 24a An Duong Vuong ☎ 097 737 1737, ⓦ facebook.com/minhducguesthousephanrang. The town's de facto Easy Rider base, which usually guarantees two things – it's cheap and reliable. The rooms are surprisingly large for the price, and it's just a short walk from the beach. Breakfast not included. $10

★**Saigon Ninhchu** Khanh Hai ☎ 0259 387 6000, ⓦ saigonninhchuhotel.com.vn. At the far north end of the bay, this hotel has nicely furnished, spacious rooms with thick carpets, and its executive suites even have beach views from each bath. There's also a big pool, tennis courts, a spa and a classy restaurant that's easily the best place to eat for miles around, and is reasonably priced to boot – a bucketful of oysters steamed over lemongrass will set you back 110,000đ. $75

TTC Resort Off Yen Ning ☎ 0259 387 4047, ⓦ ninhthuan.ttchotels.com. Based in the centre of the beach, sprawled around a wonderful swimming pool, this resort draws heavily on the region's Cham heritage for its design. Rooms are smartly decorated, if rather small, though the size of the complex as a whole can make it feel deserted outside peak season. $65

Nha Trang

4

Big enough to bustle, yet small enough to retain its relaxed air, the delightful city of **NHA TRANG** has, despite increasingly stiff competition, earned its place as Vietnam's top beach destination. A grand 6km scythe of soft yellow sand is lapped by rolling waves on one side and fringed on the other by cafés, restaurants, hotels and some unusual modern sculptures. Hawkers are on hand to supply paperbacks, fresh pineapple and massages, while **scuba-diving** classes and all kinds of **watersports** are available. Local companies also offer popular day-trips to Nha Trang's outlying **islands**, combining hiking, snorkelling and an onboard feast of seafood. Bear in mind that during the rainy season, around November and December, the sea gets choppy and the beach loses much of its appeal.

Though beach-bumming certainly takes precedence over sightseeing, there's far more to Nha Trang than sea and sand. The city itself sports a handful of attractions – the pick of which are the Yersin Museum and a couple of religious buildings – but Nha Trang's **culinary scene** stands out as particularly noteworthy, as does the range of accommodation, set among some stylish boutiques and bars. There are also a few noteworthy sights both in and around the city, though the intriguing Po Nagar Cham towers are of greatest appeal: by the time Nguyen lords wrested this patch of the country from Champa in the mid-seventeenth century, the towers had already stood here for over seven hundred years. Beyond the centre, you'll find hot springs in which you can wallow in mud, the world's longest cross-sea cable-car ride, and more besides. Last, but not least, is the city's huge and hugely photogenic **fishing fleet**, which moors just north of the centre – a place of salty, local appeal in a city that has been embracing change for decades.

City centre

Nha Trang's not all sand and sea – there's a small knot of sights near the train station, including the excellent **Nha Trang Cathedral** and **Long Son Pagoda**. Closer to the beach is the diverting **Yersin Museum**, while rising high above the waves and the rest of the city's buildings is the new **Skylight**.

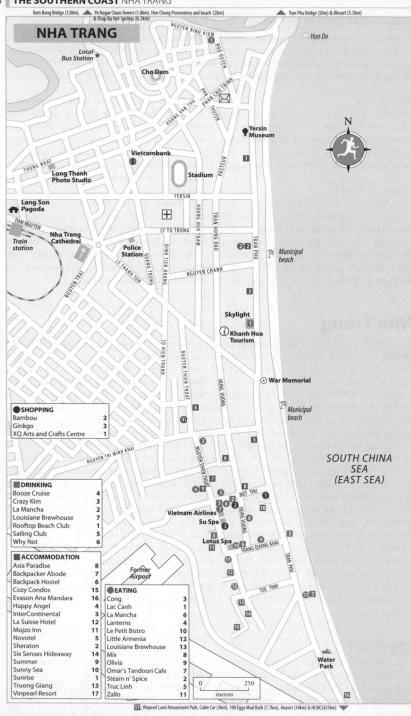

NHA TRANG

Local Bus Station ★

Cho Dam

Hon Do

Yersin Museum

Vietcombank

Stadium

Long Thanh Photo Studio

Lang Son Pagoda

Train station

Nha Trang Cathedral

Police Station

Municipal beach

Skylight

Khanh Hoa Tourism

War Memorial

Municipal beach

SOUTH CHINA SEA (EAST SEA)

● SHOPPING
Bambou	2
Ginkgo	3
XQ Arts and Crafts Centre	1

■ DRINKING
Booze Cruise	4
Crazy Kim	3
La Mancha	2
Louisiane Brewhouse	7
Rooftop Beach Club	1
Sailing Club	5
Why Not	6

Vietnam Airlines
Su Spa
Lotus Spa

■ ACCOMMODATION
Asia Paradise	8
Backpacker Abode	7
Backpack Hostel	6
Cozy Condos	15
Evason Ana Mandara	16
Happy Angel	4
InterContinental	3
La Suisse Hotel	12
Mojzo Inn	11
Novotel	5
Sheraton	2
Six Senses Hideaway	14
Summer	9
Sunny Sea	10
Sunrise	1
Truong Giang	13
Vinpearl Resort	17

Former Airport

● EATING
Cong	3	Le Petit Bistro	10
Lac Canh	1	Little Armenia	12
La Mancha	6	Louisiane Brewhouse	13
Lanterns	4	Mix	8
		Olivia	9
		Omar's Tandoori Cafe	7
		Steam n' Spice	2
		Truc Linh	5
		Zallo	11

Water Park

0   250
metres

Nha Trang Cathedral

Thai Nguyen • Daily 4am–1pm & 2–9pm; weekday Mass 4.45am & 5pm, plus five Sunday services • Free

The stolid, grey-brick **Nha Trang Cathedral**, built in the 1930s, rises up over the sloping cobbled track that winds round to its front doors from Nguyen Trai. This Gothic-style building is one of Vietnam's most passable impressions of a European cathedral; under the lofty, vaulted ceilings, vivid stained-glass windows depict Christ, Mary, Joseph, Joan of Arc and St Theresa.

Long Son Pagoda

Accessed from Thai Nguyen • Daily 7.30–11.30am & 1.30–5.30pm • Free

The **Long Son Pagoda** is a 1930s creation whose entrance is marked by stone gateposts topped by lotus buds. An impressive bronze Buddha stands at the head of the altar, and there are the usual capering dragons on the eaves, but it's the huge **White Buddha**, 180-odd steps up the hillside behind, that's the pagoda's greatest asset – and Nha Trang's most recognizable landmark. It was crafted in 1963 to symbolize the Buddhist struggle against the repressive Diem regime, and around its lotus-shaped pedestal are carved images of the monks and nuns who set fire to themselves in protest, among them Thich Quang Duc (see box, p.79). Note that the pagoda has become a popular haunt for beggars, who often use children as part of their ploys – if you do want to give a contribution to the pagoda, pop it in an official collection box.

Long Thanh Photo Studio

126 Hoang Van Thu • Mon–Sat 8am–5.30pm • Free • ☎ 0258 382 4875, ⓦ longthanhart.com

Budding culture vultures could do worse than track down the **Long Thanh Photo Studio**, a gallery filled with the monochrome works of Long Thanh, a Nha Trang native and long one of Vietnam's foremost photographers. The man himself is often around to chat, or even (if you're in luck) share some of the secrets behind his skills.

Yersin Museum

Off Tran Phu • Mon–Fri 7.30–11am & 2–4.30pm • 26,000đ

Another sight worth tracking down in central Nha Trang is the **Yersin Museum**, dedicated to the famed French scientist (see box, p.174). It's stuffed with laboratory equipment, letters, books and other paraphernalia formerly belonging to Yersin, though it shouldn't take you long to navigate the various exhibition rooms.

Skylight

38 Tran Phu • Daily 8am–2pm & 4.30pm–midnight • 50,000đ • ☎ 0258 352 8988, ⓦ skylightnhatrang.com

Nah Trang's newest draw is the **Skylight** building's "Skydeck", an observatory platform which provides truly commanding views over the city to one side, and the ocean on the other – and, from the "Skywalk", straight down 43 levels to the ground, which provides a little thrill. The building is topped with a lighthouse of sorts – not exactly a useful aid to passing mariners, but enough to be claimed as a world record. In the evening, the place morphs into the *Rooftop Beach Club* (see p.232).

North of the centre

Just to the north of Nha Trang are a couple of wonderful sights – the evocative Cham towers of **Po Nagar**, and the joyous mud-pools of the **Thap Ba Hot Springs** (see box, p.231). Heading a little further north will bring you to the **Hon Chong Promontory**, a finger of granite boulders dashed by the sea – it's quite possible to clamber down to the rocks. Immediately up the coast is **Hon Chong beach**, which is less refined than the city beach but more secluded. Cheap seafood restaurants proliferate at its far end. At night, the views from here across the bay to the central beach zone are very impressive.

ALEXANDRE YERSIN

A Swiss–French scientist who travelled to Southeast Asia in 1889 as a ship's doctor, **Alexandre Yersin** developed a great love for Vietnam and learned to speak Vietnamese fluently. He was responsible for the founding of Da Lat (he recognized the beneficial effects of the climate there for Europeans), and settled in Nha Trang in 1893. By the time of his death in 1943, Yersin had become a local hero, thanks not to his greatest achievement – the discovery of a plague bacillus in Hong Kong in 1894 (one named after him; *Yersinia pestis*) – but rather to his educational work in sanitation and agriculture, and to his ability to predict typhoons and thus save the lives of fishermen. Significantly, his name is still given to streets, not only in Nha Trang but around the country, sharing an honour generally only granted to Vietnamese heroes.

Po Nagar Cham towers

1.2km from central Nha Trang • Daily 6am–6pm • 22,000đ • Walk north from the beach and take the first left after the bridge, or hunt down a xe om (20,000–30,000đ)

The glorious **Po Nagar Cham towers** are Nha Trang's most popular sight. Of the estimated ten towers, or *kalan*, constructed here between the seventh and twelfth centuries by the Hindu Cham people (see box, p.430), only four remain. Their baked red bricks weathered so badly through the centuries that restoration work on the towers has been necessary; nevertheless, the complex manages to produce an age-old atmosphere, despite the gaggles of souvenir sellers. To access the main buildings, you'll need to don a grey cloak – they're free to rent from an easy-to-spot area up the steps, and chances are that you'll want a selfie before giving the robe back.

The northern tower

The complex's largest and most impressive tower is the 25m-high **northern tower**, built in 817 by Harivarman I and dedicated to Yang Ino Po Nagar, tutelary Goddess Mother of the Kingdom and a manifestation of Uma, Shiva's consort. Restored sections stand out due to their lighter hue, but the lotus-petal and spearhead motifs that embellish the tower are original, as is the lintel over the outer door on which a lithe four-armed Shiva dances, flanked by musicians, on the back of an ox. The two sandstone pillars supporting this lintel bear spidery Cham inscriptions.

Inside, a vestibule tapering to a pyramidal ceiling leads to the main chamber, where a fog of incense hangs in the air. The golden statue that originally stood in here was pilfered by the Khmer in the tenth century and replaced by a black stone statue of **Uma** – minus its head, which was plundered by the French and is now in a Parisian museum. A gaudy yellow robe nowadays obscures the ten arms of cross-legged Uma, and a doll-like face has been added. Yang Ino Po Nagar is still worshipped as the protectress of the city, and the statue is bathed during the Merian Festival each March.

The other towers

Possessing neither the height nor the intricacy of the main *kalan*, the **central tower**, dating back to the seventh century, is dedicated to the god Cri Cambhu, and sees a steady flow of childless couples pass through to pray for fertility at its lingam. The **southern tower** is the smallest of the four, and also features a lingam inside. Beneath its boat-shaped roof, half-formed statues in relief are still visible at the **northwest tower**, and the frontal view of an elephant is just about discernible on the western facade, its serpentine trunk now blackened with age.

South of the centre

Unmissable just south of Nha Trang, **Hon Tre** is the biggest island in the bay by far, and home to one of the country's largest amusement parks. The interesting **National Oceano-graphic Institute** is also based near the jumping-off points for the ferries and cable cars.

Vinpearl Land Amusement Park

Hon Tre Island, around 4km east of Nha Trang • Daily 8am–9pm; cable car daily 9am–10pm • 800,000đ including round-trip by cable car • ☎ 0258 3590111, ✆ nhatrang.vinpearlland.com

Hon Tre is dominated by **Vinpearl Land Amusement Park**, which includes a hotel (see p.229), a water park with slides and flumes, a mini-oceanarium, 4-D movies, a shopping mall and some rides – it's great fun, especially for those travelling with children. You can get here by cable car, and the journey, at 3.3km, is the longest over-water ride in the world. The mainland station is just south of central Nha Trang.

ARRIVAL AND DEPARTURE   NHA TRANG

By plane Cam Ranh International Airport (☎ 0258 398 9918), 35km south of the city, handles a prodigious number of Russian and Chinese tourists – there are scheduled flights to various cities across these two countries, as well as to Korea and Cambodia. From the airport, take a bus (65,000đ) or taxi (380,000đ) to Nha Trang, and keep in mind that cabs are cheaper heading to the airport.

Destinations Da Nang (1–2 daily; 1hr 15min); Hanoi (7–10 daily; 1hr 50min); HCMC (10–12 daily; 55min).

By train Nha Trang's station (ticket office daily 7.30–11am & 1.30–9pm; ☎ 0258 382 2113) is just west of the city centre on Thai Nguyen. Though the distance is walkable, it's tempting to take a cab – as always, simply stepping out of the station and flagging one down on the main road will help you avoid the cowboys. Just about any hotel or travel agency in Nha Trang will get you a train ticket, though commission rates vary widely and it pays to shop around.

Destinations Da Nang (15 daily; 9–13hr); Hanoi (13 daily; 24–31hr); HCMC (16 daily; 7–12hr); Hue (15 daily; 11hr 30min–16hr).

By bus Most visitors arrive on open-tour buses, which drop off in the centre outside affiliated offices or hotels. The long-distance bus station (☎ 0258 382 2192) sits 1km west of the city centre, and around 700m west of the train station.

Destinations Buon Ma Thuot (4hr); Da Lat (5hr); Da Nang (12hr); HCMC (10hr); Hue (15hr); Mui Ne (5hr 30min); Quy Nhon (6hr).

4

ACTIVITIES IN THE SOUTH CHINA SEA

SCUBA DIVING

Nha Trang is the **scuba centre of Vietnam**, as is well evidenced by the number of dive companies that operate here. It's best avoided October to December, when the strong currents stir up the silt and reduce visibility, but during the dry season (January to May) there are dive boats heading to the over twenty dive sites in the region every day. A typical day out, including a couple of dives and lunch, costs around $80, with snorkelling around $25; PADI courses are also available, from basic Discover packs (around $100) to four-day Open Water options ($380).

You may hear grumblings about the size of the fish you'll see in the waters around Nha Trang, and it's true that they're usually pretty small. The Hon Mun area is good for barracuda, but even there they're mostly juvenile. However, one thing the area has in spades is **hard coral**, with over 350 species found so far – it's not too far off the Great Barrier Reef, which has around 450.

There are well over a dozen **dive operators** in Nha Trang, and some are downright dangerous – there have, in the past, been cases of divers left behind. Many local outfits have licences recognized in Russia, but not anywhere else – stick with proper PADI-certified operators, including the highly reputable places listed here.

Oceans 5 49 Hung Vuong ☎ 0258 352 2012, ✆ oceans5.co.

Rainbow Divers 19 Biet Thu ☎ 0258 352 4351, ✆ divevietnam.com.

Sailing Club Divers 72–74 Tran Phu ☎ 0258 352 2788, ✆ sailingclubdivers.com.

WATERSPORTS

If you'd rather get your kicks above water, various points on the beach rent out watersports equipment (the section by *Louisiane Brewhouse* is best). Jet-skiing was recently outlawed in the waters off Nha Trang, though you'll still be able to enjoy **kitesurfing** (rental $30, 1hr lesson $60), **windsurfing** (rental $20, 2hr lesson $100) and regular **surfing** (rental $10). These days, many operators actually head down south to Long Beach, which is more appropriate for such activities.

BOAT TRIPS TO THE ISLANDS

Several companies in Nha Trang offer day-trips to a selection of **islands**, including a stop for snorkelling and a seafood lunch on board – all for around $6–8 per person. However, to fully enjoy the day you'll need to fork out for several extras, as otherwise you'll need to spend time just sitting on the boat and waiting till everyone comes back. Some boat rides, particularly those booked through backpacker guesthouses, can be quite wild and alcohol-fuelled, while other operators run gentler tours.

On a typical island day-tour, you'll be picked up from your hotel, taken to Cau Da Wharf, 6km south of the town centre, and shuffled on to one of the many boats jostling in the harbour. As the boat casts off at around 9.30am, you'll pass beneath the cable car to Hon Tre (see p.226), then chug between islands for about half an hour to **Hon Mun** (Black Island; 10,000đ entry), named after the dark cliffs that rear up from it. There's no beach to speak of on Hon Mun, but the island boasts one of the best places for snorkelling in the area, with some great coral. Boats hang around for an hour or so while people snorkel over the corals or sunbathe on deck, and there are frequently diving groups here, too. There's a 40,000đ charge to snorkel in this "protected area", though it's not clear quite how it's being protected.

After a break for lunch in the shelter of **Hon Mot**, boats head for **Hon Tam**, where there's a small beach (30,000đ entry), and you get the chance to stretch on the sand or splash about in the sea for an hour before heading for the final destination, the Tri Nguyen Aquarium (90,000đ) on **Hon Mieu**. The setting here is wonderfully kitsch: visitors approach the site through giant lobsters and past cement sharks, and the strange building that houses the aquarium looks like a galleon dragged up from the depths and draped in seaweed. Inside, the tanks feature black-tipped sharks, bug-eyed groupers, hawksbill turtles and colourful sea anemones, though as you might expect of an old aquarium in Vietnam, the tanks are a little small, and little thought is given to animal welfare. Finally the boat heads back to the mainland and visitors are whisked back to their hotels.

GETTING AROUND

On foot Nha Trang isn't a very large city, so walking everywhere is perfectly feasible – especially if a daily pilgrimage to the municipal beach marks the extent of your travels.
By bicycle Should you plan to stray a little further afield, bicycle rental is the most efficient and enjoyable way to go. Bicycles are available for around 40,000đ/day at most of the city's hotels.

By xe om Xe om are everywhere if you need them, and even if you don't.
By car Fully fledged car tours of the region (around $50/day) can be arranged by tour operators, including Khanh Hoa Tourism at 1 Tran Hung Dao (☎0258 352 8100).

ACCOMMODATION

The fact that Nha Trang is chock-full of **hotels** doesn't seem to be discouraging developers, and the city's already wide choice of accommodation just keeps on growing; already, beachfront monoliths are gradually blocking out any sea view from the backstreet mini-hotels. Even so, it's worth bearing in mind that the city draws Vietnamese as well as foreign tourists, and that there can be difficulties finding a room over **public holidays**, when prices rise.

Asia Paradise 6 Biet Thu ☎0258 352 4686, ⓦasiaparadisehotel.com; map p.224. Decent mid-ranger, right in the middle of things. Their cheapest rooms are on the small side, but shell out a bit more and you can score yourself a whopper. All are elegant affairs featuring balconies. $40
Backpacker Abode 79 Nguyen Thien Thuat ☎0258 352 9139; map p.224. Though it may look a little grubby from the outside, this hostel is a cut above the norm here – curtains on the beds add that little bit of privacy to the dorms, and evenings often see a keg of free beer opened for guests. Dorms $6, doubles $14
Backpack Hostel 92–12 Hung Vuong ☎0258 352 1140, ⓦbackpackhostel.net; map p.224. Smart hostel

option tucked into a relatively quiet side-street just a couple of blocks from the beach. The staff go out of their way to help, though private rooms are rather overpriced. Dorms $5, doubles $40
★**Cozy Condos** 92–12 Hung Vuong ☎0258 352 1001, ⓦcozy-condos.com; map p.224. This place offers impeccable apartment rooms at prices that are way too low, and is tucked into an alley whose neighbourly, everyone-knows-everyone air is quite a nice surprise in central Nha Trang. Staff are adept at organizing tours and advising on places to eat and drink. $20
Evason Ana Mandara Southern end of Tran Phu ☎0258 352 2222, ⓦsixsenses.com; map p.224. Nha Trang's most luxurious resort comes with its own slice of beach and

features dreamy bungalows with all mod cons and some traditional touches, including ethnic minority-designed tapestries. Facilities include two pools, tennis courts, a beach restaurant and the superb Six Senses spa. $400

Happy Angel 11a/3 Nguyen Thien Thuat ☎0258 352 5006; map p.224. A little way north of the hubbub, and set into a quiet back alley, this small hotel is a good place for those looking to escape Nha Trang's noise – though the bars and beach are just a short walk away, if you need them. Modern in style, the rooms are far nicer than the price may suggest. $12

★**InterContinental** 32–34 Tran Phu ☎0258 388 7777, ⊛intercontinental.com; map p.224. Newly opened at the time of research, this is the latest of the big hotel chains to hit town, and it's likely to thrive despite the intense competition. They really have lavished attention on this place – check out the artistic metalwork in the lobby, the angular fittings that your breakfast buffet sits on, or the Bluetooth-ready speakers in the rooms (which are themselves divine). From some of the shower cubicles you can see the ocean, and there's a glorious pool on site. $150

★**La Suisse Hotel** 34 Tran Quang Khai ☎0258 352 4353, ⊛lasuissehotel.com; map p.224. Perhaps the most popular budget hotel in the city, allying great service with cheap but well-appointed rooms. The semi-secluded location is also a bonus, since you're largely off the radar of hawkers and xe om drivers. $18

★**Mojzo Inn** 120/36 Nguyen Thien Thuat ☎0258 625 5568; map p.224. This is a fantastic new place that's essentially a boutique hostel. The friendly staff are full of surprises and helpful advice; rooms and common areas have been artfully decorated along a red-white-black tricolore; and you'll be able to drink in superb views over breakfast from the rooftop. The only sad thing is that they have just fifteen rooms – book early! Dorms $6, doubles $19

Novotel 50 Tran Phu ☎0258 625 6900, ⊛novotel.com; map p.224. Beautiful beachfront hotel, whose rates occasionally drop below $100 – five-star rooms at three-star prices. There's not too much in the way of facilities bar a small pool and spa, though this adds to the relaxed air. $150

★**Sheraton** 26–28 Tran Phu ☎0258 388 0000, ⊛sheraton.com; map p.224. A relative newbie and already the flashiest city-centre option by far. Rooms have been decorated with soothing colours and local art, and you'll be able to see the sea from most shower cubicles. You should be able to lop a fair chunk off the rack rates. $260

Six Senses Hideaway Ninh Van Bay ☎0258 372 8222, ⊛sixsenses.com; map p.224. Choose from beach villas, rock villas, hilltop villas, over-water villas or spa-suite villas on an idyllic island off the coast – but make sure you can handle the price tag before you come ashore. $500

Summer 34 Nguyen Thien Thuat ☎0258 352 2186, ⊛thesummerhotel.com.vn; map p.224. A cool three-star mini-hotel. The rooms are modern and comfortable, if a little on the small side, staff are helpful and there's a swimming pool on the roof. $32

Sunny Sea 64b/9 Tran Phu ☎0258 352 2286; map p.224. Set at the end of an alley that's teeming with cheap places to stay, this is a popular choice in the area, with rooms that are excellent value – if occasionally a little musty. $12

Sunrise 12–14 Tran Phu ☎0258 382 0999, ⊛sunrisenhatrang.com.vn; map p.224. Enjoying a superb location towards the northern end of the beach, this elegant, rambling hotel boasts a classical colonial design. Some rooms are a little small, but move up to a suite and you'll be drinking in the sea views from the jacuzzi on your balcony. $210

Truong Giang 3–8 Tran Quang Khai ☎0258 352 2125, ⊛truonggianghotel.hostel.com; map p.224. With professional service and clean, attractive rooms featuring small TVs, minibars and colourful bedspreads, this is a great option in the competitive budget price category. It's a good idea to book ahead. $13

Vinpearl Resort 7 Tran Phu ☎0258 391 1166, ⊛vinpearl.com; map p.224. This luxurious resort is actually located on Hon Tre out in the bay, and features nearly 500 well-equipped rooms as well as one of the biggest pools in Southeast Asia (5000sqm). It's accessed by speedboat or cable car from the southern end of Tran Phu. $260

EATING

Finding a decent place to eat presents no problem in cosmopolitan Nha Trang, which specializes in **seafood** – it's cheapest, and at its best, in the out-of-town area north of Tran Phu bridge. For something local and romantic, track down one of the seafood barbecue folk along the beach – there are no menus to speak of, but it's great fun to sit on the sand and eat goodies that were very recently hauled from the sea.

Cong 27 Nguyen Thien Thuat ☎091 181 1152; map p.224. If you're in the mood for coffee, give this artistically designed place a try – split over three levels and popular with young locals, its main wall features a retro Socialist Realist-style mural. Daily 7am–11pm.

Lac Canh 44 Nguyen Binh Kiem ☎0258 382 1391; map p.224. Some way north of the centre, this grill restaurant

has been here since the 1970s, and remains hugely popular among locals. Admittedly it's not the most salubrious place in town, but the food (around 85,000d/head) more than compensates – it's also incredibly smoky, so you'll likely crave a good wash afterwards. Daily 9am–9.30pm.

La Mancha 17 Biet Thu ☎0258 352 7978; map p.224. This is an attractive Spanish restaurant with decent food, though it's perhaps best for smaller, snackier dishes such as gazpacho (90,000đ) or a healthy range of tapas (100,000–150,000đ). Also good for evening drinks (see opposite). Daily 7am–1am.

★**Lanterns** 72 Nguyen Thien Thuat ☎058 247 1674, ⓦlanternsvietnam.com; map p.224. This charming restaurant serves delectable Vietnamese food, with burgers, pasta dishes (both from 77,000đ) and local specialities such as *com tam* (65,000đ) and snapper (175,000đ). But that's not the end of the story – their proceeds, and food, help to support over a dozen local orphanages. They also run cooking classes (daily 9am–2pm; $25). Daily 7am–11pm.

Le Petit Bistro 26b Tran Quang Khai ☎0258 352 7201; map p.224. Good-looking French bistro, doling out superb dishes at surprisingly reasonable prices. Come here for a cheap breakfast with a pain au chocolat (25,000đ) or eggs Benedict (60,000đ), or try the delicious onion soup (110,000đ) and expensive meat dishes. Daily 8am–10.30pm.

★**Little Armenia** 3/12 Tran Quang Khai ☎0258 625 2022; map p.224. Join the Russian tourists at this superb place, which sells an array of food from across the former Soviet Union as well as some Vietnamese staples. Best are the Georgian dishes – try the soup-filled *khinkali* dumplings (25,000đ each), or the Adjarian *khachapuri*, a deliciously unhealthy meal that's something like a pizza filled with butter, egg and cheese (120,000đ). Daily 10am–midnight.

★**Louisiane Brewhouse** Tran Phu Beach ☎0258 352 1948, ⓦlouisianebrewhouse.com.vn; map p.224. Eat great food with your feet buried in the sand at this big restaurant, where tables and chairs spill onto the beach every evening. The menu features an excellent range of Vietnamese and Western dishes (like red snapper for 215,000đ, fish & chips for 130,000đ and eggs Benedict for 100,000đ), as well as a sushi section, a pizza section and home-made cakes and pastries. There's also a swimming pool, which is free for customers. Daily 7am–1am.

Mix 77 Hung Vuong ☎0258 656 3231; map p.224.

Modern-looking Greek restaurant, whose food makes a great change from the norm. Try a mixed dip platter (100,000đ), a frappe (35,000đ) or a nice big slab of moussaka (110,000đ). Daily 9am–11pm.

Olivia 14b Tran Quang Khai ☎0258 352 2752; map p.224. The best of the many, many Italian restaurants huddled around this area. There's good gnocchi, tagliatelle, ravioli, penne and pizza to choose from, all from around 100,000đ. Daily 9.30am–10pm.

Omar's Tandoori Cafe 89b Nguyen Thien Thuat ☎0258 222 1625; map p.224. Not the most attractive restaurant in Nha Trang – or even on this side of the road – but this remains the place to go should you get the urge for an Indian curry. Daily set meals are 150,000đ, including a drink. Daily 7am–10pm.

★**Steam n' Spice** 26–28 Tran Phu ☎0258 388 0000; map p.224. Inside the *Sheraton* (see p.229), this stylish Hong Kong-style restaurant allows you to experience the high life on a moderate budget – you'll be able to eat well for under 150,000đ. Try a wonton soup, *char siu* pork or Sichuan spicy tofu, and wash it all down with a vanilla-mint-lime milkshake. Daily 11am–2.30pm & 6–10pm.

Truc Linh 18 Biet Thu ☎0258 352 1089; map p.224. The most atmospheric branch of a successful local chain serving a good range of Western and Vietnamese dishes, with seafood the speciality. Prices are a little above average (most dishes cost over 150,000đ) but the food is still good value – for now, since the chain's popularity has seen standards dropping. Daily 8am–10pm.

Zallo 3 Tran Quang Khai ☎0258 625 2079; map p.224. This large restaurant, right in the thick of things, came up with a winning business strategy – buffet food of a decent quality, at a low price (250,000đ, including one drink). You'll be able to pile your plate high with meat (including crocodile, which goes fast) and seafood, then grill it to the best of your abilities at your table, over the charcoal briquette provided – fantastic fun, especially if you're also taking advantage of the cheap beer. Daily 4pm–midnight.

DRINKING AND NIGHTLIFE

Nha Trang has a buzzing nightlife scene. There are plenty of chilled-out haunts and party venues around the budget district, as well as pricier nightspots along the beachfront; many have generous **happy hours**, sometimes lasting pretty much all day. Occasional **crackdowns** have the bars closing at midnight, but if they're left to their own devices most places will stay open till the wee hours.

Booze Cruise 110 Nguyen Thien Thuat ☎0286 352 1105; map p.224. There's often a raucous atmosphere at this popular venue, whose happy hour varies by drink, though the beers are particularly good as they're only

WATCH YOUR DRINKS

Nha Trang may offer some of the best nightlife in Vietnam, but from time to time locals (and even expats) take advantage of travellers and their predilection for alcoholic beverages. **Drink spiking** has long been an issue, with cocktail "buckets" making the easiest targets. Travellers have also been known to get sick after a bout of beer-pong, so consider avoiding that, too.

19,000đ each – this fact alone convinces a fair proportion of passers-by to pop in. Daily 10am–2am.

Crazy Kim 19 Biet Thu ☎0258 381 6072; map p.224. Long-running bar whose atmosphere gets pretty kicking most nights. Many opt for a three-litre beer tower, which will set you back 250,000đ, but there are plenty of other "normal" beers available, as well as cocktails from 35,000đ. Daily 6am–1am.

La Mancha 17 Biet Thu ☎0258 352 7978; map p.224. This Spanish restaurant (see p.229) is also great for evening drinks. For 200,000đ, plus a little extra per head, you can get a shisha to go with your cocktail – some of the flavours are cocktail-ey themselves, such as rose through apple juice, strawberry through sambuca, or cappuccino through milk. Daily 7am–1am.

★ **Louisiane Brewhouse** Tran Phu Beach ☎0258 352 1948, ⓦlouisianebrewhouse.com.vn; map p.224. Not just an excellent restaurant, but a terrific place to drink. They make a pilsener, a dark lager and seasonal ales, all of which can be tried in a cute sampler set (110,000đ). After that, pick a pint of your favourite one, and enjoy it on the beach or over a game of pool. Daily 7am–1am.

PAMPER YOURSELF

Besides its status as Vietnam's premier beach resort, Nha Trang's latest attractions include its **mudbath complexes** – there are now three in town, which all essentially follow the same pattern. In addition, **spas** with massage and beauty services are now big business here.

MUDBATHS

The main event at these facilities is the opportunity to wallow in baths filled with mineral-enriched mud – allegedly good for the skin, but great fun to boot. After washing off, you'll be free to have a swim in other pools, which are filled with water rich in sodium silicate chloride (said to have beneficial effects on stress, arthritis and rheumatism). There are a number of other options available at these complexes, including spa treatments, massages and meals. Note that on entry you'll be encouraged to buy a "private" bath (from around 250,000đ per person), though in practice foreigners going for the "communal" bath option (usually just over 100,000đ per person) often get exactly the same thing.

100 Egg Mud Bath 15 Ngoc Son ☎0258 383 4939, ⓦtramtrung.vn. Everything's egg-shaped at this quirky place – even some of the cocoon-like mudbaths themselves. As well as the regular range of mudbath services, their restaurant serves one hundred different egg-based dishes, and even if you're not a fan of hard-boiled, over-easy or sunny side up, you can head down to *Egg Café* for some fast food. However, it has to be said that despite such cutesiness, the complex is slightly rough around the edges. Daily 9am–7pm.

★ **iResort** 19 Suan Ngoc ☎0258 383 8838, ⓦi-resort.vn. Goodness knows how Apple Corp will feel about the name, but this is the best bathing choice in town – though a little dearer than the other two.

Centred around a pool boasting views of distant hills, its mudbaths have been stylishly designed – arrive in the hour before sundown for the best visual effects. At the time of research, they were putting the finishing touches to a water park just around the hill. Daily 7am–8pm.

Thap Ba Hot Springs 15 Ngoc Son ☎0258 383 4939, ⓦthapbahotspring.com.vn. A side-road heading west just to the north of the Po Nagar Cham towers takes you through suburban Nha Trang to this, the oldest bathing complex in town. It's still looking good; its communal pool areas are surrounded by foliage, and the VIP areas are pretty swanky. You can also stay the night here, if you so desire. Daily 7am–7.30pm.

SPAS

Some spas are more proficient than others, but the ones listed here have a decent reputation. They offer a huge range of services, including facials (from $16), body scrubs ($15) and hot-stone massages ($25); given the prodigious length of the menus, it may help to avoid any unnecessary stress by plumping for an all-in package.

Daisy 34 Nguyen Thien Thuat ☎0258 352 5929. Moderately luxurious, though with fair prices, this is a good choice. In between your welcome and goodbye drinks, you can go for a hot-stone treatment or even a full four-hour pampering session.

Sheraton 26–28 Tran Phu ☎0258 388 0000. Supremely opulent, this is the best of the high-end hotel spas, with prices that are way out of backpacker range, but still most likely far lower than you'd expect to pay at home.

Su Spa 93 Nguyen Thien Thuat ☎0258 352 3242. One of the longest running and most reputable spas in Nha Trang – prices are cheap, and the service is usually of high quality.

★**Rooftop Beach Club** 38 Tran Phu ☎0258 352 8988, ⓦskylightnhatrang.com; map p.224. By night the Skylight viewing platform (see p.225) turns into Nha Trang's "it" spot, a snazzy bar with expensive drinks and spellbinding views. The ticket (130,000đ) includes one free drink, though you'll have to pay an additional 20,000đ if you want to arrive after 8.30pm. Daily 4.30pm–midnight.

Sailing Club 72–74 Tran Phu ☎0258 352 4628; map p.224. This has been a favourite spot for an eclectic group of party animals for some years. DJs and swing chairs on the beach draw a well-heeled expat crowd and hordes of tourists to its refined beachfront bar, which gets progressively less refined as the night wears on. That said, the night-time cover charge of 150,000đ (including a drink) keeps things vaguely respectable. Try one of the signature cocktails, infused with goodies such as rose petal, ginger and chilli. Daily 7am–late.

Why Not 24 Tran Quang Khai ☎0258 352 2652; map p.224. This is a big place with inside and outside seating, a pool table, dancefloor and comfy lounge area. Serves cheap beer and spirits (happy hour 4–10pm; two-for-one cocktails 9–11pm), and there's live music some nights. Daily 9am–late.

SHOPPING

Bambou 15 Biet Thu ☎0258 352 3616; map p.224. Offers original-design T-shirts from 200,000đ each, plus other bright and colourful souvenirs. Daily 9am–9pm.

Ginkgo 99 Nguyen Thien Thuat ☎0258 352 1341; map p.224. Another good T-shirt shop, with the emphasis on goofy, Vietnam-related puns. Daily 8am–10pm.

XQ Arts and Crafts Centre 64 Tran Phu ☎0258 352 6579; map p.224. Displays and sells embroidered pictures, some of which are stunning works of art, from 350,000đ upwards. Daily 8am–8pm.

DIRECTORY

Bank Vietcombank, 17 Quang Trung, changes cash and has an ATM. There's also a convenient branch of Agribank at 2 Hung Vuong.

Hospital You'll find the hospital at 19 Yersin, below the city stadium (☎0258 382 2168).

Pharmacy There's a good pharmacy at 27 Le Thanh Ton.

Police The local police are based at 5 Ly Tu Trong (☎0258 382 2400).

Post office 4 Le Loi (daily 7am–9pm) has poste restante and a DHL courier desk (which is closed on Sundays); there are also several other small post offices scattered around town.

The north Khanh Hoa coast

Most tourists leapfrog the 400km-plus of coastline between Nha Trang and Hoi An on a tour bus, but swathes of splendid **beaches** do exist along this stretch of the country, many of which remain relatively untouched. Visitors to places like Doc Let beach, Whale Island and Dai Beach will find good accommodation options and uncrowded sand in front of their resort.

Hon Khoi Peninsula

At Ninh Hoa, about 33km north of Nha Trang, Highway 26 branches off left from Highway 1 to Buon Ma Thuot; about 5km later, a turning on the right leads 12km to the splendid **Hon Khoi Peninsula**, on which you'll find pristine **Doc Let beach**. You'll probably be keen to linger here awhile: the casuarinas and white sands of the beach are perfect for a day's beach-bumming, although you have to pay a small entrance fee for the privilege unless you are staying at one of the resorts here.

ARRIVAL AND DEPARTURE   HON KHOI PENINSULA

The turn-off to Hon Khoi is signed from the highway about 38km north of Nha Trang, just north of the village of Ninh Hoa.

By public transport Ninh Hoa itself is accessible by bus from Nha Trang (every 30min), and also has a small train station on the main line, which is served by most trains from the north and south. All resorts will be able to arrange pick-up from here, or from Nha Trang (usually $20–30/vehicle).

ACCOMMODATION

★**Jungle Beach Resort** Jungle Beach ⓣ091 342 9144, ⓦjunglebeachvietnam.com. On a separate, still-secluded beach, this place is a real find – many guests visit for a day and end up spending a week here. There are basic dorms and bungalows, as well as a/c "suite" huts; all meals are included in the price, and the food is excellent. Trails on the hillside behind are ripe for exploring and the beach is pristine. Dorms $25, bungalows $60

Paradise Resort North end of Doc Let beach ⓣ0258 367 0480, ⓦparadiseresort.vn. This cheap, markedly serene resort (which has no TVs in the rooms or at breakfast) has a few huge rooms and some simple bungalows ($80), plus a shady terrace overlooking the beach. Rates include three meals a day, and they provide free rental of kayaks, fishing rods and more. $60

★**Some Days of Silence** North end of Doc Let beach ⓣ0258 367 0952, ⓦsomedaysresort.com. Formerly the *Ki-em Art House Resort*, this place in the middle of the beach is in a class of its own. Run by artists, it's a dreamy compound with a handful of individually decorated bungalows, a meditation room, art gallery and huge picnic tables in the garden. $110

Thuy Duong Inland from Doc Let beach ⓣ0258 367 1471. The Doc Let area's best budget option, presided over by a friendly family. It's just a walk from the beach, and rooms are basic but all equipped with a/c – most are en suite, too. $15

Hon Ong

4

Some 50km or so north from the Hon Khoi Peninsula, a road branches off Highway 1 along the **Hon Gom Peninsula**, accessing the endless beaches on both sides of this swan's neck of land. A short speedboat ride will bring you to **Hon Ong**, also known as "Whale Island". Humpback whales and whale sharks are often seen in the area from May to August, and Rainbow Divers (see box, p.227) runs **scuba diving** here; off the south coast you can aim for a 7m-deep wreck, or a natural arch and tunnel. Back on dry land, you'll be able to take advantage of some delightful **walking trails** – it should only take a couple of hours to perform a full circuit of the island, and if in luck you may get to see muntjac deer and wading birds on your way around.

ARRIVAL AND DEPARTURE — HON ONG

By boat and bus Hon Ong is accessed by speedboat (5min) from the Dam Mon jetty, about 15km down the Hon Khoi Peninsula from Dai Linh, a stop on Highway 1. You can hit Dai Linh on one of the open-tour buses (see p.32) heading up and down the coast, though note that you may have to pay an additional fare and that they're far harder to pick up on your way back out. It's easier to take a bus-boat transfer from Nha Trang – *Whale Island Resort* (see below) has daily services at 9am and 2pm ($25).

ACCOMMODATION AND EATING

Whale Island Resort West coast of Hon Ong ⓣ0258 384 0501, ⓦanislandinvietnam.com. On Whale Island itself, this place has a wonderfully relaxing feel, with simple but tasteful bungalows peeking out over dense vegetation at a fabulous view of the bay. The compulsory meals (lunch and dinner both $14/person) can work out as much as your room, though they're pretty good. For a nominal fee, you'll also be able to rent catamarans, canoes and snorkelling equipment. $40

Quy Nhon and around

A likeable little seaport town, **QUY NHON** is set on a narrow stake of land spearing into the South China Sea. It's a good place to get away from tourists as few come here, thanks in no small part to the fact that the local beach is both less dazzling than others along this coast, and a bit shallow for swimming; it does make a lovely place for a breezy evening stroll, though nicer **Quy Hoa beach** is only a short xe om ride to the south. For more adventurous travellers, the lack of foreigners only adds to the town's intrigue, and there are a few places worth checking out in the nearby area, including some superbly restored Cham towers. North of Quy Nhon, and within easy day-trip distance, are two more Cham sites: the **Banh It towers** and the **Cha Ban Citadel** – both important remnants of this former civilization.

Brief history

Quy Nhon's origins lie in the Cham migration south at the start of the eleventh century, under pressure from the Vietnamese to the north. They named the empire they established in the area Vijaya, meaning "Victory"; its epicentre was the citadel of Cha Ban (see p.236), though it was the settlement of Quy Nhon – then known as Sri Bonai – that developed into its thriving commercial centre. Centuries later, the **Tay Son Rebellion** (see p.433) boiled over here; the town became the Tay Son capital after being seized in 1773, and within five years the brothers had control over most of southern Vietnam. During the American War the city served as a US port and supply centre, its population swollen by refugees fleeing from the vicious bombing meted out on the surrounding countryside.

Long Khanh Pagoda

141 Tran Cao Van • Dawn to dusk • Free

Right in the middle of the city, the **Long Khanh Pagoda** is an imposing structure, its nine-tiered roof dominating the skyline. The main building is rather sparse, bar the ornate name plaques outside its modern doors; on either side of it stand turrets – one containing a drum, the other a giant bell. The grounds are perhaps of greater interest: look out for the tall statue of Buddha, which is currently painted a rather fetching mint green.

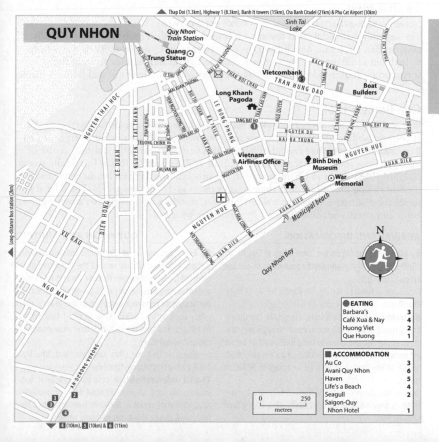

Binh Dinh Museum

28 Nguyen Hue • Tues–Sun 7–11.30am & 1.30–5pm • Free

The **Binh Dinh Museum** contains some superb examples of Cham masonry, which is exactly what you'd expect given the prevalence of such sites in the nearby area – although many have been left exposed to the elements. Other items in the collection include ethnic dress worn by minority groups in Binh Dinh province, and the usual war memorabilia, including a cannon and tank in the outer yard.

Thap Doi

2km west of the centre on Tran Hung Dao • Daily 8–11am & 1.30–6pm • 10,000đ, plus extra for your bike

The most accessible of Quy Nhon's Cham monuments are the **Thap Doi**, or "Double Towers", which have been the subject of an extensive restoration project in recent years. Their former shabby backstreet setting has been transformed into a small, green park where the slender towers, framed by palms, command attention. Both taper to an open top; you'll note that the smaller of the two is both leaning and kinked. The towers date from around the end of the twelfth century, and embellishments such as sandstone pilasters, spearhead-shaped arches and the sandstone statues of winged Garuda – the vehicle of Vishnu – give the buildings a spiritual aura.

Banh It towers

20km north of Quy Nhon • Daily 7am–11am & 1.30–5pm • 10,000đ • 100,000đ by xe om

The superbly restored **Banh It towers**, built in the twelfth century and known locally as Thap Bac, cut a gash on a hilltop over the river from Quy Nhon. Their site is little visited, but the short climb from the access road yields tremendous views of the surrounding countryside, enhanced by the giant white statue of a seated Buddha below.

Cha Ban Citadel

2km west of the highway, around 21km north of Quy Nhon; look out for a small lane on the left signposted "Canh Tien"

If you're travelling under your own steam, you could search for the last vestiges of **Cha Ban Citadel**, the erstwhile capital of Vijaya; this site constituted the political centre of Champa from the early eleventh century until 1471, when Le Thanh Ton finally seized it, killing fifty thousand Cham people in the process. The Tay Son brothers renamed the site Hoang De and made it their base in the mid-1770s (see p.433). You'll be able to see the distinctive **Canh Tien tower** from afar, standing on a slight rise: a rectangular brick and sandstone edifice framed by sandstone pilasters.

ARRIVAL AND INFORMATION

QUY NHON AND AROUND

By plane Phu Cat Airport lies 35km north of Quy Nhon. Minibuses meet flights, and shuttle passengers in and out of town (50,000đ).
Destinations Hanoi (3–4 daily; 1hr 40min); HCMC (7 daily; 1hr 10min).

By train Quy Nhon's train station is beside the Quang Trung statue at the north end of town, though very few services use this spur from the main line; you'd be better off taking a taxi (around 150,000đ) or xe om (80,000đ) to the nearby station at Dieu Tri for trains to HCMC or Hanoi.
Destinations from Dieu Tri: Da Nang (7 daily; 5hr 30min); HCMC (8 daily; 14hr); Nha Trang (9 daily; 4hr); Quang Ngai (8 daily; 3hr).

By bus Buses pull up at Quy Nhon's long-distance bus station, a short xe om ride west of the city centre at the corner of Tay Son and Nguyen Thai Hoc. Futa (⊕ futabus.vn) and other operators run services from other coastal cities, but almost all open-tour buses bypass the town – check when booking your ticket. Keep in mind that services heading to and from the highlands tend to be minibuses, rather than full-sizers.
Destinations Da Nang (8hr); Kon Tum (5hr); Nha Trang (4hr); Pleiku (4hr); Quang Ngai (4hr).

Tourist information The best place for local travel information and bicycle (50,000đ/day) or motorbike (200,000đ/day) rental is *Barbara's* (see opposite). Most hotels will also be able to get you some wheels.

ACCOMMODATION

CITY CENTRE

Au Co 24 An Duong Vuong ☎0256 374 7699; map p.235. This is the best of several mini-hotels clustered together opposite the beach to the west of town. The a/c rooms have TVs and are kept spotlessly clean, though the front desk isn't always manned – they do keep an eye on things from afar via the magic of closed-circuit television, however. $15

Saigon-Quy Nhon Hotel 24 Nguyen Hue ☎0256 382 9922, ⊛saigonquynhonhotel.com.vn; map p.235. This swanky (for Quy Nhon) hotel is centrally located, and boasts a pool and health club out back. The rooms themselves are carpetted and well equipped, as well as good value for money. $50

Seagull 489 An Duong Vuong ☎0256 384 6377, ⊛seagullhotel.com.vn; map p.235. Overlooking the beach, this high-rise hotel is a very good deal for the price – the comfy rooms are angled so that almost all get at least a little view of the sea, especially from their tiny balconies. The buffet breakfasts also go down pretty well, and there's a small fitness centre and pool. $35

SOUTH OF THE CENTRE

Avani Quy Nhon Around 18km from central Quy Nhon ☎0256 384 0132, ⊛avanihotels.com; map p.235. This is an immaculate resort, designed with thoughtful Cham touches – the bathrooms are particularly striking. Look out for the spa facilities and wonderful restaurants, or get involved with some watersports or tai chi sessions with help from the staff. Reserve online and you can get hefty discounts from the advertised rates. $165

★Haven Bai Xep ☎090 280 8949, ⊛havenvietnam.com; map p.235. This Aussie-owned spot is fantastic value for money and has just five rooms, though you may not spend much time in these simple-yet-tasteful affairs – the beach is right on your doorstep, and the views are simply wonderful. There's a decent restaurant on site, too. $30

★Life's a Beach Bai Xep ☎097 893 1085, ⊛lifesabeachvietnam.com; map p.235. This British-run establishment has proven a real hit with all sorts of travellers, thanks to a winning variety of accommodation – choose from dorm beds (in simple, colourful rooms), villas with sea views ($50), a selection of stylish apartments, or even the treehouse. You'll also be able to make use of their restaurant-bar. Dorms $7, apartments $40

EATING

Quy Nhon is perhaps best known for its **snails** – if you want to give them a try, head to Ngoc Han Cong Chia, which attracts hoards of shell-seller shacks each evening.

Barbara's 12 An Duong Vuong ☎0256 389 2921; map p.235. Now sadly without its Kiwi creator, this long-running backpacker café turns out cheap and cheerful staples such as banana pancakes (25,000đ), Vegemite sandwiches (25,000đ) and fish and chips (50,000đ). Also good for juices, smoothies and lassis, as well as cheap evening beers. Daily 7am–10pm.

Café Xua & Nay 5 An Duong Vuong ☎0256 809 4634; map p.235. Directly opposite *Barbara's* (see above), this is an intriguing little café with temple-like decorative flourishes. The coffee's cheap (from 17,000đ), and it's just a skip and a jump from the beach. Daily 6am–8pm.

Huong Viet 122 Xuan Dieu ☎0256 389 4599; map p.235. Set behind a pretty, Cham-like facade, this Chinese restaurant specializes in seafood – a seafood salad will set

you back 110,000đ, oysters cost 18,000đ each, and the seafood soup is a steal at 27,000đ. Sit in the front area and you'll see the beach and hear snatches of the sea. Daily 8am–10pm.

Que Huong 125 Tang Bat Ho ☎0256 382 1123; map p.235. This is an unassuming two-storey venue with a formidable local reputation – it's regularly full to bursting in the early evenings. Some of the dishes on the huge menu are fancifully named, such as the "fried cracky noodle and roughly fried snake head", but everything tastes great; try the *com ga* (chicken and rice; 45,000đ), pork in a clay pot (60,000đ), or one of the range of soups or hotpots. Almost all dishes can be made large or small – great for single travellers who'd like to sample a few things. Daily 8am–9pm.

Quang Ngai

Clinging to the south bank of the Tra Khuc River some 130km south of Da Nang, **QUANG NGAI** is about as pleasant as you could expect of a town that was skewered until recently by Vietnam's main highway. The area had a long tradition of resistance against French rule, one that was to find further focus during American involvement. The reward was some of the most extensive bombing meted out during the war: by 1967, American journalist Jonathan Schell was able to report that seventy percent of villages in the town's surrounding area had been destroyed. A year later, the Americans turned their focus to Son My, the site of the **My Lai massacre** (see box below). Few tourists venture this way, and even fewer stay the night – it is, however, quintessentially Vietnamese, and not a bad little place to stop by if your schedule allows.

THE MY LAI MASSACRE

The massacre of civilians in the hamlets of **Son My**, the single most shameful chapter of America's involvement in Vietnam, began at dawn on March 16, 1968. US Intelligence suggested that the 48th Local Forces Battalion of the NVA, which had taken part in the Tet Offensive on Quang Ngai a month earlier, was holed up in Son My. Within the task force assembled to flush them out was **Charlie Company**, whose First Platoon, led by Lieutenant William Calley, was assigned to sweep through My Lai 4 (known to locals as **Tu Cung Hamlet**). Recent arrivals in Vietnam, Charlie Company had suffered casualties and losses in the hunt for the elusive 48th, and had found themselves confronted with snipers and booby-traps. Unable to contact the enemy face to face in any numbers, or even to distinguish civilians from Viet Cong guerrillas, they had come to feel frustrated and impotent; in their opinion, Son My offered the chance to settle some old scores.

At a briefing on the eve of the offensive, GIs were told that all civilians would be at the market by 7am, and that anyone remaining was bound to be an active Viet Cong sympathizer. Some GIs later remembered being told not to kill women and children, but most simply registered that there were to be no prisoners. Whatever the truth, a massacre ensued, whose brutal course Neil Sheehan describes with chilling understatement in *A Bright Shining Lie*:

The American soldiers and junior officers shot old men, women, boys, girls, and babies. One soldier missed a baby lying on the ground twice with a .45 pistol as his comrades laughed at his marksmanship. He stood over the child and fired a third time. The soldiers beat women with rifle butts and raped some and sodomised others before shooting them. They shot the water buffalos, the pigs, and the chickens. They threw the dead animals into the wells to poison the water. They tossed satchel charges into the bomb shelters under the houses. A lot of the inhabitants had fled into the shelters. Those who leaped out to escape the explosives were gunned down. All of the houses were put to the torch.

In all, the Son My body count reached 500, 347 of whom fell in Tu Cung alone. Not one shot was fired at a GI in response, and the only US casualty deliberately shot himself in the foot to avoid the carnage. The 48th Battalion never materialized. The military chain of command was able temporarily to **suppress reports** of the massacre, with the army newspaper, *Stars and Stripes*, and even *the New York Times* branding the mission a success. But the awful truth surfaced in November 1969, through the efforts of former GI Ronald Ridenhour and investigative journalist Seymour Hersh, and the incontrovertible evidence of the grisly colour slides of army photographer Ron Haeberle. When the massacre did finally make the cover of *Newsweek* it was under the headline "An American Tragedy" – which, as John Pilger pointed out, "deflected from the truth that the atrocities were, above all, a *Vietnamese* tragedy".

Of the men eventually charged with murder over the massacre, or for its subsequent suppression, only Lieutenant William Calley was **found guilty**, though he had served just three days of a life sentence of hard labour when Nixon intervened and commuted it to house arrest; three years later, he was paroled.

It's all too easy to dismiss Charlie Company as a freak unit operating beyond the pale. A more realistic view may be that the very nature of the US war effort, with its resort to unselective napalm and rocket attacks, and its use of body counts as barometers of success, created a climate in which Vietnamese life was cheapened to such an extent that an incident of this nature became almost inevitable. If indiscriminate killing from the air was justifiable, then random killing at close quarters was only taking this methodology to its logical conclusion.

Michael Bilton and Kevin Sim, whose *Four Hours in My Lai* remains the most complete account of the massacre, concluded "My Lai's exposure late in 1969 poisoned the idea that the war was a moral enterprise." The mother of one GI put it more simply: "I gave them a good boy, and they made him a murderer."

Son My Memorial Park

12km east of Quang Ngai • Daily 7am–5pm • 10,000đ • Xe om 140,000đ including waiting time; taxi 380,000đ including waiting time

In the sub-hamlet of Tu Cung, the site of an infamous massacre of civilians by American soldiers (see box opposite) is remembered at the **Son My Memorial Park**. Wandering through this peaceful, almost dignified place, set within a low perimeter wall, you'll feel a palpable sense of the horrors that went on all around you. Look out for the bullet holes in the trees, the foundations of homes that were burned down (each with a tablet recording its family's losses), the blown-out bomb shelters and cement statues of slain animals. One path ends at a large, Soviet-style statue of a woman cradling a deceased baby over her left arm while raising her right fist in defiance. Once you've seen the garden, step into the museum to view the grisly display upstairs, though be warned that it's a disturbing place for anyone with a sensitive disposition. Here, beyond a massive marble plaque recording the names of the dead and a montage of rusting hardware, a **photograph gallery** documents the event.

My Khe beach

3km east of Son My • Can usually be added to a xe om trip to Son My for an extra 10,000đ

In stark contrast to the chilling sights at Son My, secluded **My Khe beach** consists of 7km of powder-soft sand, backed by casuarinas, and is a very good spot for swimming. Hamlets stand along the back of the beach, while fishing boats are sometimes moored off it, and there's a handful of restaurants that only get busy at the weekend. The area is still slowly gearing up for tourism, and may in time become the best place to stay in the Quang Ngai area.

ARRIVAL AND DEPARTURE

QUANG NGAI

By train Quang Ngai has a station on the main line about 2km west of town, and most services stop here.
Destinations Da Nang (6 daily; 2hr 40min); Dieu Tri (for Quy Nhon; 7 daily; 3hr); Nha Trang (7 daily; 7hr).

By bus The bus station is around 4km south of the centre, just off the main highway – a bit annoying if you want to buy tickets, though your accommodation may be able to assist.
Destinations Da Nang (4hr); Nha Trang (7hr); Quy Nhon (4hr).

ACCOMMODATION

Thanh Lich 310 Highway 1a ⊕ 0255 386 1046. Just over the river, this place has an inconvenient location but has still become the most popular budget guesthouse in town. The couple who run the place are cheery sorts who really try to engage with their guests, and rooms are surprisingly stylish for the price – avoid the very cheapest category, though, unless you want to sleep in a shoebox. No breakfast. $14

Thien An Riverside 1 An Duong Vuong ⊕ 0255 371 4468. Overlooking the river, this is the smartest spot in town – though admittedly, this isn't saying much. The rooms are very spacious, but it's imperative to get one on the river side for the great views – with so few staying in Quang Ngai, this isn't usually a problem. In general the hotel feels a bit empty and the rack rates are too high, but you should be able to score a discount. $65

EATING AND DRINKING

There are few good places to eat in town, but if you're up for a beer you can head for the **snack shacks** that line the river at night outside the Thien An Riverside – as well as simple food, you'll be able to sample Quang Ngai's own brews (though note that they taste little different to the "regular" beers available elsewhere).

Mi Quang Ngoc Pho 161 Phan Boi Chau ⊕ 090 514 3454. Quy Nhon is far enough north for central-Vietnamese meals to feature on menus; this small place specializes in mi quang and bun bo Hue (both 20,000đ). Daily 8am–10pm.

Nhung 2 136a Phan Dinh Phung ⊕ 0255 381 5362. Quang Ngai is known for its com ga (chicken on rice), and there's usually a crowd scoffing it down here every lunchtime for 35,000đ a pop. It's served with a broth and an odd, though tasty, kind of chilli jam. Daily 8am–9pm.

Central Vietnam

PERFUME RIVER, HUE

5

Central Vietnam

The narrowest part of the country holds an astonishingly dense collection of sights. From the south, you'll come first to the town of Hoi An, highly traditional and hugely popular on account of its wonderful old town architecture and superb culinary scene. Further north is Da Nang, whose bars, restaurants and sleek new buildings make it enjoyable in a more contemporary sense. Both places are good bases for a visit to the Cham temple complex at My Son, or for a day out at one of the local beaches. Then there's Hue, erstwhile capital of the Nguyen dynasty. A visit to the old Imperial City, with its splendid palace buildings and manicured gardens, is like a taking a step into the past. Lastly are the sights pertaining to the American War in the famed Demilitarized Zone (DMZ). The area marked the divide between North and South Vietnam, which, some would argue, still exists today.

You'll notice great differences in weather, cuisine, language and even local character to the north and south of the **Ben Hai River**, which runs through the DMZ (see box, p.295). However, Vietnam was not always divided along this point – it was previously the Hoanh Son Mountains north of Dong Hoi (see p.308) that formed the cultural and political line between the Chinese-dominated sphere to the north, and the Indianized Champa kingdom to the south. As independent Vietnam grew in power in the eleventh century, so its armies pushed southwards to the next natural frontier, the Hai Van Pass near Da Nang. Here again, the Cham resisted further invasion until the fifteenth century, when their great temple complex at **My Son** was seized and their kingdom shattered.

Since then, other contenders have battled back and forth over this same ground, among them the Nguyen and Trinh lords, whose simmering rivalry ended in victory for the southern Nguyen and the emergence of **Hue** as the nation's capital in the nineteenth century. The Nguyen dynasty transformed Hue into a stately Imperial City, whose palaces, temples and grand mausoleums now constitute one of the highlights of a visit to Vietnam, despite the ravages they suffered during successive wars. In 1954,

MY SON

Highlights

❶ Hoi An Stroll the riverside by lantern while waiting for your tailor-made clothes to measure up in this laidback city. **See p.245**

❷ Hoi An cuisine Travellers agree that central Vietnam does it best – try the assorted specialities of Hoi An and find out why. **See box, p.254**

❸ My Son Majestic Cham ruins covered in moss, grass and leaves – rise early to see them before the crowds. **See p.260**

❹ Da Nang Admire the city view from the immense Lady Buddha statue, see the Dragon Bridge breathe fire and savour gourmet seafood in central Vietnam's newest hotspot. **See p.263**

❺ Hai Van Pass The dizzying road that snakes up and over the "Pass of the Ocean Clouds" is now world-famous thanks to a *Top Gear* special. See box, p.271

❻ Hue's Imperial City Cross the Perfume River to meander through the intricately decorated buildings that emperors once called home. See p.277

❼ Vinh Moc tunnels The most interesting sight in the famed DMZ: a warren of dens where an entire village sheltered during the war. See p.295

HIGHLIGHTS ARE MARKED ON THE MAP ON P.244

5

Vietnam was divided at the Seventeenth Parallel, only 100km north of Hue, where the Ben Hai River and the **DMZ** marked the border between North and South Vietnam until reunification in 1975. Though there's little to see on the ground these days, the vast cemeteries of the DMZ are a poignant reminder of those who fought here on both sides, and to the civilians who lost their lives in the bitter conflict.

The American War has been relegated to history in modern **Da Nang**, a fast-changing city determined to emulate Singapore or Seoul. The compact historic town of **Hoi An**, meanwhile, with its core of traditional, wood-built merchants' houses and jaunty Chinese Assembly Halls, is a particularly captivating place, and for many a highlight of their trip to Vietnam. Inland from Hoi An, the Cham spiritual core, **My Son**, survives as a haunting array of overgrown ruins, some now partially but tastefully restored, while to the east and north of Hoi An you'll find a succession of beaches that are undergoing rapid development.

This region has a particularly complicated **climate** as it forms a transitional zone between the north and south of Vietnam. In general, around Da Nang and Hue the **rainy season** lasts from September to February, with most rain falling between late September and December; during this season it's not unusual for road and rail links to be cut. Hue suffers particularly badly and, even during the "**dry season**" from March to August, it's possible to have several days of torrential downpours, giving the city an annual rainfall average of three metres. Overall, the best time to visit this region is in

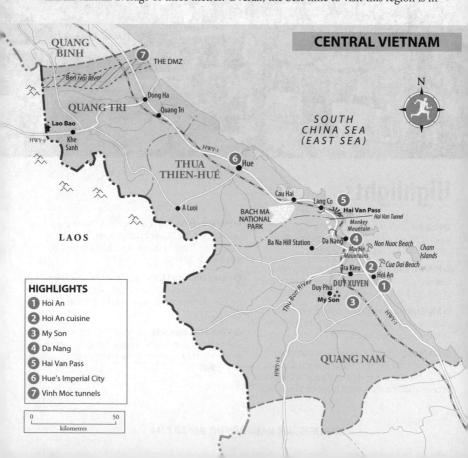

CENTRAL VIETNAM

QUANG BINH

THE DMZ

Ben Hai River

QUANG TRI

Dong Ha

Quang Tri

Lao Bao

HWY-9   Khe Sanh

SOUTH CHINA SEA (EAST SEA)

N

THUA THIEN-HUÉ

HWY-1   Hue

A Luoi

Cau Hai

Lang Co

BACH MA NATIONAL PARK

Hai Van Pass
Hai Van Tunnel

Monkey Mountain

LAOS

Ba Na Hill Station

Da Nang

Non Nuoc Beach

Cham Islands

Marble Mountains

Tra Kieu

Cua Dai Beach

Hoi An

Thu Bon River

Duy Phu

DUY XUYEN

My Son

HWY-1

QUANG NAM

HWY-14

HIGHLIGHTS

1 Hoi An
2 Hoi An cuisine
3 My Son
4 Da Nang
5 Hai Van Pass
6 Hue's Imperial City
7 Vinh Moc tunnels

0 ———————— 50
kilometres

spring, from February to late May, before both temperatures and humidity reach their summer maximum (averaging around 30°C), or just at the end of the summer before the rains break in September.

Hoi An

Wonderfully preserved and full of compelling sights, the small town of **HOI AN** exudes a laidback atmosphere and boasts a rich architectural fusion of Chinese, Japanese, Vietnamese and European influences dating back to the sixteenth century. In its heyday, the now drowsy channel of the **Thu Bon River** was a jostling crowd of merchant vessels representing the world's great trading nations (see box below), and its narrow streets comprising wooden-fronted shophouses topped with moss-covered tiles still emanate a timeless air. A concerted effort has been made to retain the town's old-world charm: by way of example, it's the only place in Vietnam that bans traffic in the town centre, and the only place that forces local businesses, by law, to dangle **lanterns** from their facades. These come to the fore as evening encroaches, and by nightfall you'll see them shining out from narrow alleys and the riverbank in their hundreds, the light reflecting in the waters of the river. Also notable are the town's many **tailors**, who will whip up made-to-measure clothes in no time – you'll find shops and workshops all over town, but the original outlet was the market, where even now rows of tailors sit at sewing machines next to rainbow-coloured stacks of material. If all the shopping has left you famished, head for the city's excellent restaurants: the **culinary scene** in Hoi An ranks among the best in Asia.

The town's most photographed sight is the beautiful **Japanese Covered Bridge**. However, the most noteworthy monuments stem from the resident ethnic Chinese, who today constitute one-quarter of Hoi An's population. **Merchant homes**, some of them more than two hundred years old, are still inhabited by the descendants of prosperous Chinese traders. Between their sober wooden facades, riotous confections of glazed roof tiles and writhing dragons mark the entrances to **Chinese assembly halls**, which still form the focal point of civic and spiritual life for a community that historically organized themselves according to their place of origin – Fujian, Guangdong, Chaozhou or Hainan. Each group maintained its own **assembly hall** as both community centre and house of worship, while a fifth hall also provided assistance to all the local groups and to visiting Chinese merchants.

Granted UNESCO World Heritage status in 1999, Hoi An is now firmly on most visitors' agendas. Many who plan to stay for a day become enamoured of the place and stay a week, but be warned that the main sights are prone at times to tourist overload and hassles from souvenir sellers. If you get frustrated by these aspects of the town, consider staying across the Thu Bon River to the south of the centre on fast-developing **An Hoi Islet**, or even on one of the nearby beaches (see p.258). If possible, try to time your visit to coincide with the **Full-Moon Festival**, on the fourteenth day of the lunar calendar every month, when traditional arts performances take place in the lantern-lit streets. However,

---

FAI FO SPRING FAIR

Hoi An owes its contemporary popularity in no small part to the legacy of the now-defunct annual spring fair of **Fai Fo** (the former name of the town), which once attracted traders from far and wide. From humble beginnings in the sixteenth century, the event grew into an exotic showcase of world produce. From Southeast Asia came silks and brocades, ivory, fragrant oils, fine porcelain and a cornucopia of medicinal ingredients. The Europeans brought their textiles, weaponry, sulphur and lead – as well as the first Christian missionaries in 1614. During the four-month fair, travelling merchants would rent local lodgings and warehouses; many went on to establish a more permanent presence through marriage to Vietnamese women, who were (and still are) renowned for their business acumen.

5

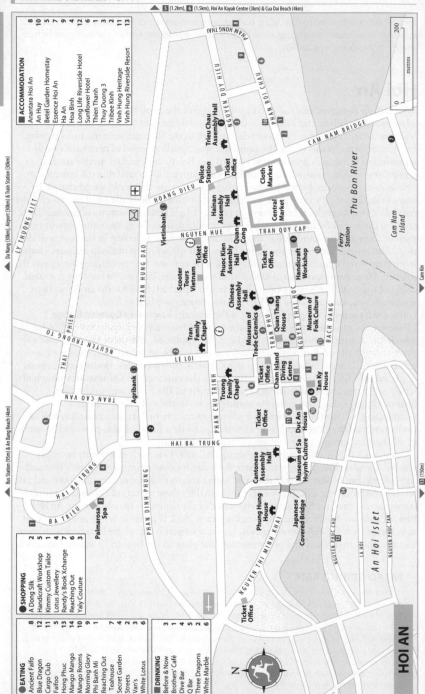

Da Nang (30m), Airport (30m) & Train Station (30m)

5 (1.2km), 6 (1.5km), Hoi An Kayak Centre (3km) & Cua Dai Beach (4km)

Bus Station (95m) & An Bang Beach (4km)

7 (1km), Hoi An Motorbike Adventures & My Son (40km)

13 (150m)

ACCOMMODATION	
Anantara Hoi An	8
An Huy	10
Betel Garden Homestay	5
Essence Hoi An	7
Ha An	9
Hoa Binh	4
Long Life Riverside Hotel	12
Sunflower Hotel	6
Thien Thanh	1
Thuy Duong 3	3
Tribee Kinh	11
Vinh Hung Heritage	2
Vinh Hung Riverside Resort	13

EATING	
Ancient Faifo	8
Blue Dragon	12
Cargo Club	11
Faifoo	5
Hong Phuc	13
Mango Mango	14
Morning Glory	9
Phi Banh Mi	1
Reaching Out	7
Secret Garden	4
Streets	3
Van's	3
White Lotus	6

SHOPPING	
A Dong Silk	2
Handicraft Workshop	12
Kimmy Custom Tailor	11
Lotus Jewellery	5
Randy's Book Xchange	7
Reaching Out	6
Yaly Couture	3

DRINKING	
Before & Now	3
Brothers' Café	1
Dive Bar	4
Q Bar	5
Three Dragons	2
White Marble	6

HOI AN

Thu Bon River

Cam Nam Island

Cam Kin

An Hoi Islet

Japanese Covered Bridge

Phung Hung House

Cantonese Assembly Hall

Museum of Sa Huynh Culture

Duc An House

Tan Ky House

Cham Island Diving Centre

Truong Family Chapel

Museum of Folk Culture

Quan Thang House

Museum of Trade Ceramics

Tran Family Chapel

Chinese Assembly Hall

Phuoc Kien Assembly Hall

Quan Cong

Hainan Assembly Hall

Handicraft Workshop

Trieu Chau Assembly Hall

Cloth Market

Central Market

Ferry Station

Police Station

Scooter Tours Vietnam

Vietinbank

Agribank

Palmarosa Spa

CAM NAM BRIDGE

Street names:
PHAM HONG THAI
NGUYEN DUY HIEU
PHAN BOI CHAU
HOANG DIEU
NGUYEN HUE
TRAN QUY CAP
TRAN HUNG DAO
NGUYEN TRUONG TO
THAI PHIEN
TRAN CAO VAN
LE LOI
PHAN CHU TRINH
HAI BA TRUNG
BA TRIEU
PHAN DINH PHUNG
NGUYEN THI MINH KHAI
LY THUONG KIET
NGUYEN THAI HOC
BACH DANG
TRAN PHU
NGUYEN PHUC CHU
NGUYEN PHUC TAN
LA HOI

Ticket Office

200
metres
0

N

it's worth making a point of avoiding the town in October and November, when Hoi An is prone to serious flooding, and the water in the streets can be knee- or waist-high.

Brief history
For centuries, Hoi An played an important role in the **maritime trade** of Southeast Asia. This goes back at least as far as the second century BC, when people of the Sa Huynh culture exchanged goods with China and India, but things really took off in the sixteenth century when Chinese, Japanese and European vessels ran with the trade winds to congregate at a port then called Fai Fo, whose annual **spring fair** brought in traders from far and wide (see box, p.245). Tax collectors arrived to fill the Imperial coffers, and the town swelled with artisans, moneylenders and bureaucrats as trade reached a peak in the seventeenth century.

Commercial activity was dominated by Japanese and Chinese merchants, many of whom settled in Fai Fo, where each community maintained its own governor, legal code and strong cultural identity. In 1639, however, the Japanese shogun prohibited foreign travel and the "Japanese street" dwindled to a handful of families, then to a scattering of monuments and a distinctive architectural style. Unchallenged, the Chinese community prospered, and its numbers grew as every new political upheaval in China prompted another wave of immigrants to join one of the town's self-governing "congregations", organized around a meeting hall and place of worship.

In the late eighteenth century, silt began to clog the Thu Bon River just as markets began to open in China, and from then on the port's days were numbered. Although the French established an administrative centre in Fai Fo, and even built a rail link from Tourane (Da Nang), they failed to resuscitate the economy, and when a storm washed away the tracks in 1916 no one repaired them. The town, renamed Hoi An in 1954, somehow escaped damage during both the French and American wars and retains a distinctly antiquated air.

Phung Hung House
4 Nguyen Thi Minh Khai • Daily 7am–6pm • Under ticket scheme (see box, p.248)
Just west of the covered bridge, **Phung Hung House** has been home to the same family since around 1780, after they moved from Hue to trade cinnamon and hardwoods from the central highlands, as well as silk and glass. The large two-storey house is Vietnamese in style, although its eighty ironwood columns and small glass skylights denote Japanese influence, and the gallery and window shutters are Chinese in style. From the upstairs windows, there are pretty views across the tiled roofs of neighbouring houses, and before leaving most visitors are invited to buy embroidery souvenirs by the staff.

Japanese Covered Bridge
Linking Nguyen Thi Minh Khai and Tran Phu • 24hr • Bridge free; temple under ticket scheme (see box, p.248)
The western extremity of Tran Phu is marked by a small arched bridge of red-painted wood, popularly known as the **Japanese Covered Bridge**, which has been adopted as Hoi An's emblem. It was known to exist in the mid-sixteenth century, and has subsequently been reconstructed several times to the same simple design. According to local folklore, the bridge was erected after Japan suffered a series of violent earthquakes which geomancers attributed to a restless monster lying with its head in India, tail in Japan and heart in Hoi An. The only remedy was to build a bridge whose stone piles would drive a metaphorical sword through the beast's heart and fortuitously provide a handy passage across the muddy creek. Inside the bridge's narrow span are a collection of stelae and four statues, two dogs and two monkeys, which suggest that work began in the year of the monkey and ended in that of the dog. The small **temple** suspended above the water is a later addition dedicated to the Taoist god Tran Vo Bac De ("Emperor of the North"), a favourite of sailors as he controls wind, rain and other "evil influences".

5

VISITING HOI AN'S SIGHTS

Hoi An has a **ticket scheme** covering the majority of its most famous sights, the proceeds of which contribute to the preservation of the old centre. A ticket costing 120,000đ (valid for 24hr), allows access to five places:

• Either Quan Cong Temple (also called Chua Ong) or the temple on the Japanese Covered Bridge (the bridge itself is free)
• One of the museums
• One of the three Chinese Assembly Halls requiring tickets
• One of the merchants' houses or family chapels requiring tickets
• The Hoi An Handicraft Workshop at 9 Nguyen Thai Hoc

Particular recommendations are the Phuoc Kien assembly hall, the Museum of History and Culture and Tan Ky House; if you want to visit more sights in the scheme, you have to fork out for another ticket. Also note that though "The Heritage Town" appears on your ticket, you can walk on any Hoi An street for free.

Tickets are on sale at four outlets: 78 Le Loi, 5 Hoang Dieu, 10 Nguyen Hue and 30 Tran Phu (see map, p.246). Groups of more than eight people are entitled to a free guide to accompany them on a tour; otherwise, you can hire one for around $15. The ticket outlets are **open** from 7am to 6pm, sometimes later, as are most of the sights included in the scheme. The price and conditions of the ticket scheme are occasionally subject to change; for the latest information, visit ⓦ hoianworldheritage.org.vn.

Cantonese Assembly Hall

176 Tran Phu • Daily 7am–6pm • Under ticket scheme (see box, p.248)

The westernmost of the Chinese assembly halls sits just east of the Japanese Bridge, and belonged to Hoi An's Cantonese population. You can't miss its gaudy entrance arch, a recent embellishment to the original late eighteenth-century hall built by immigrants from Guangdong. Though there's nothing of particular merit here, it's an appealing place, partly because of its plant-filled courtyard, ornamented with dragon and carp carvings (see box, p.251), and partly because of the fact that it's the least visited Chinese hall in Hoi An.

Museum of Sa Huynh Culture

149 Tran Phu • Daily 7am–6pm • Under ticket scheme (see box, p.248)

Occupying a tiny two-storey French-era house, the fusty **Museum of Sa Huynh Culture** focuses on a distinct culture which flourished along the coast of central Vietnam between the second century BC and the second century AD; the name comes from the town 130km south of Hoi An where evidence of the Sa Huynh was first discovered in 1902. Little is known about their culture, though they were probably the predecessors of the Cham. The most interesting exhibits are ceramic cremation jars.

Tan Ky House

101 Nguyen Thai Hoc • Daily 8am–noon & 2–5.30pm • Under ticket scheme (see box, p.248)

In the thick of things near the covered bridge, **Tan Ky House** is a beautifully preserved example of a two-storey, late eighteenth-century shophouse, amalgamating Vietnamese, Japanese and Chinese influences in an architectural style typical of Hoi An. The long, narrow building is constructed of dark hardwoods, including termite-resistant jackfruit for its main columns. Look out for two hanging poem-boards inlaid with mother-of-pearl birds in flight, and for markers showing the height of various Hoi An floods (some above your head). It can get crowded, so come early or late in the day, to appreciate the weight of history here.

Duc An House

129 Tran Phu • Daily 8.30am–noon & 1.30–5.30pm • Under ticket scheme (see box, p.248)

Duc An House is a humble building, erected in the 1850s for a family that had already been living on this site for more than two centuries. It is beautifully decorated with solid, traditional furnishings and features a plant-strewn courtyard. The owner, Mr Tram, is a direct descendant of the founding family, and is often on hand to show visitors around. In the past, it functioned as a bookshop, a medical dispensary and a meeting place for revolutionary thinkers, of whom there are a few photos on the walls.

Quan Thang House

77 Tran Phu • Daily 7am–6pm • Under ticket scheme (see box, p.248)

A modest, single-storey shophouse, **Quan Thang House** was founded in the early eighteenth century by a captain from Fujian in China, and was home to a medicine-trading business. Frankly speaking, it's a mediocre affair – you'll find far more interesting places to visit under this section of the ticket scheme.

Museum of Trade Ceramics

80 Tran Phu • Daily 7am–6pm • Under ticket scheme (see box, p.248)

The small **Museum of Trade Ceramics** is housed in a traditional timber residence-cum-warehouse. It showcases the history of Hoi An's ceramics trade, which peaked in the fifteenth and sixteenth centuries, with most of the exhibits from Vietnam, China and Japan. Unfortunately, most of these exhibits are shards or fragments of bowls and vases, and visitors will find more interest in the building itself, which is well preserved. The rear room on the ground floor houses a small display about the architecture of Hoi An.

Tran Family Chapel

21 Le Loi • Daily 7am–6pm • Under ticket scheme (see box, p.248)

The two-hundred-year-old **Tran Family Chapel** stands within a walled compound at the junction of Phan Chau Trinh and Le Loi. On the altar, oblong funerary boxes contain a name-tablet and biographical details of deceased family leaders and their wives – carved lotus blossoms indicate adherents of Buddhism. Each year the entire family – more than eighty people – gather round the altar to venerate their ancestors and discuss family affairs.

Chinese Assembly Hall

64 Tran Phu • Daily 7am–6pm • Free

Plum in the centre of town, the **Chinese Assembly Hall**, or Chua Ba, was built in 1740 as an umbrella organization for all Hoi An's ethnic Chinese population. Thien Hau graces the altar, but the hall is nowadays used mainly as a language school where local ethnic Chinese children and adults come to learn their mother tongue.

Museum of Folk Culture

33 Nguyen Thai Hoc • Daily 7am–6pm • Under ticket scheme (see box, p.248)

Housed in the largest two-storey building in town, the **Museum of Folk Culture** highlights the value of intangible culture through photographs and artefacts such as farming and household implements. If you don't find the displays exactly riveting, at least there are pleasant views of the river from the upstairs windows.

5

Handicraft Workshop

9 Nguyen Thai Hoc • Workshop daily 9am–5pm; Cultural Show daily 10.15am & 3.15pm • Under ticket scheme (see box, p.248)

Most visitors are keen to experience something of Hoi An's long-held reputation for traditional wares, and the **Handicraft Workshop** offers a good introduction to skills such as lantern-making and embroidery. It's worth timing your visit to see one of the twice-daily thirty-minute cultural shows, which feature song and dance performances accompanied by traditional instruments.

Phuoc Kien Assembly Hall

46 Tran Phu • Daily 7am–6pm • Under ticket scheme (see box, p.248)

The most populous of Hoi An's Chinese groups hailed from Fujian, or **Phuoc Kien**, and their hall is a suitably imposing edifice with an ostentatious, triple-arched gateway added in the early 1970s. The hall started life as a pagoda built in the late seventeenth century when, so it's said, a Buddhist statue containing a lump of gold washed up on the riverbank. Almost a century later, the Chinese took over the decaying structure and rededicated it as a temple to **Thien Hau**, Goddess of the Sea and protector of sailors. She stands, fashioned in two-hundred-year-old papier-mâché, on the principal altar flanked by her two assistants, green-faced Thien Ly Nhan and red-faced Thuan Phong Nhi, who between them can see or hear any boat in distress over a range of a thousand miles. A second sanctuary room behind and to the right of the main altar shelters a deity favoured by couples and pregnant women: the awesome **Van Thien** and her aides, the "twelve heavenly midwives", who decide the fundamentals of a child's life from conception onwards, including the fateful matter of gender.

Central market

Tran Phu • Daily 6am–4pm

Hoi An's **central market** retains an appealing, traditional atmosphere, and is at its best in the early morning, especially among the fresh-food stalls that line the river. Look out for jars of tiny preserved tangerines, a regional speciality, amid neat stacks of basketware, bowl-shaped lumps of unrefined cane-sugar, liniments, medicinal herbs and every variety of rice.

Around the market

Wandering down through the market square brings you out by the **ferry docks** on Bach Dang, which regularly disappears each autumn under the swollen river. For most of the year it's dry, and the spectacle of sampans bobbing on the water is best captured between 6 and 7am when the fishing boats are unloading their catch.

Quan Cong Temple

24 Tran Phu (opposite the market) • Daily 7am–6pm • Under ticket scheme (see box, p.248)

The colourful **Quan Cong Temple** is dedicated to the Chinese general Quan Cong, the deity of martial virtue who was famed for his loyalty, piety and righteousness. There's a small but attractive courtyard, lots of statues and of course, an image of Quan Cong himself on the main altar, standing nearly 3m tall. The temple dates back to 1653 and is better known to locals as "Chua Ong".

Hainan Assembly Hall

10 Tran Phu • Daily 7–11.30am & 2–5pm • Free

East of Quan Cong Temple on Tran Phu stands the hall founded by Chinese from the island of **Hainan**, or Hai Nam, and noted for its ornately carved, gilded altar table.

Its unusual history is intriguing – in 1851 a Vietnamese general plundered three merchant ships, killing 108 passengers, after which the vessels were painted black to imply they were pirate ships. A lone survivor revealed the crime to King Tu Duc, who promptly condemned the general to death and ordered that the booty be returned to the victims' families. When the hall was built later in the century, it was dedicated to the unlucky passengers.

Trieu Chau Assembly Hall

157 Nguyen Duy Hieu • Daily 7am–6pm • Under ticket scheme (see box, p.248)

The **Trieu Chau Assembly Hall** is located just east of the market, and it's worth the stroll. Built in the late eighteenth century by Chinese from the city of Chaozhou, or Trieu Chau, it's renowned for its remarkable display of woodcarving. In the altar niche sits the gilded **Ong Bon**, a deified general in the Chinese navy believed to hold sway over the wind and waves, surrounded by a frieze teeming with bird, animal and insect life so lifelike you can almost hear it buzz. The altar table itself depicts life on land and in the depths of the ocean, while panels on either side show two decorative ladies of the Chinese court modelling the latest Japanese hair fashions.

Phan Boi Chau

East of the market along the river, Hoi An takes on a distinctly European flavour – louvred shutters, balconies and stucco – along **Phan Boi Chau**, in what was the beginnings of a French quarter. The interiors of these late nineteenth-century townhouses are characterized by vast, high-ceilinged rooms and enormous roof-spaces, markedly different from the Chinese abodes. Several of them now operate as restaurants and bars, such as *Brothers Café* and *White Lotus* (see p.255).

ARRIVAL AND DEPARTURE   HOI AN

By train or plane The nearest train station and airport are both 30km away in Da Nang (see p.269), a distance easily covered by taxi (around 400,000đ) or xe om (200,000đ). It's best to negotiate a fixed fare rather than use the meter, which is usually more expensive. For a small commission, hotel booking desks and tour agents are able to arrange onward train and plane tickets from Da Nang, and handle visa extensions.

By bus Open-tour buses usually drop you at their relevant booking office (also the place to confirm your onward

---

ARCHITECTURAL MOTIFS OF HOI AN

You can't walk far in Hoi An without confronting a carving of a **mythical beast** with a fish's body and dragon's head on an ancient building; though they're found all over northern Vietnam they seem to have struck a particular chord with Hoi An's architects. One of the most prominent examples tops a weather vane in the Phuoc Kien Assembly Hall, but there are plenty of more traditional representations about, carved into lantern brackets and beam ends, or forming the beams themselves. The **carp** symbolizes prosperity, success and, here, metamorphosing into a **dragon**, serving as a reminder that nothing in life comes easily. To become a dragon, and thereby attain immortality, a fish must pass through three gates – just as a scholar has to pass three exams to become a mandarin, requiring much patience and hard work.

Another typical feature of Hoi An's architecture are *mat cua*, **"door eyes"** watching over the entrance to a house or religious building, which are often in the form of a yin and yang symbol. Two thick wooden nails about 20cm in diameter are driven into the lintel as protection against evil forces, following a practice that originated in the pagodas of northern Vietnam. Assembly halls offer the most highly ornamented examples; that of Phuoc Kien consists of yin and yang symbols with two dragons in obeisance to the sun, while the Cantonese version is a fearsome tiger. The **yin and yang** symbol became fashionable in the nineteenth century and is the most commonly used image on houses, sometimes set in a chrysanthemum flower, as at the Tan Ky House.

5

COOKERY CLASSES AROUND HOI AN

The choice of Vietnamese cooking classes in Hoi An can be overwhelming. The quality and price varies, but most will teach you how to make local specialities, and often a visit to the market to learn about local produce and pick up ingredients is included. The following classes come highly recommended.

Bamboo Home Fishing & Cooking Tours Cam Thanh ☎ 090 502 6104, ✉ dinhvuvn@yahoo.com. Vu invites guests into his home in the village of Cam Thanh, where his family have been fishermen for generations. He will collect you from Hoi An and take you to the market for fresh ingredients, before boarding a fishing boat. After a transfer in a traditional basket boat, you'll spend the morning cooking and eating. Half-day $32.

My Grandma's Home Cooking 57 Ngo Quyen ☎ 0235 386 4362, ⓦ cooking-hoian.com. Grandma doesn't run the course (she's more than ninety years old), but she lives in the family home here on An Hoi Islet. You'll grind rice to make traditional rice paper and prepare *banh xeo* and other local specialities to eat in the garden. The price includes a return trip by boat, or you can extend your morning with a cycling tour

through the countryside (for an additional $17). Half-day $30 (market tour extra $7.50).

Red Bridge Cooking School ☎ 0235 393 3222, ⓦ visithoian.com. Ferries "students" on a 4km boat cruise down the river to its hideaway school. They teach small groups here and the full-day course is particularly worthwhile. If you'd prefer to stay in the old town, they run a popular evening class at *Hai Café* (98 Nguyen Thai Hoc; ☎ 0235 386 3210; $20). Half-day $32.

Taste Vietnam 3 Nguyen Hoang ☎ 0235 224 1555, ⓦ msvy-tastevietnam.com. After outgrowing her original premises at *Morning Glory* (see p.255), Ms Vy now operates from a professional kitchen on An Hoi Islet. Classes are slick but groups can be quite large unless you pay extra for a private group. Half-day $32.

tickets), or affiliated hotel (if it is outside the old town, where cars and buses are banned). For long-distance public buses, use Da Nang bus station (see p.269); the public bus to Da Nang leaves from the small bus station 1km north of

the old town, on Le Hong Phong.

Destinations Da Nang (1–2hr); Hue (4hr); Nha Trang (12hr); Quang Ngai (4hr).

GETTING AROUND

While **bikes** are recommended for touring the outlying districts, Hoi An's central sights are all best approached **on foot**, especially since traffic restrictions apply in the town centre. The regulations are part of a much-needed effort to save the old town from the worst effects of its fame.

By bicycle or motorbike Almost every hotel and many shops and tour agents rent out bicycles (around $2/day), or can arrange motorbikes (from $5/day) – the latter are a popular way to visit My Son (see p.260). Note that

motorbikes are prohibited from the centre twice daily (9–11am & 3–9.30pm).

By taxi Reputable companies include Mai Linh (☎ 0235 392 5925) and Hoi An Taxi (☎ 0235 391 9919).

INFORMATION

Most hotels can provide you with a photocopied map of the town centre, or you can pick up a map of old town highlights from a tourist office (see below). To glean hot tips from local expats, see ⓦ hoiannow.com.

Tourist offices As well as the booths where you can buy tickets for old town attractions (see box above), there are

two useful tourist offices at 47 Phan Chau Trinh and on the corner of Phan Chau Trinh and Nguyen Hue.

TOURS AND ACTIVITIES

Bicycle or motorbike hire One of Hoi An's most popular activities is to rent a bicycle or motorbike and head off to explore the gorgeous surrounding countryside with the aid of a map; most hotels can arrange either, or contact Hoi An Motorbike Adventures (54 Hung Vuong; ☎ 0235 391 1930, ⓦ motorbiketours-hoian.com) who do

anything from a cool sunset tour of the surrounding delta (from $50) to a 5-day jungle rider adventure (from $675). If you're more interested in an eco-adventure, sign up for a tour with Scooter Tours Vietnam (19 Phan Chau Trinh; ☎ 0235 393 7838, ⓦ scootertoursvietnam.com) and ride round on a totally silent electric scooter; their most popular trip is a half-day in the countryside ($54).

Boat rides Most visitors enjoy spending an hour or two gliding along the (usually) tranquil Thu Bon River. Many hotels can organize this for around $20, or you can haggle with sampan-rowers near the market (around 100,000đ/hr). Sunrise and sunset are the most popular times. To experience splashing around in a traditional coracle basket boat, travel to Cam Thanh village where you can negotiate an hour on the water for around 100,000đ; alternatively, contact Bamboo Home Tours (see box opposite) to arrange a tour.

Diving and snorkelling From April to October is the best time to explore the depths around the offshore Cham Islands. The most reliable tour operator in town is the Cham Island Diving Centre (see p.260).

Kayaking and stand-up paddleboarding Hoi An's aquatic surroundings just beg to be explored and you can hire kayaks (single $10/hr, double $15/hr) at Hoi An Kayak Center (3km east of Hoi An in Cam Thanh village; ☎ 0979 437 338, ⓦ hoiankayak.com). They also organise kayak and SUP tours to surrounding islands (from $32). Not much fun Oct to Feb.

Spas There are some who think that visiting a spa isn't really an activity, as you just lie still and get pampered. Yet after a busy day's sightseeing and shopping, that's just what some visitors want. Recommended places include the *Anantara Hoi An* (see below) and Palmarosa Spa (90 Ba Trieu; ☎ 0235 393 3999, ⓦ palmarosaspa.com).

ACCOMMODATION

The number of **hotels** in Hoi An continues to grow at an astonishing rate. The local authorities put a block on developments in the centre – too late to prevent some eyesores in the old streets – but a whole new enclave of pleasant and cheap mini-hotels has sprung up on An Hoi Islet and to the north along Ba Trieu; some of these have **swimming pools**, which provide welcome relief in warmer months. Competition means that, in general, **prices** have come down and standards have risen; most places will bargain and there's unlikely to be a shortage of beds in peak season, though choices may be limited. If you do have difficulty, just head for the hotels further from the centre. Hotels on the beach are listed under "Around Hoi An" (see p.258).

CENTRAL HOI AN

Anantara Hoi An 1 Pham Hong Thai ☎ 0235 391 4555, ⓦ anantara.com; map p.246. Luxurious, beach-style resort (though in fact it's beside the river) in central Hoi An, blending minimalist Japanese design with maximum service and facilities; these include a fantastic pool, an excellent spa and restaurants exuding a sophisticated air. They also offer complimentary bikes, as well as free classes in yoga, lantern-making and coconut-leaf art. **$170**

An Huy 30 Phan Boi Chau ☎ 0235 386 2116, ⓦ anhuyhotel.com; map p.246. This deceptively large place in a great central location opens out behind a tiny entrance, concealing simple but well-equipped rooms. The five "superior" family rooms ($30), with solid wood floors, are a good deal, but the hotel has seen better days. **$20**

★**Ha An** 6 Phan Boi Chau ☎ 0235 386 3126, ⓦ haanhotel.com; map p.246. Welcoming, family-run hotel set back from the street in a quiet residential area. Its 24 rooms are arranged in an L-shape around a relaxing communal garden and pool; they're highly attractive, with petals strewn across the beds, and superior rooms have delightful stone-floor showers. The breakfast buffet is another big selling point. **$65**

Hoa Binh 696 Hai Ba Trung ☎ 0235 391 6838, ⓦ hoabinhhotelhoian.com; map p.246. Large, clean rooms with satellite TV at this presentable budget hotel – rarely will you get a swimming pool at this price, but there it is on the ground floor. Things can get a bit chaotic when it's full, which is often. **$18**

★**Thien Thanh** 16 Ba Trieu ☎ 0235 391 6545, ⓦ hoianthienthanhhotel.com; map p.246. Comfortable and intimate hotel with exceptionally attentive staff who try to make your stay as restful as possible. It has all mod cons, such as cable TV, a/c and small pool; the more expensive rooms have balconies overlooking water-spinach fields (great view from the restaurant too). Many guests return again and again. **$40**

Thuy Duong 3 92–94 Ba Trieu ☎ 0235 391 6565, ⓦ thuyduonghotel-hoian.com; map p.246. Well placed for open-tour bus drop-offs, the rooms here are comfortable, well maintained and reasonably priced, though those on the ground floor around the courtyard pool can be noisy, especially when a large tour group are staying. **$45**

Tribee Kinh 103 Ba Trieu ☎ 0235 386 3153, ⓔ tribeekinh@gmail.com; map p.246. New hostel offering simple doubles, twins and three-bed or four-bed dorms (not bunks) in the attic. Rooms are clean, and it's a nice place to meet fellow travellers. Dorms **$8.50**, doubles **$18**

Vinh Hung Heritage 143 Tran Phu ☎ 0235 386 1621, ⓦ vinhhungheritagehotel.com; map p.246. There are few more atmospheric places to stay in Hoi An than this broodingly dark, old Chinese shophouse – come in the evening and it'll feel like you're entering an Oriental period drama. The rooms are also traditional in style; best are the Heritage Suites (#206 & #208; they'll set you back $75), complete with balcony, wood panelling, antique furniture and four-poster beds; however, they do face the street, so are a little noisier than the standard rooms. **$65**

AN HOI ISLET AND OUTSIDE THE CENTRE

Betel Garden Homestay 161 Tran Nhan Tong ☎ 0235 392 4165, ⓦ betelgardenhomestay.com; map p.246. In

5

a small village a 15min walk from central Hoi An, this traditionally styled mini-resort is a remarkably relaxing place to stay – great for those who would like to enjoy Hoi An without the crowds. Call for a pick-up. $60

★ **Essence Hoi An** 132 Hung Vuong ☎ 0235 391 5915, ✆ essencehotels.com; map p.246. This low-key, out-of-town resort is a real find. Set among fields about 2km west of the centre, it features 70 rooms in two buildings, all tastefully furnished and well equipped, plus an appealing pool and cosy spa. If you're too lazy to walk into town, there's a regular shuttle or free bicycles for guests. $90

Long Life Riverside Hotel 61 Nguyen Phuc Chu ☎ 0235 391 1696, ✆ longliferiverside.com; map p.246. Located on An Hoi Islet, this place has a lovely little swimming pool, and staff are attentive. Though rooms are a bit dark, they're clean, have been given pleasant traditional flourishes and are tuned into the modern day with flatscreen TVs and, in most, computers. $30

Sunflower Hotel 397 Cua Dai ☎ 0235 393 9838, ✉ sunflowerhoian@gmail.com; map p.246. This budget hotel between the town and beach has become backpacker central with lots of dorm rooms with lockers. Family rooms ($36) are not such a good deal. There's a tiny pool that's often crowded when the weather is hot. Dorms $8, doubles $20

Vinh Hung Riverside Resort 110 Ngo Quyen An Hoi ☎ 0235 386 4074, ✆ vinhhungresort.com; map p.246. Part of the Vinh Hung chain, this simple resort has moderately attractive rooms, but the location is quite wonderful – quiet, and with a lovely view of the Thu Bon River. $70

EATING

Hoi An is perhaps Vietnam's best food city – nowhere else are there so many wonderful **restaurants** within walking distance of each other. The array of **local delicacies** (see box below) has been augmented by places serving Japanese, Italian, Indian, Thai, Turkish and Tex-Mex, as well as delectable French pastries. In the evenings, tables and chairs line Bach Dang, whose restaurants may look more Mediterranean than Vietnamese but largely focus on local produce; there's also a string of restaurants and cafés across the water on An Hoi Islet. In addition to cut-price **set meals** featuring local specialities, many of Hoi An's restaurants also offer **cooking classes** (see box, p.252); some establishments will help you select your ingredients at the market.

★ **Ancient Faifo** 66 Nguyen Thai Hoc ☎ 0235 391 7444; map p.246. Surrender to an evening of indulgence at this ancient house where artistic and culinary delights await. Perfectly prepared slow-caramelized pork and roasted prawns are two highly recommended dishes; most mains are 160,000–300,000đ, and four-course set menus are good value at 275,000đ. There's often a soft piano playing, and on Tues, Thurs and Sat traditional musicians perform. There's also a top-class café, bar and art gallery on site. Daily 7am–10pm.

Blue Dragon 46 Bach Dang ☎ 0235 391 1227; map p.246. Offering a similar standard of Vietnamese food and service to many other restaurants on Bach Dang, the *Blue Dragon* donates part of its profits to a charity that helps rural children stay in school. The fact that the tasty five-course meal is just 170,000đ is a bonus. Daily 8am–10pm.

Cargo Club 107–109 Nguyen Thai Hoc ☎ 0235 391 1227, ✆ msvy-tastevietnam.com; map p.246. Despite this café-restaurant having a good selection of local and international dishes, the real draw is the in-house French bakery, which offers decadent pastries (from around 40,000đ) and an array of take-to-the-beach bread rolls. The home-made ice cream also has the crowds lining up. Daily 8am–11pm.

HOI AN SPECIALITIES

Hoi An has a number of tasty specialities to sample. Most famous is *cao lau*, a mouthwatering bowlful of thick rice-flour **noodles**, bean sprouts and pork-rind croutons in a light soup flavoured with mint and star anise, topped with thin slices of pork and served with grilled rice-flour crackers or sprinkled with crispy rice paper. Legend has it that the genuine article is cooked using water drawn from one particular local well. Lovers of **seafood** should try the delicately flavoured steamed manioc-flour parcels of finely diced crab or shrimp called *banh bao*, translated as "white rose", with lemon, sugar and *nuoc mam*, complemented by a crunchy onion-flake topping, adding extra flavour. A local variation of *hoanh thanh chien* (fried wonton), using shrimp and crab meat instead of pork, is also popular. One less-heralded dish (and one of the cheapest) is *mi quang*, which sees a simple bowl of meat noodles enlivened with the addition of flavoursome oils, a quail egg and fresh sprigs of leaves. To fill any remaining gaps, try Hoi An **cake**, *banh it*, triangular parcels made by steaming green-bean paste and strands of sweetened coconut in banana leaves.

Faifoo 104 Tran Phu ☎ 0235 386 1548; map p.246. Locals rate the *banh bao* (50,000đ) at this well-established and attractive restaurant as the best in town, though many travellers choose the cheap five-course sampler (130,000đ) of Hoi An specialities (see box opposite). Daily 8am–10.30pm.

Hong Phuc 86 Bach Dang ☎ 0235 927 105; map p.246. A friendly, good-value and popular riverside place serving scrumptious local food – if you want to know the secret, you can sign up for an afternoon cookery class. They offer good-value set menus at 140,000đ; it's best to avoid the pizza. Get here early for a table on the balcony. Daily 7am–11pm.

Mango Mango 45 Nguyen Phuc Chu ☎ 0235 391 0863, ⓦ mangohoian.com; map p.246. Little sister to *Mango Rooms* (see below) and with a similarly classy menu and attentive staff, but a brighter and more contemporary style. The big difference is the stand-out view across the river to the Japanese Bridge; the perfect backdrop to sample maverick owner and celebrity chef Tran Duc's signature cocktails. Daily 9am–midnight.

Mango Rooms 111 Nguyen Thai Hoc ☎ 0235 391 0839, ⓦ mangorooms.com; map p.246. The menu at Tran Duc's original restaurant is constantly changing but always wonderfully creative – imagine red snapper with coriander and pineapple, or duck in a passion fruit and chocolate sauce (480,000đ) – and there's also an excellent wine list. Daily 9am–midnight.

★ **Morning Glory** 106 Nguyen Thai Hoc ☎ 0235 224 1555, ⓦ msvy-tastevietnam.com; map p.246. Probably Hoi An's most popular restaurant, this place can accommodate lots of customers on two floors, but it's still often packed, and for good reason – everything is delicious, beautifully presented and served with a smile. Try the roast duck with banana flower salad (145,000đ); it's a masterful blend of tastes and textures. Owner Ms Vy runs several other restaurants in town, plus the popular Taste Vietnam cookery class (see box, p.252). Daily 8am–10.30pm.

Phi Banh Mi 88 Thai Phien; map p.246. Look no further for the best *banh mi* in Hoi An (you'll spot the queue before you see the tiny street-food restaurant). Vegetarians rave about the cheese-and-tofu option (20,000đ). Daily 7am–8pm.

Reaching Out Teahouse 131 Tran Phu ☎ 0235 3910 168, ⓦ reachingoutvietnam.com; map p.246. A wonderfully tranquil spot for tea and coffee (they've got quite a selection), this café is dedicated to providing fair treatment and wages to servers who are hearing- and speech-impaired. Daily 9am–7pm.

Secret Garden 132/2 Tran Phu ☎ 0235 391 1112, ⓦ secretgardenhoian.com; map p.246. Hidden away down an alley off Le Loi (turn at no. 60), this restaurant is a gem. Dine on high-quality, thoughtfully prepared Vietnamese cuisine in a romantic candlelit garden, with live traditional music every night and excellent service. The menu is in dollars, which tells you it's pricey – mains from $12, bottles of champagne from $45. Daily 8am–midnight.

Streets 17 Le Loi ☎ 0235 391 1948, ⓦ streetsInternational.org; map p.246. As you might guess from the name, this place is all about giving street kids a chance to work as kitchen staff or waiting tables, and the enthusiasm of the staff is infectious. The short lunchtime menu covers classic Vietnamese dishes like pork and shrimp *mi quang* (110,000đ) and filling *banh mi* (from 80,000đ); in the evening you can also choose from clay pot pork or tofu (around 155,000đ). Daily noon–9.30pm.

Van's 329 Nguyen Duy Hieu ☎ 093 497 1791; map p.246. Simple, streetside café serving generous portions of yummy *cao lao* or *mi quang* for 80,000đ. Ideal for when you need a quick and filling meal, but note it's closed in the evening. Daily 8am–4pm.

White Lotus 11 Phan Boi Chau ☎ 0235 391 5545, ⓦ whitelotusrestauranthoian.com; map p.246. Operated by Project Indochina and staffed by disadvantaged kids, this smart venue is a good spot to try a tangy green papaya salad or BBQ beef in vine leaves; most main dishes are around 120,000–160,000đ, and there are some Western items too. Daily 9am–10pm.

DRINKING

Hoi An is a small town and most inhabitants are tucked up by 9pm. However, there's a growing Western contingent, leading to a gradually expanding range of options for places to spend your evenings. Particularly lively are the **late-night bars** across the Thu Bon River on An Hoi Islet, where the party starts after 11pm and the venue changes depending on the night.

Before & Now 51 Le Loi ☎ 0235 391 0599, ⓦ beforeandnow.net; map p.246. Double-storey Italian restaurant and bar inside a traditional shophouse. However, forget the food – it's far better as a venue for evening drinks, with a happy hour 9–11.30pm. Daily 9am–midnight.

Brothers' Café 27 Phan Boi Chau ☎ 0235 391 4150, ⓦ brothercafehoian.com.vn; map p.246. The garden setting on the banks of the Thu Bon River is reason enough to visit this Hoi An institution, though the food on the whole is overpriced – better to come for an atmospheric coffee or sundowner. Daily 10am–11pm.

Dive Bar 88 Nguyen Thai Hoc ☎ 0235 391 0782, ⓦ vietnamscubadiving.com; map p.246. The folks who run the Cham Island Diving Centre (see p.260) also know how to make a mean cocktail. In fact, they're so good they offer two-hour classes in making them ($30). Shisha pipes, a pool table and cool beats too. Daily 10am–midnight.

Q Bar 94 Nguyen Thai Hoc; map p.246. Trendy, gay-friendly bar that's usually busy with a good mix of locals and travellers, thanks to its expertly mixed cocktails and

5

HOI AN FESTIVALS

Once a month, coloured silk lanterns replace electric lights and shopkeepers don traditional costume to celebrate the **Full-Moon Festival** (fourteenth day of the lunar calendar). It's a tourist event, but a great occasion nonetheless: there are traditional music performances, with food stalls selling local specialities – usually veggie on this auspicious night – by the Japanese Bridge and on the waterfront.

During the **Mid-Autumn Festival**, a much bigger affair celebrated nationwide on the fourteenth or fifteenth day of the eighth lunar month, thousands of paper lanterns are floated on the river and there is a procession with fancy dress and dragon dances. Now looking like a permanent fixture – usually in June – Quang Nam province, which includes Hoi An, has also staged a week-long **cultural heritage festival** in Hoi An and My Son, including Cham dances and folk songs.

chilled-out electronica on the stereo. A little pricier than elsewhere. Daily noon–midnight.

Three Dragons 51 Phan Boi Chau ☎0235 391 4742, ⊛3dragonshoian.com; map p.246. This sports bar is the place to head for if you want to catch a live football game, an F1 Grand Prix, or other sporting event. There's a well-stocked bar and meals available too. Daily 10am–midnight.

★**White Marble** 98 Le Loi ☎0235 391 1862; map p.246. This place operates as a restaurant and bar, and it fulfils both functions very well. It has a fine menu of dishes like charcoal-grilled sesame pork (110,000đ), as well as a wide selection of wines (several by the glass; about 130,000đ), tapas-style snacks and a laidback atmosphere, making it a great spot to pass an evening. Daily 11am–11pm.

SHOPPING

While sightseeing may be the most popular activity in Hoi An, shopping comes a close second, and few visitors leave without a few extra kilos to carry in their bags. Workshops are scattered around town and you can see a range of **local crafts**, from embroidery to wood carving and pottery; visits are free, though afterwards you'll be directed to the souvenir-shop-cum-showroom, not that there's any obligation to buy. Hoi An is particularly famous for its **silk and tailoring**, with prices generally cheaper than in Hanoi or Ho Chi Minh City. You'll find shops all over town but the original outlet was the market, where even now rows of tailors sit at sewing machines next to rainbow-coloured stacks, and for a few dollars will make up beautiful garments in a matter of hours. It's worth shopping around – ask to see some finished articles before placing an order.

BOOKSHOP

Randy's Book Xchange Cam Nam Island ☎093 608 9483, ⊛bookshoian.com; map p.246. Possibly the best secondhand bookstore in Vietnam, with a huge selection in English; he deals in e-books too. Expect to pay at least $5, and be aware the book might be photocopied – a fact of life in Vietnam. Daily 8am–7pm.

HANDICRAFTS AND SOUVENIRS

Handicraft Workshop 9 Nguyen Thai Hoc; map p.246. A good place to view a variety of Hoi An handicrafts (lanterns, woodcarving, embroidery) and watch traditional artisans at their work. Included as part of the ticket scheme (see box, p.248). Daily 9am–9pm.

Lotus Jewellery 82 Tran Phu ☎0235 391 7889, ⊛lotusjewellery-hoian.com; map p.246. The hardwood display cases might make the place look intimidating, but the beautiful handcrafted silver jewellery is reasonably priced. Another location at 54a Le Loi. Daily 8am–10pm.

Reaching Out 103 Nguyen Thai Hoc ☎0235 391 0168, ⊛reachingoutvietnam.com; map p.246. Clothing and accessories, ceramics, toys, lacquerware, silver and embroidery are some of the products made by people with disabilities in this fairtrade gift shop. Ask about workshop tours. Mon–Fri 8.30am–9.30pm, Sat & Sun 9.30am–8.30pm.

SILK AND TAILORING

A Dong Silk 62 Tran Hung Dao ☎0235 391 0579, ⊛adongsilk.com; map p.246. One of the most renowned tailors in town, and in the country as a whole. Particularly good for business suits for both men and women. Another branch at 40 Le Loi. Daily 8am–9.30pm.

Kimmy Custom Tailor 70 Tran Hung Dao ☎0235 386 2063, ⊛kimmytailor.com; map p.246. Perfect English is spoken and staff take time to establish exactly what you want – they are happy to work from photos too. Great service and good-quality fabrics make this place stand out. Daily 8am–10pm.

5

Yaly Couture 358 Nguyen Duy Hieu ☎0235 391 4995, ⓦyalycouture.com; map p.246. Another revered local tailor, great for one-off pieces including clothes and bags

– highly capable staff go easy on the sales tactics. Other branches at 47 Nguyen Thai Hoc & 47 Tran Phu. Daily 8am–9.30pm.

DIRECTORY

Banks and exchange You can exchange cash and get over-the-counter cash advances on credit cards at Vietcombank, 2 Tran Cao Van, and Agribank, 6 Hoang Dieu and 92 Tran Phu. There are also several ATMs around town.
Hospital 4 Tran Hung Dao ☎0235 386 1365. Only open during the day; 24hr emergency care available in Da Nang (see p.271).

Laundry Places along Tran Hung Dao offer laundry services at around 30,000đ per kilo.
Pharmacies There are a number of small pharmacies near the hospital, including one at 4c Tran Hung Dao (daily 7am–9pm).
Police 8 Hoang Dieu ☎0235 386 1204.
Post office The unusually fancy and well-organized GPO is at 4b Tran Hung Dao (daily 8am–8pm).

Around Hoi An

From Hoi An you can bike to **Cua Dai** or **An Bang beaches** and detour along the way through the beautiful, canal-riddled Cam Thanh area, which lies to the south of the main road; head east on Nguyen Duy Hieu and take a right when the road ends a couple of kilometres east of Hoi An. Though the beaches themselves are not much fun when it's cold and rainy (any time between October and February), they are cool places to hang out on sunny days. You can also hop on a sampan to one of the low-lying, esturine **islands** of the Thu Bon River and the **craft villages** along their banks, or visit the distant **Cham Islands**, renowned for their sea swallows' nests.

Cua Dai beach

4km east of Hoi An • Taxi around 120,000đ, xe om around 60,000đ

Narrow **Cua Dai** has been heavily impacted by erosion, and the cement sea defences and sandbags lining the beach are a bit of an eyesore. Most visitors come here to stay at one of the swanky resorts or to eat at one of the busy beachfront restaurants; many serve excellent seafood – just be sure to check the prices before ordering. The harbour at the end of the beachfront road is the departure point for trips to the **Cham Islands** (see opposite).

ACCOMMODATION   CUA DAI BEACH

Hoi An Beach Resort 1 Cua Dai ☎0235 392 7011, ⓦhoianbeachresort.com.vn. Separated from the beach by a quiet road, this is slightly cheaper than nearby resorts. Rooms are elegant in cool pastels and bathrooms are generously proportioned; it's worth paying the extra for a room overlooking the river. Other attractions include two pools, a pleasant beach in front and a restaurant recommended for its well-priced local dishes. Free shuttle bus to Hoi An. **$90**

Hoi An Riverside Resort & Spa 175 Cua Dai ☎05120 386 4800, ⓦhoianriverresort.com. This attractive mid-range resort, located between the town and beach, is great value, offering the comforts of more expensive resorts at a reasonable price. Rooms in the two-storey building are comfortably furnished and have great views over rice fields from the balconies. There's a spa, fitness centre, good pool and regular shuttle buses to the town and beach. **$80**

An Bang beach

More popular for foreigners than Cua Dai is **An Bang** – follow Hai Ba Trung north out of Hoi An. Lounging on the white sand beach here is a low-key affair, though if you use an umbrella and deckchair from one of the beachfront bar-restaurants you'll be expected to buy at least a drink. The whole stretch has a pleasantly scruffy vibe that is popular with expats and backpackers.

5

ACCOMMODATION

AN BANG BEACH

An Bang Garden Homestay Lac Long Quan, An Bang ☎090 355 7974, ⓦanbanggardenhomestay.com. Friendly and family-run, this place offers just four rooms set in a beautifully tended garden a 5min walk from the beach. All rooms have a/c and either a balcony or little outside patio. **$40**

Under the Coconut Tree About 500m north of the beach road ☎0235 652 9168, ⓦunderthe coconuttreehoian.com. This laidback home-stay is a dream come true for travellers. Thatched-roof doubles or stylish dorm rooms with shared bathrooms set in a shady garden just a couple of minutes' walk from the beach. Dorms **$9**, doubles **$25**

EATING

French Bakery and Restaurant About 200m north of the beach road, tucked behind Nguyen Than Vinh ☎090 545 8043. This cute place serves inexpensive breakfast, lunch and dinner options including freshly baked croissants, *banh mi* and spring rolls (all from 35,000đ) – they're also happy to make you up a takeaway picnic for the beach. Daily 8am–11pm.

Soul Kitchen About 150m north of the beach road ☎090 644 0320, ⓦsoulkitchen.sitew.com. This cool spot is the centre of the laidback traveller scene on An Bang beach. It has an attractive thatched bar and fabulous beachfront views, plus an extensive menu that features items like beef fillet with garlic potatoes (220,000đ), salads, snacks, cocktails at around 80,000đ each, and friendly staff. Daily 8am–11pm; Mon closes early.

Cam Kim Island and the craft villages

A 10min ferry ride from the pier in Hoi An (20,000đ) or cycle across on the new bridge from the southwest of An Hoi Islet

The large island of **Cam Kim** is famed for its **craft villages**, which have been inhabited by skilled artisans since the sixteenth century. Most carpenters have moved out of the village but a handful remain, building fishing boats (you'll find one of the few surviving boatyards right beside the island's jetty) or crafting furniture for export. The work of one famous community of woodcarvers, from Kim Bong village, can be seen throughout Hoi An. Cam Kim is a nice escape from Hoi An; it's worth taking a bike over and exploring the rest of the island.

The Cham Islands

The mountainous **Cham Islands**, or Cu Lao Cham, are clearly visible 10km from the coast off Hoi An. The main island of **Hon Lao** is the only inhabited island; for the most part locals make a living from fishing or collecting highly prized birds' nests (see box below), but tourism is a growing industry, causing fears for the fragile environment. Designated a UNESCO Biosphere Reserve in 2009 for its abundant marine life – 135 species of coral, 202 species of fish and 84 species of mollusc – the vast majority of visitors come here to **dive** or **snorkel** the reefs on an organized day-trip from Hoi An. However, after years of military restrictions, it is now possible to arrange a few nights in a homestay and explore Hon Lao independently; the best accommodation is in **Bai Huong**, 5km from the small port in Bai Lang. Visit between March and September, and try to avoid holidays and weekends when domestic tourists arrive in droves.

NEST HARVESTS ON THE CHAM ISLANDS

Cham islanders have been harvesting **sea swallows' nests** since the late sixteenth century. Today the government-controlled trade contributes greatly to the local economy, with astronomical prices per kilo for the culinary delicacy, to which extraordinary medicinal virtues are also attributed. Each spring, when thousands of the tiny, grey-and-black birds nest among the islands' caves and crevices, villagers build bamboo scaffolding or climb up ropes to prise the diminutive structures, about the size of a hen's egg, off the rock.

5

ARRIVAL AND DEPARTURE   THE CHAM ISLANDS

By public ferry The usually overcrowded public ferry departs Cua Dai harbour (see p.258) at 8.30am and takes a couple of hours to reach Bai Lang. The ticket price is 100,000đ, but foreigners are routinely overcharged. The return boat is around 11.30am, so it isn't possible to take a day-trip by public ferry.

By speedboat It's best to arrange transfers through reputable agencies in Hoi An. One-day tours that throw in travel, lunch and snorkelling equipment are around $30–45 but can feel rushed.

SCUBA DIVING

★**Cham Island Diving Centre** 88 Nguyen Thai Hoc ☎ 0235 391 0782, ⓦ chamislanddiving.com. Excellent operator offering diving and snorkelling trips to the islands from Hoi An's *Dive Bar* (see p.255). Snorkel trips from $45, two dives from $85, Open-Water PADI courses from $380. They can also arrange overnight camping.

My Son

45km west of Hoi An • Daily 6.30am–5.30pm; short performances of Cham music at 9.30am, 10.30am and 2.30pm • 150,000đ • Guides are usually available for hire (around 100,000đ) at the car park

Vietnam's most evocative Cham site, **My Son** (pronounced "mee sern") lies southwest of Hoi An, in a bowl of lushly wooded hills towered over by the aptly named Cat's Tooth Mountain. A tangible sense of faded majesty still hangs over the mouldering ruins, enhanced by the assorted lingam and Sanskrit stelae strewn around and by the isolated rural setting, and it's possible, with a little stirring of the imagination, to visualize how the functioning temple complex would have appeared in My Son's heyday.

Brief history

Excavations at My Son have revealed that Cham kings were buried here as early as the fourth century, indicating that the site was established by the rulers of the early Champa capital of **Simhapura**, sited some 30km back towards the highway, at present-day Tra Kieu. The stone towers and sanctuaries whose remnants you see today were erected between the seventh and thirteenth centuries, with successive dynasties adding more temples to this holy place, until in its prime it comprised some seventy buildings. The area was considered the domain of gods and god-kings, and living on site would have been an attendant population of priests, dancers and servants.

French archeologists discovered the ruins in the late nineteenth century, when the Cham's fine **masonry** skills were still evident – instead of mortar, they used a resin mixed with ground brick and mollusc shells, which left only hairline cracks between brick courses. After the Viet Cong based themselves here in the 1960s, many unique buildings were pounded to oblivion by American B52s, most notably the once magnificent A1 tower. Craters around the site and masonry pocked with shell and bullet holes testify to this tragic period in My Son's history.

The museum

Your first stop should be the small but well-organized **museum** (same hours; included in ticket price) to get your bearings before approaching the actual site. There are permanent and thematic sections that explain the history and layout of My Son, and provide a helpful explanation of mythical beasts like the *hamsa* and the *gajasimha*, useful if you're not accompanied by a guide.

Groups H, C and B

First up is **Group H**, off to the right beside the entrance, though there's little to see here and most people head straight for **Groups C and B**, which were once divided by a wall but are now difficult to tell apart. The most impressive building in Group C is the central *kalan*, **C1**, which is standing and fairly well preserved; while in Group B, it's the **repository room**, or B5, which is of most interest for its statues of deities and bas-reliefs of elephants on the outer walls.

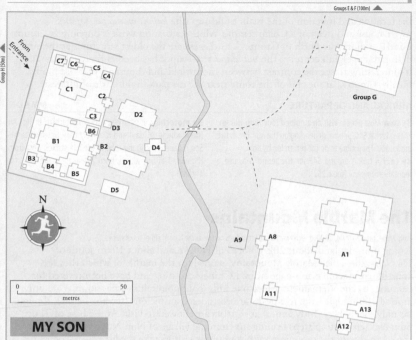

Groups E & F (100m)

From Entrance

Group H (50m)

Group G

N

0   50
metres

MY SON

A9 A8

A1

A11

A13

A12

Group D
Group D is located behind Group B but appears to be connected to it, and it's here that most visitors get their best insights into Cham culture, as the two *mandapa* (meditation halls), D1 and D2, have both been converted into modest **galleries**. They contain a lingam, the remains of a carving of Shiva, a statue of Nandi (Shiva's bull), a many-armed Shiva dancing, and an impressive statue of Vishnu's vehicle, Garuda. The ground between these two galleries was named the **Court of Stelae** by early archeologists, a reference to the stone tablets, etched with Sanskrit script, that litter it. This area gets packed with tour groups at peak times.

Other groups
From Group D, cross a stream to the east and turn right to **Group A**, where the once spectacular *kalan*, **A1**, was reduced to a heap of toppled columns and lintels by US bombs in 1969. A small amount of restoration work has been done here, but the biggest recent changes have taken place at **Group G**, just north of Group A. Originally built in the twelfth century, the small complex has been partially rebuilt to show clearly

> **EXPLORING MY SON**
> After buying a ticket and visiting the museum, cross the bridge and drive about 1km to a car park, then walk another 500m or so to the site entrance. Though groups of buildings are unimaginatively named with the letters of the alphabet, the route through them does not follow alphabetical order; groups B, C, D and G most warrant your attention. Stick to the route shown on signboards around the site, as there could be unexploded ordnance hidden in the tangled vegetation around. A visit is not much fun on a rainy day (Feb–Aug is the driest time), but in the very hottest months it's best to arrive – and leave – early. Note that most tour groups arrive around 9.30am and only stay for a couple of hours.

5

the location and function of the main buildings (the *kalan*, *mandapa*, *gopura*, tower-house and stele) of a Cham temple. More restoration work is ongoing at **Groups E and F**, a short way north of Group G, and these are the oldest structures at the site, dating to the eighth century. The *mandapa* at Group E has been entirely rebuilt, and it's interesting to see the contrast between month-old and thousand-year-old bricks. Finally, **Group K**, at the end of the route near the car park, holds little of interest.

ARRIVAL AND DEPARTURE   MY SON

By tour Most people visit on a guided tour from Hoi An. Prices start at $10/person, depending on the number in the group; you'll pay more to do the return leg by boat.

By taxi A taxi is around $45 for the round trip, use a reputable company (see p.252).

By motorbike It's easy to hire a motorbike in Hoi An (from around $6/day) and relatively easy to travel to My Son independently; the road to the site strikes west from Highway 1 at Duy Xuyen, from where there are signs for My Son.

The Marble Mountains

Daily 7am–5pm • 20,000đ, 15,000đ each way for the lift; tickets on sale at the base of either set of steps

Rising from flat land about 20km north of Hoi An and about 10km south of Da Nang, the fabled **Marble Mountains**, named for the marble of which they are constituted, resemble an image from a Chinese painting and have been revered for centuries by the Vietnamese. More like hills than mountains – the summits are only around 100m high – the five peaks are considered auspicious (see box below), though it's only the highest, **Thuy Son**, that tourists are allowed to visit. At the base of Thuy Son, two sets of steep steps leading up from the village of Non Nuoc provide access to the south side of the mountain; although most visitors take the lift.

A couple of hours allows time to both climb Thuy Son and visit its caves and pagodas, as well as wander round the marble-cutting workshops in the village at its base. It's not worth visiting when it's raining as there's nothing to see and the steps can be very slippery.

Non Nuoc village

At the foot of the mountain is the dusty, unkempt village of **NON NUOC**, set behind Non Nuoc beach (see p.267) which, since the fifteenth century, has echoed to the chink of stone masons chiselling away at religious statues, memorials and imitation Cham figures. The marble used was once quarried from the neighbouring mountains, but as this risked destroying the sacred peaks the stone is now imported from places like Thanh Hoa province and as far away as China. It's fascinating to watch the masons at work, and they produce a huge variety of subjects, ranging from mythical beasts to abstract figures. Some of the larger pieces can fetch up to $50,000, and the shopkeepers will do their best to show you round and sell you a small souvenir.

THE TURTLE GOD

Most distinctive peaks in Vietnam tend to have their creation fixed in folklore, and the Marble Mountains are no different. Local mythology tells of the **Turtle God** hatching a divine egg on the shore; the shell cracked into five pieces, represented by the five small mountains. In Vietnamese these are named Ngu Hanh Son, meaning the five ritual elements: Thuy Son (water mountain), Moc Son (wood), Tho Son (earth), Kim Son (gold or metal) and Hoa Son (fire). Historically, Cham people came here to worship their Hindu gods and then erected Buddhist altars in the caves, which became places of pilgrimage, drawing even the Nguyen kings to the sacred site.

Thuy Son

Though only 107m high, **Thuy Son** is both the highest and most important peak in the Marble Mountains. Two **staircases**, built for the visit of Emperor Minh Mang, lead up its southern flank; a lift beside the eastern staircase offers an easier ascent, but isn't always in operation. The main, westernmost entrance (furthest from Non Nuoc beach), brings you to the hollow summit, centred on pretty **Tam Thai Pagoda**, itself surrounded by jagged rocks and grottoes.

Huyen Khong Cave

Beyond Tam Thai Pagoda, a narrow defile under a natural rock arch leads to **Huyen Khong Cave**, the largest and most impressive cave on the mountain – descending steep, dark steps into the eerie half-light and swirling incense is quite an experience. Locals will point out stalactites resembling wrinkled faces and so on, but the cave's best feature is the holes in its roof through which sunlight streams like spotlights (only on a sunny day of course) – you'll catch it in the hours either side of midday. It was once used as a hospital by the Viet Cong, and some say the holes in the roof were caused by bombs in the war. A wall plaque commemorates a deadly accurate women's Viet Cong guerrilla unit, which during the war destroyed nineteen planes with just 22 rockets.

Linh Ung Pagoda and Tang Chon Cave

The path heading east from Tam Thai Pagoda ducks under a couple of rock arches, passing the missable Van Thong Cave in between, and then climbs slightly before starting to descend towards the eastern exit, affording expansive views over Non Nuoc beach, the Cham Islands and north to Monkey Mountain. About halfway down you pass **Linh Ung Pagoda** behind which lurks **Tang Chon Cave**, in this case occupied by tenth-century Cham Hindu altars and two Buddhas, one sitting and one standing. The standing Buddha is also illuminated by shafts of light in the morning. From here you can descend the eastern staircase or climb a few more steps to enjoy the views from the seven-storey Xa Loi Pagoda and then take the lift down (if it's working).

ARRIVAL AND DEPARTURE   THE MARBLE MOUNTAINS

By tour Any hotel in Da Nang or Hoi An can arrange a half-day tour to the Marble Mountains for around $20 each, depending on number in group.

By bike or motorbike The mountains are not difficult to find and the journey makes a pleasant bicycle or motorbike ride from either Hoi An or Da Nang.

By taxi or xe om You could make a deal with a taxi or xe om driver to stop by for an hour or so while travelling between Hoi An and Da Nang.

By bus The local bus that shuttles between Hoi An and Da Nang stops here (see p.252).

Da Nang and around

The largest city in central Vietnam, **DA NANG** has long been ignored as a destination in its own right, eclipsed until recently by the glories of Hue's Imperial City to the north and the nearby ancient town of Hoi An (see p.245), which lacks its own airport and train station. But things are changing fast, and the city is finally acquiring a character of its own, which, with its cafés and infrastructure of gleaming towers and bridges, is a pleasing blend of modern, cool and laidback.

The city itself occupies a small headland protruding into the southern curve of Da Nang Bay, and its elongated oval of a centre harbours a few worthwhile sights, foremost among which is the **Cham Museum** with its unparalleled collection of sculpture from the period. Other attractions include the fire-breathing **Dragon Bridge** and the riverside promenade along Bach Dang, where most of the city's bars are located, and a pale pink **cathedral**. East of the Han River and protective Son Tra Peninsula, **Da Nang's beaches** form a broad stretch of sand between **Monkey Mountain**

5

DA NANG DURING THE WAR

The city of Da Nang mushroomed after the arrival of the first American combat troops on March 8, 1965. An advance guard of two battalions of Marines waded ashore at Red Beach in Da Nang Bay (to the north of the city), providing the press with a photo opportunity that included amphibious landing craft, helicopters and young Vietnamese women handing out garlands – not quite as the generals had envisaged. The Marines had come to defend Da Nang's massive **US Air Force base**; as the troops flew in, so the base sprawled. Eventually Da Nang became "a small American city", as journalist John Pilger remembers it, "with its own generators, water purification plants, hospitals, cinemas, bowling alleys, ball parks, tennis courts, jogging tracks, supermarkets and bars, lots of bars". For most US troops the approach to Da Nang airfield formed their first impression of Vietnam, and it was here they came to take a break from the war at the famous **China Beach**.

At the same time the city swelled with thousands of **refugees**, mostly villagers cleared from "free-fire zones" but also people in search of work – labourers, cooks, laundry staff, pimps, prostitutes and drug pushers, all inhabiting a shantytown called Dogpatch on the base's perimeter. Da Nang's population rose inexorably: twenty thousand in the 1940s, fifty thousand in 1955 and, some estimate, a peak of one million during the American years. North Vietnamese mortar shells periodically fell in and around the base, but the city's most violent scenes occurred when two South Vietnamese generals engaged in a little power struggle. In March 1966 Vice Air Marshal Ky, then prime minister of South Vietnam, ousted a popular Hue overlord, General Thi, following his open support of Buddhist dissidents. Demonstrations spread from Hue to Da Nang where troops loyal to Thi seized the airfield in what amounted to a **mini civil war**. After much posturing Ky crushed the revolt two months later, killing hundreds of rebel troops and many civilians. In the preceding chaos, the beleaguered rebels held forty Western journalists hostage for a brief period in Da Nang's largest pagoda, Chua Tinh Hoi, while streets around filled with Buddhist protesters.

When the North Vietnamese Army finally arrived to **liberate** Da Nang on March 29, 1975, they had less of a struggle. Communist units had already cut the road south, and panic-stricken South Vietnamese soldiers battled for space on any plane or boat leaving the city, firing on unarmed civilians. Many drowned in the struggle to reach fishing boats, while planes and tanks were abandoned to the enemy. Da Nang had been all but deserted by South Vietnamese forces, leaving the mighty base to, according to Pilger, be "taken by a dozen NLF cadres waving white handkerchiefs from the back of a truck".

to the north and the **Marble Mountains** to the south, and are gradually being lined with top-notch resorts that attract discerning and well-heeled travellers.

Brief history

During the sixteenth and seventeenth centuries, trading vessels waiting to unload at Fai Fo (Hoi An) often sheltered in nearby Da Nang Bay, until Hoi An's harbour began silting up and Da Nang developed into a major port in its own right. After 1802, when Hue became capital of Vietnam, Da Nang naturally served as the principal point of arrival for foreign delegations to the royal court. However, the real spur to the city's growth came in the American War when the neighbouring air base spawned the greatest concentration of US military personnel in South Vietnam (see box above).

The Cham Museum

24 Tran Phu • Daily 7am–5pm • 40,000đ, audio-guide 20,000đ • ☎ 0511 388 6236

Even if you're just passing through Da Nang, try to spare an hour for the small **Cham Museum**, particularly if you plan to visit the Cham ruins at My Son (see p.260). The museum – whose design incorporates Cham motifs – sits in a garden of frangipani trees near the south end of Bach Dang, and its display of graceful, sometimes severe, terracotta and sandstone figures gives a tantalizing glimpse of an artistically inspired culture that ruled most of southern Vietnam for a thousand years. In the late

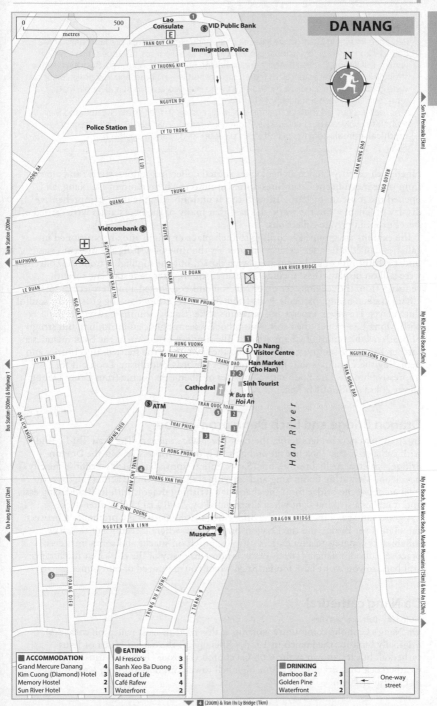

DA NANG

Lao Consulate
VID Public Bank
Immigration Police
TRAN QUY CAP
LY THUONG KIET
NGUYEN DU
Police Station
LY TU TRONG
LE LOI
DONG DA
TRUNG
QUANG
NGUYEN
Train Station (200m)
Vietcombank
HAIPHONG
LE DUAN
NGO GIA TU
NGUYEN THI MINH KHAI
LE DUAN
CHI THANH
PHAN DINH PHUNG
HAN RIVER BRIDGE
LY THAI TO
HUNG VUONG
NG THAI HOC
YEN BAI
TRANH DAO
Da Nang Visitor Centre
Han Market (Cho Han)
Sinh Tourist
Cathedral
Bus to Hoi An
ATM
TRAN QUOC TOAN
THAI PHIEN
TRAN PHU
LE HONG PHONG
HOANG DIEU
PHAN CHU TRINH
HOANG VAN THU
DANG
BACH
Han River
NGUYEN CONG TRU
TRAN HUNG DAO
NGO QUYEN
Son Tra Peninsula (3km)
My Khe (China) Beach (2km)
My An Beach, Non Nuoc Beach, Marble Mountains (15km) & Hoi An (33km)
Bus Station (500m) & Highway 1
Da Nang Airport (2km)
LE DINH DUONG
NGUYEN VAN LINH
ONG ICH KHIEM
Cham Museum
DRAGON BRIDGE
HOANG DIEU
TRUNG NU VUONG
2 THANG 9
N
0   500
metres

ACCOMMODATION
Grand Mercure Danang   4
Kim Cuong (Diamond) Hotel   3
Memory Hostel   2
Sun River Hotel   1

EATING
Al Fresco's   3
Banh Xeo Ba Duong   5
Bread of Life   1
Café Rafew   4
Waterfront   2

DRINKING
Bamboo Bar 2   3
Golden Pine   1
Waterfront   2

One-way street

4 (200m) & Tran Thi Ly Bridge (1km)

5

CHAM ART

Recurring images in Cham art are lions, elephants and Hindu **deities**, predominantly Shiva (founder and defender of Champa) expressed either as a vigorous, full-lipped man or as a lingam, but Vishnu, Garuda, Ganesha and Nandi the bull are also portrayed. **Buddhas** feature strongly in the ninth-century art of Indrapura, a period when Khmer and Indonesian influences were gradually assimilated. The most distinctive icon is **Uroja**, a breast and nipple that represents the universal "mother" of Cham kings.

As the Viets pushed south during the eleventh century, so the Cham retreated, and their sculptures evolved a bold, cubic style. Though less refined than earlier works, the chunky **mythical animals** from this period retain pleasing solidity and a playful charm.

nineteenth century French archeologists started collecting statues, friezes and altars from once magnificent Cham sites dotted around the hinterland of Da Nang, and opened the museum in 1916. Though this is undoubtedly the most comprehensive display of Cham art in the world, it's said that many of the best statues were carried off into European private collections.

The exhibits are grouped according to their place of origin and are positioned in galleries named after their excavation sites. At the time of writing the museum was under refurbishment and some areas were closed, but the highlights from the collection were still on display. These include a massive, **square altar pedestal** (late seventh century) from the religious centre of My Son and considered a masterpiece of early Cham craftsmanship, particularly its frieze depicting jaunty dancing girls, and a soulful flute player. However, experts and amateurs alike usually nominate two lithe dancers with Mona Lisa smiles, their soft, round bodies seemingly clad in nothing but strings of pearls, as the zenith of Cham artistry. The modern extension at the back includes a further 146 stone sculptures, dating from the seventh to the fourteenth centuries and depicting the Champa's shift from Hinduism towards Buddhism. Look out for the impressive bronze Tara Bodhisattva "mother of liberation" statue from Dong Duong, about 20km south of My Son.

Dragon Bridge and Bach Dang promenade

In 2013, two new bridges across the Han River were opened. The Tran Thi Ly Bridge, with cable stays that look like an orange sail, is quite impressive, but the **Dragon Bridge**, which actually breathes fire (Sat & Sun at 9pm), has quickly become the city's new icon. Measuring 666m long and carrying six lanes of traffic across the river, the steel arches of the bridge form the shape of a writhing dragon with its head facing east, and it makes a striking sight when illuminated by 2500 LED lights after dark.

A good vantage point to view the bridge from is the **Bach Dang promenade** between the Han River Bridge and the Dragon Bridge itself, where it seems half the city's inhabitants congregate after dark, to stroll, munch on snacks and sometimes even practise ballroom dancing. Bach Dang is home to many of the city's best restaurants and bars, so you won't have too far to go when you're in need of refreshment.

Da Nang cathedral

156 Tran Phu • Daily 5am–5pm • Free

Da Nang's Catholic community worship at this hard-to-miss pale pink **cathedral**, originally built for the French in 1923. Officially it's the Sacred Heart of Jesus cathedral, but it's known as the Con Ga church (Rooster church) because of the weathercock that sits atop the 70m-high bell tower. Sunday-morning **Mass** is held in English at 10am.

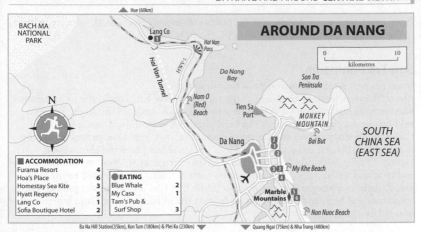

Da Nang's beaches

Just a couple of kilometres east of Da Nang's city centre lies the beginning of a 30km-long strip of sand that stretches all the way south to Hoi An. Sometimes incorrectly marked "**China Beach**" on foreign maps (see box below), it becomes less busy the further you get from the city, though also more built up with resorts, especially on Non Nuoc beach. Be warned that there's a powerful **undertow** off this coast and that when the northeasterly winter monsoon blows up, riptides become particularly dangerous. The best time to hit these beaches is from February to May.

My Khe beach

As the most easily accessible of Da Nang's beaches, **My Khe** is often crowded with large groups of locals, especially at weekends. The access road is lined with simple bars and restaurants that do a roaring trade when the weather is good. If you're here with hired transport, it's worth heading on north from the beach to explore the steep trails on the **Son Tra Peninsula** (see p.268), which has a wild feel about it.

My An and Non Nuoc beaches

At the south end of My Khe beach the road veers inland to follow behind an incredibly long stretch of luxury resorts covering several kilometres. The beaches from here are known as **My An** and further south as **Non Nuoc**, though it's difficult to tell where one ends and the other begins. The vibe here makes a marked contrast to My Khe, as security guards stand watch in front of high walls that shield shoulder-to-shoulder international hotel chains. Though the beach here is not technically private, access is very difficult to non-guests, so it gets less crowded. It's worth combining a visit to Non

---

WHERE IS CHINA BEACH?

You won't find it on any Vietnamese maps, and if you ask a local, they'll shake their head and say they've never heard of it. Yet **China Beach** still appears on many maps printed in the West and in many guidebooks, referring to the entire stretch of beach between Da Nang and Hoi An. The name was given to the area by American troops who were sent here for some welcome R&R between bouts of battle with the North Vietnamese and Viet Cong. Today, with the troops long gone, the beach names have reverted to Vietnamese: from north to south, My Khe, My An, Non Nuoc, An Bang and Cua Dai. While there's no official segregation, you'll find Vietnamese predominate at My Khe and Cua Dai, while it's mostly foreigners on My An, Non Nuoc and An Bang.

5

Nuoc beach with an exploration of the **Marble Mountains** (see p.262), which you'll see to the west of the coast road just 10km south of Da Nang.

Son Tra Peninsula

No public transport; hire a motorbike or join a tour from Da Nang (see opposite)

About 5km northeast of Da Nang at the top end of My Khe beach, the mountainous, hammerhead-shaped **Son Tra Peninsula** rises to a shade under 700m high. There's a wild feel to the peninsula, which can be explored by motorbike if you're confident riding round sharp curves and up steep slopes; the road round the perimeter and up to the summit is best circumnavigated in a clockwise loop to avoid the steepest incline. The highest peak, Nui Son Tra, is often referred to as "**Monkey Mountain**", and monkeys still inhabit the promontory, parts of which are restricted to military use, though a viewing area at the the top (Dinh Ban Co) is open to the public. There are a couple of high-end resorts that spill down the hillsides, but it's much better value to stay elsewhere.

Son Tra Nature Reserve

Around 43 square kilometres of the peninsula is set aside as the **Son Tra Nature Reserve**, specifically to protect the rare **red-shanked douc langurs** that live here. These primates are sometimes called "the costumed ape" due to their unusual appearance, with a golden face, white ruff, blue eyelids and red legs that look like stockings. They are rarely seen, however, as there are only around one hundred left in the wild here. Also in the reserve is a banyan tree believed to be a thousand years old, which has several root clusters up to a metre in diameter.

Lady Buddha statue

Erected in 2010 on the south coast of the Son Tra Peninsula at Linh Ung Pagoda (not to be confused with the Linh Ung Pagoda at Thuy Son), this enormous **Lady Buddha statue** (Quan Yin, the Goddess of Mercy) stands nearly 70m tall, and is easily visible from My Khe beach, several kilometres across the water. When it's open, which is not often, visitors can go inside and climb seventeen storeys for a dizzying view of the bay. Not surprisingly, the statue has quickly become one of Da Nang's most memorable icons.

Ba Na Hill Station

25km southwest of Da Nang • Cable car 400,000đ return • Return trip by taxi from Da Nang, including waiting time, around $60; Da Nang tour agents offer various organized bus tours, mostly in summer

Perched 1500m up a mountain to the west of Da Nang, **Ba Na Hill Station** provides a cool escape from the coast, though it is much more popular among Vietnamese than foreigners, many of whom find the experience rather tacky. The site was first developed by the French in the 1920s, who came in numbers to escape the summer heat and enjoy some cool mountain air. After a brief heyday in the 1930s the resort was abandoned and soon fell victim to the ravages of war and the encroaching jungle. Dense forest growth cloaks the mountain, which is home to over five hundred species of plant and 250 types of animal.

Local authorities have poured money into Ba Na, converting some of the old French villas into guesthouses and restaurants, laying forest trails and a new access road and even putting in a **two-stage cable car** – which has the longest nonstop single-track system in the world (5801m). The seventeen-minute ride is a great hit with the locals, who come up here at night to admire the lights of Da Nang twinkling far below. The resort at the top is something of a theme park, though the **views** are indeed spectacular, taking in the Hai Van Pass, Son Tra Peninsula and Marble Mountains (on a clear day), but you may want to avoid summer weekends, when the place can be packed out.

ARRIVAL AND DEPARTURE

BY PLANE
Da Nang International Airport is just 2km southwest of the city, and has connections to most major domestic airports as well as international services to China, South Korea, Singapore and Myanmar, among others. There are no direct flights to Laos, and for Cambodia and Thailand you'll pay more than flying from HCMC or Hanoi. A taxi to the city centre costs around 60,000đ (there isn't a bus).
Destinations Buon Ma Thuot (daily; 1hr 20min); Da Lat (daily; 1hr 35min); Hanoi (10 daily; 1hr 15min); Ho Chi Minh City (18 daily; 1hr 25min); Nha Trang (daily; 1hr 10min); Pleiku (3 weekly; 1hr).

BY TRAIN
Da Nang station is west of the city centre at 200

GETTING AROUND

By bike and motorbike Da Nang is big enough to make walking round town fairly time-consuming, though most places to stay and eat are concentrated around Bach Dang in the centre. For anywhere beachside, you'll need two wheels and most hotels either rent bicycles (around

INFORMATION AND TOURS

Da Nang Visitor Centre 108 Bach Dang ☎0511 355 0111, ⓦtourism.danang.vn/en. Provides a useful map of the city and around and will, they hope, sell you tours of the area. They also have a desk at the airport. Daily 7.30am–9.30pm.
Websites The Da Nang tourism website ⓦtourism .danang.vn/en is a great resource, but for listings, try ⓦindanang.com, which is primarily aimed at expats living in the city.
Looking Glass Jeep Tours ☎0120 440 9665,

ACCOMMODATION

The majority of Da Nang's hotels are geared to business travellers or tour groups who are likely to only stay one night. If you plan to use the city as a base to explore the surrounding area there are better-value choices – from homestays to five-star resorts – near Da Nang's beaches.

DA NANG
Grand Mercure Danang Green Island ☎0511 379 7777, ⓦmercure.com; map p.265. Sitting on a patch of reclaimed land to the south of the city centre, overlooking a grand new sports complex taking shape to the south, the *Grand Mercure* offers a glimpse of a city in transition from the windows of its 272 rooms, and for those on the upper floors it's more than a glimpse. Rooms are very stylish, in fact the whole hotel gives off a super-hip vibe, but note that superior rooms don't include breakfast. $120
Kim Cuong (Diamond) Hotel 21 Thai Phien ☎0511 356 5937, ⓦkimcuonghoteldn.com; map p.265. Tucked back from the riverfront, this welcoming budget-hotel has

Haiphong. There will be plenty of taxis (40,000đ to the centre) and xe om (about 20,000đ) vying for your attention.
Destinations Dong Hoi (4 daily; 6–7hr); Hanoi (5 daily; 15–18hr); Ho Chi Minh City (5 daily; 16–21hr); Hue (4 daily; 2hr 30min); Nha Trang (5 daily; 9–12hr).

BY BUS
Intercity bus station Public buses leave 3km west of the city centre on Dien Bien Phu. For Hoi An you can jump on a local bus from several stops in the city centre including outside the cathedral (every 20min; 1hr 30min–2hr); although overcharging is common, the official price is 18,000đ. The same bus stops at Marble Mountain.
Destinations Dong Ha (5hr); Hue (3–4hr); Quang Ngai (5hr); Quy Nhon (11hr); Savannakhet, Laos (14hr).

$2/day) or scooters (around $5–8/day), or can direct you to somewhere that does. Contact Trong at Easy Rider (☎090 359 7791, ⓦeasyridervn.com) for a one-day motorbike tour to take in Monkey Mountain and Hai Van Pass.
By taxi Try Mai Linh taxi (☎0511 356 5656).

ⓦfacebook.com/lookingglassjeeptours. Take a tour in a restored military jeep around the Son Tra Peninsula and the Hai Van Pass, or further afield to minority villages near the Laos border. Owner Jeremy is happy to customize your itinerary and it's great value if there's a few of you; expect to pay $300/day for the jeep and driver, plus drinks, lunch and admission to sights.
The Sinh Tourist 154 Bach Dang ☎0511 384 3258, ⓦthesinhtourist.vn. A busy booking office for open-tour buses and tours. Daily 7am–10pm.

bright, clean doubles with a/c, wi-fi and cable TV. Ask for a room out back to avoid street noise. $20
Memory Hostel 3 Tran Quoc Toan, ☎0511 3747797, ⓦmemoryhostel.com; map p.265. New hostel just off Bach Dang, rooms are quiet and comfortable and dorms have privacy curtains and secure lockers. Staff are super helpful but there's not much communal space for mingling. Dorms $8, doubles $18
Sun River Hotel 132–136 Bach Dang ☎0511 384 9188, ⓦsunriverhoteldn.com.vn; map p.265. This hotel is the one of the best mid-range options on the Bach Dang strip. Its modern rooms have faux-wood floors, solid furnishings and a cream-through-brown colour scheme.

5

Rooms at the front cost a little more, and have river views from the curved windows. The café/bar also makes a good place to drink, even if you're not staying here. **$45**

DA NANG BEACHES

Furama Resort Vo Nguyen Giap, My An Beach ☎0511 384 7333, ⓦfuramavietnam.com; map p.267. Set in lush gardens, this enormous development stands out as one of Vietnam's top beach resorts, and it's still growing, with new villas being offered for sale. It offers luxuriously appointed rooms, international cuisine, two swimming pools plus a guarded beach and a range of recreational activities from tennis and golf to scuba diving, ocean-kayaking and windsurfing. **$176**

Hoa's Place 9km south of Da Nang, Non Nuoc beach ☎090 564 0542, ⓔhoasplace@gmail.com; map p.267. The genial Hoa and his wife have opened a new hotel just a stone's throw from Non Nuoc beach and Marble Mountains; nightly communal dinners (80,000VND), cheap beer and friendly conversation make it the kind of place where days slip leisurely into weeks. All four rooms are en suite. **$20**

Homestay Sea Kite Lo 21, An Thuong 32, My An beach ☎0511 3958 785, ⓦbesthomestayindanang.blogspot .co.uk; map p.267. The simple, clean rooms of this four-storey family home all come with a/c and en-suite bathrooms, plus guests have access to a washing machine, kitchen and sunny terrace. The beach is within walking distance and breakfast and dinner is served on request. **$20**

Hyatt Regency Truong Sa, Non Nuoc beach ☎0511 398 1234, ⓦdanang.regency.hyatt.com; map p.267. Cut off from the outside world and occupying a huge beach frontage within walking distance of the Marble Mountains (see p.262), this stylish resort has spacious rooms with large balconies overlooking an enormous pool. There are several dining and eating options on-site and staff, as you'd expect, are efficient and helpful. **$250**

★**Sofia Boutique Hotel** 11 Pham Van Dong, My Khe beach ☎0511 394 1669, ⓦsofiahoteldanang.com; map p.267. This comfortable hotel on My Khe beach offers a good compromise if you want to stay by the sea without paying top dollar. Rooms are bright and well maintained, and staff go out of their way to be helpful. **$60**

EATING

Da Nang has no shortage of places to eat, with the majority of foreigner-friendly options clustered around Bach Dang in the centre of the city.

DA NANG

Al Fresco's 178 Tran Phu ☎0511 356 6866, ⓦalfrescosgroup.com; map p.265. If you need a break from Vietnamese fare, drop by Al Fresco's for BBQ ribs (120,000đ) or good old fish and chips (220,000đ). It's located just a block back from the Bach Dang promenade. Daily 8am–11pm.

Banh Xeo Ba Duong K280/23 Hoang Dieu; map p.265. Hidden at the end of an alley, in the evening this place buzzes with local families – and the occasional tourist – here for the cheap and delicious meat skewers and *banh xeo* (literally "sizzling cakes") stuffed with pork and shrimp. Daily 4–10pm.

Bread of Life 4 Dong Da ☎0511 356 5185, ⓦbreadoflifedanang.com; map p.265. A great place to throw down some Western comfort food. Baked goods, pancakes, pizza and a lot more are made and served by an all-deaf staff, and proceeds go towards a related food charity. Mains from 80,000đ. Mon–Sat 8.30am–9.30pm.

Café Rafew 58 Hoang Van Thu ☎0511 356 2177, ⓦrafew.vn; map p.265. This sophisticated café has three floors and a beautiful shady garden. Although the menu isn't in English, the staff will talk you through it – there's coffee, tea (try the iced strawberry tea for 30,000đ), cake and ice cream. In the evening it's the coolest spot in town, with live music at the weekend. Daily 7am–10.30pm.

★**Waterfront** 150–152 Bach Dang ☎0511 384 3373, ⓦwaterfrontdanang.com; map p.265. This two-storey restaurant and bar is probably Da Nang's most popular choice for expat diners, and the upstairs balcony seats with views of the promenade and Dragon Bridge are always first to be occupied. Sharply attired staff float around upstairs delivering burgers, seafood baskets and steaks (160,000–500,000đ). The downstairs bar is also a good place to drink (see opposite). Daily 10am–11pm.

DA NANG BEACHES

Blue Whale Son Tra-Dien Ngoc ☎0511 394 2777, ⓦbluewhale.com.vn; map p.267. With a location right on My Khe beach and set in a smartly furnished, colonial-style villa, the *Blue Whale* is one of the many touristy seafood places along this stretch. Check prices before ordering, as everything depends on the day's market prices, then settle down on the terrace to enjoy the seaside ambiance. Expect to pay 200,000–300,000đ for a meal and drink. Daily 10am–11pm.

★**My Casa** 52 Vo Nghia ☎0126 990 8903, ⓦmycasa -danang.com; map p.267. The shady garden of this Spanish-Italian restaurant is a popular retreat for travellers' and expats alike. The kitchen produces home-made pasta (200,000đ/150g), *tosta* (bruschetta; 55,000đ) and burgers (160,000đ) with a fusion of local and imported ingredients, while the bar does a roaring trade in cocktails and craft beer. Owners Jorge and Sharon were talking about moving *My Casa* at the time of our visit so do check ahead; advance reservations recommended. Mon, Tues & Thurs–Sun

11am–2pm & 5–10pm.

Tam's Pub & Surf Shop 38 An Thuong 5, My An beach ☎ 090 540 6905; map p.267. On a quiet tree-lined street not far from the beach, this great spot serves Western grub including "Tam's world famous burgers" (100,000đ).

The place for anyone interested in the American War in Da Nang; the walls are lined with memorabilia and Tam is an amazing source of local information. She also rents out scooters and surfboards (from $5/day, plus deposit). Daily 8am–7pm.

DRINKING

There are several decent **bars** in Da Nang, and more are opening all the time to cater to the growing crowd of locals and foreigners – a couple of the high-rise hotels on Bach Dang have top-floor bars where the drinks prices are as sky-high as the views. Also notable is a small selection of local beers to quaff – Da Nang Export and Bière la Rue.

★ **Bamboo Bar 2** 216 Bach Dang ☎ 090 554 4769; map p.265. One of Da Nang's most popular bars located right on the riverfront. Dim-lit and noisy, it can be tough to find a seat some nights, especially during happy hour (5.30–7pm). Live sport is on the TV most days. Daily noon–2am.

Golden Pine 52 Bach Dang ☎ 093 521 0113; map p.265. Located on Bach Dang just north of the Han River Bridge, this place attracts a young crowd of locals and foreigners, and

gets packed at weekends. You'll need to shout to hold a conversation – or try the quieter upstairs room with a pool table and a nice view of the river. Daily 2pm–2am.

Waterfront 150–152 Bach Dang ⓦ waterfrontdanang .com; map p.265. This swanky place is good for coffee during the day or alcohol by night – there's a choice of 15 different beers and 9 different wines by the glass. Live music on Fri evenings, DJ on other nights. Daily 10am–11pm.

DIRECTORY

Banks and exchange Vietcombank, 140 Le Loi; Incombank, 172 Nguyen Van Linh; VID Public Bank, 2 Tran Phu. ATMs dot the city and there are plenty in the airport.

Consulate The Lao consulate, with its visa-issuing service, is located at 12 Tran Quy Cap (Mon–Fri 8–11.30am & 2–4.30pm; ☎ 0511 382 1208). Visa applications will take around three working days.

Hospital The Family Medical Practice at 96–98 Nguyen Van

Linh (Mon–Fri 8.30am–5.30pm, Sat 8.30am–12.30pm; ☎ 0236 358 2699, ⓦ vietnammedicalpractice.com) has foreign staff and a 24hr emergency service.

Immigration police 7 Tran Quy Cap (☎ 0511 382 3383). The place to go if you've lost your passport or have similar difficulties.

Post office Main office at 60 Bach Dang, just south of the Han River Bridge (Mon–Fri 8am–7pm).

North of Da Nang

Up the coast from Da Nang, Highway 1 zigzags over the **Hai Van Pass** (see box below), a wonderfully scenic ride by road or (especially) rail. North of the pass is the small beach town of **Lang Co**, well known for its seafood restaurants and brilliant white sands – and still, as yet, comparatively undeveloped. To the west is **Bach Ma National Park**, a gorgeous place where the remains of another French-era hill station are swamped by some of the lushest vegetation in Vietnam.

UP AND OVER HAI VAN PASS

Thirty kilometres north of Da Nang, the first and most dramatic of three mountain spurs off the **Truong Son range** cuts across Vietnam's pinched central waist, all the way to the sea. This thousand-metre-high barrier forms a climatic frontier blocking the southward penetration of cold, damp winter airstreams, which often bury the tops under thick cloud banks and earn it the title **Hai Van**, or "Pass of the Ocean Clouds". These mountains once formed a national frontier between Dai Viet and Champa, and Hai Van's continuing strategic importance is marked by a succession of forts, pillboxes and ridge-line defensive walls erected by Nguyen-dynasty Vietnamese, French, Japanese and American forces.

These days, most buses and cars travel via the Hai Van Tunnel, leaving a more peaceful journey for those who choose to take on the Pass: from the top there are superb views, weather permitting, over the sweeping curve of Da Nang Bay, with glimpses of the rail lines looping and tunnelling along the cliff.

5

Lang Co

Forty kilometres north of Da Nang, Highway 1 splices through **LANG CO** village, which hides among coconut palms on the sandy peninsula, its presence revealed only by a white-spired church. The major draw here is the 10km stretch of white sand **beach** east of the highway, a popular lunch stop between Da Nang and Hue. To the west of the highway, there's a large **lagoon** with a backdrop of mountains and this is *the* place to enjoy a meal at one of the seafood restaurants on stilts. Lang Co is also worth considering as somewhere to enjoy a few days by the beach without hordes of tourists, apart from June to August when it's crowded with domestic visitors.

ARRIVAL AND DEPARTURE

LANG CO

By train The train station is south of the lagoon, a few kilometres from the beach; most trains are in the morning, so the return journey can be tricky.

Destinations Da Nang (4 daily; 2hr); Hue (4 daily; 1hr 30min).

ACCOMMODATION AND EATING

Be Than ☎0166 677 0000, ⓦnhahangbethan.vn. One of the best of the floating restaurants on the lagoon, *Be Than* is packed out at weekends with Vietnamese families enjoying steamed clams, grilled mussels or deep-fried prawns. Prices depend on the catch of the day (check out what looks fresh in the tanks lining the front of the restaurant), but expect to pay around 300,000đ per person including a cold beer or two. Daily 10am–1pm.

Lang Co Beach Resort Lang Co ☎0234 387 3555, ⓦlangcobeachresort.com.vn. Government-owned resort complex, with green-roofed, Hue-style villas, a landscaped pool and a replica covered bridge. The rooms

are big, light and well equipped and the beach here is kept scrupulously clean. You can book anything from a single "budget" room for $35 to a two-bedroom villa for $175 and prices are slashed in winter. $60

Thanh Tam Resort Lang Co, Phu Loc ☎0234 387 4456, ⓦthanhtamresort.com.vn. Good-value, mid-range option, on the highway about 1500m north of the village. It's a surprisingly large place, with two restaurants to choose from, which are popular with tour groups. The rooms themselves are smart with balconies shaded by casuarinas; all have a/c and free wi-fi; the best are the bungalows with a sea view ($64). $36

Bach Ma National Park

28km west of Lang Co and 40km southeast of Hue · 40,000đ · ⓦbachmapark.com.vn

Well off the beaten track, **Bach Ma National Park** occupies around 220 square kilometres of mountainous terrain ranging around 1450m high and stretching from near the coast to the Lao border. It is being developed as an ecotourism destination, and dedicated ornithologists and botanists may want to make the effort to get here for the chance of seeing some of the region's 330 bird species and more than 1400 species of flora. Bach Ma is also home to some rare mammals, including the Asiatic black bear, leopard, the recently discovered – and seldom seen – **saola** and **giant muntjac deer**, as well as more visible deer and macaque monkeys.

Though it's possible to make a day-trip here to tackle one of the shorter trails, nature lovers should **spend a night** or two in the park since some of the more elusive species like the crested argus (a pheasant-like peafowl) are most active at dawn and dusk. Apart from its flora and fauna, the park's greatest attraction is the cool climate near its upper reaches; in fact it's a good idea to take a jacket if staying overnight.

HIGHWAY 49B

Highway 1 links Lang Co to Hue, but if you have your own transport and are in the mood for adventure, you could turn north about 6km before Phu Loc (for Bach Ma) and follow **Highway 49B** up a little-trafficked peninsula where much of the road is bordered by elaborate tombstones. The road leads to **Thuan An beach**, then turns inland for the final 15km to Hue.

BACH MA TRAILS

Five short **nature trails** branch off the steep, tarmacked road which leads 16km from the entrance gate almost to the summit of Hai Vong Dai Mountain (1450m). Note that all marker distances refer to the distance from Highway 1 rather than from the park entrance.

Pheasant Trail (2.5km). Starts at the Km 8 marker to reach a series of waterfalls and pools, where you can swim. On the way you may hear the calls of white-cheek gibbons or some of the seven types of pheasant that inhabit the park, or see the 50cm-long earthworms which the locals cook and eat as a treatment for malaria.

Parashorea Trail (300m). At Km 14, a short but very steep trail named after this area's towering trees.

Rhododendron Trail (1.5km). Leads up 689 steps from Km 16 to a waterfall, with views over primary forest.

Five Lakes Trail (2km). Also starts at Km 16, ends at a series of five pools fed by a waterfall, where you can also swim.

Summit Trail Leads 900m from the end of the road (at Km 19) to the crest of Hai Vong Dai with good views over Cau Hai lagoon and surrounding mountains.

Bach Ma is one of the **wettest** places in Vietnam, with a staggering eight metres of rainfall a year at the summit. The best time to visit is May to early September, but even then be prepared to get wet.

ARRIVAL AND DEPARTURE
BACH MA NATIONAL PARK

By car or motorbike By far the easiest way to reach Bach Ma is with your own transport – 26km west of Lang Co, look for a big blue sign to the park pointing south off Highway 1 in Phu Loc town, then drive for another 4km to the park gate. Hiring a car and driver from Hue will cost around $100 for the return journey.

By bus Public buses will drop you at the turning in Cau Hai, from where you can pick up a xe om for the final 3km stretch to the park gates (about 30,000đ). Open tour buses should drop you right at the gate; check with The Sinh Tourist in Da Nang (see p.269) or Hue (see p.281).

GETTING AROUND

By minibus Note that, while cars are allowed inside the park, motorbikes and bicycles are not. Instead, you'll have to rent one of the park's minibuses (900,000đ for an eight-seater), which will take you to the summit and back again, but can't drop off or pick up passengers en route.

INFORMATION AND TOURS

Visitors' Centre At the entrance to the park, stop first at the Visitors' Centre (daily 7am–5pm; ☎0234 387 1330, ⊚bachmapark.com.vn) to buy your entrance tickets and arrange transport and accommodation. If you are arriving outside these hours, phone in advance. Make sure you pick up a map of the trails.

Guides Although it's not a requirement, it's definitely a good idea to take a guide ($25 for an English-speaker) when you're walking in the park, principally for your own safety – it's easy to get lost. Note that it's normal "forest etiquette" to share drinks, meals and carrying the loads.

ACCOMMODATION AND EATING

The highlands at Bach Ma were previously the location of a French summer resort, where Emperor Bao Dai also kept several luxury villas. The majority of buildings, tennis courts and rose-beds are now in ruins, but a number of villas have been restored to provide tourist accommodation. There's also a **campsite** (bring your own tent) at Km 18, though facilities are limited. There's a small **restaurant** at the park entrance, where you can also buy water and snacks. Meals have to be ordered in advance if you're staying at the summit.

Do Quyen Villa Near the summit, nestled among the trees. Especially popular for its location albeit with fairly basic facilities. It's nevertheless advisable to book in advance in peak season (June–Aug); contact the Visitors' Centre for reservations. $\overline{\underline{\$15}}$

Morin Bach Ma Just below the summit ☎0234 387 1199. This restored two-storey French-style villa is a bit classier than the *Do Quyen Villa*, with slightly higher prices too. All rooms are en suite, but fairly sparse. $\overline{\underline{\$20}}$

5 Hue

Still packed with the accoutrements of its dynastic past, **HUE** (pronounced *hoo-eh*) is one of Vietnam's most engaging cities. It boasts an unparalleled opportunity for historic and culinary exploration, thanks in no small part to its status as national capital from 1802 to 1945. Though the Nguyen dynasty is no more, Hue still exudes something of a regal, dignified air – indeed its populace is considered somewhat highbrow by the rest of the country. The city still nurtures poets, artists, scholars and intellectuals, and you'll notice, unlike elsewhere in Vietnam, that female students still wear the traditional *ao dai*.

Hue repays exploration at a leisurely pace, and contains enough in the way of historical interest to swallow up a few days with no trouble at all. The city divides into three clearly defined urban areas, each with its own distinct character, and through it all meanders the **Perfume River**, named somewhat fancifully from the tree resin and blossoms it carries. The nineteenth-century walled **citadel**, on the north bank of the Perfume River, contains the once magnificent **Imperial City** as well as an extensive grid of attractive residential streets and prolific gardens. Across Dong Ba Canal to the east lies **Phu Cat**, the original merchants' quarter of Hue where ships once pulled in, now a crowded district of shophouses, Chinese assembly halls and pagodas. What used to be called the **European City**, a triangle of land caught between the Perfume River's south bank and the Phu Cam Canal, is now Hue's modern administrative centre, where you'll also find most hotels and tourist services.

With all this to offer, plus the fact that Hue is also the main jumping-off point for day-tours of the **DMZ** (see p.295), the city is inevitably one of Vietnam's pre-eminent tourist destinations. Nevertheless, the majority of people pass through fairly quickly, partly because high entrance fees make visiting more than a couple of the major sights beyond many budgets (and touts can become an annoyance), and partly because of its wet **weather**. Hue suffers from the highest rainfall in the country, mostly falling over just three months from September to December when the city regularly floods for a few days, causing damage to the historic architecture, though heavy downpours are possible at any time of year.

Brief history

The land on which Hue now stands belonged to the Kingdom of Champa until 1306, when territory north of Da Nang was exchanged for the hand of a Vietnamese princess under the terms of a peace treaty. The first Vietnamese to settle in the region established their administrative centre near present-day Hue at a place called Hoa Chan, and then in 1558 Lord Nguyen Hoang arrived from Hanoi as governor of the district, at the same time establishing the rule of the Nguyen lords over southern Vietnam which was to last for the next two hundred years. In the late seventeenth century the lords moved the citadel to its present location where it developed into a major town and cultural centre – **Phu Xuan**, which briefly became the capital under the Tay Son emperor Quang Trung (1788–1801).

The Nguyen dynasty

However, it was the next ruler of Vietnam who literally put Hue on the map. In 1802 Prince Nguyen Anh, one of the southern Nguyen lords, defeated the Tay Son dynasty with the help of a French bishop, Pigneau de Behaine, assumed the throne under the title **Emperor Gia Long** and founded the **Nguyen dynasty**. Gia Long sought to unify the country by moving the capital, lock, stock and dynastic altars, from Thang Long (Hanoi) to the renamed city of **Hue**. Though he owed his throne to French military support, Gia Long's Imperial City was very much a Chinese concept, centred on a Forbidden City reserved for the sovereign, with separate administrative and civilian quarters.

The Nguyen emperors were Confucian, conservative rulers, generally suspicious of all Westerners yet unable to withstand the power of France. In 1884 the French were

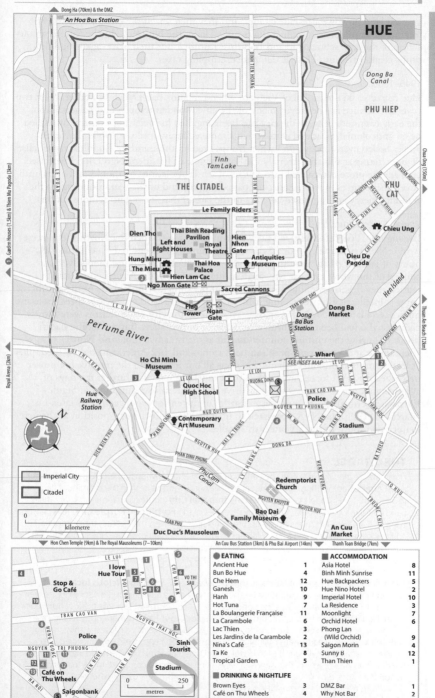

HUE

Dong Ha (70km) & the DMZ

An Hoa Bus Station

Garden Houses (1.5km) & Thien Mu Pagoda (3km)

Dong Ba Canal

PHU HIEP

Chua Ong (150km)

LE DUAN

NGUYEN TRAI

Tinh Tam Lake

THE CITADEL

DINH TIEN HOANG

PHU CAT

Thuan An Beach (12km)

NGUYEN CHI THANH
NGUYEN W BIEM
NGUYEN DINH CHIEU
MAC DANG DU
CHI LANG
BACH DANG

Chieu Ung

Dieu De Pagoda

Hen Island

Le Family Riders

Dien Tho
Thai Binh Reading Pavilion
Left and Right Houses
Royal Theatre
Hung Mieu
The Mieu
Hien Lam Cac
Thai Hoa Palace
Hien Nhon Gate
Antiquities Museum
Ngo Mon Gate
LE TRUC
Sacred Cannons

Flag Tower
Ngan Gate

Dong Ba Bus Station
Dong Ba Market

Royal Arena (2km)

Perfume River

LE DUAN
BUI THI XUAN
TRAN HUNG DAO
TRANG TIEN BRIDGE
PHU XUAN BRIDGE
DAP DA CAUSEWAY
THUAN AN

Ho Chi Minh Museum

Hue Railway Station

DIEN BIEN PHU

N

LE LOI
TRUONG DINH
LE LOI

Quoc Hoc High School

Contemporary Art Museum

PHAN BOI CHAU
NGO QUYEN
NGUYEN HUE
THAI BA TRUNG
HA NOI
PHAN DINH PHUNG

Wharf

SEE INSET MAP

P.N. LAO
DOI CUNG
CHU VAN AN

LE LOI

TRAN CAO VAN
NGUYEN THAI HOC

Police

BEN NGHE
TRAN Q. KHAI

Stadium

DONG DA
LE QUI DON

BA TRIEU

Redemptorist Church

Phu Cam Canal

LY THUONG KIET

HUNG VUONG

TO HUU

TRUONG CHINH

Bao Dai Family Museum

NGUYEN KHUYEN
NGUYEN HUE

An Cuu Market

TRAN PHU

Duc Duc's Mausoleum

Hon Chen Temple (9km) & The Royal Mausoleums (7–10km)

An Cuu Bus Station (3km) & Phu Bai Airport (14km)

Thanh Toan Bridge (7km)

Imperial City
Citadel

0   1
kilometre

INSET MAP:

LE LOI
I love Hue Tour
P.N. LAO
DOI CUNG
CHU VAN AN
VO THI SAU

Stop & Go Café

TRAN CAO VAN
NGUYEN THAI HOC

HUNG VUONG

Police

Sinh Tourist

NGUYEN TRI PHUONG
BEN NGHE
TRAN Q. KHAI

Stadium

HA NOI
Café on Thu Wheels

Saigonbank

0   250
metres

5

granted land northwest of Hue citadel, and they then seized the city entirely in 1885, leaving the emperors as nominal rulers only. Under the Nguyen, Hue became a famous centre of the arts, scholarship and Buddhist learning, but their extravagant building projects and luxurious lifestyle demanded crippling taxes.

1945–1968

Hue ceased to be the capital of Vietnam when Emperor Bao Dai abdicated in 1945; two years later a huge fire destroyed many of the city's wooden temples and palaces. From the early twentieth century the city had been engulfed in social and political unrest led by an anticolonial, educated elite, which simmered away until the 1960s. Tensions finally boiled over in May 1963 when troops fired on thousands of Buddhist nationalists demonstrating against the strongly Catholic regime of President Ngo Dinh Diem (see p.440). The protests escalated into a wave of self-immolations by monks and nuns until government forces moved against the pagodas at the end of the year, rounding up the Buddhist clergy and supposed activists in the face of massive public demonstrations.

War and reconstruction

During the 1968 **Tet Offensive** Hue was torn apart again when the North Vietnamese Army (NVA) held the city for 25 days. Communist forces entered Hue in the early hours of January 31, hoisted their flag above the citadel and found themselves in control of the whole city bar two small military compounds. Armed with lists of names, they began searching out government personnel, sympathizers of the Southern regime, intellectuals, priests, Americans and foreign aid workers. Nearly three thousand bodies were later discovered in mass graves around the city – the victims were mostly civilians who had been shot, beaten to death or buried alive. But the killing hadn't finished: during the ensuing counter-assault as many as five thousand North Vietnamese and Viet Cong, 384 Southern troops and 142 American soldiers died, plus at least another thousand civilians. Hue was all but levelled in the massive fire power unleashed on NVA forces holed up in the citadel but it took a further ten days of agonizing, house-to-house combat to drive the Communists out, in what Stanley Karnow described as "the most bitter battle" of the entire war. Seven years later, on March 26, 1975, the NVA were back to liberate Hue in its pivotal position as the first major town south of the Seventeenth Parallel.

THE CITADEL

Hue's days of glory kicked off in the early nineteenth century when Emperor Gia Long laid out a vast **citadel**, comprising three concentric enclosures, ranged behind the prominent flag tower. Within the citadel's outer wall lies the **Imperial City**, containing administrative offices, parks and dynastic temples, with the royal palaces of the **Forbidden Purple City** at its centre. Though wars, fires, typhoons, floods and termites have all taken their toll, it's these Imperial edifices, some now restored to their former magnificence, that constitute Hue's prime tourist attraction. Apart from one museum, there are no specific sights in the outer citadel, but it's a pleasant area to cycle round, especially the northern sector where you'll find many lakes and the prolific **gardens** for which Hue is famed.

In accordance with ancient tradition, the citadel was built in an **auspicious location** chosen to preserve the all-important harmony between the emperor and his subjects, heaven and earth, man and nature. Thus the complex is oriented southeast towards the low hummock of Nui Ngu Binh ("Royal Screen Mountain"), which blocks out harmful influences. Just in case that wasn't protection enough, the whole 5.2 square kilometres are enclosed within 7m-high, 20m-thick brick and earth walls built with the help of French engineers, and encircled by a moat and canal. Eight villages had to be relocated when construction began in 1805, and over the next thirty years tens of thousands of workmen laboured to complete more than three hundred palaces, temples, tombs and other royal buildings, some using materials brought down from the former Imperial City in Hanoi.

The mammoth task of **rebuilding** Hue received a boost in 1993 when UNESCO listed the city as a World Heritage Site, which served to mobilize international funding for a whole range of projects, from renovating palaces to the biennial Hue Festival.

The citadel walls, flag tower and sacred cannons

The citadel's massive, 10km-long **perimeter wall** has survived intact, as has its most prominent feature, the **flag tower**, or Cot Co (also known as Ky Dai, "the King's Knight"), which dominates the southern battlements. The tower is in fact three squat, brick terraces topped with a flagpole first erected in 1807. Ten gates pierce the citadel wall, and just inside the Ngan Gate, to the east of the flag tower, is a parade ground flanked by the nine **sacred cannons**, which were cast in the early nineteenth century. They represent the four seasons and five ritual elements of earth, fire, metal, wood and water.

The Imperial City

Daily 8am–5pm • 150,000d, combination ticket with mausoleums available (see box, p.290)

A second moat and defensive wall inside the citadel guard the **Imperial City**, which follows the same symmetrical layout as Beijing's Forbidden City – though oriented northwest–southeast, rather than north–south. The Vietnamese version, popularly known as *Dai Noi* ("the Great Enclosure"), has four gates – one in each wall – though by far the most impressive is south-facing **Ngo Mon**, the Imperial City's principal entrance. In its heyday the complex must have been truly awe-inspiring, a place of glazed yellow and green roof tiles, pavilions of rich red and gilded lacquer, and lotus-filled ponds – all surveyed by the emperor with his entourage of haughty mandarins. However, many of its buildings were badly neglected even before the battle for Hue raged through the Imperial City during Tet 1968, and by 1975 a mere twenty out of the original 148 were left standing among the vegetable plots. Some are in the midst of extensive restorations, and those which have been completed are stunning – notably **Thai Hoa Palace**, the **The Mieu** complex and **Dien Tho**. The rest of the Imperial City, especially its northern sector, is a grassed-over expanse full of birds and butterflies where you can still make out foundations and find bullet pockmarks in the plasterwork of ruined walls.

Ngo Mon Gate

In 1833 Emperor Minh Mang replaced an earlier, much less formidable gate with the present dramatic entrance-way to the Imperial City, **Ngo Mon**, considered a masterpiece of Nguyen architecture. Ngo Mon (the "Noon" or "Southwest" Gate) has five entrances: the emperor alone used the central entrance paved with stone; two smaller doorways on either side were for the civil and military mandarins, who only rated brick paving; while another pair of giant openings in the wings allowed access to the royal elephants.

Five Phoenix Watchtower

The bulk of Ngo Mon is constructed of massive stone slabs, but perched on top is an elegant pavilion called the **Five Phoenix Watchtower** as its nine roofs are said to resemble five birds in flight when viewed from above. Note that the central roof, under which the emperor passed, is covered with yellow-glazed tiles, a feature of nearly all Hue's royal roofs. Emperors used the watchtower for two major ceremonies each year: the declaration of the lunar New Year; and the announcement of the civil service exam results, depicted here in a lacquer painting. It was also in this pavilion that the last Nguyen emperor, Bao Dai, abdicated in 1945 when he handed over to the new government his symbols of power – a solid gold seal weighing ten kilos and a sheathed sword encrusted with jade.

5

Thai Hoa Palace

Walking north from Ngo Mon along the city's symmetrical axis, you pass between two square lakes and a pair of *kylin*, mythical dew-drinking animals that are harbingers of peace, to reach **Thai Hoa Palace** ("the Palace of Supreme Harmony"). Not only is this the most spectacular of Hue's palaces, its interior glowing with sumptuous red and gold lacquers, but it's also the most important since this was the throne palace, where major ceremonies such as coronations or royal birthdays took place and foreign ambassadors were received (see box opposite).

The palace was first constructed in 1805, though the present building dates from 1833 when the French floor tiles and glass door panels were added. Nevertheless, the throne room's eighty ironwood pillars, swirling with dragons and clouds, had been eaten away by termites and humidity and were on the point of collapse when rescue work began in 1991. During the restoration every column, weighing two tonnes apiece, had to be replaced manually and then painted with twelve coats of lacquer, each coat taking one month to dry.

The Forbidden Purple City

From Thai Hoa Palace the emperor would have walked north through the Great Golden Gate into the third and last enclosure, the **Forbidden Purple City**. This area, enclosed by a low wall, was reserved for residential palaces, living quarters of the state physician and nine ranks of royal concubines, plus kitchens and pleasure pavilions. Many of these buildings were destroyed in the 1947 fire, leaving most of the Forbidden Purple City as open ground, a "mood piece", haunted by fragments of wall and overgrown terraces.

The Left House and Right House

The handful of remaining buildings include the restored **Left House** and **Right House** facing each other across a courtyard immediately behind Thai Hoa Palace. Civil and military mandarins would spruce themselves up here before proceeding to an audience with the monarch. Of the two, the Right House (actually to the left – the names refer to the emperor's viewpoint) is the more complete with its ornate murals and gargantuan mirror in a gilded frame, a gift from the French to Emperor Dong Khanh.

The Royal Theatre

Northeast from the Left House is the **Royal Theatre**. Built in 1826 and restored in 2004, the opulent red-and-gold theatre hosts thirty-minute musical performances (daily 9am, 10am, 2.30pm & 3.30pm; 100,000đ).

Thai Binh Reading Pavilion

Just beyond the theatre is the **Thai Binh Reading Pavilion**, an appealing, two-tier structure surrounded by bonsai gardens. The pavilion was built by Thieu Tri and then restored by Khai Dinh, who added the kitsch mosaics. This was where the emperor came to listen to music and commune with nature, and it has once again been restored to its former splendour.

The urns and ancestral altars

The other main cluster of sights lies over in the southwest corner of the Imperial City. Aligned on a southeast–northwest axis, the procession kicks off with **Hien Lam Cac** ("Pavilion of Everlasting Clarity"), a graceful, three-storey structure with some notable woodwork, followed by the **Nine Dynastic Urns**. Considered the zenith of Hue craftsmanship, the bronze urns were cast during the reign of Minh Mang and are ornamented with scenes of mountains, rivers, rain clouds and wildlife, plus one or two stray bullet marks. Each urn is dedicated to an emperor: the middle urn, which is also the largest at 2600kg, honours Gia Long.

CEREMONIES AT THAI HOA PALACE

For state ceremonies, the emperor sat on the raised dais, wearing a golden tunic and a crown decorated with nine dragons, under a spectacular gilded canopy. He faced south across the **Esplanade of Great Salutations**, a stone-paved courtyard where the mandarins stood, civil mandarins to the left and military on the right, lined up in their appointed places beside eighteen stelae denoting the nine subdivided ranks. A French traveller in the 1920s witnessed the colourful spectacle, with "perfume-bearers in royal-blue, fan-bearers in sky-blue waving enormous yellow feather fans, musicians and guardsmen and ranks of mandarins in their curious hats and gorgeous, purple-embroidered dragons, kow-towing down, down on their noses amid clouds of incense – and all in a setting of blood-red lacquer scrawled with gold".

The urns stand across the courtyard from the long, low building of **The Mieu**, the Nguyens' dynastic temple erected in 1822 by Minh Mang to worship his father. Since then, **ancestral altars** have been added for each emperor in turn, except Duc Duc and Hiep Hoa, who reigned only briefly, and Bao Dai who died in exile in 1997; the three anti-French sovereigns – Ham Nghi, Thanh Thai and Duy Tan – had to wait until after Independence in 1954 for theirs. Take a look inside to see the line of altar tables, most sporting a portrait or photo of the monarch.

Hung Mieu

Outside The Mieu's west door, beside a 170-year-old pine tree trained in the shape of a flying dragon, a path leads north into the next compound and **Hung Mieu**. This temple is dedicated to the Nguyen ancestors and specifically to the parents of Gia Long, and is distinguished by its fine carving.

Dien Tho

Over in the northeastern side of the Imperial City, **Dien Tho**, the queen mother's residence, is worth a look. Built in a mix of Vietnamese and French architectural styles, the palace later served as Bao Dai's private residence, and the downstairs reception rooms are now set out with period furniture, echoing the photos of the palace in use in the 1930s.

Museum of Royal Antiquities

3 Le Truc • Daily 8am–5pm • Included in the cost of entrance to the Imperial City (see p.277)

From the eastern exit of the Imperial City (via Hien Nhon Gate – the "Gate of Humanity") it's a short walk to the **Museum of Royal Antiquities** (also known as the Imperial Museum or the Royal Fine Arts Museum), which boasts an interesting display of former royal paraphernalia, though there is little information about the exhibits. Objects on display include porcelain, costumes and personal items of the Nguyen emperors, but visitors are more likely to be impressed by the **Long An Palace** in which the museum is housed, with its forest of hardwood pillars, which was restored and reopened in 2012.

Dong Ba Market

Tran Hung Dao

If crossing the Perfume River on Trang Thien Bridge, you'll pass **Dong Ba Market**, a rambling covered market at the southeast corner of the citadel, and one of the epicentres of Hue's commercial life. Fruit, fish and vegetable vendors overflow into the surrounding spaces, while in the downstairs hall you'll find Hue's contribution to the world of fashion, the *non bai tho*, or **poem hat**. These look just like the normal conical hat but have a stencil, traditionally of a romantic poem, inserted between the palm fronds – only visible when held up to the light.

5

Phu Cat district

Hue's civilian and merchant quarter grew up to the east of the citadel on a triangular island now divided into **Phu Cat**, Phu Hiep and Phu Hau districts. This part of town still boasts some single-storey, wood and red-tiled houses as well as more ornate, colonial-era shophouses. The area was once home to Hue's Chinese community, and five **assembly halls** still stand along Chi Lang. Old trees shade the Dong Ba Canal on the island's southwestern side, where Bach Dang was the site of antigovernment demonstrations in the 1960s, centred around **Dieu De Pagoda**.

Chua Ong Assembly Hall

319 Chi Lang • Free

Chinese immigrants to Hue settled in five congregations around their separate **assembly halls**, of which the most interesting is **Chua Ong**. Founded by the Phuoc Kien (Fujian) community in the mid-1800s and rebuilt on several occasions, including after Viet Cong mortars hit a US munitions boat on the river nearby in 1968 and destroyed the pagoda plus surrounding houses. Surprisingly, there's no Buddha on the main altar but instead several doctors of medicine, along with General Quan Cong to the right and Thien Hau to the left, both protectors of sailors. The story goes that Quan Cong sat on the main altar until a devastating cholera epidemic in 1918 when he was displaced by the doctors, and the outbreak ended soon after.

Chieu Ung Assembly Hall

223 Chi Lang • Free

Of the other halls, **Chieu Ung** is worth dropping into. The gilded altar displays some skilled carpentry. This pagoda was also founded in the nineteenth century by ethnic Chinese from Hainan, and has been rebuilt at least twice since.

The European City

Although the French became the de facto rulers of Vietnam after 1884, they left the emperors in the citadel and settled their administration over the water on the south bank of the Perfume River. The main artery of the **European City** was riverside Le Loi where the French Resident's office stood (now *La Residence* hotel), together with other important buildings such as **Quoc Hoc High School** and the *Frères Morin* hotel (now the *Saigon Morin*). Residential streets spread out south of the river as far as the Phu Cam Canal, and are linked to the citadel by Clemenceau Bridge, renamed Trang Tien Bridge after 1954, and the Bach Ho (White Tiger) Bridge, completed in 2012. Having said all this, the district's only major sight is the **Ho Chi Minh Museum**, not just the obligatory gesture in this case, as Ho did spend much of his childhood in Hue.

REVOLUTIONARY EDUCATION

Ho Chi Minh was the most famous student to attend **Quoc Hoc High School**, which stands almost opposite his museum on Le Loi. The school was founded in 1896 as the National College, dedicated to the education of royal princes and future administrators who learnt the history of their European "motherland" – all in French until 1945. Ho studied here for at least a year before being expelled for taking part in antigovernment demonstrations. Other revolutionary names that appear on the roster are Prime Minister Pham Van Dong, General Giap and Party Secretary Le Duan, while former president of South Vietnam Ngo Dinh Diem was also a student. Even during the 1960s Quoc Hoc had a justly earned reputation for breeding dissident intellectuals, and after reunification in 1975 some staff were sent for "re-education". Quoc Hoc is still a functioning school today – and, in fact, one of the most prestigious in the whole land.

The Ho Chi Minh Museum

7 Le Loi • Tues–Sun 7.30–11am & 2–4.30pm • Free

Ho Chi Minh spent ten years at school in Hue (1895–1901 and 1906–1909) where his father worked as a civil mandarin. The **Ho Chi Minh Museum** presents these years in the context of the anti-French struggle and then takes the story on to 1960 peace protests in Hue and reunification. The most interesting material consists of family photos and glimpses of early twentieth-century Hue, but if you've visited a Ho Chi Minh Museum elsewhere on your travels, you're unlikely to find anything new here.

Redemptorist Church

Nguyen Hue • Dawn to dusk • Free

The extraordinary, tiered spire of the **Redemptorist Church** dominates the city's southern horizon with its improbable blend of Gothic and Cubism, created by a local architect in the late 1950s. The church caters to some of Hue's twenty thousand Catholics and is interesting to view in passing, though the interior is less striking.

ARRIVAL AND DEPARTURE   HUE

By plane Phu Bai Airport lies 15km southeast of the city centre. Arriving flights are met by a bus (60,000đ), which takes you to central hotels, and by metered taxis (around 300,000đ). The Vietnam Airlines office is at 23 Nguyen Van Cu (☎0234 382 4709).

Destinations Hanoi (6 daily; 1hr 10min); Ho Chi Minh City (8 daily; 1hr 20min).

By train The station lies about 1.5km from the centre of town at the far western end of Le Loi. Note that trains out of Hue get booked up, especially sleepers to Ho Chi Minh City and Hanoi, so make onward travel arrangements as early as possible (ticket office daily 7–11.30am & 1.30–8pm).

Destinations Da Nang (6 daily; 2hr 20min–3hr); Dong Ha (5 daily; 1hr–1hr 20min); Dong Hoi (6 daily; 2hr 40min–3hr 30min); Hanoi (6 daily; 13–16hr); Ho Chi Minh City (6 daily; 19–24hr); Nha Trang (6 daily; 11hr 20min–15hr); Ninh Binh (3 daily; 14hr).

By bus Public buses arrive at one of two stations – Phia Nam, 2km south of the city centre in An Cuu, for links with the south; and Phia Bac, off the citadel's northwest corner, for links with the north. It's usually far less hassle to book an open-tour bus through your hotel or a tour office.

Destinations Da Nang (3hr); Dong Ha (2hr 30min); Dong Hoi (5hr); Hoi An (4hr); Phong Nha (4hr 30min–6hr); Savannakhet, Laos (10hr).

GETTING AROUND

By bicycle Hue becomes crowded during rush hour (7–9am & 4–6pm), but generally the most enjoyable way of getting around is by bicycle. Most hotels and guesthouses,

plus a few cafés, offer bike rental (from $2/day).

By taxi Two reputable taxi companies are Mai Linh Taxi (☎0234 389 8989) and Yellow Taxi (☎0234 379 7979).

INFORMATION AND TOURS

Tourist information The best bet for tourist information is either your hotel or one of the tour agents; they all hand out photocopied maps, but for a detailed city plan try the big hotels and bookstalls on Le Loi. Tours by motorbike and car can be arranged to Hue's mausoleums (see box, p.270).

Café on Thu Wheels 3/34 Nguyen Tri Phuong, ☎0234 383 2241, ✉minhthuhue@yahoo.com. Laidback backpacker bar-restaurant (see p.285) that organizes inexpensive tours and transfers by motorbike or car.

I love Hue Tour 31 Doi Cung ☎0169 432 3030, ⊛ilovehuetour.com. Founded in 2014 to empower

women in the community, tours of the city include street food, photography or even karaoke. Upbeat and informative, you explore on foot or ride pillion with a lady biker. Tours from $28.

Le Family Riders 44 Dang Thai Tan ☎0168 926 6792, ⊛lefamilyriders.com. Recommended for guided motorcycle tours around Hue ($10–20) and further afield to the DMZ or over the Hai Van Pass to Hoi An (from $50/day).

The Sinh Tourist 37 Nguyyn Thai Hoc ☎0234 382 3309, ⊛thesinhtourist.vn. Arranges Perfume River boat trips and DMZ tours, as well as tickets for open-tour buses, including to Savannakhet in Laos.

ACCOMMODATION

Most accommodation in Hue is located south of the Perfume River; top-class establishments overlook the river, while budget hotels and guesthouses are scattered in the streets behind, particularly the backpacker enclaves around Pham Ngu Lao and Nguyen Tri Phuong.

5

Asia Hotel 17 Pham Ngu Lao ☎0234 383 0283, ⓦasiahotel.com.vn; map p.275. Tall boutique-style hotel, with attractive, generously proportioned rooms and breakfasts with a view. There's also a tiny pool, as well as sauna facilities. Book online for some healthy discounts. $75

Binh Minh Sunrise 36 Nguyen Tri Phuong ☎0234 382 5526, ⓦbinhminhhue.com; map p.275. Bright, welcoming hotel in a great location with a range of clean, homely rooms, some with balconies looking towards the mountains. A popular and good-value option, though rooms at the front will be noisy; it's worth an extra $5–10 for the better ones. $15

Hue Backpackers 10 Pham Ngu Lao ☎0234 382 6567, ⓦvietnambackpackerhostels.com; map p.275. All dorms and private rooms are en suite, with a/c and queen-sized beds on request. The ground-floor common area is always buzzing – especially in the evening (happy hour 5–6pm – and there's loads of activities on offer. Dorms $8, doubles $20

★**Hue Nino Hotel** 14 Nguyen Cong Tru ☎0234 625 2171, ⓦhueninohotel.com; map p.275. Superb value, friendly staff and mouthwatering breakfasts at this small hotel, which has become a real favourite with budget travellers to the city. Staff have a habit of welcoming you back with a glass of juice – even if you've just popped to the shops. $18

Imperial Hotel 8 Hung Vuong ☎0234 388 2222, ⓦimperial-hotel.com.vn; map p.275. The first five-star hotel in Hue dominates the skyline near the Perfume River; plush carpets lead the way to suitably well-appointed rooms, with fabulous views from the upper floors. The complex also includes a fitness centre, swimming pool and classy restaurant. Ask about discounts – the place often feels near-empty. $120

★**La Residence** 5 Le Loi ☎0234 383 7475, ⓦla-residence-hue.com; map p.275. Formerly the French governor's residence (hence the name), and overlooking the Perfume River, this M Gallery hotel blends early twentieth-century Art Deco design with excellent services. There's a palpable colonial air to the place, one best savoured with a cocktail by the riverside pool. $135

Moonlight 20 Pham Ngu Lao ☎0234 397 9797, ⓦmoonlighthue.com; map p.275. With an ideal location on Pham Ngu Lao and an enthusiastic staff, this place can do no wrong. Rooms are smallish but luxuriously furnished, some have balconies and many enjoy great views. There's a swimming pool and gym on the 5th floor, buffet breakfast is served on the 14th floor, and a hip bar, *Sirius*, is on the fifteenth floor. $70

Orchid Hotel 30a Chu Van An ☎0234 383 1177, ⓦorchidhotel.com.vn; map p.275. A strong contender for the friendliest hotel staff in the city – smiling attendants usher their customers to superbly stylish rooms, decorated with orchid petals and other attractive flourishes. Lastly, the breakfasts are astonishingly good – the staff must be tired of guests singing praises morning after morning. $50

Phong Lan (Wild Orchid) 12/66 Le Loi ☎0234 3826255, ⓔphonglanhue@gmail.com; map p.275. Tucked away at the end of a quiet cul-de-sac with several other guesthouses, this cheerful, family-run place offers pleasant, warmly decorated rooms, and pretty balconies hung with orchids. $14

Saigon Morin 30 Le Loi ☎0234 382 3526, ⓦmorinhotel.com.vn; map p.275. Hue's most famous French-era hotel has been renovated to four-star standards, but still retains some of its colonial charm, not least in the garden courtyard; swing by for a look, even if you're not staying. The rooms are a good size, if a little bland, and kitted out with all the equipment you'd expect, including minibar, bathtub and hairdryer. Facilities include a rooftop bar, two restaurants and a small pool (90,000đ to non-residents). $110

Sunny B 4/34 Nguyen Tri Phuong ☎0234 383 0145; map p.275. A wonderful place to stay – cheap, friendly and cosy. Rooms are big and bright with bamboo furnishings and the top rooms ($35) have two double beds and big balconies. If it's full, *Sunny A* and *Sunny C* are nearby with similar rooms and rates. $15

Than Thien 10 Nguyen Cong Tru ☎0234 383 4666, ⓦthanthienhotel.com.vn; map p.275. There are three types of room here – superior, deluxe and VIP – and all offer excellent value, especially the VIP rooms ($35), which are massive. All rooms have comfortable furnishings, but some of the superior rooms don't have windows, so take a look before you decide. Superior $17

EATING

If you're here for a few nights, it's worth exploring Hue's local cuisine (see box, p.284) by sampling a range of **restaurants**, both Vietnamese and colonial-style. If your visit to Hue is fleeting, you could tick off three essential Hue experiences – cuisine, *ca hue* (folk songs) and cruising on the Perfume River – all in one go. Most hotels offer such a **dinner cruise** each evening, lasting around two hours, with prices ranging around $20–40 a person. As you might expect, the quality of the boat, the food, the service and the entertainment is relative to the cost of the tour.

★**Ancient Hue** 104/47 Kim Long ☎0234 359 0356, ⓦancienthue.com.vn; map p.275. Located 2km west of the citadel, this atmospheric compound consists of five ancient wooden houses, three of which function as restaurants, one as an art gallery and one as a garden house. They serve both royal cuisine and Western fusion

5

dishes, and this is the place to go for the full "Imperial Hue" feeling. There are frequent performances of traditional music and martial arts, and cooking classes are also offered. Set menus around 250,000đ, mains 120,000–400,000đ. Daily 8am–10pm.

Bun Bo Hue 17 Ly Thuong Kiet ☎0234 382 6460; map p.275. Of all the places serving *bun bo*, this simple affair has by far the most reknown – any local will confirm this. You should definitely sample it yourself (30,000đ). Daily 6am–7.30pm.

Che Hem 29/31 Hung Vuong; map p.275. For a local speciality, there aren't as many places serving *che* as you'd expect, but this is centrally located and as tasty as you'll get. Around 10,000đ/glass. Daily 8am–9pm.

Ganesh 34 Nguyen Tri Phuong ☎0234 382 1616; map p.275. This restaurant is deservedly popular for its authentic north Indian fare, which includes a good vegetarian and *thali* selection (from 140,000đ). Daily noon–10pm.

Hanh 11 Pho Duc Chinh; map p.275. Here you'll find *banh khoai* freshly prepared throughout the day – 20,000đ will be enough for a plateful, or try a five-course meal for 100,000đ. It's a local favourite, and packed at mealtimes – many of the regulars will wonder what on earth you're doing on their turf. Daily 7am–9.30pm.

Hot Tuna 37 Vo Thi Sau ☎0234 361 6464; map p.275. A great combination of welcoming atmosphere and top-value food, covering a huge range of Vietnamese and Western dishes. Good for breakfasts, burgers (60,000đ) and hotpots. Daily 8am–11pm.

La Boulangerie Française 46 Nguyen Tri Phuong ☎0234 383 7437; map p.275. A French charity runs this café and bakery school for local orphans in the hope that they gain employment after graduation. They sell an array of light and delicious French pastries (starting at around 20,000đ), perfect for breakfast or packed away for long boat rides. A little balcony terrace makes for a nice place to relax. Daily 7am–8.30pm.

La Carambole 19 Pham Ngu Lao ☎0234 381 0491; map p.275. The original branch of foreign-owned *Les Jardins de la Carambole* (see below) still serves up great food, though service is erratic. Prices are surprisingly reasonable (mains 100,000đ and up), and the menu is full of tempting French goodies hard to find in Vietnam – cheese platters, quiche, banana flambé and so on. Daily 7am–11pm.

Lac Thien 6 Dinh Tien Hoang ☎0234 352 4674; map p.275. Restaurant run by a deaf-mute family who communicate by sign language. The food is cheap but pretty tasty, especially the Hue staples (see box below); most plump for the *banh khoai* (40,000đ), served with a mountain of leaves and lashings of peanut sauce. Daily 10am–9.30pm.

Les Jardins de la Carambole 32 Dang Tran Con ☎0234 354 8815, ⊛lesjardinsdelacarambole.com; map p.275. This upscale version of *La Carambole* (see

HUE SPECIALITY FOODS

One good argument for staying in Hue an extra couple of days is its many **speciality foods**, best sampled at local stalls and street kitchens.

BANH BEO

Order this afternoon dish and you get a whole trayful of individual plates, each containing a small amount of steamed rice-flour dough topped with spices, shrimp flakes and a morsel of pork crackling; add a little sweetened *nuoc mam* sauce to each dish and tuck in with a teaspoon. *Banh nam*, or *banh lam*, is a similar idea but spread thinly in an oblong, steamed in a banana leaf and eaten with rich *nuoc mam* sauce. Manioc flour is used instead of rice for *banh loc*, making a translucent parcel of whole shrimps, sliced pork and spices steamed in a banana leaf, but this time the *nuoc mam* is pepped up with a dash of chilli. Finally, *ram it* consists of two small dollops of sticky rice-flour dough, one fried and one steamed, to dip in a spicy sauce. You'll find good places in which to sample these dishes all over the city.

BANH KHOAI

Probably the most famous Hue dish, a small, crispy yellow pancake made of egg and rice flour, fried up with shrimp, pork and bean sprouts and eaten with a special peanut and sesame sauce (*nuoc leo*), plus a vegetable accompaniment of star fruit, green banana, lettuce and mint. Amazingly, it's even more delicious than it sounds.

BUN BO

Spicy rice-noodle beef soup flavoured with citronella, shrimp and basil; also called *bun ga* with chicken, or *bun bo gio heo* with beef and pork.

CHE

A refreshing drink made from green bean and coconut (*che xanh dua*), fruit (*chetrai cay*) or, if you're lucky, lotus seed (*che hat sen*).

THE HUE FESTIVAL

Since 1992, the city of Hue has held a biennial **nine-day-long festival** that features top musicians and artists not only from Vietnam, but also from around the world. For this spectacular event, the city's main attractions and bridges are illuminated and key events include theatrical and street performances, royal banquets and fashion parades. It's extremely photogenic though a bit crowded as all the city's inhabitants come out to join in. The event usually takes place between April and June in even-numbered years (2018, 2020, etc). For more information visit ⊚ huefestival.com.

opposite) is located in a gorgeous colonial villa on a leafy lane to the west of the citadel, and French owner Christian goes out of his way to please guests. There's a good range of French, Mediterranean and Vietnamese dishes; try the beef bourguignon (240,000đ) and the niçoise salad (120,000đ). Daily 7am–11pm.

Nina's Cafe 16/134 Nguyen Tri Phuong ☎ 0234 383 8636; map p.275. Simple, cheap and friendly affair tucked away on a little alley, with wooden chairs arrayed around a small covered courtyard. It's great for spring rolls, soups, meat and vegetarian dishes (around 40,000–60,000đ), and set menus at 140,000–200,000đ. Daily 7.30am–10.30pm.

Ta Ke 34 Tran Cao Van ☎ 0234 384 8262; map p.275. This unpretentious Japanese restaurant offers fantastic-value meals in a central location – the sushi and tempura dishes (around 70,000đ) are particularly recommended. Daily 10.30am–10pm.

Tropical Garden 27 Chu Van An ☎ 0234 384 7143; map p.275. Choose to dine in the bamboo garden or a/c interior of this upscale restaurant, which lays on perform-ances of traditional music each evening for tour groups. A choice of Hue specialities plus set menus (from 240,000đ) and plenty of seafood. Daily 10am–10pm.

DRINKING AND NIGHTLIFE

Brown Eyes 56 Chu Van An ☎ 0234 382 7494; map p.275. "Red Eyes" would be a more appropriate name for this bar – many a sozzled backpacker has stumbled from its doors into the light of early morning. Staff are fun, and there's a pool table to test your focus. Daily 5pm–late.

Café on Thu Wheels 3/34 Nguyen Tri Phuong ☎ 0234 383 2241; map p.275. Owner Thu has moved on, but her sister is doing a decent job at this tiny café-bar, which has long been a popular backpacker pit-stop. It also runs good motorbike tours around Hue (see p.281). Daily 7.30am–10pm.

DMZ Bar 60 Le Loi ☎ 0234 382 3414, ⊚ dmz.com.vn; map p.275. Exactly what you'd expect of a Western bar – pool table, cold beers, Western grub and occasional live music. The downstairs bar can get raucous, while the upstairs dining area offers excellent people-watching from the small balcony. Serves food until midnight. Daily 7am–2.30pm.

Why Not Bar? 46 Pham Ngu Lao ☎ 0234 382 4793, ⊚ whynot.com.vn; map p.275. Western food (including some good veggie pizzas), football on the big screen, a pool table, good deals on beer and streetside seating are the draws at this welcoming hostel-bar. Daily 8am–late.

DIRECTORY

Banks and exchange Vietcombank, 78 Hung Vuong, exchanges cash and has a 24hr ATM outside. There's also an exchange bureau outside the *Saigon Morin* hotel, which is open longer hours (Mon–Sat 7am–10pm), with a 24hr ATM. **Hospital** Hue Central Hospital, 16 Le Loi ☎ 0234 382 2325.

Pharmacies You'll find well-stocked pharmacies on Ngo Quyen and behind the hospital on Le Loi. **Post office** The GPO occupies a grand building at 8 Hoang Hoa Tham, and also has internet facilities (Mon–Sat 7am–7pm).

Around Hue

For the most part the Nguyen emperors lived their lives within Hue's citadel walls, but on certain occasions they emerged to participate in important rituals at symbolic locations around the city. Today these places are of interest more for their history than anything much to see on the ground, though the mouldering **Royal Arena** still hints at past spectacles. A visit to at least a couple of the **Royal Mausoleums**, however, is not to be missed – it's in these eclectic architectural confections in the hills to the south of Hue that the spirit of the Nguyen emperors lives on. Taking a boat along the **Perfume**

5

River to get to the best mausoleums also offers the chance to stop off at the **Thien Mu Pagoda** and **Hon Chen Temple** on the way (see box, p.289).

Thuan An beach is a short distance away from the city, and makes a fun contrast to slogging round historic monuments, especially on a sunny day. Though it's tempting to go by bike, the traffic can be heavy. A better bike ride is east of town to the **Thanh Toan Covered Bridge**, surrounded by paddy fields and rural scenes. Further afield, one of the most popular excursions from Hue is a whirlwind day-trip round the **DMZ** (see p.295). **Bach Ma National Park** (see p.272) is also within striking distance.

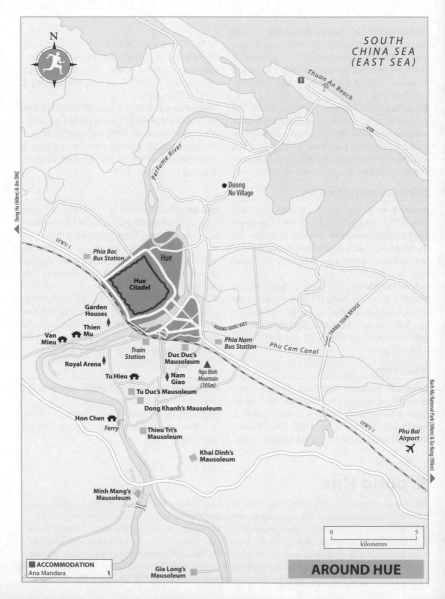

BOAT TRIPS ON THE PERFUME RIVER

A number of people still live in boats on the **Perfume River** and the waterways of Hue, such as the Dong Ba and Phu Cam canals, despite government efforts to settle them elsewhere. It's possible to join them, if only temporarily, by taking a **boat trip**, puttering about in front of the citadel on a misty Hue morning, watching the slow bustle of river life.

The standard day-long boat trip takes you to **Thien Mu Pagoda**, **Hon Chen Temple** and the most rewarding mausoleums, usually those of **Tu Duc** and **Minh Mang**, from where you return by bus. However, if you want to visit some of the others or spend more time exploring, it's usually possible to take a bicycle on the boat and cycle back to Hue, though double-check this when you book the trip.

Most tour operators (see p.281) and hotels offer river tours for about $25 per boat for a group of ten. However, all entrance fees are extra, which can work out costly at 80,000đ per mausoleum. If you'd rather do it independently, practise your bargaining skills at the boat wharf beside the Trang Tien Bridge.

West along the Perfume River

Hug the north bank of the Perfume River west of the citadel and you'll stumble across a few interesting sights, including the pagodas of **Thien Mu** and **Van Mieu**, the traditional garden houses of **Kim Long village**, and the temple of **Hon Chen**.

These sights are most easily covered on a **boat tour** (see box above), but all bar Hon Chen can be visited on an easy **bike ride** from the centre of Hue (6km; 30min), crossing the river on the new Bach Ho Bridge. If you've got time, note there is a pleasant cycle ride on from Van Mieu (see p.288) along an empty country lane beside the river.

The garden houses

Located on the north bank of the river to the southwest of the citadel is **Kim Long** village, a peaceful area of quiet lanes and canals where in the late nineteenth century, mandarins and other Imperial officials built their **houses**, surrounded by lush gardens. Some of these houses are strung along Phu Mong lane, which heads north from the riverbank just before 86 Kim Long. There is a wonderfully tranquil atmosphere along the shady lane and you can glimpse some impressive buildings, though most are closed to the public. One exception is the atmospheric restaurant *Ancient Hue* (see p.282).

An Hien

58 Nguyen Phuc Nguyen • Daily 7am–5pm • 20,000đ

One place worth visiting to get an idea of a **typical garden house** is on Kim Long's main road at **An Hien**, where there's a caretaker on duty to take your money, but no guide to show you round. Built in the late nineteenth century, An Hien has all the classical traits of a garden house – a grand archway at the entrance, a long, shaded approach path, and a brick wall concealing the main entrance, behind which is an ornamental pond. A large orchard of fruit trees surrounds the house, which features a family altar, sturdy wooden columns and beautifully carved doors.

Thien Mu Pagoda

3km west of the citadel • Dawn to dusk • Free • Best reached by bicycle or xe om (around 60,000đ return including waiting time), or as part of a boat tour

The seven-storey **Thien Mu Pagoda** ("Pagoda of the Celestial Lady") is possibly Hue's most photographed structure. In 1601 Lord Nguyen Hoang left Hanoi to govern the southern territories. Upon arriving at the Perfume River he met an elderly woman who told him to walk east along the river carrying a smouldering incense stick and to build his city where the incense stopped burning. Later Lord Hoang erected a pagoda in gratitude to the lady, whom he believed to be a messenger from the gods, on the site where they met. The pagoda was founded in 1601, making it the oldest in Hue.

5

During the 1930s and 1940s Thien Mu was already renowned as a centre of Buddhist opposition to colonialism, and then in 1963 it became instantly famous when one of its monks, the Venerable **Thich Quang Duc**, burned himself to death in Saigon, in protest at the excesses of President Diem's regime (see box, p.79); the powder-blue Austin car he drove down in is now on display just behind the main building, with a copy of the famous photograph that shocked the world.

Despite its turbulent history, the pagoda is a peaceful place where the breezy, pine-shaded terrace affords wide views over the Perfume River. Approaching by either road or river you can't miss the octagonal, seven-tier brick **stupa**, built by Emperor Thieu Tri in the 1840s; each tier represents one of Buddha's incarnations on earth. Two **pavilions**, one on each side, shelter a huge bell, cast in 1710, weighing over 2000kg and said to be audible in the city, and a large stele erected in 1715 to record the history of Buddhism in Hue.

Van Mieu Pagoda

1km further on from Thien Mu Pagoda, and 4km from the city centre • Dawn to dusk • Free • Xe om from Hue about 80,000đ return

Confucianism had been the principal state religion in Vietnam since the eleventh century and the Nguyens were a particularly traditional dynasty. Early in his reign, in1808 Gia Long dedicated a national temple to Confucius, known as **Van Mieu** or Van Thanh (the "Temple of Literature"), to replace that in Hanoi. Nothing much remains of the complex, beyond a collection of 32 stone stelae listing the names of 297 recipients of doctorates from exams held between 1822 and 1919. Two other stelae, under small shelters, record edicts from Minh Mang and Thieu Tri banning the "abuse of eunuchs and royal maternal relatives". You get a fine view of the royal landing stage and temple gate passing by on a Perfume River boat trip (see box, p.287).

Hon Chen Temple

9km downstream from Hue • Daily 8am–5pm • 40,000đ • Only accessible from the river; aside from boat tours, you can cross the river on a sampan from the ferry station directly opposite the temple (see map, p.286), but don't pay until they drop you back

Beyond Van Mieu boats stop at the rocky promontory of **Hon Chen Temple**, named "Temple of the Jade Bowl" after the concave hill under which it sits. Again it's the scenery of russet temple roofs among towering trees that is memorable, though the site has been sacred since the Cham people came here to worship their divine protectress Po Nagar, whom the Vietnamese adopted as Y A Na, the Mother Goddess. Emperor Minh Mang restored Hon Chen Temple in the 1830s, but it was Dong Khanh who had a particular soft spot for the goddess after she predicted he would be emperor. He enlarged the temple in 1886, declared himself Y A Na's younger brother and is now worshipped alongside his favourite goddess in the main sanctuary, **Hue Nam**, up from the landing stage and to the right. Keep your eyes open for some unusual, smiling figurines with clasped hands in the glass cabinets here. If you can, try to time your visit for one of the temple's biannual festivals (see box opposite).

South of the river

There are a few sights on the way south to the mausoleums (bar that of Duc Duc, which sits immediately south of the city centre). Happily, all are easily accessible by bicycle.

The Royal Arena

4km southwest from central Hue • Dawn to dusk • Free • From Hue, follow Bui Thi Xuan along the Perfume River's south bank through Phuong Duc, a famous metal-casting village; each alley on the left has a sign, and Kiet 373 is the one to look for

In Imperial times, emperors amused themselves with **fights between elephants and tigers**, originally on open ground in front of the citadel. After a tiger attacked Minh Mang they were staged in the **Royal Arena**, or **Ho Quyen**, tucked away near the south bank of the Perfume River, from 1830 until the last fight in 1904. This was not entirely sport: elephants symbolized the unequalled might of the sovereign while tigers represented rebel forces, and the arena was built on the site of an old Cham fort just to underline the message of Imperial power. It was, apparently, a pretty one-sided fight which the elephant was never allowed to lose, and contemporary accounts suggest that in later years the tigers were tied to a stake and had their claws removed first.

Unfortunately, the site has not been well looked after and there's little to see here today apart from a decaying brick stadium surrounding a grassy area. If you're lucky, it might be possible to track down a guard with the keys, but this would allow you to see little more than you can glimpse through the metal gates. However, it's possible to climb a brick staircase to get a view not much different from what the emperor would have seen over a century ago.

Long Chau Dien

After they died, fighting elephants were worshipped nearby in a small temple, **Long Chau Dien**, which stands to the west of the arena, although almost completely hidden by undergrowth and with only a couple of elephant statues to see: follow the path round the arena's south side to find the temple, overlooking a small lake.

Nam Giao esplanade

At the end of Dien Bien Phu, 3km south of central Hue • Free

First and foremost in the ceremonial and religious life of the nation was **Nam Giao** ("Altar of Heaven"), where the emperor reaffirmed the legitimacy of his rule in sacred rituals, held here roughly every three years from 1807 to 1945. The ceremonies were performed on a series of three terraces, two square-shaped and one round, symbolizing heaven, earth and man in descending order. Before each occasion the monarch purified himself, keeping to a strict regime of vegetarian food and no concubines for several days. He then carried out animal sacrifices – with the assistance of some five thousand attendants – to ensure the stability of both the country and the dynasty. Re-enactments of the sacred rituals at Nam Giao take place during the biennial **Hue Festival** (see box, p.285); otherwise, there's not much to see apart from the terraces and walkways shaded by towering pine trees, but it makes a pleasant place to stroll.

Tu Hieu Pagoda

About 1km west of Nam Giao on Le Ngo Cat • Free • Xe om from Hue about 40,000đ; by bike, take the road towards Tu Duc's Mausoleum from the Nam Giao T-junction, turn right down a dirt road near the top of the hill by two tall columns announcing "Tu Hieu", then fork left to reach the pagoda's triple-arched gate

The splendid **Tu Hieu Pagoda** is buried in the pine forests west of Nam Giao. Though not the most famous pagoda in Hue, it's one of the most attractive, and it does have an Imperial link, since this is where royal eunuchs retired to and were worshipped after their deaths. The pagoda was founded in 1843 and still houses an active community of monks who extend a warm welcome to their occasional visitors. The main altar is dedicated to Sakyamuni, with the Buddhist trinity sitting up above, while a secondary shrine room behind contains altars to several famous mandarins and the eunuchs. Between the two buildings is a small courtyard festooned with orchids, and a star-fruit vine that has been here since the reign of Thanh Thai (1889–1907).

5

TOURING THE ROYAL MAUSOLEUMS

A **motorbike tour** of the mausoleums normally includes at least three of them and costs around $10–15 (check if entrance to sites is included); there are plenty of operators in Hue to choose from (see p.281) or you can hire a scooter from $8 per day. Another popular option is a Perfume River **boat trip** (see box, p.287), though with one of these you'll face a couple of longish walks.

With your own wheels – either **bicycle or motorbike** – you'll have more time to explore and won't be restricted to the three main mausoleums. A good compromise is to take a bike on board a boat and cycle back to Hue from the last stop. If you plan to visit Tu Duc, Khai Dinh and Minh Mang, you can buy a **combination ticket** at any site that also includes the Imperial City (360,000đ; valid for 2 days). Note that you'll be charged a parking fee at each site (5000đ).

The Royal Mausoleums

Unlike previous Vietnamese dynasties, which buried their kings in ancestral villages, the Nguyen built themselves magnificent **Royal Mausoleums** in the valley of the Perfume River among low, forested hills to the south of Hue. For historical reasons only seven mausoleums were built, but each one is a unique expression of the monarch's personality, usually planned in detail during his lifetime to serve as his palace in death. More than anywhere else in Hue, it's here that the Nguyen emperors excelled in achieving a harmony between the works of man and his natural surroundings. Along with the Imperial City, these constitute Hue's most rewarding sights.

The mausoleums are intoxicating places, occasionally grandiose but more often achieving an elegant simplicity, where it's easy to lose yourself wandering in the quiet gardens. However, given the entry fee for each – except on public holidays, when entry is free – you'll want to pick the ones you visit carefully. Of the seven, the contrasting mausoleums of **Tu Duc**, **Khai Dinh** and **Minh Mang** are the most attractive and best preserved, as well as being easily accessible. These are also the three covered by the boat trips, so they can get crowded (especially at weekends); don't let this put you off – but if you do want something more off the beaten track than those of **Gia Long**, **Dong Khanh** and **Thieu Tri** are worth calling in on. Finally, **Duc Duc**'s temple and mausoleum are very modest but they are the closest to Hue and still tended by members of the royal family.

The Mausoleum of Duc Duc

Daily 7am–5pm • 100,000đ • Opposite 74 Tran Phu, head down Duong Duy Tan; the mausoleum is 100m along on the right • Unoffical guides will show you around for a small donation

Three emperors are buried at the **Mausoleum of Duc Duc**, which, although it's the closest to Hue, is rarely visited. Duc Duc (ruled 1883) and his wife are buried in a walled compound, while emperors Thanh Thai (ruled 1889–1907) and Duy Tan (ruled 1907–16) are interred in a separate row of graves behind the main temple, built in 1899. Duc Duc was forced to resign in 1883 by his senior courtiers after a mere three days as emperor, and died a year later in prison, while his son, **Thanh Thai**, was also removed in 1907 after a suspected anti-French conspiracy. The French then put Thanh Thai's 8-year-old son, **Duy Tan**, on the throne, but he fled the palace nine years later amid another revolutionary plot, and was eventually exiled with his father to the French territory of Réunion in the Indian Ocean. Duy Tan died in a World War II plane crash in 1945, fighting on the side of the Allies, but Thanh Thai was allowed back to Vietnam in 1947 and died in Saigon in the 1950s. Descendants of the Imperial family still live in the temple buildings, and possess a historic collection of family photos, including some of the funeral of Thanh Thai.

5

Mausoleum of Tu Duc

7km from central Hue by road • Daily 7am–5pm • 100,000đ • It's 2km from the boat jetty to the west; walk on the dirt track, or take one of the xe om waiting on the riverbank (about 40,000đ)

With elegant pavilions and pines reflected in serene lakes, this walled, twelve-hectare **park** is the most harmonious of all the Nguyen mausoleums. This may seem quite a claim, considering their careful design, though it's not such a surprise considering the emperor in question – Tu Duc, who ruled from 1847 to 1883, longer than any other Nguyen emperor.

Entering by the southern gate, **Vu Khiem**, brick paths lead beside a lake covered in water lilies and lotus to a small three-tiered **boating pavilion** which looks across to larger **Xung Khiem Pavilion**, where Tu Duc drank wine and wrote poetry; *khiem*, meaning "modest", appears in the name of every building. From the lake, steps head up through **Khiem Cung Gate**, the middle door painted yellow for the emperor, into a second enclosure containing the main temple, **Hoa Khiem**, which Tu Duc used as an office before his death. The royal funerary tablets here are unusual in that Tu Duc's, bearing a dragon, is smaller than the phoenix-decorated tablet of the queen. Beyond is a second temple, **Luong Khiem**, which served as the royal residence, and the elegant **royal theatre**, while behind the storerooms opposite once stood the Harem, the quarters for Tu Duc's numerous concubines.

The emperor's tomb

The second group of buildings, to the north of the royal theatre, is centred on the **emperor's tomb**, preceded by the salutation court and stele-house. Tu Duc's stele, weighing twenty tonnes, is by far the largest; unusually, Tu Duc wrote his own self-critical eulogy, running to over four thousand characters, to elucidate all his difficulties. Behind the stele is a kidney-shaped pond, representing the crescent moon, and then a bronze door leading into a square enclosure where the unadorned tomb shelters behind a screen adorned with the characters for longevity. Emperor Kien Phuc, one of Tu Duc's adopted sons, is also buried here, just north of the lake.

Mausoleum of Dong Khanh

500m from Tu Duc's mausoleum • Daily 7am–5pm • 100,000đ

Dong Khanh (ruled 1885–89) was put on the throne by the French as titular head of their new protectorate. A pliant ruler with a fondness for French wine, perfume and alarm clocks, he died suddenly at the age of 25 after only three years on the throne; having never got round to planning his final resting place he was buried near the temple he dedicated to his father. As a result this is a modest, particularly well preserved countryside **mausoleum** with a rustic charm.

The mausoleum consists of **two parts**: the main temple, and then the tomb and stele in a separate, walled enclosure on a slight rise 100m to the northwest. The complex was built mostly by Dong Khanh's son, Khai Dinh, after 1889, though has been added to since.

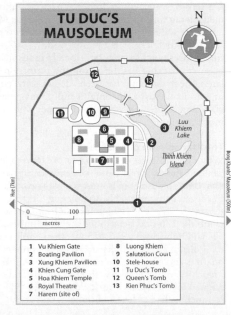

TU DUC'S
MAUSOLEUM

N

Luu
Khiem
Lake

Thinh Khiem
Island

Hue (7km)

Dong Khanh's Mausoleum (500m)

0   100
metres

1 Vu Khiem Gate	8	Luong Khiem
2 Boating Pavilion	9	Salutation Court
3 Xung Khiem Pavilion	10	Stele-house
4 Khien Cung Gate	11	Tu Duc's Tomb
5 Hoa Khiem Temple	12	Queen's Tomb
6 Royal Theatre	13	Kien Phuc's Tomb
7 Harem (site of)		

5

TU DUC

Emperor **Tu Duc** (ruled 1847–83) was a romantic poet trying to rule Vietnam at a time when the Western world was challenging the country's independence. Although he was the longest reigning of the Nguyen monarchs, he was a weak ruler who preferred to hide from the world in the lyrical pleasure gardens he created. The walled, twelve-hectare park took only three years to complete (1864–67), after which Tu Duc spent his time boating and fishing, meditating, drinking tea made from dew collected in lotus blossoms and composing some of the four thousand poems he is said to have written, besides several important philosophical and historical works. Somehow he also found time for fifty-course meals, plus 104 wives and a whole village of concubines living in the park, though – possibly due to a bout of smallpox – he fathered no children. Perhaps it's not surprising that Tu Duc was also a tyrant who pushed the three thousand workmen building his mausoleum so hard that they rebelled in 1866, and were savagely dealt with.

The main temple

The **main temple** holds most interest, especially the coloured-glass doors and windows, as well as the murals on each side-wall showing scenes of daily life. Twenty-four glass-paintings, illustrated poems of Confucian love, hang on the temple's ironwood columns and, at either end of the first row, there are two engravings of **Napoleon** and the Battle of Waterloo. The three principal altars honour Dong Khanh with his two queens to either side, while his seven concubines have a separate altar in the back room. Finally, there is an altar to Y A Na in a small side-chamber, off to the right as you enter: Dong Khanh had this built to honour her after she appeared in a dream and foretold that he would be emperor.

The Mausoleum of Thieu Tri

About 6km from central Hue • Daily 7am–5pm • 100,000đ • Head south from either Nam Giao or Tu Duc's mausoleum

Emperor **Thieu Tri** (ruled 1841–47) was the son of Minh Mang (see box, p.295) and shared his father's aversion to foreign influences – it's said he destroyed anything Western he found in the Imperial palaces – and his taste in architecture. His **mausoleum** follows the same basic pattern as Minh Mang's though without the attractive walled gardens, and is split into two sections placed side by side. As it's also smaller it took less than a year to build (1847–48), but its most distinctive feature is that it faces northwest, a traditionally inauspicious direction, and many people believed that this was the reason the country fell under the French yoke a few years later. The mausoleum has been subject to recent restoration work, and the temple is in reasonable shape. It contains numerous poems, in mother-of-pearl or painted on glass, since Thieu Tri was a prolific poet who would pen a stanza or two at a moment's notice.

The Mausoleum of Khai Dinh

10km southeast of Hue by road • Daily 7am–5pm • 100,000đ • Arriving by boat, it's a 1.5km walk, heading eastwards up a valley with a giant Quan Am statue on your right until you see the mausoleum on the opposite hillside

Khai Dinh's mausoleum is most people's favourite, with its monumental confection of European baroque, highly ornamental Sino-Vietnamese style and even elements of Cham architecture. Though it's in a beautiful setting on a wooded hill, you'll need to climb the 130-odd steps to see the most impressive aspects of the sanctuary itself.

Khai Dinh (ruled 1916–25) was the penultimate Nguyen emperor and his mausoleum is a radical departure from its predecessors, with neither gardens nor living quarters and only one main structure. Khai Dinh was also a vain man, a puppet of the French very much taken with French style and architecture, and though he only reigned for nine years it took eleven (1920–31) to complete his mausoleum, and it cost so much he had to levy additional taxes for the project.

5

> **MINH MANG**
>
> **Minh Mang**, the second Nguyen emperor (ruled 1820–41), was a capable, authoritarian monarch who was selected for his serious nature and distrust of Western religious infiltration. This revered emperor was also passionate about architecture – it was he who oversaw the completion of Hue citadel after Gia Long's death. Minh Mang's queen died at the age of 17, but despite this early loss Minh Mang managed to father 142 children with his 33 wives and 107 concubines.

The principal temple

The approach is via a series of grandiose, dragon-ornamented **stairways** leading first to the salutation courtyard, where statues of mandarins stand, and on to the stele-house. Climbing up a further four terraces brings you to the **principal temple**, built of reinforced concrete with slate roofing imported from France.

Inside, everything is decorated to the hilt, writhing with dragons and peppered with symbolic references and classic imagery such as the Four Seasons panels in the antechamber. Most of this lavish display, not as garish as it might sound, is worked in glass and porcelain mosaic – even the central canopy, which looks like fabric. A life-size gilded bronze **statue of the emperor** holding his royal sceptre sits under the canopy, while his altar table and funerary tablet are up on the mezzanine floor behind. His portrait stands on the incense table in the antechamber. Khai Dinh was a particularly flamboyant dresser and it's rumoured that he brought back a string of fairy lights from France and proceeded to wear them around the palace, twinkling, until the batteries ran out.

The Mausoleum of Minh Mang

Daily 7am–5pm • 100,000đ • From Khai Dinh's tomb, follow the road to the highway, cross over the river and turn left after 50m

Court officials took fourteen years to decide on the location for the **Mausoleum of Minh Mang** – for which the mandarin responsible was awarded two promotions; it then took only three years to build (1841–43), using ten thousand workmen. It was designed along traditional Chinese lines, with all the principal buildings symmetrical about an east–west axis. The mausoleum's stately grandeur is softened by fifteen hectares of superb landscaped gardens, almost a third of which is taken up by lakes reflecting the handsome, red-roofed pavilions.

Inside the mausoleum a processional way links the series of low mounds bearing all the main buildings. After the salutation courtyard and stele-house comes the **principal**

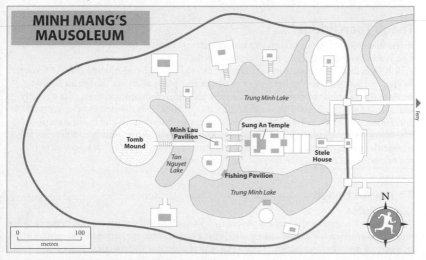

5

> ## MAUSOLEUM DESIGN
>
> It often took years to find a site with the right aesthetic requirements that would also satisfy the court cosmologists charged with interpreting the underlying supernatural forces. Artificial lakes, waterfalls and hills were added to improve the geomantic qualities of the location, at the same time creating picturesque, almost romantic, **garden settings** for the mausoleums, of which the finest examples are those of Tu Duc and Minh Mang.
>
> Though details vary, all the mausoleums consist of three elements: a **temple** dedicated to the worship of the deceased emperor and his queen; a large, stone **stele** recording his biographical details and a history of his reign, usually written by his successor; and the royal **tomb** itself at the highest spot, enclosed within a wall and a heavy, securely fastened door. Traditionally the burial place was kept secret as a measure against grave-robbers and enemies of the state, and in extreme cases all those who had been involved in the burial were killed immediately afterwards.

temple (Sung An), where Minh Mang and his queen are worshipped. Continuing west you reach **Minh Lau**, the elegant, two-storey "Pavilion of Pure Light" standing among clouds of frangipani trees, symbols of longevity; beyond, two stone gardens trace the Chinese character for long life. From here the ceremonial pathway crosses a crescent lake and ends at the circular burial mound.

The Mausoleum of Gia Long
16km south of Hue • Daily 7am–5pm • 100,000đ • Best reached by sampan from the jetty near Minh Mang's mausoleum or by road via the bridge from Minh Mang's mausoleum

As the first Nguyen ruler, **Gia Long** (ruled 1802–20) had his pick of the sites, and he chose an immense natural park 16km from Hue on the left bank of the Perfume River. Unfortunately his **mausoleum** – begun in 1814 and completed shortly after his death in 1820 – was badly damaged during the American War, but recent restoration work has revealed some fine carving, and it's worth visiting the double tomb with pitched roofs housing Gia Long and his wife. This is the least-visited of Hue's mausoleums and is recommended for the boat trip and the peaceful stroll through sandy pine forest, though some visitors complain of attracting a convoy of persistent soft-drink sellers for the duration of the 2km walk. You approach the complex from the north to find the main temple, tomb and stele-house all aligned on a horizontal axis, looking south across a lake towards Thien Tho Mountain.

Thanh Toan Bridge
6km east of Hue • A pleasant bike ride, though can be tricky to find; head east on Truong Chin, which branches east off of Hung Vuong to the south of the city centre, then cross a ring road and continue east for 3km

Thanh Toan Bridge is a beautiful structure that will remind you of the Japanese Covered Bridge in Hoi An if you've been there, though this place is, as yet, not at all touristy. Built in 1776 to honour a mandarin's wife who came from around here, it is a sturdy structure of wood pillars with ceramic tiles on the roof. It is divided into seven sections and features an altar to **Tran Thi Dao**, the woman in question, in the middle section. The other six sections are fitted with deep wooden seats, shiny with use, where locals dangle their legs over the stream and daydream. It's in a very rural area, so you're likely to see duck herders and rice farmers along the way.

Thuan An beach
15km northeast of Hue

Though Hue is one of the wettest places in Vietnam, it can get pretty hot between May and August, when it's worth calling a halt for a day to historic monument sightseeing in order to head for the **beach**. Thuan An is probably not the prettiest you've ever seen, but none too bad either, and good enough for *Ana Mandara* (see below) to build a five-star resort on. There's a broad swathe of sand and though there's little shade, there are plenty of thatched beach stalls selling food and drinks. The sea is quite clear as a rule and outside the months of September to April it's good for swimming. It gets crowded with locals at weekends and on public holidays.

The southern peninsula

With your own transport it's worth exploring the **peninsula south of Thuan An**, where Highway 49B snakes down to meet up with Highway 1 about 50km to the south, after crossing the Cua Hai Lagoon on a long bridge. The road is lined with simple houses and shops but also with extremely elaborate **tombs** and family temples; it seems that the locals have inherited the Nguyen lords' lifelong obsession with preparing for death. At times it feels like you're driving through an endless cemetery, and the tombs are mostly decorated in eye-catching combinations of pastel colours such as lilac, primrose, sky blue and soft pink.

ARRIVAL AND ACCOMMODATION	**THUAN AN BEACH**

By bike or motorbike The easiest way to get to Thuan An beach is by rented motorbike or bicycle, though you need to watch out for heavy traffic. Follow Le Loi north out of town and keep going.

Ana Mandara Thuan An beach ☎0234 398 3333, Ⓦanamandarahue-resort.com; map p.286. *Ana*

Mandara runs some of Vietnam's most luxurious hotels, and this is no exception. Villas occupy an enormous 275 square metres each, are lavishly furnished and come with swimming pools. Facilities include several dining and drinking options, a pool and spa, a kids' club and library. **$120**

The DMZ and around

During the American War, **Quang Tri** and **Quang Binh**, the two provinces either side of the **DMZ** (see box, p.298), were the most heavily bombed and saw the highest casualties – civilian and military, American and Vietnamese. Names made infamous in 1960s and 1970s America have been perpetuated in countless films and memoirs: Con Thien, the Rockpile, Hamburger Hill and Khe Sanh. For some people the DMZ will be what draws them to Vietnam, the end of a long and difficult pilgrimage; for others it will be a bleak, sometimes beautiful, place where there's nothing particular to see but where it's hard not to respond to the sense of enormous desolation.

  North of the DMZ is one of the region's main attractions – **the tunnels of Vinh Moc**, where villages created deep underground during the American War have been preserved. South of the Hien Luong Bridge over **Ben Hai River** are **Truong Son Cemetery** and the firebases of **Doc Mieu** and **Con Thien**. The area's other notable wartime locations lie west and south of **Dong Ha**, which is the closest town to the DMZ. While it's not possible to cover everything in a day, the most interesting of the places are included on **organized tours** from Dong Ha or Hue (see p.297); if you have limited time then the Vinh Moc tunnels should be high on your list, along with a drive up Highway 9 to **Khe Sanh**, both for the scenery en route and the sobering battleground itself. Note that as most sites are unmarked and unremarkable to look at, a knowledgeable local guide is indispensable. More importantly, guides know which paths are safe; in the last decade, local farmers have still occasionally been killed or injured by **unexploded ordnance** in this area.

The Vinh Moc tunnels

15km east of Ho Xa • Daily 7am–5pm • 40,000đ • 7km north of the Ben Hai River and 28km from Dong Ha is the township of Ho Xa, and the tunnels are signposted from here

Vinh Moc comprises an amazing **complex of tunnels** where over a thousand people sheltered during the worst American bombardments (see box, p.297). A section has

5

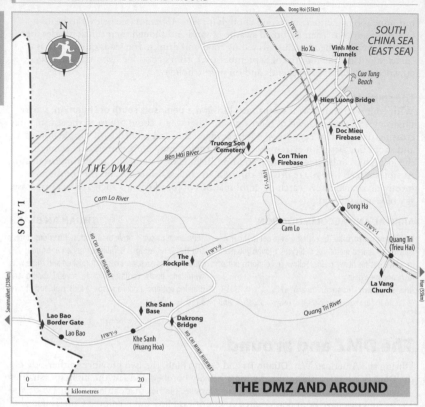

Dong Hoi (55km)

SOUTH
CHINA SEA
(EAST SEA)

N

Ho Xa

Vinh Moc
Tunnels

Cua Tung
Beach

Hien Luong Bridge

Doc Mieu
Firebase

Truong Son
Cemetery

Ben Hai River

Con Thien
Firebase

THE DMZ

Cam Lo River

L A O S

HO CHI MINH HIGHWAY

Dong Ha

Cam Lo

Quang Tri
(Trieu Hai)

HWY-9

The
Rockpile

La Vang
Church

Khe Sanh
Base

Quang Tri River

Lao Bao
Border Gate

Dakrong
Bridge

Lao Bao

HWY-9

Khe Sanh
(Huang Hoa)

HO CHI MINH HIGHWAY

Savannakhet (230m)

Hue (55km)

0   20

kilometres

THE DMZ AND AROUND

been restored and opened to visitors as a powerful tribute to the villagers' courage and
tenacity, with a small on-site **museum** providing background information.

The tunnels are on three levels at 10, 15 and 20–23m deep and to explore them
properly you'll need around one hour – although these tunnels are bigger than those of
Cu Chi (the ceiling is almost 2m high in places) a visit is not recommended for anyone
claustrophobic. The underground village was built with good ventilation, freshwater
wells and, eventually, a generator and lights; it was also equipped with a school, clinics
and a maternity room where seventeen children were born. Each family was allocated a
tiny cavern, the four-person space being barely larger than a single bed, and villagers
were only able to emerge at night.

Ben Hai River

Lying virtually on the Seventeenth Parallel is the **Ben Hai River** that once divided
north and south. You will see two bridges, the newly built one, which is open to
traffic, and the unused **Hien Luong Bridge** that runs parallel to it. Until it was
destroyed in 1967, the original Hien Luong Bridge was painted half red and half
yellow as a vivid reminder that this was a physical and ideological boundary
separating the two Vietnams. The reconstructed iron-girder bridge, now painted blue
and yellow, officially reopened in 1975 as a symbol of reunification. On the north
bank of the river, the Ben Hai River Museum (daily 7am–5pm; 20,000đ) features
some striking images of the region during wartime, as well as a few remnants such as
a US pilot's helmet, some bombs and guns. On the south bank there is a grand war

5

THE HISTORY OF THE VINH MOC TUNNELS

When American bombing raids north of the DMZ intensified in 1966 the inhabitants of Vinh Linh District began digging down into the red laterite soils, excavating more than **fifty tunnels** over the next two years. Although they were also used by North Vietnamese soldiers, the tunnels were primarily built to shelter a largely civilian population who worked the supply route from the Con Co Islands lying 28km offshore. Five tunnels belonged to **Vinh Moc**, a village located right on the coast where for two years 250 people dug more than 2km of tunnel, which housed all six hundred villagers over varying periods from early 1967 until 1969, when half decamped north to the relative safety of Nghe An province. In 1972, the villagers of Vinh Moc were finally able to abandon their underground existence and rebuild their homes, rejoined by relatives from Nghe An a year later.

monument depicting a wartime mother and child looking north for, respectively, their husband and father.

Doc Mieu Firebase

Dawn to dusk • Free • 7km south of the Hien Luong Bridge or 14km north of Dong Ha on Highway 1

Before the NVA overran it in 1972, Doc Mieu played a pivotal role in the South's defence. From here American guns shelled seaborne infiltration routes and, for a while, this was the command post for the "**McNamara Line**", calling in airstrikes from Da Nang to pound targets – both real and faked – along the Ho Chi Minh Trail. These days the site is marked by a Soviet-style memorial to fallen Vietnamese.

Con Thien Firebase

Dawn to dusk • Free • From Dong Ha, head west along Highway 9 to Cam Lo, then turn north on Highway 15 for a further 12km

There's nothing to see at **Con Thien Firebase** today, beyond a view north to what were once NVA positions, chillingly close on the opposite bank of the Ben Hai River. In the lead-up to the 1968 Tet Offensive, as part of the NVA's diversionary attacks, the base became the target of prolonged shelling, followed by an infantry assault during which it was briefly surrounded. The Americans replied with everything in their arsenal, including long-range strafing from gunships in the South China Sea and carpet-bombing by B-52s. The North Vietnamese were forced to withdraw temporarily, but then completely overran the base in the summer of 1972.

Truong Son War Martyr Cemetery

Dawn to dusk • Free • From Dong Ha, head west along Highway 9 to Cam Lo, then turn north on Highway 15 for a further 20km

Truong Son War Martyr Cemetery is dedicated to the estimated 25,000 men and women who died on the Truong Son Trail, better known in the West as the Ho Chi Minh Trail (see box, p.387). A total of 10,036 graves lie in the fourteen-hectare cemetery among whispering glades of evergreen trees. Arranged in five geographical regions, the graves are subdivided according to native province, and centred round memorial-houses listing every name and grave number in the sector. Each headstone announces *liet si*

DMZ TOURS

Considering the paucity of public transport in this area, most people opt to visit the DMZ on a **guided tour** – guides usually do a good job of relaying the essential historical information. Most tours come straight from Hue, usually costing $15–20 per person and including visits to Doc Mieu Firebase, Hien Luong Bridge, the Vinh Moc tunnels, the Rockpile, Dakrong Bridge and Khe Sanh combat base; it's a long day out starting at 6am and returning to Hue around 6pm. To take things in a more leisurely manner, you could base yourself in Dong Ha, then spend one day seeing the sights near Highway 1 and another heading west along Highway 9, either on a rented motorbike or on tours offered by places like *Tam's Café* (see p.299).

5

("martyr"), together with as many details as are known: name, date and place of birth, date of enrolment, rank and the date they died.

Dong Ha

As a former US Marine Command Post and then ARVN base, **DONG HA** was also obliterated in 1972, but unlike Quang Tri it has bounced back, thanks largely to its administrative status and location at the eastern end of Highway 9, which leads through **Laos** to Savannakhet on the Mekong River. The future looks rosy as well: a new deep-water port has been built to serve landlocked Laos, a number of special economic zones are under construction along the border, and Highway 9 has been upgraded as part of the massive Trans-Asian Highway project.

As the **closest town to the DMZ**, Dong Ha attracts a lot of tourist traffic, though few people choose to stay here, preferring the comfort and facilities of Hue. It is essentially a two-street town: Highway 1, known here as Le Duan, forms the main artery as it passes through on its route north, while Highway 9 takes off inland at a central T-junction.

Mine Action Visitor Centre

Kids First Village, 185 Ly Thuong Kiet • Mon–Fri 8am–5pm • Free • ☎ 0233 385 8445, ⓦ landmines.org.vn

Run by Project Renew, the **Mine Action Visitor Centre** makes the perfect introduction to a tour of the DMZ: you'll learn more about the reality of this region from this small museum's displays than you will at all the other sites in the DMZ. Project Renew's aim is to inform, educate and prevent further accidents caused by unexploded ordnance in the area, and the display at the centre, which is laid out clearly and

---

THE HISTORY OF THE DMZ

Under the terms of the 1954 Geneva Accords, Vietnam was split in two along the Seventeenth Parallel, pending elections intended to reunite the country. The demarcation line ran along the Ben Hai River and was sealed by a strip of no-man's land 5km wide on each side known as the **Demilitarized Zone**, or **DMZ**. All Communist troops and supporters were supposed to regroup north in the Democratic Republic of Vietnam, leaving the southern Republic of Vietnam to non-Communists and various shades of opposition. When the elections failed to take place, the river became the de facto border until 1975.

In reality both sides of the DMZ were anything but demilitarized after 1965, and anyway the border was easily circumvented – by the Ho Chi Minh Trail to the west (see box, p.387) and sea routes to the east – enabling the North Vietnamese to bypass a string of American firebases overlooking the river. One of the more fantastical efforts to prevent Communist infiltration southwards was US Secretary of Defense Robert McNamara's proposal for an **electronic fence** from the Vietnamese coast to the Mekong River, made up of seismic and acoustic sensors that would detect troop movements and pinpoint targets for bombing raids. Though trials in 1967 met with some initial success, the "McNamara Line" was soon abandoned: sensors were confused by animals, especially elephants, and could be triggered deliberately by the tape-recorded sound of vehicle engines or troops on the march.

Nor could massive, conventional bombing by artillery and aircraft contain the North Vietnamese, who finally stormed the DMZ in 1972 and pushed the border 20km further south. Exceptionally bitter fighting in the territory south of the **Ben Hai River** (I Corps Military Region) claimed more American lives in the five years leading up to 1972 than any other battle zone in Vietnam. Figures for North Vietnamese losses during that period are not known, though thousands more have died since the end of the war from inadvertently detonating unexploded ordnance. So much fire power was unleashed over this area, including napalm and herbicides, that for years nothing would grow in the impacted, chemical-laden soil; but the region's low, rolling hills are now almost entirely reforested with a green sea of pine, eucalyptus, coffee and acacia.

professionally, gives a stark impression of the enormity of their task. Quang Tri province alone was bombarded by over 350,000 tonnes of ordnance, of which thousands of tonnes failed to go off, resulting in nearly ten thousand civilian casualties here since the end of the war.

Beginning with maps showing the intensity of bombing during the war (the DMZ a glaring blotch of bright red), the display includes some graphic images and statistics of casualties in the area, a collection of home-made prosthetic limbs, as well as examples of the unexploded ordnance (UXO) recovered by the mine-clearing team.

ARRIVAL AND DEPARTURE   DONG HA

By train The station lies 1km south of town, just west of the highway.
Destinations Dong Hoi (5 daily; 1hr 20min–2hr 10min); Hanoi (5 daily; 12–15hr); Hue (5 daily; 1hr 20min).
By bus The bus station is at 68 Le Duan, 500m north of the train station and near the junction of Highways 1 and 9. It

is possible to get to Savannakhet in Laos, but you have to book in advance through a tour agency as the bus from Hue will pull over on the highway to pick you up.
Destinations Dong Hoi (2hr); Hue (2hr); Lao Bao (2hr); Savannakhet (8hr).

INFORMATION

Tourist information *Tam's Café* (see below) is a great source of information, and can help to organize onward transport and DMZ tours. Another reliable operator is Annam Tour, 207b

Nguyen Du (☎ 0233 352 2600, ⍟ annamtour.com).
Services There are several ATMs around the town centre, including one at Vietcombank, 51 Tran Hung Dao.

ACCOMMODATION

Golden Hotel 297 Le Duan ☎ 0233 379 8999. Well-priced rooms that are spacious and clean and come with a/c and satellite TV. Staff speak limited English but they are friendly and helpful. The biggest plus to the hotel is its proximity to the bus and train stations – avoid rooms at the front as Le Duan is Highway 1 through town. $20
Saigon Dong Ha 11 Bui Thi Xuan ☎ 0233 357 7888,

⍟ saigondonghahotel.com. This flashy, 4-star place looks the part, and its rooms are certainly modern, with light pine furnishings and carpeted floors. There's also a pool, sun terrace and fitness centre. Yet as in many government-run hotels, it lacks the personal touch that's so important, and service is hit-and-miss. $125

EATING AND DRINKING

The Red Lion Beer Garden 15 Le Hong Phong ☎ 0233 375 5868. This welcoming pub-restaurant in the centre of town is one of the new hip places that are changing the scene in Dong Ha. The menu has loads of Vietnamese specialities (hotpots to share are around 150,000đ) and the helpful staff will talk you through these, as well as the extensive list of beers they serve (from 30,000đ). Daily 8.30am–11.30pm.
★ **Tam's Café** 211 Ba Trieu ☎ 090 542 5912, ⍟ tamscafe .jimdo.com. Charming café serving a range of coffees,

juices, smoothies and ice cream, plus tasty main dishes at around 80,000đ. Owner Tam is your one-stop Mr Fixit for all things DMZ and as the café is a few kilometres north along the river, most people eat here pre- or post- a DMZ tour (they will transfer you from hotels across town). At the time of writing, Tam was building an extension for budget accommodation; check online for updates. Daily 7.30am–9pm.

West of Dong Ha

Heading west from Dong Ha on Highway 9 (also now known as Asian Highway 16, or AH16 for short), you begin to climb into the foothills of the Truong Son range. Where the highway veers south, a sheer-sided isolated stump 230m high dominates the valley: the **Rockpile**. For a while American troops, delivered by helicopter, used the peak for directing artillery to targets across the DMZ and into Laos, but the post was abandoned after 1968. The highway continues over a low pass and then follows a picturesque valley past the **Dakrong Bridge**, which carries a spur of the Ho Chi Minh Highway before climbing among ever more forested mountains to emerge at **Khe Sanh** (now officially rechristened **Huang Hoa**), 63km from Dong Ha. In this area you'll still see a few stilthouses from the Bru and Co minorities, most of whom have been moved

5

THE BATTLE OF KHE SANH

The **battle of Khe Sanh** was important not because of its immediate outcome, but because it attracted worldwide media attention and, along with the simultaneous Tet Offensive, demonstrated the futility of America's efforts to contain their enemy. In 1962 an American Special Forces team arrived in Khe Sanh town to train local Bru minority people in counter-insurgency, and then four years later the first batch of Marines was sent in to establish a forward base near Laos, to secure Highway 9 and to harass troops on the Ho Chi Minh Trail. Skirmishes around Khe Sanh increased as intelligence reports indicated a massive build-up of North Vietnamese Army (NVA) troops in late 1967, possibly as many as forty thousand, facing six thousand Marines together with a few hundred South Vietnamese and Bru. Both the Western media and American generals were soon presenting the confrontation as a crucial test of America's credibility in South Vietnam and drawing parallels with Dien Bien Phu (see box, p.409). As US President Johnson famously remarked, he didn't want "any damn Dinbinfoo".

The **NVA attack** came in the early hours of January 21, 1968; rockets raining in on the base added to the terror and confusion by striking an ammunition dump, gasoline tanks and stores of tear gas. There followed a seemingly endless, nerve-grinding NVA artillery barrage, when hundreds of shells fell on the base each day, interspersed with costly US infantry assaults into the surrounding hills. In an operation code-named "**Niagara**", General Westmoreland called in the air battalions to silence the enemy guns and break the siege by unleashing the most intense bombing raids of the war: in nine weeks nearly a hundred thousand tonnes of bombs pounded the area round the clock, averaging **one airstrike every five minutes**, backed up by napalm and defoliants. Unbelievably the NVA were so well dug in and camouflaged that they not only withstood the onslaught but continued to return fire, despite horrendous casualties, estimated at ten thousand. On the US side around five hundred troops died at Khe Sanh (although official figures record only 248 American deaths, of which 43 occurred in a single helicopter accident), before a relief column broke through in early April, seventy-odd days after the siege had begun. NVA forces gradually pulled back and by the middle of March had all but gone, having successfully diverted American resources away from southern cities prior to the Tet Offensive. Three months later the Americans also quietly withdrew, leaving a plateau that resembled a lunar landscape, contaminated for years to come with chemicals and explosives; even the trees left standing were worthless because so much shrapnel was lodged in the timber.

on – ostensibly for reasons of health and hygiene, though cynics would point to the fact that both the Bru and the Co helped the Americans during the war.

Khe Sanh

The bleak settlement of **KHE SANH**, its frontier atmosphere reinforced by the smugglers' trail across the border to Laos only 19km away (see box opposite), sits on the edge of a windswept plateau that was the site of a pivotal battle in the American War. Because of the high concentration of chemical and explosive contamination, it's only recently that the soil around Khe Sanh has been able to support vegetation again, and the hills are now green with coffee plantations. Nothing else remains: when American troops were ordered to abandon Khe Sanh, everything was blown up or bulldozed.

The museum

Daily 7am–5pm • 20,000đ

The only memorial is a small **museum**, 2km north of Khe Sanh town, commemorating the siege – made even more poignant by the hauntingly beautiful mountains all around. The small halls are dotted with photos and war paraphernalia, and surrounded by a reconstructed bunker, a helicopter, military vehicles and the contorted shapes of exploded bombs. Be sure to peek over the fence at the red gash of the old airstrip.

LAO BAO BORDER CROSSING

Of all the **border crossings** open to foreigners between Vietnam and Laos, the most popular is still **Lao Bao**, 90km west of Dong Ha along Highway 9. It's an attractive ride, through misty mountains on a reasonable road, and the crossing is hassle-free beyond having to walk 1km between inspection posts. However, since reports of extortion are still common with travellers trying to do this route independently, it's best to book a seat on one of the through-buses to Savannakhet from Hue.

You can obtain a thirty-day **visa** for Laos at the border ($30–42, depending on nationality; two passport photos required). Otherwise, get your visa in advance at the Lao consulates in Da Nang (see p.271) or in Ho Chi Minh City (see p.105), or at their embassy in Hanoi (see p.383).

South of Dong Ha

American troops weren't the first to suffer heavy losses in this region: during the 1950s, French soldiers dubbed the stretch of **Highway 1** north of Hue as *la rue sans joie*, or "street without joy", after they came under constant attack from elusive Viet Minh units operating out of heavily fortified villages along the coast. Later, in the 1972 Easter Offensive, Communist forces overran the whole area, capturing **Quang Tri** town, some 60km north of Hue, from the South Vietnamese Army (ARVN) and holding it for four months while American B-52s pounded the township and surrounding countryside, before it was retaken at huge cost to both sides as well as civilians caught up in the battle.

Quang Tri town

East off Highway 1 down Tran Hung Dao

Blink and you may well miss **QUANG TRI**, a town wiped off the map during the American War, and indeed now officially called **Trieu Hai**. Keep your eyes peeled for one of its few identifying features – the small, pockmarked shell of **Long Hung Church** to the east of the road, 55km from Hue, kept as a memorial to victims of 1972. Just before this, a road on the west side of the highway leads 2km to the more impressive ruin of **La Vang Church**, beside which stands an extraordinary monument of the Virgin Mary clutching baby Jesus beneath a forest of giant mushroom trees, which supposedly represents the apparition of the Virgin Mary to persecuted Catholics on this spot in 1798.

Quang Tri Citadel

Just north of town on Tran Hung Dao; entrance on Ly Thai To • Daily 7am–5pm • Free

Quang Tri's square, walled **citadel**, a smaller version of the one in Hue, was originally built from earth in 1806 by the Nguyen dynasty, fortified with bricks in 1827, and served in turn as a base for the French and the ARVN before being overrun and destroyed in 1972. Parts of the wall and moat remain, and the south gate, through which visitors enter, has been rebuilt. Inside is a war memorial, the remains of a nineteenth-century French prison consisting of fourteen tiny cells measuring 1m by 2m, and a small war **museum** with English captions. The museum houses some excellent photos of the fierce hand-to-hand fighting that took place towards the end of 1972 as ARVN troops eventually retook the city after 81 days.

The northern coast

HA LONG BAY AT SUNSET

The northern coast

Although largely devoid of beaches, Vietnam's northern coast boasts one of the country's foremost attractions, and one of the most vaunted spots in all of Southeast Asia – the mystical scenery of Ha Long Bay, where jagged emerald islands jut out of the sea in their thousands. Heading in by boat, you approach wave after wave of hidden coves, needle-sharp ridges and cliffs of ribbed limestone. The waters here are patrolled by squadrons of tourist junks, on which you'll be able to spend a night at sea. Cat Ba Island also makes a great base from which to explore Ha Long Bay, while Bai Tu Long Bay has the same dramatic views without the fleets of tourist boats. You'll find similar karst scenery inland around the small city of Ninh Binh, while other notable sights in the area are the colonial buildings of Haiphong, the ancient Ho Citadel and the monstrous caves around Phong Nha.

Heading north from the DMZ (see p.295), the first stretch is hemmed in by the jagged Truong Son Mountains, which separate Vietnam from Laos. Here, Vietnam shrinks to a mere 50km wide and is edged with sand dunes up to 80m high, marching inland at a rate of 10m per year despite efforts to stabilize them with screw-pine and cactus. The first place of note on this stretch is **Dong Hoi**, which has a decent beach and a quietly engaging feel. Inland from here is **Phong Nha** with its spectacular caves, which include **Phong Nha Cave** itself, **Paradise Cave** and **Son Doong Cave**, which at over 5km long, is the largest in the world.

The area north of Dong Hoi is one of the poorest in Vietnam, and is little developed for tourism; however, the mountains brushing the Laos border are home to a number of unique animal species, including the elusive **saola ox** and the more numerous **giant muntjac deer**. Intrepid travellers with their own transport are beginning to venture inland, but the vast majority of tourists leapfrog this long coastal stretch, with maybe a stopover in workaday **Vinh**. The town has little to offer, but you could track down **Ho Chi Minh's birthplace** in the nearby village of Kim Lien.

Back on the well-trodden trail is **Ninh Binh**, just an hour's drive from Hanoi. Ninh Binh is a rather unattractive city, but such is the wealth of nearby sights that visitors tend to stay for at least a couple of days; said attractions include more karst scenery, underground rivers that can be paddled through by boat, an ancient capital city and Vietnam's largest temple complex.

Despite the proximity of Hanoi, it's quite possible to bypass the capital and head straight for Ha Long Bay, via the buzzing city of **Haiphong** – more appealing than most northern cities thanks to great colonial-era architecture and a young, friendly populace.

Then, of course, there's **Ha Long Bay** itself. A doyen of local tourist literature, you'll most likely have seen dozens of images of this unbelievably scenic place long before your arrival – happily, it really is that pretty, though the weather doesn't always reveal it in its best light. Tourism is taking its toll too, and pollution is becoming a major issue,

CAT BA ISLAND

Highlights

❶ Phong Nha Caves Visit one or more of Phong Nha's mind-blowing caves, which include the world's biggest. **See p.309**

❷ Cycling around Tam Coc A fantasy landscape of limestone crags provides the backdrop for a leisurely cycle ride through Ninh Binh's prolific rice lands. **See p.316**

❸ Ho Citadel Marvel at the massive stones used to build this seven-hundred-year-old citadel in the middle of nowhere. **See p.319**

❹ Haiphong's colonial architecture Hectic Haiphong features a number of striking

colonial-era buildings, which give hints as to this port city's importance under French rule. **See p.322**

❺ Cat Ba Island With its nice beaches, lush interior and easy access to some of Ha Long Bay's most beguiling scenery, this is a great spot to spend a few days. **See p.327**

❻ Cruising Ha Long Bay Passing through the maze of limestone pinnacles punctuating the turquoise waters is an unmissable experience. **See p.337**

HIGHLIGHTS ARE MARKED ON THE MAP ON P.306

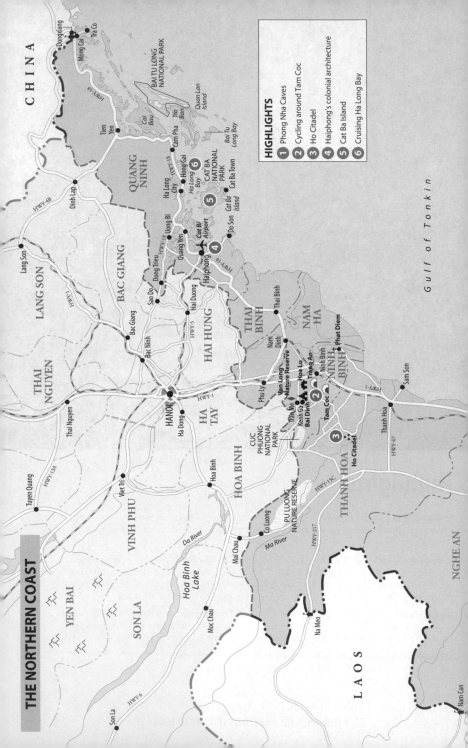

THE NORTHERN COAST

HIGHLIGHTS

1. Phong Nha Caves
2. Cycling around Tam Coc
3. Ho Citadel
4. Haiphong's colonial architecture
5. Cat Ba Island
6. Cruising Ha Long Bay

CHINA

LAOS

Gulf of Tonkin

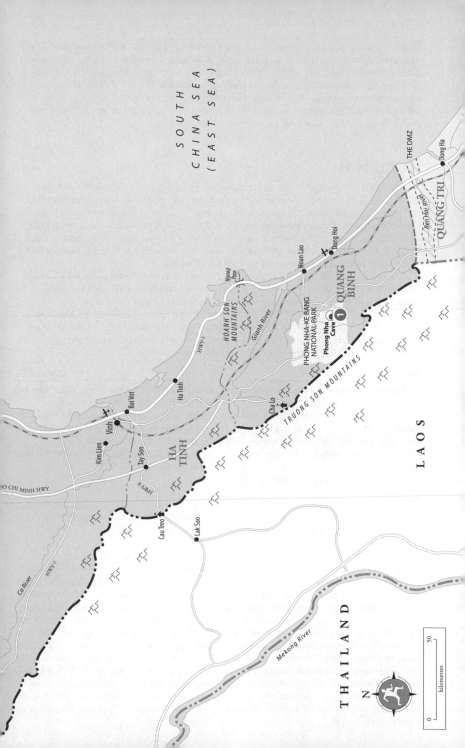

SOUTH
CHINA SEA
(EAST SEA)

THE DMZ

Dong Ha

QUANG TRI

Ben Hai RIVER

Dong Hoi

Hoan Lao

Ngang Pass

HOANH SON MOUNTAINS

Gianh River

HWY 1

QUANG BINH

PHONG NHA–KE BANG NATIONAL PARK

Phong Nha Cave

1

Ha Tinh

Bai Vot

Cha Lo

TRUONG SON MOUNTAINS

LAOS

Vinh

Kim Lien

Tay Son

HA TINH

HWY 8

HO CHI MINH HWY

Ca River

HWY 7

Cau Treo

Lak Sao

THAILAND

Mekong River

N

0   50   kilometres

so an increasing number of visitors are heading further afield to **Bai Tu Long Bay**. Many overnight aboard a traditional wooden junk; their tea-coloured sails are just for show since almost all vessels are motor-driven, but there's a timeless, romantic air to floating among pristine moonlit peaks. By far the largest island in the bay, **Cat Ba** makes an appealing base for exploring the area with some fine scenery as well as being home to **Cat Ba National Park**, a forest and maritime reserve that requires the usual mix of luck and dedication to see anything larger than a mosquito.

6

Dong Hoi

Almost entirely flattened in the American War's bombing raids, **DONG HOI** has risen from its ashes to become a prosperous, orderly provincial capital of over one hundred and sixty thousand people. Tourists who stay here usually use the town as a base for the **Phong Nha Caves**, though there are plenty of accommodation options in Phong Nha itself. However, Dong Hoi warrants a visit in itself, if only to step off the beaten track for a bit. Particularly pleasant is the esplanade along the west bank of the **Nhat Le River**, which leads to the sea and an attractive stretch of **beach**.

The city's focal point is the remnants of a Nguyen-dynasty **citadel** – the only notable part is the restored south gate, where a lively riverside **market** of covered stalls has sprung up and in summer vendors sell ice-cold glasses of sweet-bean *che*.

Crossing the Nhat Le, you'll find yourself on a small spit of land, named **My Canh**. This is also the name of the small beach rifling down the eastern edge of the isthmus. As with sandy stretches up and down the land, it's been developed as a resort area, though it attracts more Vietnamese than foreigners.

ARRIVAL AND DEPARTURE   DONG HOI

By plane Dong Hoi Airport is 6km to the north of town. Taxis into the centre cost around 120,000đ.
Destinations Hanoi (daily; 1hr 20min); Ho Chi Minh City (3 daily; 1hr 35min).
By train Dong Hoi's station is 3km out of town west along Tran Hung Dao – you'll easily find a taxi or xe om to take you into town.
Destinations Dong Ha (5 daily; 1hr 40min–2hr 35min);

Hanoi (6 daily; 10–12hr); Hue (6 daily; 3–4hr); Ninh Binh (4 daily; 9–11hr); Vinh (6 daily; 3hr 30min–5hr).
By bus The bus station is 1km west of the centre at the junction of Tran Hung Dao and Nguyen Huu Canh. There are frequent connections north and south.
Destinations Da Nang (5hr); Dong Ha (2hr); Hue (4hr); Phong Nha (1hr 30min); Vinh (4hr).

TOURS

Phongnha Discovery Tours 63 Ly Thuong Kiet ☎093 2594 126, ⓦphongnhadiscovery.com. Small outfit able

to book tickets and organize tours around Phong Nha-Ke Bang National Park (from $50).

ACCOMMODATION

Beachside Backpackers Truong Phap ☎091 8921 015 or ☎0168 5334 345, ⓦbeachsidebackpackers.com. This new hostel right on the beach is a low-key place with a big outdoor area dotted with hammocks. You could easily spend a few days here, using the free bicycles to get into town or to visit the nearby sand dunes, and drinking beer by the campfire in the evening. Dorms $6.50, doubles $20
★**Geminai Hotel & Cafe** 56 Nguyen Du ☎0232 393 8888, ⓦgeminaihotel.com. New boutique riverfront hotel run by a husband-and-wife team who care about the little details. Rooms are simple but immaculate, and some have balconies and a river view. The downstairs lounge bar is a great place to eat. $20

Nam Long Plus 28a Phan Chu Trinh ☎0232 382 6926, ⓦnamlonghotels.com. The couple (Nga and Sy) who run this hotel are incredibly switched on and can help with any travel plans, including visits to Phong Nha. They also own the nearby, slightly cheaper *Nam Long* – rooms at both places are clean and bright. Dorms $6, doubles $25
Sun Spa Resort My Canh ☎0232 384 2999, ⓦsunsparesortvietnam.com. Luxurious five-star on My Canh beach. It's easily Dong Hoi's top hotel, and worth popping into even if you're not staying – for a small fee non-guests can use the tennis courts, pool and other facilities. Rooms are often discounted, though still rather pricey. $210

EATING

QB Bar 01-03 Le Loi ☎0232 382 4694. This flashy, air-conditioned bar-restaurant opposite the south gate serves an amazing range of dishes such as hotdogs (35,000đ) and grilled lamb ribs (280,000đ). Ice creams, coffee and cocktails (50,000đ) as well. Daily 7am–10pm.

Tree Hugger Café 30 Nguyen Du ☎093 5983 831, ⓦtreehugger-cafe.com. This German-owned coffee shop with an eco-conscience uses fresh, local ingredients for everything on the simple menu. Great smoothies from 30,000VND, plus local handicrafts on sale and all the information on the area you could ever need. Daily 7am–10pm.

Tu Quy 17 Co Tam ☎0232 382 1371. On a sidestreet just east of the market, this no-frills place has an English menu and serves tasty Vietnamese staples such as *banh khoai* (a crispy pancake stuffed with prawns and pork) and *banh cuon* (rice noodle rolls with ground pork) for 35,000đ. Cheap beers too. Daily 7am–9pm.

Phong Nha-Ke Bang National Park

Admission free, though there are fees to individual attractions

There are plenty of opportunities to visit **caves** in Vietnam – especially around Ha Long Bay – but for sheer scale nothing can compare with those at **Phong Nha-Ke Bang National Park**. Designated a World Heritage Site in 2003, Phong Nha's 885 square kilometres of jungle is littered with caves and underground rivers; every year more are being discovered, surveyed and opened to the public. But don't be fooled into thinking it's all about the landscape: the park also offers opportunities for kayaking, ziplining, swimming and biking, plus it has an interesting **war history** and the rugged terrain provides an ideal habitat for many **animals**. Phong Nha is home to over one hundred species of mammal, including bears, elephants and muntjacs, as well as over eighty species of reptiles and amphibians, three hundred birds and seventy types of fish.

Located on Highway 20, which leads into the national park, little **Phong Nha town** (also known as **Son Trach**) has seen big changes recently, with a visitors' centre, several recently opened hotels and hostels as well as foreigner-friendly eateries to cater for the growing numbers of visitors, mostly backpackers, who are eager for adventure. Increasing numbers of travellers are spending a few days here, but keep in mind that **flooding** frequently occurs in October and November, when most caves become inaccessible; the best months to visit are from March to May.

Brief history

The karst formations of the Phong Nha-Ke Bang National Park constitute the **oldest karst areas** in Asia, dating back some four hundred million years, and the area has been subject to massive tectonic changes in that time. This has resulted in the creation of unique geological formations, which include underground rivers, dry caves, terraced caves, suspended caves and intersecting caves. The best known cave, Phong Nha itself, is around 44km long, though tour boats only go about 1.5km inside. The recent discovery of Son Doong (Mountain River), and Thien Dong (Paradise),

---

THE WORLD'S LARGEST CAVE

Rarely can the word "cavernous" have been used with such justification. In 2009, a group of British cavers attempted the first-ever detailed survey of the **Son Doong (Mountain River) Cave** in Phong Nha-Ke Bang National Park, finally giving up 4.5km in; they returned a year later to charter the final 2km. Their records and photographs revealed chambers large enough to swallow up whole city blocks – the largest is over 250m high, and 150m wide – plus 70m-long stalactites, gigantic shards of crystal and grapefruit-sized calcite pearls. The cave is highly remote but is now open to a limited number of visitors (around 600 a year) and despite the whacking $3000 fee for the three-night/four-day trek there and back, there's a long waiting list. Contact Oxalis (see p.311) for more information and if you want a shorter and cheaper alternative, ask them about treks to **Tu Lan and Hang En caves**.

thought to be the world's longest dry cave, has attracted a lot of attention, and considering the fact that only ten percent of the area has been fully explored, much more remains to be discovered.

Phong Nha Cave

Phong Nha town • Daily 7am–5pm • 150,000đ, additional 60,000đ for Tien Son • Dragon boat seating fourteen people 320,000đ; it's possible to join other groups at the entrance or at *Easy Tiger Hostel* (see opposite), but keep in mind that every boat that goes out is an income for a local family

The only way to visit **Phong Nha Cave** is by dragon boat, which wend their way 5km (30min) upstream to the cave entrance, after which the pilot cuts the engine and starts to paddle through. Keep your eyes open for scars on the rock in the entrance caused by an American rocket attack. You'll drift awhile between rippling walls of limestone, and see immense stalactites and stalagmites, all tastefully illuminated. The boat eventually draws into a small subterranean beach, from which you follow an easy, 500m-long trail around the cave (flip-flops will be fine) – note that visitors must stick to the path to avoid any risk of rock damage. A steep, 330-step climb beyond Phong Nha reveals a grand view of the valley, and the entrance to smaller **Tien Son Cave**. Inside there's a modern walkway and Cham inscriptions dating as far back as the ninth century.

Late afternoon on a weekday is a good time to go, when there are few other tourists about. Seasonal flooding means that Phong Nha may be closed in November and December.

Paradise Cave (Thien Duong)

14km southwest of Phong Nha town • Daily 7.30am–4pm • 250,000đ includes guide; electric cart 150,000đ • Follow Highway 20 right through town, then turn right on the Ho Chi Minh Highway (West)

Even if you're not a "cave person", the sight of **Paradise Cave** will probably leave you spellbound. You can ride to the foot of the hill where the cave is located in an electric cart, though it's a pleasant, 1.6km walk in good weather. Then you climb around 500 steps, or go up a ramp (easier), but when you see the tiny entrance, it's difficult to imagine the enormous cavern inside. You descend a dizzying staircase to the cavern floor, from where a sturdily built walkway takes you for a kilometre through a magical display of **natural sculptures** formed by mineral deposits, which are cleverly illuminated.

Most of these sculptures are in the form of colossal stalagmites (growing up from the floor) and stalactites (growing down from the roof), but no doubt your guide will also impress you with caving terminology by pointing out formations such as draperies (which look like curtains) and soda straws (which look like, er, soda straws). Not surprisingly, word of this cave's wonder has got around and sometimes it can get very busy with tour groups. This can somewhat spoil the experience, as tour guides spout forth an amplified commentary in various languages. A smart restaurant by the car park provides welcome refreshment after exploring the cave, though most of its customers are from tour groups.

Nuoc Mooc Eco-trail

Daily 7am–5pm • 180,000đ • From Paradise Cave head north on the Ho Chi Minh Highway (West) for a few kilometres and you'll find it on the right

Sprawling along picturesque riverside territory and lassoed together with bamboo bridges, the 1km-long **Nuoc Mooc Eco-trail** isn't the isolated spot it once was, but you can swim and sunbathe. It's a great spot to cool off after sweating through Paradise Cave or Dark Cave.

THE BONG LAI VALLEY

Bong Lai is a beautiful unspoiled valley just 10km east of Phong Nha town that's only just opening to tourism. It's an easy half-day loop by bicycle or motorbike on the valley's dirt roads – arm yourself with a map from your homestay and be warned it can get pretty treacherous in the rainy season. At any of the small businesses out here you'll get a friendly welcome, cold beer and menus in English. At the legendary **Pub with Cold Beer** you can fling yourself into a hammock and if you're hungry, the owner will kill and cook a chicken (for around 200,000đ). Quynh at **The Duck Stop** will show you round his family's pepper plantation and let you feed the ducks, **Moi Moi**'s speciality is slow-cooked pork in bamboo tubes (100,000đ) and finally, the remote **Wild Boar Eco Farm** has yet more river views and spit-roasted chicken. Don't forget swimwear in the summer as Bong River is great for a dip, and avoid biking back to town in the dark.

6

Dark Cave (Hang Toi)

Daily 7am–4pm • 450,000đ including cave and all activities • 2km north of the Nuoc Mooc Eco-trail on the Ho Chi Minh Highway (West)

Dark Cave (Hang Toi) is a beautiful cave to explore, but it's the 400m zipline, pitch-black squelch through thigh-deep mud, and mandatory kayak and swim that are the main attraction here. Leave all valuables in the lockers.

ARRIVAL AND DEPARTURE   PHONG NHA-KE BANG NATIONAL PARK

There's just one ATM in town – opposite the boat jetty – and it's not always reliable, so bring plenty of cash.

By bus Phong Nha is a stop on the open-tour bus route. From Hanoi, most travellers take a sleeper bus, which arrives in Phong Nha town in the early hours of the morning. The train to nearby Dong Hoi is a more comfortable option (see p.308) and frequent public buses ply the 50km route between Dong Hoi and Phong Nha. *Easy Tiger Hostel* (see below) has up-to-date public transport information.

Destinations Dong Hoi (hourly; 1hr 30min); Hanoi (2 daily;

10hr–12hr 30min); Hue (4 daily; 4hr 30min–6hr).
By taxi *Phong Nha Farmstay* (see below) operates shared taxis to and from Dong Hoi according to demand. From Dong Hoi Airport the fare is around 500,000đ.
By car or motorbike With your own wheels, from Dong Hoi take Highway 15 north for about 50km until you see a Hollywood-type sign on a mountain to the left announcing the Phong Nha-Ka Be National Park. Turn left here on Highway 20 into the town.

TOURS

Hai's Eco Conservation Tour ☎096 2606 844, Ⓦ ecophongnha.com. If you're interested in conservation and wildlife, get in touch with Hai who leads jungle treks and visits to the wildlife rescue centre. When he's not trekking, you'll find him at his de facto office, *Bamboo Café* (see p.312). Prices from 1,300,000đ.
Jungle Boss ☎094 3748 041, Ⓦ junglebosshomestay .com. A fantastic company who organize one- or two-day

treks out to Abandoned Valley and Ma Da Valley, as well as the recently opened and pristine Tra Ang Cave. Prices from 1,650,000đ.
Oxalis Highway 20, Phong Nha town ☎0232 367 7678, Ⓦ oxalis.com.vn. Runs caving tours from one to four days to Tu Lan, Hang En and Son Doong caves with highly professional staff. Prices from 2,000,000đ.

ACCOMMODATION

Great-value homestays dot the countryside around town and there's no need to book in advance. Turn up and ask around.

Easy Tiger Hostel Phong Nha town ☎0232 367 7844, Ⓦ easytigerhostel.com. Backpacker central in Phong Nha, that takes care of all needs, including comfort food, cheap cocktails, tours, bicycle and motorbike rental, transport to Dong Hoi and Hue. Part-owned by the folks at *Phong Nha Farmstay*. Dorms $\overline{\underline{\$8}}$

★**Phong Nha Farmstay** Cu Nam village, about 8km east of Phong Nha town ☎094 475 9864,

Ⓦ phong-nha-cave.com. Superb hotel run by affable Aussie Ben and his Vietnamese wife Bich. The setting is gloriously rural and highly picturesque, and though rooms are simple, there's an on-site swimming pool and chill-out area that hosts cinema nights. In addition, the kitchen serves up delectable, and fairly priced meals – a good thing, as there are no restaurants for miles around. There's daily transportation to both Dong Hoi and Hue, bicycles for

rent, and a whole raft of activities to keep you busy. $35
Phong Nha Lake House 7km east of Phong Nha town ☎ 0126 474 6876, ⊛ phongnhalakehouse.com. Besides the most luxurious dorms that you're likely to see in Vietnam, with proper two-tiered beds and mosquito nets, this Australian-Vietnamese-run guesthouse has spacious en-suite "rustic chic" villas and bungalows, the latter with own garden areas. There are expansive views over a lake from the terrace, a lively bar-restaurant and motorbikes for rent ($10/day). Dorms $8, doubles $35

EATING

Bamboo Café Opposite Easy Tiger Hostel, Phong Nha town ☎ 0232 367 8777, ⊛ phong-nha-bamboo-cafe.com. Comfy sofas, strong coffee and friendly local staff make this cool café-restaurant a great place to chill – and Western and Vietnamese dishes including mouthwatering browned pork and rice (80,000đ) will keep you here for dinner. They do cooking classes too (400,000đ). Daily 7am–10pm.

The Best Spit Roast Pork & Noodle Shop in the World (Probably) Close to the ferry dock, Phong Nha town. This long-standing local's favourite really does do the best barbecued pork in the world (probably). It's a cheap eat and the owner is super friendly. Daily 7am–10pm.

Vinh

Although a place of pilgrimage for Vietnamese tourists – Ho Chi Minh was born in the nearby village of Kim Lien – **VINH** receives very few foreign guests, most of whom simply use it as a stop on the long journey between Hue and Hanoi, or a jumping-off point for the Laos border (see box opposite). However, an overnight stay here is a chance to discover a real Vietnamese city, almost entirely unaffected by international tourism.

Brief history

Vinh fared particularly badly in the twentieth century. As an industrial port-city dominating major land routes, whose population was known for rebellious tendencies, the town became a natural target during both the French and American wars. In the 1950s French bombs destroyed large swathes of the city, after which the Viet Minh burnt down what remained rather than let it fall into enemy hands. Vinh was flattened once again during American air raids; many of these were aimed at preventing North Vietnamese troops crossing the nearby border into Laos and heading south on what later became known as the **Ho Chi Minh Trail** (see p.387). Reconstruction of the town proceeded slowly after 1975, mostly financed by East Germany, though fortunately the decrepit hulks of barrack-like apartment blocks, totally unsuited to the Vietnamese climate, have now largely been replaced by sleek high-rises; smart new villas and hotels have also sprung up, and there are even multistorey supermarkets stocked with all manner of goodies.

ARRIVAL AND DEPARTURE   VINH

By plane Vinh Airport is 6km to the north of town (100,000đ by taxi; 50,000đ by xe om).
Destinations Da Lat (3 weekly; 1hr 30min); Da Nang (3 weekly; 1hr 20min); Hanoi (2 daily; 1hr); Ho Chi Minh City (4 daily; 1hr 45min).
By train Vinh's station is in the northwest of the city, and it's an easy walk from a number of hotels.
Destinations Da Nang (4 daily; 10hr); Dong Hoi (6 daily; 4–5hr); Hanoi (6 daily; 6hr–6hr 30min); Hue (6 daily; 6–9hr); Ninh Binh (4 daily; 4hr).
By bus The long-distance bus station (Ben Xe Vinh) is in the centre of the city. Buses to Laos leave early in the morning (see box opposite). Open-tour buses can set down passengers in Vinh en route, but confirm onward travel with the relevant company beforehand.
Destinations Dong Ha (6–7hr); Dong Hoi (4hr); Hanoi (7hr); Hue (8hr); Ninh Binh (5hr); Tay Son (2hr); Vientiane (12–14hr).

ACCOMMODATION

A transport hub, Vinh has a large number of hotels, which means places are willing to bargain. Many hotels sit right on the highway, so wherever possible go for a room at the back.

BORDER CROSSINGS INTO LAOS

The **border crossings into Laos** closest to Vinh are Cha Lo, Cau Treo and Nam Can: since all are remote with haphazard bus connections, it's essential to get up-to-date advice from the bus station or local hotels before attempting any crossing. The usual opening times of central-Vietnam border crossings are daily 7am–6pm.

There is meant to be a daily 6am direct bus from Vinh to Vientiane via the **Cau Treo** border crossing, though the service is erratic and prone to over-charging. Several early morning buses depart Vinh for Tay Son, the last settlement of any size before the border, where buses leave for Lak Sao – but you must get there mid-morning in order to make the connection.

There are direct buses from Vinh to Phonsavan, via the **Nam Can** border crossing – comparatively devoid of complications, but still a rough ride. They leave from Vinh's long-distance bus station for Phonsavan (Tues–Sun at 6am; 13hr); a couple of buses per week continue straight through to Luang Prabang.

No major bus routes pass through the Cha Lo–Na Phao border. You can obtain Lao **visas** at both Cau Treo and Nam Can border posts ($30–42, depending on nationality; two passport photos required), but not at Cha Lo. If using this crossing, get your visa at the Lao consulates in Ho Chi Minh City (see p.105) or Da Nang (see p.271), or at their Hanoi embassy (see p.383).

6

Muong Thanh 1 Phan Boi Chau ☎0238 353 5666, ⓦvinh.muongthanh.com. The rooms here are smart and well equipped, and there's a swimming pool on the second floor. It's conveniently located close to the train station, and over the road is a modern shopping mall with restaurants and a coffee shop. $20
Saigon Kim Lien 25 Quang Trung ☎0238 383 8899, ⓦsaigonkimlien.com.vn. This huge hotel opened in 1990 to commemorate the hundredth anniversary of Ho Chi

Minh's birth. Prices are surprisingly affordable for comfortable and well-proportioned rooms, and staff are used to dealing with foreigners. Not far from the bus station, facilities include a recommended restaurant, bar, pool, business centre and money exchange. $50
Thanh An 158 Nguyen Thai Hoc ☎0238 358 8366. Just ten rooms in this centrally located budget hotel, where the aging facilities are well maintained. Pay a few dollars extra and you'll get a more spacious room with a balcony. $13

EATING

There's not much choice for places to eat in Vinh, although you'll find a whole host of street kitchens on Le Loi and a few modern eateries have popped up further south on Quang Trung.

Bonjour Coffee 164 Nguyen Thai Hoc ☎0238 358 6026. Tucked away around the corner from the central bus station, this little café serves the best coffee in Vinh (Vietnamese coffee is 20,000đ). The staff are friendly and helpful and the eclectic decor includes a London telephone

box. Daily 6am–11pm.
Hoa Mai 25 Quang Trung ☎0238 383 8899. The smartest option in town is this restaurant at the *Saigon Kim Lien* hotel, which serves fairly priced Asian and European dishes, starting at around 100,000đ. Daily 6am–9pm.

Kim Lien

15km west of Vinh • Both houses daily 7–11.30am & 1.30–5pm • Free • Taxi to both sites including waiting time around 300,000đ

Ho Chi Minh was born in 1890 in Hoang Tru village, **KIM LIEN** commune, which is still a quiet rural village. The two simple houses made of bamboo wattle and palm-leaf thatch are reconstructions; Ho's birthplace is said to be the hut by itself on the left as you approach, while behind stands the brick-built family altar.

At the age of 6 Ho moved 2km west, to what is now called **Lang Sen** (Lotus Village), to live with his father in very similar surroundings. The two houses here are also replicas, with nothing much to see inside, but the complex is often swarming with Vietnamese on pilgrimage. There's a **shrine** to Ho here too, built with huge wooden pillars, surrounded by bonsai trees and containing an old Russian jeep. You can pick up your Uncle Ho rubber sandals at the kitsch souvenir shops before you leave.

6

PU LUONG NATURE RESERVE

Pu Luong Nature Reserve (the "pu" is pronounced "fu") is a region of spectacular natural beauty, a pristine environment of rice terraces and minority villages that has somehow evaded tour operators. Covering an area of around 175 square kilometres in the northwest of Thanh Hoa province, it consists of two parallel mountain ridges running in a northwest–southeast direction. The valley between these ranges is not considered part of the nature reserve, and the ranges themselves are very different – the southwestern range is formed of igneous and metamorphic rocks, while the higher, northeastern range is part of a range of limestone karst that runs all the way from nearby Cuc Phuong National Park up to Son La.

Pu Luong is home to a rich variety of animals, such as the extremely rare **Delacour's leaf monkey**, of which there are an estimated forty or so in the reserve. However, what is likely to stick in the memories of most visitors are the glorious views of rice terraces cascading down the hillside, as well as the simple, thatched and stilted houses of the White Thai and Muong **minority groups**, some of which offer **home-stay accommodation** where you can sleep, eat and join in the family's daily routine. After a few days slowing down to the steady pace of life as lived by the locals, it can be tough to head back to the cacophonous city.

Simply **trekking** though the valley is a joy, with fabulous views opening up at every turn, and in the southern part of the reserve, a string of bamboo waterwheels lines the river to assist in irrigating the flatter part of the valley. None of the **reserve trails** are marked, so you really need to go with a guide (see below), and you'll need a minimum of two days to allow for getting there and away. It's possible to get to Pu Luong by car or motorbike from Hanoi (190km), Mai Chau (50km) or Ninh Binh (about 150km), though local roads can get messy after heavy rain.

TOUR OPERATORS

Though it's possible to go there independently, you'll get more out of the experience if you travel with a guide who knows the locals; Mr Xuan, who runs *Xuan Hoa Hotel* in Ninh Binh (see p.320), comes recommended. A Hanoi-based tour operator that offers several day-treks in Pu Luong is Mai Chau Trek (☎046 293 8797, ⓦ maichautrek.com).

HOMESTAYS

Several hospitable minority families in the area have adapted their houses to operate as homestays, offering sit-down loos and maybe a hot shower; these include Mr Binh at Ban Kho Muang village (☎0169 490 4372) and Mr Si at Ban Hieu village (☎0123 818 0616). Daily bed and board costs around $12.

Ninh Binh and around

The provincial capital of **NINH BINH** is an unattractive, traffic-heavy northern town with no sights of its own worth seeing. However, it makes an ideal base for trips out to the surrounding hills, which shelter several natural, historical and architectural attractions that could keep you busy for several days. A few kilometres southwest of town is **Tam Coc**, where sampans queue up to take tourists on boat trips through the limestone tunnels and between karst outcrops. West of Ninh Binh, **Trang An** offers a similar experience to Tam Coc, though boats are a bit bigger and it's generally more popular with domestic tourists. A little further north from here is one of Vietnam's ancient capitals, **Hoa Lu**, represented by two darkly atmospheric dynastic temples. Still further on is **Bai Dinh Pagoda** – though decidedly non-ancient, this ranks as the largest Buddhist complex in Vietnam, and is worth a look for its sheer scale alone. All of these places can be tackled in one day by car or motorbike, or by bicycle via the back lanes.

Northwest of Ninh Binh, more boat trips are in store at **Kenh Ga**, to visit a limestone cave, and at **Van Long Nature Reserve**, which are both on the road that leads to Cuc Phuong (see p.320). The only attraction to the southeast of Ninh Binh, the stone mass of **Phat Diem Cathedral** wallows in the rice fields, an extraordinary amalgam of Western and Oriental architecture that still shepherds an active Catholic community.

RED-SHANKED DOUC LANGUR, VAN LONG NATURE RESERVE (P.318) >

Hanoi is only a couple of hours away, and the Hoa Lu–Tam Coc–Bich Dong circuit makes a popular and inexpensive day-tour out of the capital. However, with more time, it's far better to take advantage of the **hotels** in Ninh Binh or the surrounding countryside and explore the area at a more leisurely pace.

Tam Coc and around

7km southwest of Ninh Binh • Boats 7am–5pm (go early or late to avoid the crowds; take sunscreen and an umbrella, as the boats are not shielded from the elements) • Entry 120,000đ/person, boat 150,000đ/2 people

It's hard not to be won over by the mystical, watery beauty of **Tam Coc** – the "Three Caves" – which is effectively a miniature landlocked version of Ha Long Bay, and an easy cycle ride from Ninh Binh. Be aware, however, that the excursion can seem relentlessly commercial, with many travellers having a wonderful day spoiled by hard-sell antics – persistent peddling of embroideries and soft drinks by the rowers.

The two-hour boat trip (each boat seats two people) from Dinh Cac pier in Van Lam village brings some memorable sights, especially of dumpling-shaped karst hills in a flooded landscape where river and rice paddy merge serenely into one. Sometimes the rowers switch from rowing with their arms to rowing with their legs to give their muscles a rest, which is a novel sight if you've never seen this technique before. Keep an eye open for mountain goats high on the cliffs, and bright, darting kingfishers. Journey's end is **Tam Coc** itself: three long, dark tunnel-caves (Hang Ca, Hang Giua and Hang Cuoi) eroded through the limestone hills with barely sufficient clearance for the sampan after heavy rains.

Bich Dong

2km west of Tam • Free

The cave-pagoda of **Bich Dong**, or "Green Pearl Grotto", is in fact three pagodas; one at the base, one in the middle, and one at the top of Ngu Nhac Mountain. Stone-cut steps, entangled by the thick roots of banyan trees, lead up a cliff face to the middle pagoda. Though originally built in the fifteenth century, several of the buildings you see are quite recent. Inside the cave, three Buddhas sit on lotus thrones beside a head-shaped rock, which purportedly bestows longevity if touched. Walk through the cave to emerge higher up the cliff, from where steps continue (you'll need a torch) to the third and final temple and a viewpoint from where you can gaze over the waterlogged scene.

ACCOMMODATION
Emeralda Resort	3
Hoa Lu Eco Backpackers Hostel	2
Ninh Binh Legend	1
Queen	4
Xuan Hoa	5

EATING
Chookies	1
Queen	2
Trung Tuyet	3
Xuan Hoa	4

NINH BINH

Mua Cave

3km north of Tam Coc • Daily 7am–5pm (6pm in summer) • 100,000đ

In fact, it's not **Mua Cave** (Hang Múua) that is worth the diversion, but the pagoda and its viewpoint from the hillside above. A punishing 467 steps zigzag upwards from beside the cave entrance out to a lookout across vast karst mountainscape. The land around the cave entrance has been developed into a resort, so there's an overpriced restaurant on site where you can pick up refreshments.

Trang An

9km northwest of Ninh Binh • Boats 7am–5pm (take a hat or umbrella and sunscreen, as the boats are not covered; a torch is useful for seeing stalactites in the caves) • Admission and boat hire 200,000đ; boats here need a minimum of four people, or it's 800,000đ to go alone • From Ninh Binh, head north on Tran Hung Dao, and turn left onto Trang An, a broad new highway

The boat trip around the **Trang An Scenic Landscape Complex** (its unwieldy official name), is basically the same as the one at Tam Coc, so unless you really love the experience, you wouldn't want to do both. Differences are that there are a generous **nine caves** here, the journey takes longer (about three hours), and it's a bit more expensive. Rowers steer their boats along the Sao Khe River, through the various caves and along lush valleys between them, and the trip usually includes one or more stops at **temples** to stretch your legs.

Mind your head when passing through caves as some have very low clearance; in fact, some caves have been widened or heightened to accommodate boats, which detracts somewhat from their beauty. As at Tam Coc, it's a rather commercial experience, with hundreds of boats lined up at the pier, but there's less hassle from vendors and once you're on the river you can concentrate on the natural beauty around you. If you're cycling in the area, you can see the pier and boats bobbing along the river from the main road.

Hoa Lu

12km northwest of Ninh Binh • Daily 6.30am–6pm • Admission to temples 20,000đ • From Ninh Binh, head north on Tran Hung Dao, and turn left onto Trang An, a broad new highway; pass Trang An and continue to Hoa Lu

In the tenth century, this site was the capital of an early, independent Vietnamese kingdom called **Dai Co Viet**. The fortified royal palaces of the Dinh and Le kings are now reduced to rubble, but their dynastic **temples** (seventeenth-century copies of eleventh-century originals) still rest quietly in a narrow valley surrounded by wooded, limestone hills. Though the temple buildings and attractive walled courtyards are unspectacular, the inner sanctuaries are compelling – mysterious, dark caverns where statues of the kings, wrapped in veils of pungent incense, are worshipped by the light of candles.

The temples

The more impressive of the two temples is the one dedicated to **Dinh Tien Hoang**, who seized power in 968 AD and moved the capital south from Co Loa in the Red River Delta to this secure valley, far from the threat of Chinese intervention. Dinh Tien Hoang's gilded effigy can be seen in the temple's second sanctuary room, flanked by his three sons.

The second temple, dedicated to **Le Dai Hanh**, came about as the result of the anarchy that followed the death of King Dinh Tien Hoang. Le Hoan, commander of Dinh's army and supposed lover (and eventual husband) of his queen, wrested power and declared himself King Le Dai Hanh in 980. Le Dai Hanh is enshrined in the temple's rear sanctuary with his eldest son and Queen Duong Van Nga. If you have the energy to climb the steep hill opposite the ticket office, you'll find the tomb of Dinh Tien Hoang as well as some sweeping views of the karst landscape.

Bai Dinh Pagoda

21km northwest of Ninh Binh • Pagoda 50,000đ, grounds free • Head north on Tran Hung Dao, and turn left onto Trang An, a broad new highway; past Trang An and Hoa Lu, branch left on to Highway 38B to Bai Dinh

Nine kilometres west of Hoa Lu is the jaw-dropping **Bai Dinh Pagoda**, which opened in 2010 and is only now being completed. Bai Dinh's sheer scale makes it unique among Vietnamese Buddhist complexes – its numerous halls and courtyards sprawl up the mountainside for almost a kilometre. The front courtyard is lined with over five hundred arhat statues (each individually designed), while the largest bell and Buddha statue weigh in at 36 and 100 tonnes respectively. Although the temple is a functioning place of worship, it feels like a tourist trap, albeit one laid on primarily for locals. It is nonetheless a spectacular thing to behold, particularly the wild extravagance of the three main hall interiors, all of which are filled with gigantic golden statues, and have their walls lined with dozens of smaller versions of the same.

Van Long Nature Reserve

18km northwest of Ninh Binh, 2km east of Tran Me • Daily 7am–5pm • Entry 40,000/person, 1hr 30min boat trip 60,000đ/2 people

The more beguiling of the two boat trips in the area takes you round the shallow, reed-filled lagoons of **Van Long Nature Reserve**. From the ticket office you are poled across the wetlands and among the limestone outcrops in a low-slung bamboo sampan. Take binoculars, sunscreen and an umbrella. The crags are home to Vietnam's largest population of the exceptionally rare **Delacour's langur**, and the reed beds provide refuge for migratory waterfowl. **Hawkers** are banned from using boats but they gather round the ticket office whenever a tour bus appears. All things considered, it's a much more peaceful place than Tam Coc, and if you go early or late in the day, you might not see another boat.

Kenh Ga

22km northwest of Ninh Binh • 1hr 30min boat trips 100,000đ/person (min 2 people)

The village of **Kenh Ga** sits on a canal and is accessible only by water; though the trip may not be as scenic as others in the Ninh Binh area, it's still worth the journey. Ensure you hire a boat from the official ticket office by the pier, or you might be charged an exorbitant price. Many village families live on boats and the whole place seems to be engaged in watery pursuits: boatyards turn out concrete-hulled barges to take gravel and quarried stone downstream; there are fish farms and great flocks of ducks; and sampans bustle about, often propelled by people rowing with their feet. Kenh Ga (Chicken Canal) supposedly gets its name from the nearby hot spring where chickens were soaked in the near-boiling water to make them easier to pluck.

Phat Diem

Kim Son village, 28km southeast of Ninh Binh • Daily 7.30–11.30am & 1.30–5pm, but these times are not always adhered to • Free • Frequent public buses depart from Ninh Binh bus station for the 1hr journey to Kim Son village, though note that the last bus back leaves at around 3.30pm; by rented motorbike or bicycle, take Highway 10 heading straight east from Ninh Binh's Lim Bridge and, when you get to Kim Son, 100m after passing an elegant covered bridge, take a right turn

Strike southeast from Ninh Binh and there's no mistaking that you've stumbled on a **Christian enclave**, where church spires sprout out of the flat paddy land on all sides; it's

FATHER SIX AND THE QUIET AMERICAN

The idea for Phat Diem Cathedral was conceived and carried out by Father Tran Luc (also known as **Father Six**), whose tomb lies behind the bell tower. It was more than ten years in the preparation, as stone and wood were transported from the provinces of Thanh Hoa and Nghe An, though it apparently took a mere three months to build in 1891. During the French War, the Catholic Church formed a powerful political group in Vietnam that stood virtually independent of the French administration but also opposed to the Communists. The then bishop of Phat Diem, Monseigneur Le Huu Tu, was outspokenly anti-French and an avowed nationalist, but, as his diocese lay on the edge of government-held territory, the French supplied him with sufficient arms to maintain a militia of two thousand men in return for containing Viet Minh infiltration. However, in December 1951 the Viet Minh launched a major assault on the village and took it. When paratroopers came in to regain control, the Viet Minh withdrew, taking with them a valuable supply of weapons. The author **Graham Greene** was in Phat Diem at the time, on an assignment for *Life* magazine, and watched the battle from the bell tower of the cathedral – later using the scene in his novel *The Quiet American*.

said that 95 percent of the district's population attend church regularly. These coastal communities of northern Vietnam were among the first to be targeted by Portuguese missionaries in the sixteenth century, and this area owes its particular zeal to the Jesuit Alexandre de Rhodes who preached here in 1627. The greatest monument to all this religious fervour is the stone cathedral, **Phat Diem**, built in 1891 in **Kim Son village**.

If travelling with your own transport, it's worth stopping about 5km before Phat Diem to also take in the imposing **Tran Dao Cathedral** beside the main road, with its amusing gargoyles and a lifelike statue of the Virgin Mary clutching a bloodied Jesus.

6

The cathedral

The first surprise at Phat Diem Cathedral is its monumental **bell pavilion**, whose curved roofs and triple gateway could easily be the entrance to a Vietnamese temple save for a few telltale crosses and a host of angels. The structure is built entirely of dressed stone, as is the equally impressive cathedral facade sheltering in its wake. Behind, the tiled double roof of the **nave** extends for 74m, supported by 52 immense ironwood pillars and sheltering a cool, dark and peaceful sanctuary. The **altar** table is chiselled from a single block of marble, decorated with elegant sprays of bamboo, while the altarpiece above glows with red and gold lacquers in an otherwise sober interior. Twelve priests conduct daily services here for the large community of Catholics.

Ho Citadel

60km southwest of Ninh Binh, near the junction of highways 217 and 45 (Vinh Loc is the nearest town) • Daily 7am–5pm • 10,000đ; informative booklet available for 120,000đ at the museum • No public transport

The **Ho Citadel**, built in the late fourteenth century along feng shui principles for an influential and powerful Confucian state, sits in a pretty area between the Truong Son and Don Son mountains and between the Ma and Buoi rivers. The Ho dynasty that built the place was short lived, lasting just seven years (1400–07), but their legacy lives on in this remarkable structure, designated by UNESCO as a World Heritage Site in 2011. After six centuries, its **walls** – measuring nearly a kilometre on each side, pierced by giant gateways and made of massive stones, some weighing over 20 tonnes – still stand virtually intact, though there's nothing within them now but rice paddies, which lend an enigmatic atmosphere to the place. A small **museum** near the south gate displays a few artefacts such as stone cannonballs that were found on the site; another display in a nearby thatched hut explains how the citadel was built with stone cut and transported from nearby quarries.

ARRIVAL AND DEPARTURE

NINH BINH AND AROUND

By train The train station is east of the Van River on Hang Hoa Tham.
Destinations Da Nang (5 daily; 14hr); Dong Hoi (4 daily; 10hr); Hanoi (4 daily; 2hr 30min); HCMC (5 daily; 40hr); Hue (4 daily; 13–14hr); Vinh (4 daily; 4hr).
By bus The central bus station is on Le Dai Hanh, east of the Van River. From here, public buses depart for Hanoi's Giap Bat and Luong Yen stations, as well as Haiphong and Kim Son, for Phat Diem. For all points south, including Hue, Da Nang, Hoi An and HCMC, open-tour buses en route from Hanoi (twice daily) are recommended as they pick up and drop off at their associated hotels. Public buses south stop on the new Ninh Binh bypass and need to be flagged down.
Destinations Haiphong (frequent; 3hr); Hanoi (every 20min; 2hr); Kim Son (frequent; 1hr; note that the last bus back leaves at around 3.30pm).

GETTING AROUND

Ninh Binh town is quite a sprawl, though it's easy to cover the area near the bus and train stations on foot. The best way to visit nearby sights is by motorbike or bicycle – all hotels will provide you with a photocopied map.

By motorbike and bicycle Almost every hotel can arrange motorbike rental at $5–8 per day, while bicycles cost $2–5 per day, depending on quality.
By xe om A xe om should get you anywhere in town for 20,000đ to 30,000đ. A ride to Tam Coc or Trang An (with waiting time) should be no more than 150,000đ; factor in a little more if you want to make more stops.

TOURS

Tours From Ninh Binh to either Tam Coc or Trang An start at $10 on a bike or $20/car and will likely include a stop at Hoa Lu. Hanoi tour operators (see p.367) also run day-trips, starting at $20/seat in a minibus. Check your entry fee is included in the price.

ACCOMMODATION

Emeralda Resort Van Long Reserve, Gia Van Commune, Gia Vien District, 18km northwest of Ninh Binh ☎ 0229 365 8333, ⊛ emeraldaresort.com; map p.316. This rural resort features huge rooms (the smallest are 50 square metres), equipped with natural wood furnishings and enjoying wonderful views of the surrounding countryside. There's also a spa, a large outdoor pool and heated indoor pool, kids' club, movie room and mini golf. $139

Hoa Lu Eco Backpackers Hostel Trang An village, 8km from Ninh Binh ☎ 090 439 6779, ⊛ hoaluecohomestay .com; map p.316. The real reason to come to Ninh Binh is the landscape, and this backpacker-friendly place along a bumpy track is right by Trang An Grottoes. Ideal if you have your own transport, otherwise the remote location means you'll pay a lot more for services such as onward travel or food and drink. The dorm is twelve-bed. Dorms $8, doubles $22

Ninh Binh Legend Le Thai To ☎ 0229 389 9880, ⊛ ninhbinhlegendhotel.com; map p.316. Currently Ninh Binh's most luxurious option, the eleven-floor monolith is no beauty from the outside, but the rooms are much more appealing: wood floors, solid furnishings, deep mattresses on the beds and marble counters in the bathroom. There's a pool, fitness centre, spa and tennis courts, and good views of limestone hills from some rooms. It's about 3km north of the town centre. $95

Queen 20 Hoang Hoa Tham ☎ 0229 389 3535, ⊛ queenhotel.vn; map p.316. Close to the bus station and on a street with decent restaurants, the *Queen* has been housing budget travellers for years. Flatscreen TVs and excellent en-suite facilities, with breakfast included in the rates – they also arrange tours and rent out bikes and motorbikes. $20

★**Xuan Hoa** 31d Minh Khai ☎ 0229 388 0970, ⊛ xuanhoahotel.com; map p.316. Owner Xuan and his family provide the friendliest welcome in Ninh Binh. They have two hotels, situated almost side by side just off the main drag; relatively quiet by Ninh Binh standards, they overlook a lake. The rooms are spotless, modern and well equipped, and some have views of the mountains to the west. The owners are particularly knowledgeable about the area, run excellent day-tours of the surrounding sights, and organize trips to Pu Luong Nature Reserve (see box, p.314). $15

EATING

Chookies 17 Luong Van Tuy ☎ 094 834 6026; map p.316. Pretty much the only spot in town for Western food, *Chookies* serves up excellent burgers, fat chips, milkshakes and cold beer. They have a helpful tourist office at the same address and have opened a beer garden with more veggie options near Tam Coc (on the road towards Bich Dong). Mon & Wed–Sun 11.30am–10pm.

Queen 20 Hoang Hoa Tham ☎ 0229 389 3535; map p.316. The restaurant at *Queen* hotel (see above) serves the local speciality (goat), with dishes 120,000–180,000đ, as well as pizzas and spaghetti in a modern setting. Daily 7am–10pm.

Trung Tuyet 14 Hoang Hoa Tham ☎ 094 935 8885; map p.316. This simple family restaurant almost next door to *Queen* hotel features an extensive menu of tasty Vietnamese food (most dishes 60,000–80,000đ) in four different sizes of serving. Be warned – the "small" is pretty big already. Try the beef with pineapple – yum. Daily 11.30am–9pm.

★**Xuan Hoa** 31d Minh Khai ☎ 0229 388 0970; map p.316. As with the hotel (see above), so with the restaurant – it's great value. Simple surroundings but fantastic food served by Hoa, the wife of owner Xuan. They serve goat dishes (120,000đ), as well as rabbit, frog, snail and eels. Most mains around 60,000đ, set menus upwards of 100,000đ. Daily 7am–10pm.

Cuc Phuong National Park

45km northwest of Ninh Binh • 60,000đ • ☎ 0229 384 8006, ⊛ cucphuongtourism.com.vn

In 1962 Vietnam's **first national park** was established around a narrow valley between forested limestone hills on the borders of Ninh Binh, Thanh Hoa and Hoa Binh provinces, containing over two hundred square kilometres of tropical evergreen rainforest. **Cuc Phuong** is well set up for tourism and sees a steady stream of visitors, attracted principally by the excellent **primate rescue centre**, though other attractions include one-thousand-year-old **ancient trees** (living fossils up to 70m high), tree

6

WALKING IN CUC PHUONG

Of several independent **walks** in Cuc Phuong, a couple of the most popular are to ancient trees in the interior of the park. For a steamy 7km (roughly 2hr), a well-trodden loop trail from the park centre (18km from the park gate) winds through typical rainforest and past Palace Cave (torch essential) to reach the magnificent **cho xanh tree**, a 45m-high, one-thousand-year-old specimen of *Terminalia myriocarpa* – its dignity only slightly marred by a viewing platform. Easier still, about halfway between the park gate and the park centre, are the 3km (6km return) paved trail to an ancient tree and the 200-odd steps up to the nearby **Cave of the Prehistoric Man** (torch essential).

More adventurous challenges include a tough 11km hike to **Silver Cloud Peak** (3hr; 500,000đ/group) and a 16km hike through the park to the **Muong village of Kanh**, where you spend the night in a traditional stilthouse (5hr; 770,000đ/group); for these you'll need a guide, which you can arrange at park headquarters.

ferns and kilometre-long corkscrewing lianas, as well as a treasure-trove of medicinal plants, a turtle conservation centre with over 1100 turtles confiscated from illegal wildlife traders, and a Muong minority village that can be visited on an overnight trek (see box above).

Even now Cuc Phuong National Park hasn't been fully surveyed but is estimated to contain approximately three hundred **bird species** and one hundred and thirty **mammal species**, some of which were first discovered here, such as red-bellied squirrels and a fish that lives in underground rivers. Several species of bat and monkey inhabit the park, while sadly, illegal hunting has taken its toll on the bears and leopards that once roamed its upper reaches. You're really only likely to see butterflies, birds and perhaps a civet cat or a tree squirrel, rather than the more exotic fauna.

The most enjoyable time for walking in these hills is October to January, when mosquitoes and leeches take a break and temperatures are relatively cool – but this is also peak season. Flowers are at their best February and March, while April and May are the months when lepidopterists can enjoy the "**butterfly festival**" as thousands of butterflies colour the forest. Apart from walking (see box above), you can rent mountain bikes to ride the park's trails and kayaks to paddle round **Mac Lake**.

Endangered Primate Rescue Center

60,000đ · Daily 9.30–11am & 1.30–4.30pm · ☎ 0229 384 8002, ⓦ eprc.asia

Some of the luckier victims of illegal hunting in Vietnam are now to be seen in the **Endangered Primate Rescue Center** located near the park gate. Opened in 1993, the centre not only cares for rescued animals, but also tries to rehabilitate them by releasing them into an adjacent semi-wild area. In addition, the centre runs crucial research, conservation and breeding programmes. At any one time there may be between sixty and a hundred animals here, including **Delacour's langur**, with its distinctive black body and white "shorts", the Cat Ba, or **golden-headed langur**, and the **grey-shanked douc langur**, as well as various lorises and gibbons – a unique opportunity to see these incredibly rare species at close quarters.

ARRIVAL AND DEPARTURE   CUC PHUONG NATIONAL PARK

By bus A morning bus runs from Giap Bat bus station in Hanoi directly to the park at 9am, returning at 3pm. If coming from Ninh Binh, take the public bus (20,000đ).

By motorbike From Ninh Binh you can rent a motorbike or hire a xe om (about 250,000đ return including waiting time). Head north on Highway 1 for 10km to find the sign indicating "Cuc Phuong" to the left. From the gate it's a further 18km to the heart of the forest.

By tour Day-trips from Hanoi start at $35/person (not including entrance fees) in a minibus and include lunch and guide. Or, if you are already there, it is easy to organize guided treks, including an overnight stay in a Muong village, at the park headquarters (see box above).

INFORMATION

Park headquarters The park headquarters just beyond the Cuc Phuong entrance gate hold a number of buildings including the entry ticket booth, Primate Center and accommodation. Entry tickets are on sale here (daily 7–11.30am & 1.30–4pm), and you can also arrange accommodation (here, or further into the park) and guided treks. Be aware that Cuc Phuong is some way above the plains and winter nights can get chilly.

ACCOMMODATION

Booking accommodation online is easy, and you can even arrange an airport pick up. **Homestays** at Kanh minority village can be organized at the park headquarters, but you must also pay for a guide to accompany you. **Prices** rise at weekends and food and drinks are always expensive; singles pay seventy percent of room rate.

Mac Lake 2km from the park entrance ☎0229 384 8006, ⓦ cucphuongtourism.com.vn. Detached bungalows with double room and en-suite bathroom dot the shore of Mac Lake. It's a tranquil spot, but the restaurant and snack shop is often closed. $20

Park centre 18km along the park road ☎0229 384 8006, ⓦ cucphuongtourism.com.vn. In the wild interior of the park there's a basic stilthouse. The narrow rooms squeeze in twin beds, and the shared bathrooms don't have hot water. The private bungalows (with double room and en-suite bathroom) that are scattered around only have electricity in the evening. The restaurant – which is often undersupplied – is about a 15min walk away. Bungalows $17, stilthouse $7

Park headquarters Close to the park entrance ☎0229 384 8006, ⓦ cucphuongtourism.com.vn. Unexpectedly comfortable accommodation with deluxe en-suite rooms. There is also a cheaper stilthouse where rooms have twin beds and shared bathrooms. Doubles $40, stilthouse $7

Haiphong

Buzzing **HAIPHONG** is a great place to get a handle on urban Vietnam. A city of almost two million souls, it's the third largest in the land, though with just a fraction of Hanoi's and Ho Chi Minh City's tourists and expats, your presence is likely to be greeted with genuine curiosity. Haiphong is well connected to both Hanoi and Cat Ba and can function as a good stopping-off point for those who don't fancy joining a Ha Long Bay tour; hole up here for a while and you'll uncover varied eating and drinking options, and enjoy the pleasant lack of street hustlers. Although a little scruffy around the edges, Haiphong's broad and bustling central avenues are shaded by ranks of flame trees and dotted with well-tended **colonial villas**, most of which lie along the crescent-shaped nineteenth-century core that forms a southern boundary to today's city centre.

Brief history

Haiphong lies 100km east of Hanoi on the Cua Cam River, one of the main channels of the Red River Estuary. Originally a small **fishing village** and military outpost, its development into a major port in the seventeenth century stems more from its proximity to the capital city than from favourable local conditions. In fact it was an astonishingly poor choice for a harbour, 20km from the open sea with shallow, shifting channels, no fresh water and little solid land. The first quay was only built in 1817 and it was not until 1874, when Haiphong was ceded to the French, that a town began to develop. With remarkable determination, the first settlers drained the mosquito-ridden marshes, sinking foundations sometimes as deep as 30m into huge earth platforms that passed for building plots. Doubts about the harbour lingered, but then, in 1883, the nine-thousand-strong **French Expeditionary Force**, sent to secure Tonkin, established a supply base in Haiphong and its future as the north's principal port was secured.

The twentieth century

In November 1946 Haiphong reappeared in the history books when rising tensions between French troops and soldiers of the newly declared Democratic Republic of

Vietnam erupted in a dispute about customs control. Shots were exchanged over a Chinese junk suspected of smuggling, and the French replied with a **naval bombardment** of Haiphong's Vietnamese quarter, killing many civilians (estimates range from one to six thousand), and only regained control of the streets after several days of rioting. But the two nations were now set for war – a war that ended, appropriately, with the citizens of Haiphong watching the last colonial troops embark in 1955 after the collapse of French Indochina.

Barely a decade later the city was again under siege, this time by American planes targeting a major supply route for Soviet "aid". In May 1972 President Nixon ordered the mining of Haiphong harbour, but less than a year later America was clearing up the mines under the terms of the **Paris ceasefire agreement**. By late 1973 the harbour was deemed safe once more, in time for the exodus of desperate **boat people** as hundreds of refugees escaped in overladen fishing boats (see box, p.448).

6

Haiphong Museum

66 Dien Bien Phu • Tues & Thurs–Sat 8–11am, Wed & Sun 8–11am & 7.30–9.30pm • 5000đ

On the northern side of the city centre, the wine-red **Haiphong Museum** is an attractive example of Haiphong's colonial-era structures, even if the displays themselves lack glamour. The collection spans seventeen rooms and contains around three thousand exhibits, which are divided into three sections – on natural resources, local history before 1955, and from 1955 to the present. These exhibits include ancient jewellery, household implements and colonial-era photos, and many are labelled in English. In

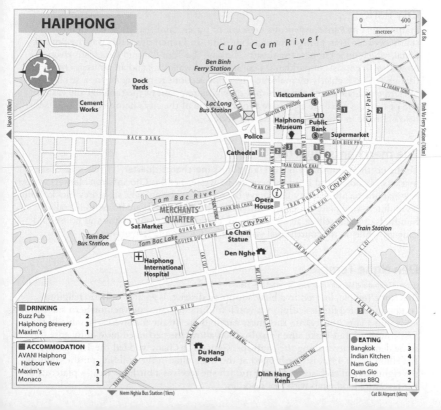

HAIPHONG

DRINKING
Buzz Pub	2
Haiphong Brewery	3
Maxim's	1

ACCOMMODATION
AVANI Haiphong Harbour View	2
Maxim's	1
Monaco	3

EATING
Bangkok	3
Indian Kitchen	4
Nam Giao	1
Quan Gio	5
Texas BBQ	2

the garden outside are war relics such as an MIC-17 aircraft and a minesweeper of the Vietnamese Navy. Note that opening hours are limited, and even during listed times it isn't always open.

Haiphong Cathedral

46 Hoang Van Thu • Dawn to dusk • Free

Just to the southwest of the Haiphong Museum is the square tower of **Haiphong Cathedral**, built in the late nineteenth century and renovated in 2010 after years of neglect; it's European in style but with an altar decorated along the same burgundy-and-gold colour scheme as a Vietnamese pagoda. Enter via the east gate.

Haiphong Opera House

27 Tran Hung Dao

South from the cathedral is the buttermilk-yellow **Haiphong Opera House**; constructed of materials shipped from France in the early 1900s, it faces onto a wide, open square – a site remembered locally for the deaths of forty revolutionaries during the street battles of November 1946 "after a valiant fight against French invaders". Unfortunately, performances here are very irregular, usually only taking place when huge tour groups are in town. There's a **flower market** just west of the opera house in the city park, and a new flag tower in front of it.

City Park

Haiphong's **City Park** consists of a crescent of public land that slices through the city centre between Tran Hung Dao and Tran Phu. In French times this was the **Bonnal Canal**, which once ran past the theatre, linking the Tam Bac and Cua Cam rivers. Nowadays it consists of parkland, pedestrianized walkways and an amusement park; though cut up regularly by major roads, some sections remain good for a stroll. To its western end is **Tam Bac Lake**, the only surviving remnant of the canal; at the eastern end of the lake you'll see a massive **bronze statue** of the city's heroine, Le Chan (see below), made in a bold Socialist Realist style.

The merchants' quarter

To the north of Tam Bac Lake is Haiphong's **merchants' quarter**, a lively area of street markets, chandlers and ironmongers. At its western end is **Cho Sat (Iron Market)** whose original nineteenth-century halls have been replaced by an ugly, six-storey block. Still, it's an interesting place to spend some time; the lower levels are home to literally hundreds of stalls, selling all sorts of food, clothing, electronic items and household gadgets, while on the fourth level you'll find a few simple restaurants.

Den Nghe Temple

Corner of Le Chan and Me Linh • Daily 7am–noon & 1.30–7pm • Free

Den Nghe Temple, located in a busy shopping district, is an atmospheric religious compound noted for its sculptures; you'll find the entrance on the northern side, which leads into a large courtyard. The finest carvings are on the massive stone table in the first courtyard, but make sure you also look above the perfumed haze of incense for some detailed friezes along the rooftops. **General Le Chan**, who led the Trung Sisters' Rebellion (see p.430), is worshipped at the main altar in the building on the right; on the eighth day of each second lunar month she receives a birthday treat – platefuls of her favourite food, crab with rice noodles.

Du Hang Pagoda

121 Du Hang, 2km south of the city centre • Dawn to dusk • Free

Located across the railway tracks in the south of town, **Du Hang Pagoda** is a rewarding attraction. In its present form, the pagoda dates from the late seventeenth century and is accessed through an imposing triple-roofed bell tower. Interestingly, the architecture reveals a distinct Khmer influence in the form of vase-shaped pinnacles ornamenting the roof and pillars of the inner courtyard – according to Buddhist legend these contain propitious *cam lo*, or sweet dew. Beside it lies a small, walled garden of burial stupas.

6

Dinh Hang Kenh

Nguyen Cong Tru • Dawn to dusk • Free

It's worth visiting **Dinh Hang Kenh**, 1km east of the Du Hang Pagoda, if you haven't yet seen a *dinh*, or communal house. This one is a low, graceful building with a sweeping expanse of tiled roof facing across a spacious courtyard to an ornamental lake. Despite the surrounding apartment blocks, it's still an impressive sight. Thirty-two monumental ironwood columns hold up the roof and populate the long, dark hall that is also noted for its carvings of 308 dragons sculpted in thirty writhing nests.

ARRIVAL AND DEPARTURE
HAIPHONG

By plane The Cat Bi Airport is 7km southeast of the city, around 130đ by taxi. Vietnam Airlines (ⓦ vietnamairlines .com), Jetstar (ⓦ jetstar.com) and VietJet (7 Tran ⓦ vietjetair.com) all operate services here.

Destinations Da Nang (3–4 daily; 1hr 15min); Ho Chi Minh City (6–8 daily; 2hr).

By train Haiphong train station is on the southeast side of town on Luong Khanh Thien, and has services to Hanoi only; note that some of these services terminate at Hanoi's lesser-used Long Bien station.

Destinations Hanoi (4 daily; 2hr 15min–3hr).

By bus Lac Long bus station is centrally located on Cu Chinh Lan (convenient for Ben Binh harbour) and receives buses from the northeast. Niem Nghia, 3km southwest, usually receives buses from the south. Tam Bac, on the edge of the merchants' quarter, is the most common arrival point for buses from the capital, Hanoi, though Hanoi-bound

minibuses also hang around the Ben Binh harbour and can be flagged down on the riverfront south of Dien Bien Phu.

Destinations Bai Chay, Ha Long City (every 30min; 2hr); Hanoi (every 10–20min; 2hr 30min); Ninh Binh (every 30min; 4hr).

By hydrofoil and ferry Ben Binh ferry station, on Ben Binh, handles departures to Cat Ba Island daily, costing around 180,000đ; avoid touts and purchase from the ticket office. Quickest is the hydrofoil (8am–4pm), which docks in the harbour at Cat Ba town, within walking distance of most hotels. Another option is to take a bus from Hai Phong's Ben Binh harbour to Dinh Vu port. Here, you take a ferry to Cat Hai Island (30,000đ), and change to a second ferry for Cat Ba's Cai Vieng harbour (40,000đ), where buses meet the ferry.

Destinations Cat Ba town (4 daily; 45min); Cat Ba Cai Vieng harbour (6–8 daily; 1hr 10min).

THE BATTLES OF BACH DANG RIVER

The **Vietnamese navy** fought its two most glorious and decisive battles in the Bach Dang Estuary, east of Haiphong. The first, in 938 AD, marked the end of a thousand years of Chinese occupation when General **Ngo Quyen** led his rebels to victory, defeating a vastly superior force by means of a brilliant ruse. Waiting until high tide, General Ngo lured the **Chinese fleet** upriver over hundreds of iron-tipped stakes embedded in the estuary mud, then counter-attacked as the tide turned and drove the enemy boats back downstream to founder on the now-exposed stakes.

History repeated itself some three centuries later during the struggle to repel **Kublai Khan**'s Mongol armies. This time it was the great **Tran Hung Dao** who led the Vietnamese in a series of battles culminating in that of the Bach Dang River in 1288. The ingenious strategy worked just as well second time round when over four hundred vessels were lost or captured, finally seeing off the ambitious Khan.

GETTING AROUND

By xe om and cyclo These are readily available and a good way of getting around the central district, although it's quite possible to tackle most of it on foot.

By taxi Haiphong Taxi ☎0225 383 8383; Mai Linh Taxi ☎0225 383 3833. The flag fare is around 12,000đ.

INFORMATION

Tourist Information Centre This is based at 56 Hoang Van Thu (Mon–Sat 8am–5pm; ☎0225 356 9600, ⓦ haiphongtourism.gov.vn). It's a fairly useful little office,

able to organize tours and sell maps of the area. There's usually an English-speaker present. If it's closed, try the office at 18 Minh Khai.

ACCOMMODATION

Haiphong has a fair number of hotels, but **budget accommodation** is hard to come by – there are no dorms or hostels here. Most hotels cluster on and around Dien Bien Phu, the city's main artery, with others dotted around town.

AVANI Haiphong Harbour View 12 Tran Phu ☎0225 382 7827, ⓦ minorhotels.com; map p.323. This mock-colonial, international-class hotel is as plush as Haiphong gets; just don't expect a view of the harbour. It boasts two restaurants, a piano bar and a pocket-sized pool, not to mention very stylish rooms, impeccable service and a superb buffet breakfast. $135

Maxim's 3k Ly Tu Trong ☎0225 374 6540, ⓦ hotelhaiphong.com; map p.323. Central, attractive and friendly, this has long been a magnet for budget travellers so you'd be wise to book ahead. It's also notable for being on what passes for a quiet road in Haiphong.

Rooms come with satellite TV, a/c and fridges; ask to look at one first as some have no windows. There is an in-house restaurant but note that the nearby bar-restaurant of the same name (see opposite) is not affiliated. Breakfast not included in the room rate. $20

Monaco 103 Dien Bien Phu ☎0225 374 6468, ⓦ haiphongmonacohotel.com; map p.323. The most attractive of Dien Bien Phu's many hotels, with an art-gallery-like reception hall. Rooms, going for up to $60, are designed with more attention than usual. Service can be a little off, but breakfast is included in the rate. $30

EATING

Haiphong is well endowed with a fair **range of places** to eat, serving everything from Indian to Italian as well as traditional Vietnamese cuisine; some (such as *Bangkok*) are quite classy. There's also good-value **seafood**.

Bangkok 22a Minh Khai ☎0225 382 3994; map p.323. Authentic Thai food served in an upmarket and stylish restaurant; the menu features dishes like *larb* (minced pork salad; 120,000đ), plus a range of spicy stir-fries and curries (most mains around 160,000đ). Good range of wines too. Look for the sign saying "BKK". Daily 10am–10pm.

Indian Kitchen 22d Minh Khai ☎0225 384 2558; map p.323. This newish place is smartly decorated and offers a broad menu of competitively priced dishes such as tandoor kebabs (70,000đ) and fish in banana leaf (150,000đ). Daily 10am–11pm.

Nam Giao 22 Le Dai Hanh ☎0225 381 0600; map p.323. Looking more like a temple or museum, this

atmospheric place has a short menu with dishes like grilled prawns for just 60,000đ, as well as teas, juices and beers. Daily 8am–10.30pm.

Quan Gio 29 Le Dai Hanh; map p.323. A step up from a street-food joint, this family-run cheap eatery serves *bun dau* (fried tofu, spring rolls and vermicelli noodles with a dipping sauce; 20,000đ) washed down with ice-cold fruit tea (5000đ). Daily 9am–7.30pm.

Texas BBQ 27 Minh Khai ☎0225 382 2689; map p.323. Hugely popular with locals and tourists alike, this place offers everything from pizzas to Thai curries and Mexican enchiladas; combo platters too, as well as cheap beer. Daily 8.30am–10.30pm.

DRINKING

Haiphong has some increasingly fancy bia hoi outlets, including the city's very own microbrewery. In the evenings, hit the cafés and small restaurants **around the theatre**, or join the throng promenading up and down the gardens, pausing at ice-cream parlours or beneath the flickering lights of popcorn vendors. If you're looking for more action, take a stroll along Minh Khai and Le Dai Hanh, both lined with restaurants and bars.

Buzz Pub 27 Hoang Van Thu ☎0225 351 5266; map p.323. Traditional Irish pub with an expat crowd who like the a/c and wide range of drinks. Live (loud) music at

weekends. Daily 10am–midnight.

Haiphong Brewery 16 Lach Tray, 2km southeast of the city centre ☎0225 364 0681; map p.323. This popular beer hall is a short taxi journey from the centre of the city. Strip lighting doesn't make for a cosy atmosphere, but the wooden tables are packed at lunchtimes. The beer and food menus are short and to the point (and available in English) and prices for a glass of draught beer start at 5500đ. Daily 11am–8pm.

Maxim's 51 Dien Bien Phu ☎ 0225 382 2934; map p.323. Decorated along contemporary Oriental lines, this restaurant-bar is a great place for a drink when there's a bit of a crowd. Cosy seating, friendly staff, and an extensive menu too in case you get peckish. There's often live music after 8.30pm. Daily 7am–11pm.

DIRECTORY

Hospital Haiphong International Hospital, 124 Nguyen Duc Canh ☎ 0225 395 5888.

Post office The GPO (daily 7.30am–7pm) is at the junction of Nguyen Tri Phuong and Ben Binh.

Cat Ba Island

Dragon-back mountain ranges mass on the horizon 20km out of Haiphong as you approach **Cat Ba Island**. The island, the largest member of an archipelago sitting on the west of Ha Long Bay, boasts only one settlement of any size – **Cat Ba town**, a buzzing tourist centre that was once a fishing village. The rest of the island is largely unspoilt and mostly inaccessible, with just a handful of paved roads across a landscape of enclosed valleys and shaggily forested limestone peaks, occasionally descending to lush coastal plains. In 1986 almost half the island and its adjacent waters were declared a **national park** in an effort to protect its diverse ecosystems, which range from offshore coral reefs and coastal mangrove swamps to tropical evergreen forest. Its value was further recognized in 2004, when the Cat Ba Archipelago was approved as a **UNESCO Biosphere Reserve**.

The wild terrain of Cat Ba Island lends itself to **adventure sports**, and many come here for rock climbing, hiking, kayaking and mountain biking, as well as cruising round **Ha Long Bay** or the nearer **Lan Ha Bay** (see p.332). With a string of mini-hotels and tourist restaurants lining the town's harbour, Cat Ba caters mostly for Western visitors to Ha Long Bay, while Ha Long City (see p.332) is the preferred base for Chinese, Korean and other Asian visitors. However, Cat Ba's appeal declines from June to August, when it's packed with domestic tourists and room rates rocket, and between November and March, when it's usually cold and damp.

Brief history

Archeological evidence shows that humans inhabited Cat Ba's many **limestone caves** at least six thousand years ago. Centuries later these same caves provided the perfect wartime hideaway – the military presence on Cat Ba has always been strong, for obvious strategic reasons. When trouble with China flared up in 1979, hundreds of ethnic Chinese islanders felt compelled to flee and the exodus continued into the next decade as "boat people" sailed off in search of a better life, depleting the island's population to fewer than fifteen thousand. Now that prosperity has come in the form of tourism, the population is growing rapidly.

Cat Ba town

Caught between green hills and a horseshoe bay alive with multicoloured fishing boats, **CAT BA TOWN**'s west-facing location makes it perfect for sunsets over outlying islands. Outside the summer peak, it retains a pretty laidback ambience despite the recent onslaught of tourism, which has seen a slew of new hotels and restaurants open along the harbour front. The town is divided into two sections: most tourist facilities are grouped around the **hydrofoil pier**, while 800m to the north lies the original, workaday **fishing village** with a bustling market and its accompanying food and bia hoi stalls. Directly behind the pier is a small hill topped by the town's **war memorial**, erected during Ho Chi Minh's visit to the island in 1953; behind this, on a higher hill, is an even better viewpoint at **Cannon Fort** (see p.331).

6

Tuan Chau & Ha Long City | Ha Long City

Titop Island

Gia Luan Port

Hang Sung Sot
Ho Dong Tien

Dong Me Cung

Cat Ba Island

Haiphong

Bridge (under construction)
Cai Vieng

CAT BA NATIONAL PARK

Park Headquarters

Ngu Lam

Viet Hai

Viet Hai Harbour

Hospital Cave (Quan Y Cave)

Dau Be Island

Lan Ha Bay

Ben Beo Tourist Wharf

Cat Ba

Monkey Island

Cat Ong Island

SEE 'CAT BA TOWN' MAP

N

ACCOMMODATION
Whisper of Nature 1

CAT BA ISLAND

0 — 4
kilometres

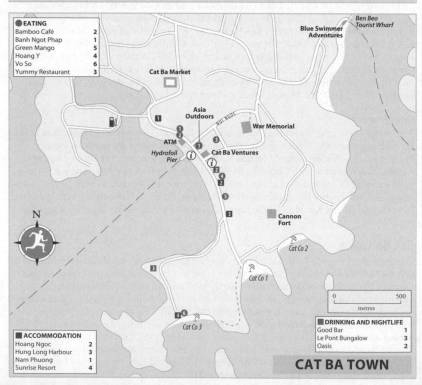

EATING
Bamboo Café	2
Banh Ngot Phap	1
Green Mango	5
Hoang Y	4
Vo So	6
Yummy Restaurant	3

Ben Beo Tourist Wharf

Blue Swimmer Adventures

Cat Ba Market

Asia Outdoors

NUI NGOC

War Memorial

ATM

Hydrofoil Pier

Cat Ba Ventures

Cannon Fort

Cat Co 2

Cat Co 1

N

Cat Co 3

0 — 500
metres

ACCOMMODATION
Hoang Ngoc	2
Hung Long Harbour	3
Nam Phuong	1
Sunrise Resort	4

DRINKING AND NIGHTLIFE
Good Bar	1
Le Pont Bungalow	3
Oasis	2

CAT BA TOWN

The beaches

To the south of town, on the far side of the peninsula, are three small, sandy **beaches**, romantically named Cat Co 1, Cat Co 2 and Cat Co 3. Cat Co 1, the middle bay, is the most popular with locals and a cliffside path links it with Cat Co 3, which makes a very pleasant walk. Cat Co 2 is quieter and cleaner.

ARRIVAL AND DEPARTURE   CAT BA TOWN

A **bridge** via Cat Hai Island is slated to join Cat Ba to the mainland in 2018, but at the time of research it was unclear if this would mean changes to ferry and hydrofoil services.

6

By tour Many people visit Cat Ba on a tour from Hanoi – several companies offer three-day tours of Ha Long Bay with one night on board and another on Cat Ba (see box, p.330). Most tours of Ha Long Bay from Cat Ba embark at Ben Beo tourist wharf, about 3km northeast of Cat Ba town.

By hydrofoil and ferry Hydrofoils (180,000đ) from Haiphong's Ben Binh ferry pier dock in Cat Ba harbour within walking distance of most hotels. Some express boats also use the harbour, while others use Cai Vieng port at the island's western point, and buses run passengers to and from here and the town. Ferries (70,000đ) from Tuan Chau (accessed from Ha Long City) land at the Gia Luan pier, in the north of the island, 40km from Cat Ba town. Public QH green buses leave Gia Luan at 9am, noon and 4pm (30,000VND) for Cat Ba town, and despite what some unscrupulous locals might tell you, foreigners are very much allowed to take the bus. Minibuses at the same price are usually there to meet ferries too.

Destinations Haiphong hydrofoil (2–4 daily; 45min); Haiphong express boat (6–8 daily; 1hr 30min); Tuan Chau–Ha Long City (3 daily; 50min).

By ferry and bus There are combined bus and ferry services to and from Hanoi Giap Bat and Nuoc Ngam bus stations run by several operators including Hoang Long Tourist Company (📞 0225 392 0920, 🌐 hoanglongasia .com; 240,000đ). These generally go via Dinh Vu ferry station in Haiphong and disembark at Cai Vieng. Getting back to Hanoi this way is easy: operators in Cat Ba town all sell tickets (with a small mark-up).

Destinations Hanoi (4 daily; 4hr 30min).

By motorbike The best route is the passenger and vehicle ferry (see p.333) from Tuan Chau (Ha Long City), to Gia Luan on the north coast of Cat Ba Island, then ride south across the island to Cat Ba town. From Haiphong, you can take motorbikes on the ferry from Dinh Vu (see p.325). You will be charged an extra 20,000đ for your motorbike on all routes.

GETTING AROUND

By bus QH green buses run between Cat Ba town and Gia Luan pier (3 daily; 30,000VND); for the latest timetables, check with the tourist office at the hydrofoil pier.

By motorbike and bicycle To explore the island independently, your best bet is to rent a motorbike with or without a driver. Xe om cruise around town and most hotels

rent motorbikes ($7/day) and mountain bikes ($4/day), but the steep hills are hard going in the heat).

By electric cars These hang around by the ferry terminal in the middle of the harbour and charge 10,000–20,000đ for short trips around town and to the beaches.

INFORMATION

Tourist information Cat Ba's information office is at 228 Harbour Road (daily 7am–8pm; 📞 0225 368 8215), with another branch at the hydrofoil pier. You can pick up

leaflets and maps, but be aware that they run their own tours and accommodation and hence can't be relied on to be impartial.

ACCOMMODATION

Thanks to a building boom, **accommodation** on Cat Ba represents good value on the whole. The exception is during the peak summer holiday period of June to Aug, when the place is absolutely packed and prices can more than double. There are few upper-range options in town, while budget hotels are popping up everywhere, especially along Nui Ngoc, where several hostels offer dorm beds at anywhere between $5 and $18. Note also that this street is home to many noisy clubs.

Hoang Ngoc 245 Harbour Rd 📞 0225 368 8788; map opposite. Rooms at this family-run guesthouse are fresh and pleasant, and there's a communal balcony on every floor; ask for a room at the front to enjoy sea views. Staff are helpful and friendly, not always a given in Cat Ba. $20

Hung Long Harbour 268 Harbour Rd 📞 0225 626 9269, 🌐 hunglonghotel.vn; map opposite. At this hard-to-miss building at the south end of the harbour road, most comfortable rooms have fabulous views of the bay. However, the staff are often busy checking tour groups in and out. $80

6

ORGANIZED TOURS IN CAT BA

Most hotels and agencies in Cat Ba town arrange **tours**, with little to choose between them on price; to ensure that you have quality to match, it pays to ask fellow travellers for up-to-date advice on the best choices – those below are certified. Tours include boat trips, of which the most pleasant is the short sail north into **Lan Ha Bay**, including a visit to a floating village, and then either walk into the national park (see opposite) or a half-day cruise around the maze of limestone islands, stopping at one of the coral-sand beaches for a spot of swimming or kayaking. You can also explore **Ha Long Bay** (see p.326) from here, either as a one- or two-day trip, with the option of returning to Cat Ba or being dropped off in Bai Chay. Other popular activities on and around Cat Ba include stand-up paddleboarding, all-day trekking and rock climbing – the karst landscape here is perfect for climbing and deep-water soloing (climbing without safety equipment until you fall into the sea).

★ **Asia Outdoors** 222 Harbour Rd (above the *Noble House*) ☎ 0225 368 8450, ⓦ asiaoutdoors.com.vn. Asia Outdoors pioneered rock climbing in Vietnam and remain the best operator for adventure activities (prices from around $58/day). They take climbers on a phenomenal network of routes and can incorporate boat trips (necessary to access some of the climbing sites), deep-water soloing, stand-up paddleboarding, kayaking, trekking, and the occasional beach party into their highly recommended, tailor-made packages. Experienced climbers can also hire gear here.

Blue Swimmer Adventures Ben Beo Pier ☎ 0225 368 8237, ⓦ blueswimmersailing.com. This outfit specializes in mountain biking on the island as well as sea-kayaking from one to three days, staying overnight on a junk or in a beach bungalow (prices from around $38/day).

Cat Ba Ventures 223 Harbour Rd ☎ 0225 388 8755, ☎ 091 246 7016, ⓦ catbaventures.com. Hands down the best operator when it comes to small-group cruises, with their highly professional management, English-speaking guides and well-organized tours that don't feel rushed or whisk you off to commission-paying pearl farms (prices from around $28 for one-day boat trip).

Nam Phuong 288 Harbour Rd ☎ 0225 388 8561; map p.328. Located towards the northern end of the harbour, this offers just a handful of small but clean rooms with good views. The novelty of this place is that the back wall of the hotel is formed by a cliff, and staff can help arrange any tour or vehicle rental. $10

★ **Sunrise Resort** Cat Co 3 beach ☎ 0225 388 7360, ⓦ catbasunriseresort.com; map p.328. If you want to feel the sand between your toes, head for this low-rise resort hotel, situated right on Cat Co 3 beach. The burgundy-trimmed rooms all have sea-view balconies; best value are the deluxe rooms, whose "Extra King Size" beds are colossal. Hotel facilities include an excellent restaurant (see below), bar, pool and sauna. $150

EATING

The number of restaurants on Cat Ba is gradually expanding, with some offering tasty food – especially **seafood** – at reasonable prices. The **floating restaurants** in Cat Ba harbour and off Ben Beo tourist wharf seem a nice idea but are to be avoided owing to the staggeringly poor value for money.

Bamboo Café 199 Harbour Rd ☎ 0225 388 7552; map p.328. Simple place with bamboo furnishings (as you might guess) that serves tasty and inexpensive Vietnamese dishes, and is particularly good for breakfast (both Western and Vietnamese) – significant in a town where many hotels don't include breakfast in the price. Daily 7am–10pm.

Banh Ngot Phap 196 Harbour Rd ☎ 0397 509 5144; map p.328. Small, family-run bakery churning out round after round of delectable croissants, brownies and brioche, as well as home-made crème caramel; all for around 20,000đ. Coffee and beer too. Daily 6am–10pm.

Green Mango 239 Harbour Rd ☎ 0225 388 7151; map p.328. One of Cat Ba's classiest restaurants, *Green Mango* has a menu that ranges from lasagna and spicy green curry to bbq pork ribs. Presentation is excellent, but sometimes the fusion-type dishes just don't work. However, the Lavazza coffee (55,000đ) is excellent and the breakfast a cut above elsewhere (eggs Benedict; 100,000đ). Daily 7am–midnight.

Hoang Y Towards the south end of Harbour Rd; map p.328. This is one of the best choices for a seafood meal, with very reasonable prices; for example, shrimp with lemon and garlic for 130,000đ and whole steamed fish with ginger for 100,000đ. Daily 7am–10.30pm.

Vo So Sunrise Resort, Cat Co 3 beach ☎ 0225 388 7360; map p.328. The restaurant at the *Sunrise Resort* (see above) has surprisingly reasonable prices given the opulent surroundings. Salads, soups and pasta dishes (from

80,000đ) are offered as well as the Vietnamese regulars, and some of the desserts are simply irresistible. Daily 6.30am–10pm.

★**Yummy Restaurant** 180 Nui Ngoc; map p.328. New on the scene and cooking up a storm, this cheap local spot is tucked away on a road behind the waterfront. Delicious plates of freshly cooked Vietnamese and Thai dishes are served – splash out for fish hotpot between two for 250,000đ. Get here early to nab a table. Daily 7am–10pm.

DRINKING AND NIGHTLIFE

In the evenings, locals and visitors stroll along the harbour front, stopping to enjoy a beer or juice at one of the many **drink stalls** that set up around sunset. If the moon is out, the path running between Cat Co 1 and Cat Co 3 makes for a spectacular place to drink. Closing time depends on how many tourists are in town – if there's enough of a crowd, things can easily go on to 4am.

6

Good Bar 221 Harbour Road ☎0225 388 8363; map p.328. Popular because of its laidback vibe, cheap beer and strong cocktails; it gets pretty wild whenever there's a crowd. Pool table and music for dancing. Daily 7.30am–late.

Le Pont Bungalow Cat Co 3 Street; map p.328. About a 10min uphill stroll west of the waterfront, *Le Pont Bungalow* has the town's best sunset view, plus a wide range of cold beers and a long happy hour. The menu and the rooms are best avoided. Daily 7am–midnight.

Oasis 228 Harbour Rd; map p.328. At the centre of Cat Ba's nightlife scene, this busy place keeps pouring drinks and playing music until the last patron stumbles out. The staff actually seem to love working here, and the service is spot on. Daily 7.30am–late.

DIRECTORY

Banks and exchange There are several ATMs in town, including Agribank just 50m north of the hydrofoil jetty on the promenade.

Post office is on the harbour front, opposite the hydrofoil pier (daily 7am–noon & 1–6pm).

Cannon Fort

2km south of Cat Ba town • Dawn to dusk • 40,000đ • A steep 15min walk, or ride a motorbike or take a xe om to the top; look out for a sign at the top of Nui Ngoc

There are amazing vistas from various points at the old hilltop **Cannon Fort**, built in 1942, even though it's only 177m high. Several remnants of the fort remain intact, including a helipad, two enormous anti-warship cannons with a 40km range (and statues of Vietnamese soldiers appearing to operate one of them), plus a few **underground tunnels** and bunkers. The best views are out to the east, gazing over limestone islands in the bay; at this viewpoint there's a telescope and a well-appointed café.

Hospital Cave (Quan Y Cave)

8km from Cat Ba town • Daily 8am–4.30pm • 40,000đ

The main cross-island road climbs sharply out of Cat Ba town, giving views over distant islands and glimpses of secluded coves, and then follows a series of high valleys. After 8km look out on the right for the distinctive **Hospital Cave**, a gaping mouth embellished with concrete, not far from the road. During the American War the cave became an army hospital big enough to treat 150 patients at a time. The entrance fee includes a guide who'll point out where the cinema and swimming pool used to be and explain what each of the seventeen spartan bunker rooms was used for. A restaurant just over the road from the entrance makes for a nice shady spot at lunchtime.

Cat Ba National Park

16km from Cat Ba town • 40,000đ • A xe om to the park headquarters should cost around 100,000đ one-way • English-speaking guides can be arranged at the park headquarters (around 270,000đ for a full day), or join an organized tour from Cat Ba town (see box opposite)

Taking up much of the island is **Cat Ba National Park**, established in 1986 and little changed in decades. Its most famous inhabitant is a subspecies of the critically endangered **golden-headed langur**, a monkey found only on Cat Ba and now probably numbering around sixty individuals. Considerably more visible will be the rich diversity of plant species, including some 350 of medicinal value, as well as birds, snakes and plenty of mosquitoes. Remember to take repellent, good boots, a hat and lots of water if you plan to do any **walks** in the park. A **compass** wouldn't go amiss either, as people have become seriously lost.

6

The short trek

There are two main **trails** through the park. The "**short trek**" (about 3hr there and back) takes you to a viewpoint at the top of Ngu Lam peak. The path is easy enough to follow, but it's a steep climb, scrambling over tree roots and rocks in places, and extremely slippery in wet weather. Not everyone agrees that the views merit the effort.

The long trek

If you've got the time and energy, the "**long trek**" (about 6hr) is a rewarding experience. It involves a strenuous 18km hike via **Frog Lake** (Ao Ech), over a steep ridge for a classic view over countless **karst towers**, then dropping down to **Viet Hai village** where groups usually stop for lunch. From there it's about an hour's walk through lush scenery to the jetty, and then it's back to Cat Ba by boat through fjord-like **Lan Ha Bay** with a stop for swimming and snorkelling or kayaking through cave tunnels to find secret lagoons.

ACCOMMODATION	CAT BA NATIONAL PARK
Whisper of Nature Viet Hai village ☎ 043 923 3706, ⓦ vietbungalow.com; map p.328. Located in the tiny village of Viet Hai, in the Cat Ba National Park, this cluster of thatch-roofed bungalows sits by a stream on the edge of	the forest; most house private en-suite rooms, with one large bungalow acting as a dorm room. The setting is unbeatable and getting there is part of the fun; contact the management before you set off. Dorms $\overline{\$15}$, doubles $\overline{\$30}$

Lan Ha Bay

One of the most rewarding ways to explore the area around Cat Ba Island is by boat, passing into the labyrinth of **Lan Ha Bay**, which is located to the northeast of Cat Ba town en route to Ha Long City. It's a miniature version of neighbouring Ha Long Bay but one which receives fewer visitors. A popular stop here is **Ho Ba Ham** (see p.338), a hidden lagoon only accessible at low tide. There are also fish farms and **oyster farms** in the area, which can be included in tour itineraries. Other options are **kayaking**, **rock climbing** and visits to isolated **beaches** where the water is noticeably cleaner than elsewhere in the bay.

Ha Long City

Vietnam evidently has grand plans for **HA LONG CITY**. South-facing, and with **Ha Long Bay** raising its limestone fingers just across the sea, this place has great potential, but unfortunately development has been haphazard. The vast majority of Western tourists hitting the bay do so on the express service from Hanoi, going straight to **Tuan Chau Island**, the new tourist wharf 10km west of the city where all boats for Ha Long Bay now embark.

Ha Long City is an amalgam of easterly **Hong Gai** and westerly **Bai Chay**, two towns each with its own distinct character, merged in 1994 and lassoed together by a bridge. For the moment, locals still use the old names – as do ferry services, buses and so on – as a useful way to distinguish between the two areas. A recent development has seen a reversible cable car built across the narrow Cua Luc channel; however, the arrival station on the Hong Gai side is an amusement complex on the top of Ba Deo mount and there's no exit here – local holidaymakers are content to ride the Ferris wheel and return to Bai Chay, which is the hub of tourist activity and accommodation. Bai Chay also boasts several huge resort-style hotels – packed out by domestic and Chinese tourists in peak season – and a \$400 million amusement park (⊕sundragonpark.com/en/).

For those in search of more local colour, or who are put off by Bai Chay's overwhelming devotion to tourism, Hong Gai provides only basic tourist facilities but has a more bustling, workaday atmosphere. It's from here that you can catch a ferry to Quan Lan Island in Bai Tu Long Bay.

6

Bai Chay

Neon signs and flashing fairy lights blaze out at night along the **BAI CHAY** waterfront, acting like a magnet to foreign visitors and advertising north Vietnam's most developed resort, with shoulder-to-shoulder hotels and a picturesque backdrop of wooded hills. While Bai Chay is swamped in summer with local holidaymakers and tourists from China, out of season it's a pretty sleepy place and decidedly less sleazy. Apart from strolling the seafront boulevard and taking a quick look at its very indifferent beach, Bai Chay has nothing to distract you from the main business of touring Ha Long Bay. If you're staying here, you can take a turn through the seafront **market**, a somewhat desultory array of stalls selling tourist tat.

Hong Gai

In contrast to Bai Chay, **HONG GAI** has a compelling, raw vitality plus an attractive harbour to the east, crowded with scurrying sampans. It's worth spending an hour or so wandering round the market and **Long Tien Pagoda**, which frequently hosts ceremonies in its small courtyard, offering fascinating glimpses into local rituals. The pagoda sits in the shadow of **Nui Bai Tho**, a limestone outcrop named after a collection of poems (*bai tho*) carved into the rock, that detail Ha Long Bay's beauty. The earliest of these poems was penned by King Le Thanh Tong in 1468.

ARRIVAL AND GETTING AROUND   HA LONG CITY

The only junk-boat launchpad for Ha Long Bay is on **Tuan Chau Island**, 10km southwest of Bai Chay and linked to the mainland by a causeway. Most tourists arrive on tours directly from Hanoi, though it's also possible to organize cruises at the wharf, or on Cat Ba Island (see box, p.330).

TO CHINA VIA MONG CAI

Of the five border crossings between Vietnam and China open to foreigners, the one at **Mong Cai**, 130km northeast of Ha Long City along Highway 18, is probably the least used, as those at Lao Cai and Dong Dang have the advantage of rail connections on the Vietnamese side. To get to Mong Cai, take a bus from either My Dinh or Gia Lam bus station in Hanoi (see p.367), from Lac Long bus station in Haiphong (see p.325) or from Ha Long City bus station in Bai Chay (see p.334).

Those who make it to Mong Cai will find a fun little frontier town, whose streets are lined with signs for karaoke and massage parlours – an interesting start or finish line to a trip through Vietnam. It thrives on cross-border trade: Vietnamese tourists flock here to snap up cheap Chinese clothes, while the Chinese come for gambling and girls. You'll find no shortage of places to stay, though local restaurant menus tend to have Chinese, rather than English, as a second language. There's also a 24hr ATM.

The border (7am–7pm) is 1km north along Tran Phu from central Mong Cai, and just over the border is the small Chinese city of **Dongxiang**, which has bus connections to Nanning and Guangzhou.

Whichever way you're going, you'll need to have your **visa** organized in advance; the nearest Chinese embassy is in Hanoi and the nearest Vietnamese one in Nanning.

6

By bus The bus station is 6km northwest of Bai Chay on Highway 18. It's around 100,000đ into central Bai Chay by taxi, 50,000đ by xe om; double that for Hong Gai.
Destinations Haiphong (frequent; 1hr 30min); Hanoi (frequent; 4hr); Mong Cai (every 45min, 6am–3pm; 4hr).
By ferry Ben Tau pier is tucked away down a sidestreet in Hong Gai, from where boats go to Quan Lan Island in Bai Tu

Long Bay (200,000đ). There's also a passenger and vehicle ferry that crosses between Tuan Chau Island and Gia Luan port on the northern tip of Cat Ba Island (70,000đ).
Destinations Gia Luan, Cat Ba Island (about 6 daily; 1hr); Quan Lan Island (about 3 daily; 1hr 30min).
Taxis Mai Linh Taxi ☎ 0203 362 8628.

ACCOMMODATION

Despite a continuing increase in the number of hotels, especially in Bai Chay, there are still temporary room shortages during the Vietnamese summer season (June to early Sept) and holiday weekends; at other times, you'll be able to get good discounts. You'll find pretty much all the more expensive places in **Bai Chay**, though there are several budget places on Vuon Dao, and plenty more in **Hong Gai**. There are also plenty of options on **Tuan Chau Island** (most Westerners who stay here do so when their cruise around Ha Long Bay is cut short due to bad weather).

BAI CHAY

Muong Thanh Quang Ninh Ha Long Rd ☎ 0203 364 6618, ⓦ quangninh.muongthanh.vn; map p.334. This 34-storey, 508-room mega-hotel is yet further proof that Muong Thanh is taking over Vietnam's hospitality industry, with classy hotels in almost every town. Rooms are fitted with deep-pile carpets and luxurious furnishings, and facilities include a pool, fitness centre and tennis courts. Though they try hard, staff are not always on the ball. $120
★**Novotel** 160 Ha Long Rd ☎ 0203 384 8108,

ⓦ novotel.com; map p.334. One of the most immaculately designed hotels in Vietnam – plush carpets lead to subtly lit and delicately scented rooms which are tastefully furnished and have great views from the upper floors. The infinity pool outside is another nice touch and the on-site restaurant serves excellent food. $145
Viet Hoa 35 Vuon Dao ☎ 0203 384 6035; map p.334. One of the better budget hotels on Vuon Dao, just 50m up the road from the seafront, this is a clean and welcoming place offering cheerful fan or a/c rooms.

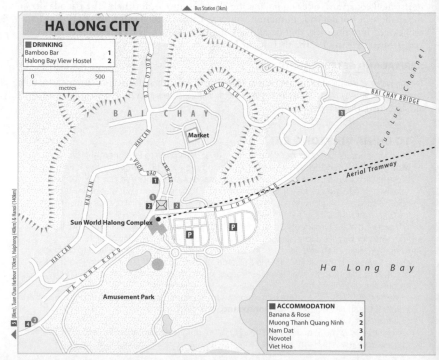

Bus Station (3km)

HA LONG CITY

■ **DRINKING**
| Bamboo Bar | 1 |
| Halong Bay View Hostel | 2 |

0 ————— 500
metres

BAI CHAY BRIDGE

Cua Luc Channel

Bai Chay Channel

B A I   C H A Y

Market

Aerial Tramway

Sun World Halong Complex

P   P

H a   L o n g   B a y

HAU CAN

VUON DAO

HA LONG ROAD

HA LONG ROAD

Amusement Park

(8km), Tuan Chau Harbour (10km), Haiphong (40km) & Hanoi (140km)

■ **ACCOMMODATION**
Banana & Rose	5
Muong Thanh Quang Ninh	2
Nam Dat	3
Novotel	4
Viet Hoa	1

They're a decent size and all come with TVs and fridges as standard. **$12**

HONG GAI

Nam Dat 8 Doan Thi Diem ☎ 0203 361 1358; map p.334. If Bai Chay is too touristy for you, head across the bridge to this newish hotel in the heart of workaday Hong Gai. Carpeted rooms are a good size, with flatscreen TVs and great en-suite facilities. **$25**

TUAN CHAU

Banana & Rose Tuan Chau Island ☎ 093 252 6789, ⓦ facebook.com/pg/bananaandroses; map p.334. Owned by an artsy Vietnamese couple who moved here to escape the city, this place feels a world away from the tourist wharf, but is only about a 30min walk. Five different rooms are all classy and cool and there's a swimming pool and plenty of communal space to take it easy. They whip up tremendous food and run bespoke tours. **$50**

6

EATING

Fresh **seafood** is the natural speciality of Ha Long Bay, with excellent lobster, crab and freshly caught fish on offer. The buzzing market near Ben Tau pier in Hong Gai is a great place to seek out local dishes like *cha muc* (squid sausage), and in the same area is the swish CGV Vincom shopping centre, with plenty of food and drink outlets including *Highland Coffee* (see below).

BAI CHAY

Novotel Ha Long Rd ☎ 0203 384 8108, ⓦ novotel.com; map p.334. The ground floor of this hotel (see opposite) has, without doubt, the best-looking restaurant in town. Lots of tempting main courses like braised lamb shanks (449,000đ), wraps and burgers, plus Vietnamese favourites, or join in the dinner buffet for 460,000đ. Daily 6–9.30pm.

Toan Huong 1 Vuon Dao ☎ 0203 384 4651; map p.334. First of a string of basic restaurants at the bottom of budget hotel street where staff almost drag passers-by in, but this one's actually worth being dragged into. Well-prepared

and well-priced seafood, plus a range of other dishes like beef sautéed with mushrooms (120,000đ). Daily 7am–10pm.

HONG GAI

Highland Coffee CGV Vincom, Tran Quoc Nghien ☎ 0203 628 8885; map p.334. Vietnam's answer to *Starbucks* might have the usual bland decor and OK Western-style coffee, but this outlet also boasts a remarkable view of the gorgeous karst landscape. A great place to chill out after a long day. Daily 7am–11pm.

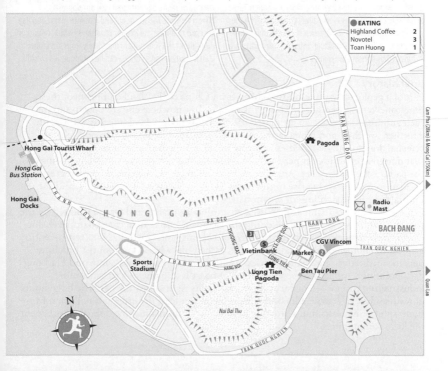

DRINKING

Bamboo Bar C 25/1 Royal Park, Ha Long Rd ☎0203 364 0899; map p.334. Good-looking bar that can be hit or miss of an evening, though even when it's a miss in terms of clientele, you can enjoy beers at 40,0000đ each, cocktails at 80,000–100,000đ as well as a good range of Western and Vietnamese cuisine, and the company of friendly, chatty staff. Daily 8am–late.

Halong Bay View Hostel 80 Ha Long Rd ☎0203 381 2988, ⓦhalongbayviewhostel.com; map p.334. The first floor of the hostel is a chilled-out pub and although the view isn't much to shout about, the drinks are cheap and the staff are friendly. Best to party here and stay elsewhere, unless you don't mind late-night noise. Happy hour 6–7pm. Daily 6.30am–midnight.

Ha Long Bay

Drifting out from Vietnam's north coast in a wooden junk, your eyes will be riveted on what, at first, appears to be a jagged wall of emerald green. After an hour or so the wall swallows you up, and you find yourself in a fairyland of otherworldly limestone peaks, jutting from the water at sheer angles – this is **Ha Long Bay**, the number-one tourist attraction in all Vietnam. Bar a clutch of impressive **caves**, specific sights are few on the ground, but even if you tire of the scenery there's a lot to do in the bay – cruises aside, there's **kayaking** across the tranquil waters, **swimming** amid the twinkles of phosphorescent plankton, or even **climbing** up a rocky cliff with your bare hands.

ARRIVAL AND INFORMATION   HA LONG BAY

By tour Every Hanoi tour agent offers Ha Long Bay excursions, travelling by road to Tuan Chau Island (8km west of Ha Long City, on the bay's northern shore), then transferring to cruise the bay on a replica wooden junk; these work out far easier – and almost invariably cheaper – than doing the same thing yourself. On all tours, check that the park fee and individual entry fees to sights are included (they almost always are).

Tourist Information Tuan Chau tourist wharf is where all junks now depart and the information desk (☎0203 3842 134, ⓦtuanchau-halong.com.vn) can help if you want to organize a private tour (see box opposite).

When to visit The splendour and romance of Ha Long Bay are hard to appreciate in poor conditions, which can occur throughout the year but are most likely from November to March – when winter drizzle can be compounded by chill.

Brief history

Part of a geological formation stretching from China to Thailand and Borneo, these limestone karst towers are by no means unique, but nowhere else are they found on such an impressive scale: an estimated 1969 islands pepper Ha Long Bay itself, with a further two thousand punctuating the coast towards China. Local legend tells of a **celestial dragon** and her children, sent by the Jade Emperor to stop an invasion, which spat out great quantities of pearls to form islands and razor-sharp mountain chains in the path of the enemy fleet. After the victory the dragons, enchanted by their creation, decided to stay on, giving rise to the name *Ha Long* ("dragon descending"), and the inevitable claimed sightings of sea monsters.

In 1469, King Le Thanh Tong paid a visit to Ha Long Bay and was so inspired by the scenery that he wrote a **poem**, likening the islands to pieces on a chessboard; ever since, visitors have struggled to capture the mystery of this fantasy world. Nineteenth-century Europeans compared the islands to Tuscan cathedrals, while a local tourist brochure opts for meditative "grey-haired fairies". With so much hyperbole, some find Ha Long disappointing, especially since this stretch of coast is also one of Vietnam's more **industrialized** regions – a major shipping lane cuts right across the bay. The huge influx of tourism has, of course, added to the problem, not least the litter and pollution from fume-spluttering boats, but a sizeable proportion of tourist income does at least benefit the local communities.

TOURS OF HA LONG BAY

There are a wide variety of **Ha Long Bay tours** available, including **day-trips**, though since the bay is an 8hr round trip from Hanoi these can feel very rushed. Most opt for a **two-day, one-night** tour, with the night spent at sea – this can be a delightful experience. However, this still means that you only spend one afternoon and one morning on the bay, so if you can spare the time, opt for a **three-day, two-night** trip, which allows you at least one full day in the bay. The **cost** depends on what kind of junk you board, which may be anything from a $500 single-cabin honeymoon cruiser serving gourmet cuisine, to a budget boat with $20 dorm-style beds and basic grub. Discounts can be negotiated off-season.

6

TOUR OPERATORS

Competition between tour operators is incredibly fierce, and you can get an overnight trip for as low as $20. However, at this price you're taking risks which may sour your appreciation of the bay: vessels can be dirty, have poor facilities or be horribly overcrowded – it's always best to ask operators if they have a **maximum group size** (sixteen is the usual upper limit), though such promises are often broken. Some junks are also simply unsafe, though regulations have been tightened up since a boat went down in early 2011, killing eleven tourists and their local guide. It is also not unusual for tours to be cut short due to bad weather; note that if your trip is cancelled completely, you are entitled to a **full refund** under Vietnamese law.

Compounding the confusion, few operators have their own vessels – travellers tend to be shunted onto whichever junk has room and you may find yourself sharing a vessel with people who have paid far more or less for the same thing. It's therefore impossible to give concrete recommendations for budget tour operators, but the following make good choices.

Buffalo Tours ☎ 024 3926 2425, ✆ buffalotours.com. Impeccable tours of both Ha Long and Bai Tu Long Bay on a range of luxurious junks. In late 2014 the company began combined seaplane and junk tours, offering an aerial perspective of the bay. The seafood is delectable, the wine list none too shabby and kayaking is included in the cost of the trip. Starts at $300/person for a 2-day, 1-night trip; add $400 for the 25min flight over the bay.

Emeraude ☎ 043 935 1888, ✆ emeraude-cruises .com. A replica of a nineteenth-century paddle-steamer, the five-star *Emeraude* is one of the most luxurious vessels on the bay. Facilities include a restaurant, two bars, beauty salon and massage rooms, and spacious sundecks where you can indulge in sunrise tai chi classes. From $250/person for a 2-day, 1-night tour.

Ethnic Travel ☎ 043 926 1951, ✆ ethnictravel.com .vn. This outfit prides itself on low-impact tours, and

has a superb reputation. Some tours head to lesser-visited Bai Tu Long Bay; a three-day trip goes from $169/person (2–9 people).

Indochina Junk ☎ 043 923 2559, ✆ indochina -junk.com. One of the most reliable outfits offering a variety of tours, with highly capable staff. The 3-day, 2-night tour of Bai Tu Long Bay on the *Dragon's Pearl* or *Dragon's Legend* (from around $380/person) is highly recommended.

Kangaroo Café ☎ 043 828 9931, ✆ kangaroocafe .com. This Aussie-owned budget outfit refuses to cut corners, and deserves its great reputation. In addition, the on-board meals are nothing short of superb. Two-day from $125/person, three-day from $175.

Vietnam Backpacker Hostels (see p.372). This hostel runs 3-day, 2-night trips that involve kayaking and swimming, and a lot of alcohol, for $219/person.

DIY TOURS FROM HA LONG CITY

Most foreigners visit the bay on tours from **Hanoi**, but it's just about possible to do the same thing independently, though you won't save much money. First of all you have to get to Ha Long City (see p.332), then head to the Tuan Chau tourist wharf, 8km west of town along Ha Long Road. From the booking desk here it's possible to take a three-hour trip for 290,000đ or six-hour trip for 390,000đ (including national park entry and a visit to a cave). These boats wait for a minimum of sixteen passengers before departing, and can get crowded; it is possible to charter a private boat for the day, but this costs up to 3,000,000đ, plus entry fees.

For the fraction of the price of a cruise, you can take the public ferry to **Cat Ba Island** (see p.329) from Tuan Chau. It's only an hour, but takes in some gorgeous views, and on Cat Ba you can arrange short cruises of Ha Long Bay or Lan Ha Bay with local operators (see box, p.330). To see **Bai Tu Long Bay**, you can take a public ferry from Ben Tau pier (see p.339) to Quan Lan Island, but unfortunately it's a closed boat and the windows barely open. The slower route between Cai Rong (50km east of Ha Long City) and Quan Lan Island is better (see p.339).

The caves

50,000đ/cave, usually included in tour prices

Organized tours to Ha Long Bay always include visits to one or more **caves**, which constitute the only actual sights in the area. Visually impressive though they are, busy days can see them rammed with tourists, which can detract from their majesty, as can the tour guides' endless comparison of particular rock formations to animals or Buddhist deities.

Hang Dau Go

The bay's most famous cave is also the closest to Tuan Chau, and therefore a favourite for day-trippers. **Hang Dau Go** – or the "Grotto of the Wooden Stakes" – is where General Tran Hung Dao amassed hundreds of stakes deep inside the cave's third and largest chamber before the Bach Dang River battle of 1288 (see box, p.325). These are now long gone, but at the entrance to the cave keep an eye out for a stone stele with Chinese inscriptions – this is a paean to the cave written by King Khai Dinh, who visited in 1929.

Hang Thien Cung

On the same island as Hang Dau Go, a steep climb to the "Grotto of the Heavenly Palace" is rewarded by a rectangular chamber 250m long and 20m high, with a textbook display of sparkling stalactites and stalagmites – supposedly petrified characters of the Taoist Heavenly Court.

Hang Sung Sot and around

The most visited of all the caves in the bay, and featuring on almost all one- and two-day itineraries, is **Hang Sung Sot**, or the "Surprise Cave". Inside its three echoing chambers, spotlights pick out the more interesting rock formations, including a "Happy Buddha" and rather surprising pink phallus. At the top you come out onto a belvedere with good views over the flotilla of junks below and sampans hawking souvenirs and soft drinks. Also in this area is **Ho Dong Tien** ("Grotto of the Fairy Lake") and **Dong Me Cung** ("Grotto of the Labyrinth") where, in 1993, ancient fossilized human remains were found; sadly, these only figure on a few tours.

Ho Ba Ham

Dau Be Island, on the southeastern edge of Ha Long Bay, encloses **Ho Ba Ham** ("Three Tunnel Lake"), a shallow lagoon wrapped round with limestone walls and connected to the sea by three low-ceilinged tunnels that are only navigable by sampan or kayak at low tide. This cave is sometimes included in day-trips out of Bai Chay but is most easily visited from Cat Ba and more commonly crops up on trips involving a stay on the island.

Bai Tu Long Bay

East of Ha Long Bay, stretching up towards the Chinese border, lies an attractive area of islands, known as **Bai Tu Long** or "Children of the Dragon". Some of the larger islands feature important forest reserves and are home to a number of rare species, such as the pale-capped pigeon, while dugong (sea cows) inhabit the surrounding waters. In 2001, **Bai Tu Long National Park** was created to protect 15,700 hectares of marine and island habitat. As Ha Long Bay begins to suffer from huge numbers of visitors, more and more tour companies are offering tours to this quieter, but equally impressive, bay. The only downside is that there are few caves to visit and it's more remote, so boats need to use more fuel, but most visitors are happy with this trade-off for a more tranquil experience.

Quan Lan Island

Though there are few specific sights in the area, the odd intrepid tourist heads as far as **Quan Lan Island**, a long skinny strip of land on the outer fringes of the bay. Although there has been much talk of developing the larger islands in Bai Tu Long as ecotourism destinations, until now Quan Lan retains a welcome "away-from-it-all" vibe.

The island's main attractions are the empty, sandy and relatively clean beaches fringing its east coast; the most attractive are **Minh Chau beach** on the northeast coast and secluded **Son Hao** to the east. A cycle ride – or better still, motorcycle ride – makes a pleasant jaunt through rice paddies and over the dunes to the north tip. Otherwise, there's not much to do apart from enjoying simply being off the tourist trail – prepare to smile and wave to every local school child. Take whatever cash you need as there is no ATM on the island, and be aware that stores don't really cater to Westerners. Take supplies.

6

ARRIVAL AND DEPARTURE
QUAN LAN ISLAND

By boat Boats leave from Ben Tau pier on the Hong Gai side of Ha Long City, arriving at Quan Lan pier at the south end of the island (200,000đ). There are also ferries to and from Cai Rong on the mainland (60,000–150,000đ), which can be reached by bus from Ha Long City or Hanoi.

Destinations Cai Rong fast boat (4 daily; 45min); Cai Rong slow boat (daily; 2hr); Ha Long City (about 3 daily; 1hr 30min).
By tour Ethnic Travel in Ha Long City (see box, p.337) offers three-day, two-night cruises that overnight on Quan Lan Island.

GETTING AROUND

By xe om There are plenty of xe om and xe may (three-wheeler motorbike taxis) that wait at Quan Lan pier, on the island's southern tip, to take people 3km north to the main Quan Lan village (about 50,000đ).

ACCOMMODATION

Be warned that **power cuts** are frequent, so take a torch and look for a room where you can open a window and catch the breeze when the a/c shuts down. Rates are higher at weekends when domestic tourists arrive. In season, guesthouses pop up in the island's second village, Minh Chau.

Ann Hotel At the junction in town ☎ 0203 387 7889, ☎ 091 651 3144, ⓦ annhotel.com.vn. Probably the most switched-on of Quan Lan's few laidback hotels. Staff speak English and can help with onward travel, rooms are big and bright, and some have sea-facing balconies. There's a decent restaurant too, and motorbikes and bikes for rent. **$30**

Ngan Ha Hotel Opposite the post office ☎ 0203 387 7296, ⓦ quanlanisland.vn. Cheap and friendly, this is the budget place of choice for most travellers. Rooms are simple but perfectly adequate (the top floor is the nicest), while the meals are about as good as you'll get in the village. Bike rental also available. **$12**

Hanoi and around

MORNING EXERCISE, HOAN KIEM LAKE

Hanoi and around

Vietnam's enigmatic capital, Hanoi provides a full-scale assault on the senses. Its mustard-hued colonial architecture is a feast for the eyes, while swarms of buzzing motorbikes invade the ears and the delicate scent of delicious street food wafts right across the city. And, unlike so many of its regional contemporaries, Hanoi is managing to modernize with a degree of grace. The city's name means "on a bend in the river", a reference to the Red River that flows through it, and it is the fertility of the Red River Delta that has enabled Hanoi to sustain a large population for over a thousand years. Despite the incessant noise drummed up by a population of around seven million, Hanoi exudes an appeal that is both intimate and urbane. It endears itself to most visitors with its unique attractions, which include the bustling Old Quarter, tranquil Hoan Kiem Lake, the atmospheric French Quarter and several museums that bring Vietnam's turbulent history to life.

7

While retaining a sense of importance of its historic heritage, Hanoi has changed almost beyond recognition in the last two decades. It now boasts glitzy megamalls and wine warehouses, while its spas attract a well-heeled clientele and some seriously expensive cars cruise the streets – though most people still zip around on motorbikes (rather than using the untrendy bicycle). The authorities are trying – with mixed success – to curb traffic anarchy and regulate unsympathetic building projects in the **Old Quarter**. Recent examples include closing most of the quarter and Hoan Kiem Lake to traffic over the weekends, plus the construction of an ambitious new metro system that aims to ease traffic congestion. With plenty of money about, wealthy Hanoians are prepared to flaunt it in the sophisticated restaurants, cafés and designer boutiques that have exploded all over the city. Nevertheless, the centre has not completely lost its old-world charm or its distinctive character.

While Hanoi itself could easily eat up a week of your time, with quirky sights like the **Ho Chi Minh Mausoleum** and **Museum of Ethnology**, there are also several out-of-town destinations that make for a good day out. Most popular is the **Perfume Pagoda**, with its spectacular setting amid limestone hills, though there are plenty of other pagodas and crafts villages nearby that also offer the chance to glimpse scenes of everyday life in rural Vietnam.

The **best time to visit** Hanoi is between October and December, when you'll find warm, sunny days and levels of humidity below the norm of eighty percent – though it

PHO BO

Highlights

1 The Old Quarter Wander through the intoxicating tangle of streets that make up Hanoi's commercial heart. **See p.350**

2 The Opera House Check out this signature piece of French colonial architecture, modelled on the one in Paris. **See p.355**

3 Ho Chi Minh's Mausoleum Visit the ghostly figure of "Uncle Ho", embalmed against his wishes and displayed in a glass casket. See p.358

4 Temple of Literature Escape the hubbub of Hanoi in the courtyards of Vietnam's foremost Confucian sanctuary and centre of learning. See p.362

5 Museum of Ethnology Discover the staggering variety and creativity of Vietnam's ethnic minorities. **See p.366**

6 Street food Join the locals squatting on tiny stools to sample some of Hanoi's best street food, such as pho, the traditional beef-and-noodle breakfast soup. **See box, p.375**

7 Bia hoi bars Look out for streetside stalls serving this mild draught beer from metal barrels at a cost of next to nothing. **See box, p.379**

8 Water puppets Marvel at the aquatic antics involved in this quirky art form, developed in the floodlands of the Red River Delta. **See p.380**

HIGHLIGHTS ARE MARKED ON THE MAP ON P.348

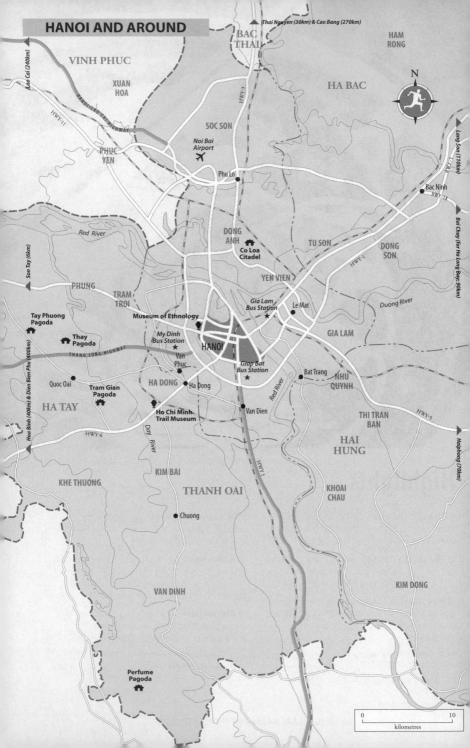

HANOI AND AROUND

Thai Nguyen (30km) & Cao Bang (270km)

HAM RONG

BAC THAI

VINH PHUC

Lao Cai (240km)

XUAN HOA

HA BAC

HWY-11

SOC SON

PHUC YEN

Noi Bai Airport

Phu Lo

Bac Ninh

HWY-18

Red River

DONG ANH

Co Loa Citadel

TU SON

DONG SON

Son Tay (6km)

YEN VIEN

Duong River

Bat Chay (for Ha Long Bay; 90km)

PHUNG

TRAM TROI

Gia Lam Bus Station

Le Mat

Tay Phuong Pagoda

Museum of Ethnology

GIA LAM

Thay Pagoda

My Dinh Bus Station

HANOI

Van Phuc

Hoa Binh (40km) & Dien Bien Phu (400km)

THANG LONG HIGHWAY

Glap Bat Bus Station

Bat Trang

NHU QUYNH

Quoc Oai

HA DONG

Ha Dong

Tram Gian Pagoda

Red River

HA TAY

Ho Chi Minh Trail Museum

Van Dien

THI TRAN BAN

Haiphong (70km)

HWY-6

Day River

HAI HUNG

KIM BAI

HWY-5

KHE THUONG

THANH OAI

KHOAI CHAU

Chuong

VAN DINH

KIM DONG

HWY-1

Perfume Pagoda

0   10
kilometres

can still be chilly at night. From January to March, cold winds from China merge with high humidity to produce a fine mist, which often hangs in the air for several days. March and early April usually bring better weather, before the extreme summer heat arrives in late April, accompanied by monsoon storms that peak in August and can last until early October, causing flooding throughout the delta.

Brief history

When Tang Chinese armies invaded Vietnam in the seventh century, they chose a small **Red River fort** as the capital of their new protectorate, named (rather optimistically) *Annam*, the "Pacified South". Three centuries later, the rebellious Vietnamese ousted the Chinese in 939 AD. After that, the citadel lay abandoned until 1010, when **King Ly Thai To**, usually credited as Hanoi's founding father, recognized the site's potential and established his own court beside the Red River. It seems the omens were on his side for, according to legend, the king spied a golden dragon soaring to the heavens as soon as he stepped from his royal barge onto the riverbank. From then on **Thang Long**, "City of the Ascending Dragon", was destined to be the nation's capital, with only minor interruptions, for the next eight hundred years.

Growth of the city

Ly Thai To and his successors set about creating a city fit for "ten thousand generations of kings", choosing auspicious locations for their temples and palaces according to the laws of **geomancy**. They built protective dykes, established a town of artisans and merchants alongside the Imperial City's eastern wall, and set up the nation's first university, in the process laying the foundations of modern Hanoi. From 1408, the country was again under **Chinese occupation**, but this time only briefly before the great hero Le Loi retook the capital in 1428. The Le-dynasty kings drained lakes and marshes to accommodate their new palaces as well as a growing civilian population, and towards the end of the fifteenth century Thang Long was enjoying a **golden era** under the great reformer, King Le Thanh Thong. Shortly after his death in 1497, however, the country dissolved into anarchy, while the city slowly declined until finally Emperor Gia Long moved the royal court to **Hue** in 1802.

International intervention

By the 1830s Thang Long had been relegated to a provincial capital renamed **Hanoi**, and in 1882 its reduced defences offered little resistance to **attacking French forces**, led by Captain Rivière. Initially capital of the French Protectorate of Tonkin, a name derived from *Dong Kinh*, meaning "Eastern Capital", after 1887 Hanoi became the centre of government for the entire Union of Indochina. Royal palaces and ancient monuments made way for grand residences, administrative offices, tree-lined

---

HANOI ORIENTATION

Hanoi city centre comprises an area known as **Hoan Kiem District**, which is neatly bordered by the Red River embankment in the east and the rail line to the north and west, while its southern extent is marked by the roads Nguyen Du, Le Van Huu and Han Thuyen. The district takes its name from its present-day hub and most obvious point of reference, **Hoan Kiem Lake**, and includes the narrow lanes of the endlessly diverting **Old Quarter** in the north, and the tree-lined boulevards of the **French Quarter**, arranged in a rough grid system, to the south. West of this central district, across the rail tracks, some of Hanoi's most impressive monuments occupy the wide open spaces around the **Hanoi Citadel**, including Ho Chi Minh's Mausoleum in Ba Dinh Square and the ancient walled gardens of the Temple of Literature. A vast body of water called **West Lake** sits to the northwest of the city, harbouring a number of interesting temples and pagodas, but the attractive villages that once surrounded it have now largely given way to upmarket residential areas and luxury hotels.

boulevards and all the trappings of a **colonial city**, more European than Asian. However, the Vietnamese community lived a largely separate, often impoverished existence, creating a seedbed of insurrection.

Modern times

During the 1945 **August Revolution**, thousands of local nationalist sympathizers spilled onto the streets of Hanoi and later took part in its defence against returning French troops, though they had to wait until 1954 for their city finally to become the **capital of an independent Vietnam**. Hanoi sustained more serious damage during the air raids of the American War, particularly the infamous Christmas Bombing campaign of 1972. The elation of reunification in 1975 was quickly dampened by mismanagement of the economy, which led to a decade of widespread unemployment, crippling inflation, lack of resources and famine, until economic reforms known as **doi moi** (renovation) came into effect in 1986. Over the next few years, these reforms had a positive effect and saved many Hanoians, who were on the brink of ruin.

Today Hanoi enjoys one of the fastest GDP growth rates in Asia. New market freedoms combined with an influx of tourists since the early 1990s have led to an explosion of privately run hotels and restaurants (several of international standard), as well as of boutiques, craft shops and tour agencies. As ancient – and antiquated – buildings give way to glittering high-rises, and as traffic congestion increases, the big question is how much of this historic and charming city will survive the onslaught of modernization.

Hoan Kiem Lake and around

Hoan Kiem Lake is the city's spiritual, cultural and commercial heart, so it makes a good place to start exploring Hanoi – especially on weekends when the lack of traffic noise makes it particularly enjoyable. The lake itself has a magical quality that fully deserves the legend of its naming (see box opposite). The streets to the east, south and west of the lake are home to the city's biggest banks, airline offices and the general post office, as well as some swanky hotels and stylish restaurants. A block west of the lake, the trendy shopping street of Nha Tho leading to **St Joseph's Cathedral** is a dedicated homage to fashion. The north end of the lake signals the beginning of the **Old Quarter**, with its maze of narrow lanes.

Hoan Kiem Lake

Early morning sees **Hoan Kiem Lake** at its best, stirring to life as walkers, joggers and tai chi enthusiasts limber up in the half-light. The lake itself is small (you can walk around it in thirty minutes) and not particularly spectacular, but to Hanoians this is the soul of their city. Space is at a premium in this crowded city, and the lake's strip of park and shady trees meets multiple needs. It's at its busiest at lunchtime when office workers and hawkers are out in force, and this slowly eases into lazy evenings filled with old men playing chess and couples seeking twilight privacy on benches half-hidden among weeping willows.

A good way to get your bearings is to make a quick **circuit of the lake**, which is a pleasant walk at any time of year and stunning when the flame trees flower in June and July. The sights here are given in a clockwise order, beginning at the iconic The Huc Bridge (which is possibly the most photographed sight in the city), at the lake's northeast corner.

Ngoc Son Temple

Mon–Fri 7am–6pm, Sat & Sun 7am–midnight • 30,000đ

Crossing over **The Huc Bridge**, an arch of red-lacquered wood poetically labelled the "place where morning sunlight rests", you find the secluded **Ngon Son Temple**, or "Temple of the Jade Mound", sheltering among ancient trees on a small island at the northeast corner of the lake. This temple was founded in the fourteenth century and is

A LEGEND COMES TO LIFE

Hoan Kiem, which means "Lake of the Restored Sword", refers to a **legend** of the great Vietnamese hero, Le Loi, who led a successful uprising against the Chinese in the fifteenth century. The story goes that while out fishing in a sampan on the lake, then known as Luc Thuy, Le Loi netted a gleaming sword, which helped him to defeat the Chinese in battle. When he returned to the lake years later as King Ly Thai To, a **golden turtle** surfaced, took the sword and disappeared with it. The king believed that the turtle had been sent by the gods to reclaim the weapon, and he renamed the lake accordingly.

The legend is not mere fantasy, as the lake is still home to one hardy giant turtle, but it is thought to be the last remaining specimen here. It was captured and examined in early 2011 when wounds on its leg and head were identified, though it still managed to elude captors twice before being netted. Its wounds were thought to be caused by the sharp edges of debris in the lake. It is an extremely rare species of enormous, **soft-shelled turtle** known as *Rafetus swinhoei*, and there are only a few other specimens remaining in Vietnam and China – it is sadly destined for extinction. This one weighed in at around 170kg and measured about 1.8 metres in length, and scientists estimate it's between eighty and a hundred years old – but of course Hanoians believe it is one and the same creature that took Ly Thai To's sword over five hundred years ago. Though you're unlikely to spot this last turtle, you can get an idea of its enormous size at Ngoc Son Temple (see opposite), where a preserved turtle is on display.

7

dedicated to **General Tran Hung Dao**, who defeated the Mongols in 1288 and whose image sits on the principal altar, **Van Xuong**, God of Literature, and **La To**, the patron saint of physicians. The temple buildings date from the 1800s and are typical of the Nguyen dynasty; in the back room, look out for a stuffed and varnished specimen of a giant turtle that once lived in the lake. On the east side of The Huc Bridge stands a nine-metre-high obelisk, the **Ink Brush Tower**, on which three outsized Chinese characters proclaim "a pen to write on the blue sky".

Statue of King Ly Thai To

On the eastern side of the lake stands an imperious statue of Hanoi's founding father, **King Ly Thai To**, which was erected in 2004 in anticipation of celebrations to mark the city's millennium in 2010. The square around it is a hive of activity in the evenings and at weekends, when you might spot groups of locals roller blading, ballroom dancing or practising laughing yoga.

Turtle Tower

A squat, three-tiered pavilion known as Thap Rua, or **Turtle Tower**, ornaments a tiny island at the southern end of Ho Hoan Kiem. It's illuminated after dark, and is another of Hanoi's most prevalent icons, with its reflection shimmering in the lake. It was built in the nineteenth century to commemorate the legend of the golden turtle and the restored sword, but is not accessible to the public.

General Post Office and Chua Bao An

At the southeast corner of the lake stands the enormous **General Post Office**, which marks the northern fringe of the French Quarter. Opposite the post office, on the shore of the lake, stands a small and ancient brick tower. This is all that remains of an enormous pagoda complex, **Chua Bao An**, after French town planners cleared the site in 1892 to construct the administrative offices and residences of their new possession.

St Joseph's Cathedral

Nha Tho • Daily 5–11am & 2–7.30pm; Mass Mon–Fri 7.30am & 12.05pm, Sat 5.15pm, Sun 8am, 10.30am, 12.30pm & 5.15pm • Free • Ⓦ saintjosephcathedral.org

Just a block west of Hoan Kiem Lake stands **St Joseph's Cathedral**, one of Hanoi's most iconic buildings. Its solemn facade makes a stark contrast to the colourful boutiques and

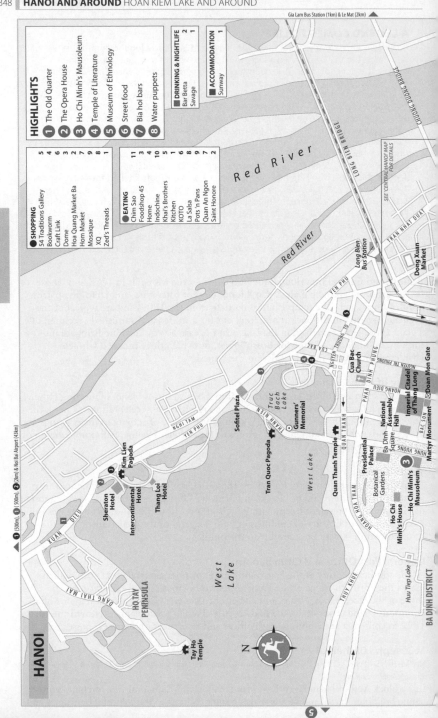

HANOI

HIGHLIGHTS
1 The Old Quarter
2 The Opera House
3 Ho Chi Minh's Mausoleum
4 Temple of Literature
5 Museum of Ethnology
6 Street food
7 Bia hoi bars
8 Water puppets

DRINKING & NIGHTLIFE
Bar Betta 2
Savage 1

ACCOMMODATION
Sunway 1

● **SHOPPING**
54 Traditions Gallery 5
Bookworm 4
Craft Link 6
Dome 3
Hoa Quang Market Ba 2
Hom Market 9
Mosaique 8
XQ 8
Zed's Threads 1

● **EATING**
Chim Sao 11
Foodshop 45 3
Home 4
Indochine 10
Khai's Brothers 5
Kitchen 1
KOTO 6
La Salsa 8
Pots 'n Pans 9
Quan An Ngon 7
Saint Honore 2

Bat Trang (7km)

National Museum
of History

Opera
House

THE OLD
QUARTER

Hoan
Kiem
Lake

Vietnam
Airlines

LY THAI TO

TRAN QUANG KHAI

LE THANH TONG

LY THUONG KIET

HANG BAI

BA TRIEU

NGO QUYEN

Hom
Market

LO DUC

HAI BA TRUNG

TRANG THI

TRAN HUNG DAO

THE FRENCH
QUARTER

NGUYEN DU

TRAN NHAN TONG

Thong Nhat Park

Bay Mau
Lake

DAI CO VIET

Hanoi
Station

LE DUAN

TRAN QUY CAP

Cot Co Flag Tower

Military
History
Museum

DIEN BIEN PHU

LE HONG PHONG

One Pillar
Pagoda

Ho Chi Minh
Museum

B52 Victory
Museum

Kim Ma
Bus Station

NGUYEN THAI HOC

CAT LINH

Goethe
Institute

Fine Arts
Museum

Temple of
Literature

NGUYEN THAI HOC

TON DUC THANG

DE LA THANH XA DAN

KHAM THIEN

DONG DA
DISTRICT

TAY SON

THAI HA

TON DUC TRANG

NGO HAO NAM

GIANG VO

LA THANH

KIM MA

DOI CAN

Family Medical Practice

VAN
PHUC

Giang Vo
Lake

GIANG VO

LA THANH

US Embassy

TRAN KHANH DU

TRAN KHAT CHAN

NGUYEN KHOAI

LO DUC

HOI MA

NGUYEN CONG TRU

PHO HUE

MAC DUC

TUE TINH

BA TRIEU

GIAI PHONG

LY NAM DE

THAN MG THACH

One-way
street

0   500
metres

7

Hanoi French Hospital (200m), Giap Bat Bus Station (1.5km), (1.2km) & Ninh Binh (90km)

Ha Dong (5km), Perfume Pagoda (50km) & Hoa Binh (700m)

Lotte Observation Deck (500li) & My Dinh Bus Station (8km)

cafés that line fashionable Nha Tho ("Big Church") street in front of it. The cathedral was completed in 1886, partly financed by two lotteries, and though the exterior is badly weathered, its high-vaulted interior is still imposing. Among the first things you notice inside are the ornate altar screen and the stained-glass windows, most of which are French originals. Over the black marble tomb of a former cardinal of Vietnam is one of several statues commemorating martyred Vietnamese saints, in this case André Dung Lac, who was executed in 1839 on the orders of the fervently anti-Christian emperor Minh Mang.

The cathedral's main door is sometimes open; at other times, you can walk round to the small door in the southwest corner. **Mass** is conducted several times each day, with Sunday evening Mass at 5.15pm attracting big crowds.

Ba Da Pagoda
3 Nha Tho

Hidden down a narrow alley at the eastern end of Nha Tho, **Chua Ba Da**, or the Stone Lady Pagoda, makes a delightful contrast to the grandeur of St Joseph's Cathedral. A temple has stood on this site for a thousand years, but it acquired its current name when a stone statue of a woman was discovered during reconstruction in the fifteenth century. These days, it is the headquarters of the Municipal Buddhist Association. A recent restoration has left the pagoda in fine shape, and a wander through its halls lined with Buddha images can be a serene experience. It's not visible from the street – look for a narrow alley and sign beside no. 3 Nha Tho.

The Old Quarter

North of Hoan Kiem Lake are the tumultuous streets of the **Old Quarter**, also known as "**the 36 Streets**" after the guilds that once operated here, though there are many more than 36 streets these days. It occupies a congested square kilometre that was closed behind massive ramparts and heavy wooden gates until well into the nineteenth century. Apart from one **gate**, at the east end of Hang Chieu, the walls have been dismantled, though the crowded enclave still has its own distinct character. To explore it, the best approach is simply to dive into the maze of twisted lanes and wander at will, equipped with a map to find your way out again. Alternatively, you might like to see it first from the seat of a cyclo or one of the electric cars that zigzag through (see p.369), to help you pinpoint places you'd like to come back to.

Everything spills out onto pavements that double as workshops for stone-carvers, furniture-makers and tinsmiths, and as display space for merchandise ranging from pungent therapeutic herbs and fluttering prayer flags to ranks of Remy Martin and shiny-wrapped chocolates. With so much to attract your attention at ground level, it's easy to miss the **architecture**, which reveals fascinating glimpses of the quarter's history, starting with the fifteenth-century merchants' houses otherwise found only in Hoi An (see p.345). As you explore the quarter you'll come across some sacred sites – temples, pagodas, *dinh* and venerable banyan trees – tucked away between the houses.

OLD QUARTER ARCHITECTURE

The most distinctive buildings in the Old Quarter are the aptly named **tube-houses**, which evolved from market stalls into narrow single-storey shops, with windows no higher than a passing royal palanquin, under gently curving, red-tiled roofs. The moniker comes from their narrow facades (some are just two metres wide), which are the result of **taxes** levied on street frontages, and deep interiors that accommodate a succession of storerooms and living quarters up to 60m in length, interspersed with open courtyards to give them access to light and air. As royal palanquins no longer pass through the Old Quarter, many owners have now added several storeys, giving rise to a new architectural term – **rocket houses**.

WHAT'S IN A NAME?

The Old Quarter's **street names** date back five centuries to when the area was divided among 36 artisans' guilds, each gathered around a temple or a *dinh* dedicated to the guild's patron spirit. Even today many streets specialize to some degree, and a few, such as **Hang Bac** ("Silver Street"), are still dedicated to the original craft or its modern equivalent. The most colourful examples are **Hang Quat**, full of bright-red banners and lacquerware for funerals and festivals, and **Hang Ma**, where paper products have been made for at least five hundred years. Nowadays gaudy tinsel dances in the breeze above brightly coloured votive objects, which include model TVs, dollars and cars to be offered to the ancestors. A selection of the more interesting streets with an element of specialization is listed below. Note that *hang* means "merchandise", not "street".

STREET NAME	MEANING	MODERN SPECIALITY
Hang Trong	Drum skin	Bag menders, upholsterers
Hang Bo	Bamboo baskets	Haberdashers
Hang Buom	Sails	Imported foods and alcohol, confectionery
Hang Chieu	Sedge mats	Mats, ropes, bamboo blinds
Hang Dau	Oil	Shoes
Hang Dieu	Pipes	Cushions, mattresses
Hang Duong	Sugar	Clothes, general goods
Hang Gai	Hemp goods	Silks, tailors, souvenirs
Hang Hom	Wooden chests	Glue, paint, varnish
Hang Ma	Paper votive objects	Paper goods
Hang Quat	Ceremonial fans	Religious accessories
Hang Thiec	Tin goods	Tin goods, mirrors
Hang Vai	Fabrics	Bamboo ladders

Heritage House

87 Ma May • Daily 8am–noon & 1.30–5pm • 10,000đ

To get a better idea of the layout of tube-houses, pop into the beautifully restored **Heritage House** (sometimes called "Memorial House"). There's usually a volunteer on hand to show you through the various rooms and courtyards, who will point out the elegant carvings on the doors and balustrades, as well as examples of traditional fine arts and handicrafts such as ceramics and silk paintings on display. You might also see a calligrapher practising his art in a corner or a seamstress working on an embroidered painting. Some items are on sale, and might make a distinctive souvenir.

Dinh Kim Ngan

42–44 Hang Bac • Daily 7.30–11.30am & 2–5.30pm • Free

Hang Bac ("Silver Street") retains its own *dinh*, or communal house, which has long been home of the silversmiths' guild. The entrance to **Dinh Kim Ngan** is similar to that of a temple, with huge walls and wooden gates leading on to a courtyard, where a large urn holds burning incense sticks. Information panels provide the background to communal houses in general and this one in particular, including its restoration in 2009; though its exact age is unknown, references on a stele in the grounds suggest that it was established in the eighteenth century. The altar in the main hall is dedicated to the worship of Hien Vien, a legendary figure believed to be the founder of all crafts. You'll find some interesting books and pamphlets about Vietnamese architecture and crafts on sale, and there are performances of *ca tru* music here some evenings (see p.379).

▲ Gia Lam Bus Station (1km)

CENTRAL HANOI

7

N

▲ Noi Bai Airport (43km)

EATING

Avalon Café Lounge	23
Al Fresco's	36
Banh Mi 25	1
Bittet Ong Loi	3
Blue Butterfly	7
Café de Paris	5
Café Dinh	24
Café Lam	17
Cha Ca Thang Long	18
Chops	12
Com Chay Nang Tam	37
Cong Caphe	11
Eden Coffee	32
Essence	8
Fanny	33
Gecko	13
Green Tangerine	19
Hanoi Social Club	30
Highlands Coffee	22
Highway 4	15
Hue Café	4
La Place	28
La Verticale	38
Little Hanoi	20
Loft Stop Café	26
Mam	14
Moca	31
Moose & Roo	2
New Day	6
Nola	10
Pane e Vino	35
Pho Co	21
Press Club	34
Puku	27
Red Bean	9
Tandoor	16
Thuy Ta	25
Xofa Cafe	29

SHOPPING

Collective Memory	15
Dong Xuan Market	1
Flora Boutique	14
Ginkgo	4
Hanoi Moment	8
Ipa-Nima	13
Kenly Silk	9
Khai Silk	10
Love Planet Travel	2
Mekong Quilts	3
Ngoc Diep Silk	11
Pham Bich Huong	6
Tan My Design	7
Thai Khue Music Shop	5
Things of Substance	12

Quan Chuong Gate

Dong Xuan Market

THE OLD QUARTER

Bach Ma Temple

Dinh Kim Ngan

Heritage House

Golden Bell Theatre

Dien Dam Gallery

Suong Pho

Weekend Night Market

Thang Long Art Gallery

Thang Long Water Puppet Theatre

The Huc Bridge

Ngoc Son Temple

Apricot Gallery

Hong Ha Theatre

Hang Da Market

TRAN QUANG KHAI

HANG TRE

NGUYEN HUU HUAN

HANG BE

HANG DAU

LY THAI TO

LO SU

HANG THUNG

PHUC TAN

HANG MUOI

PHAT LOC

MA MAY

DAO DUY TU

HANG BUOM

TA HIEN

HANG GIAY

HANG BAC

NGO TRUNG YEN

GIA NGU

CAU GO

DINH

LUONG NGOC QUYEN

HANG NGANG

HANG DAO

LUONG VAN CAN

HANG BO

HANG CAN

HANG QUAT

HANG GAI

LY QUOC SU

CHAN CAM

HANG TRONG

HANG HANH

BAO KHANH

HANG NON

HANG HOM

THUOC BAC

HANG GA

BAT SU

BAT DAN

YEN THAI

HANG THIEC

HANG BONG

HANG MANH

HANG DIEU

DUONG THANH

PHUNG HUNG

CUA DONG

LAN ONG

CHA CA

NGO GACH

HANG DUONG

HANG MA

HANG CHAI

HANG LUOC

HANG COT

HANG VAI

HANG LO

HANG BE

HA

HONG

BAO LINH

THANH HA

TRAN NHAT DUAT

NGUYEN SIEU

CHIEU

NGUYEN KHOAI

NGUYEN THIEN THUAT

CAU DONG

GAM CAU

HANG GIAY

DONG XUAN

HANG DAU

HANG CHINH

PHUC TAN

TRAN QUANG KHAI

NGUYEN HUU HUAN

PHUNG HUNG

LE VAN LINH

HANG DA

NGO TRAM

HA TRUNG

HANG BONG

DUONG THANH

LY NAM DE

LY NAM DE

HAI TUONG

NGUYEN KHAC

HONG PHUC

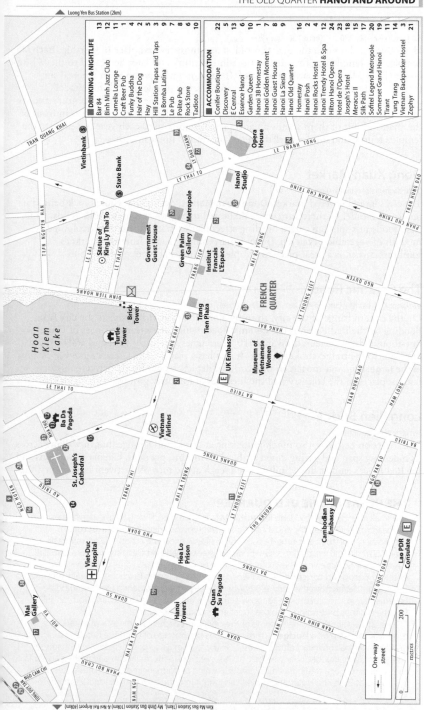

Bach Ma Temple

Hang Buom • Tues–Sun 7.30–11.30am & 1.30–6pm • Free

Hang Buom is home to the quarter's oldest and most revered place of worship, **Bach Ma Temple**. The temple was founded in the ninth century and later dedicated to the White Horse (Bach Ma), the guardian spirit of Thang Long who posed as an ethereal site foreman and helped King Ly Thai To overcome a few problems with his citadel's collapsing walls. The present structure dates largely from the eighteenth century and its most unusual features are a pair of charismatic, pot-bellied Cham guardians in front of the altar. In front of them stands an antique palanquin, used each year to celebrate the temple's foundation on the twelfth day of the second lunar month.

Dong Xuan Market

On the northern side of the Old Quarter

The city's largest covered market, **Dong Xuan Market**, occupies a whole block behind its renovated facade. Its three storeys are dedicated to clothes and household goods, while fresh foodstuffs spill out into a bustling street market stacked with multicoloured mounds of vegetables. Nguyen Thien Thuat, running south from the market's southeast corner, is a great place to sample some unusual types of street food.

The Ceramic Road

Tran Quang Khai, Tran Nhat Duat, Yen Phu, Nghi Tam and Au Co streets

On the eastern fringe of the city, running along the dyke that protects the city from flooding by the Red River, is the **Ceramic Road**, which was created as part of Hanoi's one-thousand-year celebrations in 2010. It stretches for nearly 4km and adds a splash of colour to the traffic-choked streets. It also has a place in the *Guinness Book of Records* as the **largest ceramic mosaic** in the world. It depicts scenes from Vietnam's history, famous places in the country and the lifestyles of minority groups.

Long Bien Bridge

Just north of the Old Quarter

The attraction here is not so much in looking at this historic bridge, but in walking across its mile-long span and gazing down at the chicken runs, pig pens, banana plantations and the Red River's endless flow. Built by the French at the turn of the twentieth century, the

---

THE HEART OF THE OLD QUARTER

The small area enclosed by Hang Buom, Ma May, Hang Bac and Hang Ngang constitutes the heart of the Old Quarter, and it contains a delightful patchwork of **architecture**, superimposed on the basic tube-house design: simple one-storey shophouses, some still sporting traditional red-tiled roofs; elaborate plasterwork and Art Deco styling from colonial days; and the Soviet chic of the 1960s and 1970s. Nowadays, the majority of facades bear distinctly **European touches** – faded wooden shutters, sagging balconies and rain-streaked moulding – dating from the early 1900s when the streets were widened to accommodate pavements. Some occupants were too wealthy or influential to be shifted, and you can still find their houses protruding onto the street and standing out of line.

These streets are also home to some of the city's most popular lodgings and restaurants, especially for those on a **budget** – though there's no shortage of boutique hotels as well. It's a good area to soak up local culture, whether in the form of a cup of super-strong Vietnamese coffee, a glass of draught beer (see box, p.379), a live rock performance in one of the bars on Ta Hien (see p.378), or a traditional music show. Evening performances of *ca tru* music (see p.379) are staged at Dinh Kim Ngan, and provide an insight into the uses of traditional Vietnamese instruments.

> **WEEKEND NIGHT MARKET**
>
> From around 7pm every Friday, Saturday and Sunday, Hang Dao and its northerly continuation as far as Dong Xuan Market is closed to traffic, and vendors set up stalls selling all kinds of trinkets at the **Weekend Night Market**. Though it's a fun place to experience modern Hanoi, there's not much on sale that would interest Western visitors – most shoppers are Vietnamese youngsters snapping up fashion accessories like mobile phone covers. It can get very crowded at times (so watch out for pickpockets), but winds down after 11pm. Sections of Ha Tien, Hang Buom and Ma May are also technically closed to traffic on weekend evenings, though many motorbikes ignore this.

bridge was a favourite target for US bombers during the American War, and is now a popular spot among Hanoians who like to shoot pictures against its distinctive background. Make sure you keep an eye out for mad motorbike riders.

7

The French Quarter

The first French concession was granted in 1874, and was a mosquito-infested plot of land on the banks of the Red River, southeast of where the **Opera House** stands today. Once in full possession of Hanoi, after 1882, the French began to create a city appropriate to their new protectorate, starting with the area between the old concession and the train station, 2km to the west. In the process they destroyed many ancient Vietnamese monuments, which were replaced with Parisian-style buildings and boulevards. Elegant villas gradually filled plots along the grid of tree-lined avenues, then spread south from Hoan Kiem Lake in the 1930s and 1940s towards what is now **Thong Nhat Park**, a peaceful but rather featureless expanse of green marking the French Quarter's southern boundary. The streets south of Le Lai on the east side of Hoan Kiem Lake, which include the *Metropole Hotel* and the Government Guest House, are also generally considered part of the French Quarter because of their architectural features.

The Opera House

Near the eastern end of Trang Tien • Open during performances only • ☎ 024 3993 0113, ⓦ hanoioperahouse.org.vn

A grand example of the Parisian-style architecture for which the quarter is famous, the stately **Opera House** (now officially known as the Municipal Theatre) is modelled on the neo-Baroque Paris Opera, complete with Ionic columns and grey slate tiles imported from France. The theatre was erected on reclaimed land and opened in 1911 after ten years of construction; it was regarded as the jewel in the crown of French Hanoi, the colonial town's physical and cultural focus, until 1945 when the Viet Minh proclaimed the **August Revolution** from its balcony. After Independence, audiences were treated to a diet of Socialist Realism and revolutionary theatre, but now the building has been restored to its former glory after a massive face-lift. Crystal chandeliers, Parisian mirrors and sweeping staircases of polished marble have all been beautifully preserved, although, unfortunately, there's no access to the public unless you attend a performance (see p.379). Otherwise, feast your eyes on the exterior, which is particularly stunning under evening floodlights or, better still, the soft glow of a full moon.

National Museum of History

1 Trang Tien • Daily 8am–noon & 1.30–5pm; closed first Monday of each month • 40,000đ; with camera 55,000đ • ☎ 024 3824 1384, ⓦ baotanglichsu.vn

One block east of the Opera House, the building that houses the **National Museum of History** is a fanciful blend of Vietnamese palace and French villa, which came to be

COLONIAL ARCHITECTURE

After the hectic streets of the Old Quarter, the grand boulevards and wide pavements of Hanoi's **French Quarter** are a welcome relief. Again it's the **architecture** that's the highlight, running the gamut of early twentieth-century European styles from elegant Neoclassical through to 1930s Modernism and Art Deco, with an occasional Oriental flourish. One of the most splendid examples is the former residence of the governor of Tonkin, now the Government Guest House at the junction of Ngo Quyen and Le Thach. There are several other elegant colonial mansions along Phan Dinh Phung and Dien Bien Phu in Ba Dinh District, which is sometimes referred to as Hanoi's "other" or "second" French Quarter.

called "Neo-Vietnamese" style. The museum was founded in the 1930s by the École Française d'Extrême Orient, but after 1954 changed focus to reflect Vietnam's evolution from paleolithic times to Independence. Exhibits, including many plaster reproductions, are arranged in chronological order across two floors, covering everything from prehistory to 1945, while the building across the street at 216 Tran Quang Khai covers the post-1945 era.

The ground floor

On the ground floor, the museum's prize exhibits are those from the **Dong Son culture**, a sophisticated Bronze Age civilization that flourished in the Red River Delta from 1200 to 200 BC. The display includes a rich variety of implements, from arrowheads to cooking utensils, but the finest examples of Dong Son creativity are several huge, ceremonial **bronze drums**, which were used to bury the dead, invoke the monsoon or celebrate fertility rites. The remarkably well-preserved **Ngoc Lu Drum** is the highlight, where advanced casting techniques are evident in the delicate figures of deer, birds and musicians ornamenting the drum's surface. Other notable exhibits on this floor include finds from excavations in Hanoi's citadel, a willowy **Amitabha Buddha** of the eleventh century, pale-green celadon ware from the same era and a group of wooden stakes from the glorious thirteenth-century battle of the Bach Dang River (see box, p.325).

The second floor

Displays on the museum's **second floor** illustrate the great leap in artistic skill that took place in the fifteenth century following a period of Chinese rule. Pride of place goes to a 3m-tall stele inscribed with the life story of Le Loi, who spearheaded the resistance against the Chinese and founded the Later Le dynasty, which ruled the country from 1428 to 1788. Also on display is an extensive collection of ceramics and exhibits relating to the nineteenth-century **Nguyen dynasty** and the period of French rule. A series of ink-washes depicting Hue's Imperial court in the 1890s is particularly eye-catching, as are the embroidered silks and inlaid ivory furniture once used by the emperors cloistered in the citadel.

216 Tran Quang Khai

The former Museum of Vietnamese Revolution is now a part of the History Museum, and catalogues the "Vietnamese people's patriotic and revolutionary struggle" from the first anti-French movements of the late nineteenth century to post-1975 reconstruction. Much of the tale is told through documents, including the first clandestine newspapers and revolutionary tracts penned by Ho Chi Minh, and illustrated with portraits of Vietnam's most famous revolutionaries – among them are many photos you won't see elsewhere. There's good coverage of Dien Bien Phu and the War of Independence, and a small but well-presented exhibition on the American War, a subject that is treated in greater depth at the Military History Museum (see p.361).

Trang Tien

Trang Tien, the main artery of the French Quarter, is still a busy shopping street where you'll find bookshops and art galleries, as well as **Trang Tien Plaza** with its flash boutiques. South of Trang Tien you enter French Hanoi's principal **residential quarter**, consisting of a grid of shaded boulevards whose distinguished villas are much sought after for restoration as embassies and offices, or as desirable, expatriate residences. To take a swing through the area, drop down **Hang Bai** onto **Ly Thuong Kiet** and start heading west.

Museum of Vietnamese Women

36 Ly Thuong Kiet · Daily 8am–5pm · 30,000đ; audio-tour 30,000đ · ☎ 024 3825 9936, ⓦ womenmuseum.org.vn

The **Museum of Vietnamese Women** has undergone a complete overhaul in recent years and is now one of Hanoi's most interesting attractions, with good audio-tours available as well as detailed video presentations on each floor about different aspects of the lives of Vietnamese women. It starts off with a look at street vendors, whose presence on the streets of the city with their baskets of goods suspended from bamboo poles is one of the country's most indelible icons. The role of women in the country's wars is the focus of the second floor, while the third floor focuses on family life and the top floor features an eye-catching display of ethnic minority costumes.

7

Hoa Lo Prison

1 Hoa Lo · Daily 8am–5pm · 30,000đ

The Hanoi Towers complex looms over the sanitized remnants of French-built **Hoa Lo Prison**, nicknamed the "Hanoi Hilton" by American prisoners of war as a wry comment on its harsh conditions and brutal treatment. The jail became famous in the 1960s when the PoWs, mostly pilots and crew, were shown worldwide in televised broadcasts. There's a heavy dose of propaganda in the two rooms dedicated to the PoWs, peddling the message that they were well treated, clothed and fed.

The museum mostly concentrates on the pre-1954 colonial period, when the French incarcerated many nationalist leaders at Hoa Lo, including no fewer than five future general secretaries of the Vietnamese Communist Party. Some of the cells – which were still in use up to 1994 – have been preserved, along with rusty shackles, a guillotine and instruments of torture. Other rooms display photos and information on the more famous political prisoners.

THE METROPOLE LEGEND

The bright, white Neoclassical facade of the **Metropole** – nowadays *Sofitel Legend Metropole* hotel – opened in 1901 as the Grand Metropole Palace, and soon became one of Southeast Asia's great hotels. Even during the French War, Bernard Fall, a journalist killed by a landmine near Hue in 1967, described the hotel as the "last really fashionable place left in Hanoi", where the barman "could produce a reasonable facsimile of almost any civilized drink except water". After Independence it re-emerged as the Thong Nhat or Reunification Hotel, but otherwise stayed much the same, apart from the resident rats and lethal wiring, until 1990 when Sofitel transformed it into Hanoi's first international-class accommodation (see p.373). The *Metropole*'s illustrious visitors' book includes Charlie Chaplin and Paulette Goddard on honeymoon in 1936, as well as Graham Greene, who first came here in 1952. Twenty years later, Jane Fonda stayed for two weeks while making her famous broadcast to American troops.

Quan Su Pagoda

73 Quan Su, near the junction with Tran Hung Dao • Daily 7.30–11am and 1.30–5.30pm

The **Quan Su Pagoda**, also known as the Ambassadors' Pagoda, was founded in the fifteenth century as part of a guesthouse for officials from neighbouring Buddhist countries, though the current building dates only from 1942. Nowadays Quan Su is one of Hanoi's most active pagodas: on the first and fifteenth days of the lunar month, worshippers and mendicants throng its forecourt; inside, an iron lamp ornamented with sinuous dragons hangs over the crowded prayer-floor, and ranks of crimson-lacquered Buddhas glow through a pungent haze of burning incense. The compound, shaded by ancient trees, is the headquarters of the officially recognized Central Buddhist Congregation of Vietnam and is a centre of Buddhist learning, hence the well-stocked library and classrooms at the rear.

7 Ba Dinh District

Hanoi's most important cultural and historical monuments are found in the **Ba Dinh District**, immediately west of the Old Quarter, where the Ly kings established their Imperial City in the eleventh century. The venerable **Temple of Literature** and the picturesque **One Pillar Pagoda** both date from this time, but nothing else remains of the Ly kings' vermilion palaces, whose last vestiges were cleared in the late nineteenth century to accommodate an expanding French administration. Most impressive of the district's colonial buildings is the dignified residence of the governor-general of Indochina, now known as the **Presidential Palace**; part of its former gardens now house two great centres of pilgrimage – **Ho Chi Minh's Mausoleum** and **Museum**.

East of Ba Dinh Square, the **Hanoi Citadel** was the seat of power for all Vietnamese dynasties apart from the Nguyen dynasty. To the south of the Citadel stands the **Cot Co Flag Tower**, which is accessed via the **Military History Museum**.

There's a lot to see in this area, and though it's possible to cover everything described below in a single day, in order to digest everything it's best to spend one day exploring the sites around Ba Dinh Square and the Citadel, then return another day to see the Temple of Literature, the **Fine Arts Museum** and the Military History Museum.

Ba Dinh Square

Two kilometres west of Hoan Kiem Lake, the wide, open spaces of **Ba Dinh Square** are the nation's ceremonial centre. It was here that Ho Chi Minh read out the Declaration of Independence to half a million people on September 2, 1945, and here that Independence is commemorated each National Day with military parades. You'll see the **National Assembly Hall**, the venue for Party congresses, standing on the square's east side.

Ho Chi Minh's Mausoleum

Ba Dinh Square • April–Oct Tues–Thurs 7.30–10.30am, Sat & Sun 7.30–11am; Nov–March Tues–Thurs 8–11am, Sat & Sun 8–11.30am • Free

In the tradition of great Communist leaders, when Ho Chi Minh died in 1969 his body was **embalmed**, though it was not put on public view until after 1975. The mausoleum is probably Hanoi's most popular sight for domestic tourists, attracting hordes of visitors at weekends and on national holidays; from school parties to ageing confederates, all come to pay their respects to "Uncle Ho".

Visitors to the mausoleum (note the very limited opening hours) must leave bags and cameras at a kiosk by the entrance, and are escorted by soldiers in immaculate uniforms. Respectful behaviour is requested, which means **appropriate dress** (no shorts, sleeveless vests or hats) and keeping silent within the sanctum. Note that each September and October the mausoleum usually closes while work is done to preserve the body.

Inside the mausoleum

Inside the building's marble entrance hall, Ho Chi Minh's most quoted maxim greets you: "Nothing is more important than independence and freedom." Then it's up the stairs and into a cold, dark room where the charismatic hero lies under glass, a small, pale figure glowing in the dim light, his thin hands resting on black covers. Despite the rather macabre overtones, it's hard not to be affected by the solemn atmosphere, though in actual fact Ho's last wish was to be cremated and have his ashes divided between the north, centre and south of the country, with each site marked only by a simple shelter. The grandiose building where he now lies seems sadly at odds with this unassuming, egalitarian man.

Presidential Palace

Just north of Ho's mausoleum lie the grounds of the **Presidential Palace**. The palace was built in 1901 as the home of the governor-general of Indochina – all sweeping stairways, louvred shutters and ornate wrought-iron gates of the belle époque – and these days is used to receive visiting heads of state. It's closed to the public, but you can still admire the outside as you walk through the palace gardens to Ho Chi Minh's house.

7

Ho Chi Minh's House

Ba Dinh Square • April–Oct: Mon 7.30–11am, Tues–Sun 7.30–11am & 1.30–4pm; Nov–March: Mon 8–11am, Tues–Sun 8–11am & 1.30–4pm • 40,000đ

Ho Chi Minh's House, built in 1954 and modelled on an ethnic minority stilthouse, is a simple structure with open sides and split-bamboo screens. Since it stands almost next to the grandiose Presidential Palace where Ho declined to live, it's tempting to see it as a succinct comment by him on the excesses of colonialism – and it certainly looks like a cosier place to call home. Ho and his Politburo used to gather in the ground-level meeting area, while his study and bedroom upstairs are said to be as he left them, sparsely furnished, unostentatious and very highly polished. Ho lived here for the last eleven years of his life, even during the American War, tending his garden and fishpond; it's said that he died in the small hut next door.

Hanoi Botanical Gardens

3 Hoang Hoa Tham, between West Lake and the mausoleum • Daily 7am–10pm • 4000đ

After the rather solemn sights around Ba Dinh Square, particularly the mausoleum, many visitors feel in need of a breath of fresh air, and the **Botanical Gardens** (signed Vuon Bach Tao at the entrance) is just the place for that. Established by the French in 1890, it's more of a park than a botanical garden, but it does have tall, shady trees, grassy lawns, a couple of small lakes, a network of footpaths, benches to rest on, and some intriguing modern sculptures.

One Pillar Pagoda

Ong Ich Khiem

Just south of the Ho Chi Minh Mausoleum, the **One Pillar Pagoda** rivals the Turtle Tower as a symbol of Hanoi. It is the most unusual of the hundreds of pagodas sponsored by devoutly Buddhist Ly-dynasty kings in the eleventh century, and represents a flowering of Vietnamese art. The tiny wooden sanctuary, dedicated to **Quan Am** whose statue nestles inside, is only three square metres in size and is supported by a single column rising from the middle of an artificial lake, and the whole structure is designed to resemble a lotus blossom, the Buddhist symbol of enlightenment. In fact this is by no means the original building – the concrete pillar is a real giveaway – and the last reconstruction took place after departing French troops blew up the earlier structure in 1954.

Ho Chi Minh Museum

19 Ngoc Ha • Mon & Fri 8am–12pm, Tues–Thurs, Sat & Sun 8am–12pm & 2–4.30pm • 40,000đ • ⓦ baotanghochiminh.vn

The angular, white building housing the **Ho Chi Minh Museum** was built with Soviet aid and inaugurated on May 19, 1990, the hundredth anniversary of Ho's birth. The museum celebrates Ho Chi Minh's life and the pivotal role he played in the nation's history; not surprisingly, this is also a favourite for school outings. Exhibits around the hall's outer wall focus on Ho's life and the "Vietnamese Revolution" in the context of socialism's international development, including documents, photographs and a smattering of personal possessions, among them a suspiciously new-looking disguise Ho supposedly adopted when escaping from Hong Kong. Running parallel on the inner ring are a series of heavily metaphoric "spatial images", six tableaux portraying significant places and events, from Ho's birthplace in Nghe An to Pac Bo cave and ending with a symbolic rendering of Vietnam's reunification. Go in for the surreal nature of the whole experience, but don't expect to come away having learned much more about the man.

7

Imperial Citadel of Thang Long

9 Hoang Dieu • Tues–Sun 8am–5pm • 30,000đ • ☏ 024 3734 5927, ⓦ hoangthanhthanglong.vn

While not as impressive a sight as the Hue Citadel, the **Imperial Citadel of Thang Long** (Hanoi's former name) is still of sufficient interest to warrant its World Heritage status (granted in 2010 to coincide with the city's one-thousandth birthday) and to feature on any visitor's itinerary. It comprises **two sections** – the Central Sector of the citadel to the east of Hoang Dieu, and the archeological site on the west side of Hoang Dieu. Note that two other surviving fragments of the citadel are accessed separately: the flag tower, or **Cot Co**, through the nearby Military History Museum, and the northern gate, or **Cua Bac** (which still bears huge scars from cannon fire), from Phan Dinh Phung.

A citadel was first erected here in the eighth century by the Chinese, though nothing remains from that time, and Ly Thai To is usually credited as the founder of the Imperial Citadel, which was then added to by succeeding dynasties – Tran, Le, Mac and Nguyen – until the capital was moved to Hue in 1802. Though most of its buildings were subsequently razed by the French, enough remains in the twelve-acre complex to keep visitors busy for at least a couple of hours.

The central sector

The central sector of the citadel is accessed through the **Doan Mon Gate**, where you'll find the ticket desk. This huge wall, topped with a double-roofed pavilion and with five arches leading through it, was once the main entrance to the king's forbidden realm. Inside the gate is an excavated area that reveals an ancient irrigation system.

The next building, **Kinh Thien Palace**, was once the grandest structure in the citadel, but all that remains today are two beautiful stone dragons flowing down a flight of steps that lead to the building. Among these ancient remains, it comes as a shock to encounter the **D67 Building**, which dates from 1967 and functioned as command centre for the Northern forces during the American War. The name of military mastermind Vo Nguyen Giap, among others, still sits on the conference table here, and the reinforced underground bunker acts as a reminder of the threat of aerial bombardment in that era.

The final building in this complex is the Hau Lau, or "back pavilion", a mix of Eastern and Western styles. It is sometimes referred to as the "princess pavilion", as it once housed concubines of the Nguyen kings.

The archeological dig

Once you've seen the central sector, it's worth retracing your steps to the west of Kinh Thien Palace and crossing Hoang Dieu through a side gate to visit the **archeological dig** on the other side of the road. This huge site was discovered in 2002 when foundations were being dug for a new National Assembly, and it has revealed the remains of more grand palaces and relics from various dynasties, some of which are now on display in the National Museum of History (see p.355).

The Military History Museum

28a Dien Bien Phu • Tues–Thurs, Sat & Sun 8–11.30am & 1–4.30pm • 40,000đ • ⓦ btlsqsvn.org.vn

Dien Bien Phu, a road lined with gnarled trees and former colonial offices, interspersed with gingerbread villas, is home to the white, arcaded building of the **Military History Museum**, opposite a small park with a statue of Lenin. The museum chronicles national history from the 1930s to the present day, a period dominated by the French and American wars, though it's noticeably quiet on China and Cambodia.

The forecourt

The museum **forecourt** is full of weaponry: pride of place goes to a Russian MiG-21 fighter, alongside artillery from the battle of Dien Bien Phu (see box, p.409) and a tank from the American War, while the second courtyard is dominated by the mangled wreckage of assorted American planes piled against a tree.

7

Inside the museum

The exhibition proper starts on the building's second floor and runs chronologically from the 1930 Nghe Tinh Uprising, through the August Revolution to the "People's War" against the French, culminating in the decisive **battle of Dien Bien Phu**. If there's sufficient demand, they'll show an English-language video to accompany the battle's diorama; despite the heavy propaganda overlay, the archive footage is fascinating, including Viet Minh hauling artillery up mountain slopes and clouds of French parachutists. Naturally, General Giap and Ho Chi Minh make star appearances – after the ubiquitous still images, it's a shock to see Ho animated. The American War, covered in a separate hall at the rear, receives similar treatment with film of the relentless drive south to "liberate" Saigon in 1975.

Cot Co

In the northwest corner of the museum compound stands the 30m **Cot Co** (Flag Tower), one of the few remnants of Emperor Gia Long's early nineteenth-century citadel, where the national flag now billows in place of the emperor's yellow banner. Built in 1812, it features 36 flower-shaped and six fan-shaped windows. When the French flattened the ramparts in the 1890s, they kept Cot Co as a handy lookout post. It is possible to climb a spiral staircase inside for a view of the surrounding area, though the door to the upper part is sometimes locked. There's also a convenient café at its base.

Vietnam Fine Arts Museum

66 Nguyen Thai Hoc • Daily 8.30am–5pm • 40,000đ; guided tour 150,000đ • ⓦ vnfam.vn

A couple of blocks southwest of the Military History Museum, a three-storey colonial block with chocolate-brown shutters houses the **Vietnam Fine Arts Museum**. It not only boasts the country's most comprehensive collection of fine art, but it is also unusually well presented, with plenty of information in English. Arranged chronologically, the museum illustrates the main themes of Vietnam's artistic development, kicking off with a collection of **Dong Son drums** and statues of graceful Cham dancers. Though many items are reproductions, there are some fine pieces, notably among the seventeenth- and eighteenth-century **Buddhist art**, which spawned such masterpieces as Tay Phuong's superbly lifelike statues. Other highlights include extensive collections of folk art and ethnic minority art, and an interesting exhibition of twentieth-century artists charting the evolution from a solidly European style through Socialist Realism to the emergence of a distinct Vietnamese school of art.

The Temple of Literature

Nguyen Thai Hoc, entrance on Quoc Tu Giam • Daily: April–Oct 7.30am–6pm; Nov–March 8am–6pm • 30,000đ

Hanoi's most revered temple complex, the **Temple of Literature**, or Van Mieu, is both Vietnam's principal Confucian sanctuary and its historical centre of learning. The temple is also one of the few remnants of the Ly kings' original city and retains a strong sense of harmony despite reconstruction and embellishment over the nine hundred years since its dedication in 1070.

Entry is through the two-tiered **Van Mieu Gate**. The temple's ground plan, modelled on that of Confucius's birthplace in Qufu, China, consists of a succession of five walled courtyards. The first two are havens of trim lawns and trees separated by a simple pavilion.

The third courtyard

You enter the third courtyard via the imposing **Khue Van Cac** (the Constellation of Literature), a double-roofed gateway built in 1805, its wooden upper storey ornamented with four radiating suns. If it looks familiar, it's because it's frequently used as a symbol of the city on websites and in tourist brochures. Central to this section of the complex is the **Well of Heavenly Clarity** – a rectangular pond – to either side of which stand the temple's most valuable relics – 82 stone **stelae** mounted on tortoises. Each stele records the results of a state examination held at the National Academy between 1442 and 1779, though the practice only started in 1484, and gives brief biographical details of successful candidates. It's estimated that up to thirty stelae have gone missing or disintegrated over the years, but the two oldest, dating from 1442 and 1448, occupy centre spot on opposite sides of the pond.

The fourth courtyard

Passing through the **Gate of Great Synthesis** brings you to the fourth courtyard, the **Courtyard of Sages**, and the main temple buildings. Two pavilions on either side once contained altars dedicated to the 72 disciples of Confucius, but now house souvenir shops. During Tet this courtyard is the scene of calligraphy competitions and "human chess games", with people instead of wooden pieces on the square paving stones.

The House of Ceremonies

This long, low building, whose sweeping tiled roof is crowned by two lithe dragons bracketing a full moon, stands on the courtyard's north side. Here the king and his

---

BECOMING A MANDARIN

Examinations for admission to the **Imperial bureaucracy** were introduced by the Ly kings in the eleventh century as part of a range of reforms that served to underpin the nation's stability for several centuries. Vietnam's exams were based on the Chinese system, though they also included Buddhist and Taoist texts along with the Confucian classics. It took until the fifteenth century, however, for academic success, rather than noble birth or patronage, to become the primary means of entry to the civil service. By this time the system was open to **all males**, excluding "traitors, rebels, immoral people and actors", but in practice very few candidates outside the scholar-gentry class progressed beyond the lowest rung.

First came **regional exams**, *thi huong*, after which successful students (who could be any age from 16 to 61) would head for Hanoi, equipped with their sleeping mat, ink-stone and writing brush, to take part in the second-level *thi hoi*. These **national exams** might last up to six weeks and were as much an evaluation of poetic style and knowledge of the classic texts as they were of administrative ability. Those who passed all stages were granted a doctorate, *tien si*, and were eligible for the third and final test, the *thi dinh*, or **palace exam**, set by the king himself. Some years as few as three *tien si* would be awarded whereas the total number of candidates could be as high as six thousand, and during nearly three hundred exams held between 1076 and 1779, only 2313 *tien si* were recorded. Afterwards the king would give his new mandarins a cap, gown, parasol and a horse on which to return to their home village in triumphal procession.

mandarins would make sacrifices before the altar of Confucius, accompanied by booming drums and bronze bells echoing among the magnificent ironwood pillars. Within the ceremonial hall lies the **temple sanctuary**, at one time prohibited even to the king, where a large and striking statue of Confucius sits with his four principal disciples, resplendent in vivid reds and golds. Between the altar and sanctuary is a Music Room, where musicians playing traditional instruments sometimes provide a great opportunity for photos.

The fifth courtyard

The fifth and final courtyard once housed the **National Academy**, regarded as Vietnam's first university, which was founded in 1076 to educate princes and high officials in Confucian doctrine. In 1947 French bombs destroyed the academy buildings but they have now been painstakingly reconstructed, including an elegant two-storey pavilion housing a small museum and an altar dedicated to a noted director of the university in the fourteenth century, Chu Van An. Upstairs, three more statues honour King Ly Thanh Tong (the founder of Van Mieu), Ly Nhan Tong (who added the university) and Le Thanh Tong (instigator of the stelae). The pavilion is flanked by an imposing drum tower as well as a bell tower.

7

B-52 Victory Museum

157 Doi Can, Ba Dinh District • Tues–Thurs, Sat & Sun 8–11am & 1.30–4.30pm • Free

For war buffs, it's worth checking out this intensely patriotic museum that commemorates the shooting down of fifteen **B-52 bombers** during the US's Operation Linebacker II in December 1972. This operation is often referred to in the West as "the Christmas bombings", as President Nixon initiated them between December 18 and 29 (with a day off for Christmas). Over 15,000 tonnes of ordnance was dumped on industrial and military targets in and around Hanoi, with a few stray bombs destroying hospitals and schools, causing untold damage and loss of life. However, the event is remembered by Vietnamese as "Dien Bien Phu in the air", since it did not bring about the capitulation of Viet Cong forces so dearly sought by the US.

The museum is located between Ba Dinh Square and the Museum of Ethnology, so can be combined with a visit to either of these attractions to the west of the city centre. It is also just a short distance from **Huu Tiep Lake**, where one of the bombers came down, and the exhibits, as you'd guess, include the wreckage of B-52 bombers.

Lotte Observation Deck

54 Lieu Giai, Ba Dinh District • Daily 8.30am–11pm (last entry 10pm) • 230,000đ, but 150,000đ after 5.30pm • ☎ 024 3333 6000, ⓦ lottecenter.com.vn

Located on the 65th floor of the **Lotte Center**, at a height of 253m, this observation deck features 360-degree views over Hanoi and the chance to test your mettle with a "sky walk", which involves stepping out onto a glass floor to admire the view straight down. That said, you might find the experience a bit of a letdown, as there are very few distinctive landmarks to see in Hanoi, the city is often cloaked in smog, and reflections of ambient lighting and handprints on the glass make it difficult to take a good photo.

West Lake and around

As in the days of Vietnam's emperors, **West Lake** (Ho Tay), to the northwest of the city centre, has once again become Hanoi's most fashionable neighbourhood. It's particularly popular among the city's expats, who tend to hone in on Xuan Dieu, and you'll find a wealth of exclusive residential developments, lakeside clubs and spas, as well as a clutch of luxury hotels.

> ## THE WEST LAKE CIRCUIT
>
> A track runs right around the 17km circumference of **West Lake**, which is ideal for a long walk (3–4hr), bike ride (about 1.5hr) or a tour in an electric car (1.5hr; see p.369). The electric cars (80,000đ per person or 330,000đ for the whole car) depart from Tran Quoc Pagoda every half an hour and pass around twenty different sights along the route, including the Quan Thanh and Tay Ho temples. There's often a fresh breeze coming off the lake, though admittedly it suffers badly from pollution due to the dense human habitation beside its shores.

In the seventeenth century, villagers built a causeway across the lake's southeastern corner, creating a small fishing lake that's now known as **Truc Bach** and ringed with little cafés. Attractions around West Lake include several temples and pagodas as well as the excellent **Museum of Ethnology**, a short distance from the lake's southwest corner.

Truc Bach Lake

The name **Truc Bach** derives from an eighteenth-century summer palace built by the ruling Trinh lords; it later became a place of detention for disagreeable concubines and other "errant women", who were put to work weaving fine white silk, or *truc bach*. The causeway, or **Thanh Nien**, is an avenue of flame trees and a popular picnic spot in summer, when a cooling breeze comes off the water and hawkers set up shop along the grass verges. Many Vietnamese rent swan-shaped pedalboats (100,000đ per hour for two people) on Truc Bach Lake and pedal across the waters.

Quan Thanh Temple

Quan Thanh • Daily 7.30am–5pm • 10,000đ

Although the summer palace no longer exists, the eleventh-century **Quan Thanh Temple** still stands on the lake's southeast bank, erected by King Ly Thai To and dedicated to the Guardian of the North, Tran Vo, who protects the city from malevolent spirits. Quan Thanh has been rebuilt several times, most recently in 1893, and has lost nearly all its original features along the way.

Tran Vo statue

It's well worth wandering into the shady courtyard to see the 334-year-old black bronze **statue of Tran Vo**, seated on the main altar. The statue, nearly 4m high and weighing four tonnes, portrays the Taoist god accompanied by his two animal emblems, a serpent and a turtle. It was the creation of a craftsman called Trum Trong, whose own statue, fashioned in stone and sporting a grey headscarf, sits off to one side.

The shrine room

The **shrine room** also boasts a valuable collection of seventeenth- and eighteenth-century poems and parallel sentences (boards inscribed with wise maxims and hung in pairs on adjacent columns), most with intricate, mother-of-pearl inlay work.

Gunners' Memorial

North of Quan Thanh Temple, where Thanh Nien bears gently right, the small **Gunners' Memorial** stands on the eastern side of the road, which is dedicated to the teams of antiaircraft gunners that were stationed here during the American War. In particular the memorial commemorates the downing of Navy Lieutenant Commander John McCain, who parachuted into Truc Bach Lake in October 1967 and survived more than five years in the "Hanoi Hilton". He went on to run for US president in 2008, only to be beaten by Barack Obama.

Tran Quoc Pagoda

Thanh Nien • Daily 7.30–11am & 1.30–5pm • Free • Visitors are requested not to wear shorts

Tran Quoc Pagoda, Hanoi's oldest religious foundation, occupies a tiny spur of land off Thanh Nien, which separates West Lake from Truc Bach. The pagoda's exact origins are uncertain, but it's usually attributed to the Early Ly dynasty in the sixth century, during a brief interlude between ten centuries of Chinese domination. In the early seventeenth century, when Buddhism was enjoying a revival, the pagoda was moved from its original location beside the Red River to its present, less vulnerable spot.

Entry is along a narrow, brick causeway lying just above the water, past a collection of imposing brick stupas, the latest of which – towering over its more modest neighbours – was erected in 2003 on the death of the then master of the pagoda. The sanctuary's restrained interior and general configuration are typical of northern Vietnamese pagodas, though there's nothing inside of particular importance.

Kim Lien Pagoda

Dawn to dusk • Free

About a kilometre north of the causeway, the red-tiled roofs of **Kim Lien Pagoda** provide an incongruous neighbour for the *Intercontinental Hotel*. Though it may appear to be closed, you can usually enter through a small gate to the left of the main building. The pagoda's best attributes are its elaborate carvings and unplastered brick walls, which date from an eighteenth-century rebuild.

Tay Ho Temple

Dawn to dusk • Free

The **Tay Ho Temple**, located at the end of the Ho Tay Peninsula on the east side of the lake, is dedicated to Thanh Mau, the Mother Goddess, who in the seventeenth century appeared as a beautiful girl to a famous scholar out boating on the lake. She refused to reveal her name and just smiled enigmatically, recited some poetry and disappeared. But when the scholar worked out her identity from the poem, local villagers erected a temple on the shore where they still worship the goddess today – particularly on the first and fifteenth day of each lunar month, when the place takes on a carnival atmosphere and vendors line the approach roads. At other times, Tay Ho Temple attracts few tourists, and the petitioners here are mostly women and young people asking for favours by burning fake dollars under the banyan trees.

THE LEGEND OF WEST LAKE

Way back in the mists of time, a gifted **monk** returned from China bearing quantities of bronze as a reward for curing the emperor's illness. The monk gave most of the metal to the state, but decided to fashion a bell with a small lump, and its sound was so pure that it resonated throughout the land and beyond the far-off mountains. The sound reached the ears of a golden **buffalo calf** inside the Chinese Imperial treasury, and the creature followed the bell, mistaking it for the call of its mother. When the bell fell silent, the calf spun round and round, not knowing which way to go. Eventually it had trampled a vast **hollow**, which filled with water and became West Lake. Some say the golden buffalo is still there, at the bottom of the lake, but can only be retrieved by a man assisted by his ten natural sons.

More prosaically, West Lake is a shallow **lagoon**, left behind as the Red River shifted course eastward to leave a narrow strip of land separating the lake and the river, reinforced over the centuries with massive embankments. The lake was traditionally an area for royal recreation or spiritual pursuits, where monarchs erected summer palaces and sponsored religious foundations, among them Hanoi's most ancient pagoda, Tran Quoc.

Museum of Ethnology

Nguyen Van Huyen • Tues–Sun 8.30am–5.30pm; water puppet shows Sat & Sun 10am, 11.30am, 2.30pm & 4pm • 40,000đ; with guide 50,000đ; with camera 50,000đ • ☎ 024 3756 2193, ⓦ vme.org.vn • City bus #14 from Dinh Tieng Hoang, just north of Hoan Kiem Lake, to Nghia Tan; taxi from the Old Quarter 120,000đ

The **Museum of Ethnology** is 7km west of the city centre and about 1km southwest of West Lake, though it more than repays the effort of getting there, particularly if you'll be visiting any of Vietnam's minority areas. Spread across two floors, the displays are well presented and there's information in English on all the major ethnic groups. The musical instruments, games, traditional dress and other domestic items that fill the displays are brought to life through musical recordings, photos and plenty of life-size models, as well as captivating videos of festivals and shamanistic rites (but don't watch the one on buffalo sacrifice if you're squeamish). This wealth of creativity amply illustrates some of the difficulties ethnologists are up against – the museum also acts as a **research institute** charged with producing ethnologies for Vietnam's 54 main groups, plus their profusion of subgroups. The grounds contain a collection of **minority buildings** relocated from all over Vietnam, dominated by a beautiful example of a Bahnar communal house.

Southeast Asia Museum

Entry included in Museum of Ethnology ticket

Right next door to the Museum of Ethnology, the striking, kite-shaped **Southeast Asia Museum** is one of the city's newest. Displays focus on the daily life, social activities, garments, performing arts and religions in eleven countries across the region, and rotating exhibitions cover topics such as Indonesian glass paintings.

ARRIVAL AND DEPARTURE   **HANOI**

As a major gateway into Vietnam and a transit hub for the country, Hanoi is well served by **long-distance transport**. It's also easy to arrange onward transport from here to some of north Vietnam's most popular destinations – among them Ha Long Bay, Sa Pa and the Dong Van Karst Plateau Geopark in Ha Giang province. For those eager to see as much of the country as they can in a single visit, the next step is a plane or train ride south to the Imperial City of Hue, the beaches of Nha Trang, and eventually the sensory overload of Vietnam's second city, Ho Chi Minh City. Note that travellers planning on crossing the Lao, Cambodian or Chinese **borders** should first read the information in Basics on p.26.

BY PLANE

Noi Bai Airport is based 45km north of the city (☎ 024 3886 5047, ⓦ noibaiairport.vn). It boasts an international terminal, which opened in April 2015, and has all the usual facilities, including sleeping pods that cost 170,000đ/hour (ⓦ hanoiairporthotels.vn).

Destinations Buon Ma Thuot (2 daily; 1hr 40min); Da Lat (daily; 1hr 40min); Da Nang (26 daily; 1hr 15min); Dien Bien Phu (2 daily; 1hr); Dong Hoi (2 daily; 1hr 30min); HCMC (frequent; 2hr); Nha Trang (12 daily; 1hr 40min); Phu Quoc (2 daily; 2hr).

ONWARD TRANSPORT

By bus The #86 bus operates every thirty minutes from 6am–11pm between the airport and Hanoi railway station, with convenient stops at Long Bien bus station and at the north end of Hoan Kiem Lake for hotels in the Old Quarter. The buses have lots of space for luggage, and cost just 30,000đ. City bus #17 (9000đ) runs every twenty minutes between 5.30am–10.30pm from the airport to Long Bien station, but has less luggage room.

By shuttle bus The shuttle minibuses are run by Vietnam Airlines (45min–1hr; 40,000đ) and leave when full from outside the terminal; you'll be dropped off near the airline's main office, just south of Hoan Kiem Lake.

By taxi Taxis from the airport cost around 350,000đ, but beware of scams (see p.49). The safest option is to get your hotel to send a taxi to meet you.

BY TRAIN

Hanoi train station is roughly 1km west of centre, at 120 Le Duan. Note there are two gateways: if you're arriving from or departing for HCMC and all points south, or from China, you'll use the main station platforms on Le Duan. However, trains arriving and departing from the east and north (Haiphong, Sa Pa and Lao Cai) pull into platforms at the rear of the main station, bringing you out among market stalls on a narrow street called Tran Quy Cap.

Tickets You can purchase tickets in the main station building (daily 7.30am–12.30pm & 1.30–7.30pm). It's best to make onward travel arrangements well in advance, especially for sleeper berths to Lao Cai, Hue and Ho Chi Minh City. If you don't want to go to the station, you can also book online with a website like ⓦ baolau.com, which will be able to sort it but will charge you a couple of dollars' commission. Current timetables and prices can be found at ⓦ vietnam-railway.com.

Destinations Da Nang (6 daily; 14–20hr); Dong Dang (daily; 6hr); Dong Ha (3 daily; 12–16hr); Dong Hoi (4 daily; 9–13hr); Haiphong (4 daily; 2–3hr); HCMC (4 daily; 30–40hr); Hue (5 daily; 11–16hr); Lao Cai (6 daily; 7–9hr); Ninh Binh (3 daily; 2hr 20min); Thanh Hoa (3 daily; 3–4hr); Vinh (5 daily; 6–7hr).

BY BUS

By long-distance bus Hanoi's three main long-distance bus stations are all located several kilometres from the centre, and you'll need to catch a city bus (see p.368) or hop on a xe om to get to them. From the south, buses generally terminate at Giap Bat station, which is 6km south of the city on Giai Phong. From the north and northeast, buses from Lang Son, Ha Long and Haiphong usually arrive at Gia Lam station, 4km away on the east bank of the Red River. From the north and northwest, services from Cao Bang, Son La, Mai Chau and Lao Cai arrive at either Giap Bat or My Dinh, about 10km west of the centre. Buses from Ha Giang arrive either at My Dinh or Gia Lam. The bus from Cat Ba operated by Hoang Long company stops at the smaller Nuoc Ngam terminal, about 10km south of the city centre. Note that some buses from Mai Chau and Hoa Binh

---

TOUR AGENTS

7

Hanoi's tourist-service industry has become increasingly diversified over the years, and now comprises a dizzying array of companies – many of which, it has to be said, are dubious, **fly-by-night operators** who specialize in ripping off foreign tourists. There were so many outfits claiming to be affiliated to Sinh Café, for example, that the original Sinh Café was forced to change its name to The Sinh Tourist. To be on the safe side, it's best to go to one of the longer-established and more **reliable agents** such as those listed here. Most also arrange day-long city tours, from around $20 per person for a half-day tour up to $150 for a luxury option, including meals.

★ **Buffalo Tours** 70–72 Ba Trieu ☎ 024 3828 0702, ⓦ buffalotours.com. Long-established experts in organizing tailor-made private tours throughout Indochina, with a particular focus on adventure and special interest holidays; prices are a little high but the service is extremely professional.

Cuong's Motorbike Adventures 122 Pho Vinh Tuy ☎ 091 876 3515, ⓦ cuongs-motorbike-adventure .com. Group and custom tours on modern or classic Ural bikes to all parts of the country, including the wild landscapes of Ha Giang province.

Ethnic Travel 35 Hang Giay ☎ 024 3926 1951, ⓦ ethnictravel.com.vn. Popular operation with a genuine passion for low-impact, environmentally conscious travel; a five-day hiking trip through Ha Giang province costs $498/person for up to six people.

Far East Tours 3b Thi Sach ☎ 024 3747 5876, ⓦ fareastour.asia. Reputable company offering everything from one-day city trips to three-week tours of the whole country. A three-day tour of rice terraces in the north costs $156/person.

Handspan Travel 78 Ma May ☎ 024 3926 2828, ⓦ handspan.com. Environmentally conscious adventure-tour specialist. Options range from sea-kayaking in Ha Long Bay to exploring the north on foot or by mountain bike, staying in minority villages. A one-day craft village tour costs $65/person for a group of two. The tours are well organized and come with plenty of good equipment, and they're also restricted to small groups.

Lotussia 1 Co Nhue, Bac Tu Liem ☎ 024 6673 7596, ⓦ vietnamcycling.com. Offers bike tours to attractions around Hanoi such as Bac Trang village and the Tay Phuong Pagoda, with daily rates of $40–100. Kids' bikes available, too.

Mr Linh's Adventures 83 Ma May ☎ 024 3642 5420, ⓦ mrlinhadventure.com. Offering everything from street-food tours in Hanoi to explorations near the Chinese border, Mr Linh has earned a reputation for reliability and helpful guides.

The Sinh Tourist 52 Luong Ngoc Quyen ☎ 024 3926 1568, ⓦ thesinhtourist.vn. Perhaps Vietnam's most famous tour operator, frequently imitated but still reliable, especially for open-tour bus journeys.

Tonkin Travel 164 Xuan Dieu ☎ 024 3719 1184, ⓦ tonkintravel.com. Established company offering a range of tours, from Vespa sunset trips in Hanoi to adventures across the beautiful landscapes of Pu Luong Nature Reserve.

★ **Vietindo Travel** CT2B Building, Thach Ban ☎ 024 3636 5365, ⓦ vietindotravel.com. An enthusiastic company offering a wide range of travel services and customized tours countrywide. Offers one-day tours to the Perfume Pagoda ($35/person) or to the Thay, Tay Phuong and Tram Gian pagodas, as well as Chuong village ($40/person).

Vietnam in Focus 46 Hang Vai ☎ 012 1515 0522, ⓦ vietnaminfocus.com. If you fancy a photography tour, look no further. In such a photogenic city, it makes sense to explore it with these knowledgeable pros.

terminate in Ha Dong, a suburb of Hanoi also roughly 10km west on Highway 6 – you can jump on one of the waiting buses for the forty-minute ride into the centre.

Gia Lam destinations Bai Chay (Ha Long City; every 30min; 4hr); Ha Giang (3 daily; 8hr); Haiphong (every 30min; 2hr 30min); Lang Son (every 30min; 3hr); Thai Nguyen (every hour; 3hr).

Giap Bat destinations Hue (20 daily; 10hr); Mai Chau (6 daily; 4hr); Ninh Binh (every hour; 2hr); Son La (10 daily; 8hr); Thanh Hoa (every 30min; 3hr).

My Dinh destinations Cao Bang (10 daily; 8hr); Dien Bien Phu (20 daily; 12hr); Ha Giang (14 daily; 8hr); Hoa Binh (15 daily; 2hr); Lao Cai (every 30min; 5hr).

Nuoc Ngam destinations Cat Ba (4 daily; 4hr).

By open-tour bus Open-tour buses can be booked through any tour agent, but many companies have a bad reputation; the most reliable are Mai Linh, Hoang Long and The Sinh Tourist. These buses, many of which offer sleeper berths, allow passengers to hop off and on where they like. It's a cheap, but not always enjoyable, way to travel (see p.32).

Destinations Da Lat (35hr); HCMC (42hr); Hoi An (17hr); Hue (12hr); Nha Trang (28hr); Ninh Binh (2hr).

GETTING AROUND

Despite the chaotic traffic, getting around **on foot** in Hanoi remains the best way to do justice to Hanoi's central district, taking an occasional motorbike taxi to scoot between more distant places. Alternatively, enjoy a leisurely tour by **cyclo**. Bicycle and **motorbike** hire is not recommended for the city itself, since traffic discipline is an unfamiliar concept in Hanoi: teenagers on their Hondas ride without fear, and everyone drives without signalling, preferring to sound the horn constantly to warn others of their presence. If you prefer something solid between you and the maelstrom, there are numerous **taxi** companies operating in Hanoi, and tariffs aren't exorbitant. Finally, the much improved city **buses** are mainly useful for getting out to the long-distance bus stations, and a new **metro** system is on the horizon.

By bus Bus Rapid Transit (BRT) buses were introduced in Hanoi in 2016 in a bid to tackle pollution. They run in lanes clear of other traffic – though the only route up and running at the time of research was going from Kim Ma to Yen Nghia (7000đ). Seven other routes are expected to launch by 2030. Regular buses are mostly only used by travellers as a means to get to or from Noi Bai Airport (see p.366), but other useful routes connect the far-flung long-distance bus stations. These buses run approximately every fifteen to twenty minutes between 5am–9pm, and are fairly empty except during the rush hours (7–9am and 4–6pm) when some routes can be hideously overcrowded. The fares are heavily subsidized, with a flat rate of 7000đ within the city centre and 9000đ to the airport and the outer suburbs; pay the ticket collector on board. Route #3 runs between Gia Lam and Giap Bat (30min), with stops on Hang Tre (or Tran Quang Khai, heading south), Tran Hung Dao and outside the train station; #34 covers Gia Lam and My Dinh (40min) via Hai Ba Trung and the Opera House.

By xe om These hover at every major intersection in Hanoi and provide the main form of cheap, inner-city transport, though they are now getting stiff competition from motorbikes operated by Grab (ⓦgrab.com), which are generally a bit cheaper. An average journey within the city centre should cost around 20,000đ, and a trip out to Ho Chi Minh's Mausoleum or West Lake will be in the region of 40,000đ. Always negotiate a fare before setting off. Drivers are obliged to carry spare helmets for passengers, but it can still be a hair-raising ride.

By cyclo These days, cyclo mainly cater to tour groups taking leisurely ambles around the Old Quarter. If you fancy doing the same, the simplest option is to get your hotel to

arrange it for you. Otherwise, be prepared to bargain hard, aiming at around $7/person ($10 for two) for an hour. Cyclo are banned from certain roads in central Hanoi, so don't be surprised if you seem to be taking a circuitous route or are dropped off around the corner from your destination.

By motorbike Motorbikes in the inner city are only for the brave, but they're definitely worth considering for exploring sights further afield; some agencies will even arrange for you to pick one up somewhere like Mai Chau or Ninh Binh. Most rental outlets are located in the Old Quarter – especially along Ta Hien and Hang Bac – and offer a standard 110cc Honda Wave for around $5/day, with the helmet thrown in. Cuong's Motorbike Adventure (see box, p.367) buys, sells, rents out and repairs bikes, while Rentabike (27/52 To Ngoc Van; ⓣ090 439 2423, ⓦ rentabikehanoi.com) offers bikes at reasonable rates (from $45/month). Staff at the Minsk Club (ⓦminskclubhanoi.wordpress.com) are also an invaluable source of information, and occasionally arrange one-off motorbiking excursions and other events. Make sure you always use the designated parking areas (*gui xe may*); the rate for motorbikes should be 5000đ or under.

By bicycle As with riding a motorbike, you need nerves of steel to pedal a bicycle around Hanoi. However, a bike can be useful for a jaunt round West Lake or a ride to the craft villages or ancient temples around the city. The Hanoi Bicycle Collective at 29 Nhat Chieu (Tues–Sun 9am–7pm; ⓣ024 3718 3156, ⓦthbc.vn) is conveniently located near West Lake and offers city bikes for around $5/day or mountain bikes for around $10/day.

By car Though traffic congestion makes renting a car a cumbersome method of sightseeing in the central districts, it does offer greater flexibility for day-trips out of Hanoi. Virtually every tour agency (see box, p.367) can arrange an a/c car with driver, starting at around $80/day; as few drivers speak English, you may also want to hire a guide for an extra $20–30/day.

By electric car An alternative way to explore the Old Quarter is in an electric car, which follows a route along the narrow streets and round neighbouring Hoan Kiem Lake. The tours last just over half an hour (200,000đ/car; maximum five people) or an hour (300,000đ), with brief stops at a dozen sights en route. You can hire one in front of Dong Xuan Market (see p.354) or opposite the water puppet theatre on the northeast corner of Hoan Kiem Lake.

By taxi With a short ride across the city centre averaging 40,000đ, and around 80,000đ to the suburbs, taxis are definitely worth considering for hopping around the city.

Ask your hotel to call one for you, or call them yourself – try Hanoi Taxi (☎024 3853 5353), CP Taxi (☎024 3826 2626) or Mai Linh Taxi (☎024 3822 2666), which all have a decent reputation. Note that prices are metered in dong, though it looks like dollars – 20.00 on the meter means 20,000đ, not $20. Alternatively, you could try Uber (⊛uber.com) or Grab (⊛grab.com), which are challenging the local taxis with their cheap and efficient services. Download their apps and tap in your destination to find the fare and availability of vehicles.

By metro The new metro wasn't up and running at the time of research, but work is well advanced on it. It will run partly under- and partly over-ground along nine routes connecting key areas of the capital. The first line is scheduled to begin operation in 2018, and the project should be complete by 2021 – but don't bet on it.

INFORMATION

Listings These are carried in several publications, but the most useful are *The Word: Hanoi* (⊛wordhanoi.com), *AsiaLife* (⊛asialifemagazine.com) and *Citypass Guides* (⊛citypassguide.com). Check them out online, or look out for free copies in tourist-oriented establishments.

Maps Most hotels give out free maps of the Old Quarter, but for an in-depth exploration of the city you can't beat *Nancy Chandler's Map of Hanoi* ($17; ⊛nancychandler.net).

ACTIVITIES

If you tire of sightseeing in Hanoi, there are plenty of other activities to keep you occupied, ranging from Vietnamese **cooking classes** to pampering sessions in the city's luxurious **spas**. The big state-run tour agencies such as Vietnam Tourism at 80 Quan Su (☎024 3942 3760, ⊛vietnamtourism.com), are more interested in signing you up for a tour than dishing out information. A far better option is to try one of the well-established and reliable private agencies (see box, p.367), which can provide information on visas, tours, transport and so forth.

ART TOURS
Sophie's Art Tour ☎0168 796 2575, ⊛sophiesarttour.com. Runs tours (Tues–Sat 9am–1pm; $65) of the Fine Arts Museum, private collections and contemporary art spaces, and offers insights into the development of Hanoi's various art scenes over the last century.

COOKING CLASSES AND FOOD TOURS
Blue Butterfly 61 Hang Buom ⊛bluebutterfly restaurant.com. This centrally located restaurant in the Old Quarter offers morning and afternoon cookery classes at $55/person.
Hanoi Cooking Centre 44 Chau Long ⊛hanoicooking centre.com. This school offers a range of classes, from Vietnamese street food to regional cuisine, at $60/person.
Hidden Hanoi 147 Nghi Tam, near the Sheraton Hotel ⊛hiddenhanoi.com.vn. Classes are held Mon–Sat at 11am–2pm and cost $45/person (minimum three people).
Highway 4 31 Xuan Dieu ⊛highway4.com. After a trip to the market, students are shown to their own cooking station at the school, and then spend two hours learning how to make four dishes. Prices start at $40/person, depending on the number in the group (maximum ten).
Street Eats Hanoi ☎090 451 7074, ⊛streetfoodtourshanoi.blogspot.com. Street-food tours are all the rage in Hanoi these days, and it's worth paying $75/person to join Tu or Mark Lowerson (aka Sticky) on a morning, afternoon or evening trip to discover the city's tastiest food stalls.

GOLF
Dao Sen Driving Range 125 Nguyen Son ☎024 3872 6602, ⊛daosen.com.vn. This sixty-lane driving range (100,000đ/100 balls) is located about 3km from the city centre.
Hanoi Club 76 Yen Phu ☎024 3829 3829, ⊛thehanoiclub.com. This club includes the Arena Golf Driving Range, where you can drive floating balls (100,000đ/100 balls) out over West Lake.
The Kings' Island Golf Course 36km west of Hanoi in Dong Mo, Ho Tay province ☎024 3368 6555, ⊛kingsisland golf.com. Kings' Island has two eighteen-hole courses open to non-members, though members get priority at weekends. The weekday walk-in fee for eighteen holes is $100.

LANGUAGE COURSES
123Vietnamese 173 Xuan Thuy ⊛123vietnamese.com, ☎024 9632 9475. Offers individual instruction from

> ## BEWARE THE COPYCAT SCAM
>
> Be warned that **copyright** counts for nothing in Vietnam, so as soon as someone starts a successful business, the copycats jump on the bandwagon. This is especially true of hotels, so for example there are multiple *Queen, Prince* and *Camellia* hotels. However, they are not all under the same management, so you'll need to insist on being taken to the hotel you've specified; check the address with staff when you arrive. Some **taxi drivers**, especially those at Noi Bai Airport, will try to persuade you that your chosen hotel has closed, moved or changed name, or they will simply take you to a place with the same name and a different address, in order to get a commission. If this happens, make a note of the vehicle registration number and report it to the hotel you were aiming for, so that they can make a complaint.

7

$10/hour or group classes from $6/hour. It's located west of the centre.

Hidden Hanoi 147 Nghi Tam ☎091 225 4045, ⓦhiddenhanoi.com.vn. Hidden Hanoi runs a range of language classes, from a survival basic course to an advanced course (twenty classes for $200–250). They also offer private tuition.

SPAS AND SALONS

Salon 15 Ma May ☎024 3926 2036. This is a handy beauty salon in the Old Quarter, where you'll pay from around $10 for a foot massage and $14 for an oil massage (1hr).

SF Spa 30 Cua Dong ☎024 3747 5301, ⓦsfintercare .com. This highly rated spa on the western fringe of the Old Quarter offers a range of treatments, from their signature $42 package (2hr) to an hour-long foot massage for $17. The price includes a free taxi ride.

Zen Spa 164 Tu Hoa ☎024 3719 9889, ⓦzenspa.vn. For pure pampering, you can indulge yourself at Zen Spa near West Lake. The treatments, which include facials, flower baths and foot and body massages, are derived from traditional ethnic minority therapies and come complete with wooden tubs and mood music. Go for a 1hr hot stone massage ($60), or splash out on the $200 "Together Forever" session for couples (4hr 30min), which includes a foot treatment, a body scrub, a herbal steam bath, herbal therapy and a collagen facial treatment.

SWIMMING

All the five-star hotels have swimming pools and fitness centres, which are sometimes open to non-guests for a daily fee of $4–20.

Army Guest House 33c Pham Ngu Lao. This place has a large, open-air saltwater pool ($4), which is significantly cheaper than other hotel pools, and popular in summer. It's quietest in the mornings.

WALKING TOURS

Hanoi Free Walking Tours 79 Ly Nam De ☎097 199 9014, ⓦhanoifreewalkingtours.com. Run by students who are eager to practise their English, these tours take in all the city's main sights. Apart from getting a free tour, you're likely to end up making a long-term local friend.

ACCOMMODATION

The best place to find **budget accommodation** is in the Old Quarter, and to the west of Hoan Kiem Lake, where you'll find dozens of hotels and hostels ranging from the most basic dormitories to increasingly ritzy places with air-conditioning and satellite TV. For the cheapest of the cheap, look around Ngo Huyen, just north of the cathedral, where dorm rooms go for $5 per night. The city's most-sought-after addresses are in the French Quarter, headed up by the venerable *Sofitel Legend Metropole* and its neighbour, the *Hilton Hanoi Opera*. Northwest of the centre, there are also a few **high-end hotels** on the eastern shores of West Lake. Some of the best deals to be found throughout the city are in the **mid-range** mini-hotels, where you can often find four-star facilities and service at two-star prices.

THE OLD QUARTER AND WEST OF HOAN KIEM LAKE

Discovery 22 Luong Ngoc Quyen ☎024 3926 2462, ⓦdiscoveryhotel.com.vn; map p.352. This tiny hotel, hidden up an alley off Luong Ngoc Quyen, is one of the best budget deals in the Old Quarter. Its ten rooms come with fridges, phones, TVs, a/c and minuscule en-suite bathrooms, though some rooms have no windows. Step outside and you'll find yourself in the heart of the action. $17

E Central 18 Lo Su ☎024 3938 0175, ⓦelegance hospitality.com; map p.352. With an excellent location near Hoan Kiem Lake, top-notch service and stylish rooms, *E Central* is one of the best boutique choices in the Old Quarter. $50

★**Essence Hanoi** 22 Ta Hien ☎024 3935 2485, ⓦessencehanoihotel.com; map p.352. The comfortable rooms, ideal location and flawless service at *Essence Hanoi* make this one of the best in the Old Quarter. Add the fact

HO CHI MINH'S MAUSOLEUM (P.358) >

that on the ground floor you have one of the best restaurants in the whole city (see p.374), and you know you're onto a winner. Reservations highly recommended. **$60**

Garden Queen 65 Hang Bac ☎024 3826 0860, ⓦhotelgardenqueen.com; map p.352. In the heart of the Old Quarter, this homely hotel (with only eight rooms) stands out for its eye-catching entrance hall lined with vintage bicycles and mopeds, and for its friendly atmosphere. The rooms are decked out in calming creams and beiges, which are offset by the dark wooden floorboards and bamboo furniture. There's also a wonderful little Zen garden on the roof. **$50**

Hanoi 3B Homestay 67 Hang Than ☎024 3266 8892, ⓦhanoi3bhomestay.com; map p.352. This place is more like a hotel than a homestay, but that doesn't prevent the staff from acting like family. All rooms are good value, particularly the family room that comes with a kitchen, and the penthouse that has a balcony and great views over the city. **$25**

Hanoi Golden Moment 15 Hang Can ☎024 3923 1508, ⓦhanoigoldenmomenthotel.com; map p.352. This boutique hotel in the Old Quarter makes good use of limited space, with sixteen tiny but tastefully equipped rooms. All have double-glazing (a definite plus), and some even have glass-roofed balconies that look a bit like conservatories. **$45**

Hanoi Guest House 85 Ma May ☎024 3935 2571, ⓦhanoiguesthouse.com; map p.352. On popular Ma May, this guesthouse has friendly staff and smart but compact rooms, as well as an elevator and computers for guests' use. They even have a honeymoon suite. Doubles **$25**, suites **$40**

Hanoi La Siesta 94 Ma May ☎024 3926 3641 ⓦhanoilasiestahotel.com; map p.352. This is one of the Old Quarter's newest and most successful boutique hotels, which is not surprising given its fantastic service, beautifully designed rooms, great spa and unbeatable location. One of the Old Quarter's best restaurants, *Red Bean* (see p.376) is located on the ground floor. **$95**

Hanoi Old Quarter Homestay 39 Ngo Huyen ☎090 555 5369 ⓦhanoioldquarterhomestay.com; map p.352. Luan and his family offer a warm welcome in this comfortable homestay, and the rooms have been decked out with modern furnishings. Bigger family rooms are also available, which come equipped with bunk beds ($60). **$35**

Hanoi Posh 4a Hang Giay ☎024 3927 6088, ⓦhanoiposhhotel.com; map p.352. This place isn't exactly posh, but it does offer a range of good-value lodgings, ranging from simple dorm beds to a $45 honeymoon suite. The location on the northern fringe of the Old Quarter is perfectly fine, and the friendly staff go out of their way to help. Dorms **$7**, doubles **$28**

Hanoi Rocks Hostel 56 Hang Duong ☎090 488 4121, ⓦhanoirockshostel.com; map p.352. This place is party central in Hanoi's Old Quarter, and its motto is rather fitting: "If we don't have it, you don't need it". It offers several mixed and single-sex dorms, buffet breakfasts, free beers each evening and awesome trips. Its location, bang in the centre of the weekend night market, fits its free-spirited vibe. Dorms **$5**

Hanoi Trendy Hotel & Spa 65 Hang Dieu ☎024 3923 3868, ⓦhanoitrendyhotel.com; map p.352. Formerly the Art Hotel, *Hanoi Trendy* has 25 cosy rooms that are kitted out with all the latest gadgetry (including two-way a/c units), as well as soft headboards for the beds and separate shower cubicles in the bathrooms. **$60**

Joseph's Hotel 5 Au Trieu ☎024 3938 1048, ⓦjosephshotel.com; map p.352. On a quiet street behind St Joseph's Cathedral, this well-appointed hotel has comfy rooms, helpful staff and a good range of choices for breakfast. **$40**

Meracus II 32 Hang Trong ☎024 3938 2526, ⓦmeracushotels.com; map p.352. This is the newer of the two branches of *Meracus* (the older one is based at 11 Hang Dzau, on the east side of the Old Quarter). Its thirteen rooms are beautifully appointed with deep mattresses and restful decor, and the whole place is based in a great location between Hoan Kiem Lake and St Joseph's Cathedral. Staff are incredibly friendly. **$60**

Silk Path 195–199 Hang Bong ☎024 3266 5555, ⓦsilkpathhotel.com; map p.352. Located in the southwest corner of the Old Quarter, this four-star business hotel offers supreme comfort, with thick-piled carpets, tasteful furnishings and a totally relaxed vibe. **$85**

Tirant 36–38 Gia Ngu ☎024 6265 5999, ⓦtiranthotel .com; map p.352. The *Tirant* stands out from the crowd with its spacious rooms, well-equipped gym and rooftop pool. Staff quickly learn guests' names and enjoy helping out with things like restaurant bookings and calling taxis. Go for a front-facing room on the top floor for views of Hoan Kiem Lake. **$65**

★**Tung Trang** 13 Tam Thuong ☎024 3828 6267, ⓦtungtranghotel.com; map p.352. This recently renovated, family-run place is a little gem, hidden in a backstreet right opposite Yen Thai Temple. It offers a range of rooms, from small doubles to big family options ($47), but the best is number 401 ($39) that comes with a lovely, big balcony. **$23**

Vietnam Backpacker Hostel 9 Ma May ☎024 3935 1891, ⓦvietnambackpackerhostels.com; map p.352. This popular hostel is usually packed to the rafters with fun-seeking backpackers, as is its sister branch at 48 Ngo Huyen (☎024 3828 5372). As this place has friendly staff, long happy hours, comfort food and dorm rooms, budget travellers have all they need here under one roof. There are also regular barbecue nights, and staff organize hugely popular – some might say debauched – tours of Ha Long Bay (see p.337). Dorms **$6**, doubles **$50**

THE FRENCH QUARTER

Conifer Boutique 9 Ly Dao Thanh ☎ 024 3266 9999 ⓦ coniferhotel.com.vn; map p.352. This newish boutique hotel has a great location and lots of character, as well as reasonable rates. Add a good restaurant and the lovely *Terrace Café*, and you've got a good base from which to explore the city. Go for a Deluxe Room with a balcony ($140) if you fancy watching the street action. $85

Hilton Hanoi Opera 1 Le Thanh Tong ☎ 024 3933 0500, ⓦ hilton.com; map p.352. Arguably Hanoi's top city-centre address for all-round value, this five-star hotel is carefully designed to blend in with the neighbouring Opera House. There are a total of 269 cheerful rooms, which feature excellent bathrooms as well as local touches in the ceramics, contemporary paintings and chunky furniture. In-house services include three restaurants, a business centre and a fitness room with outdoor swimming pool. $150

Hotel de l'Opera 29 Trang Tien ☎ 024 6282 5555, ⓦ hoteldelopera.com; map p.352. If the nearby *Metropole*'s room rates seem a bit steep, consider this stylish alternative, a recently opened top-class hotel operated by M Gallery. It has a fantastic location, just down the road from the Opera House, and rooms are beautifully designed with unbelievably deep mattresses and a choice of five different pillow styles. There's a gym, a small pool and a sun terrace, as well as two classy restaurants. $150

★ **Sofitel Legend Metropole** 15 Ngo Quyen ☎ 024 3826 6919, ⓦ sofitel.com; map p.352. Opened in 1901, and host to numerous illustrious guests over the years, the *Metropole* remains the most sought after hotel in Hanoi despite increasingly fierce competition. Though the rooms in the modern Opera Wing exude international-class luxury, they lack the old-world charm of the original building, which has wooden floorboards and louvred shutters. In-house services include a business centre, a small open-air swimming pool, a fitness centre and a choice of bars and restaurants, notably *Spices Garden* and its upmarket Vietnamese fare. $220

Somerset Grand Hanoi 49 Hai Ba Trung ☎ 024 3934 2342, ⓦ somerset.com; map p.352. These serviced apartments, with up to three bedrooms and fully equipped kitchens, can be rented by the night and make a more homely alternative to an upmarket hotel. They also represent surprisingly good value, including access to facilities such as an open-air pool, a gym and a creche. Make sure you book well in advance, as this place is popular. $130

Sunway 19 Pham Dinh Ho ☎ 024 3971 3888, ⓦ hanoi .sunwayhotels.com; map p.348. An award-winning, four-star boutique hotel whose consistently high standards of service and comfortable rooms make up for a slightly inconvenient location to the south of the French Quarter, from where it's quite a trek to the city's major sights. There's an in-house restaurant and a health spa. $60

★ **Zephyr** 4–6 Ba Trieu ☎ 024 3934 1256, ⓦ zephyrhotel.com.vn; map p.352. This three-star place offers value for money with its 44 spacious and carpeted rooms, based in a prime location just a stone's throw from Hoan Kiem Lake. It also features a stylish restaurant, a café and a bakery. $70

7

EATING

The choice of eating options in Hanoi is staggering and you could easily plan your entire stay in the city around a tour of its restaurants and street food outlets. You'll find everything from humble **food stalls** and street kitchens, the best dishing out top-quality food for next to nothing, to a dizzying range of stylish **international restaurants**. Hanoi's French legacy is particularly apparent in the city's adoption of café culture. The city boasts hundreds of **cafés**, all offering great coffee – usually small, strong shots of the local brew. **Juice stalls** are wonderful places to sample Vietnam's wide range of tropical fruits – just look out for the glass cabinets on the street displaying fruit, then take a seat on a stool and wait for them to whip up your selection.

THE OLD QUARTER AND WEST OF HOAN KIEM LAKE

Avalon Café Lounge 73 Cau Go ☎ 024 3926 0801; map p.352. This is the place to go for the best views of Hoan Kiem, based on the fifth floor of the tall building at the northern end of the lake. Look for the entrance on Cau Go, take the lift up and bag a seat overlooking the peaceful waters and frantic traffic below. Fruit shakes and beers come at reasonable prices, but the food is pricey, such as burgers for 188,000đ. Daily 10am–11pm.

Banh Mi 25 25 Hang Ca ☎ 097 766 8895, ⓦ facebook .com/banhmi25; map p.352. This place occupies two adjacent shophouses: order a stuffed baguette at the stall at number 25, then sit down in number 23 and enjoy a filling meal – expect crispy, fresh bread and yummy fillings for 25,000đ. Mon–Sat 7am–7pm, Sun 7am–5pm.

Bittet Ong Loi 51 Hang Buom ☎ 024 3825 1211; map p.352. Hidden down a long, dark passage, this small, bustling restaurant serves platters of *bittet* – a Vietnamese corruption of French *biftek* – with lashings of garlic and chips for 220,000đ. Alternatively, you can opt for roast chicken, roast pigeon, crab or prawns. Daily 5–9pm.

★ **Blue Butterfly** 69 Ma May ☎ 024 3926 3845, ⓦ bluebutterflyrestaurant.com; map p.352. This place has everything – classic tube-house architecture, super-friendly and helpful staff, excellent Vietnamese cuisine, traditional musicians and cooking classes. Try the steamed fish in banana leaf (125,000đ) and fried morning glory

7

(65,000đ). Daily 9am–11pm.

Café de Paris 12 Luong Ngoc Quyen ☎ 024 3926 1327; map p.352. This tiny French bistro, complete with black-and-white-tiled floors and a brass rail round the bar, serves up a short but excellent range of Western dishes such as *hachis Parmentier* (a French version of shepherd's pie; 170,000đ) as well as good breakfasts for 120,000đ. It's based right in the heart of the Old Quarter. Daily 7.30am–11pm.

Café Dinh 13 Dinh Tien Hoang ☎ 024 3824 2960, ⓦ facebook.com/cafe13dinh; map p.352. As with several of Hanoi's coolest cafés, finding this place can be tricky. Go to the north end of the lake and look for number 13 on Dinh Tien Hoang, then walk through the luggage shop and up the narrow stairs to the atmospheric café above. It's one of the longest-running cafés in town, and claims to be the originator of egg coffee (17,000đ), which is now sold everywhere. It's certainly a hip joint, with smooth jazz in the background, monochrome photos on the walls and a tobacco haze hanging in the air. Daily 8am–9pm.

Café Lam 60 Nguyen Huu Huan ☎ 024 3824 5940; map p.352. This shabby yet atmospheric one-room café made its name in Hanoi's lean years as a place for artists and young intellectuals to hang out, and subsequently has a bohemian vibe – a few customers even paid their bills with paintings, which still adorn the walls. If you're not an artist, a coffee will cost you around 35,000đ. Daily 7am–10pm.

Cha Ca Thang Long 21 Duong Thanh ☎ 024 3824 5115; map p.352. Patronized by locals, this is the best place to sample tasty, inexpensive *cha ca*, which is fried fish with turmeric, dill and other condiments (120,000đ) – it's one of Hanoi's most famous dishes. Daily 11am–9pm.

Chops 12 Hang Bac ☎ 024 6686 7885, ⓦ chopsvietnam .com; map p.352. "Hops, wheat and meat" are the specialities here, in the form of local craft beers and burgers with whacky names like "The Abattoir" (double beef, cheese, bacon, tobacco onions, pickles and *Chops* mayo; 220,000đ) and "Dirty Tree & A Turd" (110,000đ) – an "adult milkshake" combining Jameson whisky, Baileys, chocolate ice cream and bacon bits. It gets packed at lunchtimes, when they offer a burger, side and drink for 165,000đ. Daily 9am–midnight.

Cong Caphe 35a Nguyen Huu Huan ⓦ congcaphe.com; map p.352. This branch is a good option from the café chain whose premises are designed like Viet Cong bunkers, complete with bullet holes in the walls, staff wearing Viet Cong gear and coffee served in war-style enamel mugs (35,000đ) – all very 1970s. Daily 7am–11.30pm.

Eden Coffee 2 Nha Tho ☎ 090 343 6880; map p.352. Tucked away to the left of the cathedral, this super-cool café serves imaginative beverages such as a spicy mango Americano (60,000đ). Choose from soft armchairs and sofas, or head up to the third-floor terrace for views of the cathedral square. Daily 8am–11pm.

★**Essence** 22 Ta Hien ☎ 024 3935 2485; map p.352. Hotel restaurants can sometimes be rather bland, but the one in

Essence Hanoi offers some of the best gourmet food in Hanoi – both Vietnamese and Western – at reasonable prices. Go for the delicious beef in bamboo or the duck in coconut – most mains around 200,000đ. Daily 11.30am–10pm.

Gecko 85 Hang Bac ☎ 024 3935 1392; map p.352. There seems to be a branch of this self-styled "cheap and cheerful" eatery on every street in the Old Quarter, and while you shouldn't expect gourmet food, you should expect prompt and friendly service, a cosy, a/c environment and rock-bottom prices. The menu at 85 Hang Bac covers everything from spring rolls (49,000đ) to pancakes (35,000đ) to cocktails (68,000–78,000đ). This centrally located branch features soft lighting, comfortable seating, contemporary artwork on the walls and a soundtrack of modern music. Daily 9am–midnight.

★**Green Tangerine** 48 Hang Be ☎ 024 3825 1286, ⓦ greentangerinehanoi.com; map p.352. The setting for this delightful restaurant is a 1920s Art Deco villa and a lovely, plant-filled courtyard. It's worth reserving a table to sample the Vietnamese–French fusion cuisine: expect rich and unusual flavour combinations such as smoked duck breast with goat's cheese and red tuna carpaccio with frozen yoghurt and lime (though the menu changes regularly). The two-course set lunch (265,000đ) is excellent value. Otherwise, this is definitely one for a splurge – a meal for two will set you back 800,000đ or more. Daily 11am–11pm.

Hanoi Social Club 6 Hoi Vu ☎ 024 3938 2117; map p.352. Set in an atmospheric building that was built in 1924, this is a great place to hang out. Choose between three floors of quirky seating (including a rooftop garden), and order porridge (120,000đ), pumpkin salad (115,000đ), potato pancakes with chorizo (140,000đ) or, of course, coffee. The vibe is so laidback that sometimes the staff forget to work. Daily 8am–11pm.

Highlands Coffee 1-3-5 Dinh Tien Hoang ☎ 024 3936 3228, ⓦ highlandscoffee.com.vn; map p.352. This is a Vietnamese *Starbucks* clone with an increasing number of outlets; this is the best location, based on the third floor of a building overlooking the north end of Hoan Kiem Lake, though the one outside the Hanoi Opera House is also good. Prices are higher than you'll find elsewhere, but quality coffee and comfy seating make it worthwhile. Daily 7am–9pm.

Highway 4 5 Hang Tre ☎ 024 3926 4200, ⓦ highway4 .com; map p.352. With several locations scattered around town, *Highway 4* offers moderately priced North Vietnamese favourites such as hotpots (from 350,000đ) and caramelized braised pork and coconut in an earthen pot (80,000đ), as well as more innovative fare such as their famous catfish spring rolls (70,000đ). This branch is set in a colonial house with bamboo lightshades and low tables for sitting on the floor as you dine. There's also a range of traditional rice wine liquors, which come in more than thirty varieties – the medicinal benefits are explained on the English-language menu. Food served until 11pm. Daily 10am–1am.

Hue Café 26 Hang Giay ☎024 3828 2507; map p.352. This tiny store sells strong coffee from the central highlands. The quality is high, as every cup is freshly ground, and prices are very low (30,000–50,000đ). Also available is "weasel coffee", though this unusual beverage has its downsides (see box, p.42). Daily 8am–10pm.

La Place 6 Au Trieu ☎024 3928 5859; map p.352. This is a sweet little place with views of the cathedral square. The dishes here are small but well prepared, and the coconut chicken curry is a deservedly popular choice (95,000đ). Daily 7.30am–10.30pm.

Little Hanoi 23 Hang Gai ☎024 3828 8333; map p.352. This a/c place comes as a welcome relief after walking round Hoan Kiem Lake or shopping for gifts on Hang Gai. Munch on a baguette (95,000đ) and sip a fresh fruit juice (55,000đ) while watching the traffic chaos around the crossroads out front. Daily 8am–11pm.

Loft Stop Café 11b Bao Khanh ☎024 3928 9433; map p.352. An ideal spot for refreshment while slogging round the lake and the Old Quarter, this recently renovated café provides a cheaper alternative to its sister restaurant upstairs (the *Millennium*), serving good juices and coffees and a decent range of Western and Vietnamese dishes (most mains 120,000đ–150,000đ). Daily 8am–11pm.

Mam 11–13 Hang Mam ☎024 3935 2888, ⓦmamrestaurant.vn; map p.352. Excellent Vietnamese cuisine, efficient service and a refined ambience combine to make dining at *Mam* an enjoyable experience. Go for one of the set menus (from $25 for two) and wash it down with a reasonably priced bottle of wine. Daily 9am–10pm.

Moca 14–16 Nha Tho ☎024 3825 6334; map p.352. Located in the hip cathedral area, *Moca*'s huge picture windows are ideal for people-watching over a mug of frothy caffé latte (49,000đ), and the prices aren't steep either. In winter, hunker down here by the open fire. Daily 8am–10pm.

Moose & Roo 42b Ma May ☎024 3266 8081, ⓦmooseandroo.com; map p.352. This Canadian- and Aussie-run gastropub is a bit pricier than most places in the Old Quarter, but it seems there are plenty of visitors willing to splash out on a steak, burger or home-made pie (most mains 200,000–300,000đ) – including backpackers from the hostel opposite. The short menu includes some unusual but tasty items, such as a beetroot and goat cheese salad (175,000đ) and pulled pork sandwich (165,000đ), so this is a good spot for a break from Vietnamese fare. Daily 11am–midnight.

New Day 72 Ma May ☎024 3828 0315, ⓦnewdayrestaurant.com; map p.352. This no-frills

7

STREET FOOD

For sheer value for money and atmosphere, your best bet is to eat either at the rock-bottom, stove-and-stools **food stalls** or at the slightly more upmarket **street kitchens**, most of which specialize in just one or two types of food. You'll find both of these sorts of places scattered across the city, often with no recognizable name and little to identify individual establishments, but there are a few that stand out from the crowd – we've listed some of the best here.

Banh cuon is a Hanoi snack consisting of almost transparent rice-flour pancakes that are usually stuffed with minced pork and black mushrooms, sprinkled with fried shallots. Give it a try at 68 Hang Cot.

Banh goi, sometimes called "pillow cake", is a fried pastry, somewhat like a samosa, filled with vermicelli, minced pork and mushrooms, and eaten with a thin sweet sauce, parsley and chilli. Sample a serving of two per plate (18,000đ) at 52 Ly Quoc Su.

Bun bo nam bo is a southern dish, and a hot favourite with most Westerners. It consists of lean beef with noodles and beansprouts, topped with roasted peanuts, garlic and basil. Join the lunchtime queue at 67 Hang Dieu, throw on a spoonful of chilli sauce, stir it up and fill your belly for 60,000đ.

Bun cha, consisting of pork patties served with cold rice noodles and dipping sauce (about 40,000đ), is a popular lunchtime dish and can be found all over the city. Our favourite spot is at 34 Hang Than.

Bun rieu cua, a crab noodle soup laced with tomatoes, tofu, spring onions and fried shallots, is another popular breakfast dish, especially on cold winter mornings. Try it at 34 Cau Go.

Nem vuong is a square spring roll stuffed with crabmeat, glass noodles, minced pork, carrots and mushrooms, and served with a sweet and sour dip.

Pho bo is Vietnam's national dish, a beef noodle soup served with chopped spring onion, usually eaten for breakfast and costing around 40,000đ. Novels have been written extolling its virtues, and the addresses to head for are 10 Ly Quoc Su, 49 Bat Dan and our favourite, *Suong Pho* at 24b Ngo Trung Yen.

7

diner turns out consistently delicious Vietnamese staples for rock-bottom prices, and customers are welcome to wander in the kitchen to select from pre-prepared dishes. If it's full out front, make sure you muscle your way in as they'll find a spot for you somewhere. Daily 10am–10.30pm.

★**Nola** Alley beside 89 Ma May ☎ 024 3926 4669; map p.352. This is a rather difficult place to find, despite being almost next door to Heritage House (see p.351) – though it's well worth the effort. Head down the twisting alley and up the stairs, and you'll find a variety of cosy, high-ceilinged rooms with retro decor, cool music (Louis Armstrong, vintage Dylan), interesting snacks and cheap beers (30,000–50,000đ). Daily 10am–11pm.

Pho Co 11 Hang Gai ☎ 024 3928 8153; map p.352. As with *Nola*, finding this fascinating place is half the fun: go through the souvenir shops at number #11, then along a narrow passage and into a hushed courtyard, where you can place your order. Head up the stairs, past the family altar, then up a spiral staircase and one more flight of steps, and you'll finally reach a roof terrace high above Hoan Kiem Lake, where you can sample coffee with added egg white, if you dare (40,000đ). Daily 8am–11pm.

★**Red Bean** 94 Ma May ☎ 024 3926 3641, ⊛ redbean restaurant.com; map p.352. On the ground floor of *La Siesta Hotel*, this place welcomes diners with plenty of comfortable seating. Dishes like grapefruit salad and beef in coconut (180,000đ) are elegantly presented and well prepared, and the service is flawless. Daily 11.30am–11pm.

Tandoor 24 Hang Be ☎ 024 3824 5359, ⊛ tandoor vietnam.com; map p.352. A perennially popular Indian restaurant with simple decor but cracking curries, including a Goan fish curry, mutton vindaloo and an extensive range of mouthwatering vegetarian dishes. The *thali* set meals (Mon–Fri only) offer reasonable value at 135,000–185,000đ. Daily 10.30am–10.30pm.

Thuy Ta 1 Le Thai To ☎ 024 3825 1907; map p.352. A breezy lakeside café that's a great spot for breakfast, afternoon tea, ice cream or an evening beer, though the food is only average quality. Very popular among tourists and a bit pricey (lemon chicken, for example, is 115,000đ), but you pay for the great location. Daily 7am–10pm.

Xofa Café 14 Tong Duy Tan ☎ 024 3717 1555, ⊛ facebook.com/xofacafe; map p.352. *Xofa* serves a wide range of Vietnamese and Western dishes (most mains 120,000–180,000đ), and is open 24 hours a day, but the big attraction here is the cosy atmosphere both inside the old colonial house and in the cute courtyard outside. Kick back on a sofa and enjoy. Daily 24hr.

THE FRENCH QUARTER

Al Fresco's 23l Hai Ba Trung ☎ 024 3826 7782, ⊛ alfrescos.com.vn; map p.352. This is the place to head for when you're really hungry, as portions are huge. A café,

bar and grill in one, its menu includes good-quality Aussie and international fare, including great ribs, salads, steaks and a choice of thin- or thick-crust pizzas from 140,000đ and up. There are several other locations around town, including on Nha Tho near the cathedral – see the website for details. Daily 8.30am–11pm.

★**Chim Sao** 65 Ngo Hue ☎ 024 3976 0633, ⊛ chimsao .com; map p.352. It's worth hunting down this quirky restaurant for its laidback atmosphere (dining upstairs is on floor cushions around low tables), and its menu of unusual items such as buffalo sautéed with morning glory (120,000đ), pomelo salad (75,000đ) and crab and spinach broth (60,000đ). The menu changes according to availability of ingredients in the market, so everything is fresh. Daily 8am–10pm.

Com Chay Nang Tam 79a Tran Hung Dao ☎ 024 3942 4140, ⊛ nangtam.com.vn; map p.348. Small, vegetarian restaurant down a quiet alley off Tran Hung Dao and named after the Vietnamese Cinderella character. *Goi bo*, a main-course salad of banana flower, star fruit and pineapple, is recommended, or you could try one of the well-priced set menus (60,000–100,000đ/person). The food's all tasty and MSG-free, though purists may not like the way some dishes (mostly made of tofu) emulate meat. Daily 9am–9pm.

Fanny 2 Hang Bai ☎ 024 3937 8170, ⊛ fanny.com.vn; map p.352. Hanoi's top ice-cream parlour serves up a bewildering array of flavours, such as cinnamon, avocado and durian, but it's pricey, with most items around 100,000đ. It's handy for Hoan Kiem Lake, too. Daily 7am–11pm.

Indochine 38 Thi Sach ☎ 024 3942 4097, ⊛ indochinehanoi.com; map p.348. Consistently high-quality food keeps this well-established restaurant up there with its younger rivals, though its prices are still a bit expensive. The classic Vietnamese cuisine includes seafood spring rolls, steamboat and the famous prawn on sugar cane (140,000–300,000đ), or you could try the set meals from 340,000đ. Evenings are popular with tour groups, so reservations are recommended. Daily 11am–2pm & 5.30–10pm.

La Salsa 5 Bui Thi Xuan ☎ 024 3828 9052, ⊛ lasalsa -hanoi.com; map p.348. Now relocated from its spot near the cathedral to the French Quarter, this place serves up decently priced tapas (35,000–75,000đ), paella (260,000đ) and French cuisine, too. Daily 8.30am–10.30pm.

La Verticale 19 Ngo Van So ☎ 024 3944 6317, ⊛ verticale-hanoi.com; map p.352. Spice is the word at this colonial outlet, the venue for the creations of French chef Didier Corlou. Featuring on the ever-changing menu is red tuna on lemongrass with passion fruit sauce (350,000đ). The open top level is perfect for an evening drink. Set lunch 230,000đ, à la carte 540,000–900,000đ. Daily 11am–2pm, 6–9.30pm.

Pane e Vino 3 Nguyen Khac Can ☎ 024 3826 9080; map p.352. This place is popular with the local Italian

HANOI'S UNUSUAL EATS

In addition to the traditional **street food**, it's not uncommon to find dishes featuring goat, dog, rat and snake in Hanoi. Many find this ethically challenging, though the eating of animals is deeply entrenched in Vietnamese culture, and an invitation to share in the feast is considered an honour.

Dog meat (*thit cho*) is a northern speciality, eaten mostly in winter but never during days one to ten of the lunar calendar month. If you'd like to try it, you can head along the Red River dyke to Nghi Tam Avenue, where there are dozens of stilthouse restaurants to choose from. The meat comes boiled (*luoc*) or grilled (*cha nuong*) and served with green banana and tofu (*rua man*), and is washed down with rice wine.

Le Mat snake village – 4km over Chuong Duong Bridge in the Gia Lam District – is home to a slew of **snake-meat** restaurants. Be aware that some of these places play to the crowd with gory theatrics, including killing the snake in front of you. The meat is then served up in every possible form, from soup and crispy-fried skin accompanied by rice wine liquors laced with blood and bile. The guest of honour eats the heart – but keep in mind that it's alleged to have amphetamine properties. Though it's not the cheapest of Le Mat's restaurants, *Quoc Trieu* (74/161 Hoa Lam; daily 10am–10pm; ☎024 3827 2988) has a reliable reputation and leaves out the gory bits.

7

community for its authentic cuisine and relaxed atmosphere. The menu ranges from favourites like the *caprese* salad and minestrone soup through to *osso buco* and roast lamb to *zabaglione* and the obligatory tiramisu – not to mention the gourmet pasta and pizza dishes. Count on around 700,000đ/head for three courses, and 150,000–250,000đ for a pizza. Daily 8am–10pm.

Pots 'n Pans 57 Bui Thi Xuan ☎024 3944 0204, ⓦpotsnpans.vn; map p.348. This slick venue with minimalist decor is run by graduates of *KOTO* (see p.378). While many chefs tend to make a mess of fusion food, this place produces some innovative twists on classics like duck breast and beef tenderloin. It isn't cheap, but you get what you pay for – set menus are 500,000–700,000đ. Daily 11.30am–9.30pm.

Press Club 59a Ly Thai To ☎024 3934 0888, ⓦhanoi-pressclub.com; map p.352. If you're looking to splurge on a meal in Hanoi, you could do worse than the *Press Club*, which has an exclusive feel about it with plush leather chairs and starched tablecloths. The menu, featuring mostly fusion and international dishes (mains around 700,000đ), is constantly changing, according to the whim of two-star Michelin chef Alain Dutournier. There's also a good bar, *La Plume*, on the third floor. Daily 11am–2pm & 6–10.30pm.

Puku 16–18 Tong Duy Tan ☎024 3938 1745, ⓦpukukafe.com; map p.352. This popular café, located a couple of blocks north of the railway station, offers round-the-clock service, so it's handy for early arrivals looking for a 4am breakfast (omelettes 85,000đ). It's one of the main hangout venues for Hanoi expats, and deservedly so as it offers "couch-surfing food and wi-fi-enabled coffee", plus sports on TV. Not cheap, but worth it for the ambience. Daily 24hr.

★**Quan An Ngon** 18 Phan Boi Chau ☎024 3942 8162, ⓦngonhanoi.com.vn; map p.348. One of the city's most popular restaurants, *Ngon* (meaning "delicious") is often

packed full – and service can get a little erratic during peak hours. The goal is simple: to provide upmarket street food in pleasant surroundings at easily affordable prices. Choose from the menu or see what takes your fancy on the stalls, which cook up Hanoi and Hue specialities around the garden seating area – there are more tables in the colonial villa behind. Daily 6.30am–10pm.

WEST AND NORTH OF THE CENTRE

★**Foodshop 45** 59 Truc Bach ☎024 3716 2959, ⓦfoodshop45.com; map p.348. Don't be fooled by the name; this former foodshop is now located in an elegantly decorated, three-storey house, which has a roof terrace with views over Truc Bach Lake. Service is excellent too, but the clincher here are the lip-smacking curries (from 100,000đ), bhajis (from 55,000đ) and breads (from 25,000đ) on the extensive menu, which make it a must-visit for lovers of Indian food. They deliver as well, and have a smaller, less atmospheric outlet at 32 Hang Buom. Daily 10am–10.30pm.

Home 34 Chau Long ☎024 3939 2222, ⓦhome hanoirestaurant.vn; map p.348. Set in a stunning colonial villa to the north of the Old Quarter and near Truc Bach Lake, this place lives up to its claim of being "a fusion of old world splendour and cutting edge sophistication". The menu features dishes like stewed beef with starfruit (255,000đ) and Hanoian roast duck with five spices (275,000đ), and the service is spot-on. Daily 11am–1pm & 6–9pm.

Khai's Brothers 26 Nguyen Thai Hoc ☎024 3733 3866; map p.348. Through a traditional entranceway on a busy main road, you'll find this peaceful courtyard restaurant with tables set out under the trees. They only serve buffets, consisting mostly of Vietnamese dishes but with some Western options like cheesey mashed potatoes, which are well priced at $15 for lunch and $20 in the evening (weekends are $23, with wine thrown in). Daily 11.30am–2pm & 6.30–10pm.

Kitchen 30 To Ngoc Van, Tay Ho District ☎ 024 3719 2679; map p.348. This place has a shady patio and an a/c interior, and is a handy spot for refreshment if you're exploring the West Lake area. They serve Mexican dishes, sandwiches, salads and pasta (all 120,000–220,000đ), as well as yummy juices and shakes. Mon 7am–2.30pm, Tues–Sun 7am–10pm.

★**KOTO** 59 Van Mieu ☎ 024 3747 0337, ⓦ koto.com .au; map p.348. This is a deservedly popular restaurant that's staffed by erstwhile street kids, who are being trained in hospitality under a charity project. Start the day with muesli and fresh fruits or a full buffet breakfast, or stop by later for a gourmet sandwich or a barbecued duck salad (most main courses are around 110,000–200,000đ) – but make sure you leave room for dessert. The views from the rooftop terrace overlook the Temple of Literature. All proceeds are ploughed back into the charity, and they offer cooking classes too. Daily 7am–9.30pm.

Saint Honore 5 Xuan Dieu ☎ 024 3933 2373, ⓦ sainthonore.com.vn; map p.348. Excellent patisserie and bistro in the West Lake area, serving delicious cakes and main dishes such as steak tartare (230,000đ). There's another branch in the Old Quarter at 33 Hang Buom. Daily 6.30am–10pm.

DRINKING AND NIGHTLIFE

For a capital city, Hanoi goes to bed pretty early, though the authorities seem to be gradually relaxing their midnight curfew and there are now several bars serving until the early hours. The choice of nightspots is constantly increasing, particularly on **Ta Hien**, a street packed with lively, dimly lit bars, and nearby **Dau Duy Ta**, where lots of locals come to hang out. Nevertheless, the busiest venues are without doubt the bia hoi outlets selling pitchers of the local brew (see box, p.379).

Bar 84 23 Ngo Van So ☎ 093 735 8484, ⓦ facebook .com/bar84hanoi; map p.352. This trendy spot has two floors and features live music from around 9pm every night on a rotating schedule – blues on Tuesdays, jazz on Thursdays, and so on. Expect reasonably priced beers, wines and cocktails at around 100,000đ. Daily 9am–2am.

Bar Betta 34c Cao Ba Quat ☎ 024 3734 9134; map p.348. This quirky bar near the Fine Arts Museum is worth tracking down for its retro decor and cozy rooftop terrace (open in the evenings only). Offers a good range of beers (70,000–100,0000đ), cocktails, shishas and music, and there's also free beer from 8–9pm on Wednesdays and Sundays. Daily 9am–midnight.

Binh Minh Jazz Club 1 Trang Tien ☎ 024 3933 6555, ⓦ minhjazzvietnam.com; map p.352. Hanoi's premier jazz club is located in a narrow street right behind the Opera House – look for the dimly lit lane with a small sign on Trang Tien. It's run by Hanoi's living jazz legend, the charismatic and highly accomplished saxophonist Quyen Van Minh. Sit back and enjoy a 2hr set of mainstream classics every night between 9–11pm, but be prepared for a smoky ambience. No cover fee, but pricey drinks (beers from 100,000đ). Daily 8pm–midnight.

Camelia Lounge 3F Melia Hotel, 44B Ly Thuong Kiet ☎ 093 969 3223, ⓦ facebook.com/camelialoungehanoi; map p.352. Good music, great decor and well-prepared cocktails (from 150,000đ) make this one of Hanoi's classiest nightspots. Expect guest DJs and occasional events, such as the Latin Fiesta with free-flowing wine. Daily 8pm–2am.

Craft Beer Pub 26 Hang Buom ☎ 096 312 4838, ⓦ facebook.com/craftbeerpubhanoi; map p.352. Craft beers are all the rage in Hanoi these days, and this smart place offers eight beers on tap (25,000–95,000đ) and over thirty international brews, as well as a decent menu of Tex-Mex and Asian food. There's sports on the TV as well. Daily 8.30am–2am.

Funky Buddha 2 Ta Hien ☎ 097 465 3972, ⓦ facebook .com/funkybuddhahn; map p.352. A focus on pulsating lighting has made this one of Hanoi's most popular lounge bars, with beers costing around 68,000–90,000đ. There's an excellent sound system that plays great dance music – it attracts lounge lizards of every nationality. Daily 6pm–1am.

Hair of the Dog 32 Ma May ☎ 094 789 3232, ⓦ facebook.com/hairofthedogbarhanoi32mamay; map p.352. Classic nightclub with flashing lights and a dancefloor downstairs and a chill-out area with shisha pipes upstairs. It attracts plenty of young locals, as well as backpackers from the hostel across the street. Cocktails around 100,000đ. Daily 9pm–2am.

Hay 12 Ta Hien ☎ 090 499 6585, ⓦ facebook.com /haybar12tahien; map p.352. This place stands out from other Ta Hien bars for its live music, which features talented locals playing original compositions. On weekends you may need to fight your way along Ta Hien to get in. Beers around 40,000–50,000đ. Daily midday–midnight.

Hill Station Tapas and Taps 2T Ta Hien ☎ 016 537 84927, ⓦ thehillstation.com; map p.352. This place is an enclave of sanity in the madness of Ta Hien, with craft beers and cider on tap (95,000đ) as well as homemade rice wines and locally sourced tapas (60,000–130,000đ). Daily 11am–midnight.

La Bomba Latina 46 Ngo Huyen ☎ 090 406 3468, ⓦ labombalatina.com; map p.352. This music club is a must-visit for lovers of merengue, bachata, zouk, reggaeton or salsa. Located along a narrow lane of budget hotels near the cathedral, it attracts a mixed crowd of Vietnamese and foreigners with one thing in common –they all love to dance. Cocktails from 100,000đ. Daily 6pm–2am.

Le Pub 25 Hang Be ☎024 3926 2104, ☞facebook.com /LePub; map p.352. This place is based in an Old Quarter tube-house, and its good range of drinks at reasonable prices (including genuinely cold beers from 25,000đ) and above-average food, music and bar staff ensure it has a real pub atmosphere. Daily 7am–2am.

Polite Pub 5b Bao Khanh ☎090 419 8086, ☞facebook .com/politepubhanoi; map p.352. This place claims to be the oldest pub in town, and it has a loyal clientele who drop in after work for a beer or a single malt scotch, and maybe a cigar. Cocktails 70,000–90,000đ. Expect a pool table, cool tunes and ice-cold drinks. Daily 4pm–midnight.

Rock Store 61 Ma May ☎096 396 6616, ☞facebook .com/rockstorehanoi; map p.352. With a choice location on Ma May, this two-floor bar always has some event going on, whether it's a "sexy nurse" party, a live music performance or a visiting DJ. Cocktails are around 100,000đ. It's run by Link Hanoi, which now operates around half a dozen bars in the Old Quarter. Daily 10am–2am.

Savage 112 Xuan Dieu ☎024 6686 6150, ☞facebook .com/savagehanoi; map p.348. Savage by name, savage by nature. This is one of the wildest spots for a night out in Hanoi, with two distinct areas – one for chilling out and one for dancing. Local and international DJs regularly make an appearance, and the sound system is spot on. Cocktails from 100,000đ. Daily 6pm–4.30am.

Tadioto 24b Tong Dan ☎024 6680 9124, ☞facebook .com/tadiototongdan; map p.352. This gem of a place has a relaxing vibe as befits a venue "for thinkers and drinkers", and it's a place to strike up intriguing conversations. Offers a short but adequate menu of beers (from 45,000đ), cocktails and snacks – try the ramen (90,000đ). Daily 8am–midnight.

7

ENTERTAINMENT

Hanoi offers an unusual mix of highbrow entertainment, from traditional Vietnamese **water puppetry** to performances of **traditional music**, such as *ca tru*, and theatres featuring **classical opera**. The shows at the Golden Bell and Hong Ha theatres offer a glimpse of traditional Vietnamese folk music and drama, but apart from these and a few tourist-oriented restaurants (such as *Indochine*; see p.376), there are no other venues regularly showcasing Vietnamese traditional culture in Hanoi. However, things are changing fast, so it's worth asking the concierge at your hotel if there's anything interesting happening in your part of town, and you should check out ☞hanoigrapevine.com for news of upcoming arts events. For movie buffs, there are **cinema complexes** in shopping malls that screen English-language films.

CA TRU

Dinh Kim Ngan 42 Hang Bac ☎097 132 9646, ☞catru .vn. Recognized by UNESCO in 2009 as an intangible heritage in need of safeguarding, *ca tru* music is performed by an ensemble consisting of just three musicians, one of whom is a female singer. The haunting sounds are not everyone's cup of tea, but if you can open your ears and close your eyes for an hour, you might just find it very moving. The venue changes occasionally so check the website for the latest info. Tickets cost 270,000đ. Wed, Fri & Sun from 8pm.

CINEMA

Megastar Vincom Center, 191 Ba Trieu ☎024 3974 3333, ☞cgv.vn. Shows English-language films with tickets priced at $3–5. Daily 11am–11pm.

OPERA

Hanoi Opera House 1 Trang Tien ☎024 3933 0113, ☞hanoioperahouse.org.vn. Hanoi's Opera House makes a grand setting for performances of classical music and opera; this historic building features a truly sumptuous interior of plush red fabrics, mirrors and

---

A BOOZER'S GUIDE TO BIA HOI

Bia hoi stalls or shophouses generally open from midafternoon to mid-evening, and serve fresh **draught beer** poured straight from the barrel – just look for the tell-tale metal barrel and patrons sitting on stools and clutching greenish glass tumblers. The alcohol content is low, but it's tasty, refreshing and only 5000–7000đ per glass, so you can sink a few without fear of falling off your stool. Enjoying a spot of bia hoi is a great way to start an evening, and as essential to Hanoi culture as the city's street food – though it can be difficult to find a space to sit at the stalls that line Hang Buom, Ma May and Luong Ngoc Quyen in the Old Quarter. Locals tend to patronize branches of **Lan Chin**, where they'll order snacks such as spring rolls and fermented sausage in banana leaf to nibble on as they quaff the brew. The main branch is directly opposite the History Museum at 2 Trang Tien, but there's a more convenient branch at 22 Hang Tre on the east side of the Old Quarter, and a new outlet at 14 Tang Bat Ho (off Hai Ba Trung) in the French Quarter.

chandeliers. Tickets are available from the foyer between 8am–6pm (200,000–700,000đ), or they can be booked by phone or online. Check the website for upcoming events.

Hong Ha Theatre 51 Duong Thanh ☎024 3825 2803, ⓦvietnamtuongtheatre.com. Hosts performances of Vietnamese classical opera (*hat tuong*; 150,000đ). Show times can vary, so it's best to call ahead and check. Mon & Thurs 6pm–7pm.

THEATRE
Golden Bell Theater 72 Hang Bac ☎098 112 1872, ⓦnhahatcailuonghanoi.com.vn/goldenbellshow. This theatre is housed in a beautiful colonial building in the heart of the Old Quarter. Its one-hour shows are geared towards tourists, and present eight performances of traditional folk styles (130,000–180,000đ). Thurs 8–9pm.

WATER PUPPETS
Thang Long Water Puppet Theatre 57b Dinh Tien Hoang ☎024 3824 9494, ⓦthanglongwaterpuppet .org. The Thang Long Water Puppet Troupe is by far the most popular, and polished, of Hanoi's water-puppeteers; though aimed at tourists, their shows (100,000đ) feature modern stage effects to create an engaging spectacle. Catch them at this small, a/c theatre, located by the northeast corner of Hoan Kiem Lake. Mon–Sat 3pm, 4.10pm, 5.20pm, 6.30pm, 8pm & 9.15pm, Sun also 9.30am.

SHOPPING

When it comes to shopping for crafts, silk, accessories and souvenirs, Hanoi offers the best overall choice, quality and value for money in the country. **Specialities** of the region are embroideries, wood- and stone-carvings, inlay work and lacquerware; the best areas to browse are the south end of the Old Quarter, such as along Hang Gai and the streets around St Joseph's Cathedral. Though smarter establishments increasingly have fixed prices, you'll be expected to **bargain** in many shops (see box, p.55), and the same goes for market stalls. Hanoi has over fifty **markets**, selling predominantly foodstuffs – you'll rarely be far from one.

ANTIQUES AND INTERIORS
It's illegal to export antiques from Vietnam, but you'll find plenty of fake "antique" jewellery and watches on sale, and beautifully crafted copies of ancient religious statues. The following outlets supply elegant if pricey home accessories and gifts.

54 Traditions Gallery 30 Hang Bun ☎024 3715 0194, ⓦ54traditions.com.vn; map p.348. This place deals in genuine antiques and artefacts from the ethnic minority groups, and provides full documentation for each item. These items include tribal textiles, tribal tools for living and shamanic arts. It's worth a visit to their gallery, even if you're not buying. Daily 8.30am–6pm.

Collective Memory 20 Nha Chung ☎098 647 4243, ⓦcollectivememory.vn; map p.352. This "house of curios" is exactly that, and you could lose track of time browsing the eclectic range of items here, from books to bags to kitschy paraphernalia. Daily 9am–10pm.

Dome 10 Yen The ☎024 3843 6036, ⓦdome.com.vn; map p.348. The tempting displays here show off luxurious items of home decor such as rugs, lamps and paintings. Daily 9am–5.30pm.

Hanoi Moment 101 Hang Gai ☎024 3928 7170, ⓦhanoimoment.vn; map p.352. Classy souvenirs are laid out in an uncluttered manner, unlike at most souvenir shops, so it's easy to see products like tea sets, original jewellery and bags. Daily 9am–6pm.

Mosaique 7 Alley 218, Hoang Mai ☎024 3971 3797, ⓦmosaiquedecoration.com; map p.348. It's worth heading to this showroom south of the city centre to view gorgeous interiors that feature elegant drapes, vases, silk hangings, lamps, ready-to-wear items and silver jewellery. Daily 9am–5pm.

BOOKS AND NEWSPAPERS
There's not a great choice of English-language reading material in Hanoi, though wandering vendors in the Old Quarter and near the lake sell pirated English-language publications, including guides, phrasebooks and novels.

Bookworm 44 Chau Long ☎024 3715 3711, ⓦbookwormhanoi.com; map p.348. Located to the north of the Old Quarter, this is probably Hanoi's best bookshop with a great selection of new and secondhand English-language books for sale or exchange. Daily 9am–7pm.

Love Planet Travel 25 Hang Bac ☎091 484 6452; map p.352. This place buys and sells used books, and also stocks a few guidebooks, but it's only open for limited hours. Daily 10.30am–noon & 3–8pm.

CLOTHES AND ACCESSORIES
Although the selection is limited, you'll find no shortage of places to buy embroidered and printed T-shirts, notably along Hang Gai and Hang Dao. To complete your look, head for Hang Dau, near the northeast corner of the lake, and pick up a pair of sneakers or high heels.

Flora Boutique 62 Au Trieu ☎042 3928 8338, ⓦfacebook.com/floraboutique62; map p.352. Expect light and loose tops, many in modern floral designs, as well as bags and cushions at this trendy boutique near the cathedral. Daily 9.30am–8pm.

Ginkgo 44 Hang Be ☎024 3926 4769, ⓦginkgo
-vietnam.com; map p.352. This store is worth checking
out for its eye-catching designs on T-shirts, trousers and
shorts. See their website for other branches in the Old
Quarter. Daily 8am–10pm.
Ipa-Nima 5 Nha Tho ☎024 3928 7616, ⓦipa-nima
.com; map p.352. If you're looking for a handbag that'll
make heads turn, this is your place – though they don't
come cheap. Daily 9am–8pm.
Things of Substance 5 Nha Tho ☎097 238 0888,
ⓦfacebook.com/thingsofsubstance; map p.352. This
Aussie-run store features clothing designs for Western
sizes, mostly in soft cotton jersey and linen. Daily
9am–9pm.
Zeds Threads 36 To Ngoc Van, Tay Ho District ☎024
6258 0208, ⓦzedsthreads.com; map p.348. The tailored
and ready-made garments at this store are so popular that
they've developed a loyal clientele, and employees are
treated fairly. Mon–Sat 8am–5.30pm.

EMBROIDERY

Embroideries and drawn threadwork make eminently
packable souvenirs. Standard designs range from traditional
Vietnamese to Santa Claus, but you can also take along your
own artwork for something different. Many of the silk and
accessories shops also sell embroidered items.
Mekong Quilts 13 Hang Bac ☎024 3926 4831,
ⓦmekong-plus.com; map p.352. Mekong Quilts is a
non-profit organization that raises funds for a variety of
causes through the sale of bright, patterned quilts, oven
gloves and more unusual items like bamboo bikes; the
quilts are around $400 each, but they are all unique and
made by women in rural provinces. Daily 9am–9pm.
Tan My Design 61 Hang Gai ☎024 3938 1154,
ⓦtanmydesign.com; map p.352. This is the place to go
for the very finest, albeit expensive, embroidered
bedlinens, tablecloths, cushion covers and so forth. Daily
8am–8pm.

FOOD AND FLOWER MARKETS

Dong Xuan Market Dong Xuan; map p.352. This is
Hanoi's largest covered market, spread across two
enormous floors with numerous sections to explore; items
on sale include shoes, rolls of cloth, fashion accessories,
hats, watches and bags. It's the most convenient market for
the Old Quarter and also the starting point of electric car
tours of the area. Daily 8am–5pm.
Hoa Quang Market Ba 236 Au Co; map p.352. This
flower market, sometimes called Quang An Market, is
located near West Lake at the northern junction of Au Co
with Xuan Dieu; it's at its busiest from midnight to the early
hours, though some stalls open all day. It's where hotels,
restaurants and street vendors go to stock up for each day,
and the air is thick with the scent of tropical blooms. It's

particularly busy in the weeks before Tet (Jan/Feb), when
everyone wants flowers to brighten their home. Daily
midnight–5pm.
Hom Market Pho Hue; map p.352. Though it's quite a
trek from the Old Quarter, this market is one of the best
places to buy fabrics in the city, and it functions as a fresh
market as well. Daily 6am–5pm.

HANDICRAFTS

Silk lanterns, water puppets and silver items – both plated
and solid silver – make good souvenirs, as do hand-painted
greetings cards, which usually depict scenes of rural life or
famous beauty spots on paper or silk and sell for next to
nothing. Most ordinary souvenir shops also stock ethnic
minority crafts, particularly the Hmong and Dao bags, coats
and jewellery that are so popular in Sa Pa. Though it's
virtually impossible to tell, the majority of these are now
made in factories around Hanoi. Of course, everyone will
insist their goods are genuine, and they are very well made,
but it's something to be aware of.
Craft Link 43–51 Van Mieu ☎024 3733 6101,
ⓦcraftlink.com.vn; map p.348. One of the more
interesting craft outlets, Craft Link is a not-for-profit
organization working with small-scale producers of
traditional crafts (particularly ethnic minorities), which
helps develop increasingly high-quality modern designs.
Products include tops and dresses, bags and wallets, as
well as items of home decor such as sets of lacquerware.
Daily 9am–6pm.
XQ 138 Pho Hue ☎024 3938 1905, ⓦxqvietnam.com;
map p.352. This place produces exquisite silk embroidered
paintings that make distinctive souvenirs, and it's
fascinating to watch the painstaking process to make
them. Daily 8.30am–6pm.

LACQUERWARE

Lacquerware makes a pretty portable souvenir: chopsticks,
boxes, bowls, vases – the variety of items coated in lacquer
is endless. Natural lacquer gives a muted finish, usually in
black or rusty reds. However, lacquerware in a rainbow
array of colours – made from imported synthetic products
– is now very popular in Old Quarter souvenir shops,
especially on Hang Be and Ma May. Some designs
incorporate eggshell to give a crazed finish, and gold leaf
on black lacquer for a more dramatic effect.

MUSICAL INSTRUMENTS

For more unusual mementoes, have a look at the traditional
Vietnamese musical instruments on sale in a clutch of little
workshops on Hang Non and round the corner on Hang Manh.
Pham Bich Huong 11a Hang Non ☎024 3828 7412;
map p.352. Sells tiny percussion instruments and jew's
harps, which make great little gifts, as well as bamboo
xylophones and the classic *dan bau*. Daily 8am–7pm.

7

Thai Khue Music Shop 1a Hang Manh ☎024 3828 9469; map p.352. This tiny but excellent shop sells a range of unusual instruments, from packable pipes and flutes to lithophones and bronze gongs from the central highlands. Daily 8am–8pm.

PROPAGANDA
Several small shops on Hang Bong supply Communist Party banners and badges as well as Vietnamese flags. Reproduction posters are another popular souvenir from the Communist days, and you'll find these in shops throughout the Old Quarter.

SILK
Hanoi has so many silk shops concentrated on Hang Gai, at the southern edge of the Old Quarter, that it's now referred to as "Silk Street". Competition is fierce, and you should take care since you'll find a fair amount of shops selling tat alongside more reputable outlets. Classy designer boutiques offering excellent quality at premium prices now also concentrate around the cathedral. Most big places have multilingual staff, accept credit cards and also offer less expensive souvenirs, such as ties, purses, mobile-phone holders and sensuous silk sleeping bags.

Kenly Silk 108 Hang Gai ☎024 3826 7236, ⓦkenlysilk.com; map p.352. Kenly specializes in expensive but high-quality Vietnamese silks (raw, taffeta, satin and even knitted) as well as other fabrics. It also stocks ready-made clothes and has a reputation for reliable tailoring. Daily 9am–6pm.

Khai Silk 113 Hang Gai ☎024 3928 9883, ⓦkhaisilkcorp.com; map p.352. Exclusive and expensive silk creations from Vietnam's leading fashion designer. Daily 10am–8pm.

Ngoc Diep Silk 9 Bao Khanh ☎024 3824 7215; map p.352. This place is filled with a colourful array of silk items at very reasonable prices. Well worth rooting around. Daily 9am–8pm.

SUPERMARKETS
For general supplies, there are lots of small convenience stores scattered around the Old Quarter, and there are also two well-stocked and easily accessible supermarkets: one is Fivimart at 27a Ly Thai To to the east of Hoan Kiem Lake, and the other is Intimex at 22 Le Thai To, on the west side of Hoan Kiem Lake near the junction with Hang Trong.

GALLERIES AND EXHIBITIONS

As Vietnamese art continues to attract international recognition, ever more **art galleries** are appearing on the streets of Hanoi. Many of these are merely souvenir shops selling reproduction paintings of variable quality but usually at affordable prices, while some of the big galleries (such as Apricot Gallery and Thang Long Art Gallery) deal with the country's top artists. A number of the galleries listed here showcase more **experimental work** and promote promising newcomers, and ⓦhanoigrapevine.com is one of the best sources of up-to-date information. A few **photographers** have also set up shops that double as exhibition spaces. To get an overview of the Hanoi art scene, sign up for Sophie's Art Tour (see p.369).

Apricot Gallery 40b Hang Bong ☎024 3828 8965, ⓦapricotgallery.com.vn. This is a great place to get an idea of the latest trends in Vietnamese art, but if you ask the prices the answer will probably make your hair stand on end – there's nothing for less than $1000. Daily 8am–8pm.

Dien Dam Gallery 4b Dinh Liet ☎024 3825 9881, ⓦdiendam-gallery.com. The shop-cum-gallery of award-winning photographer Lai Dien Dam. Daily 8.30am–8.30pm.

Goethe Institute 56–58 Nguyen Thai Hoc ☎024 3734 2251, ⓦgoethe.de/ins/vn. Puts on an interesting programme of films, concerts and exhibitions. Daily 9am–5pm.

Green Palm Gallery 15 Trang Tien ☎024 3936 4757, ⓦgreenpalmgallery.com. Big, well-established gallery showcasing established names alongside lesser-known artists. Daily 8am–8pm.

Hanoi Studio 13 Trang Tien ☎024 3934 4433, ⓦarthanoistudio.com.vn. Commercial gallery hosting up to four interesting and well-displayed exhibitions a year, which promote young local artists. Daily 9am–7pm.

Institut Français L'Espace 24 Trang Tien ☎024 3936 2164, ⓦinstitutfrancais-vietnam.com. Extensive programme of films (subtitled in English), concerts and exhibitions, plus a members-only media centre. Mon–Fri 8am–8.30pm.

Mai Gallery 113 Hang Bong ☎024 3938 0568, ⓦmaigallery-vietnam.com. This commercial contemporary art gallery, which also fosters new talent, was actually the first private art gallery to be established in Hanoi, back in 1993. Daily 9am–6pm.

Thang Long Art Gallery 41 Hang Gai ☎024 3825 0740, ⓦthanglongartgallery.com. Like Apricot Gallery, Thang Long represents both established artists and up-and-coming newcomers, and often displays large canvases with dramatic compositions in its exhibition space. Daily 8am–8pm.

DIRECTORY

Banks and exchange 24hr ATMs are widespread throughout the city; those operated by Vietcombank and HSBC accept the most overseas cards. The Vietcombank's head office, 198 Tran Quang Khai (foreign exchange services Mon–Fri 8–11.30am & 1–3.30pm; all other services Mon–Fri 7.30–11.30am & 1–5pm), handles all services including cash withdrawals on credit cards and telegraphic transfers. It has branches at 32 Quang Trung, 31 Hang Khoai and 29 Hang Phen, among other locations.

Dentists The Family Medical Practice Dental Clinic in the Van Phuc Diplomatic Compound, 298 Kim Ma (Mon–Fri 8.30am–4.30pm; ☎024 3843 0748, ⓦvietnammedical practice.com), has a 24hr emergency service. The Hanoi French Hospital (ⓦhfh.com.vn) and International SOS (ⓦinternationalsos.com) also provide dental care.

Embassies and consulates Australia, 8 Dao Tan, Van Phuc ☎024 33774 0100, ⓦvietnam.embassy.gov.au; Cambodia, 71a Tran Hung Dao ☎024 33942 4789, ⓔcamemb.vnm@mfa.gov.kh; Canada, 31 Hung Vuong ☎024 3734 5000, ⓦcanadainternational.gc.ca; China, 46 Hoang Dieu ☎024 3845 3736, ⓦvn.china-embassy.org; Lao PDR, 22 Tran Binh Trong ☎024 3942 4576, ⓦlaoembassyhanoi.org.vn; Malaysia, 43–45 Dien Bien Phu ☎024 3734 3836, ⓦkin.gov.my/web/vnm_hanoi; Myanmar, A3 Van Phuc Compound, Kim Ma ☎024 3845 3369, ⓔmevhan@fpt.vn; New Zealand, 63 Ly Thai To ☎024 3824 1481, ⓦnzembassy.com; Singapore, 41–43 Tran Phu ☎024 3848 9168, ⓦmfa.gov.sg; Thailand, 26 Phan Boi Chau ☎024 3823 5092, ⓦthaiembassy.org; UK, 31 Hai Ba Trung ☎024 3936 0500, ⓦwww.gov.uk; US, Rose Garden Tower, 170 Ngoc Khanh ☎024 3850 5000, ⓦvietnam.usembassy.gov. For information on visas for China, Laos and Cambodia, see p.28.

Emergencies Dial ☎113 to call the police, ☎114 in case of fire and ☎115 for an ambulance; better still, get a Vietnamese-speaker to call on your behalf.

Hospitals and clinics The Hanoi French Hospital, 1 Phuong Mai, Dong Da District, offers facilities of an international standard including a 24hr emergency service (☎024 3574 1111), an outpatients clinic (Mon–Fri 8.30am–5.30pm, Sat 8.30am–noon; ☎024 3577 1100, ⓦhfh.com.vn), dental and optical care, and surgery. Alternatively, the Family Medical Practice, Van Phuc Compound, 298 I Kim Ma, is well known for its reasonable pricing (Mon–Fri 8.30am–5.30pm, Sat 8.30am–12.30pm; ☎024 3843 0748, ⓦvietnammedicalpractice.com). It has an outpatient clinic and a 24hr emergency service. International SOS, at 72 Xuan Dieu, provides routine care (Mon–Fri 8am–7pm, Sat 8am–2pm; ☎024 3718 6390, ⓦinternationalsos.com).

Laundry Most hotels have a laundry service, while the top hotels also offer dry cleaning, but prices can be steep. Alternatively, try one of the low-priced laundries (*giat la*) in the Old Quarter. Look for laundry signs along Hang Be, Ma May or Ta Hien; the standard rate is around 25,000đ per kilo for a one-day service.

Pharmacies The Hanoi French Hospital, Family Medical Practice and International SOS (see above) all have pharmacies. Of the local retail outlets, those at 37a Ta Hien and 4a Dinh Liet stock a selection of imported medicines. Traditional medicines can be bought on Lan Ong.

Post offices The GPO occupies a whole block at 75 Dinh Tien Hoang (daily 6.30am–9pm). The main entrance leads to general mail and telephone services, while international postal services, including parcel dispatch (Mon–Fri 7.30am–9pm), are located in the southernmost hall.

Around Hanoi

When you've taken in Hanoi's main sights, there are plenty more places waiting to be explored in the surrounding area, including the cave-shrine of the **Perfume Pagoda**, which is one of the country's most sacred locations. There are dozens of other historic buildings, of which the most strongly atmospheric are the **Thay Pagoda** and **Tay Phuong Pagoda**, buried deep in the Red River Delta – both are fine examples of traditional Vietnamese architecture. You could also spend months exploring the delta's villages, in particular the **craft villages**, which retain their traditions despite a constant stream of tourists passing though. The **Ho Chi Minh Trail Museum**, southwest of the centre, is also well worth a visit, especially if you're heading out of town on Highway 6 to Mai Chau or elsewhere. Finally, the ancient citadel of **Co Loa**, just north of the Red River, merits a stop in passing, mostly on account of its historical significance – today, barely a hint of its former grandeur remains. One of the best ways to visit these out-of-town sights (though not the Perfume Pagoda) is to sign up for a day-trip (see p.367).

The Perfume Pagoda complex

Huong Son, My Duc, 60km southwest of the city · 78,000đ; return boat ride 100,000đ · Boats run 8am–4pm (maximum 4/boat)

To the southwest of Hanoi, steep-sided **limestone hills** rise from the paddy fields. The most easterly of these forested spurs – known as Nui Huong Tich (the "Mountain of the Perfumed Traces") – shelters north Vietnam's most famous pilgrimage site, the **Perfume Pagoda** (Chua Huong), which is named after the spring blossoms that scent the air.

One of more than thirty peppering these hills, the Perfume Pagoda is in fact an impressive **grotto** over 50m high, with altars in its recesses at which devotees pray and make offerings. The start of the journey there involves an hour's ride in metal **rowboats** propelled by local women up a silent, flooded valley, amid the karst hills where fishermen and farmers work their fields. The boats drop visitors beside a string of restaurants that hang out deer, weasels and other animals to tempt customers in – which works well with Vietnamese visitors, but horrifies most foreigners. From here a stone-flagged path shaded by gnarled frangipani trees brings you to the foot of the hill, from where thousands of steps lead to the grotto.

Note that **respectful attire** – meaning long trousers, skirts below the knee and no sleeveless tops – should be worn for this trip; nobody will berate you for not doing so, but you might be the subject of unflattering comments. A hat or umbrella will also help, as the boats have no shelter. While the karst scenery is undoubtedly memorable, and a visit gives the chance to see the Vietnamese in festive mood, many find the trip here a long and tiring day (starting around 8am and returning after dark) with little reward, so think carefully before signing up for a tour or heading out on your own. If you don't like crowds, then avoid coming here at weekends or during the annual Perfume Pagoda Festival from February to April.

Chua Thien Chu

A magnificent, triple-roofed bell pavilion stands in front of the **Chua Thien Chu**, ("Pagoda Leading to Heaven"), the first of several pagodas at the site. Quan Am, Bodhisattva of Compassion, takes pride of place on the pagoda's main altar, though the original bronze effigy was stolen by Tay Son rebels in the 1770s, and some say they melted it down for cannonballs.

Uphill to the Perfume Pagoda

Cable car 100,000đ one-way, 160,000đ return

To the right of Chua Thien Chu, steps lead steeply uphill for two kilometres (about 1hr) to the Perfume Pagoda, also dedicated to Quan Am. The **cable car** may appeal despite the expense, as the hike is not especially interesting and can be hard going, especially in hot or wet weather; you'll need good walking shoes and to remember to drink plenty of water (bring your own, or be prepared to pay above the odds at drinks stalls along the route). During festival time, the path is lined all the way with stalls selling tacky souvenirs and refreshments, giving the place more of a commercial than spiritual atmosphere.

The Perfume Pagoda

However you reach it, the grotto that functions as the **Perfume Pagoda** reveals itself as a gaping cavern on the side of a deep depression filled with vines and trees, which reach for light beneath the Chinese inscription "supreme cave under the southern sky". Another flight of 120 steps descends into the dragon's-mouth-like entrance, where gilded Buddhas emerge from dark recesses wreathed in clouds of incense that is lit as an offering by Vietnamese visitors.

ARRIVAL AND DEPARTURE

THE PERFUME PAGODA

By tour The easiest and most popular way to visit the pagoda is on an organized tour out of Hanoi ($30–50/person, including the boat ride, lunch and entry fee) with a

company like Vietindo Travel (see box, p.367). One big advantage of this is that your guide will shield you from the persistent hawkers who want to sell you cold drinks and souvenirs, as well as from the boat rowers who demand huge tips at the end of the ride.

By motorbike It's not advised, but if you'd rather go it alone, it's a two- to three-hour ride to the Perfume Pagoda. To get there, you can rent a motorbike in Hanoi (see p.368) and follow Highway 6 through Ha Dong, from where a sign points you left down the QL21B, heading due south through Thanh Oai and Van Dinh to My Duc village and the Ben Yen (Yen River boat station). You'll need to bargain hard to get a boat ride for a reasonable fee (around 100,000đ/person), and you should memorize your boat number for the return journey, as there are hundreds of identical craft and you'll need to take the same one back.

Thay Pagoda

30km west of Hanoi • Daily 7am–5pm • 10,000đ

Thay Pagoda, or the "Master's Pagoda" – also known as Thien Phuc Tu ("Pagoda of the Heavenly Blessing") – was founded in the reign of King Ly Nhan Ton (1072–1127) and is an unusually large complex fronting a picturesque lake in the lee of a limestone crag.

Despite many restorations over the centuries, the pagoda's dark, subdued interior retains a powerful atmosphere. Nearly a hundred **statues** fill the prayer halls: the oldest dates back to the pagoda's foundation, but the most eyecatching are two seventeenth-century giant **guardians** made of clay and papier-mâché, which weigh a thousand kilos apiece and are said to be the biggest in Vietnam. Beyond, the highest altar holds a Buddha trinity, dating from the 1500s, and a thirteenth-century wooden statue of the Master (see box below).

The grounds

In front of the pagoda are two attractive **covered bridges**, which have arched roofs built in 1602 (though recently renovated) and dedicated to the sun and moon: one leads to an islet where spirits of the earth, water and sky are worshipped in a diminutive Taoist temple; the other takes you to a well-worn flight of steps up the limestone hill. In the middle of the lake is an ancient pavilion, which is still occasionally used for performances of water puppets.

THE MASTER

The Master was the ascetic monk and healer **Tu Dao Hanh** who "burned his finger to bring about rain and cured diseases with holy water", in addition to countless other miracles. He was head monk of the pagoda and an accomplished water-puppeteer – hence the dainty theatre-pavilion in the lake – and, according to legend, he was reincarnated first as a Buddha and then as **King Ly Than Tong**, the adopted son of King Ly Nhan Tong, whom he succeeded to the throne of the Ly dynasty in 1127. To complete an uncanny cycle, in 1136 Ly Than Tong was cured of a severe disease by a monk named Nguyen Minh Khong, who had been a disciple of Tu Dao Hanh. The Thay Pagoda is dedicated to the cult of Tu Dao Hanh in his three incarnations as monk (the Master), Buddha and king.

The highest **altar** in the pagoda holds a thirteenth-century wooden statue of the Master as a Bodhisattva, dressed in yellow garb and perched on a lotus throne. On a separate altar to the left he appears again as King Ly Than Tong, also in yellow, accompanied by two dark-skinned, kneeling figures, who are said to be Cambodian slaves, while to the right sits a mysterious, lavishly decorated wooden chamber. The monk's mortal remains and a sandalwood statue with articulated legs repose in this final, securely locked sanctuary – though a **photo** on the altar shows the statue's beady eyes staring out of a gaunt, unhappy face. This room is only revealed once a year: at 1pm on the fifth day of the third lunar month, the village of Sai Son's oldest male bathes the statue of Tu Dao Hanh with fragrant water and helps him to his feet.

Traditionally, this event was for the monks' eyes only, but nowadays anyone can see as long as they're prepared to put up with the scrum. The celebrations, attended by thousands, continue for three days and include daily processions as well as a famous **water-puppet festival**, held on the lake on the fifth to seventh days of the third lunar month.

By tour The pagoda lies in the village of Sai Son, and the best way to get there is to join a tour taking in other sights around Hanoi as well. Since the pagoda is packed with significant artefacts, it's helpful to go in the company of a guide who can explain things for you. Vietindo Travel (see box, p.367) offer a tour combining all three out-of-town pagodas as well as Chuong village for $40/person.

By bicycle Companies like Lotussia (see box, p.367) offer one-day cycling trips to the Thay and Tay Phuong pagodas ($110).

By motorbike You can rent a motorbike and follow the new Thang Long Highway, heading west out of Hanoi; after about 25km, look out for a right turn to Chua Tay and Sunny Garden City, a new satellite development. Note that this is a popular weekend jaunt for domestic visitors, at its busiest on Sundays.

Tay Phuong Pagoda

36km west of Hanoi • Daily 7am–5pm • 10,000đ • Tay Phuong Pagoda is only 6km west of Thay Pagoda, but a complex network of lanes makes it difficult to find – It's best to arrange a customized tour (see box, p.367)

Known as the "Pagoda of the West", small **Tay Phuong Pagoda** perches atop a 50m-high limestone hillock that's supposedly shaped like a buffalo. Among the first pagodas built in Vietnam, Tay Phuong's overriding attraction is its invaluable collection of jackfruit-wood **statues**, some of which are now on display at Hanoi's Fine Arts Museum (see p.361). The highlights here are the **eighteen arhats**, disturbingly lifelike representations of Buddhist ascetics as imagined by eighteenth-century sculptors, grouped around the main altar – a torch would help pick out the finer details.

As Tay Phuong is also an important **Confucian sanctuary**, disciples of the sage are included on the altar, each carrying a gift to their master – some precious object, a book or a symbol of longevity – alongside the expected Buddha effigies. Tay Phuong's most notable architectural features are its heavy double roofs, whose graceful curves are decorated with phoenixes and dragons, and an inviting approach via 237 time-worn, red-brick steps.

Tram Gian Pagoda

25km southwest from Hanoi • Daily 8am–5pm • Free • Signed to the right of Highway 6 at the Km21 marker; several companies in Hanoi offer bicycle tours here

With time to spare, you could combine a day's outing to the Thay and Tay Phuong pagodas with a quick detour to the **Tram Gian Pagoda**. Again, the large, peaceful temple sitting on a wooded hill is best known for its rich array of statues. Though not as fine as those at Tay Phuong, they are numerous, and include more *arhats* in the side corridors alongside some toe-curling depictions of the underworld and an impressive group on the main altar. Among them sits the pot-bellied, laughing Maitreya, the carefree Buddha, who stands in stark contrast to the black, emaciated figure behind him. According to legend, this is the mummified and lacquered body of **Duc Thanh Boi** (St Boi), who was born nearby in the thirteenth century. He is credited with numerous miracles, including the ability to fly, and with saving the country from a catastrophic drought by summoning rain – though he had to wait a century after death for his sainthood, when devotees disinterred his body to find it in a perfect state of preservation.

Ho Chi Minh Trail Museum

14km southwest of Hanoi • Mon–Sat 7.30–11.30am & 1.30–2.30pm • 20,000đ; with camera 10,000đ • To the right of Highway 6, just beyond the Km14 marker as you leave Hanoi

While this museum is not really worth making a special trip, with a bit of forethought it can be combined with visits to the Perfume Pagoda, the Tram Gian Pagoda or the Tay Phuong Pagoda, or visited on the way to Mai Chau. Once you're there you'll learn a lot, including the fact that the **Ho Chi Minh Trail** was never a single trail, but a complex network of muddy tracks that crisscrossed the border with Laos and Cambodia.

THE HO CHI MINH TRAIL

At the end of its "working" life, the **Ho Chi Minh Trail** had grown from a rough assemblage of animal tracks and jungle paths to a highly effective logistical network stretching from near Vinh, north of the Seventeenth Parallel, to Tay Ninh province on the edge of the Mekong Delta. Initially it took up to six months to walk the trail from north to south. By 1975, however, the trail – comprising at least three main arteries plus several feeder roads leading to various battlefronts and totalling over **15,000km** – was wide enough to take tanks and heavy trucks, and could be driven in just one week. It was protected by sophisticated antiaircraft emplacements and supported by regular service stations (fuel and maintenance depots, ammunition dumps, food stores and hospitals), often located underground or in caves and all connected by field telephone. Eventually there was even an oil pipeline constructed alongside the trail to take fuel south from Vinh to a depot at Loc Ninh.

The trail was conceived in early 1959, when **General Giap** ordered the newly created Logistical Group 559 to reconnoitre a safe route along which to direct men and equipment down the length of Vietnam, in support of Communist groups in the south. Political cadres blazed the trail, followed in 1964 by the first deployment of ten thousand regular troops, and culminating in the trek south of 150,000 men in preparation for the **1968 Tet Offensive**. It was a logistical feat that rivalled Dien Bien Phu (see box, p.409) in both scale and determination – this time it was sustained over fifteen years and became a symbol to the Vietnamese of their victory and sacrifice. For much of its southerly route, the trail ran through Laos and Cambodia, sometimes on paths forged during the war against the French, sometimes along riverbeds, and always through the most difficult, mountainous terrain plagued with leeches, snakes, malaria and dysentery.

On top of all this, people on the trail had to contend with almost constant bombing. By early 1965, **aerial bombardment** had begun in earnest, using napalm and defoliants as well as conventional ordnance, and this was joined later by carpet-bombing B-52s. Every day in the spring of 1965, the US Air Force flew an estimated three hundred bombing raids over the trail, and in eight years dropped over two million tonnes of explosives (mostly over Laos) in an effort to cut the flow. Later they experimented with seismic and acoustic sensors, to eavesdrop on troop movements and pinpoint targets, but the trail was never completely severed and supplies continued to roll south in sufficient quantities to sustain the war.

7

Visitors are currently shown an informative, twenty-minute **video** about the construction of the trail, though this may change after a renovation of the premises in late 2017. Exhibits include equipment used in the trail's construction, along with some of the horrific shrapnel-, nail- and cigarette-bombs that were employed to slow down the trail's progress. Outside are a few vehicles that once used the trail, and behind the museum is a forgettable mock-up of an underground operations centre.

The craft villages

For centuries, the **villages** around Vietnam's major towns have specialized in single-commodity production, initially to supply the local market, and sometimes going on to win national fame for the skill of their artisans. A few communities continue to prosper, of which the best known near Hanoi are **Bat Trang** for pottery, **Van Phuc** for silk and **Chuong** for conical hats. These feature well-run, commercial operations where family units turn out fine, hand-crafted products, and they are used to foreigners coming to watch them at work. Most other villages are far less touristy, and the more isolated ones may treat visitors with suspicion. Nevertheless, it's worth taking a guide for the day to gain a rare glimpse into a way of life that continues to follow the ancient rhythms, using craft techniques handed down the generations virtually unchanged.

Bat Trang

16km southeast of Hanoi

BAT TRANG village, across the Red River in Hanoi's Gia Lam District, has been producing **bricks** and **earthenware** since the fifteenth century, and the oldest quarter beside the river has an almost medieval aura, with its narrow, high-walled alleys spattered with handmade coal-pats (used as fuel in the kilns) drying in the sun. Through tiny doorways, you catch glimpses of courtyards stacked with moulds and hand-painted pots, while all around rise the squat brick chimneys of the traditional coal-fired kilns.

Around two thousand families live in Bat Trang, producing time-honoured **blue and white ceramics** alongside more contemporary designs, as well as mass-produced floor tiles and balustrades to feed Hanoi's building boom. Some workshops also allow visitors to try their hand at the potter's wheel. Showrooms along Bat Trang's main drag offer a bewildering choice of pottery. Prices are not necessarily any cheaper than in Hanoi itself, though the range is superior and it's easier to bargain. At some of the bigger workshops (such as Hoa Lan Ceramics, 81 Duong Giang Cao), you can paint your own design and have the piece delivered to your hotel once it's fired.

The village has **expanded** rapidly in recent years, thanks largely to a healthy export market, and now boasts some 2500 kilns. Most are now gas-fired, but air pollution and respiratory infections remain a problem.

Van Phuc
11km southwest of Hanoi

In the silk village of **VAN PHUC**, the clatter of electric looms from the thirty-odd workshops fills the air. You're welcome to wander into any of them, and will be given a brief explanation, but there's nothing much to detain you unless you're shopping for silk. Material is a shade cheaper than in Hanoi, while finished items such as scarves and clothes can be as little as half the city price.

Chuong
30km south of Hanoi

Conical hats are the staple product of **CHUONG** village (also known as Phuong Trung), which is best visited on market days (held six times each lunar month), when hats are piled high in golden pyramids. At other times it's possible to see artisans deftly assembling the dried leaves on a bamboo frame. Traditionally the designs varied according to the different needs: thick and robust for working in the fields, more delicate for outings to the temple and other special occasions, and flat, ornamented hats for fashion-conscious aristocrats.

ARRIVAL AND DEPARTURE   THE CRAFT VILLAGES

A number of Hanoi tour agents (see box, p.367) offer organized day-trips to a selection of craft villages for $40–70, or can include some in a visit to the various pagodas.

BAT TRANG

By car or motorbike Bat Trang is an easy jaunt by car or motorbike; go over Chuong Duong Bridge from Hanoi, then immediately right along the levee. Once in the village, to reach the old quarter of narrow lanes and workshops, park up and walk straight ahead at the end of Duong Giang Cao, and keep going west.

By bicycle Cyclists have to use Long Bien Bridge, which is a short distance further north from the Chuong Duong Bridge. After 10km of heading south, following signs to Xuan Quan, a right turn indicates the village entrance.

By bus Bus #47 departs from Long Bien bus station every fifteen minutes or so, and the journey takes about 30 minutes. Bat Trang is the last stop (8000đ).

VAN PHUC

By bicycle or motorbike Van Phuc lies to the north of Highway 6, about a kilometre north of Ha Dong post office on the Quoac Hai Road.

By bus Take bus #1 from Long Bien station, which costs 7000đ and takes around half an hour.

CHUONG

By bicycle or motorbike Chuong lies about 30km southwest of Hanoi, just off Highway 21B a couple of kilometres south of Thanh Oai, on the road to the Perfume Pagoda.

By bus and xe om Take bus #94 from Giap Bat to Kim Bai (9000đ), then a xe om for the last 1.5km.

THE HISTORY OF THE CITADEL

King An Duong Vuong built his **citadel** inside three concentric ramparts, which spiralled like a snail's shell, separated by moats large enough for ships to navigate; the outer wall was 8km long, 6–8m wide and at least 4m high, topped off with bamboo fencing. After the Chinese invaded in the second century BC, Co Loa was abandoned until 939 AD, when **Ngo Quyen** established the next period of independent rule from the same heavily symbolic site.

Archeologists have found rich pickings at Co Loa, including thousands of **iron arrowheads**, displayed in Hanoi's History Museum (see p.355), which lend credence to at least one of the Au Lac legends. The story goes that the sacred **Golden Turtle** gave King An Duong Vuong a magic crossbow made from a claw that fired thousands of arrows at a time. A deceitful Chinese prince married An Duong Vuong's daughter, Princess My Chau, persuaded her to show him the crossbow and then stole the claw before mounting an invasion. The king and his daughter were forced to flee, whereupon My Chau understood her act of betrayal and nobly told her father to kill her. When the king beheaded his daughter and threw her body in a well, she turned into lustrous, pink pearls.

7

Co Loa Citadel

13km north of Hanoi • Daily 7.30am–5.30pm • 10,000đ • Bus #46 from My Dinh bus station (45min; 7000đ)

The earliest independent Vietnamese states grew up on the Red River flood plain, atop low hills or crouched behind sturdy embankments. First to emerge from the mists of legend was **Van Lang**, presided over by the Hung kings from a knob of high ground marked today by a few dynastic temples north of Viet Tri (Vinh Phu province), known as the Hung Kings Temple. Then the action moved closer to Hanoi when King An Duong Vuong defeated the last of the Hung kings and ruled Au Lac (258–207 BC) from an immense citadel at **Co Loa** (Old Snail City). At the time it was the first fortified Vietnamese capital, but these days the once massive **earthworks** are barely visible and all that remains are a couple of quiet temples with interesting histories set amid the streets of modern Co Loa.

Den An Duong Vuong

The principal temple, **Den An Duong Vuong**, faces a lake, with a graceful stele-house to one side. Looking across the fields from the stele-house, you can just make out the earthen ramparts of the former citadel. Inside the rebuilt temple, a sixteenth-century black-bronze **statue** of King An Duong Vuong resides on the main altar, resplendent in a double crown, while a subsidiary altar is dedicated to Kim Quy, the Golden Turtle.

Other buildings

About 100m east of Den An Duong Vuong, a **statue** of King An Duong Vuong holding his magic crossbow (see box above) stands in a small pond. The lane beside the pond leads to a second group of buildings, where a large walled courtyard contains the beautifully simple, open-sided **Dinh Da Quy**, furnished with huge ironwood pillars, and containing ornate palanquins. Next door is a small temple, **Den My Chau**, dedicated to An Duong Vuong's daughter, the Princess My Chau. Inside, she is still honoured in the surprising form of a dumpy, armchair-shaped stone clothed in embroidered finery and covered in jewels – but lacking a head.

The far north

FLOWER HMONG PEOPLE

The far north

As Vietnam fans out above Hanoi towards the Chinese and Lao borders, it attains its maximum width of 600km, most of it a mountainous buffer zone wrapped around the Red River Delta. This wild, remote region contains some of Vietnam's most awe-inspiring scenery, sparsely populated by a fascinating mosaic of ethnic minorities. Most visitors gravitate to the northwest, where the country's highest mountain range and its tallest peak, Mount Fan Si Pan, rise abruptly from the Red River Valley. Within its shadow lies Sa Pa, a former French hill station and the base for trekking through superb scenery to isolated minority hamlets. To the east of the Red River, Bac Ha's major draw are the Flower Hmong, whose markets are great fun. These two towns – and the historic battlefield of Dien Bien Phu, the site of the Viet Minh's decisive victory over French forces in 1954 – are the most visited places in the north. From Dien Bien Phu, it's worth considering the scenic route back to Hanoi, passing though Son La, with its forbidding penitentiary, and Mai Chau, with its gorgeous scenery.

The little-travelled provinces of **Ha Giang** and **Cao Bang** also deserve attention, especially the stunning scenery and ethnic minorities in the **Dong Van Karst Plateau Geopark**, which occupies over 2300 square kilometres of Ha Giang province. Cao Bang's attractions include the pretty Ban Gioc Falls and Hang Pac Bo, where Ho Chi Minh plotted his country's liberation. The northeast region also features **Ba Be National Park**, where Vietnam's largest natural lake nestles amid forested limestone crags and impenetrable jungle.

Not surprisingly, **infrastructure** throughout the northern mountains is poor: facilities tend to be thin on the ground, and some roads are in terrible condition. However, this area is becoming increasingly popular with tourists as Hanoi's tour agents organize new tours and independent travellers venture into uncharted terrain by jeep or motorbike. New homestays are also opening all the time, especially in Ha Giang province.

The **best time** to visit the northern mountains is from September to November or from March to May, when the weather is fairly settled with dry, sunny days and clear, cold nights. **Winter** can be decidedly chilly, especially in the northeast where night frosts are not uncommon from December to February, but the compensation is daybreak mists and breathtaking sunrise views high above valleys filled with early-morning lakes of cloud. The **rainy season** lasts from May to September, peaking in July and August, when heavy downpours wash out bridges, turn unsealed roads into quagmires and throw in the occasional landslide for good measure. Peak season for

CABLE CAR FROM SA PA

Highlights

❶ Mount Fan Si Pan Ride the record-breaking cable car from Sa Pa and stand on top of Mount Fan Si Pan, Vietnam's highest mountain. **See p.402**

❷ Bac Ha Sunday market Have your camera ready for the Sunday market in Bac Ha, which is frequented by the Flower Hmong – perhaps the most flamboyant dressers in the country. **See p.404**

❸ Thai minority villages Sleep in a Thai stilthouse in Mai Chau, cycle or trek through the rice fields in the valley and watch traditional dance performances. **See p.414**

❹ Dong Van Karst Plateau Geopark Vietnam's first geopark, recognized by UNESCO for its unique geological significance, harbours some of the country's most spectacular scenery. **See p.419**

❺ Ba Be Lake Glide around in a boat on the lake's glassy waters or hike to minority villages near the shore, and spend a night in a welcoming homestay. **See p.423**

❻ Ban Gioc Falls Take a ride amid karst landscapes from Cao Bang to the Chinese border to reach these attractive falls, an image of which adorns the walls of cafés throughout the country. **See p.426**

HIGHLIGHTS ARE MARKED ON THE MAP ON P.394

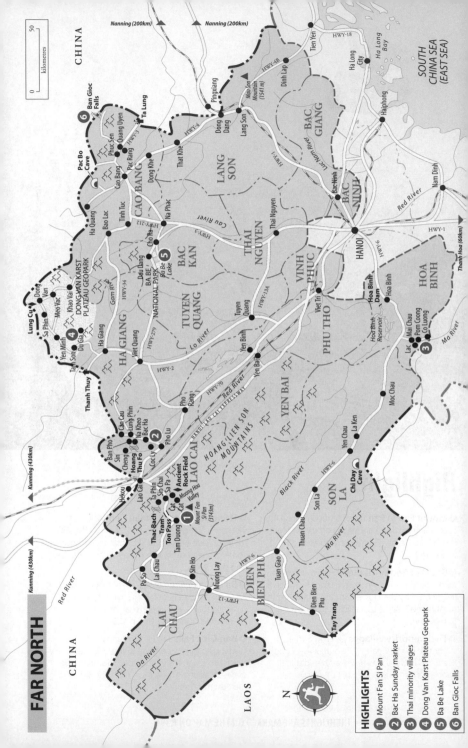

foreign tourists is from September to November, while the rainy summer months of July and August are when Hanoians head up to the mountains to escape the stifling heat of the delta.

GETTING AROUND   THE FAR NORTH

However you choose to travel, you'll need to allow around a week to cover the northwestern region, or two weeks to cover both the northwest and northeast. When planning your **route**, base your itinerary on an average speed of about 40km/hour, but bear in mind that these roads are unpredictable, and become downright dangerous during the rains. If you've got only limited time, Sa Pa, Mai Chau and Ba Be National Park make rewarding two- or three-day excursions out of Hanoi.

By tour It's worth joining a tour for short trips to places like Mai Chau, especially if you're travelling alone. Joining a motorbike tour is one of the best ways to see the Dong Van Karst Plateau Geopark, but you'll need to be an experienced rider. For recommended agencies in Hanoi, see box, p.367.

By car or motorbike Most visitors hire a motorbike or car and driver to travel around the Northwest or Northeast loops from Hanoi – and these options give you more freedom to stop at villages or wander off along side tracks. The cost of hiring a car and driver (for 3–4) in Hanoi averages around $100/day, while scooters and motorbikes go for between $5–$8/day.

By bus Travelling through the northern provinces using local buses is possible, though it's an uncomfortable experience – only the hardiest adventurers bother to take them.

Brief history

Though Vietnam's far north has been inhabited for thousands of years, as evidenced by the **Ancient Rock Field** in the Sa Pa Valley (see p.402), little of its history was documented until the French and Chinese came to blows over control of northern Vietnam during the 1880s. By the 1920s, the French had established a hill station at Sa Pa, but their tenure was brief; remote uplands, dense vegetation and rugged terrain suited to guerrilla activities, plus a safe haven across the border, made this region the perfect place from which to orchestrate Vietnam's independence movement. For a short while in 1941, **Ho Chi Minh** hid in the Hang Pac Bo on the Chinese frontier, later moving south to the province of Tuyen Quang, from where the Viet Minh launched their August Revolution in 1945. These northern provinces were the first to be liberated from French rule, but over in the northwest some minority groups, notably from among the Thai, Hmong and Muong, supported the colonial authorities – it took the Viet Minh until 1952 to gain control of the area. Two years later, they staged their great victory over the French at **Dien Bien Phu**, close to the Lao border.

During the late 1970s **Sino–Vietnamese** relations became increasingly sour for various reasons, not least due to Vietnam's invasion of Cambodia, whose genocidal regime was supported by China (see p.447). Things came to a head on February 17, 1979, when the Chinese sent two hundred thousand troops into northern Vietnam, destroying most of the border towns; seventeen days later, however, the invasion force was driven out, some twenty thousand short. Though much of the infrastructural and political damage from the war has been repaired, unmarked minefields along 1000km of frontier pose a more intractable problem. Most areas – including all that regularly receive tourists – have been cleared and declared safe, but in the more remote areas it's sensible to stick to well-worn paths.

Sa Pa

The tourist capital of Vietnam's mountainous north, **SA PA** is perched dramatically at an elevation of around 1600 metres on the western edge of a high plateau, facing the hazy blue peak of **Mount Fan Si Pan**, Vietnam's highest mountain, across the Muong Hoa Valley. The refreshing climate and alpine landscape struck a nostalgic chord with European visitors, who dubbed these mountains the "Tonkinese Alps". The French travelled up from Lao Cai by sedan chair in the early twentieth century, and by 1930 a flourishing hill station had developed here, complete with tennis court, church and over two hundred villas. Nowadays only a handful of the old buildings remain, the rest lost to time and the 1979 Chinese invasion, as well as the ongoing hotel development spree. With new hotels constantly rising, Sa Pa's days as an idyllic haven in the hills have been concreted over.

Sa Pa is surrounded by **ethnic minorities**, notably the Red Dao and Black Hmong, and trekking to their villages is the primary objective of many visitors. Sa Pa itself is ethnically Vietnamese, but minority groups are still likely to catch your eye as you're wandering around town. Women typically come dressed in their finery – the most striking are the **Red Dao**, who wear scarlet headdresses festooned with woollen tassels and silver trinkets. **Black Hmong** are the most numerous group – they make up over a third of the district's population – and the most commercially minded, peddling their embroidered indigo-blue waistcoats, bags, hats and heavy, silver jewellery at all hours. It's common to see young Hmong girls walking hand-in-hand with Westerners they have befriended prior to making their sales pitch. By contrast, the Red Dao are generally shy about being photographed, despite their eye-catching dress.

Sa Pa's invigorating air is a real tonic after the humidity of Hanoi, though **cold nights** make warm clothes essential throughout the year – the sun sets early behind Mount Fan Si Pan, and temperatures fall rapidly after dark. During the coldest months (December to February), night temperatures often drop below freezing and winter brings some snow, but most hotel rooms now have heating. However, Sa Pa's best-known climatic feature is a thick fog straight out of a Sherlock Holmes story, which sweeps up from the valley below and blots out the whole town, lending a spooky feel to the streets. You'll find the best **weather** from September to November and March to May, though even during these months the cold, damp clouds can descend, blotting out the views for several days.

8

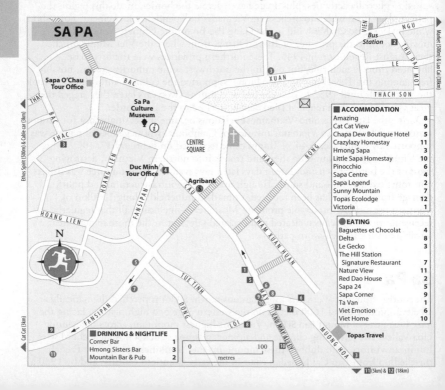

SA PA

Sapa O'Chau Tour Office

Sa Pa Culture Museum

CENTRE SQUARE

Duc Minh Tour Office

Agribank

Bus Station

■ ACCOMMODATION
Amazing	8
Cat Cat View	9
Chapa Dew Boutique Hotel	5
Crazylazy Homestay	11
Hmong Sapa	3
Little Sapa Homestay	10
Pinocchio	6
Sapa Centre	4
Sapa Legend	2
Sunny Mountain	7
Topas Ecolodge	12
Victoria	1

● EATING
Baguettes et Chocolat	4
Delta	8
Le Gecko	3
The Hill Station Signature Restaurant	7
Nature View	11
Red Dao House	2
Sapa 24	5
Sapa Corner	9
Ta Van	1
Viet Emotion	6
Viet Home	10

Topas Travel

■ DRINKING & NIGHTLIFE
Corner Bar	1
Hmong Sisters Bar	3
Mountain Bar & Pub	2

0   100
metres

THE NORTHERN MINORITIES

Around seven million **minority people** (nearly two-thirds of Vietnam's total minority population) live in the northern uplands, mostly in isolated villages. The largest ethnic groups are Thai and Muong in the northwest, Tay and Nung in the northeast and Hmong and Dao dispersed throughout the region. Historically, all these peoples migrated from southern China at various times throughout history: those who arrived first, notably the Tay and Thai, settled in the fertile valleys where they now lead a relatively prosperous existence, while late arrivals, such as the Hmong and Dao, took to living on the higher slopes. Despite government efforts to integrate them into the Vietnamese community, most continue to follow a way of life that's changed very little over the centuries. For an insight into the minorities' traditional cultures and highly varied styles of dress, visit Hanoi's informative **Museum of Ethnology** (see p.366) before setting off into the mountains.

VISITING MINORITY VILLAGES

A popular, hassle-free way to visit minority villages is to join one of the **organized trips** offered by tour agencies in Hanoi, Sa Pa, Bac Ha and Ha Giang (see respective sections for recommended companies). Generally, you're better off going with local companies, as they are more familiar with the villages visited. While it's possible to go alone to places like Cat Cat near Sa Pa, independent trekking is generally frowned upon and locals may not be as welcoming as they are to groups.

ETIQUETTE

Behaviour that we take for granted may cause offence to some ethnic minority people – remember that you are a guest. Apart from being sensitive to the situation and keeping an open mind, the following rules should be observed when visiting the ethnic minority areas.

- **Dress modestly**, in long trousers or a skirt and a T-shirt or shirt.
- Be sensitive when taking **photographs**, particularly of older people who are generally suspicious of the camera – always ask permission first.
- Only enter a house when you've been invited, and be prepared to **remove your shoes**.
- Small **gifts**, such as fresh fruit from the local market, are always welcome, and it's also a good idea to buy **craft work** produced by the villagers – most communities have some embroidery, textiles or basketry for sale.
- As a mark of respect, learn the local **terms of address**, either in a dialect or at least in Vietnamese, such as *chao ong, chao ba* (see p.490).
- Try to **minimize your impact** on the fragile local environment: take litter back to the towns with you and be sensitive when using wood and other scarce resources.
- Growing and using **opium** is illegal in Vietnam and is punishable with a fine or prison sentence – do not encourage its production by buying or smoking it.

The market

Dawn to dusk

What initially attracted visitors to Sa Pa was the weekend **market** (now a daily market), which added a blaze of colour to the steep lanes and stairways around Cau May, the town's main street. Recently it was moved a couple of kilometres east of the town centre to a custom-built, two-storey edifice, though half the stalls remained empty at the time of research. The souvenir stalls here offer an unappealing range of tacky mementoes, so instead make a beeline for the fresh market and food stalls at the back of the building, where there's always a crowd of elaborately attired minority groups. More authentic markets can be found on the other side of the Red River on Saturdays at **Can Cau** (see p.405) and on Sundays in **Bac Ha** (see p.404).

Sa Pa Culture Museum

2 Fansipan (behind the tourist office) • ☎ 0214 387 1975 • Daily 7.30–11.30am & 1.30–5pm • Free

The small **Sa Pa Culture Museum** features video presentations and wall displays about Sa Pa's history and the lifestyles of the local hill tribes, but exhibits are dimly lit and the captions are unclear – you might not learn much here. Other exhibits include a mock-up of a Hmong wedding ceremony and a run-down of the social architecture of ethnic minority groups.

Ham Rong Mountain Park

Dawn to dusk • 70,000đ

To get in shape for a trek through the valley, try taking a short but steep hike to the top of **Ham Rong Mountain**, which overlooks the town from an elevation of around 2000m. Stone steps lead up to the peak where there are fine, panoramic views on a clear day. The pathway is lined with potted orchids, landscaped gardens and depictions of cartoon characters like Mickey Mouse. To find the entrance to the park, follow Ham Rong to the north of the church in the town centre.

ARRIVAL AND DEPARTURE   SA PA

Previously, the journey by bus from Gia Lam bus station in Hanoi to the centre of Sa Pa took just as long as the train and bus combination (about 10hr), but the completion of a new highway between Hanoi and Lao Cai has cut that time by about 4 hours – making the bus journey a more appealing alternative.

By bus Sa Pa's bus station is by the lake in the northeast of town, though many buses, such as the shuttle buses to and from the railway station in Lao Cai, drop passengers off in front of the church; buses to Hanoi leave from the main square in front of the church in the morning and evening. Note that if you're heading to Bac Ha, you'll need to change buses in Lao Cai and consequently endure a rather slow journey, though there are tour buses that go directly from Sa Pa on Sundays only for the market – ask at your hotel about these. There's also a daily sleeper bus directly to Bai Chay for Ha Long Bay.

Destinations Bai Chay (daily; 10hr); Dien Bien Phu (3 daily; 10hr); Hanoi (about 10 daily; 6hr); Lao Cai (every 30min; 1hr); Lai Chau (hourly; 2hr 30min).
By train There's no railway station in Sa Pa, yet most people still come here by train from Hanoi via the border town of Lao Cai (see box below), located on the east bank of the Red River, 38km from Sa Pa. They then take a shuttle bus (around 50,000đ) from the station up the winding, switchback road to Sa Pa, which takes about an hour and drops passengers off on Cau May, Sa Pa's main street.

GETTING AROUND

By motorbike Motorbikes, with or without a driver, can be arranged through hotels in Sa Pa; self-drive is available (from around $7/day) but you will need to be an experienced biker to tackle the stony mountain tracks; make sure you test the bike for faults before leaving town. A bike with a driver will cost around $10/day.

By car It's also possible to hire your own jeep and driver (around $100/day) via Sa Pa's tour operators (see below), depending on availability, but if you want to tackle the whole northwestern circuit you'll find cheaper long-term prices in Hanoi.

INFORMATION AND TOURS

Maps The tourist office can provide a map of the town and surrounding area, while most hotels provide guests with a simple sketch map of the town centre.
Tourist information There's a dedicated and helpful tourist office facing across the square to the church at 2

Fansipan (daily 7.30–11.30am & 1.30–5.30pm; ☎ 0214 387 1975, ⓦ sapa-tourism.com), though their tour prices tend to be inflated. Sa Pa's hotels remain the best source of advice on visiting minority villages.
Tour operators Duc Minh Travel at 10 Cau May

INTO CHINA FROM LAO CAI

The **border crossing** from Lao Cai (see p.403) into China, 38km northeast of Sa Pa, is popular with travellers heading to Kunming. Hekou Bridge border gate, which is 3km north of the bus and train stations in Lao Cai, is open daily from 7am–10pm; you can expect the journey across to take about an hour. After crossing the border you can travel on to Kunming, the capital of Yunnan province, by train (four per day) from Hekou North station, or by bus (regular departures). The 450km journey takes from six to ten hours, and you'll need to have arranged your Chinese visa beforehand.

(☎0214 387 1881, ⓦducminhtravel.com) provides tours to hill tribe markets, villages near Sa Pa, as well as car and motorbike rental. Sapa O'Chau at 8 Thac Bac (☎0214 377 1166, ⓦsapaochau.org) is run by a Hmong woman who can organize welcoming homestays, treks in the Muong Hoa Valley and volunteer experience for visitors. Ethos Spirit at 79 Nguyen Chi Thanh (☎0166 689 2536, ⓦethosspirit.com) offers a variety of authentic experiences that support local ethnic cultures, including treks and motorbike trips. Prices range from $40–60/day, depending on the number in the group and the activities included.

ACCOMMODATION

Despite the glut of guesthouses and hotels in Sa Pa, rooms can still be in **short supply** in the summer months, pushing up prices by as much as fifty percent. Most hotels bump up prices over weekends too, when the town is crawling with Vietnamese tourists, so it's worth considering a midweek visit. Most places offer some kind of heating, such as electric blankets, but it's best to check rather than risk shivering all night. Foreigners can also now stay in many of Sa Pa's surrounding **minority villages**, though you'll need to arrange this through guesthouses and travel agencies, as independent trekking and village visits are frowned upon.

Amazing Dong Loi ☎0214 386 5888, ⓦamazinghotel .com.vn; map p.396. The rooftop pool and fitness centre, stylish spa and the 100-square-metre penthouse on the sixth floor with dizzying views are all amazing, but the prices bring a bump back down to earth. $120

★**Cat Cat View** 46 Fansipan ☎0214 387 1946, ⓦcatcathotel.com; map p.396. One of the town's longest-standing mini-hotels, *Cat Cat* has a building on each side of the road and a huge variety of rooms, some with private terraces and fantastic panoramic views across to Mount Fan Si Pan. The rooftop restaurant is an added attraction. $35

Chapa Dew Boutique Hotel 34 Cau May ☎0214 377 1999, ⓦchapadewhotel.vn; map p.396. Set back from Sa Pa's main street, this boutique hotel has a lot going for it – a good range of rooms, some with spectacular views, as well as very helpful staff and a filling buffet breakfast. $35

Crazylazy Homestay Lao Chai village, near Ta Van (10km from Sa Pa) ☎0163 980 9197, ⓦlazy crazyhomestay.com; map p.396. "There's no rush here" is the byline of this neat rural getaway, and if lounging in a hammock, gazing across a beautiful valley and splashing in the local river appeals, this is your spot. Enjoy meals with the family and local treks. Dorms $6, doubles $16

Hmong Sapa 10 Thac Bac ☎0214 377 2228, ⓦhmongsapahotel.com; map p.396. It's worth the uphill, kilometre-long walk from the city centre for this welcoming hotel in the northwest outskirts of town, which has rooms that are full of character and fabulous views. Rooms are decorated in vibrant colours and most have canopied beds and balconies, and there's also a lovely communal terrace. $45

Little Sapa Homestay 42 Cau May Alley ☎098 889 7711, ⓦlittlesapahomestay.com; map p.396. Located off the stairway to the south of Cau May, this place has small but cozy rooms named after the different ethnic groups, and very helpful owners. $12

Pinocchio 15 Muong Hoa ☎0214 387 1876, ⓦpinocchiohotel.com; map p.396. This place has stood the test of time, and offers rooms that have great views and balconies, as well as comfortable dorm beds. The breakfast is decent. Dorms $5, doubles $12

Sapa Centre 10–12 Cau May ☎0214 387 2881, ⓦsapacentrehotel.com; map p.396. Located right at the top of Cau May and overlooking the Centre Square, this place has something for everybody, from dorm beds with comfortable mattresses to small doubles and suites with spacious balconies. Dorms $5, doubles $25

★**Sapa Legend** 1 Thu Dau Mot ☎0214 382 8888, ⓦsapalegendhotel.com; map p.396. This recently opened hotel just south of the lake is giving stiff competition to the *Victoria* with its sumptuous rooms and suites, superb spa, excellent buffet breakfast and competitive rates. $75

Sunny Mountain 10 Muong Hoa ☎0214 378 7998, ⓦsunnymountainhotel.com; map p.396. This efficiently run hotel has 75 well-designed rooms, most with mountain views, and all have comfortable beds, cable TV and minibars. There's a decent restaurant on the top floor and a travel desk that can help plan exploration of the local area. $35

Topas Ecolodge Lech Dao village, Thanh Kim ☎0214 387 2404, ⓦtopasecolodge.com; map p.396. Situated a 45min drive from Sa Pa, the *Topas Ecolodge* is made up of luxurious yet rustic alpine lodge-style cottages, set on a clifftop with spectacular views looking down over a glorious valley and the ethnic minority village of Ban Ho. The older buildings are ecofriendly, meaning no a/c, TV or wi-fi in rooms, while the refurbished rooms are less so, featuring a/c and even hairdryers. Their office in Sa Pa (21 Muong Hoa) offers transport to the lodge and a number of tours. $160

Victoria Xuan Vien ☎0214 387 1522, ⓦvictoriahotels -asia.com; map p.396. The *Victoria*'s 77 rooms bring a touch of luxury to Sa Pa, and attract a regular clientele of expat residents from Hanoi looking for an accessible weekend away. Tennis courts, a sauna and jacuzzi are on site, as well as an excellent restaurant and a spa with heated pool on a hilltop. $150

8

EATING

Sa Pa has the widest range of **food** in the north outside Hanoi; one benefit of the building boom is that there is plenty of choice, with many places serving a mixture of local cuisine and foreign dishes. To go where the locals are, try the **street stalls** along Pham Xuan Huan, parallel to Cau May, which serve pho and rice; some stay open late into the night, when the focus shifts to barbecued meat and rice wine.

Baguettes et Chocolat 11 Thac Bac ☎ 0214 387 1766; map p.396. Part of a chain that trains disadvantaged children in hospitality, this place offers excellent pastries and, as the name suggests, filling baguettes and chocolate sweets, in a comfortable colonial setting. Mains 80,000–120,000đ. Daily 7am–9.30pm.

Delta 33 Cau May ☎ 0214 387 1799; map p.396. With a prime location and a good wine list, the *Delta* is better known for its pizzas than its pasta (180,000–280,000đ), and the soft lighting creates an intimate atmosphere. Daily 7.30am–midnight.

Le Gecko 33 Xuan Vien ☎ 0214 387 1898, ⊚ geckosapa .com; map p.396. It's moved from one side of the road to the other, and is now under Vietnamese rather than French management, but it's kept the high standards of its forerunner. Its two small terraces are a good place to enjoy a pizza (130,000–170,000đ), a cake or a glass of wine. Daily 6.30am–10pm.

The Hill Station Signature Restaurant 37 Fansipan ☎ 0214 388 7111, ⊚ thehillstation.com; map p.396. The striking design of this restaurant combines traditional and modern features – think stone walls with mat cushions around low tables. The cuisine is inspired by local ethnic gastronomy and features dishes like ash-baked rainbow trout wrapped in banana leaves. Most dishes 100,000–200,000đ. Daily 7am–10.30pm.

Nature View 51 Fansipan ☎ 0214 377 1707; map p.396. You could pay for the views alone here and still feel that you'd got value for money; throw in a selection of reasonably priced Vietnamese and Western dishes and it's a really good deal. The *pho bo* is a good choice on a chilly morning. Mains 60,000–115,000đ. Daily 7.30am–10.30pm.

★ **Red Dao House** 4b Thac Bac ☎ 0214 387 2927; map p.396. Located in a wooden building full of character, this welcoming place ticks all the boxes—good ambience, good food and good service. It has a wide range of Vietnamese and Western dishes, including pastas and pizzas (most mains 100,000–160,000đ). Staff are all Red Dao. Daily 8am–10pm.

Sapa 24 24 Fansipan ☎ 091 542 2268; map p.396. Though the facade and decor are nothing special, the food is excellent (warming pumpkin soup and sizzling hot plates) and prices are cheaper than at most places in town. Daily 7am-11pm.

Sapa Corner 38 Cau May ☎ 0214 387 1238; map p.396. This quiet but classy restaurant features starched tablecloths and dishes like *tartiflette de Sapa* (potato, bacon, onion, cheese and wine in a clay pot; 150,000đ) as well as a good range of wines. Daily 6.30am–10.30pm.

Ta Van Victoria Hotel, Xuan Vien ☎ 0214 387 1522, ⊚ victoriahotels-asia.com; map p.396. This place specializes in French cuisine with locally grown produce, and the meals, service and quality are sumptuous – but with a price to match. Also offers an excellent breakfast buffet that is perfect fuel for early morning treks. Mains 200,000–480,000đ. Daily 6.30am–10pm.

Viet Emotion 27 Cau May ☎ 0214 387 2559; map p.396. Spanish tapas, tempting main courses and a healthy range of cocktails are on the menu at this place – try the salmon with steamed rice (169,000đ) or the pork grilled with cardamom (129,000đ), or start the day with a filling set breakfast. Daily 7.30am–10pm.

Viet Home 40 Cau May ☎ 091 306 9423; map p.396. This unpretentious place serves an enormous range of dishes, including exotics like fried deer and wild pork, as well as set menus from 120,000–160,000đ. If it's crowded downstairs, head up to the quieter first floor. Daily 8am–9.30pm.

DRINKING AND NIGHTLIFE

It's worth taking a walk to **Centre Square** at around 6pm, as there are frequently performances of ethnic music and dance taking place there.

Corner Bar 24 Cau May ☎ 091 605 3009; map p.396. It's not on a corner, but it is a choice spot from which to watch the action on Sa Pa's main street while nursing a bottle of beer or puffing on a shisha pipe. Daily 2pm–2am.

Hmong Sisters Bar 31 Muong Hoa; map p.396. One of Sa Pa's most popular late-night bars, complete with up-to-date music and a pool table – though it can be quiet midweek. The spacious, dimly lit interior also has a fireplace for chilly evenings. Daily 4pm–2am.

Mountain Bar & Pub 4 Muong Hoa ☎ 098 388 9798; map p.396. Popular bar with a good range of beers and cocktails, as well as sports showing on TV. They sometimes serve mulled wine on cold nights and it can get packed at weekends. Daily 11am–1am.

DIRECTORY

Banks There are several ATMs dotted around Sa Pa, and the Agribank (Mon–Fri 7.30–3.30pm) on Cau May can exchange cash.

Post office You can find a post office at Ham Rong (Mon–Fri 8–11.30am & 1–4pm), though service is poor and mail delivery times are exceptionally long.

Around Sa Pa

Most visitors come to Sa Pa to **trek to minority villages** in the Muong Hoa Valley, which separates Sa Pa from Mount Fan Si Pan. Until 2016, only a few hardy trekkers each year were ever successful in scaling Vietnam's highest peak, but thousands now head there each day thanks to the completion of a controversial seven-kilometre, three-wire cable car from Sa Pa to the top (see p.402).

About 12km south of town, the **Ancient Rock Field** is an area of huge boulders with carvings made by humans thousands of years ago. Other possible targets for a half-day outing include the roadside **Thac Bach** (Silver Falls) and **Tram Ton Pass**, both of which are on the way to Lai Chau.

Cat Cat

The nearest village to Sa Pa is **CAT CAT**, which lies in the valley immediately below. Here chickens and pot-bellied pigs scavenge through trailing pumpkin vines, though the sheer number of visitors makes the experience feel less authentic than it really is. Look out for tubs of **indigo dye**, used to colour the hemp cloth typical of Hmong dress, and for interlocking bamboo pipes that supply the village with both water and power for de-husking rice. Cat Cat **waterfall** is just below the village, and is a pleasant spot to rest before tackling the homeward journey.

Sin Chai and Ta Phin

About 4km north of Cat Cat is **SIN CHAI**, another large Hmong settlement spread out along the path. Some tours include an overnight stop here in a tribal house, and you will also have the chance to watch weavers at work and listen to performances of traditional music. Further north, about 10km from Sa Pa, lies the village of **TA PHIN**, populated by Red Dao and another popular overnight stay.

VISITING VILLAGES AND TREKKING AROUND SA PA

While it's possible to wander into the Muong Hoa Valley, pass through a couple of minority villages and return to Sa Pa in a day, for the full-on Sa Pa trekking experience you'll want to **overnight in a home-stay** and get to know something about your hosts. The cost to enter most villages is 50,000đ, though this is included in the price of organized treks; expect to pay $40–60 per day per person for these, depending on the number of people in the group.

TREKKING PRACTICALITIES

It's important to wear the right **clothing** when walking in these mountains: strong boots with ankle support are the best footwear, though you can get away with training shoes in the dry season. Choose thin, loose clothing (long trousers offer some protection from thorns and leeches); wear a hat and sunblock; take plenty of water; and carry a basic medical kit. If you plan on spending the night in a village, you'll need warm clothing as temperatures can drop to around freezing, and you might want to take a **sleeping bag**, mosquito net and food, though these are usually provided on organized tours. Finally, aggressive **dogs** can be a problem when entering villages, so it's a good idea to carry a strong stick when trekking, and always be watchful for the **venomous snakes** that are common in this area.

The Muong Hoa Valley

Heading southeast from Sa Pa along the beautiful **Muong Hoa Valley**, after passing a viewpoint with a fantastic view over rice terraces, the road leads to other **villages** popular for treks such as Ta Van, home to the Dao and Giay minorities, Lao Chai (Hmong), Giang Ta Chai (Dao) and Ban Ho (Tay).

Ancient Rock Field

Follow the Muong Hoa Road southeast of Sa Pa for 12km to the museum

Discovered in the 1920s, the **Ancient Rock Field** is a curious region of inscribed rocks, covering an area of around eight square kilometres between the villages of Ta Van, Hau Thao and Su Pan. It consists of around two hundred large, smooth boulders, buried in the middle of rice paddies or at the roadside, which are clearly carved by human hand; while many of the carved patterns are unfathomable, some pictographs like human or bird forms are easy to decipher. Because of the nature of the motifs, archeologists estimate these carvings to be around 2500 years old. The small **museum** on site documents the stones' discovery, locations and dimensions, with a few samples of carved rocks beside the road and in the neighbouring field.

Mount Fan Si Pan

At 3143m, **Mount Fan Si Pan** (also spelled Fan Xi Pan) is not only Vietnam's highest mountain, but also the tallest in Indochina. It lies around 7km west of Sa Pa across the Muong Hoa Valley. If you like a challenge, it's worth contacting one of the tour operators in Sa Pa like Sapa O'Chau (see p.399), who can arrange one-, two- or three-day **guided treks** to the summit – but you'll need to be in good physical shape to do it. Near the top, you'll see several unusual flowers and trees, such as rhododendrons, and temperatures up here are considerably colder than in Sa Pa itself.

Until 2016, less than two thousand people reached the mountain's summit each year, but since the opening of a record-breaking **cable car** that crosses the valley to the summit, that same number arrives at the top of the mountain each hour.

Fansipan Legend cable car

3km north of Sa Pa on Nguyen Chi Thanh • Daily 7.30am–5.30pm • 600,000đ return or 700,000đ with a funicular ride to the top; taxi from town 80,000đ

Stretching 6292m, **Fansipan Legend** (ⓦfansipanlegend.sunworld.vn) is the longest three-rope cable car in the world, and its altitude gain of 1410m is also the world's highest for a three-rope cable car. Though this enormous project (costing $210 million) was strongly criticized by environmentalists for threatening the continued existence of rare species of flora and fauna, most visitors find it an exciting experience.

Gondolas hold up to thirty people, and the journey up takes around twenty minutes and offers eye-popping views of rice terraces in the valley, churning rivers, waterfalls and dense woodland near the summit. Unfortunately, the **summit** itself is cloaked in cloud more often than not, but there's still no shortage of visitors queuing to snap a selfie at the top. There are souvenir shops and restaurants at the lower and upper terminals. Take a couple of extra layers to put on when you get out of the cable car at the top, allow a few hours for the round trip and be prepared to stand in long queues to get on board at weekends.

Thac Bach

12km from Sa Pa along the westbound road to Lai Chau • Dawn to dusk • 10,000đ

If you plan to ride the Northwest Loop back to Hanoi, you'll pass **Thac Bach**, or Silver Falls, along the way. The waterfall itself is quite impressive during the rainy season from June to October, but as every passing tour group makes a stop here, and roadside vendors are particularly aggressive, you shouldn't expect a quiet time. Follow the steep trail beside the falls to escape from the crowds.

Tram Ton Pass
Just 3km beyond the falls, the 1900m **Tram Ton Pass** is the highest in Vietnam, and when the weather is clear there are fabulous views west towards Lai Chau – but again you'll have to fend off the pestering vendors.

Lao Cai

For most people, the frontier town of **LAO CAI** is just a staging point between Sa Pa and Hanoi or Kunming in China (see box, p.398), and there's nothing to see unless you get a kick out of watching people crossing a border. There are, however, a couple of useful places to sleep or eat, should you get stuck in transit.

ARRIVAL AND DEPARTURE   LAO CAI

By train Most people arrive in Lao Cai by train from Hanoi. If you choose the night service, you'll arrive in Lao Cai in the early morning, saving on both time and accommodation, though a daylight journey offers great views along the Red River Valley and arrives at a more convenient time. Once you've reached Lao Cai's train station, you can hop on one of the shuttle buses waiting at the station for the hour's winding, uphill run to Sa Pa.
Destination Hanoi (5 daily; 8–9hr).

By bus Lao Cai's bus station is just 200m west of the train station, and operates services to towns throughout Lao Cai province, though only a few interest most travellers.
Destinations Bac Ha (10 daily; 2hr); Hanoi (about 10 daily; 5–6hr); Sa Pa (every 30min; 1hr).

On foot If you've just walked across the border from China, you can take a xe om or taxi to the train station, where you can catch a train to Hanoi or shuttle bus up to Sa Pa.

ACCOMMODATION AND EATING

Pineapple 47 Phan Dinh Phung ☎0214 383 5939. Just a few steps west of the *Thien Hai* hotel, between the train and bus stations, *Pineapple* is a welcome sight for hungry travellers, serving *banh mi* (85,000VND), breakfasts, ice cream and beer in a cozy setting. Opens early to catch passengers off the night train from Hanoi. Daily 5am–10pm.

Thien Hai 306 Khanh Yen ☎0214 383 3666, ⓦthienhaihotel.com. This three-star hotel is an uninspiring but clean and adequate spot to rest your head right beside the train station. $30

Bac Ha

Around 110km northeast of Sa Pa, across the Red River, the small town of **BAC HA** nestles in a high valley, 1200m above sea level. This bustling agricultural community enjoys a scenic backdrop of cone-shaped mountains popping up out of the mist; sights revolve around a lively **Sunday market** and **trekking opportunities**, though infrastructure is limited – which in many ways is the key to Bac Ha's charm. One pleasing development has been the clearing of the area around the town's small lake, which backs onto the market and makes for a good, short stroll; another is the opening of some friendly homestays in the area.

Bac Ha gets most of its visitors on a Sunday, when convoys of minibuses arrive from Sa Pa for the market, though Saturdays are also busy with tour buses arriving for the colourful market at **Can Cau** – it's advisable to book accommodation in advance for the weekend. Bac Ha also makes a good base for trips out to the surrounding Flower Hmong villages of **Ban Pho** and **Coc Ly**. If you happen to be in town in early June, ask about the **annual horse races** that take place by the stadium to the north of the town centre. Bac Ha has a formidable reputation for producing war horses, so the local breed should have plenty of stamina.

The Sunday market

Sun 8am–5pm

Bac Ha's **Sunday market**, the town's one big attraction, gradually swells between 8am and 10am, with ethnic minorities arriving from the hills alongside camera-toting tourists visiting with minibuses and SUVs. Until lunchtime it's a jostling mass of colour, mostly provided by the stunningly dressed **Flower Hmong** women looking for additional adornments. The market sprawls over a huge area, and the scene is filled out with a sizeable livestock market (selling horses, water buffalo, dogs, ducks and pigs), meat and vegetable sellers, orchid dealers, rice wine sellers and vendors of backpacks and farming implements. Another section of the market is stocked with ethnic fabrics and other souvenirs aimed at foreign visitors. The town returns to a dusty shadow of its former self by 5pm, when people head home to their outlying villages.

Hoang A Tuong's Palace

Daily 7.30–11.30am & 1.30–5pm • Free

At the northern end of town, on the left along the main road, you'll find the remarkable folly of **Hoang A Tuong's Palace**, formerly known as Vua Meo or Cat King House. Two storeys of pure wedding cake surround a courtyard built in 1921 by the French as a palace for Hmong leader Hoang A Tuong, whom they had installed as the local "king" ("Meo", or "Cat" in Vietnamese, is a disparaging term formerly applied by the Vietnamese and French to the Hmong). The building now houses a tourist information office, with a few displays of local ethnic dress and a shop selling hill-tribe gear.

ARRIVAL AND DEPARTURE
BAC HA

By bus Bac Ha's bus station is beside the southeast corner of the lake. There are nightly sleeper buses to and from Hanoi, along with regular buses to Lao Cai, from where you can catch alternative connections to Hanoi or Sa Pa. Destinations Hanoi (4 daily; 7hr); Lao Cai (10 daily; 2hr).

By tour Your best bet for a quick visit is to take a tour from one of Sa Pa's guesthouses for around $20, which includes spending the morning at the market, a trek in the afternoon and a ride back to Sa Pa, with the option of being dropped off at Lao Cai station on the way back if you're heading for Hanoi.

INFORMATION

Tourist information There's no tourist office in town, but you can find out anything you want about the area from helpful Dong (☎ 0127 780 1988, ⊛ bachatrip.com) at the

Ngan Nga hotel (see opposite). He also offers cheap and rewarding tours of the local area.
Services Bac Ha has a couple of ATMs on the main street.

ACCOMMODATION

The range of accommodation available in Bac Ha is limited, with few people spending more than one night in town.

Bac Ha Homestay About 2.5km southeast of the town centre ☎ 091 468 3833, ⊛ bachahomestay.com. Enjoying

an idyllic rural location and overlooking pathways through rice, corn and soya fields that just beg to be explored, this

---

SOME BACKROADS FROM BAC HA

If you'd like to embark on the Northeast Loop from Bac Ha, or just head for the wonders of the Dong Van Karst Plateau Geopark, there are **two different routes** you could take. The most thrilling – only possible by 4WD or motorbike in the dry season – is to head north from Bac Ha to Lung Phin, then go east to Viet Quang via Xin Man and Huong Su Phi; the road is awful, but the views are nothing short of spectacular. An easier route is to head back down out from Bac Ha towards Lao Cai, turn left on Highway 70 and follow it about 40km to Pho Rang. Turn left just before the bridge and follow Highway 279 to Viet Quang, then left again on Highway 2, which takes you into Ha Giang. The trip takes about six hours in good conditions, but also becomes impassable after heavy rain – in which case you're faced with a long, southward detour on Highway 70 to Yen Binh, then east on Highway 370 and finally north on Highway 2.

traditional house run by members of the Tay minority offers simple lodgings (with mattresses and mosquito nets) plus meals with the family included in the price. $\underline{\$15}$

Cong Fu 152 Ngoc Uyen ☏ 0214 388 0254. The *Cong Fu* has bright rooms with big windows, some of which directly overlook the lake and market. They are equipped with spartan furnishings and clean, tiled floors, as well as smart bathrooms (someb with bathtubs as well as showers). They also arrange local tours to places like Can Cau and Coc Ly markets. $\underline{\$30}$

★**Ngan Nga** 115–117 Ngoc Uyen ☏ 0214 388 0286, ⓦ nganngabachahotel.com. Rooms here are rather plain

but have two-way a/c (hot and cold), and some have balconies. The big advantage of staying here is that Dong, who runs the place, will help you plan a fun trip. Advance booking necessary at weekends. $\underline{\$15}$

Sao Mai Off Ngoc Uyen, west of the main junction ☏ 0214 388 0288, ⓦ saomaibacha.com. The Sao Mai is probably the biggest place in town with three different buildings. It's quieter than hotels on the main road, but service can be hit and miss and rooms vary a lot, from small and dingy to big and plush, so look at a few before deciding. $\underline{\$20}$

EATING

Bac Ha's restaurants are bursting with tourists on Sundays and practically deserted at all other times. Don't expect the same variety that you'd find in Sa Pa.

Cong Fu 152 Ngoc Uyen. The restaurant in the *Cong Fu* hotel produces reasonable Vietnamese dishes for 100,000–200,000đ and has good views of the surrounding countryside. Daily 7am–9pm.

Ngan Nga 115–117 Ngoc Uyen. The *Ngan Nga* has an

extensive menu of Vietnamese and Western fare like spaghetti (120,000đ) as well as Dalat wine at 200,000đ a bottle. The barbecue dishes, served on sizzling hot plates, are particularly popular. Daily 7am–10pm.

Around Bac Ha

8

The area around Bac Ha is not only blessed with picturesque landscapes, but also with villages inhabited by a variety of **ethnic minorities**, including the Flower Hmong, the Nung, the Black Dao, the Tay and the Phu La. Some villages, such as Ban Pho and Na Kheo, are within walking distance of Bac Ha, while others need some form of transport to get there. It's worth timing your visit to attend one or more of the weekly markets, in villages such as Can Cau (Saturday) and Coc Ly (Tuesday), or Lung Phin (Sunday) and Sin Cheng (Wednesday). Contact Dong at the *Ngan Nga* hotel (see above) for more details.

Ban Pho and Na Kheo

It's only a 3km stroll from Bac Ha to the picturesque Flower Hmong hamlet of **BAN PHO**, but the route is not clearly marked so it's best to go with a guide (see opposite). Along the way you'll pass fields planted with potatoes, artichokes, pumpkins, corn and the like. The village consists of simple, wooden houses, and its people have a reputation for making powerful corn wine, so don't be surprised if you're offered a glass. A short way beyond Ban Pho, a country lane leads to the idyllic Nung village of **Na Kheo**, from where it is possible to follow a different route back to Bac Ha. The total distance is about 7km. Beyond Na Kheo there's a waterfall at Hoang Thu Pho where you can swim, about 12km from Bac Ha.

Can Cau

The village of **CAN CAU**, 18km north of Bac Ha, hosts a Saturday market, which is every bit as colourful as that in Bac Ha and located in a fairy tale-like setting amid rolling hills. In recent years this place has attracted the attention of foreign tourists, and the number of minivans here on Saturdays now rivals Bac Ha on a Sunday. The **market** consists of a disparate mix of livestock on sale – including horses, ponies, buffalo and cattle – with traders trekking in from as far afield as China in search of bargains, plus many vendors selling bright pieces of cloth, which attract the Flower Hmong women, already resplendent in their bright outfits. A special section of the market is aimed at tourists, and there are some beautiful clothes, bedspreads and cushion covers on sale – though expect to bargain hard to get a good price. Things are generally busiest between 10am and lunchtime. Other than the market, there's not really much else to see in Can Cau, but the ride there across a high, empty range (with panoramic views on either side) is glorious.

Coc Ly

One spot that's rarely visited by foreigners is the Tuesday flower market at **COC LY**, about 20km southwest of Bac Ha on Highway 154, where Nung, Flower Hmong and Dao women stand side by side selling carefully selected flowers to neighbouring minority groups. A visit here is usually preceded by a night in a homestay at the Nung village of **Nam Mon**, and followed with a boat ride on the Chay River to Bao Nhai. For more information, see ⓦbachatravel.com.

GETTING AROUND   **AROUND BAC HA**

By tour The best way to visit villages around Bac Ha is on an organized tour, which can be arranged through your accommodation or with Dong (☎0127 780 1988) at the *Ngan Nga* hotel. Prices are around $10 for a half-day walk or $30/day depending on the number of people in your group.

By motorbike You can rent motorbikes at any of the hotels in town for $5–6/day. One journey that could be made by rented motorbike without a guide is to Can Cau, as it's on the road directly north of Bac Ha, but you'll need to be a confident rider to deal with the rugged terrain.

The Northwest Loop

Vietnam's topography west of the Red River Valley is dominated by the country's highest range, Hoang Lien Son. From Sa Pa a road loops west across the immense flank of **Mount Fan Si Pan** to join the Song Da (Black River) Valley running south, through the old French garrison towns of **Muong Lay** (formerly Lai Chau) and **Son La**, via a series of dramatic passes to the town of **Hoa Binh** on the edge of the northern delta. The only real sight is the historic battlefield of **Dien Bien Phu**, close to the Lao border, but the scenery makes the diversion worthwhile. Throughout the region, sweeping views and mountain grandeur contrast with ribbons of intensively cultivated valleys, and here more than anywhere else in Vietnam the **ethnic minorities** have retained their traditional dress, architecture and languages. After Sa Pa, the most popular tourist destination in these mountains is **Mai Chau**, an attractive area inhabited by the White Thai minority, within easy reach of Hanoi.

The best way to tackle this **Northwest Loop** is with a rented car (and driver) or motorbike, though it's possible by public transport if you have plenty of patience. You'll need a minimum of three days for this journey, but allowing time for photo stops and exploring places along the way, five to six days is more realistic.

Lai Chau

About two hours' drive west from Sa Pa, the new town of **LAI CHAU** is getting uglier by the minute despite being surrounded by immaculate mountain scenery. Expect to see huge boulevards with hardly any traffic and characterless office blocks, which are of little interest to travellers. That said, save some time to see the lively market in the old town, where various ethnic groups turn up to trade each morning. This town was formerly known as Tam Duong, and is not to be confused with the former Lai Chau that's now called Muong Lay (see box opposite).

ARRIVAL AND DEPARTURE	**LAI CHAU**

By bus Lai Chau's bus station is off Tran Hung Dao to the west of the town centre.
Destinations Dien Bien Phu (8 daily; 7hr); Hanoi (5 daily;

12hr); Muong Lay (8 daily; 3hr); Sa Pa (hourly; 2hr 30min); Sin Ho (2 daily; 3hr).

ACCOMMODATION AND EATING	

Muong Thanh 113 Le Duan ☎0213 379 0555, ⓦlaichau.muongthanh.vn. This is the best of a bad bunch of accommodation options in Lai Chau. It's situated between the old and new towns, but is quite self-contained, with a good restaurant and even tennis courts. Rooms are big and well equipped, though they could do with a fresh lick of paint. It's surrounded by tea fields and

affords fantastic views from the upper floors. $\overline{\$37}$
Tuan Anh Restaurant 83 Tran Hung Dao ☎0213 387 5217. This is about the only foreigner-friendly restaurant in town, situated on the main road by the market. It has an English menu with dishes like fried beef and potatoes for 180,000đ. Daily 7.30am–10pm.

Sin Ho

From Lai Chau the main route veers north to Pa So (sometimes called Phong Tho), after which it swings south on Highway 12 to Muong Lay. However, there's a more challenging, **less-travelled route** (TL128) that heads southwest out of Lai Chau and climbs up to the market town of **SIN HO** before descending to join up with Highway 12 just north of Muong Lay. Set at an elevation of 1500m, Sin Ho is worth visiting for several reasons: there's a small but bustling and colourful **market** on Saturday and Sunday that attracts diverse ethnic minorities; the climate is cool and fresh; there are superb views on the way up and down; and it's not swarming with tourists. Accommodation is very limited and there are no organized treks, but there's nothing to stop you hiking the steep trails around town.

ARRIVAL AND ACCOMMODATION	**SIN HO**

By bus There's no official bus station in Sin Ho, but buses still pull up and leave from the square in the centre of town. Destinations Dien Bien Phu (daily; 6hr); Lai Chau (2 daily; 3hr); Muong Lay (daily; 3hr).

Thanh Binh Zone 5 Sinho ☎0213 387 0366. This is the best of a mediocre bunch of hotels in Sin Ho that provide all the basics (a/c, TV, hot water), but make sure you lock your room securely as thefts have been known to occur. $\overline{\$30}$

Muong Lay

MUONG LAY was virtually wiped off the map when the old town was submerged beneath a new **reservoir**, the result of a dam being built downstream on the Da River. Most of the town's old buildings were lost, though several wooden stilthouses were taken apart and reassembled higher up the banks on both sides of the water. A huge bridge now connects Highway 12 on the east side with the new town on the west side. The *Lan Anh Hotel*, once a popular haunt of travellers, has reappeared in a more luxurious incarnation on the west side of the bridge, offering treks, tours and boat rides on the newly formed reservoir. However, there's nothing to see in the town itself, and Muong Lay is now nothing more than a convenient stopover between Sa Pa and Dien Bien Phu.

> #### WHAT'S IN A NAME?
> Only in Vietnam can things become so confusing. Some years ago, the government decided to **change the names** of certain towns in the northwest region, which is not that uncommon. However, when places began adopting the old names of nearby towns that already had changed their names, travelling became much harder than it needed to be. While some signs have been slow to change on the ground, the new names are used throughout this chapter.
> In Lai Chau province, Binh Lu has changed to Tam Duong, and Tam Duong to Lai Chau. In Dien Bien province, Lai Chau town has changed to Muong Lay town, and Moung Lay to Muong Tra.

8

ARRIVAL AND ACCOMMODATION   MUONG LAY

By bus Muong Lay's small bus station is located in the new town, about a kilometre north of the *Lan Anh Hotel*.
Destinations Dien Bien Phu (2 daily; 3hr); Lai Chau (8 daily; 7hr); Sin Ho (daily; 3hr).

Lan Anh 9 Song Da ☎ 0215 350 9577, ⍵ lananhhotel .com. Muong Lay's legendary hotel offers good views from

its hilltop perch. Rooms are tastefully designed with stone floors and four-poster beds, and there's even a small swimming pool. The restaurant, a cavernous, alpine-style hall, still turns out some of the tastiest food this side of Hanoi. All things considered, it's not a bad spot to rest up. $\underline{$25}$

Dien Bien Phu

South of Muong Lay the road splits: Highway 6 takes off southeast towards Tuan Giao and Son La (see p.411), while Highway 12 ploughs on south for 100km to the town of **DIEN BIEN PHU**, whose heart-shaped valley was the setting during the 1950s for a key **battle** that signalled the beginning of the end for France's empire in Indochina (see box opposite). The town's trickle of tourists tends to be history buffs, and if you're not interested in sites connected to the war there's little else to attract you. That said, the valley's population is predominantly White and Black Thai, and the nearby open border provides an alternative **gateway to Laos** (see p.410).

Dien Bien Phu Victory Museum
Daily 7.30–11am & 1.30–5pm • 15,000đ

To commemorate the sixtieth anniversary of the victory at Dien Bien Phu, this museum exchanged its former premises, which looked like a derelict school surrounded by rusting guns and tanks, for something out of a *Star Wars* film – a futuristic, cone-shaped building with three times as much space for displays. Another subtle change was the addition of the word "victory" to the museum's title, giving a hint at the perspective of events presented within. The thousand or so exhibits focus on the strategic location of Dien Bien Phu, French plans to control the region, Viet Minh preparations for the final siege, the impact of the battle outcome at home and abroad, and the town as it is today. Pride of place goes to an 83-centimetre-tall **bronze statue of General Vo Nguyen Giap**, who masterminded the victory and whose death at the age of 102 in 2013 sparked a national outpouring of grief.

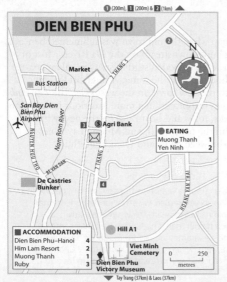

Viet Minh Cemetery
Dawn to dusk

Directly opposite the museum, some of the fallen heroes are buried under grey-marble headstones marked only with a red and gold star, and the stark simplicity of the scene makes it probably the most moving reminder of the battle. In 1993 an imposing Imperial gateway and white-marble wall of names was added in time for the fortieth anniversary of the battle. The exterior of this wall features bas-reliefs in gold-painted concrete of battle scenes.

Hill A1
Daily 7.30–11am & 1.30–5pm • 15,000đ

A small hill overlooking the cemetery, known as **Hill A1** to the Vietnamese and as Eliane 2 to French defenders,

THE BATTLE OF DIEN BIEN PHU

In November 1953, General Navarre, Commander-in-Chief in Indochina, ordered the French Expeditionary Force's parachute battalions to establish a base in Dien Bien Phu. Taunted by Viet Minh incursions into Laos, with which France had a mutual defence treaty, Navarre asserted that this would block enemy lines through the mountains, force the Viet Minh into open battle and end the war in Indochina within eighteen months – which it did, but not quite as Navarre intended. His deputy in Dien Bien Phu was **Colonel de Castries**, an aristocratic cavalry officer and dashing hero of World War II, supposedly irresistible to women, although Graham Greene, visiting the base in January 1954, described him as having the "nervy histrionic features of an old-time actor".

Using bulldozers dropped in beneath seven parachutes apiece, the French cleared two airstrips and then set up nine heavily fortified positions on low hills in the valley floor, reputedly named after de Castries' mistresses – Gabrielle, Isabelle, Béatrice and so on. Less than a quarter of the garrison in Dien Bien Phu were mainland French: the rest were either from France's African colonies or the Foreign Legion (a mix of European nationalities), plus local Vietnamese troops including three battalions drawn from the Thai minority.

Meanwhile, **General Giap**, Commander of the People's Army, quietly moved his own forces into the steep hills around the valley, mobilizing an estimated three hundred thousand porters, road gangs and auxiliary soldiers in support of up to fifty thousand battle troops. Not only did they carry in all food and equipment, often on foot or bicycle over vast distances, but they also hauled antiaircraft guns up the slopes, hacking paths through the dense steamy forest as they went. Ho Chi Minh described the scene to journalist Wilfred Burchett by turning his helmet upside down: "Down here is the valley of Dien Bien Phu. There are the French. They can't get out. It may take a long time, but they can't get out."

French commanders continued to believe their position was impregnable until the first shells rained down on March 10, 1954. Within five days Béatrice and Gabrielle had fallen, both airstrips were out of action and the siege had begun in earnest; the French artillery commander, declaring himself "completely dishonoured", lay down and took the pin out of a grenade. All French supplies and reinforcements now had to be parachuted in, frequently dropping behind enemy lines, and when de Castries was promoted to general even his stars were delivered by parachute; at the end of the battle, 83,000 parachutes were strewn across the valley floor. The **final assault** began on May 1, by which time the rains had arrived, hindering air support, filling the trenches and spreading disease. Waves of Viet Minh fought for every inch of ground, until their flag flew above de Castries' command bunker on the afternoon of May 7. The following morning, the day talks started in Geneva, the last position **surrendered** and the valley at last fell silent after 59 days. A ceasefire was signed in Geneva on July 21, and ten months later the last French troops left Indochina.

The Vietnamese paid a high price for their victory, with an estimated twenty thousand dead and many thousands more wounded. On the French side, out of a total force of 16,500, some ten thousand were captured and marched hundreds of kilometres to camps in Vietnam's northeastern mountains; less than half survived the rigours of the journey, diseases and horrendous prison conditions.

Over sixty years on, the Battle of Dien Bien Phu remains one of the most significant military conflicts of the twentieth century, with its importance in Vietnam's struggle for independence commemorated in nearly every town by a street named in honour of this famous victory.

8

was the scene of particularly bitter fighting before it was eventually overrun towards the end of the battle. You can inspect a reconstructed bunker on the summit and various memorials, including the grave of a Viet Minh hero who gave his life while disabling the French tank standing next to him, and you also get a panorama over the now peaceful, agricultural valley.

De Castries' bunker

Daily 7.30–11am & 1.30–5pm • 15,000đ

There's little to see at the last battle site, a reconstruction of **de Castries' bunker**, located on a dusty country road across the river a couple of kilometres from central

ONWARDS TO LAOS

Dien Bien Phu is only 35km by road from the **border with Laos** at Tay Trang. It's possible to get a visa at the border (prices dependent on nationality), though to be sure, this is best done in advance in Hanoi (see p.383). Buses to **Muang Khoua**, a further 70km over the border in Laos (115,000đ), leave Dien Bien Phu at 5.30am every morning; at other times you can get a xe om to the border (about 250,000đ), though it's a 3km checkpoint-to-checkpoint walk and you may find it hard to get onward transport.

Dien Bien Phu, and now capped by an ugly shelter. Captured tanks, antiaircraft guns and other weaponry rust away in the surrounding fields. Carry on past the bunker and you'll come to a concrete enclosure with a memorial to "Those who died here for France".

ARRIVAL AND DEPARTURE   DIEN BIEN PHU

By plane Two daily flights from Hanoi arrive at the airport, 1.5km north out of town. The journey takes just over an hour, rather than 12 hours by bus, and costs around $80. The Vietnam Airlines office on Nguyen Huu Tho (☎0215 382 4948) is next door: it's a ten-minute walk into town from here, or you can take a xe om (30,000đ).
Destinations Hanoi (1–2 daily; 1hr 15min).

By bus The bus station is located at the T-junction a couple of hundred metres from the centre on the western edge of town. This is also where you catch the numerous mini-buses for Son La and beyond (the first one departs at 6am). The journey to Hanoi is interesting but gruelling.
Destinations Hanoi (several daily; 12hr); Muong Lay (2 daily; 3hr); Sa Pa (3 daily; 10hr); Son La (4 daily; 5hr).

8

ACCOMMODATION

Dien Bien Phu–Hanoi 849 7 Thang 5, south of the roundabout towards the museum ☎0215 382 5103, ✉dienbienphuhotel@gmail.com; map p.408. This place sees few foreigners, though it has simple but acceptable rooms (the VIP choices are good value) as well as helpful staff. $30
Him Lam Resort Him Lam ☎0215 381 1856 ⓦhimlamresort.vn; map p.408. Dien Bien Phu's most extravagant accommodation, complete with swan-shaped pedal boats on a lake, lies a kilometre out of town in a peaceful setting. The rooms are good and the location is superb, though staff are more used to dealing with

Vietnamese tour groups than independent foreigners. $30
Muong Thanh 514 7 Thang 5 ☎0215 381 0043, ⓦdienbienphu.muongthanh.vn; map p.408. This long-running favourite, located to the northeast of the town centre, represents DBP's top lodgings in town, with 150 spacious and comfortable rooms, a decent restaurant, tennis courts and a small swimming pool. $50
Ruby Nguyen Chi Thanh ☎091 365 5793; map p.408. With a central location, and set on a side street off the main road, this place has well-equipped rooms and friendly staff, making it a good choice in DBP. $20

EATING

Locals tend to patronize the **com pho stalls** around the roundabout and along the main roads – it's worth wandering around and choosing the one with the biggest crowd. Look out for the region's speciality dish, which is the Thai minority's black rice (*com gao cam*).

Muong Thanh 514 7 Thang 5 ☎0215 381 2556, ⓦdienbienphu.muongthanh.vn; map p.408. This hotel's restaurant gets the nod simply for its English menu and English-speaking staff, which are difficult to find in this town. There's a reasonable choice of stir-fries and soups, priced from 65,000đ, though it's not exactly gourmet standard. Daily 6.30am–10pm.

Yen Ninh On a small lane running south from 7 Thang S ☎098 988 7513, ⓦdbpcity.wixsite.com/yenninh; map p.408. It's worth hunting down this place for the delicious vegetarian food. Try the Vietnamese eggplant salad (35,000đ) and the fried tofu rolled in seaweed (40,000đ) – you won't be disappointed. Daily 10am–9pm.

DIRECTORY

Bank Head south from the busy roundabout and market to find an Agribank (Mon–Fri 8am–3.30pm), which has an

ATM and can change US dollars.
Post office Located one block south of the Agribank.

Highway 6

East of Dien Bien Phu, Highway 279 heads through lush countryside, where ancient waterwheels still turn beside rivers and streams, then it climbs into steep mountains to **TUAN GIAO**, where Highway 6 takes off north to Muong Lay or south to Son La. From here, it goes over the Pha Din ("Heaven and Earth") Pass, one of the highest in the north. If you're lucky there are great views from the top, but more often than not it's enveloped in clouds. Highway 6 then drops down to the small town of **Thuan Chau**, where there's a lively market of predominantly Black Thai people each morning until 9 or 10am. The last stretch passes through a valley bordered by massive karst pillars before reaching a softer landscape of paddy fields and banana plantations, where more waterwheels feed sculpted terraces, to the industrious town of **Son La**.

EATING   HIGHWAY 6

Thanh Thuy Highway 6 ☏ 0215 386 2408. On the south side of the main road, about halfway through Tuan Giao, the *Thanh Thuy* restaurant is located in a large stilted house and features an English menu. It's a good spot for a lunch break when travelling between Dien Bien Phu and Son La, with main dishes costing 60,000–150,000đ. Daily 7am–10pm.

Son La and around

The welcoming, low-key charm of **SON LA**, the bulk of which straggles for little more than a kilometre along the west bank of the Nam La River, is enhanced by its valley-edge setting, and it merits more than the usual overnight stop. If time allows, there's enough of interest to occupy a few days, taking in the **old French prison** and making forays to nearby **minority villages** on foot or by motorbike.

8

The French prison
Bao Tang Son La • Daily 7–11am & 1–4.30pm • 30,000đ

Son La's principal tourist sight is the **French prison**, which occupies a wooded promontory above To Hieu and offers good views over town. This region was a hotbed of anti-French resistance, and a list of political prisoners interred here reads like a roll call of famous revolutionaries – among them Le Duan and Truong Chinh, veteran Party members who both went on to become general secretary. Local hero **To Hieu** was also imprisoned for seditionary crimes, but he died from lung cancer while in captivity in 1944.

The two turnoffs from the highway are both marked with chunky stylized signs suggesting incarceration; walk uphill to find the prison gates and an arched entrance, still announcing "Pénitencier", leading into the main compound. Most of the buildings lie in **ruins**, destroyed by a French bombing raid in 1952, but a few were restored in 2007, including a two-storey block beneath which were seven punishment cells. Political prisoners were often incarcerated in brutal conditions: the two larger cells (then windowless) held up to five people shackled by the ankles. Behind this block, don't

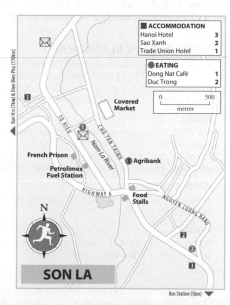

miss the well-presented **collection of prison memorabilia.** Enter the second arched gate and upstairs in the building on your right you'll find a display about the dozen or so **minorities** who inhabit the area, including costumes, handicrafts, jewellery and photos.

Ban Hin

The Black Thai village of **BAN HIN** is located off to the right of the Son La–Dien Bien Phu highway about 7km north of town. The village consists of traditional stilthouses, and most of the women wear the colourful headdresses for which they are well known. The hillsides are covered with plum trees, coffee bushes and stands of bamboo. Some minority villages such as Ban Hin occasionally stage events for tour groups, such as **traditional Thai dancing** or tastings of the local home brew, a sweet wine made of glutinous rice – it's drunk from a communal earthenware container using bamboo straws, and hence named *ruou can*, or stem alcohol.

ARRIVAL AND DEPARTURE	SON LA AND AROUND
By bus Son La's bus station is located 5km southwest of town, so it's necessary to take a xe om into the centre (about 40,000đ).	Destinations Dien Bien Phu (5 daily; 4hr); Hanoi (several daily; 7hr); Hoa Binh (5 daily; 5hr), via the Mai Chau junction (3hr).

GETTING AROUND AND INFORMATION

By motorbike Motorbikes are available for rent in many hotels for around $7/day.

Tourist information The best place for information is the helpful *Trade Union Hotel*, where you can also hire transport and organize village visits with English-speaking guides ($20–30/day), or arrange to see Thai dancing and sample rice wine.

ACCOMMODATION

Hanoi Hotel 228 Truong Chinh ☎0212 375 3299; map p.411. Son La's most appealing hotel (which isn't saying much) has spacious, comfortable doubles and affordable suites on the upper floors, which offer spectacular views of the countryside. Doubles $30, suites $55

Sao Xanh 1 Quyen Thang ☎0212 378 9999; map p.411. The *Sao Xanh* is a centrally located hotel with decent-sized rooms, all with a/c and cable TV. There's even a lift and staff are very helpful, if limited with their English. $20

Trade Union Hotel 4 Xuan Thuy ☎0212 385 2244, ⊚sonlatradeunionhotel.com; map p.411. The rooms here are quite appealing, with canopies over the beds and tubs in bathrooms, though the beds are a bit hard for some. It's the best place in town to find local information. $25

WHITE THAI OR BLACK THAI?

The villages around Mai Chau are predominantly populated by **White Thai**, and those around Son La and Dien Bien by **Black Thai**, but how do you tell the difference? Unfortunately it's not a simple matter that one group wears white and the other black, though the Black Thai definitely have a preference for a black background to tunics and trousers. Here are a few useful pointers:

DRESS
The White Thai don't usually wear traditional dress (black dress and pastel-coloured blouse), except for dance performances and special family occasions, while the Black Thai are renowned for the intricately embroidered and colourful headdresses. Incongruously, many women have a penchant for wearing a crash helmet perched on top.

HANDICRAFTS
The White Thai sell their handicrafts, usually in the form of colourful textiles, while for the most part the Black Thai don't.

ROOFS
Both groups live in stilted houses, but the roofs of White Thai houses are usually thatched, while those of the Black Thai are usually tiled.

EATING

Both the *Hanoi* and *Trade Union* hotels have passable restaurants, but the latter is open to hotel guests only. If you have yet to try Thai speciality black rice (*com gao cam*), then look for it at one of the com pho stalls at the south end of town.

Dong Nat Café 27 Ngo Quyen, off To Hieu ☎ 097 585 8989; map p.411. A neat and relaxing café just off the main drag that serves good coffee and a small range of Vietnamese dishes. Daily 8am–9pm.

Duc Trong 147 Truong Chinh ☎ 097 380 6076; map

p.411. Located right in front of the *Hanoi Hotel*, this welcoming place serves a wide range of Vietnamese staples, such as pho for breakfast and plenty of stir-fries and soups. Daily 5.30am–midnight.

DIRECTORY

Banks There are several banks in town, including the Agribank at 8 Chu Van Thinh, which also has an ATM.

Post office On the main drag, To Hieu.

Yen Chau and around

Halfway between Son La and Moc Chau along Highway 6, the town of **YEN CHAU** is famed for its fruit and surrounded by some very pretty Black Thai villages. One such village is **La Ken**, about 15km south of Yen Chau, which can be visited by crossing swaying suspension bridges over a narrow stream on the west side of the road. With your own transport, you could make a detour about 20km over rolling hills to the **Chi Day Cave**, a popular pilgrimage site for Vietnamese – look for a turning to the west, about 20km north of Yen Chau.

Moc Chau

Around 120km southeast of Son La, the sprawling market town of **MOC CHAU** provides a convenient place for a break. The **cool climate** of this thousand-metre-high plateau favours tea and coffee cultivation, mulberries to feed the voracious worms of Vietnam's silk industry and herds of dairy cattle, initially imported from Holland, to quench Hanoi's thirst for milk, yoghurt and ice cream. Just out of town towards Hanoi, the road is dotted with stalls selling local **milk products** such as three kinds of flavoured milk, thick home-made yoghurt and blocks of condensed milk (which they advertise as chocolate when cocoa is added), as well as green tea. The rigid lines of tea bushes that border the road around Moc Chau create curious patterns, and though there are few side roads, this is a region in which some might want to linger.

Mai Chau Valley

The minority villages of the **Mai Chau Valley**, inhabited mainly by White Thai, are close enough to Hanoi (135km) to make this a popular destination, particularly at weekends when it's often swamped with large groups of students. The valley itself, however, is still largely unspoiled, apart from the appearance of a few new resorts that are popping up between the rice paddies. The bucolic scene of pancake-flat rice fields trimmed with jagged mountains is incredibly photogenic, particularly when the rice fields flourish.

MAI CHAU is the valley's main settlement – a friendly, quiet place that has a bustling morning **market** frequented by minority people who trek in to haggle over buffalo meat, star fruit, sacks of tea or groundnuts. However, most visitors see little of the town, as they are bussed straight into the nearby White Thai villages of **Lac** and **Pom Coong** to spend the night in a homestay.

ARRIVAL AND DEPARTURE   **MAI CHAU VALLEY**

By tour Most people visit Mai Chau on an organized tour out of Hanoi, which usually includes overnighting in a minority

village, or as part of a longer trip into the northwest mountains by jeep or motorbike. Some companies offer day tours from Hanoi but these are not recommended as you'll spend most of the day on the bus. Tour groups tend to stay in the villages of Lac and Pom Coong to the west of Mai Chau and go on organized walks around the valley.

By bus Buses in Mai Chau pull up and leave from the main road in front of the market.
Destinations Hanoi (3 daily; 4hr); Son La (3 daily; 4hr).

ACCOMMODATION

Ban Van Homestay Van village, 1km east of Mai Chau ☎0218 386 7182. This traditional stilthouse has an attractive setting next to rice fields, and its main appeal is that this village is much less touristy than Lac and Pom Coong. $12
Mai Chau Ecolodge Na Thia village, Na Phon ☎0218 381 9888, ⓦmaichau.ecolodge.asia. The most salubrious accommodation in Mai Chau by far is the *Mai Chau Ecolodge*, which sits on a low hill overlooking bucolic scenery. The nineteen bungalows are built using only natural materials, and each has a private garden.

Swimming pool, restaurant, cooking classes, guided hikes and more. $160
★**Mai Chau Valley View** Just south of Mai Chau on the main road ☎0218 386 7080, ⓦmaichauvalleyview .com. Enjoying similar idyllic views to the *Mai Chau Ecolodge* but with smaller rooms at a fraction of the price, *Valley View* offers a sensible compromise between comfort and luxury. Its eight rooms are clean and well furnished, and feature knock-out views from the small balconies. The staff are also helpful (but not pushy) and the restaurant serves a good range of tasty food. $55

EATING

There are a couple of options in Mai Chau, but most visitors eat a simple set dinner with their hosts in their stilthouse accommodation, with the cost included as part of the tour.

Mai Chau Ecolodge The Ecolodge's restaurant serves a fusion of traditional Vietnamese and tribal food, with most main dishes costing 150,000–250,000đ. The setting is quite romantic, with views over rice paddies stretching across the valley. Daily 7am–9.30pm.

Mai Chau Valley View Some of the best food in town is dished up here, including tasty steamed fish in banana leaves. Set lunches 240,000đ, set dinners 300,000đ. Daily 7am–9pm.

8

Lac and Pom Coong

Just south of Mai Chau's centre, a lane to the west leads across a few paddy fields to **LAC** and **POM COONG**, neighbouring villages that are home to prosperous communities of **White Thai** – though these days their wealth is derived more from tourist dollars than from farming. Most **overnight tours** include a guided trek around the valley, which for many is the highlight of their visit. In the evenings, the **traditional dance performances** staged for tour groups after dinner are also interesting, with coy, long-haired girls acting out agricultural chores in a graceful manner. After the show, the audience is invited to join them in a dance and enjoy local wine from a big bowl through a bamboo straw. While too touristy for some, there is at least the chance to stay in a genuine **stilthouse** – a true taste of rural Vietnam, particularly at dawn if your sleeping quarters happen to be above the henhouse. Avoid a weekend visit if possible, when the village is overrun with students from Hanoi.

During the day the lanes between houses are draped with scarves, bags and dresses, with villagers urging passers-by to stop for a quick look. Though it seems a bit commercial, the vendors are not as pushy as their Black Hmong counterparts in Sa Pa, and if it does get tiring then a few minutes' walk in any direction from the centre leads out to paddies and a view of the ring of purple mountains that make for some of north Vietnam's most classic scenery.

GETTING AROUND | LAC AND POM COONG

By bicycle Many houses in Lac and some in Pom Coong rent out mountain bikes for 50,000–100,000đ/day, which

are an ideal way to explore the Mai Chau Valley.

ACCOMMODATION

Most people on a two-day tour from Hanoi overnight in a **homestay**, but you shouldn't expect much interaction with your hosts. Just about every house in both villages doubles as a guesthouse, and all have sit-down toilets fitted below. Some house owners have even changed their roofs from tile back to the original thatch, perhaps to fulfil visitors' expectations.

Mai Chau Nature Place Lac 2 village, 1km west of the main Lac village ☎ 091 478 8884, ⓦ maichaunatureplace .com. If the thought of sleeping on a thin mattress in a room with twenty snorers puts you off, here's a good alternative. You can choose between having a bed in a dorm or an individual bamboo bungalow with private balcony overlooking a stream. They also serve decent set dinners at around 140,000–170,000đ per person. Dorms $\overline{\underline{\$5}}$, bungalows $\overline{\underline{\$30}}$

Around Mai Chau

One interesting route from Mai Chau is to cycle 12km south on Highway 15 to **Co Luong**, passing timeless rural scenes and reflections of mountains in the flooded paddy fields. At Co Luong, the Ma River joins the road, and huge limestone walls and dense bamboo growth adorn the riverbank. The active **market** here on Saturday mornings is worth the trip to see the array of handicrafts and fish.

Some 25km further south from Co Luong along Highway 15 lies the **Pu Luong Nature Reserve** (see box, p.314), over the provincial boundary in Thanh Binh province, though this journey is better tackled by car or motorbike. It's an hour or two's drive to the south, and one that features yet more bucolic scenery, including rice terraces cascading down hillsides and remote homestays – as well as fewer tourists.

Hoa Binh

Northeast of Mai Chau, Highway 6 traverses one final pass before leaving the northwest mountains. It's a steady climb along precipitous hillsides up to a col at 1200m, and then an ear-popping descent through sugar-cane plantations on the east side to **HOA BINH**, on the edge of the Red River plain. The main highway thunders straight past the centre of town on a by-pass, but a hint of quieter days lingers in its shaded main boulevard, Cu Chin Lan, where there are a few simple restaurants. There's little to detain you here, but you could stretch your legs while taking a look at the dam wall southeast of the centre, before pushing on for a couple more hours to either Hanoi or Mai Chau.

Hoa Binh Dam

Daily 8–11am & 2–5pm • Tunnel admission 30,000đ

Less than 2km to the west of the city, the 620m-wide **Hoa Binh Dam** chokes the Da River to create a lake over 200km long, stretching most of the way to Son La. The reservoir is a beautiful place for a boat ride, but its main purpose is to feed Vietnam's largest hydroelectric plant, which came into being in 1994 and has gone some way to solving Vietnam's chronic power shortage.

You can get a worm's-eye view of the dam from the bridge that links Hoa Binh's main street (Cu Chin Lan) with the industrial suburbs across the Da River, or you can drive right up to it – follow Cu Chin Lan to its southeastern end, and continue round to the right. If you're interested in the workings of the dam, it's possible to go right inside the **tunnels** for a small fee. Staff at Hoa Binh Tourism (see opposite) can also arrange homestays in nearby Muong villages as well as boat trips on the reservoir behind the dam.

Muong Cultural Heritage Museum

28 Thai Binh, about 1km south of the town centre • Tues–Sun 7.30am–4.30pm • 20,000đ • ☎ 091 309 5689

This fascinating **museum**, opened in 2015, is clearly a labour of love, and offers insights into the lives of the Muong people, whose villages are scattered throughout Hoa Binh province. It consists of five stilthouses displaying gongs, ceramics, basketware, ancient

HOA BINH DURING THE FRENCH WAR

During the French War Hoa Binh was the scene of a disastrous **French raid** into Viet Minh-held territory, which reads like a dress rehearsal for the epic rout of Dien Bien Phu. In November 1951, French paratroop battalions seized Hoa Binh in a daring attempt to hamper enemy supply routes. They were met with little resistance and dug in, only to find themselves marooned as Giap's forces cut both road and river access. In February the following year, the French fought their way out towards Hanoi in a battle that came to be known as the "hell of Hoa Binh".

rifles and shamanistic paraphernalia. If you're lucky, you might get an explanatory tour from one of the staff there.

ARRIVAL AND INFORMATION   HOA BINH

By bus Hoa Binh's main bus station lies on the eastern edge of town, where you'll find the usual gaggle of xe om drivers waiting to take you 1km into the centre (20,000đ). Buses for Hanoi leave regularly, but note that some terminate at Ha Dong where you will have to pick up a Hanoi city bus.
Destinations Hanoi (every 15min; 2hr); Mai Chau

(5 daily; 2hr).
Tourist information Hoa Binh Tourism at the *Hoa Binh Hotel* (see below) offers boat tours of the dam and hydroelectric plant, as well as of the Muong, Thai, Hmong and Dao minority villages on the shores of the reservoir. They can also help arrange homestays in Muong villages.

ACCOMMODATION AND EATING

As well as the restaurant at the *Hoa Binh* hotel, there's also a group of local restaurants, cafés and ice-cream parlours at the west end of Cu Chin Lan, about 50m before the T-junction.

Hoa Binh 367 An Duong Vuong, about 2km south of the town centre ☎ 0218 385 2001, ⓦ hoabinhhotel .net.vn. The most popular place to stay for foreigners is the *Hoa Binh*, which consists of about forty well-equipped rooms in long, thatched stilthouses. It has a good

restaurant with an English menu, which serves up dishes such as grilled chicken and pork with tomato sauce (100,000–160,000đ), and often features folk dancing, music displays and tastings of Thai rice wine from the communal pot. $60

The Northeast Loop

The provinces of northeast Vietnam, looping eastwards from Ha Giang to Lang Son, are less frequented than their counterparts west of the Red River Valley, though the area is growing in popularity, especially around the fabulous landscapes of the **Dong Van Karst Plateau Geopark** in Ha Giang province. With the notable exception of the geopark, the peaks in the northeast are lower and the views smaller-scale and of an altogether softer quality; there are also less minority folk wearing traditional dress. Getting to see everything is not as straightforward as in the northwest either, though the upgrading of the road between Meo Vac and Cao Bang means it's possible to visit Ha Giang province, as well as **Ba Be Lake** and the region around **Cao Bang**, without backtracking.

Highlights of the northeast are its **rural landscapes**, from traditional scenes of villages engulfed in forest to dramatic limestone country, typified by pockets of cultivated land squeezed among rugged outcrops whose lower slopes are wrinkled with terraces. However, population densities are still low, leaving huge forest reserves and high areas

ONWARDS TO CHINA

In 2014 the border with China at **Thanh Thuy**, just 22km northwest of Ha Giang, opened to foreigners (daily 7.30–11am & 1.30–5pm) carrying a valid visa. This has not resulted in long queues of Western visitors, as the region of China beyond – the first town is Malipo, en route to larger Weshan – is currently as unexplored as the Dong Van region of Vietnam was until recently. However, adventurous types might like to consider this as a less-travelled route to Kunming.

of wild, open land inhabited by **ethnic minorities** practising swidden farming. While many have adopted a Vietnamese way of life, in remoter parts the minorities remain culturally distinct – particularly evident when **local markets**, their dates traditionally set by the lunar calendar, are in full swing.

Ha Giang

HA GIANG is the capital of the north's most remote and least-visited province, just over 300km north of Hanoi, where Vietnam's border juts into China and almost reaches the Tropic of Cancer. Until the early 1990s, this region was the scene of fierce fighting between Vietnam and China, and it is still considered a "sensitive area" even though its inhabitants nowadays are peaceful and welcoming.

Ha Giang itself is a sizeable town, and though its buildings are of no great architectural merit and there's little to see, its setting is very impressive, hemmed in by the imposing Mo Neo and Cam **mountains**. The ochre waters of the **Lo River** curve southward through the centre of town, and traffic is thick on the two bridges that connect the west and east districts. The town is a jumping-off point for a journey into the **Dong Van Karst Plateau Geopark** (see opposite).

Ha Giang Museum
Mon–Fri 7.30–11am & 1.30–4pm • Free

The **Ha Giang Museum**, located just west of the northern bridge, is well worth a visit if you're interested in getting a preview of the many different minority groups who inhabit the province (there are over twenty), or seeing artefacts such as bronze drums and ancient axe-heads that have been unearthed by digs in the area. Archeological evidence shows there has been a settlement here for tens of thousands of years, and the region seemingly flourished during the Bronze Age judging by the number of beautifully designed drums that have been found.

ARRIVAL AND INFORMATION   HA GIANG

By bus The bus station is a couple of kilometres to the southwest of the town centre, just off Nguyen Trai that runs along the west side of the Lo River. Xe om are on hand to run passengers into the centre for around 30,000đ.
Destinations Dong Van (6 daily; 8hr); Hanoi (frequent; 8hr); Lao Cai (2 daily; 6hr); Meo Vac (6 daily; 8hr).
By car or motorbike If you hired a car and driver or rented a motorbike in Hanoi, it's possible to approach Ha Giang from Bac Ha (see box, p.404) as well as directly from

Hanoi on Highway 2. To rent in Ha Giang, contact Vision Travel (see below).
Tourist information The best source of information for Ha Giang province is Vision Travel at 453 Nguyen Trai (☎091 470 1033 or ☎090 209 3223, ⓦ visiontravelagent.com), which is run by James Anh, who can help organize transport and treks in the region. In general, tours should be booked several days in advance, and you should make sure to ask to see the guide's licence – there are several unlicensed operators in town.

ACCOMMODATION AND EATING

There are plenty of **places to stay** in town, though few people speak English in the hotels. It's a different story in the hostels, which have opened to accommodate backpackers heading for the Dong Van Karst Plateau Geopark. There are also several **restaurants** along Nguyen Van Linh, which runs beside the west bank of the river just north of the museum, and you can find the usual soup and rice places around the market on the east side of the river.

Bong Hostel 63–65 Minh Khai ☎091 512 1987, ⓦ bonghostel.wordpress.com. This popular hostel has two ten-bed dorms with shared bathrooms, as well as a private room with an en-suite bathroom. Dorms $5, doubles $10
Ha An 168 Tran Hung Dao ☎0219 386 6242. With its big, bright lobby and welcoming staff, the *Ha An* is about as good as it gets in town itself – it's probably your best choice if you don't have a rented vehicle. Expect spacious, well-furnished

rooms with reasonably soft beds, some with balconies. $17
Highland Hostel 173 Ly Tu Trong ☎0219 949 6888, ⓦ highlandhostel.co. This seems the most laidback of Ha Giang's backpacker hostels, with good-sized bunk beds, comfortable mattresses and reading lights, as well as helpful staff. Dorms $5
Huy Hoan 395 Nguyen Trai ☎0219 386 1288, ⓦ huyhoanhotel.com. This place is one of Ha Giang's

8

GETTING A TRAVEL PERMIT

Foreigners currently must obtain a **permit** (220,000đ) to travel through the Dong Van Karst Plateau Geopark. It's easiest to get one through the hotel you're staying at, but they're also available from Ha Giang's **immigration office** at 415a Tran Phu, at the northern end of the street opposite the stadium (7.30–11.30am & 1.30–5pm; ☎069 242 9184). You should apply for as many days as possible, as you won't be able to extend it – and given the beauty of the area, you may well want to stay longer than planned. In reality, very few if any officials ask to see the permit apart from hotel staff, and in future this requirement may be dropped.

longest-standing hotels. Although it's not much from the outside, it does have clean rooms with traditional furnishings, and the staff are always eager to help. $\overline{17}$

Quan An Ngon 461 Nguyen Trai. This no-frills place serves a range of typical Vietnamese dishes (50,000–100,000đ). They are displayed in a glass-fronted case, so you can just point to whatever you fancy. Daily 7am–8pm.

★ **Truong Xuan Resort** Km5, Nguyen Van Linh Rd

☎0219 386 2268, ⓦhagiangresort.com. Though it's a few kilometres from the town centre, this is by far Ha Giang's best place to rest your head, with rustic, thatched cabins nestled beneath towering trees amid landscaped gardens. Go for a river-view room and soak up the wonderful scenery. They also provide motorbike and kayak rental, and are able to arrange tours of Dong Van Karst Plateau Geopark. $\overline{25}$

DIRECTORY

Bank There are several banks in town, including a branch of Agribank on Nguyen Trai with an ATM just south of the museum.

Post office Located along Nguyen Trai, to the south of the southern bridge.

Dong Van Karst Plateau Geopark

Travel permit 220,000đ (see box above) • ⓦdongvangeopark.com

The main reason for a trip to Ha Giang province is to gaze across the stunning scenery at the **Dong Van Karst Plateau Geopark**, to the northeast of Ha Giang town, which was designated Vietnam's first geopark by UNESCO in 2010. The geopark consists of four districts of Ha Giang province – Quan Ba, Yen Minh, Dong Van and Meo Vac – covering an area of 2350 square kilometres. The region's newfound status has been accompanied by the erection of **information boards** in places with unique geological formations, and though they employ a lot of "geospeak", these boards help visitors appreciate the special nature of the landscape.

The two biggest towns in the geopark are **Dong Van** and **Meo Vac**, both set in valleys surrounded by forbidding peaks and connected by a hair-raising road with spectacular views. The trip from Ha Giang to Dong Van, then on to Cao Bang via Bao Lac, is about 300km and takes at least two (more often three) full days of driving along narrow, bumpy roads, which may become impassable during the rainy season. This border area is home to several **minority groups**, including the White Hmong and the Lo Lo – the latter has only a few thousand members. Most towns along the route, including Dong Van and Meo Vac, have a **Sunday market** attended by villagers from the surrounding valleys.

There's adequate **accommodation** in the region, including some rustic homestays where you can eat with your hosts, but note that **restaurants** are noticeably expensive here, especially in Dong Van – justified, no doubt, by the long haul to get supplies in. Be prepared to pay 200,000đ for a chicken dish or 500,000đ for a big hotpot.

GETTING AROUND

By car or motorbike The best way to explore the geopark is to hire a car and driver or, if you're an experienced rider, rent a motorbike (though it's best to choose a model that's used to dealing with rugged terrain). Rentals are available in Hanoi or at Vision Travel in Ha Giang (see opposite).

DONG VAN KARST PLATEAU GEOPARK

By bus Buses travel between Ha Giang's bus station and Dong Van, passing through Tam Son and Yen Minh. There's a similar service to and from Meo Vac, though at present there is no public bus connecting Dong Van and Meo Vac; a xe om along this hair-raising stretch should cost around 200,000đ.

Tam Son

Roughly 40km north of Ha Giang, after passing a huge, Hollywood-type sign announcing the beginning of the geopark, Highway 4C crosses Quan Ba Pass ("Heaven's Gate"). Just beyond the pass is a pull-off where steps lead up to a delightful view – when the weather is clear – over the town of **TAM SON** and the patchwork fields and dramatic hills around it. Two perfectly rounded karst hills that stand out are dubbed "Fairy Bosom", a typical example of the fanciful terms that Vietnamese, like the Chinese, like to apply to natural phenomena. Unlike most karst outcrops, which weather into contorted and tortured shapes, these perfectly rounded hills have weathered evenly, as a result of their composition – a form of hard-crushed limestone. There's a **market** in Tam Son on Sundays where, apart from the White Hmong, who are the biggest group in this region, you might see Red Dao, Tay, Giay, Co Lao, Pu Peo and Lo Lo people. The valley is great fun to trek or cycle around, and there are a few decent hotels to choose from.

ACCOMMODATION   TAM SON

Hotel Tam Son On the north side of Highway 4C in the centre of town ☎ 097 719 8333. This newish hotel has four types of room, with the biggest containing four beds and representing good value for a group of friends. $̄12

Ly Quoc Thang Homestay Nam Dam village, 3km east of Tam Son ☎ 0164 367 2893. This is one of several homestays in a Red Dao village near Tam Son, and has two houses with basic accommodation, sharing an outside toilet and shower. You can choose to have all meals included for $10. $̄4

Nui Doi Motel Opposite the Hotel Tam Son in the centre of town ☎ 0219 651 0789. This place offers eight spotless doubles and triples, and the friendly owner goes out of her way to help guests. $̄12

Du Gia and around

With an early start from Ha Giang, it's possible to make a side-trip south to **DU GIA** (pronounced "zoozah") and still arrive in Dong Van on the same day. However, there are places to eat and sleep in Du Gia, so it's possible to stay overnight as well. Du Gia itself is a scruffy, unremarkable village, but the main reason for taking this detour is for the unforgettable scenery. About 10km east of Tam Son, look out for a right turn on to Highway 181 heading south. The route passes through the Lo River Valley and the towns of **Lung Tam** (where there's a hemp weaving co-operative that you can visit) and **Duong Thuong**, where the sheer sides of the mountains hem in the narrow valley. A right turn south on Highway 176 then leads to Du Gia, passing several distinctive geological formations such as an "orphan rock", a pillar of limestone protruding from a hillside and capped with a few trees. From Du Gia, head north back up Highway 176 to the junction with Highway 182, and then take a left turn to get back on to Highway 4C at Yen Minh, from where you can continue to Dong Van.

ACCOMMODATION   DU GIA AND AROUND

Du Gia Backpackers' Hostel Highway 176, Du Gia ☎ 091 284 9915, ⓦ facebook.com/dugiabackpacker hostel. There's nothing special about this dorm-style hostel, but it has a convenient location in the middle of Du Gia and offers a meals-included option for $10. $̄4

★ **Du Gia Homestay** Coc Pang village, about 1km south of Du Gia, east of the main road ☎ 0615 772 0252, ⓦ dugiahomestay.com. This is just as you might dream a homestay to be: a beautiful wooden stilted house set amid green fields and away from the hustle and bustle. Outside, there are clean showers and toilets. As with most homestays in the region, $10 gets you full board. $̄3

Yen Minh

Beyond Tam Son, Highway 4C follows a pretty stream for some distance, with steep mountain flanks rising on both sides. After climbing over treeless, terraced hills, which serve to increase the feeling of remoteness, the road then descends into **YEN MINH**. This makes a good lunch stop, especially since there is a reasonable restaurant here and a passable hotel located in the centre of town.

Phuc Cai North of the main road, opposite the Tha Nguyen Hotel ☎ 0219 385 2050. This simple eatery serves a good range of soups and stir-fries. Daily 6am–10pm.

Thao Nguyen On the main road in the centre of town ☎ 0219 385 2297, ✉ khachsanthaonguyen2011@gmail .com. This 54-room, centrally located hotel has clean, bright rooms with flatscreen TVs and smart bathrooms. The carpeted VIP rooms are worth the bit extra. **$17**

Yen Minh to Dong Van

The road splits 4km east of Yen Minh, and whether you go north to Dong Van or south to Meo Vac, the scenery is universally spectacular. Still, the Dong Van stretch is slightly more worthwhile, as it features a Hmong palace along the way. There's very little traffic on the road, which passes through rugged limestone landscapes that gradually get wilder and more dramatic, and there are few settlements at the roadside. For much of the way, the terrain is pocked with blackened knuckles of rock that must make for difficult farming, though small fields of corn are planted here and there, and cone-shaped bundles of stalks, used for fodder and fuel, are scattered across the rock-strewn landscape. The locals, for the most part White Hmong, stoop low under heavy burdens of wood – and it's all too evident that life here is tough.

The Vuong Palace

Sa Phin • Daily 7am–5pm • 20,000đ

At **Sa Phin**, about 15km west of Dong Van, look out for the sturdy building of the People's Committee on the south side of the road. A turning here leads 400m down to **Vuong Palace**. The palace is a large, two-storey residence with three courtyards that was built by the French for the local Hmong king. In 2006 it was subject to sensitive renovation, which replaced many collapsing beams but has retained the integrity of the original building. The thick walls show intricate craftsmanship, and have slits set into them that were used to defend the place with rifles in bygone days. In the shade of pine trees beside the gateway to the palace are several impressive tombs of members of the Vuong family. A newly built **market**, which attracts crowds of colourfully dressed minorities, is held every six days at the junction just west of the People's Committee building. The road north from this market leads to Lung Cu flag tower (see below).

Dong Van and around

East of Sa Phin, the scenery is superb – a constant string of cone-shaped peaks standing over fields in the valley below. Your destination in this direction is **DONG VAN**, the northernmost major town in Vietnam, and arriving here is something of an achievement itself.

Towards the eastern end of town, Pho Co, a road on the north side of the main road through town, features some impressive architecture, particularly in the building that houses the *Pho Co Café* (see p.422). It's also worth hiking up the hill behind, where you'll find the ruins of an **old French fort** and sensational views over town (follow the road heading north from the *Hoa Cuong* hotel). Apart from that, most people visit to witness the cacophonous and colourful **Sunday market** on the street opposite *Pho Co*, where hill-tribe people dressed in their best come to buy and sell pigs, farming implements and rice wine. The town is also the jumping-off point for the **flag tower at Lung Cu**, the northernmost point in the country.

Lung Cu

Daily 7am–6.30pm • 25,000đ

If you have time, head north out of Dong Van and continue 22km to Lung Cu. There's nothing here except a **flag tower**, built in 2010, which marks the northernmost point in the country. Set on top of a hill, the flag tower is reached by a long flight of steps, and the views into China from the top over thatched huts and fields being ploughed by buffalo have probably remained unchanged for centuries.

Hoa Cuong On the north side of Highway 4C in the centre of town ☎0166 319 7888. This towering, 81-room hotel is evidence that Dong Van is finally on the map. All rooms are spacious and comfortable, especially the VIP rooms on the top floor that have fabulous views ($60). $30

Hoang Ngoc On the south side of Highway 4C in the town centre ☎0219 385 6020, ✉hoangngochotel2 @gmail.com. This friendly and clean guesthouse features brightly lit rooms, marble bathrooms and helpful staff. Discounts available during quiet periods. $18

Lam Tung Vao Cho, opposite Pho Co leading down to

the market ☎0219 385 6789, ⓦfacebook.com /lamtunghotel. This place has a welcoming staff, well-equipped rooms and a good restaurant next door. $17

Ma Le Homestay Ma Le village ☎0162 898 6678. Nestled high in the mountains just south of the Lung Cu tower, this homestay is based in a lovely stilted house. It's a great place to sample local cuisine as well as "happy water" (corn wine), and you can also spend time swimming in the local stream. For your money, you get a mattress on the floor and lots of new friends. $2

Au Viet Next door to the Hoang Ngoc hotel ☎094 290 5888. This place has an extensive menu of Vietnamese dishes that are generally very tasty. Though it's foreigner-friendly, it's very popular among Vietnamese visitors too. Main dishes 100,000–500,000₫. Daily 6.30am–11.30pm.

Lam Tung Next door to Lam Tung hotel ☎0165 418 3178. This place has a (sort of) English menu featuring local specialities such as fried stream fish (120,000₫),

which you can crunch through – heads, tails and all. Daily 5.30am–11pm.

Pho Co Café At the north end of Pho Co St ☎0166 420 0511. A wonderfully atmospheric café providing delicious coffee and juices at cheap prices around a courtyard, where you'll probably spend your time taking photos of the bare brickwork and carved wooden balconies on the upstairs terrace. Daily 6am–midnight.

8

Meo Vac

The next stage of the journey, covering just 36km on the way to Meo Vac, is perhaps the most spectacular part of the whole trip. The road clings to the side of a massive canyon and crosses the **Ma Pi Leng Pass** at around 1500m. The views down to the Nho Que River, snaking through a canyon far below, are dizzying. There's a pull-in spot at around the 8km marker, but the best views (right down the canyon) are a couple of kilometres further on. There's little to see in **MEO VAC** itself, apart from a small statue of Uncle Ho and the town's market that overflows on Sundays, but it's the setting, with a ring of mountains forming a bowl around it, that's the most impressive.

Auberge de Meo Vac North of Meo Vac ☎0219 387 1686. Set in an ancestral Hmong house built in the 1930s, this unusual place features mud walls, tasteful furnishings and a big fireplace. Dorms $15, doubles $60

Hoa Cuong Next to the market ☎0219 387 1888. Meo Vac's most popular hotel has good-sized rooms, which come with cable TVs and minibars. $20

Mai Dao On the road into town from Dong Van ☎0219 387 1294. This is the best of several mini-hotels in town, providing decent a/c rooms. $11

May Co Quan Round the corner from the Hoa Cuong hotel ☎096 355 1991. Very popular among locals for dishes like bamboo shoots with beef (100,000₫) and stuffed vine leaves (5000₫/piece). To order, just go to the fridge and point at your choice. Daily 6am–9pm.

Xuan Hac Roughly opposite the Mai Dao hotel ☎091 598 0560. This restaurant is the biggest and fanciest dining venue in town, serving dishes like beef noodles (60,000₫) and mushroom omelette with chicken (200,000₫). Daily 6am–10pm.

Bao Lac and around

From Meo Vac, Highway 217 descends from the karst plateau, passing Tay villages and the small Hmong village of **Khau Vai**, where the annual **love market** on the 27th day of the third lunar month (late April or early May) attracts busloads of domestic tourists, inevitably debasing the event. Snaking its way south, the route passes through the large market town of **BAO LAC**, where there are a few basic hotels. It's worth taking a walk around Bao Lac's market, where you might spot people from the Red Dao, Giay and Black Lolo minorities.

Continuing south on Highway 34, the scenery continues to be impressive, particularly near the mining town of **Tinh Tuc**. If you're heading for **Ba Be National Park**, look for a turn to the south shortly after Tinh Tuc onto Highway 212, which carries you up and over Phia Den Pass at around 1200 metres before dropping down to the valley floor. At the junction with Highway 279, turn west for the last few kilometres to the lake.

ARRIVAL AND ACCOMMODATION

By bus Buses stop on the main road (Highway 34) in front of Bao Lac's market, heading for Cao Bang and Bao Lam (for Ha Giang).
Destinations Bao Lam (5 daily; 1hr); Cao Bang (4 daily; 4hr).

BAO LAC AND AROUND

Song Gam 1km north of the bridge near the centre of town ⊙ 0206 387 0269. This place was under renovation at the time of research, as its friendly owners were in the middle of adding new rooms and a swimming pool. There are lovely views across the river from the back. **$10**

Ba Be National Park

46,000đ

Designated Vietnam's eighth national park in 1992 and covering an area of about one hundred square kilometres, **Ba Be National Park** is a region of astounding beauty, from the lush vegetation mirrored in the still waters of **Ba Be Lake**, to the towering limestone pinnacles that reach over 1500m high. Black bears, palm civets and flying squirrels are known to inhabit the park, but nearer the lake there's a better chance of spotting the more common macaques, herons and garrulous, colourful flocks of parrots. Few people are around to disturb the wildlife, and outside the months of July and August (when Hanoians take their holidays) you'll usually find only a handful of tourists.

Ba Be Lake

Vietnam's largest natural lake, **Ba Be Lake** forms the core of the national park. Enclosed by steep, densely wooded slopes breaking out here and there into white limestone cliffs, the lake is 7km long, up to 30m deep and 1km wide in parts. A few islands dot the surface. Kayaks are available to rent to explore the lake – ask at your homestay or hotel.

ARRIVAL AND DEPARTURE

By tour Hanoi tour agencies (see box, p.367) can arrange three-day tours to Ba Be for around $120/person. Ba Be is about a five-hour drive from Hanoi.
By car or motorbike A car or motorbike rented in Hanoi allows maximum flexibility; good roads connect Ba Be with

BA BE NATIONAL PARK

Hanoi, Cao Bang and Meo Vac to the north.
By bus and xe om This is just about possible – infrequent buses leave from Gia Lam bus station in Hanoi and pull up in Cho Ra, from where a xe om to Ba Be Lake (17km) will cost around 150,000đ.

INFORMATION AND TOURS

Tourist information On arrival, independent travellers should head either for a homestay or for park headquarters

to get the latest information about the two- to five-day tours available in the park – the boat trips to the caves and

---

BA BE ITINERARIES

The Ba Be itinerary usually begins with a boat trip along the Nang River to **Hang Puong**, where the waters have tunnelled a 300m-long, bat-filled cave through a mountain. From here they go on to the **Dau Dang Waterfall**, a stretch of beautiful but treacherous rapids. Take care if you walk on the slippery rocks around the falls, as there has been at least one tourist fatality here. Next up is a visit to a Tay village on the lakeside, and on longer trips an overnight stay in a stilthouse. A road around the south end of the lake has made **Pac Ngoi** less of an isolated Tay community than it used to be; in fact these days its multiple homestays make it tourist central, but several other less-visited villages in the area, such as **Buoc Luom**, **Ban Vang** and **Bo Lu**, can accommodate visitors too. Few Tay still wear traditional dress, and you're most likely to see it only at a minority show at the *National Park Guest House* (see p.424).

waterfalls are the most popular.

Boat trips Most trips are in narrow, covered motorboats, but it's also possible to be rowed around parts of the lake in a narrow dugout canoe. A tour in either costs $20–40.

ACCOMMODATION AND EATING

If you're staying in a **homestay**, your hosts will generally provide well-prepared, though not very exciting, set **meals**. Snacks and drinks are available at the boat jetty by Ba Be Lake, while restaurants in the nearby town of Cho Ra specialize in cooking fish caught from the lake.

Ba Be National Park Guest House ☎0209 389 4026. This government-run hotel (known as *Vuon Quoc Gia Ba Be* in Vietnamese) offers smart but pricey rooms, a restaurant and occasional minority shows. In the summer months (June–Aug) it is often booked out by party cadres, who have deemed it a good location for meetings. $25

Duc Khuyen's Homestay Pac Ngoi village, 7km from the park headquarters ☎0209 389 4140. This is the best of several places within the park where you can spend a night in a stilthouse at a lakeside Tay village. Meals are included in the rate. $12

Viet Trinh Cho Ra, 17km from the park ☎0209 387 6354. The *Viet Trinh* has large, clean rooms and expansive views from the back, plus friendly staff who can help arrange tours on Ba Be Lake. $20

Cao Bang

CAO BANG is Vietnam's northeasternmost province near the border with China, and makes a fine alternative destination for adventurous travellers who want to avoid the crowds in Sa Pa. The province's major attractions are **Hang Pac Bo**, where Ho Chi Minh holed up briefly on his return to Vietnam in 1941, and **Ban Gioc Falls**, Vietnam's highest waterfall, right on the border with China (see p.426). Many who come here are also interested in visiting the markets and homestays in **ethnic minority villages**, particularly those of the Dao, Nung and Tay, who still maintain their traditional way of life in the more remote uplands.

The eponymous provincial capital of Cao Bang itself is a likeable place: its centre may be dusty and noisy, but its riverside setting, with dense clumps of bamboo backed by sugar-loaf mountains, helps to blur the edges. The town is built on the southwestern bank of the **Bang Giang River**, on a spur of land formed by the confluence with the Hien River. The narrow, shady park on top of the low hill in the centre of town is worth a wander, and the **statue of Uncle Ho** is a reminder of the fact that this region was vital to the thrust for independence that he led.

The market

Held daily, the enormous **market** to the northwest of the bridge forms the town's focal point, though there are plenty of vendors selling their produce on the narrow road by the river to the south of the bridge too. It's at its liveliest around sunrise, when locals buy and sell items like honey, sweet potatoes and fish.

ARRIVAL AND INFORMATION   CAO BANG

By bus Cao Bang's bus station is on Pac Bo, on the east side of the river, near the Bang Giang Bridge.

Destinations Ban Gioc (2 daily; 2hr 30min); Bao Lac (2 daily; 4hr); Hang Pac Bo (every 30min; 2hr 30min); Hanoi (hourly; 7hr); Lang Son (4 daily; 4hr).

Tourist information The tourist office is based on Pac Bo, just north of the bus station (daily 7–11.30am & 1–5pm; ☎0206 385 8229). The helpful staff here can provide information about attractions and homestays in the province.

ACCOMMODATION

Bang Giang Kim Dong ☎0206 385 3431, ✉banggiang .tkv@gmail.com; map opposite. Located right next to the bridge, this place has a grand lobby, though the uninspiring rooms are rather overpriced and beds are on the hard side. $24

★**Hoang Anh** 131 Kim Dong ☎0206 385 8969, ✉hoanganh131kdcb@yahoo.com.vn; map opposite. Compared with other options in Cao Bang, the *Hoang Anh* is a standout. Its tastefully furnished rooms are spacious, some with picture-postcard views, and all amenities are clean and in working order. Ask for a room in the new wing next door ($18), where facilities are

even better. $\overline{\$12}$
Huong Sen 100 Kim Dong ☎0206 385 4654; map below. The *Huong Sen* is good value, with river views from most rooms, cable TV, friendly staff and an excellent restaurant in the lobby. The rooms vary in style and size, so

ask to see at least a couple. $\overline{\$14}$
Jeanne 99 Kim Dong ☎0206 385 4187; ⓦ caobanghotel.com; map below. This new place has just ten smartly furnished rooms, which are compact but clean. Helpful staff too. $\overline{\$18}$

EATING

Few restaurants cater to **foreigners** in Cao Bang. If none of the options here appeal, your best bet is heading to the market to track down a steaming bowl of pho. For something a bit more familiar, stop by one of the many bakeries in front of the market, or look out for stalls selling doner kebabs.

Bang Giang Kim Dong ☎0206 385 3431; map below. *Bang Giang* has an English menu and serves reasonable food, with most main dishes costing around 120,000–200,000đ. Daily 6am–9pm.
Café Pho 140 Vuon Cam ☎0206 395 0240; map below. This attractive café has two floors linked by a spiral staircase, and serves delicious coffee (30,000đ) plus fresh juice and beer. Since there's no nightlife to speak of in Cao Bang, this place is fine to while away an hour or two in the evening. Daily 7am–11pm.
Com Phuot Vuon Cam, just north of the market ☎094 844 4123; map below. This simple restaurant is hugely popular with locals for its sausage and fish dishes (most mains 50,000–100,000đ). Go take a look at what's cooking

and point at what you fancy. Daily 11am–9pm.
Huong Sen 100 Kim Dong ☎0206 385 4654; map below. *Huong Sen* has no English menu, but since most of the dishes (50,000–100,000đ) are on display in glass cabinets it's easy to see what's on offer. Daily 7am–9pm.
Nhat Lau 27 Kim Dong ☎091 711 7771; map below. There's nothing like a hotpot to warm you up on a cold evening, and this is the best place in town to get one. Choose from chicken, duck or seafood, served with lots of veggies and noodles, for 200,000–400,000đ. Daily 5–11pm.
Pizza Chi 85 Vuon Cam ☎091 459 3569; map below. The menu here is unconventional, with several Vietnamese dishes like pho and baguettes mixed among the pizzas (60,000–100,000đ). Daily 8am–9pm.

DIRECTORY

Banks There are a few dotted around town – the easiest to find is the Agribank, opposite the *Bang Giang* hotel.
Immigration office If you're going to Ban Gioc Falls without a guide, stop by the Immigration Office at 54 Kim Dong (Mon–Fri 7–11.30am and 1.30–5pm; ☎069 240 9240) to pick up a permit, which costs $10.
Post office Based on a hill in the centre of town, the post office is recognizable from its radio mast.

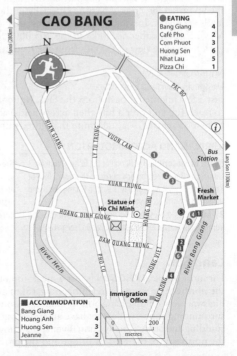

Around Cao Bang

The countryside around Cao Bang is peppered with limestone outcrops and minority villages, several of which provide the opportunity to overnight in a homestay. While the landscape is not quite as dramatic as that around Dong Van, a trip out to **Hang Pac Bo** or **Ban Gioc Falls** will make the journey out here worthwhile.

Hang Pac Bo
Museum open daily 8–11.30am & 1–4.30pm • 20,000đ
Hang Pac Bo ("Waterwheel Cave") is situated right on the border with China, and would attract little

attention today had Ho Chi Minh not plotted the liberation of his country here in 1941. If you're not a fan of Ho memorabilia then it's hard to justify the 50km excursion from Cao Bang, as the cave itself is unimpressive – though the first stage of the journey, passing minority villages moored in rice-paddy seas and tobacco fields against craggy blue horizons, is a memorable ride.

When Ho Chi Minh walked over from China's Guangxi province in January 1941, he took his first steps on Vietnamese soil for thirty years. Later that same year he went back to China, to drum up support for his nascent army, and when he next returned to Hang Pac Bo it was after Independence, as a tourist, in 1961. The **cave** today is a strange mixture of shrine and picnic spot, while exhibits in the small **museum** include Ho's Hermes Baby typewriter, bamboo suitcase and Mauser pistol.

Ban Gioc Falls and around
Dawn to dusk • 45,000đ • Permit required, see p.419

The journey from Cao Bang to **Ban Gioc Falls** takes around two hours and is extremely picturesque, passing several minority villages along the way. After 32km, the route passes the forging village of **Phuc Sen**, where you'll see locals hammering new blades into shape on ancient anvils. Just beyond Phuc Sen down a right turn, **Pac Rang** is a Nung village with traditional stilthouses, and is well worth exploring. If you'd like to spend more time in this area, the scruffy town of **Quang Uyen** is based around the 38km mark and has a friendly homestay (see below). About six kilometres before arriving at the falls, look out for the delightful scenes to the north across the Quay Son River, complete with waterwheels, grazing horses and rugged karst mountains.

At the falls themselves, there are plenty of vendors selling snacks, and it's a pleasant spot to enjoy a picnic on the riverbank if the weather is good. Bamboo rafts offer rides right up by the falls (50,000đ), so you can feel the spray on your face and take lots of dramatic selfies. Though the falls are not particularly high, the broad curtain of water spilling over the lip makes for a pretty picture, especially in the rainy season (June–Oct) when water levels are higher. Inevitably, the falls are less than spectacular in the dry season (Nov–May). If you'd rather not fork out the 265,000đ for a permit and admission, you can still get a reasonable view of the falls from the road outside the entrance for free.

Nguom Ngao Cave
Turn right 3km before Ban Gioc Falls • 40,000đ

Just a few kilometres back from the falls, **Nguom Ngao Cave** requires quite a long trek to reach (up and over a hill, then across fields) and there's nothing unusual inside apart from a "silver tree" – a stalagmite that glitters under the lights.

ARRIVAL AND ACCOMMODATION
AROUND CAO BANG

By car or motorbike For Hang Pac Bo, follow Highway 3 east of Cao Bang, then branch north on Highway 205. For Ban Gioc Falls, follow Highway 3 east to Quang Uyen and then branch north on Highway 206.

By bus Buses to destinations across the province leave from the bus station in Cao Bang on Pac Bo (see p.424).

Kieu-Chinh Homestay 95 Hong Thai, Quang Uyen ☎ 0127 845 4383. This homestay is on the way to the falls and offers simple but clean accommodation (think mattress and mosquito net with shared hot showers). The price includes tasty meals and treks across the area. **$14**

Lang Son

For most people, **LANG SON** is just a meal stop or overnight rest on the journey through the northeast or en route to China, only 18km away to the north. And with a fast highway now linking Lang Son to Hanoi, reasons to linger are even fewer, though the surrounding countryside does have an endearing quality in the form of karst outcrops studding the plain. The **Ky Cung River** splits Long Son in two, leaving the main bulk on the north side of the Ky Lua Bridge and the provincial offices to the south.

The area around **Mau Son Mountain**, just east of town, is good hiking country, and Lang Son is also the start of Highway 4B, a little-travelled back road that cuts across 100km of empty country to Tien Yen on the east coast, offering a route to (or from) Ha Long Bay.

Ky Lua Market

You'll find **Ky Lua Market**, the town's main attraction, along Tran Dang Ninh just east of the highway. This is well worth investigating in the evening when Tay, Nung and Dao women come to trade. Items on sale include food, clothing and household goods.

Dong Kinh Market

The three-storey **Dong Kinh Market** is a temple to Chinese kitsch, where illuminated Buddhas sit in front of posters of Huangguoshu Falls, China's largest waterfall. The broad boulevards south of the bridge are also worth exploring, as the atmosphere is less frenetic than in the centre, and there are some interesting colonial buildings.

Nhi Thanh Cave and Tam Thanh Cave

Daily 7am–5.30pm • 20,000đ each

Nhi Thanh Cave, located off Tam Thanh, follows the Ngoc Tuyen River underground and is worth a look. **Tam Thanh Cave**, a little further along Tam Thanh, features fake stalactites around a temple altar and chambers linked by illuminated paths. One path on the right leads out to a so-so view over town.

ARRIVAL AND INFORMATION   LANG SON

By bus The bus station in Lang Son is on Ngo Quyen, which branches off Le Loi just west of the train station.
Destinations Cao Bang (5 daily; 4hr); Hanoi (every 30min; 3hr).

By train The train station in Lang Son is located just a block north of the bus station on Le Loi.
Destinations Hanoi (5 daily; 5hr 30min).
Information Staff at the *Van Xuan* are helpful.

ACCOMMODATION AND EATING

Muong Thanh 68 Ngo Quyen ☎0205 386 6668, ⊛langson.muongthanh.vn. Part of the *Muong Thanh* hotel empire, which now seems to have reached every corner of the country. The facilities here are very impressive (spa, pool, gym, etc), but the service is a bit of a let-down. $30
New Century Phai Loan Lake opposite the Ky Lua Market ☎098 373 6678. Surrounded by a lake, this fancy restaurant has an English menu – though prices are not

marked, so check as you order. There's a huge range of standard Vietnamese fare such as spring rolls and clay pot dishes, but there are also unusual items such as snake and turtle. Mains 60,000–160,000đ. Daily 7.30am–11pm.
Van Xuan 147 Tran Dang Ninh ☎0205 371 0440, ✉lsvanxuanhotel@yahoo.com.vn. The city's best accommodation, based just north of the market overlooking Phai Loan Lake, has attentive staff and a range of rooms. $18

DIRECTORY

Bank The Vietinbank at 51 Le Loi changes dollars and has an ATM.

Post office The post office is based at 49 Le Loi, next to the Vietinbank.

ACROSS THE BORDER TO CHINA

The majority of people taking this route into China travel **by train**, using one of the two weekly services direct from Hanoi to Beijing. Note that you can only board this train in Hanoi (and not at Dong Dang), though on the Chinese side it's possible to disembark up the line – pleasant Nanning is the first major city.

Alternatively, you can use the **road crossing** known as the **Huu Nghi border gate**, which lies 18km north of Lang Son and 4km from Dong Dang at the end of Highway 1 – it's open between 7am and 6pm. On the Chinese side, infrequent minibuses head to Pingxiang (15km), where you'll find the nearest accommodation. Note that China is **one hour ahead** of Vietnam, and that you must already have a Chinese **visa** (available from the embassy in Hanoi; see p.383) whichever way you choose to cross the border.

STATUE AT THE TAY PHUONG PAGODA

Contexts

History

As a unified state within its present geographical boundaries, Vietnam has only existed since the early nineteenth century. The national history, however, stretches back thousands of years to a legendary kingdom in the Red River Delta. From there the Viet people pushed relentlessly down the peninsula of Indochina on the "March to the South", Nam Tien. The other compelling force, and a constant theme throughout its history, is Vietnam's ultimately successful resistance to all foreign aggressors.

The beginnings

The earliest evidence of human activity in Vietnam can be traced back to a paleolithic culture that existed some five hundred thousand years ago. These hunter-gatherers slowly developed agricultural techniques, but the most important step came about four thousand years ago when farmers began to cultivate irrigated rice in the Red River Delta. The communal effort required to build and maintain the system of dykes and canals spawned a stable, highly organized society, held to be the original Vietnamese nation. This embryonic kingdom, **Van Lang**, emerged sometime around 2000 BC and was ruled over by the semi-mythological Hung kings from their capital near today's Viet Tri, northwest of Hanoi. Archeological finds indicate that by the first millennium BC these people, the Lac Viet, had evolved into a sophisticated Bronze Age culture whose influence spread as far as Indonesia. Undoubtedly their greatest creations were the ritualistic **bronze drums**, discovered in the 1920s near Dong Son, and revered by the Vietnamese as the first hard evidence of an indigenous, independent culture.

Early kingdoms

In the mid-third century BC a Chinese warlord conquered Van Lang to create a new kingdom, **Au Lac**, with its capital at Co Loa, near present-day Hanoi. For the first time the lowland Lac Viet and the hill peoples were united. After only fifty years, around 207 BC, Au Lac was itself invaded by a Chinese potentate and became part of **Nam Viet** (Southern Viet), an independent kingdom occupying much of southern China. For a while the Lac Viet were able to maintain their local traditions and an indigenous aristocracy. Then, in 111 BC the Han emperors annexed the whole Red River Delta and so began a thousand years of Chinese domination.

Chinese rule

A millennium under Chinese rule had a profound effect on all aspects of Vietnamese life, notably the social and political spheres. With the introduction of **Confucianism** came the growth of a rigid, feudalistic hierarchy dominated by a mandarin class. This innately conservative elite ensured the long-term stability of an administrative system that continued to dominate Vietnamese society until well into the nineteenth century.

c. 3000 BC	c. 2000 BC	257 BC
First evidence of cultivation in Red River Delta	Birth of Van Lang, first Vietnamese kingdom	Beginning of Au Lac kingdom

FUNAN AND CHAMPA

While China has always exerted a strong influence over north Vietnam, in the south it was initially the Indian civilization that dominated, though as a cultural influence rather than as a ruling power. From the first century AD Indian traders sailing east towards China established **Hindu enclaves** along the southern coast of Indochina. The largest and most important of these city-states was **Funan**, based on a port city called Oc Eo, near present-day Rach Gia in the Mekong Delta (see box, p.140). By the early third century, Funan had developed into a powerful trading nation with links extending as far as Persia and even Rome. But technological developments in the fifth century enabled larger ships to sail round Indochina without calling at any port, and Funan gradually declined.

At around the same time, another Indianized kingdom was developing on the central Vietnamese coast. Little is known about the origins of **Champa**, but its economy was based on agriculture, wet-rice cultivation, fishing and maritime trade, which it carried out with Indians, Chinese, Japanese and Arabs through **ports** at Hoi An and Quy Nhon. Champa was ruled over by divine kings who first worshipped Shiva and later embraced Buddhism – a fact made apparent in the deities manifest in the extravagant religious edifices that they sponsored, many of which still pepper the Vietnamese coast today (see box, p.220).

Concertinaed between the Khmer to the south and the clans of the Vietnamese (initially under Chinese rule) to the north, Champa's history was characterized by consistent **feuding** with the neighbours. By the end of the eleventh century Champa had lost its territory north of Hue; wars raged with the **Khmer** in the twelfth and thirteenth centuries, one fateful retaliatory Cham offensive culminating in the **destruction of Angkor**. With the installation on Champa's throne of warmongering Binasuor in 1361, three decades of Cham expansionism ensued; on his death in 1390, though, the Viets regained all lost ground, and soon secured the region around Indrapura (near today's Da Nang). In a decisive push south, the Viets, led by **Le Thanh Tong**, overran Vijaya in 1471. Champa shifted its capital south again, but by now it was becoming profoundly marginalized.

For a few centuries more, the Cham kings still claimed nominal rule of the area around Phan Rang and Phan Thiet, but in 1697 the last independent Cham king died, and what little remained of the kingdom became a Vietnamese vassal state. **Minh Mang** dissolved even this in the 1820s, finally absorbing Champa into Vietnam, and the last Cham king fled to Cambodia. Most of the estimated one hundred thousand **descendants** of the Cham kingdom reside around Phan Rang and Phan Thiet, though there are also tiny pockets in Tay Ninh and Chau Doc.

The Chinese also introduced technological advances, such as writing, silk production and large-scale hydraulic works, while Mahayana Buddhism first entered Vietnam from China during the second century AD.

At the same time, however, the Viet people were forging their national identity in the continuous struggle to break free from their powerful northern neighbour; on at least three occasions the Vietnamese ousted their masters. The first and most celebrated of these short-lived independent kingdoms was established by the **Trung sisters** (Hai Ba Trung) in 40 AD. After the Chinese murdered Trung Trac's husband, she and her sister rallied the local lords and peasant farmers in the first popular insurrection against foreign domination. The Chinese fled, leaving Trung Trac ruler of the territory from Hue to southern China until the Han emperor dispatched twenty thousand troops and a fleet of two thousand junks to quell the rebellion three years later. The sisters chose to drown themselves in a river rather than be captured, and the Chinese quickly set about removing

111 BC	40 AD	166
Chinese invade; would rule Vietnam, on and off, for nearly one thousand years	The Trung sisters (Hai Ba Trung) overthrow the Chinese	First envoys arrive from Roman Empire

the local lords. Though subsequent uprisings also failed, the sisters had demonstrated the fallibility of the Chinese and earned their place in Vietnam's pantheon of heroes.

Over the following centuries Vietnam was drawn closer into the political and cultural realm of China. The seventh and eighth centuries were particularly bleak as the powerful Tang dynasty tightened its grip on the province it called **Annam**, or the "Pacified South". As soon as the dynasty collapsed in the early tenth century a series of major rebellions broke out, culminating in the battle of the **Bach Dang River** in 938 AD (see box, p.325). Ngo Quyen declared himself ruler of **Nam Viet** and set up court at the historic citadel of Co Loa, heralding what was to be nearly ten centuries of Vietnamese independence.

Dynastic rule

The period immediately following **independence from Chinese rule** in 939 AD was marked by factional infighting. Ngo Quyen died after only five years on the throne, and Nam Viet dissolved in anarchy while twelve warlords disputed the succession. In 968 one of the rivals, Dinh Bo Linh, finally united the country and secured its future by paying tribute to the Chinese emperor, a system that continued until the nineteenth century. Dinh Bo Linh took the additional precaution of moving his capital south to the well-defended valley of Hoa Lu, where it remained during the two short-lived Dinh and Early Le dynasties.

These early monarchs laid the framework for a centralized state. They reformed the administration and the army, and instigated a programme of road building. But it was the following **Ly dynasty**, founded by **Ly Thai To** in 1009, that consolidated the independence of **Dai Viet** (Great Viet) and guaranteed the nation's stability for the next four hundred years. One of the first actions of the new dynasty was to move the capital back into the northern rice-lands, founding the city of Thang Long, the precursor of modern Hanoi.

Ly Thai To's successor, **Ly Thai Tong** (1028–54), carried out a major reorganization of the national army, turning it into a professional fighting force, able to secure the northern borders and expand southwards. So confident was this new power that in 1076 the army of Dai Viet, under the revered General Ly Thuong Kiet, launched a pre-emptive strike against the Sung Chinese and then held off their counterattack.

Mongol and Ming invasions

Having ousted the declining Ly clan in 1225, the following **Tran dynasty** won spectacular military victories against the **Mongol invasions** of 1257, 1284 and 1288. On the first two occasions, Mongol forces briefly occupied the capital before having to withdraw, while the last battle is remembered for a rerun of Ngo Quyen's ploy in the Bach Dang River. This time it was General Tran Hung Dao, a prince in the royal family, who led Viet forces against the far superior armies of Kublai Khan. While the Mongol navy foundered in the Bach Dang River, its army was also being trounced and the remnants driven back into China; soon after, the khan died, and with him the Mongol threat.

In the confusion that marked the end of the Tran dynasty, an ambitious court minister, Ho Qui Ly, usurped the throne in 1400. Though the **Ho dynasty** lasted only seven years, its two progressive monarchs launched a number of important reforms. They tackled the problem of land shortages by restricting the size of holdings and then rented out the excess to landless peasants; the tax system was revised and paper money replaced

544–602	907	938
Early Ly dynasty; brief respite from Chinese rule	Chinese Tang dynasty collapses	State of "Nam Viet" declares independence

THE VIETNAMESE DYNASTIES

Ngo	939–68	Ho	1400–07
Dinh	968–80	Ming (Chinese)	1407–28
Early Ly	980–1009	Later Le	1428–1788
Ly	1009–1225	Tay Son	1788–1802
Tran	1225–1400	Nguyen	1802–1945

coinage; ports were opened to foreign trade; and public health care introduced. Even the education system was broadened to include practical subjects along with the classic Confucian texts. Just as the Ho were getting into their stride, the new **Ming dynasty** in China were beginning to look south across the border. Under the pretext of restoring the Tran, Ming armies invaded in 1407 and imposed **direct Chinese rule** of Vietnam a few years later. The Chinese tried to undermine Viet culture by outlawing local customs and destroying Vietnamese literature, works of art and historical texts.

Le Loi

This time, however, the Chinese occupation faced a much tougher problem, as the Viet people were now a relatively cohesive force. Vietnamese resistance gravitated towards the mountains of Thanh Hoa, south of Hanoi, where a local landlord and mandarin, **Le Loi**, was preparing for a war of national liberation. For ten years Le Loi's well-disciplined guerrilla force harassed the enemy until he was finally able to defeat the Chinese army in open battle in 1427.

Le Loi, as King Le Thai To, founded the third of the great ruling families, the **Later Le dynasty**, and set in train the reconstruction of Dai Viet, though he died after only five years on the throne. Initially the Le dynasty reaped the economic rewards of its expanding empire, but eventually their new provinces spawned wealthy semi-autonomous rulers strong enough to challenge the throne. As the Le declined in the sixteenth century, two such powerful clans, the **Nguyen** and **Trinh**, at first supported the dynasty against rival contenders. Towards the end of the century, however, they became the effective rulers of Vietnam, splitting the country in two. The Trinh lords held sway in Hanoi and the north, while the Nguyen set up court at Hue; the Le, meanwhile, remained monarchs in name only.

The first Westerners

The first Western visitors to the Vietnamese peninsula were probably **traders** from ancient Rome, who sailed into the ports of Champa in the second century AD. Marco Polo sailed up the coast in the thirteenth century on his way to China, but more significant was the arrival of a Portuguese merchant, Antonio Da Faria, at the port of Fai Fo (Hoi An) in 1535. The Portuguese established their own trading post at Fai Fo, then one of Southeast Asia's greatest ports, crammed with vessels from China and Japan, and were soon followed by other European maritime powers.

With the traders came **missionaries**, who found a ready audience, especially among peasant farmers and others near the bottom of the established Confucian hierarchy. It didn't take long before the ruling elite felt threatened by subversive Christian ideas; missionary work was banned after the 1630s and many priests were expelled, or even

968	**1009**	**1076**
Nam Viet unified by Dinh dynasty	Ly Thai To inaugurates Ly dynasty; Vietnam now "Dai Viet"	Major battle with Chinese Sung dynasty

executed. But enforcement was erratic, and by the end of the seventeenth century the Catholic Church claimed several hundred thousand converts. At this time Vietnam was breaking up into regional factions and the Europeans were quick to exploit growing tensions between the Nguyen and Trinh lords, providing weapons in exchange for trading concessions. However, when the civil war ended in 1674 the merchants lost their advantage. Gradually the English, Dutch and French closed down their trading posts, until only the Portuguese remained in Fai Fo.

Towards the end of the eighteenth century, the remaining Catholic missions provided an opening for French merchants wishing to challenge Britain's presence in the Far East. When a large-scale rebellion broke out in Vietnam in the early 1770s, these entrepreneurs saw their chance to establish a firmer footing on the Indochinese peninsula.

The Tay Son rebellion

As the eighteenth century progressed, insurrections flared up throughout the countryside. Most were easily stamped out, but in 1771 three brothers raised their standard in Tay Son village, west of Quy Nhon, and ended up ruling the whole country. The **Tay Son rebellion** gained broad support among dispossessed peasants, ethnic minorities, small merchants and townspeople attracted by the brothers' message of equal rights, justice and liberty. As rebellion spread through the south, the Tay Son army rallied even more converts when they seized land from the wealthy and redistributed it to the poor. By the middle of 1786 the rebels had overthrown both the Trinh and Nguyen lords, again leaving the Le dynasty intact. When the Le monarch called on the Chinese in 1788 to help remove the Tay Son usurpers, the Chinese happily obliged by occupying Hanoi. At this the middle brother (Nguyen Hue) declared himself **Emperor Quang Trung** and quick-marched his army 600km from Hue to defeat the Chinese at Dong Da, on the outskirts of Hanoi. With Hue as his capital, Quang Trung set about implementing his promised reforms, but when he died prematurely in 1792, aged 39, his 10-year-old son was unable to hold onto power.

One of the few Nguyen lords to have survived the Tay Son rebellion in the south was Prince Nguyen Anh. The prince made several unsuccessful attempts to regain the throne in the mid-1780s. After one such failure he fled to Phu Quoc Island where he met a French bishop, Pigneau de Béhaine. With an eye on future religious and commercial concessions, the bishop offered to make approaches to the French on behalf of the Nguyen. A treaty was eventually signed in 1787, promising military aid in exchange for territorial and trading concessions, though France failed to deliver the assistance due to a financial crisis preceding the French Revolution. The bishop went ahead anyway, raising a motley force of four thousand armed mercenaries and a handful of ships. The expedition was launched in 1789 and Nguyen Anh entered Hanoi in 1802 to claim the throne as **Emperor Gia Long**. Bishop de Béhaine didn't live to see the victory or to enforce the treaty: he died in 1799 and received a stately funeral.

The Nguyen dynasty

For the first time **Vietnam**, as the country was now called, fell under a single authority from the northern border all the way down to the point of Ca Mau. In the hope of promoting unity, Gia Long established his capital in the centre, at Hue, where he built a

1225	1257	1288
Tran dynasty pushes the Ly out of power; Vietnam now "Dai Ngu"	First Mongol invasion	Third Mongol invasion

ALEXANDRE DE RHODES

Portuguese Dominicans had been the first European missionaries to arrive in Vietnam in the early sixteenth century, but it wasn't until 1615, when Jesuits set up a small mission in Fai Fo, that the Catholic Church gained an established presence. The mission's initial success in the Nguyen territory encouraged the Jesuits to look north. The man they chose for the job was a 28-year-old Frenchman, **Alexandre de Rhodes**, a gifted linguist who, only six months after arriving in Fai Fo, in 1627, was preaching in Vietnamese. His talents soon won over the Trinh lords in Hanoi, where de Rhodes gave six sermons a day and converted nearly seven thousand Vietnamese in just two years. During this time he was also working on a simple **romanized script** for the Vietnamese language, which otherwise used a formidable system based on Chinese characters. De Rhodes merely wanted to make evangelizing easier, but his phonetic system eventually came to be adopted as Vietnam's national language, *quoc ngu*.

magnificent citadel in imitation of the Chinese emperor's Forbidden City. The choice of architecture was appropriate: Gia Long and the **Nguyen dynasty** he founded were resolutely Confucian. The new emperor immediately abolished the Tay Son reforms, reimposing the old feudal order; land confiscated from the rebels was redistributed to loyal mandarins, the bureaucracy was reinstated and the majority of peasants found themselves worse off than before. Gradually the country was closed to the outside world and to modernizing influences that might have helped it withstand the onslaught of French military intervention in the mid-nineteenth century. On the other hand, Gia Long and his successors did much to improve the infrastructure of Vietnam, developing a road network, extending the irrigation systems and rationalizing the provincial administration. Under the Nguyen, the arts, particularly literature and court music, also flourished.

By refusing to grant any trading concessions, Gia Long disappointed the French adventurers who had helped him to the throne. He did, however, permit a certain amount of religious freedom, though his successors were far more suspicious of the missionaries' intentions. After 1825 several edicts were issued forbidding missionary work, accompanied by sporadic, occasionally brutal, persecutions of Christians, both Vietnamese converts and foreign priests. Ultimately, this provided the French with the excuse they needed to annex the country.

French conquest and rule

French governments grew increasingly imperialistic as the nineteenth century wore on. In the Far East, as Britain threatened to dominate trade with China, France began to see Vietnam as a potential route into the resource-rich provinces of Yunnan and southern China. Not that France had any formal policy to colonize Indochina; rather it came about in a piecemeal fashion, driven as often as not by private adventurers or the unilateral actions of French officials. In 1847, two French naval vessels began the process when they bombarded Da Nang on the pretext of rescuing a French priest. Reports of Catholic persecutions were deliberately exaggerated until Napoleon III was finally persuaded to launch an armada of fourteen ships and 2500 men in 1858. After capturing Da Nang in September, the force moved south to take Saigon, against considerable opposition, and the whole Mekong Delta over the next three years. Faced with serious unrest in the north, Emperor Tu Duc signed a treaty in 1862 granting

1400–07	1407–27	1427
Short-lived Ho dynasty	Short period under rule of Chinese Ming dynasty	Le Loi defeats Chinese, inaugurates Later Le dynasty

France the three eastern provinces of the delta plus trading rights in selected ports, and allowing missionaries the freedom to proselytize. Five years later, French forces annexed the remaining southern provinces to create the colony of **Cochinchina**.

France became embroiled in domestic troubles and the French government was divided on whether to continue the enterprise, but their administrators in Cochinchina had their eyes on the north. The first attempt to take Hanoi and open up the Red River into China failed in 1873; a larger force was dispatched in 1882 and within a few months, France was in control of Hanoi and the lower reaches of the Red River Delta. Spurred on by this success, the French parliament financed the first contingents of the **French Expeditionary Force** just as the Nguyen were floundering in a succession crisis following the death of Tu Duc. In August 1883, when the French fleet sailed into the mouth of the Perfume River, near Hue, the new emperor was compelled to meet their demands. **Annam** (central Vietnam) and **Tonkin** (the north) became protectorates of France, to be combined with Cochinchina, Cambodia and, later, Laos to form the **Union of Indochina** after 1887.

The anticolonial struggle and Ho Chi Minh

For a population brought up on legends of heroic victories over superior forces, the ease with which France had occupied Vietnam was a deep psychological blow. The earliest resistance movements focused on the restoration of the monarchy, such as the "Save the King" (Can Vuong) movement of the 1890s, but any emperor showing signs of patriotism was swiftly removed by the French administration. Up until the mid-1920s, Vietnam's fragmented anticolonial movements were easily controlled by the Sûreté, the formidable French secret police. On the whole, the nationalists' aims were political rather than social or economic, and most failed to appeal to the majority of Vietnamese. Gradually, however, the nationalists saw that a more radical approach was called for, and an influential leader named **Phan Boi Chau** finally called for the violent overthrow of the colonial regime.

Meanwhile, over the border in southern China, the **Revolutionary Youth League** was founded in 1925. Vietnam's first Marxist–Leninist organization, its founding father was a certain **Ho Chi Minh**. Born in 1890, the son of a patriotic minor official, Ho was already in trouble with the French authorities in his teens. He left Vietnam in 1911, spending several years wandering the world; he worked in the dockyards of Brooklyn and as pastry chef in London's *Carlton Hotel*, then turned up in Paris after World War I under one of his many pseudonyms, Nguyen Ai Quoc ("Nguyen the Patriot"). In France, Ho became increasingly active among other exiled dissidents exploring ways to bring an end to colonial rule. At this time one of the few political groups actively supporting anticolonial movements were the Communists; in 1920 Ho became a founding member of the French Communist Party and by 1923 he was in Moscow, training as a Communist agent. A year later he went to southern China, where he later set up Vietnam's first Marxist–Leninist organization, the Revolutionary Youth League, which attracted a band of impassioned young Vietnamese.

Although many other subsequently famous revolutionaries worked with Ho, it was largely his fierce dedication, single-mindedness and tremendous charisma that held the nationalist movement together and finally propelled the country to independence. The first real test of Ho's leadership came in 1929 when, in his absence, the League split into three separate Communist parties. In Hong Kong a year later, Ho persuaded the

1535

1627

Portuguese create trading post at Fai Fo (now Hoi An)

French missionary Alexandre de Rhodes arrives in Vietnam – his romanized version of Vietnamese script remains in use today

LIFE UNDER FRENCH RULE

Despite much talk of the "civilizing mission" of Imperial rule, the French were more interested in the economic potential of their new possession. Governor-general Paul Doumer launched a massive programme of **infrastructural development**, constructing railways, bridges and roads and draining vast areas of the Mekong Delta swamp, all funded by raising punitive taxes, with state monopolies on opium, alcohol and salt accounting for seventy percent of government revenues. During the Great Depression of the 1930s markets collapsed; peasants were forced off the land to work as indentured labour in the new rubber, tea and coffee estates or in the mines, often under brutal conditions. Heavy taxes exacerbated **rural poverty** and any commercial or industrial enterprises were kept firmly in French hands, or were controlled by the small minority of Vietnamese and Chinese who actually benefited under the new regime.

On the positive side, mass vaccination and health programmes did bring the frequent epidemics of cholera, smallpox and plague under control. **Education** was a thornier issue: overall, education levels deteriorated during French rule, particularly among unskilled labourers, but a small elite from the emerging urban middle class received a broader, French-based education and a few went to universities in Europe. Not that it got them very far: Vietnamese were barred from all but the most menial jobs in the colonial administration. Ironically, it was this frustrated and alienated group, imbued with the ideas of Western liberals and Chinese reformers, who began to challenge French rule.

rival groups to unite into one **Indochinese Communist Party** whose main goal was an independent Vietnam governed by workers, peasants and soldiers. In preparation for the revolution, cadres were sent into rural areas and among urban workers to set up party cells. The timing couldn't have been better: unemployment and poverty were on the increase as the Great Depression took hold, while France became less willing to commit resources to its colonies. For his efforts, the French authorities placed a death sentence on Ho's head; he was arrested and imprisoned in the British Colony of Hong Kong. His release was later arranged by his counsel, who circulated confusion about his identity and rumours that he had died of tuberculosis.

Throughout the 1930s Vietnam was plagued with strikes and labour unrest, of which the most important was the **Nghe Tinh uprising** in the summer of 1930. French planes bombed a crowd of twenty thousand demonstrators marching on Vinh; within days, villagers had seized control of much of the surrounding countryside, some setting up revolutionary councils to evict wealthy landlords and redistribute land to the peasants. The uprising demonstrated the power of socialist organization, but proved disastrous in the short term – thousands of peasants were killed or imprisoned, the leaders were executed and the Communist Party structure was badly mauled. Most of the ringleaders ended up in the notorious penal colony of Poulo Condore (see p.203), which came to be known as the "University of the Revolution". It's estimated that the French held some ten thousand activists in prison by the late 1930s.

World War II

The German occupation of France in 1940 suddenly changed the whole political landscape. Not only did it demonstrate to the Vietnamese the vulnerability of their colonial masters, but it also overturned the established order in Vietnam and ultimately provided Ho Chi Minh with the opportunity he had been waiting for. The immediate

1771

Beginning of Tay Son rebellion, in a village near Quy Nhon

1802

Proclamation of Nguyen dynasty, with Hue chosen as the national capital repercussion was the **Japanese occupation** of Indochina after Vichy France signed a treaty allowing Japan to station troops in the colony, while leaving the French administration in place. By mid-1941 the region's coalmines, rice fields and military installations were all under Japanese control. Some Vietnamese nationalist groups welcomed this turn of events as the Japanese made encouraging noises about autonomy and "Asia for the Asians". Others, mostly Communist groups, declared their opposition to all foreign intervention and continued to operate from secret bases in the mountainous region that flanks the border between China and Vietnam.

By this time, Ho Chi Minh had reappeared in southern China, from where he walked over the border into Vietnam, wearing a Chinese-style tunic and rubber-tyre sandals, and carrying his rattan trunk and trusty Hermes typewriter. The date was February 1941; Ho had been in exile for thirty years. In **Pac Bo Cave**, near Cao Bang, Ho met with other resistance leaders, including Vo Nguyen Giap and Pham Van Dong, to start the next phase in the fight for national liberation; the League for the Independence of Vietnam, better known as the **Viet Minh**, was founded in May 1941.

Over the next few years Viet Minh recruits received military training in southern China; the first regular armed units formed the nucleus of the **Vietnamese Liberation Army** in 1945. Gradually the Viet Minh established liberated zones in the northern mountains to provide bases for future guerrilla operations. With Japanese defeat looking ever more likely, Ho Chi Minh set off once again into China to seek military and financial support from the Chinese and from the Allied forces operating out of Kunming. Ho also made contact with the American Office of Strategic Services (forerunner of the CIA), which promised him limited arms, much to the anger of the Free French who were already planning their return to Indochina. In return for **American aid** the Viet Minh provided information about Japanese forces and rescued Allied pilots shot down over Vietnam. Later, in 1945, an American team arrived in Ho's Cao Bang base, where they found him suffering from malaria, dysentery and dengue fever – it's said they saved his life.

Meanwhile, suspecting a belated French counterattack, Japanese forces seized full control of the country in March 1945. They declared a nominally independent state under the leadership of Bao Dai, the last Nguyen emperor, and imprisoned most of the French army. The Viet Minh quickly moved onto the offensive, helped to some extent by a massive famine that ravaged northern Vietnam that summer. Then, in early August, US forces dropped the first atom bomb on Hiroshima, precipitating the **Japanese surrender** on August 14.

Independence and division

The Japanese surrender left a power vacuum that Ho Chi Minh was quick to exploit. On August 15, Ho called for a national uprising, which later came to be known as the **August Revolution**. Within four days Hanoi was seething with pro-Viet Minh demonstrations, and in two weeks most of Vietnam came under their control. Emperor Bao Dai handed over his Imperial sword to Ho's provisional government at the end of August, and on September 2, 1945, Ho Chi Minh proclaimed the establishment of the **Democratic Republic of Vietnam**, cheered by a massive crowd in Hanoi's Ba Dinh Square. For the first time in eighty years Vietnam was an independent country.

1858	**1867**	**1887**
Napoleon dispatches an armada to Vietnam	Outright French annexation of Cochinchina	Cochinchina becomes part of wider French Union of Indochina

THE NORTH–SOUTH DIVIDE

Although Vietnam was reunified in 1975, there still exists a palpable north–south divide, one that many tourists pick up on as they head across the DMZ. Of course, many of the differences stem from the **ideological division** that followed World War II, and the protracted, bloody war between the two sides; however, there have long been other factors at work.

One of these is the relative **fertility of the soil** – parts of the south get three rice harvests per year, while in the north it's usually one. This leads to a difference in character between north and south – northerners are typically more frugal and southerners more laidback, partly because the latter have historically had less work to do for the same reward.

There are also notable differences in **tradition**. Ho Chi Minh City flaunts its Westernization, while Hanoians are just as proud of their city's colonial- and dynastic-era structures.

Then there are **dialectical** differences – ask a traditionally clad Hanoian girl what she's wearing, and she'll say it's "*ao zai*". Ask a woman from Ho Chi Minh City the same thing, and it would be an "*ao yai*". Trained ears will also hear that there's another dialect at work in the centre of Vietnam.

However, for visitors, the most enjoyable aspect of the north–south divide is likely to be the **food**. The quintessential northern food is *pho bo* – this beef noodle soup is found throughout Vietnam, but originated in Hanoi, where it's still at its best. Other northern dishes include hotpots, rice gruels and sweet and sour soups. Southern flavours include curries and spicy dipping sauces, often married with a touch of sugar and coconut milk to balance the heat. However, most renowned nationwide is central cuisine – both Hoi An and Hue boast dishes of astonishing variety.

Famously, Ho's Declaration of Independence quoted from the American Declaration: "All men are created equal. They are endowed by their Creator with certain inalienable rights, among these are life, liberty and the pursuit of happiness." But this, and subsequent appeals for American help against the looming threat of recolonization, fell on deaf ears as America became increasingly concerned at Communist expansion.

The **Potsdam Agreement**, which marked the end of World War II, failed to recognize the new Republic of Vietnam. Instead, Japanese troops south of the Sixteenth Parallel were to surrender to British authority, while those in the north would defer to the Chinese Kuomintang. Nevertheless, by the time these forces arrived, the Viet Minh were already in control, having relieved the Japanese of most of their weapons. In the **south**, rival nationalist groups were battling it out in Saigon, where French troops had also joined in the fray. The situation was so chaotic that the British commander proclaimed martial law and, amazingly, even deployed Japanese soldiers to help restore calm. Against orders, he also rearmed the six thousand liberated French troops and Saigon was soon back in French hands. A few days later, General Leclerc arrived with the first units of the French Expeditionary Force, charged with reimposing colonial rule in Indochina.

Things were going more smoothly in the north, though the two hundred thousand Chinese soldiers stationed there acted increasingly like an army of occupation. The Viet Minh could muster a mere five thousand ill-equipped troops in reply; forced to choose between the two in order to survive, Ho Chi Minh finally rated French rule the lesser of the two evils, reputedly commenting, "I prefer to smell French shit for five years, rather than Chinese shit for the rest of my life." In March 1946, Ho's government signed a treaty allowing a limited French force to replace Kuomintang soldiers in the north. In return, France recognized the Democratic Republic as a "free state" within the proposed French Union; the terms were left deliberately vague. The treaty also

1890	1925	1940
Birth of Ho Chi Minh	Ho founds anticolonial Revolutionary Youth League in southern China	Japanese occupy Indochina during World War II

provided for a referendum to determine whether Cochinchina would join the new state or remain separate.

While further negotiations dragged on during the summer of 1946, both sides were busily rearming as it became apparent that the French were not going to abide by the treaty. By late April the Expeditionary Force had already exceeded agreed levels, and there was no sign of the promised referendum. In September 1946 the talks effectively broke down. Skirmishes between Vietnamese and French troops in the northern delta boiled over in a dispute over customs control in Haiphong; to quell the rioting, the French navy bombed the town on November 23, killing thousands of civilians. This was followed by the announcement that French troops would assume responsibility for law and order in the north. By way of reply, Viet Minh units attacked French installations in Hanoi on December 19, and then, while resistance forces held the capital for a few days, Ho Chi Minh and the regular army slipped away into the northern mountains.

The French War

For the first years of the **war against the French** (also known as the First Indochina War, or Franco-Viet Minh War) the Viet Minh kept largely to their mountain bases in northern and central Vietnam. While the Viet Minh were building up and training an army, the Expeditionary Force was consolidating its control over the Red River Delta and establishing a string of highly vulnerable outposts around guerrilla-held territory. In October 1947 the French attempted an ambitious all-out attack against enemy headquarters, but it soon became obvious that this was an unconventional "war without fronts" where Viet Minh troops could simply melt away into the jungle when threatened. In addition, the French suffered from hit-and-run attacks deep within the delta, unprotected by a local population who either actively supported or at least tolerated the Viet Minh. Although the French persuaded Bao Dai to return as head of the Associated State of Vietnam in March 1949, most Vietnamese regarded him as a mere puppet and his government won little support.

The war entered a new phase after the Communist victory in China in 1949; America was drawn in and funded the French military to the tune of at least $3 billion by 1954. The Viet Minh, under the command of General Giap, recorded their first major victory, forcing the French to abandon their outposts along the Chinese border and gaining unhindered access to sanctuary in China. Early in 1951, equipped with Chinese weapons and confident of success, the Viet Minh launched an assault on Hanoi itself, but in this first pitched battle of the war, suffered a massive defeat, losing over six thousand troops in a battle that saw napalm deployed for the first time in Vietnam. But Giap had learnt his lesson, and for the next two years the French sought in vain to repeat their success.

By now France was tiring of the war and in 1953 made contact with Ho Chi Minh to find some way of resolving the conflict. The Americans were growing increasingly impatient with French progress, and the Russians and Chinese were also applying pressure to end the fighting. Eventually, the two sides agreed to discussions at the Geneva Conference, due to take place in May the next year to discuss Korean peace. Meanwhile in Vietnam, a crucial battle was unfolding in an isolated valley on the Lao border, near the town of **Dien Bien Phu**. Early in 1954 French battalions established a massive camp here, deliberately trying to tempt the enemy into the open. Instead the Viet Minh surrounded the valley, cut off reinforcements and slowly closed in. After 59 days of bitter

1941	**1945**	**1946**
Ho re-enters Vietnam; founds the Viet Minh	Ho proclaims establishment of Democratic Republic of Vietnam	Beginning of the French War

fighting the French were forced to surrender on May 7, 1954, the eve of the Geneva Conference. The eight years of war proved costly to both sides: total losses on the French side stood at 93,000, while an estimated 200,000 Viet Minh soldiers had been killed.

The Geneva Conference

On May 8, a day after the French capitulation at Dien Bien Phu, the nine delegations attending the **Geneva Conference** trained their focus upon Indochina: hampered by distrust, the conference succeeded only in reaching a necessarily ambiguous compromise which, however, allowed the French to withdraw with some honour and recognized Vietnamese sovereignty at least in part. Keen to have a weak and fractured nation on their southern border, the Chinese delegation spurred the Viet Minh into agreeing to a division of the country; reliant on Chinese arms, the Viet Minh were forced to comply.

Under the terms of July 1954's **Geneva Accords** Vietnam was divided at the Seventeenth Parallel, along the Ben Hai River, pending nationwide free elections to be held by July 1956; a demilitarized buffer zone was established on either side of this military front. France and the Viet Minh, who were still fighting in the central highlands even as delegates machinated, agreed to an immediate ceasefire, and consented to a withdrawal of all troops to their respective territories – Communists to the north, non-Communists plus supporters of the French to the south. China, the USSR, Britain, France and the Viet Minh agreed on the accords, but crucially neither the US nor Bao Dai's government endorsed them, fearing that they heralded a reunited, Communist-ruled Vietnam.

A country divided

In the long term, the Geneva Accords served to cause a deep polarization within the country and to widen the conflict into an ideological battle between the superpowers, fought out on Vietnamese soil. The immediate consequence, however, was a massive exodus from the north during the stipulated three-hundred-day period of **"free movement"**. Almost a million (mostly Catholic) refugees headed south, their flight aided by the US Navy, and to some extent engineered by the CIA, whose distribution of scaremongering, anti-Communist leaflets was designed to create a base of support for the puppet government it was concocting in Saigon. Approaching a hundred thousand **anti-French guerrillas** and sympathizers moved in the opposite direction to regroup, though, as a precautionary measure, between five and ten thousand Viet Minh cadres remained in the south, awaiting orders from Hanoi. These dormant operatives, known to the CIA as **"stay-behinds"** and to the Communists as "winter cadres", were joined by spies who infiltrated the Catholic move south. In line with the terms of the ceasefire, Ho Chi Minh's army marched into Hanoi on October 9, 1954, even as the last French forces were still trooping out.

The Geneva Accords were still being thrashed out as Emperor Bao Dai named himself president and **Ngo Dinh Diem** ("Zee-em") prime minister of South Vietnam, on July 7. A Catholic, and vehemently anti-Communist, Diem knew that Ho Chi Minh would win the lion's share of votes in the proposed elections, and therefore steadfastly refused to countenance them. His mandate "strengthened" by an October 1955 **referendum** (the prime minister's garnering of 98.2 percent of votes cast was more indicative of the blatancy of his vote-rigging than of any popular support), Diem promptly ousted Bao Dai from the chain of command, and declared himself president of the Republic of Vietnam.

1949	**1951**	**1953**
Bao Dai becomes head of Associated State of Vietnam	Viet Minh launches attack on Hanoi	French approach Ho Chi Minh for ceasefire

STREET NAMES

In travelling around Vietnam, it doesn't take long before you can recite the **street names**, a litany of the principal characters in Vietnamese history. Just a few from this cast list of famous revolutionaries, party leaders, legendary kings and peasant heroes are given below. Other favoured names commemorate the glorious victories of Bach Dang and Dien Bien Phu, and the momentous date when Saigon was "liberated" in 1975: 30 Thang 4 (30 April).

Hai Ba Trung The two Trung sisters led a popular uprising against the Chinese occupying army in 40 AD and established a short-lived kingdom (see p.430).

Hoang Hoa Tham (or De Tham) Famous pirate with a Robin Hood reputation and anti-French tendencies, assassinated in 1913.

Hung Vuong The semi-mythological Hung kings ruled an embryonic kingdom, Van Lang, around 2000 BC.

Le Duan General Secretary of the Communist Party, 1960–86.

Le Hong Phong Leading Communist and patriot who died from torture in Poulo Condore prison (Con Son Island) in 1942.

Le Loi One of the most revered Vietnamese heroes, Le Loi defeated the Ming Chinese in 1427, and then ruled as King Le Thai To.

Ngo Quyen First ruler of an independent Vietnam following his defeat of the Chinese armies in 938 AD (see box, p.325).

Nguyen Hue Middle member of the three Nguyen brothers who led the Tay Son rebellion in the 1770s (see box, p.433), and then ruled briefly as Emperor Quang Trung.

Nguyen Thai Hoc Founding member of the Vietnam Nationalist Party (VNQDD), executed in 1930 following the disastrous Yen Bai uprising.

Nguyen Thi Minh Khai Prominent anticolonialist revolutionary of the 1930s, the wife of Le Hong Phong and sister-in-law of General Giap.

Nguyen Trai Brilliant strategist who helped mastermind Le Loi's victories over the Chinese. His ideas on the popular struggle ("it is better to conquer hearts than citadels") were used to good effect by Northern leaders in the French and American wars.

Pham Ngu Lao General in the army of Tran Hung Dao.

Phan Boi Chau Influential leader of the anticolonial movement in the early twentieth century.

Tran Hung Dao Thirteenth-century general who beat the Mongols twice in the space of four years, and reached the ripe old age of 87.

Tran Phu Founding member and first General Secretary of the Indochinese Communist Party, he died in prison in 1931 at the age of 27.

Diem's heavy-handed approach to Viet Minh dissidents still in the South was hopelessly misguided: although the subsequent **witch-hunt** decimated Viet Minh numbers, the brutal and indiscriminate nature of the operation caused widespread discontent – all dissenters were targeted, Viet Minh, Communist or otherwise. As the supposed "free world democracy" of the South mutated into a police state, over fifty thousand citizens died in Diem's pogrom.

Back in Hanoi…

In Hanoi, meanwhile, Ho Chi Minh's government was finding it had problems of its own as, aided by droves of Chinese advisers, it set about constructing a socialist society. Years of warring with France had profoundly damaged the country's infrastructure, and

1954	1954
End of French War – almost three hundred thousand lives had been lost, the majority Vietnamese	Geneva Accords divide Vietnam at the Seventeenth Parallel

now it found itself deprived of the South's plentiful rice stocks. Worse still, the **land reforms** of the mid-1950s, vaunted as a Robin Hood-style redistribution of land, saw thousands of innocents "tried" as landlords by ad hoc **People's Agricultural Reform Tribunals**, tortured and then executed or set to work in labour camps. "Reactionaries" were also denounced and punished, often for such imperialist "crimes" as possessing works of the great French poets and novelists. The **Rectification of Errors Campaign** of 1956 at least released many victims of the reforms from imprisonment, but as Ho Chi Minh himself said, "one cannot wake the dead".

With Hanoi so preoccupied with getting its own house in order, Viet Minh guerrillas south of the Seventeenth Parallel were for several years left to fend for themselves. For the most part, they sat tight in the face of Diem's reprisals, although guerrilla strikes became increasingly common towards the end of the 1950s, often taking the form of assassinations of government officials. Only in 1959 did the erosion of their ranks prompt Hanoi to shift up a gear and endorse a more overtly military stance. Conscription was introduced in April 1960, cadres and hardware began to creep down the **Ho Chi Minh Trail** (see box, p.387), and at the end of the year Hanoi orchestrated the creation of the **National Liberation Front** (NLF), which drew together all opposition forces in the South. Diem dubbed its guerrilla fighters **Viet Cong**, or VC (Vietnamese Communists) – a name which stuck, though in reality the NLF represented a united front of Catholic, Buddhist, Communist and non-Communist nationalists.

The American War

American dollars had been supporting the French war effort in Indochina since 1950. In early 1955 the White House began to bankroll Diem's government and the training of his army, the **ARVN** (Army of the Republic of Vietnam). Behind these policies lay the fear of the chain reaction that could follow in Southeast Asia, were South Vietnam to be overrun by Communism – the so-called **Domino Effect** – and, more cynically, what this would mean for US access to raw materials, trade routes and markets. Though President John F. Kennedy baulked at the prospect of large-scale American intervention, by the summer of 1962 there were twelve thousand American advisers in South Vietnam.

Despite all these injections of money, Diem's incompetent and unpopular government was losing ground to the Viet Cong in the battle for the hearts and minds of the population. Particularly damaging to the government was its **Strategic Hamlets Programme**. Formulated in 1962 and based on British methods used during the Malayan Emergency, the programme forcibly relocated entire villages into fortified stockades, with the aim of keeping the Viet Cong at bay. Ill-conceived, insensitive and open to exploitation by corrupt officials, the programme had the opposite effect, driving many disgruntled villagers into the arms of the resistance.

Militarily, things were little better. If America needed proof that Diem's government was struggling to subdue the guerrillas, it came in January 1963, at the **Battle of Ap Bac**, where incompetent ARVN troops suffered heavy losses against a greatly outnumbered Viet Cong force. Four months later, Buddhists celebrating Buddha's birthday were fired upon by ARVN soldiers in Hue, sparking off riots and demonstrations against religious repression, and provoking **Thich Quang Duc**'s infamous self-immolation in Saigon (see box, p.79). Fearing that the Communists would gain further by Diem's unpopularity,

1956	1959	1960
Rectification of Errors Campaign begins	Hanoi adopts tougher military stance against guerrillas	Conscription introduced

> **THE HUMAN COST OF THE WAR IN VIETNAM**
> The **toll** of the American War in human terms is staggering. Of the 3.3 million Americans who
> served in Vietnam between 1965 and 1973, some 58,000 died and more than 150,000 received
> wounds that required hospital treatment. The ARVN lost 250,000 troops, while perhaps two
> million **civilians** were killed in the South. Hanoi declared that over two million North
> Vietnamese civilians and one million troops died during the war. Many more on both sides are
> still listed as "missing in action" (MIA). Since 1975, an estimated 35,000 people – a third of them
> children – have been killed by leftover ordnance, while **contamination** from Agent Orange
> (see p.470) and other chemicals continues to cause health problems. In the US, some half a
> million veterans suffer from post-traumatic stress disorder, while **veteran suicides** have now
> exceeded the total number of US fatalities during the conflict.

America tacitly sanctioned his ousting in a **coup** on November 1; Diem escaped with
his brother to Cho Lon, only to be shot the following day.

The capital staggered from coup to coup, but corruption, nepotism and dependence
upon American support remained constant. In the countryside, meanwhile, the Viet
Cong were forging a solid base of popular support. Observing Southern instability,
Hanoi in early 1964 proceeded to send battalions of **NVA** (North Vietnamese Army)
infantrymen down the Ho Chi Minh Trail, with ten thousand Northern troops hitting
the trail in the first year. For America, unwilling to see the Communists granted a say
in the running of the South, yet unable to envisage Saigon's generals fending them off,
the only option seemed to be to "**Americanize**" the conflict.

In August 1964, a chance came to do just that, when the American destroyer USS
Maddox allegedly suffered an unprovoked attack from North Vietnamese craft; two
days afterwards, the *Maddox* and another ship, the *C Turner Joy*, reported a second
attack. Years later it emerged that the *Maddox* had been taking part in a covert mission
to monitor coastal installations, and that the second incident almost certainly never
happened. Nevertheless, reprisals followed in the form of 64 **bombing** sorties against
Northern coastal bases. And back in Washington, senators voted through the **Tonkin
Gulf Resolution**, empowering Johnson to deploy regular American troops in Vietnam,
"to prevent further aggression".

Operation Rolling Thunder
An NVA attack upon the highland town of Pleiku in February 1965 curtailed several
months of US procrastination about how best to prosecute the war in Vietnam, and
elicited **Operation Flaming Dart**, a concerted bombing raid on NVA camps above the
Seventeenth Parallel. **Operation Rolling Thunder**, a sustained carpet-bombing campaign,
kicked in a month later; by the time of its suspension three and a half years later, its
350,000 sorties had seen twice the tonnage of bombs dropped (around eight hundred
daily) as had fallen on all World War II's theatres of war. Despite such impressive
statistics, Rolling Thunder failed either to break the North's sources and lines of supply,
or to coerce Hanoi into a suspension of activities in the South. Bombing served only to
strengthen the resilience of the North, whose population was mobilized to rebuild
bridges, roads and railways as quickly as they were damaged. Moreover, NVA troops
continued to infiltrate the South in increasing numbers.

1962	1963
12,000 American advisers in Vietnam	Buddhists killed in Hue; Thich Quang Duc sets fire to himself in protest

WAR TERMINOLOGY

A wholly unconventional conflict at the time, the American War gave birth to a raft of new terms, many of which have been reinforced through movies and other wars. Missions to flush active Viet Cong soldiers out of villages, which were initiated towards the end of 1965, became known as **Search and Destroy** operations; the most infamous of these resulted in the My Lai massacre (see p.238). In the highlands, **firebases** were established, from where howitzers could rain fire upon NVA troop movements; elsewhere, **free fire zones** – areas cleared of villagers to enable bombing of their supposed guerrilla occupants – were declared. In addition, **scorched earth**, the policy of denuding and razing vast swathes of land in order to rob the Viet Cong of cover, was introduced. One such way of doing this was with the use of **Agent Orange**, another term that has gone down in infamy, as have specific missions such as **Operation Rolling Thunder**. And all the while, generals in the field were quick to establish that most symbolic arbiter in this bitter war, the **body count**, according to which missions succeeded or failed.

As far back as 1954, the American politician William F. Knowland had warned that "using United States ground forces in the Indochina jungle would be like trying to cover an elephant with a handkerchief – you just can't do it". His words fell on deaf ears. The first regular **American troops** from the 3rd US Marine Division landed at Da Nang in March 1965; by the end of the year, two hundred thousand GIs were in Vietnam, approaching half a million by the winter of 1967. In addition, there were large numbers of Australians and South Koreans, plus smaller units of New Zealanders, Thais and Filipinos. The war these troops fought was a dirty, dispiriting and frustrating one: for the most part, it was a guerrilla conflict against an invisible enemy able to disappear into the nearest village, leaving them unable to trust even civilians.

In the **North**, outrage at the merciless bombing campaign meted out by a remote foreign aggressor engendered a sense of anticolonial purpose; in the **South**, there was only disorientation. To some, the immensity of the US presence seemed to preclude the possibility of a protracted conflict, and was therefore welcome; to others, it felt so much like an invasion, especially when GIs began to uproot them and destroy their land, that they supported or joined the NLF. The Viet Cong themselves were no angels, though, often imposing a reign of terror, augmented by summary executions of alleged traitors. What's more, successive Saigon governments were corrupt and unpopular, but the alternative was the Northern Communists so gruesomely depicted by American propaganda.

To survive, villagers quickly learned to react, and to say the right thing to the right person. Trying to appease the two sets of soldiers they encountered in the space of a day was like treading a tightrope, creating a climate of hatred and distrust that turned neighbours into informants. Since children were conscripted by whichever side reached them first, brothers and sisters often found themselves fighting on opposing sides.

The Tet Offensive

On January 21, 1968, around forty thousand NVA troops laid siege to a remote American military base at **Khe Sanh**, near the Lao border northwest of Hue. Wary that the confrontation might become an American Dien Bien Phu – an analogy that in reality held no water, given the US's superior air power – America responded, to borrow the military jargon of the day, "with extreme prejudice", notching up a Communist body

1965	1969	1973
US Army launches massive carpet-bombing campaign known as Operation Rolling Thunder	Death of Ho Chi Minh	Peace treaty ends American War; millions died in the conflict, the vast majority of them Vietnamese

count of over ten thousand in a carpet-bombing campaign graphically labelled "Niagara". However, such losses were seen as a necessary evil by the Communists, for whom Khe Sanh was primarily a decoy to steer US troops and attention away from the **Tet Offensive** that exploded a week later. In the early hours of January 31, a combined force of seventy thousand Communists (most of them Viet Cong) violated a New Year truce to launch offensives on over a hundred urban centres across the South. The campaign failed to achieve its objective of imposing Viet Cong representation in the Southern government; only in Hue did Viet Cong forces manage to hold out for more than a few days.

But success did register across the Pacific, where the offensive caused a sea change in popular perceptions of the war. Thus far, Washington's propaganda machine had largely convinced the public that the war in Vietnam was under control; events in 1968 flew in the face of this charade. Around two thousand American GIs had died during the Tet Offensive, but symbolically more damaging was the audacious assault mounted, on the first day of the offensive, by a crack Viet Cong commando team on the compound of the **US Embassy in Saigon**.

On March 31, President Johnson announced a virtual cessation of bombing; a month later, the first bout of diplomatic sparring that was to grind on for five years was held in Paris; and, before the year was out, a full end to bombing had been declared.

Nixon's presidency

Richard Nixon's term of office commenced in January 1969, on the back of a campaign in which he promised to "end the war and win the peace". His quest for a solution that would facilitate an American pull-out without tarnishing its image led Nixon to pursue the strategy of "**Vietnamization**", a gradual US withdrawal coupled with a stiffening of ARVN forces and hardware. Though the number of US troops in Vietnam reached an all-time peak of 540,000 early on in 1969, 60,000 of these were home for Christmas, and by the end of 1970 only 280,000 remained. Over the same time period, ARVN numbers almost doubled, from 640,000 to well over a million.

However, the NVA had for several years been stockpiling both men and supplies in **Cambodia**, and in March 1969 US covert bombing of these targets commenced. Code-named **Operation Menu**, it lasted for fourteen months, yet elicited no outcry from Hanoi since they had no right to be in neutral Cambodia in the first place. The following spring, an American-backed coup replaced Prince Sihanouk of Cambodia with Lon Nol and thus eased access for US troops, and a **task force** of twenty thousand soldiers advanced on Communist installations there. The American public was outraged: dismayed that Nixon, far from closing down the war, was in fact widening the conflict, they rallied at mass antiwar demonstrations.

After **Ho Chi Minh's death** on September 2, 1969, the stop-start **peace talks** in Paris dragged along with Le Duc Tho representing the North, and Nixon's national security adviser Henry Kissinger at the American helm. Two stumbling blocks hindered any advancement: the North's insistence on a coalition government in the South with no place for then-president Thieu, and the US insistence that all NVA troops should move north after a ceasefire. Tit-for-tat military offensives launched early in 1972 saw both sides attempting to strengthen their hand at the bargaining table: Hanoi launched its **Easter Offensive** on the upper provinces of the South; while Nixon countered by resuming the **bombing of the North**. Towards the year's end, negotiations

1976	**1978**
Declaration of the unified Socialist Republic of Vietnam	Vietnam invades Cambodia in order to remove Khmer Rouge from power

recommenced, this time with Hanoi in a mood to compromise – not least because Nixon let rumours spread of his **Madman Theory**, which involved the use of nuclear weaponry – but the draft agreement produced in October (Nixon was keen to see a resolution before the US elections in November) was delayed by President Thieu in Saigon. By the time it was finalized in January 1973 Nixon had flexed his military muscles one last time, sanctioning the eleven-day **Christmas Bombing** of Hanoi and Haiphong in which 20,000 tonnes of ordnance was dropped.

Under the terms of the **Paris Accords**, signed on January 27 by the United States, the North, the South and the Viet Cong, a ceasefire was established, all remaining American troops were repatriated by April, and Hanoi and Saigon released their PoWs. The Paris talks failed to yield a long-term political settlement, instead providing for the creation of a **Council of National Conciliation**, comprising Saigon's government and the Communists, to sort matters out at some future date. The agreements allowed the NVA and ARVN troops to retain whatever positions they held. For this fudged deal, Kissinger and Le Duc Tho were awarded the Nobel Prize for peace, though only Kissinger accepted.

The fall of the South

The Paris Accords accomplished little beyond smoothing the US withdrawal from Vietnam: with the NVA allowed to remain in the South, it was only a matter of time before **renewed aggression** erupted. Thieu's ARVN, now numbering a million troops and in robust shape thanks to its new US-financed equipment, soon set about retaking territory lost to the North during the Easter Offensive. The Communists, on the other hand, were still reeling from losses accrued during that campaign. By 1974, things were beginning to sour for the South. An economy already weakened by heavy **inflation** was further drained by the **unemployment** caused by America's withdrawal; corruption in the military was rife, and unpaid wages led to a burgeoning desertion rate. By the end of the year, the South was ripe for the taking.

Over the Christmas period of 1974, an **NVA drive** led by General Tran overran the area north of Saigon now called Song Be Province. Duly encouraged, Hanoi went into action, and towns in the South fell like ninepins under the irresistible momentum of the **Ho Chi Minh Campaign**. Within two months, Communist troops had occupied Buon Ma Thuot, taking a mere 24 hours to finish a job they'd anticipated would require a week. Hue and Da Nang duly followed, and by April 21 Xuan Loc, the last real line of defence before Saigon, had also fallen. ARVN defiance disintegrated in the face of the North's unerring progress: a famous image from these last days shows a highway scattered with the discarded boots of fleeing Southern soldiers. President Thieu fled by helicopter to Taiwan, and leadership of Saigon's government was assumed by **General Duong Van Minh** ("Big Minh"). Minh held the post for just two days before NVA tanks crashed through the gates of the Presidential Palace and Saigon fell to the North on April 30. Only hours before, the last Americans and other Westerners in the city had been **airlifted out** in the frantic helicopter operation known as "Frequent Wind" (see p.80).

Socialist Vietnam

By July 1976, Vietnam was once again a **unified nation** for the first time since the French colonization in the 1850s. At first the new leaders trod softly, in order to

1979

The "boat people" start to flee Vietnam in large numbers, and would continue to do so until the 1990s

1979

Chinese launch invasion of northern Vietnam, but retreat after only sixteen days impress the international community, but Southerners eyed the future with profound apprehension. Their fears were well founded, as Hanoi was in no mood to grant Saigon autonomy: the Council of National Reconciliation, provided for by the Paris Accords, was never established, and the NLF's **Provisional Revolutionary Government** worked beneath the shadow of the Military Management Committee, and therefore Hanoi, until the **Socialist Republic of Vietnam** was officially born, in July 1976. The impression of a conquering army was exacerbated when Northern cadres – the *can bo* – swarmed south to take up all official posts.

Monumental **problems** faced the nascent republic. For many years, the two halves of Vietnam had lived according to wildly variant political and economic systems. The North had no industry, its agriculture was based on cooperative farms, and much of its land had been ravaged during the war. In stark contrast, American involvement in the South had underwritten what John Pilger describes as "an 'economy' based upon the services of maids, pimps, whores, beggars and black-marketeers", buttressed by American cash that dried up when the last helicopter left the embassy in Saigon.

The changes that swept the country weren't limited to economics. Bitterness on Hanoi's part towards its former enemies was inevitable, yet instead of making moves towards national conciliation – and despite the fact that many families had connections in both camps – recriminations drove further wedges between the peoples of North and South. Anyone with remote connections to America was interned in a **re-education camp**, along with Buddhist monks, priests, intellectuals and anyone else the government wanted to be rid of. Hundreds of thousands of Southerners were sent to these camps, without trial. Some were to remain incarcerated for over a decade. The quagmire Vietnam found itself in after reunification prompted many of its citizens to flee the country in unseaworthy vessels, an exodus of humanity known as the **boat people** (see box, p.448).

While all this was going on, just three weeks before the fall of Saigon in 1975 **Pol Pot**'s genocidal regime seized power in Cambodia; within a year, his troops were making **cross-border forays** into regions of Vietnam that had once fallen under Khmer sway, around the Mekong Delta and north of Ho Chi Minh City (as Saigon had been renamed). One such venture led to the massacre at **Ba Chuc** (see p.134), in which almost two thousand people died. Reprisals were slow in coming, but by 1978 Vietnam could stand back no longer; on Christmas Day of that year 120,000 **Vietnamese troops invaded Cambodia** and ousted Pol Pot. Whatever the motives for the invasion, and even though it brought an end to Pol Pot's reign of terror, Vietnam was further ostracized by the international community. In February 1979, Beijing's response came in the form of a punitive **Chinese invasion** of Vietnam's northeastern provinces; Chinese losses were heavy, and after sixteen days they retreated. Meanwhile, Pol Pot had withdrawn across the Thai border, from where he commanded his army in their continued attack on the occupying Vietnamese forces. The Vietnamese remained in Cambodia until September 1989, by which time they had defeated the Khmer Rouge at the expense of fifty thousand soldiers, the majority of them Southern conscripts.

Doi moi

A severe famine in 1985 and the 775 percent inflation that crippled the country in 1986 were just two of the many symptoms of the **economic malaise** threatening to tear

1986	1989
Nguyen Van Linh becomes General Secretary of Socialist Party; inaugurates *doi moi* policy	Vietnamese soldiers withdraw from Cambodia after more than a decade of occupation

THE "BOAT PEOPLE"

In 1979 the attention of the world was caught by images of rickety fishing boats packed with Vietnamese **refugees**, seeking sanctuary in Hong Kong and other Southeast Asian harbours. An untold number – some say a third – fell victim to typhoons, starvation and disease or pirates, who often sank the boats after raping the women and seizing the refugees' meagre possessions. Others somehow landed on the coast of Australia or were picked up by passing freighters. The prime destination, however, was Hong Kong, where 68,000 asylum-seekers arrived in 1979 alone. The exodus was at its peak in 1979, but it had been going on, largely unnoticed, since reunification four years earlier, and continued up to the early 1990s. Over this period an estimated 840,000 boat people arrived safely in "ports of first asylum", of whom more than 750,000 were eventually resettled overseas.

The first refugees were mostly **Southerners**, people who felt themselves too closely associated with the old regime or their American allies, and feared Communist reprisals. Some were former nationalists and a few were even ex-Viet Cong, disillusioned with the new government's extremism. Then, in early 1978, nationalization of private commerce was instituted in the South, hitting hard at the **Chinese** community, which controlled much Southern business and the all-important rice trade. As anti-Chinese sentiment took hold, thousands made their escape in fishing boats followed in the late 1970s by more Vietnamese, driven by a series of bad harvests, severe hardship and the prospect of prolonged military service in Cambodia.

By 1979 the situation had become so critical that the international community was forced to act, offering asylum to the more than two hundred thousand refugees crowding temporary camps around Southeast Asia. Under the auspices of the UN, the **Orderly Departure Program** (ODP) also enabled legal emigration of political refugees to the West, resettling over half a million in more than forty Western countries.

In 1987, the South China Sea was once again full of Vietnamese people in overcrowded boats. This **second wave** were mostly Northerners fleeing desperate poverty rather than fear

Vietnam apart during the late 1970s and early 1980s. An experimental hybrid of planned and market economies tried out in 1979 came to nothing, and by the early 1980s the only thing keeping Vietnam afloat was Soviet aid. Treaties made it illegal for Americans to do business with the Vietnamese, who, largely due to American pressure, were unable to look to the IMF or World Bank for development loans.

In 1986 **Nguyen Van Linh** took over as general secretary, and a raft of market-based economic reforms, known as **doi moi** or "renovation", followed. This encompassed limited moves towards decentralization and privatization, collectivized agriculture was abandoned in favour of individual land-holdings and attempts were made to attract foreign capital by liberalizing foreign investment regulations. Political reforms came a poor second, although the congress did instigate purges on corrupt officialdom and gave the press freer rein to criticize. With the **collapse of Communism** across Europe in 1989, though, the press was again silenced, and in a keynote speech Nguyen Van Linh rejected the concept of a multiparty state; all economic reforms, however, remained in place, and the government set in motion efforts to end Vietnam's isolation.

International rehabilitation, which had already begun with the withdrawal of troops from Cambodia in 1989, gathered momentum in the 1990s, as efforts to aid the US search teams looking for remains of the two thousand-plus American soldiers still unaccounted for (MIAs, or Missing in Action) were stepped up. In 1993, a year after the reformist **Vo**

1990	**1993**
Government relaxes laws governing establishment of private businesses	At the Cannes Film Festival, *The Scent of Green Papaya* wins Vietnam's first major movie award

of persecution, with Hong Kong again bearing the brunt of new arrivals. Governments were less sympathetic this time round and, in an attempt to halt the flow, from early 1989 boat people were denied automatic refugee status. Instead, a screening process was introduced to identify "genuine" refugees; the rest, designated "economic migrants", were encouraged to return under the **Voluntary Repatriation Scheme**, which offered concrete assistance with resettlement.

Then, in early 1996, all parties finally agreed that the only "viable solution" was to send the remaining forty thousand failed asylum-seekers still in Southeast Asian camps back home. In theory deportations were to take place "without threat or use of force", though clashes with security forces became more violent as it gained momentum. The situation was worst in **Hong Kong**, where there was pressure to clear the camps before the handover to China in 1997. The rate of repatriation – both voluntary and, increasingly, forced – was stepped up throughout the region and by mid-1997 nearly all the boat people had been either resettled or returned to Vietnam.

The UN High Commission for Refugees (UNHCR), which monitored returnees in Vietnam up until 2000, said there was little evidence of persecution or discrimination. Others, however, claimed that the monitoring was inadequate and ineffective, and cited examples of returnees being imprisoned. At the same time, various international bodies, such as the European Union, helped returnees reintegrate into the community through job creation schemes, vocational training programmes and low-interest loans. In 1998, a scheme known as **ROVR** got under way, resettling mostly Southerners who were able to prove some sort of relationship with the Americans during the war.

As the Vietnamese economy improved and as relations between America and Vietnam started to thaw around the turn of the millennium, so the ODP and ROVR programmes were gradually wound up. Their completion marked the end – at least as far as officialdom was concerned – of the whole sorry saga of the boat people.

Van Kiet became prime minister, the Americans duly lifted their veto on aid, and Western cash began to flow. By the year's end, inflation was down to five percent. The rapprochement with the US continued into 1994, as the US trade embargo was lifted by President Clinton, and in February 1995 the two countries opened liaison offices in each other's capitals. Vietnam was admitted into **ASEAN** (the Association of Southeast Asian Nations) in July 1995, and the same month saw full **diplomatic relations restored** with the US.

During the next two years foreign investment continued to flood in, pushing economic growth rates close to ten percent per annum. Revenues from oil, manufacturing and tourism took off and everyone was forecasting Vietnam as the next **Asian tiger**. For all the optimism, however, cracks were beginning to appear: the economic upturn was benefiting city-dwellers (particularly in Ho Chi Minh City) far more than the rural population; top bureaucrats were openly criticized in **corruption** scandals; and an alarmed government launched a campaign against "**social evils**" – videos, advertising, pornography and other Western imports that were seen to be undermining traditional society.

By 1997 the honeymoon period was definitely over. Economic growth flagged as foreign companies scaled back, or pulled out altogether, frustrated by an overblown bureaucracy, miles of red tape and regulations in a constant state of flux. Vietnam's mostly inefficient, state-run industries became increasingly uncompetitive, and

1995	2000	2002
Full diplomatic relations restored with the US	At the Sydney games, Tran Hieu Ngan wins Vietnam's first ever Olympic medal – a silver for taekwondo	Opening of first branch of *Highland Coffee*, Vietnam's first Western-style café chain

HUMAN RIGHTS ISSUES

Despite what the world community expected of a younger and "more enlightened" government, in 2008 measures were put in place to prevent bloggers from posting "inappropriate content", while two local **journalists were arrested** and imprisoned after their exposure of a corruption scandal. One of them, Nguyen Van Hai, was freed after pleading guilty, while the other, Nguyen Viet Chien, was one of more than 15,000 released from prison as part of a wide-ranging amnesty early in 2009. Later that year, however, seven **pro-democracy activists** were jailed for antigovernment activities, with another following in early 2010. One was Le Cong Dinh, a local lawyer who had been involved with a number of high-profile human rights cases; his detention was roundly criticized by Amnesty International, while Human Rights Watch also chimed in with criticism of the country's suppression of online content. In 2013, a further 22 were arrested for antigovernment activities, before a decree was passed banning the online discussion of "current affairs" – a wide-ranging topic, indeed. The arrest of two more prominent bloggers followed in 2014, and in 2016 "Mother Mushroom" (the political blogger's online pseudonym) was handed an unusually lengthy sentence of ten years for "defaming" the regime; she received the International Women of Courage Award, conferred by US First Lady Melania Trump.

The suppression of dissent has not only been limited to perceived antigovernment activities – in 2013 alone at least fifty Christians were arrested, and Open Doors International ranked Vietnam as one of the worst nations worldwide for religious freedom.

smuggling grew at an alarming rate. In May 1997, widespread corruption, growing agricultural unemployment and the ever-widening gulf between urban and rural Vietnam sparked off **demonstrations** by thousands of dissatisfied farmers in Thai Binh province, part of the traditionally Communist north.

National **elections** in July 1997 brought a long-awaited change of government, ushering in a band of younger, more worldly-wise ministers under Prime Minister **Phan Van Khai**. His tenure, however, got off to a shaky start, with Pham The Duyet, a senior member of the Politburo, arrested for corruption in 1998. Compounding this was the Asian Financial Crisis, which hit the same year; Vietnam's economy, on the face of things, handled it fairly well, with GDP growth barely dipping below five percent; such statistics, however, disguised harsh economic realities for the majority of the population, with the burgeoning middle-class feeling most of the benefits.

The twenty-first century

Phan Van Khai was re-elected in 2002. There then followed further signs of improved US–Vietnam relations – in 2004, a United jet touched down in Ho Chi Minh City, in the process becoming the first direct American passenger service to Vietnam since the war (though this route ended in October 2016 with no other service taking its place at present). Pham Van Khai made a visit to the US in 2005, and 2006 saw a second wave of younger leaders elected to top posts. Khai's "chosen one" **Nguyen Tan Dung** took over as prime minister, continuing his predecessor's economic reforms – no simple task given the inherent constraints of a "state capitalism" system – and the battle against corruption. In early 2007, following more than a decade of intense negotiations, Vietnam gained membership of the **World Trade Organization** (WTO). Nguyen Tan Dung was reappointed

2007	2011	2014
Vietnam joins the WTO	Completion of Landmark Tower in Hanoi, the country's tallest building	Wave of anti-China protests, in response to Chinese deployment of oil rig in disputed seas

Prime Minister in 2011, but in 2016 when he attempted to challenge party boss **Nguyen Phu Trong** – effectively the most powerful man in Vietnam – he lost. Trong kept his position as general secretary and congress elected new prime minister **Nguyen Xuan Phuc**.

All the while, the old beast of **corruption** was regularly rearing its ugly head. In 2000, senior government officials were investigated over the embezzlement of millions of dollars of state funds and ten years later a major scandal almost sank shipbuilder Vinashin, one of the largest state-owned enterprises; its chairman was arrested and jailed. The Communist Party chief was forced to publicly apologize for a raft of other scandals at state-run companies, but in 2014 there was yet another mammoth fraud trial, this time revolving around state-run Vietinbank – 23 were jailed.

Relations with China and the US

Ties between Vietnam and China have been fraught for centuries, but in 2011 both sides signed an agreement pertaining to the resolution of the long-running dispute in the South China Sea, whose waters are contested by another four countries in the area (in Vietnam this stretch of water is known as the East Sea). It wasn't long before relations took a turn for the worse – in 2014, Vietnamese state media marked, for the first time, the anniversary of the 1974 clashes with China over the disputed **Paracel Islands**. This may have had something to do with the protests that swept the country later that year, after the repositioning of a Chinese oil rig – Chinese homes and businesses were attacked across Vietnam, leading to twenty deaths, and the evacuation of three thousand ethnic Chinese. Hundreds of Vietnamese were held as the government tried to put a lid on the protests, though the nation's ire was stoked once more when a Chinese ship hit, and sank, a small Vietnamese fishing boat just a week later.

The deep mistrust of China might in some ways have brought the US and Vietnam closer together. When former president Obama visited Vietnam in 2016, he lifted the decades-old arms embargo and entered into negotiations for a Trans-Pacific Partnership trade deal. President Trump's administration put paid to this, as one of his first acts in office was to abandon the deal; however a new trade agreement reputedly worth billions was announced in 2017, after talks in Washington between Prime Minister Phuc and Trump.

Reasons to be cheerful

Despite the regular stories of corruption, increasing repression of human rights, dubious religious freedom and a stumbling economy, life is not all bad for the average Vietnamese. Many quality-of-life indicators seem to be heading the right way, albeit from very low bases: according to World Bank figures, the number of Vietnamese living in poverty has dropped from seventy percent in the 1980s to under fifteen percent today, child mortality has fallen, literacy levels are well over ninety percent, and the average life expectancy is now around 75 years, compared with 65 in 1990. All in all, it's important to remember what a state the country was in at the beginning of independence – divided, damaged and destitute – and how strangely normal life now seems after the atrocities that took place here only a generation ago.

2016	2016	2017
Vietnam's population passes the ninety-five million mark, leaving it ranked fourteenth worldwide	Environmental disaster as seventy tonnes of dead fish wash ashore on central Vietnam's coastline; Taiwanese-owned company admits responsibility	Hanoi launches first BRT (Bus Rapid Transit) system in bid to tackle pollution. Both Hanoi and HCMC plan a Metro system

Religion and beliefs

The moral and religious life of most Vietnamese people is governed by a complex mixture of Confucian, Buddhist and Taoist philosophical teachings interwoven with ancestor worship and ancient, animistic practices. Incompatibilities are reconciled on a practical level into a single, functioning belief system whereby a family may maintain an ancestral altar in their home, consult the village guardian spirit, propitiate the God of the Hearth and take offerings to the Buddhist pagoda.

The primary influence on Vietnam's religious life has been Chinese. However, in southern Vietnam, which historically fell within the Indian sphere, small communities of Khmer and Cham still adhere to Hinduism, Islam and Theravada Buddhism brought direct from India. From the fifteenth century on, **Christianity** has also been a feature, represented largely by Roman Catholicism but with a small Protestant following in the south. Vietnam also claims a couple of home-grown religious **sects**, both products of political and social turmoil in the early twentieth century: Cao Dai and Hoa Hao.

The **political dimension** has never been far removed from religious affairs in Vietnam, as the world was made vividly aware by Buddhist opposition to the oppressive regime of President Diem in the 1960s. After 1975, the Marxist–Leninist government of

VIETNAMESE DEITIES

BUDDHIST DEITIES

A Di Da or **Amitabha** The Historical Buddha, the most revered member of the Buddhist pantheon in Vietnamese pagodas.

Avalokitesvara A Bodhisattva often represented with many arms and eyes, being all-powerful, or as Quan Am (see below).

Di Lac or **Maitreya** The Future Buddha, usually depicted as chubby, with a bare chest and a huge grin, sitting on a lotus throne.

Ong Ac or **Trung Ac** One of the two guardians of the Buddhist religion, popularly known as Mister Wicked, who judges all people. He has a fierce red face and a reputation for severity – of which badly behaved children are frequently reminded.

Ong Thien or **Khuyen Thien** The second guardian of Buddhism is Mister Charitable, a white-faced kindly soul who encourages good behaviour.

Quan Am The Goddess of Mercy, adopted from the Chinese goddess, Kuan Yin. Quan Am is a popular incarnation of Avalokitesvara. She is usually represented as a graceful white statue, with her hand raised in blessing.

Thich Ca Mau Ni or **Sakyamuni** The Present Buddha, born Siddhartha Gautama, who founded Buddhism.

OTHER CHARACTERS

Ngoc Hoang The Jade Emperor, ruler of the Taoist pantheon who presides over heaven.

Ong Tau God of the Hearth, who keeps watch over every family and reports on the household to the Jade Emperor every New Year.

Quan Cong A Chinese general of the Han dynasty, revered for his loyalty, honesty and exemplary behaviour. Usually flanked by his two assistants.

Thanh Mau The Mother Goddess.

Thien Hau Protectress of Sailors.

Tran Vo Properly known as Tran Vo Bac De, Taoist Emperor of the North, who governs storms and generally harmful events.

reunified Vietnam declared the state atheist, while theoretically allowing people the right to practise their religion under the constitution. In reality, churches and pagodas were closed down, religious leaders sent for re-education, and followers discriminated against if not actively persecuted.

In 1992 the situation changed, with the right to **religious freedom** being reaffirmed in a new constitution. A number of high-profile prisoners held on religious grounds were released, while party leaders publicly demonstrated the new freedoms by visiting pagodas and churches. Despite such moves, however, the government continues to exercise close control on religious groups, and came in for particularly severe criticism for its crackdown on ethnic minority Christians following widespread unrest in the central highlands in 2001 and 2004; international human rights organizations continue to criticize the Vietnamese government for its record on religious freedom.

Ancestor worship

One of the oldest cults practised in Vietnam is that of ancestor worship, based on the fundamental principles of filial piety and of obligation to the past, present and future generations. No matter what their religion, virtually every Vietnamese household, even hardline Communist, will maintain an **ancestral altar** in the belief that the dead continue to live in another realm. Ancestors can intercede on behalf of their descendants and bring the family good fortune, but in return the living must pay respect, perform prescribed ceremonies and provide for their ancestors' wellbeing. At funerals and subsequent anniversaries, quantities of paper money and other **votive offerings** (these days including television sets and cars) are burnt, and choice morsels of food are regularly placed on the altar. Traditionally this is financed by the income from a designated plot of land, and it is the responsibility of the oldest, usually male, member of the family to organize the rituals, tend the altar and keep the ancestors abreast of all important family events; failure in any of these duties carries the risk of inciting peeved ancestors to make mischief.

The ancestral altar occupies a central position in the home. On it are placed several wooden tablets, one for each ancestor going back five generations. One hundred days after the funeral, the deceased's spirit returns to reside in the tablet. People without children to honour them by burning incense at the altar are condemned to wander the world in search of a home. Some childless people make provision by paying a temple or pagoda to observe the rituals, while the spirits of others may eventually take up residence in one of the small shrine houses (*cuong*) you see in fields and at roadsides. Important times for remembering the dead are **Tet**, the lunar New Year, and **Thanh Minh** ("Festival of Pure Light"), which falls on the fifth day of the third lunar month.

Spirit worship

Residual animism plus a whole host of spirits borrowed from other religions have given Vietnam a complicated mystical world. The universe is divided into **three realms**: the sky, earth and man, under the overall guardianship of Ong Troi, Lord of Heaven, assisted by spirits of the earth, mountains and water. Within the hierarchy are four **sacred animals** who appear everywhere in Vietnamese architecture: the dragon, representing the king, power and intelligence; the phoenix, embodying the queen, beauty and peace; the turtle, symbol of longevity and protector of the kingdom; and the mythical *kylin*, usually translated as unicorn, which represents wisdom.

In addition each village or urban quarter will venerate a **guardian spirit** in either a temple (*den*) or communal house (*dinh*). In either case people will propitiate these tutelary spirits – represented on the altar by a gilded throne – with offerings, and will consult them in times of need.

> **THE DINH**
>
> A *dinh* is a kind of **communal house** that can be found all over Vietnam. They often look like temples, and indeed they operate as places of worship with altars and urns to hold incense. However, they also serve as administrative centres and as training centres for the various guilds, which is why there are so many in Hanoi's Old Quarter (see p.350). Another use is as a meeting place for local communities, and some are open to the public, while others only open on special occasions.

Buddhism

The Buddha was born **Siddhartha Gautama** to a wealthy family sometime during the sixth century BC in present-day Nepal. At an early age he renounced his life of luxury to seek the ultimate deliverance from worldly suffering and strive to reach **nirvana**, an indefinable, blissful state. After several years Siddhartha attained enlightenment while sitting under a bodhi tree, and then devoted the rest of his life to teaching the **Middle Way** that leads to nirvana. The Buddha preached that existence is a cycle of perpetual reincarnation in which actions in one life determine one's position in the next, but that it is possible to break free by following certain precepts, central to which are nonviolence and compassion. The Buddha's doctrine was based on the **Four Noble Truths**: existence is suffering; suffering is caused by desire; suffering ends with the extinction of desire; the way to end suffering is to follow the eightfold path of right understanding, thought, speech, action, livelihood, effort, mindfulness and concentration.

It's estimated that up to two-thirds of the Vietnamese population consider themselves Buddhist. The vast majority are followers of the Mahayana school, which was introduced to northern Vietnam via China in the second century AD.

The history of Buddhism in Vietnam

In fact Buddhism first arrived in southern Vietnam nearly one hundred years earlier as **Theravada**, or the "Lesser Vehicle", introduced via the Indian trade routes through Burma and Thailand. Theravada is an ascetical form of the faith based on the individual pursuit of perfection and enlightenment, which failed to find favour beyond the Khmer communities of the Mekong, where it still counts roughly one million followers. One of the salient features of **Mahayana** Buddhism, in contrast, is the belief that intermediaries – **Bodhisattvas** – have chosen to forgo nirvana to work for the salvation of all humanity, and it was this that enabled Mahayana to adapt to a Vietnamese context by incorporating local gods and spirits into its array of Bodhisattvas. Mahayana Buddhism spread through northern Vietnam until it became the **official state religion** after the country regained its independence from China in the tenth century, but by the mid-fourteenth century Buddhism had lost its political and economic influence and, when the Later Le dynasty came to power in 1427, Confucianism finally eclipsed it as the dominant national philosophy.

But by then Buddhism was too deeply rooted, particularly in the folk religion of the countryside, to lose its influence completely. It enjoyed further brief periods of **royal patronage**, notably during the seventeenth and eighteenth centuries when new pagodas were built and old ones repaired. Since then the Buddhist community has been a focus of **dissent**, not least in the 1960s when images of self-immolating Buddhist monks focused world attention on the excesses of South Vietnam's Catholic President Diem. At the time, protesting Buddhists were accused of being pro-Communist, although their standpoint was essentially neutral. In the event they experienced even greater repression after reunification when pagodas were closed, and monks and nuns were sent to re-education camps.

The situation has eased considerably in recent years, and pagodas affiliated to the officially recognized Vietnam Buddhist Sangha (VBS) have been allowed to resume their social and educational programmes to a certain extent. Many pagodas, now bustling with life again, have been renovated after years of neglect.

Confucianism

The teachings of Confucius provide a guiding set of moral and ethical principles, an **ideology** for the state's rulers and subjects onto which ritualistic practices have been grafted.

Confucius is the Latinized name of Kongfuzi (Khong Tu in Vietnamese), who was born into a minor aristocratic family in China in 551 BC. At this time China was in turmoil as the Zhou dynasty dissolved into rival feudal states battling for supremacy. Confucius worked for many years as a court official, where he observed the nature of power and the function of government at close quarters. At the age of 50, he packed it all in and for the next twenty years wandered the country spreading his ideas on social and political reform in an effort to persuade states and individuals to live peacefully together for their mutual benefit. His central tenet was the importance of **correct behaviour** and **loyal service**, reinforced by ceremonial rites whereby the ruler maintains authority through good example rather than force. Important qualities to strive for are selflessness, respectfulness, sincerity and nonviolence; the ideal person should be neither heroic nor extrovert, but instead follow a "golden mean". Confucius remained silent on spiritual matters, though he placed great emphasis on observing ancient rituals such as making offerings to heaven and to ancestors.

Confucian **teachings** were handed down in the *Analects*, but he is also credited with editing the Six Classics, among them the *Book of Changes* (*I Ching*) and the *Book of Ritual* (*Li Chi*). Later these became the basic texts for civil service examinations, ensuring that all state officials had a deeply ingrained respect for tradition and social order. Though Confucianism ultimately led to national inflexibility and the undermining of personal initiative, its positive legacy has been an emphasis on the value of education and a belief that individual merit is of greater consequence than high birth.

After the death of Confucius in 478 BC the doctrine was developed further by his **disciples**, the most famous of whom was Mencius (Mengzi). By the first century AD, Confucianism, which slowly absorbed elements of Taoism, had evolved into a cult and also become the state ideology whereby kings ruled under the Mandate of Heaven. Social stability was maintained through a fixed hierarchy of interdependent relationships encapsulated in the notion of filial piety. Thus children must obey their parents without question, wives their husbands, students their teacher and subjects their ruler. For their part, the recipient, particularly the king, must earn this obedience;

PAGODA OR TEMPLE?

The Vietnamese word *chua*, translated as "pagoda", is an exclusively Buddhist term, whereas a temple (*den* or *mieu*) may be Taoist, Confucian, Hindu, Buddhist, or house a guardian spirit. In a pagoda, Buddha is worshipped, but in a temple, gods and real historical figures such as emperors and national heroes are honoured as deities. It can be difficult for an outsider to differentiate between the two, as confusingly you'll find temples inside a pagoda, or a complex that is a mix of both. Pagodas are often single-storey pavilions laid out in either an inverse T or three parallel lines. Other typical elements are a **bell tower**, either integral to the building or standing apart, and a **walled courtyard** containing ponds, stone stelae and, particularly in Mahayana pagodas, the white figure of Quan Am symbolizing charity and compassion. In the south, you'll also find Cham temples, incorporating Hindu, Indian and Khmer elements.

The **best times to visit** a temple or pagoda are the first and fifteenth days of the lunar month (new moon and full moon), and during festivals or at Tet (New Year), when they are at their busiest.

if the rules are broken, the harmony of society and nature is disturbed and authority loses its legitimacy. Therefore, by implication, revolution was justified when the king lost his divine right to rule.

The history of Confucianism in Vietnam

Confucian thinking has pervaded Vietnamese society ever since Chinese administrators introduced the concepts during the second century BC. Reinforced by a thousand years of Chinese rule, Confucianism (*Nho Giao*) came to play an essential role in Vietnam's political, social and educational systems. The philosophy was largely one of an intellectual elite, but Confucian teaching eventually filtered down to the village level where it had a profound influence on the Vietnamese family organization.

The arrival of Western ideas and French rule in the late nineteenth century finally undermined its political dominance, though Confucianism managed to survive as the court ideology until well into the twentieth century. The cult of Confucius (*Van Mieu*) continues in a few temples dedicated to the sage, and he also appears on other altars as an honoured ancestor, an exemplary figure remembered for services to the nation.

Many **Confucian ideals** have been completely assimilated into Vietnamese society. After Independence, the Communist Party struggled against inherent conservatism and the supremacy of the family as a political unit; indeed, leaders can still be heard railing against the entrenched "feudal" nature of rural Vietnam. But the party was also able to tap into those elements of the Confucian tradition that suited their new classless, socialist society: conformity, duty and the denial of personal interest for the common good. Today, however, Confucian ideals are being seriously undermined by the invasion of materialism and individual ambition.

Taoism

Taoism is based on the **Tao-te-Ching**, the "Book of the Way", traditionally attributed to **Lao-tzu** (meaning "Old Master"), who is thought to have lived in China in the sixth century BC. The Tao, the Way, emphasizes effortless action, intuition and spontaneity; the Tao is invisible and impartial; it cannot be taught, nor can it be expressed in words. It is the one reality from which everything is born, universal and eternal. However, by virtuous, compassionate and nonviolent behaviour, it is possible to achieve ultimate stillness, through a mystical and personal quest. Taoism thus preached nonintervention, passivity and the futility of academic scholarship; Confucians viewed it as suspiciously subversive.

Chinese immigrants brought Taoism (*Dao Giao*) to Vietnam during the long period of Chinese rule (111 BC to 939 AD). Between the eleventh and fourteenth centuries the philosophy enjoyed equal status with Buddhism and Confucianism as one of Vietnam's three "religions", but Taoism gradually declined until it eventually became a strand of folk religion. A few Taoist temples (*quan*) exist in Vietnam but on the whole its deities have been absorbed into other cults. The Jade Emperor, for example, is frequently part of the Buddhist pantheon in Vietnamese pagodas.

Central to the Tao is the **duality** inherent in nature; the whole universe is in temporary balance, a tension of complementary opposites defined as **yin** and **yang**, the male and female principles. Yang is male, the sun, active and orthodox; yin is female, the earth, flexible, passive and instinctive. Harmony is the balance between the two, and experiencing that harmony is the Tao. Accordingly all natural things can be categorized by their property of yin or yang, and human activity should strive not to disrupt that balance. In its pure form Taoism has no gods, only emanations of the Tao, but in the first century AD it corrupted into an organized religion venerating a deified Lao-tzu. The new cult had popular appeal since it offered the goal of immortality

RELIGION AND BELIEFS **CONTEXTS** 457

GEOMANCY

The **practice of geomancy** is a pseudoscientific study, much like astrology or reading horoscopes, which was introduced to Vietnam from China. The underlying idea is that every location has harmful or beneficial properties governed by its physical attributes, planetary influences and the flow of natural energy through the earth. Geomancy is used mainly in **siting buildings**, particularly tombs, palaces, temples and the like, but also ordinary dwellings.

Geomancers analyze the general **topography** of the site, looking at the location of surrounding hills, as well as rivers, streams and other bodies of water, to find the most auspicious situation and orientation. They may suggest improving the area by adding small hills or lakes; if a family suffers bad fortune, a geomancer may be called in to divine the cause of the imbalance and restore the natural harmony.

---

through yogic meditation and good deeds. Eventually the practice of Taoism developed highly complex **rituals**, incorporating magic, mysticism, superstition and the use of geomancy (see box above) to ensure harmony between man and nature, while astrology might be used to determine auspicious dates for weddings, funerals, starting a journey or even launching a new business. Ancient spirit worship, the cult of ancestors and the veneration of legendary or historic figures all fused happily with the Taoist idea of a universal essence; Confucius is also honoured as a Taoist saint.

Christianity

Vietnam's **Catholic community** is the second largest in Southeast Asia after the Philippines. Exact figures are hard to come by but estimates vary between six and eight million (seven to ten percent of the population), of which perhaps two-thirds live in the south. The south is also home to the majority of the one million or so adherents to the **Protestant** faith, known as *Tin Lanh*, or the Good News, which was introduced by Canadian and American missionaries in the early twentieth century. Perhaps two-thirds of Protestants belong to ethnic-minority groups in the central highlands and northwest mountains. There's evidence that the number of adherents has been growing rapidly, despite government restrictions on proselytizing.

The first Christian **missionaries** to reach Vietnam were Portuguese and Spanish Dominicans who landed briefly on the north coast in the sixteenth century. They were followed in 1615 by French and Portuguese Jesuits, dispatched by the Pope to establish the first permanent missions. Among the early arrivals was the Frenchman Alexandre de Rhodes (see box, p.434), a Jesuit who impressed the northern Trinh lords and won, by his reckoning, nearly seven thousand converts. The inevitable **backlash** against Christianity, which opposed ancestor worship and espoused subversive ideas such as equality, was not long in coming. In 1630 the Trinh lords expelled all Christians, including de Rhodes, who returned to France where he helped create the Society of Foreign Missions (*Société des Missions Étrangères*). This society soon became the most active proselytizing body in Indochina; by the end of the eighteenth century it had claimed thousands of converts, particularly in the coastal provinces.

Official attitudes towards Christianity fluctuated over the centuries, though the Vietnamese kings were generally suspicious of the Church's increasingly political role. The most violent **persecutions** occurred during the reign of Minh Mang (1820–41), an ardent Confucian, and reached a peak after 1832. Churches were destroyed, the faces of converts were branded with the words *ta dao*, meaning "false religion", and many of those refusing to renounce their faith were killed; 117 martyrs, both European and Asian, were later canonized. Such repression, much exaggerated at the time, provided the French with a pretext for greater involvement in Indochina, culminating in full colonial rule at the end of the nineteenth century.

European influence

Not surprisingly, Catholicism **prospered** under the French regime. Missions reopened and hundreds of churches, schools and hospitals were built. Vietnamese Catholics formed an educated elite among a population that counted some two million faithful by the 1950s. When partition came in 1954 many Catholics chose to move south, partly because of their opposition to Communism and partly because the new leader of South Vietnam, President Ngo Dinh Diem, was a Catholic. Of the estimated nine hundred thousand Vietnamese who left the North in 1954, it's said that around two-thirds were Catholic; many of these became refugees a second time in the 1970s.

Diem actively discriminated in favour of the Catholic community, which he viewed as a bulwark against Communism. As a result he alienated large sections of the population, most importantly Buddhists whose protests eventually contributed to his downfall. Meanwhile in North Vietnam the authorities trod fairly carefully with those Catholics who had chosen to stay, allowing them freedom to practise their religion, but the Church was severely restricted and reports of persecution persisted.

After reunification, churches were permitted to function but still came under strict **surveillance**, with all appointments controlled by the government, and members of the Church hierarchy frequently received heavy jail sentences for opposition to the regime. Since 1986, relations between the two continue to improve. A senior Vatican emissary visited Hanoi in 2005 and Vietnam's then prime minister visited the Pope in Rome in 2014; it will undoubtedly be several years before the much-hoped-for papal visit occurs.

Protestant problems

The situation is not quite so rosy as regards Vietnam's **Protestant** communities. While the government now officially recognizes the Southern Evangelical Church of Vietnam (SECV) and the smaller Evangelical Church of Vietnam (ECVN), based in the north, it remains deeply suspicious of another evangelical branch known as "Dega Protestantism" practised mainly by the ethnic minorities of the **central highlands**. It's not so much the belief system itself that the authorities are concerned about, but the movement's potential as a political force and, specifically, its alleged association with demands from certain minority groups for greater autonomy. There have been (sometimes violent) clashes between ethnic minorities in the central highlands and the authorities in recent years (see box, p.171). While the protests were generally sparked by disputes over land and continued poverty, some demonstrators also cited **religious persecution** among their grievances. As a result, the government imposed significant restrictions on all Protestant churches in the region. The government continues to keep a close eye on all Christian activity in the central highlands – as recently as 2010 propaganda campaigns were launched against Catholic sects, and forced renunciation ceremonies took place in Gia Lai province.

Cao Dai

Social upheaval coupled with an injection of Western thinking in the early twentieth century gave birth to Vietnam's two indigenous religious sects, **Cao Dai** and Hoa Hao. Of the two, Cao Dai claims more adherents, with an estimated following of around two million in south Vietnam, plus a few thousand among overseas Vietnamese in America, Canada and Britain. The sect's headquarters, the **Holy See**, resides in a flamboyant cathedral at Tay Ninh (see p.108), where it also maintains a school, agricultural cooperative and hospital. Vietnam's most northerly Cao Dai congregation worships in Hue.

The basic tenets of Cao Dai were first revealed to **Ngo Van Chieu**, a civil servant working in the criminal investigation department of the French administration on Phu Quoc Island, at the beginning of the 1920s. A spiritualist, Ngo was contacted during a seance by a superior spirit calling itself Cao Dai, or "high place". This spirit communicated to him the basics of the Cao Dai creed, and instructed him to adopt the **Divine Eye** as a tangible representation of its existence. Posted back to Saigon soon afterwards, Ngo set about preaching that Cao Dai had already revealed itself to mankind using such vehicles as Lao-tzu, Christ, Mohammed, Moses, Sakyamuni and Confucius to propagate systems of belief tailored to suit localized cultures. Such religious intolerance had resulted from this multiplicity, that for the **third alliance** it would do away with earthly messengers and convey a universal religion via spirit intermediaries, including Louis Pasteur, William Shakespeare, Joan of Arc, Sir Winston Churchill and Napoleon Bonaparte. The revelations of these "saints" were received using a planchette (a pencil secured to a wooden board on castors, on which the medium rests his hand, sometimes known as a *corbeille-à-bec*).

Though a fusion of Oriental and Occidental religions, propounding the concept of a universal god, Cao Dai is primarily entrenched in Buddhism, Taoism and Confucianism, to which cause-and-effect creeds, elements of Christianity, Islam and spirituality are added. By following its five commandments – Cao Dai followers must avoid killing living beings, high living, covetousness, verbal deceit and the temptations of the flesh – adherents look to hasten the evolution of the soul through reincarnation.

Borrowing the structure and terminology of the Catholic Church, Cao Dai began to grow rapidly, its emphasis on simplicity appealing to disaffected peasants, and by 1930 there were five hundred thousand followers. In 1927, Tay Ninh became the religion's **Holy See**; Ngo opted out of the papacy, and the first pope was Le Van Trung, a decadent mandarin from Cho Lon who saw the error of his ways after being visited by the Cao Dai during a seance.

Inevitably in such uncertain times, Cao Dai developed a political agenda. Strongly anti-French during World War II, subsequently the Cao Dai militia turned against the Viet Minh, with whom they fought, using French arms, in the French War. By the mid-Fifties, the area around Tay Ninh was a virtual fiefdom of Cao Dai followers. In *The Quiet American*, Graham Greene describes the Cao Dai militia as a "private army of 25,000 men, armed with mortars made out of the exhaust-pipes of old cars, allies of the French who turned neutral at the moment of danger". Even then, however, they were feuding with the rival Hoa Hao sect, and in a few years their power had waned.

Post-liberation, the Communist government closed down Cao Dai temples and schools, and sent priests for re-education. However, Cao Dai survived as a religion and has gained some new adherents since 1990, when its temples and mansions, approximately four hundred in all, were allowed to reopen, albeit under strict control.

Practising Cao Dai

The **rituals** of Cao Dai are a complex mixture of Buddhist and Taoist rites, including meditation and seances. Prayers take place four times a day in the temples, though ordinary members are only required to attend on four days per month and otherwise can pray at home. At the start of the thirty-minute-long ceremony, worshippers file into the temple in three columns, women on the left, men in the middle and on the right; they then kneel and bow three times – to the Supreme Being, to the Earth and to mankind. Cao Dai's most important **ceremony**, a sort of feast day for the Supreme Being, takes place on the ninth day of the first lunar month; other special observances are the day of Taoism (fifteenth day of the second month), Buddha's birthday (fifteenth of the fourth lunar month), the day of Confucius (28th of the eighth lunar month) and Christmas Day.

Hoa Hao

The second of Vietnam's local sects, **Hoa Hao**, meaning "peace and kindness", emerged in the late 1930s near Chau Doc in the Mekong Delta (see box, p.138). The movement was founded by a young mystic, **Huynh Phu So**, who disliked mechanical ritual and preached a very pure, simple form of Buddhism that required no clergy or other intermediaries, and could be practised at home by means of meditation, fasting and prayer. Gambling, alcohol and opium were prohibited, while filial piety was once more invoked to promote social order.

As a young man Huynh Phu So was cured of a mysterious illness by the monks of Tra Son Pagoda near his hometown of Chau Doc. He continued to live at the pagoda, studying under the monk Xom, but returned to his home village after Xom died. During a storm in 1939, So entered a trance from which he emerged to develop his own Buddhist way. The sect quickly gained followers and, like Cao Dai, was soon caught up in **nationalist politics**. To the French, So was a mad but dangerous subversive; they committed him to a psychiatric hospital (where he promptly converted his doctor to Hoa Hao), and then placed him under house arrest. During **World War II** Hoa Hao followers were armed by the Japanese and later continued to fight against the French while also opposing the Communists. At the end of the war Hoa Hao members formed an anti-Marxist political party, prompting the Viet Minh to assassinate So in 1947.

However, the movement continued to grow, its **private army** equalling the Cao Dai's in size, until Diem came to power and effectively crushed the sect's political and military arm. The sect then splintered, with some members turning to the National Liberation Front, while most sided with the Americans. As a result, when the Communists took over in 1975 many Hoa Hao leaders were arrested and its priesthood was disbanded. Nevertheless some claim that there are now over 1.5 million Hoa Hao practising in the Mekong Delta. The government recognized the principal Hoa Hao sect in 1999, although its more radical offshoots, which are accused of antigovernment activities, remain outlawed.

Vietnam's ethnic minorities

The population of Vietnam currently numbers just over ninety-five million people, of whom around 86 percent are ethnic Vietnamese (known as Viet or Kinh), while almost nine hundred thousand are Chinese, or Hoa, in origin. The remaining eleven million people comprise 53 ethnic minority groups divided into dozens of subgroups, some with a mere hundred or so members, giving Vietnam the richest and most complex ethnic make-up in the whole of Southeast Asia. The vast majority of Vietnam's minorities live in the hilly regions of the north and central highlands – all areas that saw heavy fighting in recent wars – and several groups straddle today's international boundaries.

Little is known about the origins of many of these people, some of whom already inhabited the area before the ancestors of the **Viet** arrived from southern China around four to five thousand years ago. At some point the Viet emerged as a distinct group from among the various indigenous peoples living around the Red River Delta, and then gradually absorbed smaller communities until they became the dominant culture. Other groups continued to interact with the Viet people, but either chose to maintain their independence in the highlands or were forced up into the hills, off the ever-more-crowded coastal plains.

Vietnamese legend accounts for this fundamental split between **lowlanders** and **highlanders** as follows: the Dragon King of the south married Au Co, a beautiful northern princess, and at first they lived in the mountains where she gave birth to a hundred strong, handsome boys. After a while, however, the Dragon King missed his watery, lowland home and decamped with half his sons, leaving fifty behind in the mountains – the ancestors of the ethnic minorities.

Vietnam's ethnic groups are normally differentiated according to three main **linguistic families** – Austronesian, Austro-Asian and Sino-Tibetan – which are further subdivided into smaller groups, such as the Viet-Muong and Tay-Thai language groups. Austronesians, related to Indonesians and Pacific Islanders, were probably the earliest inhabitants of the area, but are now restricted to the central highlands. Peoples of the two other linguistic families originated in southern China and at different times migrated southwards to settle throughout the Vietnamese uplands.

Despite their different origins, languages, dialects and hugely varied traditional dress, there are a number of similarities among the highland groups that distinguish them from Viet people. Most immediately obvious is the **stilthouse**, which protects against snakes, vermin and larger beasts as well as floods, while also providing safe stabling for domestic

---

VIETNAM'S MINORITY PEOPLE

Below is a list of Vietnam's most colourful minority groups, and where best to come into contact with them:
Bahnar Kon Tum (see p.194)
Black Hmong Sa Pa (see p.395)
Black Thai Son La (see p.411)
Cham Phan Rang (see p.219)
Flower Hmong Bac Ha (see p.403)
Jarai Pleiku (see p.190)
Red Zao Sa Pa (see p.395)
White Thai Mai Chau (see p.414)

animals. The communal imbibing of **rice wine** is popular with most highland groups, as are certain **rituals** such as protecting a child from evil spirits by not naming it until after a certain age. Most highlanders traditionally practise **swidden farming**, clearing patches of forest land, farming the burnt-over fields for a few years and then leaving it fallow for a specified period while it recovers its fertility. Where the soils are particularly poor, a seminomadic lifestyle is adopted, shifting the village location at intervals as necessary.

Recent history

Traditionally, Viet kings demanded tribute from the often fiercely independent ethnic minorities, but otherwise left them to govern their own affairs. This relationship changed with the arrival of Catholic missionaries, who won many converts to Christianity among the peoples of the central highlands – called **montagnards** by the French. Under colonial rule the minorities gained a certain degree of local autonomy in the late nineteenth century, but at the same time the French expropriated their land, exacted forced labour and imposed heavy taxes. As elsewhere in Vietnam, such behaviour sparked off rebellions, notably among the Hmong in the early twentieth century.

The northern mountains

The French were quick to capitalize on ancient antipathies between the highland and lowland peoples. In the northwest mountains, for example, they set up a semiautonomous Thai federation, complete with armed militias and border guards. When war broke out in 1946, groups of Thai, Hmong and Muong in the northwest sided with the French and against the Vietnamese, even to the extent of providing battalions to fight alongside French troops. But the situation was not clear-cut: some Thai actively supported the Viet Minh, while Ho Chi Minh found a safe base for his guerrilla armies among the Tay and Nung people of the northeast. Recognizing the need to secure the minorities' allegiance, after North Vietnam won independence in 1954 Ho Chi Minh created two **autonomous regions**, allowing limited self-government within a "unified multinational state".

The central highlands

The minorities of the **central highlands** had also been split between supporting the French and Viet Minh after 1946. In the interests of preserving their independence, the ethnic peoples were often simply anti-Vietnamese, of whatever political persuasion. After partition in 1954, anti-Vietnamese sentiment was exacerbated when President Diem started moving Viet settlers into the region, totally ignoring local land rights. The Bahnar, Jarai and E De joined forces in an organized opposition movement and this well-armed coalition developed into the United Front for the Liberation of Oppressed Races, popularly known by its French acronym, **FULRO**. They demanded greater autonomy for the minorities, including elected representation at the National Assembly, more local self-government, school instruction in their own language and access to higher education. While FULRO met with some initial success, the movement was weakened after a number split off to join the Viet Cong. An estimated ten thousand or more remained, fighting first of all against the South Vietnamese and the Americans, and then against the North Vietnamese Army until 1975. After this, FULRO rebels and other anti-Communist minority groups, mainly E De, operated out of bases in Cambodia. The few who survived Pol Pot's killing fields later fled to Thailand and were eventually resettled in America.

Post-reunification

After reunification promises of greater autonomy came to nothing; even the little self-government the minorities had been granted was removed. Those groups who had opposed the North Vietnamese were kept under close observation and their leaders sent for re-education. The new government pursued a policy of **forced assimilation** of the

ETHNIC MINORITIES AND THE AMERICAN WAR

During the **American War**, those minorities living around the Seventeenth Parallel soon found themselves on the front line. The worst fighting occurred during the late 1960s and early 1970s, when North Vietnamese troops were based in these remote uplands and American forces sought to rout them. Massive bombing raids were augmented by the use of defoliants and herbicides which, as well as denuding protective forest cover, destroyed crops and animals; this chemical warfare also killed an unknown number of people and caused severe long-term illnesses. In addition, villages were often subject to night raids by Viet Cong and North Vietnamese soldiers keen to "encourage" local support and replenish their food supplies.

It's estimated that over two hundred thousand minority people in the central highlands, both civilian and military, were **killed** as a result of the American War, out of a population of around one million. By 1975, 85 percent of villages in the highlands had been either destroyed or abandoned, while nothing was left standing in the region closest to the Demilitarized Zone. At the end of the war thousands of minority people were living in temporary camps, along with Viet refugees, unable to practise their traditional way of life.

minorities into the Vietnamese culture and glossed over their previous anti-Viet activities: all education was conducted in the Vietnamese language, traditional customs were discouraged or outlawed, and minority people were moved from their dispersed villages into permanent settlements. At the same time the government created **New Economic Zones** in the central highlands and along the Chinese border, often commandeering the best land to resettle thousands of people from the overcrowded lowlands.

Doi moi brought a shift in policy in the early 1990s, marked by the establishment of a central office responsible for the ethnic minorities. Minority languages are now officially recognized and can be taught in schools, scholarships enable minority people to attend institutes of higher education, television programmes are broadcast in a number of minority languages, and there is now greater representation of minorities at all levels of government. Indeed, in 2001 Nong Duc Manh, a member of the Tay ethnic group, became the first non-Viet secretary general of the Communist Party (though some rumours, which refuse to go away, suggest that his father was a certain Ho Chi Minh). Cash crops such as timber and fruit are being introduced as an alternative to illegal hunting, logging and opium cultivation. Other income-generating schemes are also being promoted and healthcare programmes upgraded.

All this has been accompanied by moves to preserve Vietnam's **cultural diversity**, driven in part by the realization that ethnic differences have greater appeal to tourists. However, in many areas the minorities' traditional lifestyles are fast being eroded and extreme **poverty** is widespread; while minorities constitute around fourteen percent of Vietnam's population, they account for one-third of those living under the poverty line.

Minorities in the northern highlands

The mountains of northern Vietnam are home to a large number of ethnic groups, all of them originating from southern China. The dominant minorities are the Tay and Thai, both feudal societies who once held sway over their weaker neighbours. These powerful, well-established groups farm the fertile, valley-bottom land, while Hmong and Dao people, who only arrived in Vietnam at the end of the eighteenth century, occupy the least hospitable land at the highest altitudes. These isolated groups have been better able to lead an independent life and to preserve their traditional customs, though most exist at near-subsistence levels. Local **markets**, usually held at weekly intervals, fulfil an important role in social and economic life in the highlands; the best known are at Sa Pa and Bac Ha, though there are others throughout the area. Most groups maintain a tradition of **call-and-response singing**, which is performed at ceremonies and festivals.

Dao

Population: 500,000 · Based in: Lao Cai, Ha Giang

The **Dao** (pronounced "Zao") ethnic minority is incredibly diverse in all aspects of life: social and religious practices, architecture, agriculture and dress. For several centuries, small, localized groups have settled in the northern border region after crossing over from China; there are related groups in Laos, Thailand and China.

The Dao boast a particularly striking traditional dress, the most eye-catching element of which is a bulky red turban. Dao people live at all altitudes, their house style and agricultural techniques varying accordingly. While groups living at lower levels are relatively prosperous, growing rice and raising livestock, those in the high, rocky mountains live in considerable poverty.

Giay

Population: 50,000 · Based in: Lao Cai, Lai Chau, Ha Giang

The **Giay** (pronounced "Zay") are a relatively small minority group. Traditional society is feudal, with a strict demarcation between the local aristocracy and the peasant classes. All villagers work the communal lands, living in closely knit villages of stilthouses. A few Giay women still wear the traditional style of dress, distinguished by the highly coloured, circular panel sewn around the collar and a shirt-fastening on the right shoulder; the shirt itself is often of bright green, pink or blue. On formal occasions, women may also wear a chequered turban.

Hmong

Population: 800,000 · Based in: the north, villages at high altitude

Since the end of the eighteenth century, groups of Miao people have been fleeing southern China, heading for Laos, Myanmar, Thailand and Vietnam. Miao meant "barbarian", whereas their adopted name, **Hmong**, means "free people". Poor farming land, geographical isolation and their traditional seclusion from other people have left the Hmong one of the most impoverished groups in Vietnam; standards of health and education are low, while infant mortality is exceptionally high. Hmong farmers grow maize, rice and vegetables on burnt-over land, irrigated fields and terraced hillsides. Traditionally they also grew poppies, though this is now discouraged by the government. Hmong people raise cattle, buffaloes and horses, and have recently started growing fruit trees, such as peach, plum and apple. They are also skilled hunters and gather forest products, including honey, medicinal herbs, roots and bark, either for their own consumption or to trade at weekly markets. Hmong houses are built flat on the ground, rather than raised on stilts.

Until recently there was no written Hmong language, but a strong oral tradition of folk songs, riddles and proverbs. Perhaps the Hmong are best known, however, for their handicrafts, particularly weaving hemp and cotton, cloth that is then coloured with indigo dyes. Many Hmong women, and some men, still wear traditional indigo apparel and chunky silver jewellery. The main subgroups are **White**, **Red**, **Green**, **Black** and **Flower Hmong**; though the origin of the names is unknown, there are marked differences in dialect and social customs as well as dress and hairstyle, especially among the women.

Muong

Population: 1.2 million · Based in: Yen Bai, Son La, Thanh Hoa

The lower hills from the Red River Valley are the domain of the **Muong** ethnic minority, with the majority now living in Hoa Binh province. The Muong are believed to share common ancestors with the Viet. It's thought that the two groups split around two thousand years ago, after which the Muong developed relatively independently in the highlands. Society is traditionally dominated by aristocratic families, who distribute communal land to the villagers in return for labour and tax contributions; the symbols of their authority are drums and bronze gongs.

Muong stilthouses are similar to those built by the Thai, and the main staple is rice, though fishing, hunting and gathering are all still fairly important. Muong people have varied cultural traditions, including call-and-response singing and epic tales, and they are famed for their embroidery, typically creating bold geometric designs in black and white. Older Muong women continue to wear the traditional long, black skirt and close-fitting shirt; a broad, heavily embroidered belt is the main accessory, and many women also wear a simple white headscarf.

Nung
Population: 750,000 • Based in: Cao Bang, Lang Son

Nung people are closely related to the Tay, sharing the same language and often living in the same villages. Nung farmers terrace the lower slopes to provide extra land, and are noted for the wide variety of crops they grow, including maize, groundnuts and a whole host of vegetables. In fact, the Nung are reckoned to be the best horticulturalists in Vietnam, while their blacksmiths are almost as renowned. Unusually, the traditional Nung house has clay walls and a tiled roof, and is built either flat on the ground or with only one section raised on stilts.

Most Nung are Buddhist, worshipping Quan Am, though they also honour the spirits and their ancestors. They are particularly adept at call-and-response singing, relishing the improvised double entendre. Not surprisingly, Nung traditional dress is similar to that of the Tay, though hemmed with coloured bands. Women often sport a neck scarf with brightly coloured fringes and a shoulder bag embroidered with the sun, stars and flowers, or woven in black and white interspersed with delicately coloured threads.

Tay
Population: 1.5 million • Based in: Cao Bang, Lang Son, Bac Kan

The **Tay** are Vietnam's largest minority group living in the highlands, and are concentrated in the northeast, from the Red River Valley east to the coastal plain, where they settled over two thousand years ago. Through centuries of close contact with lowlanders, Tay society has been strongly influenced by Viet culture, sharing many common rituals and Confucian practices.

Many Tay have now adopted Viet architecture and dress, but it's still possible to find villages of thatched stilthouses, characterized by a railed balcony around the building. Nowadays it's largely the women who still wear the Tay's traditional long, belted dress of indigo-dyed cloth, with a similarly plain, knotted headscarf peaked at the front and set off with lots of silver jewellery. Tay farmers are famous for their animal husbandry, and they also specialize in fish-farming and growing high-value crops, such as anise, tobacco, soya and cinnamon.

The Tay have developed advanced irrigation systems for wet-rice cultivation, including the huge waterwheels found beside rivers in the northeast. They have had a written language – based on Chinese ideograms – since the fifteenth century, fostering a strong literary tradition; call-and-response singing is also popular, as are theatrical performances, kite-flying and a whole variety of other games.

Thai
Population: 1.3 million • Based in: Dien Bien Phu, Son La, Mai Chau

The **Thai** minority is the dominant group in the northwest mountains from the Red River south to Nghe An, though most live in Lai Chau and Son La provinces. They are distantly related to the Thai of Thailand and to groups in southern China, their ancestral homeland. However, Thai people have been living in Vietnam for at least two thousand years and show similarities with both Viet and Tay cultures. Traditional Thai society was strongly hierarchical, ruled over by feudal lords who controlled vast land-holdings worked by the villagers. Their written language, which is based on Sanskrit, has furnished a literary legacy dating back five centuries, including epic poems, histories and a wealth of folklore. The Thai are also famous for their unique dance repertoire and finely woven brocades decorated with flowers, birds and dragons, which are on sale in local markets. From their early teens women learn how to weave and embroider, eventually preparing a set of blankets for their dowry. Thai houses are often still constructed on stilts, with wood or bamboo frames, though the architecture varies between regions.

There are two main subgroups: **Black Thai** (around Dien Bien Phu, Tuan Giao and Son La) and **White Thai** (Mai Chau, Muang Lay), whose names are often attributed to the traditional colour of the women's shirts, though this is open to dispute. Both groups wear long, narrow skirts and fitted shirts, topped with an intricately embroidered headdress.

Minorities in the central highlands

Nearly all minority groups living in the central highlands are indigenous peoples; most are matrilineal societies with a strong emphasis on community life and with some particularly complex burial rites. Catholic **missionaries** enjoyed considerable success in the central highlands, establishing a mission at Kon Tum in the mid-nineteenth century; then early in the twentieth century Protestantism was also introduced to the region. Likewise, **Vietnamese influence** has been stronger here than in northern Vietnam, while the **American War** caused severe disruption. Nevertheless, their cultures have been sufficiently strong to resist complete assimilation. For how much longer is a matter of debate, as thousands of lowland Viets, plus significant numbers of northern minorities, are moving into the region, clearing huge swathes of land for coffee plantations on the back of a booming export market.

Bahnar (Ba Na)

Population: 170,000 • Found in: Kon Tum

Now a highland people, the **Bahnar** trace their ancestry back many centuries to communities coexisting on the coastal plains with the Cham and Jarai. The most distinctive aspect of a Bahnar village is its *rong*, or communal house, the roof of which may be up to 20m high. This is the centre of village cultural and ceremonial life, and also the home of adolescent boys, who are taught Bahnar history, the skills of hunting and other manly matters. Village houses grouped around the *rong* are typically stilthouses with a thatched or tiled roof, and are often decorated with geometric motifs.

The Bahnar people are skilled horticulturalists, growing maize, sweet potato or millet, together with indigo, hemp or tobacco as cash crops. Bahnar groups also erect funeral houses decorated with elaborate carvings, although they are less imposing than those of the Jarai. Sometime after the burial, wooden statues, gongs, wine jars and other items of family property are placed in the funeral house.

E De

Population: 270,000 • Found in: Dak Lak

People of the **E De** minority live in stilthouses grouped together in a village, or *buon*. These longhouses, which can be up to 100m in length, are boat-shaped with hardwood frames, bamboo floors and walls, and topped with a high thatched roof. As many as a hundred family members may live in a single house, under the authority of the oldest or most respected woman, who owns all family property, including the house and domestic animals; wealth is indicated by the number of ceremonial gongs. Other much-prized heirlooms are the large earthenware jars used for making the rice wine drunk at festivals. Like the Jarai, E De people worship the kings of Fire and Water among a whole host of animist spirits, and also erect a funeral house on their graves. Both the original longhouse and its grave-site replica are often decorated with fine carvings.

The E De homeland lies in a region of red soils on the rolling western plateaux. In the nineteenth and twentieth centuries French settlers introduced coffee and rubber estates to the area, often seizing land from the local people they called Rhadé. Traditional swidden farming has gradually been disappearing, a process accelerated by the American War and the forced relocation of E De into permanent settlements.

Jarai (Gia Rai)
Population: 300,000 • Based in: Gia Lai

The **Jarai** are the largest minority group in the central highlands. It's thought that they left the coastal plains around two thousand years ago, settling on the fertile plateau around Pleiku. Some ethnologists hold that Cham people are in fact a branch of the Jarai, and they certainly share common linguistic traits and a matrilineal social order. Young Jarai women initiate the marriage proposal and afterwards the couple live in the wife's family home, with children taking their mother's name. Houses are traditionally built on stilts, facing north. The focus of village life is the communal house, or *rong*, where the council of elders and their elected chief meet.

Animist beliefs are still strong, and the Jarai world is populated with spirits, the most famous of which are the kings of Water, Fire and Wind, represented by shamans who are involved in rain-making ceremonies and other rituals. Funeral rites are particularly complex and expensive: each family maintains a funeral house that they ornament with evocative sculptures of people, birds and objects from everyday life. The Jarai also have an extensive musical repertoire, the principal instruments being gongs and the unique *k'long put*, made of bamboo tubes into which the players force air by clapping their hands. During the American War the majority of Jarai villagers moved out of their war-torn homeland, many being resettled in Pleiku; only in recent years are some slowly returning.

Koho (Co Ho) and Lat
Population: 130,000 • Based in: Da Lat

The **Koho** minority is subdivided into six highly varied subgroups, including the **Lat**. The typical Koho house is built on stilts with a thatched roof and bamboo walls and flooring. Although many Koho were converted to Christianity in the early twentieth century, spirit worship is widely practised and each family adopts a guardian spirit from the natural world. Catholic missionaries developed a phonetic script for the Koho language, but the oral tradition remains strong. Unlike many minorities in this region, the Koho incorporate dance into their religious rites, and it is an important element of them; a variety of musical instruments, such as gongs, bamboo flutes and buffalo horns, are also involved. Subgroups of the Koho minority are famed for their pottery and ironwork, whereas Lat farmers have a reputation for constructing sophisticated irrigation systems.

Mnong
Population: 90,000 • Based in: Dak Lak, Da Lat

The **Mnong** ethnic minority is probably best known for its skill in hunting elephants and domesticating them for use in war, for transport and for their ivory. Mnong people are also the creators of the lithophone, a kind of stone xylophone thought to be among

---

THE VIET KIEU

Overseas Vietnamese are known in their homeland as **Viet Kieu**. There are over two million worldwide, the figure rocketing up in the 1980s as 750,000 fled Vietnam by boat (see box, p.448). Many settled in America, Australia and France, but in recent years the Vietnamese government has gradually made it easier for Viet Kieu to return; procedures for sending money back to family members from overseas were also simplified, providing an important source of extra income for individuals and becoming increasingly valuable in the wider economy, especially in the south. Not surprisingly, however, the attitudes of those who stuck it out in Vietnam towards Viet Kieu are ambivalent, and the government itself is unsure about how to handle relations with the Viet Kieu; in general their money and expertise are welcomed but not necessarily their politics, nor their Western ways.

the world's most ancient musical instruments; an example is on show at the Ethnographic Museum in Buon Ma Thuot (see p.366). Mnong houses are usually built flat on the ground and, though the society is generally matrilineal, village affairs are organized by a male chief. Mnong craftsmen are skilled at basketry and printing textiles, while they also make the copper, tin and silver jewellery worn by both sexes. In traditional burial rituals a buffalo-shaped coffin is placed under a funeral house, which is peopled with wooden statues and painted with black, red or white designs.

Sedang (Xo Dang)

Population: 130,000 • Based in: Kon Tum

The **Sedang** were traditionally a warlike people whose villages were surrounded with defensive hedges, barbed with spears and stakes, and with only one entrance. Inter-village wars were frequent, and the Sedang also carried out raids on the peaceable Bahnar, mainly to seize prisoners rather than territory. In the past, Sedang religious ritual involved human sacrifices to propitiate the spirits – a practice that was later modified into a profitable business, selling slaves to traders from Laos and Thailand.

In the early twentieth century, the French authorities conscripted Sedang labour to build Highway 14 from Kon Tum to Da Nang; conditions were so harsh that many died, provoking a rebellion in the 1930s. Soon after, the Viet Minh won many recruits among the Sedang in their war against the French. In the American War some Sedang groups fought for the Viet Cong, while others were formed into militia units by the American Special Services. But when fighting intensified after 1965, Sedang villagers were forced to flee, and many now live in almost destitute conditions, having lost their ancestral lands.

Each Sedang extended family occupies a longhouse, built on stilts and usually facing east; central to village life is the communal house where young men and boys sleep, and where all the major ceremonies take place. Because villages historically had relatively little contact with each other, there are marked variations between the social customs of the subgroups,

---

VIETNAM'S REAL-LIFE KURTZ

The Sedang played their part in one of colonial Vietnam's oddest interludes and one which finds echoes in Joseph Conrad's novella *Heart of Darkness*, in which a mysterious voyager named Kurtz proclaims himself king, deep in the Belgian Congo – a story later borrowed by Francis Ford Coppola for his film *Apocalypse Now* (see p.486).

The career of French rogue **Marie-David de Mayréna** was a chequered one to say the least. After a stint with the French army in Cochinchina in the mid-1860s, he made his way back to Paris, only to return to the East after having failed as a banker. Back in Vietnam by the 1880s, he established himself as a planter around Ba Ria, until 1888 when the governor sent him to explore the highlands. Of the hundred or so porters and soldiers who accompanied him, only one, a Frenchman named Alphonse Mercurol, remained by the time he reached Kon Tum. Through the contacts of the French missionaries based there, Mayréna was able to arrange meetings with local tribal chiefs; soon the leaders fell under the spell of his "blue eyes" and "bold, confident stare", and he conspired to proclaim himself **King Marie I of Sedang**, while Mercurol adopted the title "Marquis of Hanoi". For three months, Mayréna ruled from a straw hut flying the national flag (a white cross on a blue background, with a red star in the centre), legislating, creating an army and even declaring war on the neighbouring Jarai people.

But Mayréna was more interested in money than sovereignty, and within months he had decamped, setting off in the hope of getting some mileage from his "title". In his book *Dragon Ascending* Henry Kamm quotes an erstwhile manager of Saigon's *Continental*, where Mayréna boarded on credit with assorted courtiers: "Alas, when, several days later, Mayréna moved out of the hotel, nothing was left to Laval [the then hotel manager] as payment for his services, except for a decoration, that of the National Order of the Kingdom of the Sedangs, which the king gave him before departure." Returning to Europe, Mayréna took to selling fictitious titles and mining concessions to raise cash but, inevitably, cracks began to appear in his story, and he fled back to Southeast Asia in 1890 where he died in penury on Malaya's Tioman Island, supposedly of a snake bite.

and so far seventeen Sedang dialects have been identified. Agricultural techniques are more consistent, mainly swidden farming supplemented by horticulture and hunting.

Minorities in the southern lowlands

As the Viet people pushed down the coastal plain and into the Mekong Delta they displaced two main ethnic groups, the Cham and Khmer, whose descendants remain today.

Cham

Population: 130,000 • Based in: Ninh Thuan, Binh Thuan, Cambodian border area

Up until the tenth century powerful **Cham** kings had ruled over most of southern Vietnam (see box, p.430). Today's surviving coastal communities are still largely Hindu worshippers of Shiva and follow the matrilineal practices of their Cham ancestors; they earn a living from farming, silk-weaving and crafting jewellery of gold or silver. Groups along the Cambodian border are Islamic and, in general, patrilineal. They engage in river fishing, weaving and cross-border trade, with little agricultural activity. On the whole, Cham people have adopted the Vietnamese way of life and dress, though their traditional arts, principally dance and music, have experienced a revival in recent years.

Hoa

Population: 800,000 • Based in: Mekong Delta

Ethnic Chinese people, known in Vietnamese as **Hoa**, form one of Vietnam's largest minority groups. Throughout the country's history, Chinese people, mostly from China's southern provinces, have been emigrating to Vietnam as administrators and merchants or as refugees from persecution. In the mid-seventeenth century the collapse of the Ming dynasty sent a human deluge southwards, and there were other large-scale migrations in the nineteenth century and then the 1940s. Until the early nineteenth century all Hoa, even those of mixed blood, were considered by the Viets to be Chinese. After that date, however, they were admitted to public office and gradually became integrated into Vietnamese society. Nevertheless, the Hoa remain slightly apart, living in close communities according to their ancestral province in China.

The Hoa have tended to settle in urban areas, typically becoming successful merchants, artisans and business people, and playing an important role in the economy. Viet people have tended to distrust the Hoa, mainly because of their dominant commercial position and their close links with China. After 1975 the Hoa were badly hit when socialist policies were enforced, in what amounted to an anti-Chinese persecution. Tensions rose even further when China invaded Vietnam in 1979 and thousands of Hoa left the country to escape reprisals, forming a large majority of the "boat people" (see box, p.448). It's estimated that up to one third of the Hoa population eventually left Vietnam.

Khmer

Population: 1,000,000 • Based in: Mekong Delta

Ethnic **Khmer** (known in Vietnam as *Kho Me Khrom*) are the indigenous people of the Mekong Delta, including Cambodia; some arrived in Vietnam in the late 1970s as refugees from Pol Pot's brutal regime in Cambodia. Khmer farmers are noted for their skill at irrigation and wet-rice cultivation; it's said that they farm nearly 150 varieties of rice, each suited to specific local conditions. Traditionally, the Khmer live in villages of stilthouses erected on raised mounds above the floodwaters, but these days are more likely to build flat on the earth, along canals and roadways. The pagoda, however, is still a distinctive feature of Khmer villages, its brightly patterned roofs decorated with images of the sacred ancestral dragon, the *neak*. Although ancient beliefs persist, since the late thirteenth century the Khmer have been devout followers of Theravada Buddhism, as practised in Cambodia, Laos and Thailand. They produce fine silk and basketry, and wear distinctive red and white scarves.

Environmental issues

Vietnam is endowed with a wide variety of fauna and flora, including an unusually high number of bird species and a rich diversity of primates. Current estimates suggest there are over 12,000 plant species, around three hundred mammals and 850 birds, though remote areas are still being explored. Over recent years, particularly in the forest reserves bordering Laos, the identification of several species of plants, butterflies, snakes, birds and even mammals that were previously unknown has caused a sensation in the scientific community.

Such diversity is largely attributable to Vietnam's **range of habitats**, from the north's subalpine limestone mountains to the Mekong Delta's mangrove swamps and the country's 3400km of coastline. However, the list of endangered and **critically endangered species** is also long – over 880 types of animal and plant – as their domains are threatened by population pressure, widespread logging and pollution, particularly along the coastal zone. One of the biggest environmental challenges facing Vietnam is to preserve its rapidly diminishing forest areas by establishing methods of sustainable use.

Happily, the government does at least seem to recognize the value of Vietnam's biodiversity and the need to act quickly. It has now put in place a number of **laws** dealing with environmental issues, the most important being the Environmental Protection Law, revised in 2015, which sets out national policy covering the prevention and control of pollution, the protection, conservation and sustainable use of natural resources and improving environmental quality. The promulgation of a law on tourism contains provisions on sustainable tourism from an environmental and social perspective, aiming to encourage greater community participation and spreading the benefits more widely. The law also includes tougher regulations on tourism-related pollution, though ensuring these laws are effectively implemented is a problem.

Ecological warfare

The word "**ecocide**" was coined during the American War, in reference to the quantity of herbicides dropped from the air to deprive the Viet Cong of their safe areas, deep under the triple-canopy forest, and their food crops. The most notorious defoliant used was **Agent Orange**, along with agents Blue and White, all named after the colour of the respective storage containers. Their active ingredient was **dioxin**, a slowly dissolving poison that has a half-life of seven to eleven years in human tissue. It's estimated that over eighty million litres of chemical defoliants were sprayed from American planes crisscrossing the forests and mangrove swamps of South Vietnam and the Demilitarized Zone between 1961 and 1971. Figures vary, but somewhere between twenty and forty percent of the South's land area was sprayed at least once and in some cases more frequently, destroying up to a quarter of the forest cover.

The environmental impact was perhaps greatest on the **mangrove forests**, which are particularly susceptible to defoliants. Spraying destroyed about half of all Vietnam's mangrove forests, and since they don't regenerate naturally, they have to be replanted by hand, a slow operation with a low success rate. The herbicides also had a severe impact on **soldiers**, both Vietnamese and American, and **villagers** who were caught in the spraying or absorbed dioxins from the food chain and from drinking water. Children and the elderly were the worst affected: some died immediately from the poisons, while others suffered respiratory diseases, skin rashes and other ailments. Soon it became apparent that the dioxins were also causing abnormally high levels of

THE SARUS CRANE

A symbolically significant success of local environmentalists has been the return of the **Sarus crane** to the Mekong Delta, near the Cambodian border, though the success promises to be short-lived. The crane, a stately bird with an elaborate courtship dance, abandoned its nesting grounds when the Americans drained the wetlands and dropped herbicides and then napalm in their attempts to rout Viet Cong soldiers from the marshes. After the war thousands of landless farmers were settled in the area, but the acidic soils proved difficult to farm so the provincial governor re-established a portion of the wetlands, thus restoring the cranes' natural habitat. The first Sarus cranes reappeared in 1986, after which Tam Nong Bird Sanctuary, now the **Tram Chim National Park** (see p.131), was set up to protect the crane and other returning species. Though the population increased initially, in recent years no more than a few dozen have returned to spend the dry season in the delta's wetlands.

miscarriage, birth defects, neurological disease and cancers. Surveys suggest that over three million Vietnamese may be affected, many of whom now receive a tiny monthly allowance from the government. The chemical companies themselves and the US government have so far resisted claims to pay compensation.

Apart from using herbicides, American and South Vietnamese troops cut down swathes of forest with specially adapted bulldozers, called **Rome Ploughs**. These vehicles were capable of slicing through a three-metre-thick tree trunk, and were used to clear roadsides and riverbanks against ambushes, or to remove vestiges of undergrowth and trees left after the spraying. Finally, there were the **bombs** themselves: an estimated thirteen million tonnes of explosives were dropped during the course of the war, leaving a staggering 25 million bomb craters, the vast majority in the South. In addition to their general destructive power, explosions compact the soil to the point where nothing will grow, and napalm bombs sparked off forest fires. The worst single incident occurred in 1968 when U Minh forest, at the southern tip of Vietnam, burned for seven weeks – 85 percent of its trees were destroyed. It's estimated that overall more than 20,000 square kilometres of Vietnam's forests were destroyed during the American War as a result of defoliation, napalm fires and bombing.

Since the war, Vietnamese environmentalists led by Professor Vo Quy, founder of the Center for Natural Resources and Environmental Studies at Hanoi University, have instigated **reforestation programmes**, slowly coaxing life back into even the worst-affected regions. This has involved pioneering work in regenerating tropical forest, planting native species under a protective umbrella of acacia and eucalyptus.

Postwar deforestation

Originally, perhaps 75 percent of Vietnam's land area would have been covered by forest. By 1945 it had dwindled to 43 percent, and was down to just 24 percent (roughly 80,000 square kilometres) in 1975. Since then, at least another 30,000 square kilometres of forest have been lost to commercial **logging**, agricultural **clearance**, forest **fires**, firewood collection and **population pressure**. Cover has now edged back up to 40 percent, however, thanks to one of the world's most ambitious reforestation programmes, launched in 1998, to replant 50,000 square kilometres. Although an impressive 1300 square kilometres are planted each year, this only just exceeds the area being lost to clearance, and the new growth is largely fast-growing acacia and eucalypt, rather than native species. The area under "high-quality" native forest continues to shrink, and primary forest constitutes less than one percent of the total.

The **worst-affected areas** are Vietnam's northern mountains, the central province of Nghe An and around Pleiku in the central highlands. In these areas soil erosion is a major problem, and countrywide floods are getting worse as a result of deforestation along the watersheds. Many rare hardwoods are fast disappearing, and the fragile

CONSERVATION AND THE NATIONAL PARKS

Vietnam recognized the need for conservation relatively early, establishing its first national park (Cuc Phuong) in 1962 and adopting a **National Conservation Strategy** in 1985. The most accessible or interesting of Vietnam's thirty **national parks** are listed below, but unless you're prepared to spend a lot of time in them, it's unlikely that you'll see many animals. Birds, insects and butterflies are more readily visible, and often the dense tropical vegetation or mountain scenery are in themselves worth the journey. To learn more about Vietnam's protected areas, and how to access them, Fauna and Flora International's *Ecotourism Map of Vietnam* is quite useful, though it hasn't been updated since 2005; all proceeds go to support Vietnamese primate conservation.

Ba Be (see p.423). A park of 80 square kilometres, containing Vietnam's largest natural lake and over 350 butterfly species. The park has limited tourist facilities, but boat trips, jungle walks and homestays in minority villages are possible.

Bach Ma (see p.272). This park of 220 square kilometres sits on the climatological divide between the tropical forests of the south and the northern subtropical zone, and contains Vietnam's lushest tropical rainforests. It is also home to a wide variety of bird species, including several rare pheasants, and over 1400 recorded plants.

Cat Ba (see p.331). The park covers only 152 square kilometres, but 5400 of these are important marine reserves, including areas of coral reef. The limestone island supports a broad range of habitats, a wealth of medicinal plants and a critically endangered population of golden-headed langurs.

Cat Tien (see p.172). The wetlands at this 740square-kilometre park are a haven for water birds, including the critically endangered white-winged duck and white-shouldered ibis, as well as the equally rare Siamese crocodile.

Cuc Phuong (see p.320). Vietnam's first national park, Cuc Phuong was established in 1962 in an area of limestone hills relatively close to Hanoi. The park covers 220 square kilometres and contains a number of unique, ancient trees and provides excellent birdwatching, as well as an opportunity to see some of the world's rarest monkeys in its Endangered Primate Rescue Center.

Phong Nha-Ke Bang (see p.309). Established in 2002, this 860square-kilometre park along the mountain chain bordering Laos is best known for its extensive underground river system. The park itself is home to more than sixty different animal species, including several types of langur.

Tram Chim (see p.131). One of Vietnam's most important wetlands ecosystems, comprising 75 square kilometres in the Mekong Delta and providing haven to thousands of overwintering water birds. Its most famous visitors are the critically vulnurable Sarus crane (see box, p.471).

Yok Don (see p.189). Lying on the border with Cambodia, Yok Don constitutes 1115 square kilometres carved out of Vietnam's most extensive forests. The area is also one of the most biologically diverse in the whole of Indochina, supporting rare Indochinese tigers and Asian elephants.

To support environmental programmes already taking place in Vietnam, contact the following organizations:

BirdLife International UK ☎0122 327 7318, ⊛birdlife.org. Trip reports are welcomed by their Hanoi office (✉birdlife@birdlife.org.vn).

Fauna and Flora International UK ☎0122 357 1000, ⊛fauna-flora.org.

International Crane Foundation US ☎608 356 9462, ⊛savingcranes.org.

WWF International Switzerland ☎22 364 9111, ⊛wwf.panda.org.

ecosystems are no longer able to support a wildlife population forced into ever-smaller pockets of undisturbed jungle. Much of the blame for this rapid reduction in the forest cover is often laid on the **ethnic minorities** who traditionally clear land for farming and rely on the forests for building timber and firewood. However, lowland Vietnamese settling in the mountains have also put pressure on scant resources.

Both lowland Vietnamese and minority people have cleared huge swathes of the central highlands for **coffee plantations,** while the carefully replanted coastal mangrove forest is threatened by uncontrolled development of intensive **prawn farming**. Another significant threat to the forests is the highly lucrative **timber trade**, both legal and illegal. By **replanting**, it's hoped to create sustainable forests for commercial logging and to protect the tiny remaining areas of primary forest, but **enforcement** is hampered by lack of resources. The authorities have devolved the management and protection of the forest reserves to local communities, with some success.

Wildlife

Forest clearance, warfare, pollution and economic necessity have all contributed to the loss of natural habitat and reduced Vietnam's broad species base. In 1994, when Vietnam signed the **Convention on International Trade in Endangered Species** (CITES), which bans the traffic in animals or plants facing extinction, the species list identified 365 animal species in need of urgent protection. Among these, the Javan rhino, possibly the world's rarest large mammal, has already become extinct in the country, while no fewer than five of the world's most endangered primate species, including the golden-headed (or Cat Ba) langur and the Tonkin snub-nosed langur, survive in small isolated communities in the northern forests. Other severely endangered species include the Indochina tiger and Asian elephant. Vietnam is also home to around 850 species of **bird**, with the highest number of endemic species in mainland Southeast Asia. Again, many of these are under threat of extinction, including the Vietnamese pheasant, small numbers of which have been recorded in Ha Tinh and Quang Binh provinces.

Hunting continues to be a vital source of local income, as a walk round Vietnamese markets soon reveals. Wild animals and birds are sought for their meat or to satisfy the demand for **medicinal products** and live specimens, an often illegal (but extremely lucrative) business. Since the border with China was reopened in the early 1990s, smuggling of rare species has increased, among them the Asiatic black bear, whose gall bladder is prized as a cure for fevers and liver problems; relentless hunting has decimated the population to small numbers in the north. Similarly, Vietnam's population of wild Asian elephants is now reduced to fewer than one hundred individuals, down from two thousand in the 1970s. Not only has their habitat along the Cambodian border declined, but poachers have been hunting the elephants for their tusks since 1975. At least ten elephants were killed in Dak Lak and Dong Nai provinces during 2010 and 2011, and wildlife experts are warning that the Asian elephant could be extinct in Vietnam within a decade.

Fortunately, quite large areas of the Vietnamese interior remain amazingly untouched, especially the Truong Son Mountains north of the Hai Van Pass, the southern central highlands and lowland forests of the Mekong Delta. These isolated areas are rich in **biodiversity** and have yielded spectacular discoveries in recent years. In 2015, 87 new species were identified in Vietnam, including the **wooly-headed bat** and the **orange-eyed litter frog**, both found in the Central Highlands.

Protected areas, with buffer zones and corridors linking reserves to conservation areas across borders, have been set up. The task is fraught with difficulties, such as achieving cross-border cooperation and establishing effective policing of reserves – especially against poaching and illegal logging – with inadequate personnel and financial resources. At the same time, the authorities have been working to find alternative sources of income and food for people living in or near protected areas, and carrying out educational work on the importance of conservation and its relevance to their daily lives.

The government has also been adding to the number of national parks and nature reserves over a number of years, but the most recent were in 2006: U Minh Ha National Park, near the southernmost tip of the Mekong Delta, and Xuan Nha Nature Reserve, in Son La province in the country's northwest. As a further boost to conservation efforts, in 2000 UNESCO recognized an area of mangrove forest at Can Gio in the Mekong Delta and Cat Tien National Park as Vietnam's first "Man and Biosphere" reserves. Since then another half-dozen sites have been added.

Sustainable tourism

There's a growing awareness among tourists and travel companies of the negative impact tourism can have on the environment and local culture – the very things most people come to see. All too often the terms **ecotourism** and **sustainable tourism** are reduced to mere marketing gimmicks. Mass tourism didn't really get going in Vietnam until the mid-1990s. From just over one million in 1995, the number of foreign visitors (including business trips) topped 10 million in 2016, while the number of domestic holidaymakers currently stands at around 62 million, and is growing even faster. Not surprisingly, the Vietnamese government is eager to promote tourism as a **key revenue-earner** and has significantly eased visa regulations, among other things, in the hope of attracting more foreign visitors. This sudden influx of sightseers, coupled with a lack of effective planning or control, is putting pressure on some of the country's most famous beauty spots.

In response, the government has gradually introduced a number of laws and initiatives placing greater emphasis on the conservation of the nation's natural – and cultural – heritage. Local authorities in **Hoi An** have banned cars from the centre and put a block on further hotel construction in addition to introducing restrictive pricing to control the flow of tourists. Some of this revenue is being ploughed back into improving the townscape – for example, renovating the old houses, hiding television aerials and burying cables. In **Ha Long Bay**, the problems of notoriously haphazard hotel development are exacerbated by **pollution** from tourist boats (plastic bags and bottles floating on the water tend to spoil otherwise idyllic views), fish farms and nearby coalfields, and by the presence of a major port. Concern over the future of this World Heritage Site, however, means that the issues are at least being discussed, and various measures, such as more effective management of the caves, have been put in place.

Perhaps the key areas, however, are the **uplands** of north and central Vietnam. These are increasingly popular destinations, both for their outstanding natural beauty and their communities of **ethnic minority people**. In the honey-pot market town of **Sa Pa**, for example, the number of hotels and guesthouses has mushroomed – from none before 1991 to around 180 in 2013 – and the town's famous market attracts more tourists than minority people. Some of these people, disturbed by the unwanted attention and intrusive cameras, now shy away from Sa Pa completely, in favour of more inaccessible markets. The challenge is how to achieve **responsible tourism** (see box, p.53) that contributes to the **long-term development** of the local community while also preserving cultural and biological diversity.

Music and theatre

The binding element in all Vietnam's traditional performing arts is music, and particularly singing (*hat*), which is a natural extension to an already musical language. The origins of Vietnamese music can be traced back as far as the bronze drums and flutes of Dong Son, and further again to the lithophone (stone xylophone) called the *dan da*, the world's oldest known instrument. The Chinese influence is evident in operatic theatre and stringed instruments, while India bestowed rhythms, modal improvisations and several types of drum. Much later, especially during the nineteenth century, elements of European theatre and music were coopted, while during the twentieth century most Vietnamese musicians received a classical, Western training based on the works of Eastern bloc composers such as Prokofiev and Tchaikovsky.

Traditionally, the professions of artists or performers were hereditary, but the wars and political upheavals of the twentieth century have contributed to the loss of much of this largely oral tradition. While certain art forms continue to attract new talent, the younger generation is, on the whole, more interested in higher-paid professions and Vietnamese pop. As revolutionary ("red") music has waned since 1986, so pre-1975 music from the South, previously outlawed as "decadent and reactionary", is back with a vengeance, mixed with a sprinkling of artists from other Asian countries and the West.

Traditional theatre

Vietnam's **traditional theatre**, with its strong Chinese influence, is more akin to opera than pure spoken drama. A musical accompaniment and well-known repertoire of songs form an integral part of the performance, where the plots and characters are equally familiar to the audience. Nowadays, however, the two oldest forms, **Cheo** and **Tuong**, are struggling to survive, while even the more contemporary **Cai Luong** is losing out to television and video. However, other traditional arts have seen something of a revival, most notably **water puppetry** and folk-song performances. The stimulus for this came largely from tourism, but renewed interest in the trance music of **Chau Van** and the complexities of **Tai Tu** chamber music has been very much home-grown.

Hat Cheo

Vietnam's oldest surviving stage art, **Hat Cheo**, or "Popular Opera", has its roots in the Red River Delta where it's believed to have existed since at least the eleventh century. Performances consist of popular legends and everyday events, often with a biting satirical edge, accompanied by a selection of tunes drawn as appropriate from a common fund. Though the movements have become highly stylized over the centuries, Cheo's free form allows the actors considerable room for interpretation; the audience demonstrates its approval, or otherwise, by beating a drum.

Cheo has the reputation of being anti-establishment, thanks in part to its buffoon character who comments freely on the action, the audience and current events. It is promoted as the country's national theatre, although its local popularity continues to decline despite a body of new work dealing with contemporary issues.

Hat Tuong

Hat Tuong (also known as Hat Boi or Hat Bo), probably introduced from China around the thirteenth century, evolved from classical Chinese opera, and was originally for royal entertainment before being adopted by travelling troupes. Its story lines are mostly historic events and epic tales dealing with such Confucian principles as filial piety and relations between the monarch and his subjects. Tuong, like Cheo, is governed by rigorous rules in which the characters are rendered instantly recognizable by their make-up and costume. Setting and atmosphere are conjured not by props and scenery but through nuances of gesture and musical conventions with which the audience is completely familiar – and which they won't hesitate to criticize if badly executed. Of the clutch of Tuong troupes still in existence, Hanoi's Vietnam Tuong Theatre is one of the most active.

Hat Cai Luong

While performances of Tuong are comparatively rare events these days, it's still possible to catch an occasional performance of **Hat Cai Luong**, or "Reformed Theatre". Cai Luong originated in southern Vietnam in the early twentieth century, showing a French theatrical influence in its spoken parts, with short scenes and relatively elaborate sets. The action is a tangle of historical drama (such as *The Tale of Kieu*) and racy themes from the street (murder, drug deals, incest, theft and revenge). Its music is a similar hodgepodge: eighteenth-century chamber music played on amplified traditional instruments for the set pieces; electric guitar, keyboards and drums during the scene changes. Cai Luong's constant borrowing from contemporary culture – from language and plots to the incorporation of hit songs – has enabled it to keep pace with Vietnam's social changes. Around thirty professional Cai Luong troupes are currently performing, of which the best known are the Golden Bell Theatre in Hanoi (see p.380) and Ho Chi Minh City's Tran Huu Trang Cai Luong Theatre.

Water puppetry

The origin of **water puppetry** (*mua roi nuoc*) is obscure, beyond that it developed in the flooded rice paddies of the Red River Delta and usually took place in spring when there was less farm work to be done. The earliest record is a stele in Ha Nam province dated 1121 AD, suggesting that by this date water puppetry was already a regular feature at the royal court.

The art of water puppetry was traditionally a jealously guarded secret handed down from father to son; women were not permitted to learn the techniques in case they revealed them to their husbands' families. This contributed to its decline until the art seemed in danger of dying out altogether. Happily, a French organization, the Maison des Cultures du Monde, intervened and, since 1984, with newly carved puppets, a revamped programme and more elaborate staging, Vietnam's water-puppet troupes have played various international capitals to great acclaim – and can be seen daily in Hanoi (see p.380) and Ho Chi Minh City (see p.79). Where before gongs and drums alone were used for scene-setting and building atmosphere, today's national troupes often maintain a larger ensemble, similar to Hat Cheo, including zithers and flutes. The songs are also borrowed from the Cheo repertoire, particularly declamatory styles and popular folk tunes, and the show often includes a short recital of traditional music before the puppets emerge to create their own unique illusion.

Music, dance and song

Vietnamese artists have generated a variety of musical forms over the centuries, though the **voice** and its inherent melodic information is integral, and most instruments are, to some extent, made to do what voices do: delicate pitch bends, ornaments and subtle slides. The folk tradition is particularly rich, with its improvised courtship songs and the strident, sacred music of trance dances, to which the more than fifty ethnic minorities add their own repertoire of songs and instruments. Surprisingly, **dance** is less developed than in neighbouring Thailand, Cambodia and Laos.

Quan Ho

One of Vietnam's oldest song traditions is that of **Quan Ho**, or "call-and-response singing", a form that thrives in the Red River Delta, particularly Bac Giang province, and has parallels among the north's ethnic minorities. These unaccompanied songs are usually heard in spring, performed by young men and women bandying improvised lyrics back and forth. Quan Ho traditionally played a part in the courtship ritual and performers are applauded for their skill in complimenting or teasing their partner, earning delighted approval as the exchange becomes increasingly bawdy.

Hat Chau Van

Found in north and central Vietnam, **Hat Chau Van** is a form of ancient, sacred ritual music used to invoke the spirits during **trance possession ceremonies**. Statues of a pantheon of goddesses are placed in shrines to the Mother Goddess, Thanh Mau, found in Buddhist pagodas and village temples. Throughout the performance of hypnotically rhythmic music (the performers may be one or many, male or female) a medium enters a trance state and is possessed by a chosen deity. Because of the antireligious stance of the Vietnamese government until 1986, the style was practised in secret, though some pieces were adapted for inclusion in state-sponsored Cheo theatre. Chau Van is currently being revived by older practitioners in its original religious setting, promoted by a class of *nouveau riche* keen for the goddesses to intercede and protect their business interests.

Ca Tru

Although the song tradition known as **Ca Tru**, or Hat A Dao, dates back centuries, it became all the rage in the fifteenth century when the Vietnamese regained their independence from China. According to legend, a beautiful young songstress, A Dao, charmed the enemy with her songs of the verdant countryside and the way of life in the villages. Fascinated by her voice, the soldiers were encouraged to drink until they became incapacitated and could be pushed into the river and drowned.

The **lyrics** of Ca Tru are often taken from famous poems and are traditionally sung by a woman. The singer also plays a bamboo percussion instrument, and is accompanied by a three-string lute (*dan day*) and drum. This beguiling genre has undergone a strong revival in Hanoi in recent years, and was recognized by UNESCO as a form of Intangible World Heritage in 2009. It's well worth catching the performances at the Heritage House or the Dinh Kim Ngan in Hanoi (see p.351). In Hue excerpts from the closely related **Ca Hue** song tradition are performed for tourists on sampans on the Perfume River (see p.287).

Nhac Tai Tu

The traditional music accompanying Cai Luong theatre originated in eighteenth-century Hue. Played as pure chamber music, without the voice, it is known as **Nhac Tai Tu**, or "skilled chamber music of amateurs". This is one of the most delightful and challenging of all Vietnamese genres. The players have a great degree of improvisational latitude over a fundamental melodic skeleton; they must think and respond quickly, as in a game, and the resulting independently funky rhythms can be wild.

Nha Nhac

It was also in Hue under the Nguyen emperors that the specialized body of **royal music and dance** reached its peak of sophistication. These solemn ceremonial dances again owed their origins to the Chinese courtly tradition and were categorized into a highly complex system according to the occasion on which they would be performed: ritual dances to be held in temples or pagodas, during feasts or at various civil and military functions, and dances to mark particular anniversaries were just some of the distinctions.

TRADITIONAL INSTRUMENTS

STRING INSTRUMENTS

Many instruments whose strings are now made of steel, gut or nylon originally had **silk** strings; silk is now out of fashion, more for acoustic than ecological reasons. The most famous of these, and unique to Vietnam, is the monochord **dan bau** (or *dan doc huyen*), an ingenious invention perfectly suited to its job of mimicking vocal inflections. It is made from one string (originally silk obtained by yanking apart the live worm), stretched over a long amplified sounding box, fixed at one end. The other end is attached to a buffalo-horn "whammy bar" stalk that can be flexed to stretch or relax the string's tension. Meanwhile the string is plucked with a plectrum at its harmonic nodes to produce overtones that swoop and glide and quiver over a range of three octaves. Other "silk-stringed" instruments include the *dan nguyet* (moon-shaped lute), the *dan tranh* (sixteen-string zither), *dan nhi* (two-string fiddle with the bow running between the strings), *dan day* (a three-stringed lute with a long fingerboard used in Ca Tru and also unique to Vietnam) and *dan luc huyen cam* (a regular guitar with a fingerboard scalloped to allow for wider pitch bends).

PERCUSSION INSTRUMENTS

The *dan da* **stone** lithophone is the world's oldest instrument, consisting of six or more rocks (most commonly eleven) struck with heavy wooden mallets. Several sets have been found originating from one slate quarry in the central highlands, where the stones sing like nowhere else. The oldest *dan da* is now in Paris, but other sets exist in museums throughout Vietnam, such as the Ethnographic Museum in Buon Ma Thuot (see p.366).

Various kinds of **drum** (*trong*) are used, played with acrobatic use of the sticks in the air and on the sides. Some originated in China, while others were introduced from India via the Cham people, such as the double-headed "rice drum" (*trong com*), which was developed from the Indian *mridangam*; the name derives from thin patches of cooked rice-paste stuck on each membrane.

Representing **clay**, four thimble-size teacups are held in the fingers and often played as percussion instruments for Hue chamber music. Representing **metal**, the *sinh tien*, **coin clappers**, are another invention unique to Vietnam, combining in one unit a rasping scraper, wooden clapper and a sistrum rattle made from old coins. Bronze **gongs** are occasionally found in minority music, but Vietnam is the only country in Southeast Asia where tuned gamelan-type gong-chimes are not used.

WIND INSTRUMENTS

Air, **wood** and **bamboo** furnish a whole range of wind instruments, such as the many side- and end-blown flutes used for folk songs and to accompany poetry recitals; or the *ken*, a double-reed oboe common across Asia and played, appropriately, in funeral processions and other outdoor ceremonies. Five thin bones often dangle from the *ken* player's mouthpiece to suggest the delicate fingers of a young woman, while disguising the hideous grin necessary to play the instrument. The *song lang* is a slit drum, played by the foot, used to count the measures in Tai Tu skilled chamber music; while the *k'long put*, consisting of racks of bamboo pipes, is the only percussion instrument you don't actually touch but clap in front of. Another instrument from the same folk tradition is the *t'rung*, a type of xylophone made of ladders of tuned bamboo. Some of these instruments can be seen and heard in musical recitals at the Temple of Literature in Hanoi (see p.362).

As the Imperial court fell under European sway in the twentieth century, so the taste – and opportunity – for such music waned, until the late 1980s when it was revived by the provincial authorities with assistance from UNESCO. Hue's former Royal Theatre has now been renovated and is the venue for occasional performances of courtly music and dance by students of Hue University of Fine Arts. In 2003 UNESCO recognized **Nha Nhac** ("refined music") as a Masterpiece of Oral and Intangible Heritage.

New folk

Turn on the TV during the Tet Lunar New Year festivities and you can't miss the public face of Vietnamese traditional music: ethnic-costumed dancers, musicians and singers smilingly portraying the happy life of the worker. Fancy arrangements of well-known tunes from all over the country, including some token minorities' music, are spiced up with fancy hats and bamboo pianos. This choreographed entertainment known as **Modernized Folk Music** (Nhac Dan Toc Cai Bien) has only been "traditional" since 1956, when the Hanoi Conservatory of Music was founded and the teaching of folk music was deliberately "improved".

For the first time, music was learned from written Western notation (leading to the neglect of improvisational skills while opening the way for huge orchestras), and conductors were employed. Trained conservatoire graduates have spread throughout the country and been promoted through competitions and state-sponsored ensembles on TV, radio and even in the lobbies of classier hotels. The new corpus of music and song arrangements has become an emblem of national pride and scientific improvement. Folk songs, melodies from the ethnic minorities, Mozart and Chinese tunes are all ripe fodder for the arranger's pen. Much to the chagrin of the few remaining traditional musicians outside this system, this is now the predominant folk-based music generally heard in public.

Music for new folk is entertaining and accessible, albeit risking tawdriness; at its best, though, it can be an astonishing display of a lively new art form. Circular breathing and lightning-speed virtuosity are just some of the dazzling features of a performance.

V-pop

Though not as popular throughout East Asia as J-pop (from Japan), K-pop (from Korea) and C-pop (from China), **V-pop** has a huge following among young Vietnamese, and the top artists often perform sell-out shows in the country's biggest stadia. Many composers have tried their hand at writing a pop hit, but only about three are acknowledged masters: **Van Cao** (who died in 1995 and also wrote the national anthem), **Pham Duy** (who died in 2013 after many years of writing pointed political songs from the safe distance of California) and **Trinh Cong Son** (whose life of wine, women and song ended in 2001, with over six hundred songs to his credit).

Though many of the top names these days are home-grown, from 1975 to 1995 pop music was suppressed by the government, and during that period the most successful singers and songwriters were those who had fled to the US during or after the war. The main Vietnamese community there is based in **Orange County**, California, which has produced a string of successful pop artists, including Khanh Ha, Don Ho, Lam Nhat Tien, Nhu Quynh, Y Lan, Khanh Ly, Tuan Ngoc, Jimmi Nguyen, Trizzie Phuong Trinh and Thanh Ha. Though many of these are now ageing, they maintain a strong following in their homeland. For example, Khanh Ly performed sell-out concerts in 2014 in Hanoi and Da Nang at the age of 69.

Among Vietnam-based performers, legends include My Linh, Phuong Thanh, Hong Nhung, Lam Truong, Thanh Lam, Dam Vinh Hung, Thu Minh and My Tam, plus there's a host of younger stars, including Son Tung MT-P, Soobin Hoang Son, Noo Phuoc Thinh, Dong Nhi and Isaac (formerly of Vietnam's most successful boy band 365DaBand). My Tam is currently the country's foremost diva, having won a string of awards and hosted *Vietnam Idol* and *The Voice of Vietnam*.

The ubiquitous **pop-rock band** comprises a singer, bass guitar and one or two electronic keyboards, hailed throughout the country as the greatest labour-saving device, despite their cheesy sound. All the rhythm buttons on these portable keyboards that are so rarely used elsewhere – rumba, tango, bossa nova and surf-rock – are employed liberally here. The slap-echo on the singer's microphone is intentional; without it, they say, it sounds "unprofessional". Each evening, when the traffic noise dies down, you can hear the mournful laments of neighbouring karaoke bars mingling together, the ghostly echoes of lonely pop singers reverberating from another dimension.

Books

Of the vast canon of books written on the subject of Vietnam, the overwhelming majority concern themselves, inevitably, with the American War. Some indigenous attempts to come to terms with the conflicts that have caused Vietnam such pain have also filtered through the country's overcautious censorship. Some of the few novels that have reached the West are also reviewed here. Particularly recommended titles are marked with a ★ symbol.

For a decent copy of a book on Vietnam, your best bet is to scour bookshops before you set off from home – only Hanoi and Ho Chi Minh City have ranges of literature of any breadth, and then often only in photocopied offprint form. The exceptions to this are books produced by local presses, notably The Gioi Publishers, which you'll have difficulty finding outside Vietnam.

TRAVEL WRITING

Maria Coffey *Three Moons in Vietnam*. A delightfully jolly jaunt around Vietnam by boat, bus and bicycle. Coffey conspires to meet more locals in one day than most travellers do in a month, making this a valuable snapshot of modern Vietnam.

Sue Downie *Down Highway One*. In 1988 Sue Downie was one of the first Westerners since the American War to travel the length of Highway 1. Returning in the early 1990s, she witnesses the changes – not all good – transforming the country and people's daily lives.

Graham Greene *Ways of Escape*. Greene's global travels in the 1950s took him to Vietnam for four consecutive winters; the coverage of Vietnam in this slim autobiographical volume is intriguing, but tantalizingly short, its memories of dice-playing with French agents over vermouths and opium-smoking in Cho Lon are evidently templates for scenes in *The Quiet American* (see p.489).

Christopher Hunt *Sparring with Charlie*. Hunt can be a maddening travelling companion, but this account of his jaunt down the Ho Chi Minh Trail on a Russian-made motorbike is undeniably a page-turner.

★ **Norman Lewis** *A Dragon Apparent*. When in 1950 Lewis made the journey that would inspire his seminal Indochina travelogue, the Vietnam he saw was still a land of longhouses and Imperial hunts, though poised for renewed conflict; the erudite prose of this doyen of travel writers reveals a Vietnam now long gone.

W. Somerset Maugham *The Gentleman in the Parlour*. The fruit of Maugham's grand tour from Rangoon to Haiphong to recharge his creative batteries, *The Gentleman in the Parlour* finds him less than enamoured with Vietnam, his last stop. Nevertheless, his accounts of the Hue court teetering on the brink of extinction, and of a run-in with an old acquaintance in a Haiphong café, are vintage Maugham.

Karin Muller *Hitchhiking Vietnam*. A feisty American, Karin Muller went searching for the "real Vietnam", a Vietnam untouched by commercialism and Western culture. On the way she gets deported, is arrested on numerous occasions and meets some motley characters, but eventually finds what she's looking for among the minorities of the northwest mountains. Beautifully told, with great compassion and a never-failing sense of humour.

Andrew X. Pham *Catfish and Mandala*. After twenty years in America, Pham takes a gruelling bike ride through Vietnam to rediscover the country, his family and – in the process – himself. A compelling insight into the frustrations and fascinations of Vietnam.

Gontran de Poncins *From a Chinese City*. Believing that "the ancient customs of a national culture endure longer in remote colonies than in the motherland", de Poncins opted for a sojourn in Cho Lon as a means to a better understanding of the foibles of the Chinese; the resulting document of life in 1955 Cho Lon is a lively period piece, backed up by fluid illustrations.

Pam Scott *Hanoi Stories* and *Life in Hanoi*. Hanoi and its inhabitants – both local and expat, from its celebrities to its cyclo drivers – viewed through the lens of an Australian who came on business and stayed ten years.

James Sullivan *Over the Moat*. Cultures collide as Sullivan courts a Hue shopgirl he met while cycling through Vietnam in 1992. Part love story, part travelogue.

Paul Theroux *The Great Railway Bazaar*. His elaborate circumnavigation of Europe and Asia by train took Theroux, in 1973, to a South Vietnam still bewildered by the recent American withdrawal. In bleak soundbite accounts of rides from Saigon to Bien Hoa and Hue to Da Nang, he describes the war's awful legacy of poverty, suffering and infrastructural breakdown, but marvels at the country's unbowed, and unexpected, beauty.

Gabrielle M. Vassal *On and Off Duty in Annam*. An enchanting wander through early twentieth-century southern Vietnam, penned by the intrepid wife of a French army doctor. A stint in Saigon is followed by a boat trip to Nha Trang (where she was carried ashore "on the backs of natives through the breakers") and a gutsy foray into the central highlands; amazing prints of the Vietnamese and *montagnards* she encountered further enhance the account.

Justin Wintle *Romancing Vietnam*. Wintle's genial but lightweight yomp upcountry was one of the first of its kind, post-*doi moi*, and remains a pleasing aperitif to travels in Vietnam.

VIETNAMESE ABROAD

Donald Anderson (ed) *Aftermath: An Anthology of Post-Vietnam Fiction*. As the war's tendrils crept across the Pacific to America, they touched not only the people who fought, but also those who stayed at home. In their depictions of Americans, Amerasians and Asians regathering the strands of their lives, these short stories run the gamut of emotions provoked by war.

★**Robert Olen Butler** *A Good Scent from a Strange Mountain*. Pulitzer Prize-winning collection of short stories that ponder the struggles of Vietnamese in America to maintain the cultural ley lines linking them with their mother country, and the gulf between them and their Americanized offspring. War veteran Olen Butler's assured prose ensures the voices of his Vietnamese characters find perfect pitch.

★**Le Ly Hayslip** *Child of War, Woman of Peace*. In this follow-up to *When Heaven and Earth Changed Places* (see p.483), Hayslip's narrative shifts to America, where the cultural disorientation of a new arrival is examined.

VIETNAMESE LITERATURE

John Balaban and Nguyen Qui Duc (eds) *Vietnam: A Traveller's Literary Companion*. The editors of this entertaining volume of short stories, written by Vietnamese writers based both at home and abroad, chose to avoid tales of war and politics during their selection process, though both themes inevitably make their presence felt.

★**Bao Ninh** *The Sorrow of War*. This is a groundbreaking novel, largely due to its portrayal of Communist soldiers suffering the same traumas, fear and lost innocence as their American counterparts.

Steven Bradbury *Poems from the Prison Diary of Ho Chi Minh*. This beautifully rendered selection of the poems Ho penned while behind bars in 1942, in which he looks to birdsong and moonlight to ease the loneliness of prison life, provide a touching glimpse of the man behind the myth.

Alastair Dingwall (ed) *Traveller's Literary Companion to South-East Asia*. Among the bite-sized essays inside this gem of a book is an enlightening thirty-page segment on Vietnam, into which are crammed biopics, a recommended reading list, historical, linguistic and literary backgrounds. Excerpts range from classical literature to the writings of foreign journalists in the 1960s.

★**Duong Thu Huong** *Novel Without a Name*. A tale of young Vietnamese men seeking glory but finding only loneliness, disillusionment and death, as war abridges youth and curtails loves. A depiction of dwindling idealism, and a radical questioning of the political motives behind the war. Other highly acclaimed works by the same author include *Paradise of the Blind* and *Memories of a Pure Spring*.

★**Duong Van Mai Elliot** *The Sacred Willow*. Mai Elliot brings Vietnamese history to life in this compelling account of her family through four generations.

Wayne Karlin, Le Minh Khue and Truong Vu (eds) *The Other Side of Heaven*. A unique anthology of postwar fiction by Vietnamese and American authors. Though written by former enemies from all sides of the conflict, these stories echo back and forth the unifying themes of sorrow, pain and survival.

Le Minh Khue *The Stars, The Earth, The River*. Fourteen short stories by one of Vietnam's leading contemporary writers, an ex-sapper who gently details the seesaw of "tragedy and hope" which defines her war-torn generation.

Nguyen Du *The Tale of Kieu*. Epic poem of the ill-starred love between Kim and Kieu, a beautiful and educated girl who is forced to become a prostitute in order to free her parents from jail. She eventually escapes and marries Kim, but is now unable to return his affections. Seen as an allegory of Vietnamese history – or simply of the timeless conflict between duty and desire – the poem is widely held to represent the zenith of Vietnamese literature.

★**Nguyen Huy Thiep** *The General Retires and Other Stories*. Perhaps Vietnam's pre-eminent writer, Nguyen Huy Thiep articulates the lives of ordinary Vietnamese in these short stories – instead of following the prevailing trend of reimagining the lives of past heroes.

NOVELS SET IN VIETNAM

Marguerite Duras *The Lover*. Young French girl meets wealthy Chinese man on a Mekong Delta ferry; the ensuing affair initiates her into adulthood, with all its joys and responsibilities. The novel's depiction of a dysfunctional, hard-up French family in Vietnam provides an interesting slant on colonial life, showing it wasn't all vermouths and tennis.

★**Camilla Gibb** *The Beauty of Humanity Movement*. Gibb's deft characterization creates an endearing and poignant, contemporary tale that revolves around Hung, an old man whose life is dedicated to making pho even when there are no ingredients to be had in post-reunification Hanoi.

★**Graham Greene** *The Quiet American*. Greene's prescient and cautionary tale of the dangers of innocence in uncertain times, which anticipated America's boorish manhandling of Vietnam's political situation by several years, is still the best single account of wartime Vietnam. Its regular name-drops of familiar locales – Tay Ninh, the *Continental*, Dong Khoi – make it doubly enjoyable.

★**Anthony Grey** *Saigon*. Vietnamese history given a blockbuster makeover: a rip-roaring narrative, whose Vietnamese, French and American protagonists conspire to be present at all defining moments in recent Vietnamese history, from French plantation riots to the fall of Saigon.

Nguyen Kien *Tapestries*. This rich and beautifully woven novel is based on the extraordinary real-life story of the author's grandfather, who eventually became an embroiderer in the royal court of Hue. The context is a country on the cusp of change as French influence gains the upper hand.

★**Tim O'Brien** *Going After Cacciato*. A highly acclaimed, lyrical tale of an American soldier who simply walks out of the war and sets off for Paris, pursued by his company on a fantastical mission that takes them across Asia. The savage reality of war stands out vividly against a dream world of peace and freedom.

HISTORY

William J. Duiker *The Communist Road to Power in Vietnam*. One of America's leading analysts of the political context in Vietnam takes a long close look at why Communist Vietnam won its wars – as opposed to why France and America lost.

William J. Duiker *Ho Chi Minh: A Life*. Duiker turns his spotlight on the patriot and revolutionary who led Vietnam to independence. It's a thoroughly researched and exhaustive tome, particularly good on Ho's political evolution, though fails to get under the skin of this enigmatic man.

Bernard Fall *Hell in a Very Small Place*. The classic account of the siege of Dien Bien Phu, capturing the claustrophobia and the fear, written by a French-born American journalist.

★**Bernard Fall** *Street Without Joy*. Another masterpiece by Fall, charting the French debacle in Indochina, which became required reading for American generals and GIs – though it didn't prevent them committing exactly the same mistakes just a few years later.

David Halberstam *Ho*. Diminutive, sympathetic and highly readable biography of Vietnam's foremost icon, though no attempt is made to apportion blame for the disastrous land reforms of the 1950s.

★**Stanley Karnow** *Vietnam: A History*. Weighty tome that elucidates the entire span of Vietnamese history.

Michael Maclear *Vietnam: The Ten Thousand Day War*. A solid introductory account of the French and American wars, from Ho's alliance with Archimedes Patti, to the fall of Saigon.

Nguyen Khac Vien *Vietnam: A Long History*. Published by Hanoi's The Gioi Publishers, and therefore heavily weighted in favour of the Communists, but easier to get hold of in Vietnam than most histories.

Keith Weller Taylor *The Birth of Vietnam*. As a GI, Taylor was struck by the "intelligence and resolve" of his enemy. This meticulous account of the dawn of Vietnamese history, trawling the past from the nation's first recorded history up to the tenth century, is the result of his attempt to uncover their roots.

★**Martin Windrow** *The Last Valley: Dien Bien Phu and the French Defeat in Vietnam*. This meticulously researched and detailed account of the battle of Dien Bien Phu gives a brutally realistic picture of what it was like for the French

soldiers (many actually Vietnamese, Thai and North African) trapped in what came to be known as the "toilet bowl". Windrow's sympathy and admiration for the soldiers – on both sides – comes across loud and clear.

THE AMERICAN WAR

Mark Baker *Nam*. Unflinching firsthand accounts of the GI's descent from boot camp into the morass of death, paranoia, exhaustion and tedium. Gut-wrenchingly frank at times, the book depicts war as a rite of passage, and moral deterioration as a prerequisite to survival.

Tad Bartimus (ed) *War Torn: Stories of War from the Women Reporters Who Covered Vietnam*. Nine pioneering women journalists who covered the American War tell their tales, from the struggle to get there in the first place and be recognized in what was then an almost exclusively male profession to their reactions to the war itself and coming to terms with the aftermath.

★**Michael Bilton and Kevin Sim** *Four Hours in My Lai*. Brutally candid and immaculately researched reconstruction of the events surrounding the My Lai massacre of 1968; as harrowing a portrayal of the depths plumbed in war as you'll ever read.

★**Philip Caputo** *A Rumour of War*. One of the classics of the American War, Caputo's straightforward narrative is a powerful account of the numbing daily routine of the ordinary US soldier's life, the strange exhilaration of combat and the brutalization that accompanies war.

★**Denise Chong** *The Girl in the Picture*. Kim Phuc was the little girl running naked away from her napalm-bombed village in what is arguably the most famous – and most harrowing – photo taken during the American War. Not only did she survive the burns, just, but her resilience and capacity for forgiveness are remarkable. Denise Chong tells Kim's story simply, letting the horrific events speak for themselves.

Michael Clodfelter *Mad Minutes and Vietnam Months*. Combat reminiscences from a man who found war's false promise of "courage, sacrifice, glory and adventure" displaced by monotony and, occasionally, atrocity.

★**Horst Faas and Tim Page** (eds) *Requiem*. Turning

through this compendium of shots by photographers who subsequently lost their lives in Vietnam, Laos or Cambodia will haunt you for weeks. Never was a book more aptly named.

James Fenton *All the Wrong Places*. In Vietnam at the moment of Saigon's liberation, Fenton somehow managed to hitch a lift on the tank that rammed through the palace gates; his easy prose and poet's eye for detail make his account an engrossing one.

★**Frances Fitzgerald** *Fire in the Lake*. Pulitzer Prize-winning analysis of the historical, political and cultural context of the war, this time told from the Vietnamese perspective.

Albert French *Patches of Fire*. Examining his experiences of the infantryman's life in Vietnam and his attempts to exorcise his war-conjured demons back in the US, French's autobiography is at once moving and engrossing.

★**Le Ly Hayslip** *When Heaven and Earth Changed Places*. Giving a human face to the Vietnamese people, a stark contrast with the inherently racist American writing on Vietnam, this heart-rending tale of villagers trying to survive in a climate of hatred and distrust is perhaps more valuable than any history book.

★**Michael Herr** *Dispatches*. Infuriatingly narcissistic at times, Herr's spaced-out narrative still conveys the mud, blood and guts of the American war effort in Vietnam. Herr's distinctive tone is also evident in the classic war movie *Apocalypse Now* (see p.489), for which he wrote the screenplay.

John Laurence *The Cat from Hue*. Highly acclaimed for his coverage of the Vietnam conflict for CBS News from 1965 to 1970, Laurence has written not only an evocative memoir but also a moving testimony to the courage of the American troops who, like him, came of age in the battlefields of Vietnam.

Tom Mangold and John Penycate *The Tunnels of Cu Chi*. The most thorough and captivating account yet written of the guerrilla resistance mounted in the tunnels around Cu Chi.

★**Karl Marlantes** *Matterhorn*. It took Marlantes 35 years to complete this novel about young marines dropped into the jungle and their subsequent battles with the enemy, disease and each other, but it was worth the wait for its mature perspective of the conflict.

★**Robert Mason** *Chickenhawk*. Few people can be better qualified than Mason to deliver an account of the American War: a helicopter pilot with over a thousand missions under his belt, his blood-and-guts, bird's-eye account of the war is harrowing but compelling.

Harold G. Moore and Joseph Galloway *We Were Soldiers Once...and Young*. This blow-by-blow account of the ferocious battle of the Ia Drang valley, among the earliest encounters of the American War, makes compelling reading as the authors recapture the chaos and fear alongside moments of incredible courage and the sheer determination to survive.

★**Tim O'Brien** *The Things They Carried* and *If I Die in a Combat Zone*. Through a mix of autobiography and fiction O'Brien lays to rest the ghosts of the past in a brutally

honest reappraisal of the war, his own actions and the events he witnessed (see also O'Brien's novel *Going After Cacciato*; opposite).

★**John Pilger** *Heroes*. Journalist Pilger's systematic dismantling of the myth that America's role was in any way a justifiable "crusade" makes his Vietnam reportage required reading.

William Prochnau *Once Upon a Distant War*. Now that all the journos ever to set foot in Vietnam have published memoirs, Prochnau presents a new twist – the intriguing story of the people (among them Neil Sheehan, David Halberstam and Peter Arnett) who wrote the stories of Vietnam.

★**Neil Sheehan** *A Bright Shining Lie*. This monumental and fluently rendered account of the war, hung around the life of the soldier John Paul Vann, won the Pulitzer Prize for Sheehan; one of the true classics of Vietnam-inspired literature.

Justin Wintle *The Vietnam War*. Written in reaction to the shelves of long-winded texts available on the subject, Wintle's succinct overview manages to condense this mad conflict into fewer than two hundred pages.

Tobias Wolff *In Pharaoh's Army*. A former adviser based in My Tho, Wolff's honest, gentle autobiographical tale takes a wry look at life away from the "front line".

POSTWAR VIETNAM

Bui Tin *Following Ho Chi Minh*. An erstwhile colonel in the North Vietnamese Army, Bui Tin effectively defected to the West in 1990, since when he has been an outspoken critic of Vietnam's state apparatus. These memoirs don't flinch from addressing the underside – corruption, prejudice, naivety and insensitivity – of the Party.

Adam Fforde and Stefan de Vylder *From Plan to Market*. Highbrow, laudably researched book plotting the route Vietnam has taken from Stalinist central planning to market economy. Fforde and de Vylder hold the fabric of *doi moi* up to the light for examination in the mid-1990s.

David Lamb *Vietnam, Now: A Reporter Returns*. War journalist David Lamb returned to Vietnam for a four-year stint in 1997. While the war is a constant presence, this is primarily a commentary on contemporary Vietnam and its prospects for the future. Lamb is ultimately optimistic, though his criticisms of the government – notably its failure to reconcile the still-deep divisions between North and South – were sufficient to get the book banned.

Tim Page *Derailed in Uncle Ho's Victory Garden*. The war photographer with a legendary ability to defy death returns to Vietnam in the 1980s. Buried among the flashbacks and meandering discourse, Page's eye for detail and his delight in the bizarre give a flavour of postwar Vietnam.

Neil Sheehan *Two Cities: Hanoi and Saigon*. Sheehan returned to Vietnam in 1989 to witness firsthand the legacy of the war. Down south, the memories really begin to flow as encounters and travels trigger wartime flashbacks, interspersed with commentary on re-education camps and other deprivations of the dark, pre-*doi moi* years.

★ **Robert Templer** *Shadows and Wind*. This hard-hitting book casts a critical eye over Vietnam's decades of reform, from corruption and censorship to the emergence of a consumer-oriented youth culture. Though written in the late 1980s, the informative and balanced analysis still holds true today.

CULTURE AND SOCIETY

James Goodman *Uniquely Vietnamese*. Asia-based author Goodman has produced an informative catalogue of Vietnamese ingenuity, ranging from conical hats to Cheo theatre, from local festivals to water puppets and the haunting, one-stringed *dan bau*.

Gerald Cannon Hickey *Shattered World*. Detailed but readable account of ethnic minorities living in Vietnam's central highlands by one of the region's leading ethnologists. A fascinating analysis of the minorities' tragic struggle to survive both war and peace.

Henry Kamm *Dragon Ascending*. Pulitzer Prize-winning correspondent Kamm lets the Vietnamese – art dealers, ex-colonels, academics, doctors, authors – speak for themselves. This they do eloquently, resulting in a convincing portrait of contemporary Vietnam.

Norma J. Livo and Dia Cha *Folk Stories of the Hmong*. The Hmong's fading oral tradition is captured in this unique collection, gleaned from US immigrants, while its scene-setting introduction offers a valuable overview of Hmong culture, accompanied by illustrations of traditional costume and embroidered "storycloths".

William S. Logan *Hanoi: Biography of a City*. A heritage adviser, Logan peels back the layers of history revealed in Hanoi's architecture and streetscapes to provide an academic but engaging account of the city. In doing so, he also examines the challenges facing Hanoi at the start of the new millennium as it strives to preserve its unique heritage while also meeting the needs of its citizens.

Robert S. McKelvey *The Dust of Life*. Moving oral histories by Vietnamese Amerasians abandoned by their American fathers and discriminated against by the Vietnamese.

Mai Pham *Pleasures of the Vietnamese Table*. Saigon-born chef and restaurateur rediscovers her Vietnamese culinary roots and puts together one of the best Vietnamese cookbooks.

Nguyen Van Huy and Laurel Kendall (eds) *Vietnam: Journeys of Mind, Body and Spirit*. A broad range of contemporary commentators present an evocative snapshot of Vietnamese society and culture at the start of the new millennium.

★ **Christina Noble** *Bridge Across My Sorrows*. Life-affirming autobiography by a Dublin woman spurred by a dream to channel her considerable strengths into helping Ho Chi Minh City's *bui doi*, or street children. In her sequel, *Mama Tina*, Noble continues the story of her work in Vietnam, and describes her more recent campaign for children's rights in Mongolia.

VIETNAM ON FILM

Gilbert Adair *Hollywood's Vietnam: From the Green Berets to Full Metal Jacket*. Adair's excitable prose guides you past the firefights, f-words and R&R hijinks, to a real appreciation of how Hollywood reflected shifting American attitudes to the war.

Jeremy Devine *Vietnam at 24 Frames a Second*. The most wide-ranging analysis of Vietnam movies, covering more than four hundred films, including many obscure or forgotten titles.

Linda Dittmar and Gene Michaud (eds) *From Hanoi to Hollywood*. Collected essays on the way the American War encroached on Hollywood.

Vietnam in the movies

The embroilment of France and the US in Vietnam has spawned hundreds of movies, ranging from soft-focused, fond colonial reminiscences to blood-and-guts depictions of the horrors of war. As a means of brushing up on your Indochinese history, their value is questionable: for the most part, they're hardly objective. Yet, through the reflections they cast of the climates in which they were created, these films amplify the West's efforts to come to terms with what went on there, and for this reason they demand attention.

Early depictions

Hollywood was setting movies in Indochina long before the first American troops splashed ashore at Da Nang. As early as 1932, Jean Harlow played a sassy Saigon prostitute to smouldering Clark Gable's rubber-plantation manager, in the steamy pot-boiler **Red Dust**. At this early stage, however, Vietnam was no more than an exotic backdrop.

Even by the mid-1950s, as the modest beginnings of American involvement elicited from Hollywood its first real moves to acquaint itself with Vietnam, the country was often treated less as a nation with its own discernible identity and unique set of political issues, and more as a generic Asian theatre of war, in which the righteous **battle against Communism** could be played out. In its portrayal of noble and libertarian French forces, aided by American military specialists, confronting the evil of Communism, **China Gate** (1957) is an early example of this trend.

Vietnam provided Hollywood with a golden opportunity to project its militaristic fantasies, and a chance to tap into the prejudices brought to the surface by more than a decade of anti-Japanese World War II movies. Rather more depth of thought went into the making of **The Quiet American** (1958); but to author Graham Greene's chagrin, "hero" Pyle was depicted not as a representative of the American government, but of a private aid organization – something which Greene felt blunted his anti-American message. Nevertheless, the movie retained its source's sense of the futility of attempting to rationalize Vietnam's political quagmire.

Post-1965: American troops deployed

The military mandarins who led America into war failed to get the message, though: with American troops duly deployed in a far-flung corner of the globe by 1965, it was only a matter of time before **John Wayne** produced a patriotic movie to match. This came in the form of the monumentally bad **The Green Berets** (1968), in which a paunchy Wayne starred as "Big" Bill Kirby, a loveable colonel leading an adoring team of American soldiers into the central highlands. That Wayne, while on a promotional trip out to Vietnam, handed out cigarette cases inscribed with his signature and the message "Fuck Communism" speaks volumes about the film's subtlety. Kicking off with a stirring marching song ("Fighting soldiers from the sky, Fearless men who jump and die..."), the movie depicts American soldiers in spotless uniforms and perma-grins fighting against no less a threat than total "Communist domination of the world", yet still abiding, as the critic Gilbert Adair has it, "by Queensberry rules". In stark contrast to the squeaky-clean GIs are the barbaric Viet Cong, depicted as child-abusing rapists who whoop and holler like madmen as they overrun a US camp, all to the strains of suitably eerie Oriental music.

The war in Vietnam was a much dirtier affair than *The Green Berets* made it seem, its politics far less cut and dried. As the struggle turned into tragedy and popular support for it soured, movie moguls sensed that the war had become **taboo**. "Vietnam is awkward", said the journalist Michael Herr, "and if people don't even want to hear about it, you know they're not going to pay money to sit there in the dark and have it brought up." It was to be a full decade before another major combat movie was released. Instead, film-makers trained their gaze upon returning Vietnam veterans' doomed attempts to ease back into society. The resulting pictures were low in compassion: America's national pride had been collectively compromised by the failure to bring home a victory, and sympathy and forgiveness were at a premium.

A raft of **exploitation movies** was churned out, boasting names such as *Born Losers* (1967), *Angels from Hell* (1968) and *The Ravager* (1970), in which the mental scars of Vietnam provided topical window-dressing to improbable tales of martial arts, motorbikes and mayhem. At best, vets were treated as dysfunctional vigilantes acting beyond the pale of society – most famously in **Taxi Driver** (1976) – at worst, they were wacko misfits posing a threat to small-town America. With veterans being portrayed as anything but heroes, it was left to the stars of the **campus riot movies** and films lionizing **draft-dodgers** to provide role models.

Coming to terms with the war

Only in 1978 did Hollywood finally pluck up enough courage to confront the war head-on, and so aid the nation's healing process – **movies-as-therapy**. In the years since John Wayne's *Green Berets* had battened down the hatches against Communism, America had first lost sight of justification for the war, and then effectively lost the war itself. Movies no longer sought to make sense of past events, but to highlight their futility; for the generation of young Americans unfortunate enough to live through Vietnam, mere survival was seen as triumph enough. As audiences were exposed to their first dramatized glimpses of the war's unpalatable realities, they were confronted by shocking examples of soldiers' fraying moral fibre.

Coming Home (1978) was significant for its sensitive consideration of the emotional and physical tolls exacted by the war, and initiated the trend for more measured and intelligent vet movies. Similarly concerned with the ramifications of the war, both home and away, was **The Deer Hunter** (1978), in which the conscription of three friends fractures their Russian Orthodox community in Pennsylvania. The picture's ending, with its melancholy rendition of *God Bless America* by the central characters, is only semi-ironic, and alludes to the country's regenerative process. For all its power, *The Deer Hunter* is marred by overt racist stereotyping of the Vietnamese who, according to John Pilger, are dismissed as "sub-human Oriental barbarians and idiots". The Vietnamese we see are grotesque caricatures interested only in getting their kicks from gambling and death, and there's a strong sense that American youths ought never to have been exposed to such primordial evil as existed across the Pacific.

Francis Ford Coppola's hugely indulgent but visually magnificent **Apocalypse Now** (1979) rounded off the vanguard of postwar Vietnam combat movies. Described by one critic as "Film as opera… it turns Vietnam into a vast trip, into a War of the Imagination", the picture's Dantean snapshots of the war rob Vietnam of all identity other than as a "heart of darkness". Fuelled by his desire to convey the "horror, the madness, the sensuousness, and the moral dilemma of the Vietnam war", Coppola totally mythologizes the conflict, rendering it not so much futile as insane. However, with its stylized representation of *montagnards* as generic savages deifying Westerners, and its depiction of the Viet Cong as butchers who happily lop the arms off children who have had "American" inoculations, *Apocalypse Now* is little more enlightened than *The Deer Hunter*. Coppola subsequently compared the creation of the film itself to a war: "We were in the jungle, there were too many of us. We had access to too much money and too much equipment and little by little we went insane" – a process graphically depicted in **Hearts of Darkness: A Filmmaker's Apocalypse** (1991).

Returning home

The precedent set by *Coming Home* of sympathetic consideration for **returning veterans**' mindsets spurred many movies along similar lines in subsequent years. These focused on the disillusionment and disorientation felt by soldiers coming back not to heroes' welcomes, but to indifference and even disdain.

One of the first of these movies was **First Blood** (1982), which introduced audiences to Sly Stallone's muscle-bound super-vet John Rambo. As we witness Rambo's torment in small-town America, the picture is more "shoot 'em up" than cerebral. Yet its climax, in which Rambo's former colonel becomes a surrogate father figure to him, underscores the tender ages of the troops who fought the war. Other movies of the genre – among them Alan Parker's **Birdy** (1984) and Oliver Stone's **Born on the 4th of July** (1989) – reiterated the message of stolen youth and innocence by screening idyllic, elegiac scenes of childhood. Stone has his hero (played by Tom Cruise) swallowing the anti-Communist line, and returning to an indifference symbolized by the squalor of the army hospital in which he recuperates and by the breakdown of his relationship with his mother. In *Birdy*, doctors at a loss as to how to treat a catatonic patient turn to a fellow vet for help – this sense of America's inability to relate to returnees subsequently resurfaces in **Jacknife** (1989).

1980s

Not content with squaring up to the war in Vietnam, Hollywood during the 1980s attempted, bizarrely, to rewrite its script in a series of **revisionist movies**. Richard Gere had made the armed forces hip again in 1982's weepie *An Officer and a Gentleman*; a year later the first of an intriguing subgenre of films hit cinemas, in which Americans returned to Vietnam, invariably to rescue MIAs, and "won".

The mother of them all, was **Rambo: First Blood, Part II** (1985), in which the hero of *First Blood* gets to settle some old scores. "Do we get to win this time?" asks Rambo, at the top of the movie. As he riots through the Vietnamese countryside in order to extricate a band of American PoWs, he answers his own question by slaying Vietnamese foes at an approximate rate of one every two minutes.

The backlash to the patent nonsense of the revisionist films came in the form of a series of shockingly realistic movies which attempted, in the words of the director Oliver Stone, to "peel the onion" and reveal the **real Vietnam**, routine atrocities, indiscipline and all. There are no heroes in these GI's-view movies, only fragile, confused-looking young men in fatigues, emphasizing that this was a war that affected a whole generation – not just its most photogenic individuals.

In **Platoon** (1986), Oliver Stone, himself a foot soldier in Vietnam, created the most realistic cinematographic interpretation of the American involvement yet. Filmed on location in the Philippines, this movie reminded audiences that killing wasn't as straightforward as *Rambo* made it seem. As well as portraying the depths to which humankind can sink, Stone shows the circumstances under which it was feasible for young American boys to become murderers of civilians.

If *Platoon* portrays a dirty war, in **Hamburger Hill** (1987), which dramatizes the taking of Ap Bia hill during May 1969's battle for the A Shau valley, it has degenerated into a positive mud bath. As troops slither and slide on the flanks of the hill in the highland mists, they become indistinguishable, and the image of an entire generation stumbling towards the maws of death is strengthened by the fact that the cast includes no big-name actors – the men who fall on the hill are neighbours, sons or brothers, not film stars. American losses are taken in order to secure a useless hill, a potent symbol of the futility of America's involvement in the war; as one soldier says, time after time, in a weary mantra, "It don't mean nothing, not a thing."

Stanley Kubrick's **Full Metal Jacket** (1987) picks up *Hamburger Hill*'s theme of the war's theft of American youth in its opening scene, as the camp barber strips conscripts of their hair and, by implication, their individuality. However, as US troops plod wearily through a smouldering Hue in the movie's final scene, the usual macho marching tunes are replaced with a plaintive echo of youth: "Who's the leader of the club that's made for you and me? M-I-C, K-E-Y, M-O-U-S-E."

1990s–present day

In the majority of Hollywood movies about Vietnam, Vietnamese people have mostly been noticeable by their absence, or through the filter of blatant stereotyping. **Heaven and Earth** (1993), the final part of Oliver Stone's Vietnam trilogy, went some way towards rectifying this imbalance by following the true story of Vietnamese village girls – a timely reminder that not only Americans suffered during the struggle.

Only in the late 1990s were American movie-makers allowed to shoot on location in Vietnam again. Filmed in Ho Chi Minh City, **Three Seasons** (1999) was directed by Vietnamese-Californian Tony Bui, and features Harvey Keitel at the head of a predominantly local cast. It provides a lyrical and graceful portrayal of a city trying to come to terms with the return of the West.

Perhaps the best-known Vietnam-based movie of the new millennium is Philip Noyce's atmospheric remake of **The Quiet American** (2002). Its portrayal of the Vietnamese struggle as a patriotic fight against colonial oppression, earned the film official approval, allowing it to be screened widely within Vietnam – a first for a major Hollywood production. In the same year (2002), Randall Wallace made **We Were Soldiers**, his adaptation of Lt Col Hall Moore and Joe Galloway's blow-by-blow account of the catastrophic battle of Ia Drang, with Mel Gibson as the caring commander. Though the movie made some effort to be impartial, it did not meet with Vietnamese approval: the government banned the film, saying it distorted Vietnamese history, and branded actor Don Duong a "traitor" for his portrayal of the NVA leader pitting his wits – and his men – against the Americans.

More recently, the lauded director Werner Herzog turned his attention to the American War with **Rescue Dawn** (2007), based on the true story of Dieter Dengler, a pilot who was shot down over Laos in 1966. Herzog's unique spin on the nightmarish situation makes it appear that there is little to choose between the lives of the captives and the captors.

VIETNAMESE FILM-MAKERS

Among **Vietnamese film-makers**, probably the best known is Tran Anh Hung, whose **The Scent of Green Papaya** (1993), filmed entirely in Paris, is a fondly nostalgic period piece in which the East's languorous elegance and beauty are shown, minus its squalor – it won two awards at the Cannes Film Festival. His second film, *Cyclo* (1996), is an altogether different matter, a grimy tale of murder and prostitution set in a bleak rendition of Ho Chi Minh City – so bleak that the film is banned in Vietnam. Nevertheless, Tran Anh Hung obtained permission to shoot **At the Height of Summer** (aka *The Vertical Ray of the Sun*, 2000) on location in Hanoi. It's a gentler film with the same languid, dream-like quality of *Cyclo*, in which three sisters prepare to commemorate their parents' deaths.

Vietnamese censors are infamously strict concerning topics broached in Vietnam-based movies, but they lightened up a little in allowing Vietnamese director Dang Nhat Minh to make his ground-breaking **The Season of Guavas** (2001), which deals with the extremely sensitive issue of 1950s Communist land reforms; however, the film has yet to be released in Vietnam. Other **Vietnamese directors** beginning to attract an international audience include Tran Van Thuy (*Sand Life*, 2000), Bui Thac Chuyen (*Course de Nuit*, 2000) and **Le Hoang**, whose stark portrayal of prostitutes in **Bar Girls** (2003) caused a major stir. That the film was made at all is thanks to a radical change of policy at Vietnam's Ministry of Culture, which in 2002 stopped vetting scripts and allowed private film studios to start making films. A sign of growing confidence in the Vietnamese film industry was the release in 2007 of **The White Silk Dress**, directed by **Luu Huynh** with a record budget of $2 million, about the struggles of an impoverished couple in the 1950s to provide their daughters with *ao dai* to wear to school.

VIETNAM IN THE FRENCH MOVIES

French cinema only began to tackle the subject of Vietnam in the 1990s. If in **Dien Bien Phu** (1992) it confronted its own ghosts, on the whole its output has been limited to visually captivating colonial whimsies, to which the Vietnamese setting merely adds an exotic tang. For example, **The Lover** (1992) works not because it does justice to Marguerite Duras' poignant rites-of-passage novella, but because its extended interludes of heaving flesh are cloaked with a veneer of Oriental mystique created by location filming in Ho Chi Minh City, Sa Dec and Can Tho. The same dreamy, sweeping landscape is the backdrop for grand melodrama **Indochine** (1993) starring Catherine Deneuve as a beautiful plantation owner in the dying days of colonial rule.

1950–1960

China Gate (1957). Dedicated to the French *colons* who "advanced this backward society to its place as the rice bowl of Asia", *China Gate's* laboured plot, concerning an attempt to destroy a Viet Minh arms cache, is of much less interest than its heavy-handed politics.

The Quiet American (1958). Michael Redgrave plays the British journalist and cynic Fowler, while Audie Murphy (America's most decorated soldier in World War II) plays Pyle, the eponymous "hero" of Graham Greene's novel.

The Green Berets (1968). John Wayne stars and co-directs this formulaic propaganda flick, with Japanese-American George Takei cast as a southern-Vietnam captain. Critics gave it a cold reception when it was released, but it amassed $11 million at the box office.

1970–1980

Hearts and Minds (1974). Peter Davis's searing and emotional Oscar-winning documentary drives home truths about the horror of a meaningless war. A precursor to Michael Moore's style of film-making.

Taxi Driver (1976). Robert De Niro's disturbed insomniac returnee, Travis Bickle, embarks on a one-man moral crusade to purge the streets of a hellish New York.

Coming Home (1978). Jane Fonda as a military career-man's wife who falls in love with a wheelchair-bound veteran (Jon Voight).

The Deer Hunter (1978). Three friends from the same community are conscripted, and their "one-shot" code of honour, espoused on a last pre-Vietnam hunting trip, contrasts wildly with the moral vacuum of the war, whose random brutality is embodied in the movie's central scenes of Russian roulette.

Apocalypse Now (1979). The usual elements of needless death, casual atrocity, moral decline and spaced-out soldiers leaning heavily on substance abuse are all here, played out against a raunchy soundtrack.

Good Morning Vietnam (1986). A warm-hearted film that is ultimately a vehicle for the genius of Robin Williams, who plays a military DJ stationed in Saigon who doesn't toe the government line. Zany comedy is interspersed with some poignant moments.

Platoon (1986). Its oppressive sensory overload powerfully conjures the paranoiac near-hysteria spawned by fear, confusion, loss of motivation and inability to discriminate between friend and foe. Inherent in its shadowy, half-seen portrayal of the enemy is a grudging respect for their expertise in jungle warfare.

Full Metal Jacket (1987). A brutal drill-sergeant sets about expunging the humanity of young conscripts, on the grounds it will only hamper them when they experience first-hand the insanity of the war.

Hamburger Hill (1987). Capturing the futility of ground combat in Vietnam, *Hamburger Hill* is a bloody account of the 1969 ten-day battle for Ap Bia hill. Four hundred American lives were lost, the hill was abandoned to the enemy and public opinion back home turned against the war.

1990–PRESENT

Heaven and Earth (1993). A Vietnamese girl's odyssey (based on the life of Le Ly Hayslip), from idyllic early childhood to the traumas of life as a wife in San Diego.

Three Seasons (1999). Ex-marine (Harvey Keitel) returns to Vietnam to look for the Amerasian daughter he abandoned decades before.

The Quiet American (2002). Sticks much more closely than the original to Graham Greene's novel in its indictment of American involvement in Vietnam.

The Fog of War: Eleven Lessons from the Life of Robert S. McNamara (2003). Director Errol Morris interviews former Secretary of Defense Robert S. McNamara about his role in the Vietnam War. The political game-playing – even now, decades later – is fascinating.

Rescue Dawn (2007). Based on the true story of a pilot shot down in Laos and then captured and tortured by villagers sympathetic to the Pathet Lao (Lao communists).

Vietnamese

Linguists are uncertain as to the exact roots of Vietnamese, though the language betrays Thai, Khmer and Chinese influences. A tonal language, it's extremely tricky for Westerners to master, though the phrases below should help you get by. English superseded Russian as *the* language to learn following the sweeping changes of *doi moi*, and as a visitor you'll generally find that being able to speak Vietnamese isn't called for. Then again, nothing will endear you to locals as much as showing conversational ability – or even willingness.

Vietnamese was set down using Chinese characters until the fourteenth century, when an indigenous **script** called *chu nom* was created. This, in turn, was dropped in favour of *quoc ngu*, a Romanized script developed by a French missionary in the seventeenth century, and it's this form that's universally used today – though you'll still occasionally spot lavish *chu nom* characters daubed on the walls of more venerable pagodas and temples.

Three main **dialects** – northern, central and southern – are used in Vietnam today, and although for the most part they are pretty similar, pronunciation can be so wildly variant that some locals have trouble understanding each other; in the words and phrases listed below, we indicate important differences between variants used in the north and south. Bear in mind, too, that Vietnam's minority peoples have their own languages, and may look blankly at you as you gamely try out your Vietnamese on them.

If you want more scope than the expressions below allow and are determined to master the basics of spoken Vietnamese, try one of the **self-teaching packs** on the market, such as those produced by Audio-Forum (🌐audioforum.com).

Pronunciation

The Vietnamese language is a **tonal** one, that is, one in which a word's meaning is determined by the pitch at which you deliver it. Six tones are used – the mid-level tone (syllables with no marker), the low falling tone (syllables marked à), the low rising tone (syllables marked ả), the high broken tone (syllables marked ã), the high rising tone (syllables marked á) and the low broken tone (syllables marked ạ) – though you'll probably remain in the dark until you ask a Vietnamese person to give you spoken examples of each of them. Depending on its tone, the word *ba*, for instance, can mean three, grandmother, poisoned food, waste, aunt or any – leaving ample scope for misunderstandings and diplomatic faux pas.

With tones accomplished, or at least comprehended, there are the many vowel and consonant sounds to take on board. These we've listed below, along with phonetic renderings of how they should be pronounced.

VOWELS

a "a" as in f**a**ther	**o** "o" as in h**o**t
ă "u" as in h**u**t (slight "u" as in unstressed English "a")	**ô** "aw" as in **aw**e
â "uh" sound as above only longer	**ơ** "ur" as in f**ur**
e "e" as in b**e**d	**u** "oo" as in b**oo**
ê "ay" as in p**a**y	**ư** "oo" closest to French "u"
i "i" as in -**i**ng	**y** "i" as in -**i**ng

VOWEL COMBINATIONS

ai	"ai" as in Th**ai**	oa	"wa"
ao	"ao" as in M**ao**	oe	"weh"
au	"a-oo"	ôi	"oy"
âu	"oh" as in **oh**	ơi	"uh-i"
ay	"ay" as in h**ay**	ua	"waw"
ây	"ay-i" (as in "ay" above but longer)	uê	"weh"
		uô	"waw"
eo	"eh-ao"	uy	"wee"
êu	"ay-oo"	ưa	"oo-a"
iu	"ew" as in f**ew**	ưu	"er-oo"
iêu	"i-yoh"	ươi	"oo-uh-i"

CONSONANTS

c	"g"	ng/ngh	"ng" as in si**ng**
ch	"j" as in **j**ar	nh	"n-y" as in ca**n**yon
d	"y" as in **y**oung	ph	"f"
đ	"d" as in **d**ay	q	"g" as in **g**oat
g	"g" as in **g**oat	t	"d" as in **d**ay
gh	"g" as in **g**oat	th	"t"
gi	"y" as in **y**oung	tr	"j" as in **j**ar
k	"g" as in **g**oat	x	"s"
kh	"k" as in **k**eep		

Useful words and phrases

How you greet and then speak to somebody in Vietnam depends very much on their sex, and on their age and social standing relative to your own. As a general rule of thumb, if you address a man as *ông*, and a woman as *bà*, you can be sure you aren't being impolite. If you find yourself in conversation, either formally or informally, with someone of your approximate age, you can use *anh* (for a man) and *chi* (for a woman). You can also use the same formula to address someone when you know their name. Vietnamese names are traditionally written with the family name first (Nguyen, Tran, Le and Pham are among the most common) and the given name last and between them a qualifying name, which often indicates a person's sex or the particular branch of the family to which they belong. People are usually referred to by their given name so, for example, you would address an older man called Nguyen Van Hai as Ong Hai.

GREETINGS AND SMALL TALK

Hello	chào ông/bà	My name is...	tên tôi là...
How are you?	ông/bà có khỏe không?	Where do you come from?	ông/bà ở đâu đến?
Fine, thanks	toè, cảm ơn.	I come from...	tôi ở . . .
Pleased to meet you	hân hạnh gặp bạn ông/bà	...England	. . . nước Anh
Goodbye	chào, tạm biệt	...America	. . . nước Mỹ
Good night	chúc ngủ ngon	...Australia	. . . nước Úc
Excuse me (to say sorry)	xin lỗi	What do you do?	ông/bà làm gì?
Excuse me (to get past)	xin ông/bà thứ lỗi	Do you speak English?	ông/bà biết nói tiếng Anh không?
Please	làm ơn		
Thank you	cảm ơn ông/bà	I don't understand	tôi không hiểu
Thank you very much	cảm ơn bạn rất nhiều	Could you repeat that?	xin ông/bà lặp lại?
Don't mention it	không có chi	Yes	vâng (north); dạ (south)
What's your name?	ông/bà tên gì?	No	không

EMERGENCIES

Can you help me?	ông/bà có thể giúp tôi không?	Please call a doctor	làm ơn gọi bác sĩ
		hospital	bệnh viện
There's been an accident	có một vụ tai nạn	police station	đồn công an

GETTING AROUND

Where is the...?	ở đâu...?	bus station	bến xe buýt
How many kilometres is it to...?	bao nhiêu cây số thì đến...?	train station	bến xe lửa/ga
		taxi	tắc xi
How do I get to...?	tôi phải đi...bằ`ng cách nào?	car	xe hơi
		filling station	trạm xăng
We'd like to go to...	chúng tôi muốn đi...	bicycle	xe đạp
To the airport, please	làm ơn đưa tôi đi sân bay	baggage	hành lý
Can you take me to the...?	ông/bà có thể đưa tôi đi...?	bank	nhà băng
Where do we catch the bus to...?	ở đâu đón xe đi...?	post office	sổ bưu điện
		passport	hộ chiếu
When does the bus for Hoi An leave?	khi nào xe Hội An chạy?	hotel	khách sạn
		restaurant	nhà hàng
Can I book a seat?	tôi có thể đặt ghế trước không?	Please stop here	xin dừng lại đây
		over there	bên kia
How long does it take?	phải tốn bao lâu?	here	đây
ticket	vé	left/right	bên trái/bên phải
aeroplane	máy bay	north	phía bắc
airport	sân bay	south	phía nam
boat	tàu bè	east	phía đông
bus	xe buýt	west	phía tây

ACCOMMODATION AND SHOPPING

Do you have any rooms?	ông/bà có phòng không?	room with a private bathroom	một phòng tắm riêng
How much is it per night?	mỗi đêm bao nhiêu?		
How much is it?	bao nhiêu tiền?	cheap/expensive	rẻ/đắt
How much does it cost?	cái này giá bao nhiêu?	single room	phòng một người
Can I have a look?	xem có được không?	double room	phòng hai người
Do you have...?	ông/bà có không...?	single bed	giường một người
I want a...	tôi muốn một...	double bed	giường đôi
I'd like...	cho tôi xin một...	air-conditioner	máy lạnh
How much is this?	cái này bao nhiêu?	fan (electric)	quạt máy
That's too expensive	đắt quá	mosquito net	cái màn
Do you have anything cheaper?	ông/bà còn gì rẻ hơn không?	toilet paper	giấy vệ sinh
		telephone	điện thoại
Could I have the bill please?	làm ơn tính tiền?	laundry	quần ào dơ
		blanket	chăn (north); mền (south)
room with a balcony	một phòng có ban công	open/closed	mở cửa/đóng cửa

TIME

What's the time?	mấy giờ rời?	year	năm
noon	buổi trưa	today	hôm nay
midnight	nửa đêm	tomorrow	mai
minute	phút	yesterday	hôm qua
hour	giờ	now	bây giờ
day	ngày	next week	tuần tới
week	tuần	last week	tuần vừa qua
month	tháng	morning	buổi sáng

afternoon	buổi chiều	night	ban đêm
evening	buổi tối		

NUMBERS

Note that for numbers ending in 5, from 15 onwards, **nhăm** is used in northern Vietnam and **lăm** in the south, rather than the written form of **năm**. Also, bear in mind that an alternative for numbers that are multiples of ten is **chục** – so, for example, ten would be **một chục**, twenty would be **hai chục**, etc.

zero	không	fifteen	mười lăm/nhăm
one	một	sixteen	mười sáu
two	hai	seventeen	mười bảy
three	ba	eighteen	mười tám
four	bốn	nineteen	mười chín
five	năm	twenty	hai mười
six	sáu	twenty-one	hai mười một
seven	bảy	twenty-two	hai mười hai
eight	tám	thirty	ba mười
nine	chín	forty	bốn mười
ten	mười	fifty	năm mười
eleven	mười một	one hundred	một trăm
twelve	mười hai	two hundred	hai trăm
thirteen	mười ba	one thousand	một ngàn
fourteen	mười bốn	ten thousand	mười ngàn

EATING AND DRINKING

USEFUL PHRASES

bát (north); **chén** (south)	bowl	**phở**	flat rice noodle soup
bao nhiêu?	how much is it?	**phở bò**	noodle soup with beef
cạn chén (north); **cạn ly** (south)	cheers!	**phở với trứng**	noodle soup with eggs
chúc sức khỏe	to your good health	**FISH, MEAT AND VEGETABLES**	
cúp	cup	**cá**	fish
đá	ice	**cá rán** (north); **cá chiên** (south)	fried fish
không có đá cảm ơn	no ice, thanks	**cua**	eel
đũa	chopsticks	**con lươn**	crab
ít đường	a little sugar	**mực**	squid
lạnh	cold	**tôm**	shrimp or prawn
chay	vegetarian	**tôm hùm**	lobster
tôi không ăn thịt	I don't eat meat	**thịt**	meat
nóng	hot	**bít tết**	beefsteak
rất ngon	delicious	**bò**	beef
		gà	chicken
RICE AND NOODLES		**lợn** (north); **heo** (south)	pork
bún	round rice noodles	**vịt**	duck
bún bò	beef with bun noodles	**rau cỏ or rau các loại**	vegetables
bún chả	vermicelli noodles with pork and vegetables	**bắp cải**	cabbage
bún gà	chicken with bun noodles	**cà chua**	tomato
cơm	cooked rice	**cà tím**	aubergine
cơm rang (north); **cơm chiên** (south)	fried rice	**đậu**	beans
		giá	beansprouts
cơm trắng	boiled rice	**khoai tây**	potato
cháo	rice porridge	**khoai lang**	sweet potato
mì xào	fried noodles	**măng**	bamboo shoots
		ngô (north); **bắp** (south)	sweet corn

rau xào các loại	stir-fried vegetables
xà lách	salad
xà lách cà chua	tomato salad
xà lách rau xanh các loại	green salad

DESSERTS AND FRUIT

bánh ngọt	cakes and pastries
đường	sugar
kem	ice cream or cream
mật ong	honey
sữa chua	yoghurt
trái cây	fruit
bưởi	pomelo/grapefruit
cam	orange
chanh	lemon/lime
chôm chôm	rambutan
chuối	banana
dâu tây	strawberry
dừa	coconut
dứa (north); **thơm** (south)	pineapple
dưa hấu	watermelon
đu đủ	papaya
khế	star fruit
măng cầu (north); **quả na** (south)	custard apple
măng cụt	mangosteen
mít	jackfruit
nhãn	longan
quả bơ	avocado
sầu riêng	durian
xoài	mango
táo tây	apple
thanh long	dragon fruit
vải	lychee

MISCELLANEOUS

bánh	cake (sweet or savoury)
bánh mì	bread
bơ	butter
pho mát	cheese

lạc (north); **đậu phộng** (south)	peanuts (groundnuts)
muối	salt
mứt	jam
ớt	chilli
tàu hũ (north); **đậu phụ** (south)	tofu
tiêu	pepper
trứng	egg
trứng tráng or **trứng ốp lếp**	omelette
trứng rán (north) or **trứng chiên** (south)	fried eggs

DRINKS

bia	beer
cà phê	coffee
cà phê đá	iced coffee
cà phê đen	black coffee
cà phê đen không đường	black coffee without sugar
cà phê nóng	hot coffee
cà phê sữa	coffee with milk
cà phê sữa nóng	hot milk coffee
trà	tea
trà với chanh	tea with lemon
trà với sữa	tea with milk
không đá	no ice
nước	water
nước khoáng	mineral water
nước xô-đa	soda water
nước cam	orange juice
nước chanh	lime juice
nước dừa	coconut milk
rượu rắn	snake wine
rượu cơm	rice alcohol
xô-đa cam	orange soda
xô-đa chanh	lime soda
sữa	condensed milk
sữa tươi	fresh milk

Glossary

Agent Orange Defoliant herbicide used by the Americans during the American War to deprive guerrillas of forest cover

Annam ("Pacified South") A term coined by the Chinese to refer to their protectorate in northern Vietnam before 939 AD; the French later applied the name to the middle reaches of their protectorate, from the southern central highlands to the edge of the Red River Delta

ao dai Traditional Vietnamese dress for women, comprising baggy pants and a long, slit tunic

arhat Ascetic Buddhist saint, whose statues are found in northern pagodas

ARVN (Army of the Republic of Vietnam) The army of South Vietnam

ben xe Bus station

bo doi Northern soldiers

boat people Ethnic Chinese who fled Vietnam by boat in the late 1970s to escape persecution at the hands of the Communists and, later, Vietnamese escaping poverty (see box, p.448)

Bodhisattva An intermediary who has chosen to forgo Buddhist nirvana to work for the salvation of all humanity

body count Term coined by the Americans to measure the success of a military operation, determined by the number of dead bodies after a battle

bonze Buddhist monk

buu dien Post office

Cao Dai Indigenous religion, essentially a hybrid of Buddhism, Taoism and Confucianism, but hinged around an attempt at unification of all earthly codes of belief (see p.458)

Champa Indianized Hindu empire that held sway in much of the southern half of Vietnam until the late seventeenth century (see box, p.430)

Charlie Nickname for the VC ("Vietnamese Communists") used by American soldiers

cheo Form of classical theatre (see p.475)

cho Market

chu nom Classic Vietnamese script, based on Chinese

chua pagoda Buddhist place of worship

Cochinchina A Portuguese term adopted by the French colonial government for its southern administrative region

colon French colonial expatriate

com pho Literally, "rice noodles", often used to indicate restaurant serving basic dishes

cyclo Three-wheeled bicycle with a carriage on the front

dao Island

den Temple (Taoist or other non-Buddhist place of worship)

dinh Communal meeting hall

DMZ ("dee-em-zee") The Demilitarized Zone along the Seventeenth Parallel, marking the border between North and South Vietnam from 1954 to 1975

doi moi Vietnam's economic restructuring programme, begun in 1986

DRV (Democratic Republic of Vietnam) The North Vietnamese state established by Ho Chi Minh following the August Revolution in 1945

duong Avenue

FULRO (United Front for the Liberation of Oppressed Races) An opposition movement formed by the ethnic minorities of the central highlands, demanding greater autonomy

Funan Indianized empire, a forerunner of the great Khmer empires

GI (General Infantryman) Soldier in the US Army

gopuram Bank of sculpted deities over the entrance to a Hindu temple

"grunt" American infantryman

gui xe Bicycle compound

hang Cave

ho Lake

Ho Chi Minh Trail Trail used first by the Viet Minh and later by the North Vietnamese Army to transport supplies to the South, via Laos and Cambodia

Hoa Ethnic Chinese people living in Vietnam

Honda om Literally "Honda embrace" – a motorbike taxi

"Huey" Nickname given to American helicopter, the HU-1

Indochina The region of Asia comprising Vietnam, Laos and Cambodia

kalan Sanctuary in a Cham tower

khach san Hotel

Khmer Ethnic Cambodian

kylin Mythical, dew-drinking animal (often translated as unicorn); a harbinger of peace

Lien Xo Translating as "Soviet Union", this is also used as a term of abuse – and may very occasionally be hurled at foreigners in more remote regions

lingam A phallic statue representing Shiva, often seen in Cham towers

mandapa Meditation hall in Cham temple complex

MIAs (Missing in Action) Soldiers who fought – on both sides – in the American War, but have still not been accounted for

monkey bridge Basic log bridge over a stream or small river

montagnards French term for Vietnam's ethnic minority peoples

mua roi nuoc Water-puppet show

mui Cape

mukha lingam Lingam fashioned into the likeness of a deity

napalm Jellied fuel dropped by US forces during the American War, and capable of causing terrible burns

ngo Alley

NGO Non-governmental organization

nha hang Restaurant

nha khach Hotel or guesthouse

nha nghi Guesthouse

nha tro Basic dormitory accommodation, usually found near stations

NLF (National Liberation Front) Popular movement formed in South Vietnam in 1960 by opponents of the American-backed Southern regime

nui Mountain

nuoc mam Fish sauce

NVA (North Vietnamese Army) The army of the Democratic Republic of Vietnam

Oc Eo Ancient seaport of the Funan empire, east of modern-day Rach Gia in the Mekong Delta

ODP (Orderly Departure Programme) A United Nations-backed scheme enabling legal emigration of Vietnamese refugees

paddy Unharvested rice

pagoda Not just a tower, but an entire Buddhist temple complex

PoW Prisoner of war

quan District

R&R ("Rest and Recreation") Term coined during the American War to describe a soldier's temporary leave of duty

roi nuoc See *mua roi nuoc*

rong Communal house of ethnic minorities in the central highlands

RVN (Republic of Vietnam) The official name for South Vietnam from 1954 to 1976

sampan Small, flat-bottomed boat

song River

SRVN (Socialist Republic of Vietnam) The post-liberation amalgamation of the DRV and RVN, and the official name of modern Vietnam

tai chi Chinese martial art, commonly performed as early-morning exercise

Tet Vietnam's lunar New Year

thung chai Coracle

Tonkin One of the three administrative regions of French colonial Vietnam, from Ninh Binh northwards

tunnel rats American soldiers trained for warfare in tunnels such as those at Cu Chi

VC (Viet Cong) Literally "Vietnamese Communists"; term used by the Americans to describe the guerrilla forces of the NLF

Viet Kieu Overseas Vietnamese

Viet Minh Shortened version of Viet Nam Doc Lap Dong Minh, the League for the Independence of Vietnam, established by Ho Chi Minh in 1941

VNQDD Abbreviation for Viet Nam Quoc Dan Dang, the Vietnam Nationalist Party, founded in 1927

xe lam Motorized three-wheeler buggy carrying numerous passengers

xe om Northern equivalent of the Honda om, a motorbike taxi

Small print and index

A ROUGH GUIDE TO ROUGH GUIDES

Published in 1982, the first Rough Guide – to Greece – was a student scheme that became a publishing phenomenon. Mark Ellingham, a recent graduate in English from Bristol University, had been travelling in Greece the previous summer and couldn't find the right guidebook. With a small group of friends he wrote his own guide, combining a contemporary, journalistic style with a thoroughly practical approach to travellers' needs.

The immediate success of the book spawned a series that rapidly covered dozens of destinations. And, in addition to impecunious backpackers, Rough Guides soon acquired a much broader readership that relished the guides' wit and inquisitiveness as much as their enthusiastic, critical approach and value-for-money ethos. These days, Rough Guides include recommendations from budget to luxury and cover more than 120 destinations around the globe, from Amsterdam to Zanzibar, all regularly updated by our team of roaming writers.

Browse all our latest guides, read inspirational features and book your trip at **roughguides.com**.

Rough Guide credits

Editors: Brendon Griffin and Georgia Stephens
Layout: Jessica Subramanian
Cartography: Animesh Pathak
Picture editor: Marta Bescos Sanchez
Proofreader: Diane Margolis
Managing editor: Andy Turner
Assistant editor: Payal Sharotri

Production: Jimmy Lao
Cover photo research: Sarah Stewart Richardson
Photographer: Tim Draper
Editorial assistant: Aimee White
Senior DTP coordinator: Dan May
Programme manager: Gareth Lowe
Publishing director: Georgina Dee

Publishing information

This ninth edition published March 2018 by
Rough Guides Ltd,
80 Strand, London WC2R 0RL
11, Community Centre, Panchsheel Park,
New Delhi 110017, India
Distributed by Penguin Random House
Penguin Books Ltd, 80 Strand, London WC2R 0RL
Penguin Group (USA), 345 Hudson Street, NY 10014, USA
Penguin Group (Australia), 250 Camberwell Road,
Camberwell, Victoria 3124, Australia
Penguin Group (NZ), 67 Apollo Drive, Mairangi Bay,
Auckland 1310, New Zealand
Penguin Group (South Africa), Block D, Rosebank Office
Park, 181 Jan Smuts Avenue, Parktown North, Gauteng,
South Africa 2193
Rough Guides is represented in Canada by DK Canada, 320
Front Street West, Suite 1400, Toronto, Ontario M5V 3B6
Printed in Singapore
Rough Guides 2018
Maps © Rough Guides

MIX
Paper from
responsible sources
FSC www.fsc.org FSC™ C018179

Help us update

We've gone to a lot of effort to ensure that the ninth
edition of **The Rough Guide to Vietnam** is accurate
and up-to-date. However, things change – places get
"discovered", opening hours are notoriously fickle,
restaurants and rooms raise prices or lower standards. If
you feel we've got it wrong or left something out, we'd like
to know, and if you can remember the address, the price,
the hours, the phone number, so much the better.

Please send your comments with the subject line
"**Rough Guide Vietnam Update**" to mail@uk.roughguides
.com. We'll credit all contributions and send a copy of the
next edition (or any other Rough Guide if you prefer) for
the very best emails.

Acknowledgements

Ron Emmons thanks fellow authors Rachel Mills and
Martin Zatko for their useful tips, and editors Helen
Abramson and Georgia Stephens for their sharp-eyed
editing. Thanks also to the generous people who shared
their time and expertise on Hanoi and the far north,
including Tony Nong, Tuyen, Dang Duc Thuc, Mark
Lowerson, Minh and James Anh.

Rachel Mills would like to thank Andy Turner, Helen
Abramson, Georgia Stephens and Brendon Griffin at
Rough Guides HQ, plus Ben and Bich at Phong Nha

Farmstay, Tonkin Travel, TravelLocal, Tam's Cafe in Dong
Hoi and Anh and Michaella at Beachside Backpackers in
Dong Hoi.

Martin Zatko would like to thank the many people
who made his latest trip around Vietnam so pleasurable,
including Kim Hang, Mia Tran and Mark in Saigon, and Felix
in Nha Trang – and, of course, the staff at Hoan My Hospital
in Da Lat, who ensured that his first-ever hospitalisation
(over Christmas, no less) was actually rather pleasant.

ABOUT THE AUTHORS

Ron Emmons (@ronemmons.com) has been based in Chiang Mai, Thailand, since the late 1980s. He has contributed to several editions of *The Rough Guide to Vietnam* and *The Rough Guide to Thailand*, and has updated guidebooks to Southeast Asian destinations for National Geographic, Frommer's and DK Books. His travel articles and images appear regularly in international publications.

Rachel Mills is a freelance writer and editor based on the Kent coast, or in her campervan somewhere in the UK. She is a co-author for the Rough Guides to India, Ireland and England, as well as Vietnam.

Martin Zatko has authored or co-authored over thirty Rough Guides, including those to Korea, Japan, China, Myanmar, Taiwan, Fiji, Morocco, Turkey, Greece and Europe. After making the mistake of skipping Vietnam during his first trip around Southeast Asia back in 2003, he now regards it as something of a home.

Readers' updates

Thanks to all the readers who have taken the time to write in with comments and suggestions (and apologies if we've inadvertently omitted or misspelt anyone's name):

Francesco De Kunert, Dan Duperron, Darren Ensley, Marco Gallico, Jonathan Ghari, Friedel Geeraert and Frédéric De Rycke, Dustin Gerding, Freya Godfrey, Ha Thi Thu Hang, David L Hagen, Julia Hanson-Abbott (and Mish), Hoa Hoolihan, Hong Nu, Stephen Jones, Johannes Kellner, Maria and Steffen, Anna Nguyen, Will Reeve, Mila Rodriguez, Miriam Schmitz, Robbie Thompson, Robert Villa, Matthew Williams.

Photo credits

Index

Maps are marked in grey

Map symbols

The symbols below are used on maps throughout the book

▬▬··	International boundary	✈	International airport	⊤	Gardens	■	Tower
▬ ▬ ▬	Chapter division boundary	✖	Domestic airport	☼	Viewpoint	🏛	Monument
▬▬ ··	State boundary	⊘	Airline office	☩	Lighthouse	✚	Buddhist temple/Pagoda
▤▤▤	Pedestrianized road	★	Bus stop/taxi pick-up	⚘	Waterfall	🏰	Mosque
▬▬▬	Road	⛽	Petrol station	◔	Cave	⚜	Hindu temple
▭▭▭	Steps	@	Internet access	≈	Swimming area	◉	Cao dai temple
-○-○-	Unpaved road	ⓘ	Information office	✕	Dive site	⊞	Hospital
▬▬▬	Motorway	Ⓢ	Bank	⛴	Boat	▢	Building
▬▬▬	Wall	✉	Post office	〰	Spring/spa	⇨	Church
●---●	Cable car	E	Embassy	▲	Mountain peak	▢	Market
- - -	Footpath	◆	Place of interest	⏙	Mountain range	⬭	Stadium
▬ ▬	Ferry route	∴	Ruin	⚑	Border crossing	▢	Park
▬▬▬	Railway	☉	Statue	⛳	Golf course	🏖▢	Beach
⤞	Bridge	⊠	Gate	⚱	Museum	⊞	Cemetery
⫽	Pass	P	Parking				

Listings key

■ Accommodation

● Eating

■ Drinking/nightlife

● Shopping

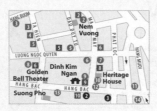

Buffalo tours
Discover Your Asia
www.buffalotours.c
EXPERIENCE LOCAL LIFE
IN VIETNAM WITH
BUFFALO TOURS